A

MODERN GRAMMAR

FOR

BIBLICAL
HEBREW

DUANE A. GARRETT

AND

JASON S. DeROUCHIE

ACADEMIC

Nashville, Tennessee

A Modern Grammar for Biblical Hebrew

Published by B&H Publishing Group
Nashville, Tennessee

ISBN: 978-0-8054-4962-4

Dewey decimal classification: 492.4
Subject heading: HEBREW LANGUAGE—GRAMMAR

Hebrew Scripture quotations are from *Biblia Hebraica Stuttgartensia*, edited by Karl Elliger and Wilhelm Rudolph, Fourth Revised Edition, edited by Hans Peter Rüger, © 1977 and 1990 Deutsche Bibelgesellschaft, Stuttgart. Used by permission.

Printed in the United States of America
1 2 3 4 5 6 7 8 9 10 · 15 14 13 12 11 10 09
BP

TABLE OF CONTENTS

A. Orthography and Phonology

1. The Hebrew Alphabet and Vowels 1

2. Pointed Vowel Letters and the Silent Shewa 12

3. Daghesh Forte, Mappiq, Metheg, and Rules for Gutturals 18

4. Accent Shift and Vowel Changes 23

B. Basic Morphology and Syntax

5. Gender and Number in Nouns 28

6. Hebrew Verbs 33

7. The Directive ה, Negative לֹא, and Interrogative ה 42

8. The Definite Article 45

9. Roots, Stems, and the Qal *Qatal* 50

10. The Conjunction and the Qal *Yiqtol* and *Weqatal* 58

11. The Qal Infinitive Construct and *Wayyiqtol* 68

12. The Construct Chain 74

13. Prepositions 83

14. Pronominal Suffixes on Nouns and Prepositions 89

15. Adjectives and the Qal Participles 99

16. Geminate and Segholate Nouns 106

17. Pronouns 116

18. More About יֵשׁ and אֵין and the Qal Imperative 122

19. Numbers 127

20. Stems, Roots, and Principal Parts of Weak Roots with Gutturals in the Qal Stem 134

21. Principal Parts of Other Weak Roots in the Qal Stem 144

22. Characteristics of the Niphal, Piel, and Hiphil 150

23. Characteristics of the Pual, Hophal, and Hithpael 161

24. Principal Parts of Weak Roots in the Derived Stems 167

25. Pronominal Suffixes on Verbs 178

26. The Qal Infinitive Construct with Suffixes, the Qal Infinitive Absolute, and הִנֵּה 186

C. Detailed Study of the Qal Verb

27. The Qal *Yiqtol* and *Wayyiqtol* with Weak Roots 196

28. The Qal Imperative and Participle with Weak Roots 206

29. The Qal *Qatal* with Weak Roots, Qal Statives, and the Qal Passive Participle 212

30. The Qal Cohortative, Jussive, and *Weyiqtol* 220

D. Detailed Study of the Derived Stems

31. The Niphal 226

32. The Piel and Pual 235

33. The Hiphil and Hophal..246

34. The Hithpael..261

35. The Alternative Doubled Stems..267

E. The Masoretic Text, Detailed Study of Syntax, and Poetry

36. The Cantillation Marks and Other Masoretic Conventions 273

37. An Overview of Text Syntax and Literary Structure....................................283

38. More on Historical Discourse and Paragraphs, Connectors, and Subordination..........296

39. More on Anticipatory and Descriptive Discourse 312

40. Discourse Markers and More on Directive Discourse...................................321

41. An Overview of Poetry 336

F. Appendixes

Appendix 1: Basics for Using Your Hebrew Bible 349

Appendix 2: Noun Types and Basics for Using Your Hebrew Lexicon..............366

Appendix 3: Distinguishing Subject and Predicate in Nominal Clauses............371

Appendix 4: Connection, Offline Clauses, and Text Type Predicate Patterns ...373

Appendix 5: Glossary for the Study of Hebrew Grammar 375

Appendix 6: Hebrew-English Vocabulary—By Chapter 385

Appendix 7: Hebrew-English Vocabulary—By Alphabet 398

Appendix 8: Principal Parts and Finite Verb Paradigms 411

Preface

A Modern Grammar for Biblical Hebrew and its accompanying materials are designed for a two-semester course of study. The textbook's structure, however, is intentionally set up to allow maximal use in both traditional and non-traditional academic settings. The format of the material gives instructors numerous options for customizing their syllabi.

1. Possible Tracks

Looking at the Table of Contents, you can see that the grammar is organized in the following manner:

- A. Orthography and Phonology (chapters 14)
- B. Basic Morphology and Syntax (chapters 5–26)
- C. Detailed Study of the Qal Verb (chapters 27–30)
- D. Detailed Study of the Derived Stems (chapters 31–35)
- E. The Masoretic Text, Detailed Study of Syntax, and Poetry (chapters 36–41)

It is important to realize that the student is introduced to all essential elements of biblical Hebrew grammar, including the derived stems, by the end of chapter 26. The grammar provides the following four options for a full course of study:

(1) *Chapter 26:* Ending here enables professors to cover nearly all traditional first-year grammar, including an introduction to weak verbs and derived stems. Students will have studied the Qal strong verb and III-ה verb with full inflections, but they will have also become acquainted with weak verbs and derived stem verbs by means of inflected vocabulary, principal parts, and translation practice. Two extra topics on which first-year professors may want to comment are the jussive and cohortative forms in chapter 30 and the alternative doubled stems in chapter 35.

(2) *Chapter 30:* This ending point allows professors to address all traditional first-year grammar, with all Qal weak forms being taught through full inflections and with the derived stems being taught through principal parts. The one additional topic that professors may want to address is the alternative doubled stems in chapter 35.

(3) *Chapter 35:* By this point, all traditional first-year grammar has been thoroughly covered, with all stems being taught through full inflections along with full discussions of the derived stem verbs in weak roots.

(4) *Chapter 41:* Completing the whole book allows instructors to cover all traditional first-year grammar, along with an introduction to essential intermediate issues like the Hebrew cantillation system, text syntax (as opposed to sentence syntax), literary structure, discourse markers, poetry, textual criticism, and lexicography. Students will have translated over 300 verses of actual biblical Hebrew (plus numerous practice sentences) and memorized nearly all words used 79 times or more in the Hebrew Bible (plus some extras), including 510 core vocabulary and 155 proper names.

Some instructors may choose to take their students through all 41 chapters in a three-semester program. There may also be those who do not have enough time to complete the book but who still desire to incorporate some intermediate-level material into a first-year course. For these, the grammar is very usable since, so long as students have learned to use their lexicons, professors can jump to specific textbook chapters and readings without in any way jeopardizing the students' mastery of the basics. Since most teachers of first-year Hebrew will want students to become acquainted with basic guidelines for using the Hebrew Bible and the lexicon, and also with noun types, information on these topics is provided in Appendixes 1 and 2.

2. A Note on Vocabulary

Accompanying this material are "Third Semester Hebrew Catch-up Lists" that will allow students to master vocabulary down to 100 uses, regardless of which of the four termination options were used in the first year. If you skip chapters, we encourage you to have students continue to work on vocabulary in the consecutive chapters, so as to enable the use of these catch-up lists.

3. Ancillary Materials

The CD in the back of this volume contains many helpful materials for the student, including audio files for the alphabet and vocabulary. Additional ancillary materials for students and teachers are available on the publisher's Web site at http://www .bhacademic.com/A-Modern-Grammar-for-Biblical-Hebrew/.

4. Acknowledgements

With profound appreciation, we here offer our thanks to those who toiled for hours in proofreading, evaluating, and correcting this work. Responsibility for any remaining errors is entirely ours. Special thanks are extended to Anna Strom, Jason Andersen, Sarah Lysaker, Dr. Rebekah Josberger, and Dr. David Stabnow. Their thoroughness, enthusiasm, and honesty are deeply appreciated. We also thank Dr. Kenneth Turner of Bryan College and Brian Tabb and Ryan Griffith of Bethlehem College and Seminary for trying early drafts of this material in the classroom. We must also voice the deepest gratitude to our own Hebrew students at The Southern Baptist Theological Seminary and Northwestern College (MN), who patiently bore with the early manuscript versions of this grammar while kindly making suggestions for its improvement.

Finally and chiefly, we joyfully give praise to God, whose clear and sufficient disclosure of himself and his will through the Scripture makes such a grammar possible and necessary. Being confident in all God's past and future grace won for us through Messiah Jesus, we pray our grammar will help equip the next generation to study, practice, and teach all of God's Word in God's world for God's glory.

Duane A. Garrett and Jason S. DeRouchie
Easter Week 2009

CHAPTER 1
THE HEBREW ALPHABET AND VOWELS

The Hebrew alphabet consists entirely of consonants, the first being א (Aleph) and the last being ת (Taw). It has 23 letters, but שׂ (Sin) and שׁ (Shin) were originally counted as one letter, and thus it is sometimes said to have 22 letters. It is written from right to left, so that in the word written אשׁ, the letter א is first and the letter שׁ is last. The standard script for biblical Hebrew is called the **square** or **Aramaic script**.

A. The Consonants
1. The Letters of the Alphabet

Table 1.1. The Hebrew Alphabet

1	א	Aleph	7	ז	Zayin	13	מ	Mem	19	ק	Qoph
2	ב	Beth	8	ח	Heth	14	נ	Nun	20	ר	Resh
3	ג	Gimel	9	ט	Teth	15	ס	Samek	21	שׂ	Sin
4	ד	Daleth	10	י	Yod	16	ע	Ayin	22	שׁ	Shin
5	ה	Hey	11	כ	Kaph	17	פ	Pe	23	ת	Taw
6	ו	Waw	12	ל	Lamed	18	צ	Tsade			

To master the Hebrew alphabet, first learn the signs, their names, and their alphabetical order. Do not be concerned with the phonetic values of the letters at this time.

2. Letters with Final Forms

Five letters have **final forms**. Whenever one of these letters is the last letter in a word, it is written in its final form rather than its normal form. For example, the final form of Tsade is ץ (contrast צ). It is important to realize that the letter itself is the same; it is simply written differently if it is the last letter in the word. The five final forms are as follows.

Table 1.2. Consonants with Final Forms

Normal Form	כ	מ	נ	פ	צ
Final Form	ך	ם	ן	ף	ץ

(1) In מלך (*mlk*), מ (the first letter, reading the Hebrew right to left) has the normal form, but the last letter in the word is כ in its final form (ך).

(2) In לכם (*lkm*), the כ has the normal form, but the מ has the final form (ם).

Blackboard 1.1. The Use of Final Forms of Letters

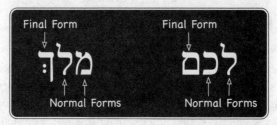

3. Confusing Letters

Hebrew can be difficult to read because many letters look very similar. Observe the letters in the following chart. In each box, you see a series of letters that look similar to one another. Be sure that you can distinguish which letter is which.

Table 1.3. Easily Confused Letters

ע צ	ס מ ט ם	י ו ז ן	ד ר ךָ
ב כ פ	ה ח ת	נ ג ו	

4. The Phonetic Value of the Alphabet

For learning the alphabet, Hebrew consonants can be divided conveniently into six groups: **begadkephat** letters, sibilants, שׂ and ק, gutturals, liquids, and nasals. These six groups are not built around phonetic definitions of the Hebrew consonant system, although some phonetic terminology is used. These groups simply provide a framework for learning to pronounce the letters of the Hebrew alphabet.

a. Begadkephat Letters

Referred to as the begadkephat letters (from the artificial memory words בְּגַד כְּפַת), the letters ב, ג, ד, כ, פ, and ת are unique in that each has two distinct phonetic values. Each of these may be found with a dot called a **Daghesh Lene** (e.g., בּ) or without the Daghesh Lene (e.g., ב).

(1) If the Daghesh Lene is present, the letter is a **plosive**, like the English *B*.

(2) If there is no Daghesh Lene, the sound is a **fricative** or **spirant** (there is a strong breathing sound, as with the English *V* sound).

Table 1.4. The "Begadkephat" Letters

	בּ	גּ	דּ	כּ	פּ	תּ
With Daghesh Lene	*B* as in *boy*	*G* as in *good*	*D* as in *dot*	*K* as in *kite*	*P* as in *paste*	*T* as in *tin*
	ב	ג	ד	כ	פ	ת
Without Daghesh Lene	*V* as in *very*	*GH* as in *dog house*	voiced *TH* as in *then*	*C* as in *cool*	*F* as in *fix*	unvoiced *TH* as in *thin*

Do not think of the begadkephat letters as twelve different letters. There are only six. In a given word the same begadkephat letter will be written sometimes with and sometimes without a Daghesh Lene, according to rules we will learn in the next chapter. The Daghesh Lene is used only with these six begadkephat letters.

b. The Gutturals

Hebrew has four guttural letters: א, ע, ה, and ח. The sounds of these letters are made at the back of the throat. For English speakers, the "sounds" of א and ע are especially odd. The letter א is a mild "glottal stop," the tiny sound made by the tightening of the throat before the *oh* sound in *uh-oh*. But for all practical purposes, א has no sound at all. א was necessary, however, because originally Hebrew was written with no vowels. Writing without vowels obviously posed a problem if, for example, a word began with a vowel sound. Some letter had to be an "empty" consonant to show that there was a vowel there, and א had that role. The ע is a strong "glottal stop," and it has a much stronger guttural sound. It is important to try to pronounce the letters distinctly. Today, people frequently treat א and ע as redundant (both having no sound) and also treat ה and ח as redundant (both having an H sound). Biblical Hebrew does not confuse these letters.

Table 1.5. The Gutturals

א	Almost no sound; a weak glottal stop. The tiny sound made by the tightening of the throat before the *oh* sound in *uh-oh*.
ע	A strong glottal stop. Exaggerate the sound made by the tightening of the throat before the *oh* sound in *uh-oh*, and add a slight but hard *G* sound. Somewhat similar to the final guttural sound of the English -*ING* ending.
ה	*H* as in *hot*.
ח	Like *H* but with friction at the back of throat; like the *CH* in Scottish *loch*.

c. The Sibilants

These are the S-type letters. They are created by passing air between the teeth. These letters differ from one another in several respects as described in the chart below.

(1) **Voiced** refers to a consonant that is pronounced while using the voice (e.g., the sound of *Z*); **unvoiced** refers to a consonant pronounced without using the voice (e.g., the sound of *S*).

(2) To English speakers, ס and שׂ appear to be redundant letters, but probably most speakers of biblical Hebrew could distinguish the two.

Table 1.6. The Sibilants

ז	*Z* as in *Zion*; voiced
ס	*S* as in *sack*; a sharp *S* made with teeth; unvoiced
צ	*TS* as in *hats*; unvoiced but emphatic

| שׂ | *S* as in *seen*; a softer *S* than the Samek; unvoiced and slightly aspirated |
| שׁ | *SH* as in *sheen*; unvoiced and strongly aspirated |

d. Velar (Emphatic) T and K

The letter ט is a *T* sound that may have been pronounced more on the palate than was the case with its counterpart ת (the ת seems to have been pronounced with the tongue on the back of the teeth). The letter ק is a *K* that was probably pronounced further back in the throat, more in the back of the palate, than כ. These two consonants are pronounced more emphatically and are called **velars**. The צ is also a velar.

Table 1.7. ט and ק

| ט | a *T* made more on the palate, as in *tot*; may have had a glottal sound |
| ק | a *K* sound at the back of the throat; no English analogy |

e. The Nasals

A **nasal** is a sound made by vibrating the vocal chords while obstructing the flow of air through the mouth with the lips or tongue with the result that air and its sound comes out the nose instead of the mouth. Hebrew has two nasals: מ (which obstructs airflow with the lips) and נ (which obstructs airflow with the tongue on the palate). These are like their English counterparts *M* and *N*.

Table 1.8. The Nasals

| מ | *M* as in *miss* |
| נ | *N* as in *now* |

f. The Linguals

A **lingual** is a consonant sound made by causing the airstream the flow over the sides of the tongue, as in the English *L* and *R*.

Table 1.9. The Liquids

| ל | *L* as in *look* |
| ר | *R* as in *read* |

g. The Glides (Semivowels)

A **semivowel** or **glide** is a consonant with a vowel-like sound; sometimes they are actually used as vowels. For example, English *Y* is a consonant in *yoke* but a vowel in *easy*. Hebrew has two semivowels: ו and י.

| ו | *W* as in *wish* (modern pronunciation: like *V* in *very*) |

׳	*Y* as in *yes*

h. Phonetic Classification of the Letters

The velars ק and ט are also plosive like כ, not fricative like כ. Notice also that the begad-kephat letters are in three classes: labials (made with the lips), palatals (made on the palate), and dentals (made with the front teeth). As you can see, the begadkephat letters are subdivided by whether they are voiced or unvoiced and whether they are fricative or plosive.

In the table below, unvoiced consonants are italicized, and voiced consonants are bold.

Table 1.10. Letters Phonetically Classified

Class	Fricative	Plosive	Velars	Nasals	Glides	Other
Labials	**ב** *פ*	**בּ** *פּ*		**מ**	**ו**	
Palatals	**ג** *כ*	**גּ** *כּ*	*ק*		**י**	
Dentals	**ד** *ת*	**דּ** *תּ*	*ט*	**נ**		
Gutturals						**ע** *ח ה* **א**
Sibilants			*צ*			**ז** *ס שׁ שׂ*
Linguals						**ל ר**

i. Summary of the Pronunciation of the Hebrew Consonants

The following chart summarizes the phonetic values of the Hebrew alphabet.

Table 1.11. Pronunciation of the Hebrew Consonants

א almost silent	ח *CH* of *loch*	פּ *P* of *paste*
בּ *B* of *boy*	ט *T* of *tot*	פ *F* of *fix*
ב *V* of *very*	י *Y* of *yes*	צ *TS* of *hats*
גּ *G* of *good*	כּ *K* of *kite*	ק *K* at back of throat
ג *GH* of *dog house*	כ *C* of *cool*	ר *R* of *read*
דּ *D* of *dot*	ל *L* of *look*	שׂ *S* of *seen*
ד *TH* of *the*	מ *M* of *miss*	שׁ *SH* of *sheen*
ה *H* of *hot*	נ *N* of *now*	תּ *T* of *tin*
ו *W* or *V*	ס *S* of *sack*	ת *TH* of *thin*
ז *Z* of *zoo*	ע strong glottal stop	

5. Writing Hebrew Letters

You obviously will want to learn to write Hebrew letters. Everyone develops his or her particular style for writing Hebrew letters, but use the following guidelines.

(1) Remember that Hebrew is written from right to left. Thus, the general motion of your hand should be right to left rather than left to right.

(2) Be sure that your letters are standard and recognizable to all people who know Hebrew. Do not develop an eccentric style.

(3) Make your writing clear by including the small marks that distinguish similar letters. Your ב should not look like כ. Final Nun (ן) should drop below the rule line; Waw (ו) should not.

(4) On the other hand, you do not need to imitate the very formal style of the Hebrew letters found in a Hebrew Bible. Simple lines, as found in the letters below, suffice. The stroke order found in the letters below will help you write clear letters that move from right to left.

B. The Concept of Vowel Points

1. Background

Biblical Hebrew was originally written without vowels; the tradition of how to vocalize correctly the Hebrew text was passed down orally from one generation to the next. But eventually, the scribes realized that some way of writing down the vowels had to be devised if the correct pronunciation was not to be lost or corrupted. They were not willing, however, to deface the sacred text by inserting large vowels (like the Roman letters A, E, or U) that would require moving aside the received letters. Instead, they created a system of dots and lines to represent vowels. They were able to insert these minute vowels around the Hebrew letters of the text without having to move the letters. The vowel signs are called **vowel points**. By about the seventh century A.D., the current system of vowel pointing was made the standard. The scribes who devised this system are commonly called the Masoretes, and thus the standard text they produced is called the **Masoretic Text** (MT).

2. Simple Vowels and Their Classes

(1) Hebrew vowel points are written below the consonants, or to the left of the consonants, or raised and to the left of the consonants, as in the examples below.

    (a) The vowel Hireq is a small dot written under a consonant. It is pronounced like the English *I* in *hit*. Thus, מִ is *MI* as in *miss*.

    (b) The vowel Holem is a small, raised dot slightly to the left of its consonant. It is pronounced like the *O* in *hole*. מֹ would be pronounced *MO*.

(2) A vowel is pronounced *after* the consonant that it is with. Thus, מִ is *MI* and not *IM*.

(3) Hebrew vowels may be described in three categories: simple vowels, pointed vowel letters, and reduced vowels. All make use of vowel points (reduced vowels are described below; pointed vowel letters are described in chapter 2).

(4) Hebrew has long and short vowels, but the quantity of a vowel in a given word can change depending on what happens to that word. If a word is altered (for example, by the addition of a suffix), a long vowel may be replaced by a short vowel, or a short vowel by a long one. A vowel that can undergo this kind of change can be called **changeable**. We learn how vowels change in chapter 4.

(5) The Hebrew vowels are divided into three classes called a-class, i-class, and u-class. Generally, vowels change within their classes (this is not an invariable rule). A long a-class vowel (Qamets) might become a short a-class vowel (Pathach) but will not normally become a short u-class vowel (e.g., Qibbuts).

Table 1.12. The Simple Vowel Points

Class	Symbol		Name	Quantity	Sound
A	-	בַּ	Pathach	short	*A* of *cat*
A	ָ	בָּ	Qamets	long	*A* of *father*
I	ִ	בִּ	Hireq	short	*I* of *hit*
I	ֶ	בֶּ	Seghol	short	*E* of *set*
I	ֵ	בֵּ	Tsere	long	*E* of *hey*

U	ֻ	בֻ	Qibbuts	short	*U* of *cut*
U	ֹ	בֹ	Holem	long	*O* of *whole*
U	ָ	בָ	Qamets Hatuph	short	*O* of *tote*

Under the column "Symbol," you can see both how the vowel looks when written with a consonant (in this case, ב) and how it looks by itself. There are three ambiguities in the vowels listed above.

(1) A single vowel symbol ָ is used for both the Qamets and Qamets Hatuph. In order to distinguish the two, you must know how to tell a short syllable from a long syllable. This is discussed in chapter 3.

(2) The vowel Holem written with the letter Shin or Sin is confusing. A Shin with Holem looks like this: שֹ. A Sin with Holem looks like this: שֹ. Sometimes a single dot does double duty, so that Sin with Holem looks like this: שֹ.

(3) Holem is in some words "unchangeable." When unchangeable, it stays the same and will not be transformed into a different vowel. For example, in שֹׁפֵט ("judge") it is unchangeably long. In different words, however, Holem will change. The reason for this is described in the next lesson.

3. The Reduced Vowels

Sometimes a simple long or short vowel will become an extremely short or "reduced" vowel. Hebrew has four such "reduced" vowels. These are analogous to the very short sound for the *E* many people use when pronouncing "because" (as b*ᵉ*cause).

Table 1.13. The Reduced Vowels

Name	Symbol		Sound	Transliteration
Shewa	ְ	בְ	*E* of *because*	ĕ
Hateph Pathach	ֲ	אֲ	*A* of *aside*	ă
Hateph Seghol	ֱ	אֱ	*E* of *mechanic*	ĕ
Hateph Qamets	ֳ	אֳ	first *O* of *tomato*	ŏ

The three vowels with the name Hateph are also called **composite Shewas**. They are almost always found with gutturals and not with the other letters.

C. Other Introductory Matters

1. Basic Transliteration

From time to time, you will see Hebrew words written in transliteration, that is, written with Roman characters. The following chart gives you standard transliterations for the consonants and vowels you have learned. By practicing transliterating Hebrew words in the early stage of your learning, you can better associate the Hebrew letters with their phonetic values. At the same time, you should never rely on transliteration for reading and pronunciation. Learn to read and pronounce Hebrew letters. Using the following table, the word אָדָם would be transliterated as *'āḏām*, and שַׂר would be transliterated as *śar*.

Table 1.14. Transliterations for Consonants and Basic Vowels

א	'	ו	*w*	מ	*m*	ר	*r*	◌ֲ	*a*
בּ	*b*	ז	*z*	נ	*n*	שׂ	*ś*	◌ָ	*ā*
ב	*ḇ*	ח	*ḥ*	ס	*s*	שׁ	*š*	◌ִ	*i*
ג	*g*	ט	*ṭ*	ע	*ʿ*	תּ	*t*	◌ֶ	*e*
ג	*ḡ*	י	*y*	פּ	*p*	ת	*ṯ*	◌ֵ	*ē*
דּ	*d*	כּ	*k*	פ	*p̄*			◌ֻ	*u*
ד	*ḏ*	כ	*ḵ*	צ	*ṣ*			◌ֹ	*ō*
ה	*h*	ל	*l*	ק	*q*			◌ָ	*o*

2. Reading a Hebrew Word

Read the word from right to left and pronounce the consonant before you pronounce a vowel that is below or to the left of that consonant.

Blackboard 1.2. Pronouncing Hebrew with Vowel Points

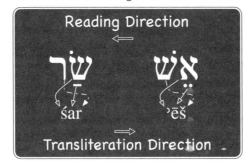

3. Basic Accentuation

In Hebrew, words are normally accented on the last syllable of the word (the ultima). Not infrequently, however, the accent is on the second to last syllable (the penult). In this textbook, words accented on the ultima have no special mark, but words accented on the penult are marked with the ˋ sign, as follows: מֶֽלֶךְ.

4. Gender in Nouns

Every noun in Hebrew is masculine or feminine. There is no neuter gender. We will learn more about gender in nouns in chapter 5. Every noun in the vocabulary is marked with Ⓜ

for masculine nouns and ☐F☐ for feminine nouns. If a noun has both ☐M☐ and ☐F☐ with it, that means that it could be either gender.

5. Nouns in Construct

The normal or **lexical** form of a noun is called the **absolute** form in Hebrew. For example, דָּבָר is an absolute noun and means "word" or "a word." There is also a form of the noun called the **construct**. Think of the construct form as always having the English "of" after it. The construct form of דָּבָר is דְּבַר, and it means "word of." Notice in דְּבַר the Shewa under the ד and the Pathach under the ב.

A construct noun followed by an absolute noun forms a **construct chain**. For example, the phrase דְּבַר מֶלֶךְ means "a word of a king" (that is, "a king's word"). *The construct noun is always in front of the absolute noun.*

Blackboard 1.3. The Basic Construct Chain

(1) In some cases, the absolute noun and the construct look exactly the same; in other cases, they are different. You will learn about this in chapter 12.

(2) For now, focus on memorizing the absolute form of each noun and on familiarizing yourself with the construct forms. Exercises in the workbook will help you get used to seeing construct forms.

(3) In the vocabulary lists, you will see the construct singular form of each noun given between two vertical lines like |דְּבַר|.

Below is an example of how a noun is listed in the vocabulary.

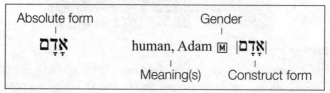

D. Vocabulary

Learn the following vocabulary words and use these words to practice the pronunciation of Hebrew words with simple vowels. Distinguish the sounds of begadkephat letters with Daghesh Lene from those without it. In all of the words given in the list below, ◌ָ is Qamets and not Qamets Hatuph.

In this textbook, there are four categories of vocabulary.

(1) *Core Vocabulary*: These are the essential words for memorization. Each of these words appears frequently in the Hebrew Bible, and some appear hundreds of times.

(2) *Inflected Vocabulary*: In the early chapters, some words will be given in an inflected form (like the English *saw* from the verb *see*). These words will enable you to begin reading simple sentences and will serve as reference points as you progress in the grammar.

(3) *Proper Names*: The names of people and places; these are easy to recognize.

(4) *Reading Vocabulary*: These are words that you need in order to read a specific biblical passage in the lesson. These words either are inflected in a pattern that you have not yet studied or are relatively uncommon words and therefore not in the core vocabulary.

1. Core Vocabulary

אָדָם	human, Adam Ⓜ |אָדָם|
אֶ֫רֶץ	earth, land Ⓕ |אֶרֶץ|
אֵשׁ	fire Ⓕ |אֵשׁ|
דָּבָר	word, thing Ⓜ |דְּבַר|
דַּ֫עַת	knowledge Ⓕ |דַּעַת|
זָקֵן	old (adjective); elder, old man (noun) Ⓜ |זְקַן|
חָצֵר	village, courtyard ⒻⓂ |חֲצַר|
מֶ֫לֶךְ	king Ⓜ |מֶלֶךְ|
עֶ֫בֶד	servant, slave Ⓜ |עֶבֶד|
צֹאן	flock (of sheep or goats) (s or p collective) Ⓕ |צֹאן|
שַׂר	ruler, leader, prince Ⓜ |שַׂר|
שֹׁפֵט	judge, leader Ⓜ |שֹׁפֵט|

CHAPTER 2
POINTED VOWEL LETTERS AND THE SILENT SHEWA

A. The Pointed Vowel Letters

Before vowel points were invented, Hebrew scribes used the consonants י, ו, and ה to mark some of the vowels in a text. When used as vowels, these are called **vowel letters**. Vowel letters are not consonants. For example, the ה has no *H* sound if it is used as a vowel letter; it is strictly a vowel. After vowel points were invented, the points were inserted with the vowel letters. Thus, they are called "pointed vowel letters." They are also called *matres lectionis*, Latin for "mothers of reading."

Table 2.1. The Vowel Letters

Letter	Symbol		Class	Name	Sound	Quantity	Comments
י	יִ	בִּי	I	Hireq-Yod	*EE* in *seek*	long	unchangeable[1]
	יֵ	בֵּי	I	Tsere-Yod	*EY* in *hey*	long	unchangeable; used in specific conditions
	יֶ	בֶּי	I	Seghol-Yod	*E* in *set*	short	unchangeable; used in specific conditions
ו	וֹ	בּוֹ	U	Holem-Waw	*O* in *hole*	long	unchangeable
	וּ	בּוּ	U	Shureq	*OO* in *mood*	long	unchangeable
ה	הָ	בָּה	A	Qamets-Hey	*A* in *father*	long	only at end of word
	הֵ	בֵּה	I	Tsere-Hey	*EY* in *hey*	long	only at end of word
	הֶ	בֶּה	I	Seghol-Hey	*E* in *set*	short	only at end of word
	הֹ	בֹּה	U	Holem-Hey	*O* in *hole*	long	only at end of word

The Waw is sometimes left out of Holem-Waw. When this happens, the vowel is said to be written **defectively**. Thus, שׁוֹפֵט is often written simply as שֹׁפֵט. In either case, the vowel is **unchangeable**. But if a Holem is not a "defective" Holem-Waw but a "normal" Holem, it is changeable. Concerning pointed vowel letters, remember:

(1) Vowel letters are not consonants. The word בִּי has one consonant (בּ) and one vowel (יִ).

---

1.   The significance of unchangeable vowels is discussed in chapter 4.

(2) Three vowels above are marked "unchangeable." This does not mean that they never change under any circumstances. However, they are not normally subject to the kinds of changes that the changeable "simple vowels" of chapter 1 undergo. The changeable vowels readily become longer or shorter whenever the position of the accent shifts (rules for this are given in chapter 4). "Unchangeable vowels" like Shureq (וּ) tend to remain long in situations where the changeable vowels would become short.

(3) The other pointed vowel letters are not like the changeable vowels either. They tend to appear only in specific conditions, such as in certain suffixes, in specific kinds of words, or at the end of certain words. They are not unchangeable, but because they are used in special circumstances, they are not subjected to the rules of vowel transformation (chapter 4) in the way that the changeable vowels are.

B. The Silent Shewa

1. What is the Silent Shewa?

A complicating factor is that the Shewa is sometimes **vocal** and sometimes **silent**. When *vocal*, it is pronounced as described in chapter 1 and constitutes a separate syllable. For example, בְּרִית, "covenant," is two syllables (בְּ/רִית). But when *silent*, it has no sound at all and it simply closes a syllable, as in מַלְכָּה, "queen" (מַלְ/כָּה).

To understand this, think of the word *chapter*. Its syllables are *chap/ter*. If it were written with Hebrew vowels, there would be a silent Shewa under the letter *p*. The Shewa with the *p* would not be pronounced; it would only show that the *p* closes the syllable *chap-*. Thus, the silent Shewa is not a vowel at all but is a marker that indicates the close of a syllable. In transliteration, therefore, you do not mark a silent Shewa.

2. Distinguishing Vocal Shewa from Silent Shewa

(1) In the first letter of a word, Shewa is vocal, as in בְּרִית (*bĕ/rît*) or כְּסִיל (*kĕ/sîl*).

(2) At the end of a word, Shewa is silent, as in מֶלֶךְ (*me/lek̲*).

(3) In the middle of a word:

    (a) after a short vowel or an accented long vowel, it is silent, as in תִּקְטֹלְנָה (*tiq/ṭōl/ nâ*, with a short, unaccented, closed syllable /תִּק/ and a long, closed, accented syllable /טֹל/) and מַלְכָּה (*mal/kâ*, with a short, unaccented, closed syllable /מַלְ/);

    (b) after an unaccented long vowel, it is vocal, as in שֹׁפְטִים (*šō/pĕ/ṭîm*).

    (c) If two Shewas are side-by-side in a word, the first is silent and the second is vocal, as in יִקְטְלוּ (*yiq/ṭĕ/lû*).

These rules for distinguishing vocal from silent Shewa are summarized in the diagram below. Be sure that you sound out the words and observe how the rules function in the pronunciation of the words.

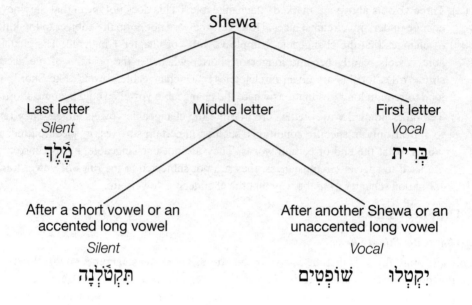

3. Silent Composite Shewas

A composite Shewa can be silent. This happens when, at the beginning of a word, a short vowel is followed by the composite Shewa that corresponds to that short vowel. For example, יַעֲקֹב, "Jacob," is two syllables (יַעְ/קֹב) and the Hateph Pathach is silent.

C. Summary of Hebrew Vowels

(1) The Hebrew vowels are in three classes: a-class, i-class, and u-class.

(2) Simple vowels may lengthen, shorten, or reduce. Reduced vowels can become longer. Generally, vowels lengthen or shorten within their classes.

(3) The pointed vowel letters are not subject to the general rules of vowel transformation. Either they are unchangeably long, or they appear only in specific situations where specific rules apply.

(4) In addition, the vowel classes subdivide into types. These types are similar to the vowel types a, e, i, o, and u.

    (a) I-class vowels include both i- and e-type vowels.

    (b) U-class vowels include both u- and o-type vowels.

    (c) A-class vowels are of the a-type.

(5) Unfortunately, Hebrew vowel types do not correspond to how English pronounces vowels.

    (a) In English, we think of the vowel sound in *way* as being a long letter *A*. In Hebrew, that sound is made by the Tsere, an i-class vowel. The Hebrew long a-type vowel has the sound of the *A* in the English *father*.

(b) English thinks of the long *E* as the vowel sound of *seek*, but Hebrew uses the i-type vowel Hireq-Yod for that sound. Other languages, such as French and German, are more like Hebrew in how they pronounce their vowels.

(6) Vowel letters are not consonants even though they contain letters. Notice that the word סוּסָה contains only two consonants.

Blackboard 2.1. Vowel Letters Are Not Consonants

D. Transliteration for Vowel Letters

The vowels with vowel letters are transliterated according to the table below. You can see that there is some ambiguity in the transliterations. For example, *ê* could be either Tsere-Yod or Seghol-Yod.

The transliterations for Tsere-Hey, Seghol-Hey, and Holem-Hey have the letter *h* in parentheses. This is done to avoid ambiguity. For example, in the transliteration of Tsere-Yod (as opposed to Tsere-Hey), it would be confusing if both were transliterated as *ê*. But different scholars may follow different conventions.

Table 2.2. Transliteration for Vowel Letters

ִי	*î*	וֹ	*ô*	הָ	*â*
ֵי	*ê*	וּ	*û*	הֵ	*ē(h)*
ֶי	*ê*			הֶ	*e(h)*
				הֹ	*ō(h)*

E. The Basics of Syllable Division

The basic rules of syllable division in Hebrew are as follows.

(1) A syllable always begins with a consonant and never with a vowel. (One possible exception occurs with special cases of the Hebrew conjunction being attached to the front of certain word forms, but we will examine this feature in chapter 10.)

(a) In דָּבָר the syllables are divided בָר / דָּ and *never* ר / דָּב.

(b) The first consonant may be א, as in דָם / אָ; the word still begins with a consonant and not a vowel.

(2) A syllable may be closed or open.

    (a) An open syllable is one consonant followed by one vowel (abbreviated CV). Put another way, an open syllable ends with a vowel. In דָּבָר, /דָּ/ is an open syllable.

    (b) A closed syllable is two consonants with a vowel in the middle (abbreviated CVC). A closed syllable both begins and ends in a consonant. In דָּבָר, /בָר/ is a closed syllable.

(3) Except at the end of a word, a closed syllable has a silent Shewa with its second consonant.

    (a) In מַלְכָּה (מַלְ/כָּה), /מַלְ/ is a closed syllable and ends in a silent Shewa.

    (b) In דָּבָר, בָר is a closed syllable at the end of a word and thus does not take the silent Shewa.

(4) A pointed vowel letter (*mater lectionis*) is simply a vowel; it does not count as a consonant or close a syllable.

    (a) אֵין is a closed syllable with one vowel and two consonants.

    (b) In מַלְכָּה (מַלְ/כָּה), /כָּה/ is an open syllable; the ה is a mater lectionis.

F. More on Construct Chains: Construct Nouns Used with Proper Names

Whenever a construct noun is placed in a construct chain with a proper name, the construct noun is regarded as definite (i.e., as having the definite article "the"). Thus, אִישׁ שִׁלֹה means "the man of Shiloh" and *not* "a man of Shiloh."

G. More on the Daghesh Lene

Remember that a Daghesh Lene appears only in a begadkephat letter (בנדכפת).

(1) A begadkephat letter has a Daghesh Lene if it begins a syllable and does not follow a vowel, as in the ד of דָּבָר.

    (a) If it follows a vowel within a word, it does not have a Daghesh Lene, as in the ב of דָּבָר.

    (b) If it follows a silent Shewa, it will have a Daghesh Lene, as in the פ of מִשְׁפָּט.

(2) A begadkephat letter at the beginning of a word has a Daghesh Lene, but if the previous word ends in a vowel, the Daghesh Lene may be dropped.

    (a) "Dan" is normally written as דָּן. Notice the Daghesh Lene.

    (b) "In Dan" would normally be written as בְּדָן. Notice that the Daghesh Lene in דָ has dropped out because it follows a vocal Shewa in בְּ (silent Shewa does not cause a Daghesh Lene to drop).

    (c) But "a queen in Dan" could be written as מַלְכָּה בְדָן (the word מַלְכָּה ends in a vowel, and thus בְדָן is preceded by a vowel). Hebrew is not consistent about this, however. "A queen in Dan" could be written as מַלְכָּה בְּדָן, with the Daghesh Lene in place in the בְּ. As with any language, you must be prepared for some inconsistency with Hebrew!

H. Vocabulary

Again, no word below has a Qamets Hatuph.

1. Core Vocabulary

אֹהֶל   tent M |אֹהֶל|

אֵין   there is no (Note: אֵין is used with a noun to indicate that the noun does not exist. The noun follows אֵין, thus אֵין מֶלֶךְ means "There is no king.")

אִישׁ   man, husband M |אִישׁ| (plural = אֲנָשִׁים)

אֱלֹהִים   God, gods M |אֱלֹהֵי|

בְּ   in, with, by, among (directly attached to a noun, as in בְּאָשֵׁר, "in Asher")

בְּרִית   covenant F |בְּרִית|

יֵשׁ   there is (יֵשׁ is used with a noun to say that the noun exists. The noun follows יֵשׁ, so יֵשׁ מֶלֶךְ means "There is a king.")

כְּלִי   vessel, tool, weapon, thing M |כְּלִי|

מַלְכָּה   queen F |מַלְכַּת|

מִשְׁפָּט   judgment, justice M |מִשְׁפַּט|

סוּס   horse M |סוּס|

עִיר   city F |עִיר|

2. Inflected Vocabulary

מְלָכִים   kings (the plural of מֶלֶךְ)

סוּסָה   mare (the feminine of סוּס)

שֹׁפְטִים   judges (the plural of שֹׁפֵט)

3. Proper Names

אָשֵׁר   Asher

שִׁלֹה[1]   Shiloh

---

1.   This is an example of defective writing. The Hireq is actually long, and the "full writing" of the name is שִׁילֹה, as in Gen 49:10.

CHAPTER 3
DAGHESH FORTE, MAPPIQ, METHEG, AND RULES FOR GUTTURALS

A. Daghesh Forte

1. An Overview of the Doubling Dot

In addition to the Daghesh Lene, Hebrew also has the **Daghesh Forte**. The Daghesh Forte is a simple dot inside a letter, just like a Daghesh Lene. The difference is in where it occurs and what it does.

(1) A Daghesh Forte can occur in almost any letter and is not confined to a begadkephat letter.

(2) The function of the Daghesh Forte is to indicate that a letter is doubled. Hebrew writes the same letter twice side-by-side only in special cases. Usually, it uses the Daghesh Forte instead. For example, in אִשָּׁה, the שׁ stands for two letters שׁ (a doubled שׁ). However, a begadkephat letter can also be doubled, as in גִּבּוֹר, where the בּ is doubled.

How do you tell a Daghesh Lene from a Daghesh Forte?

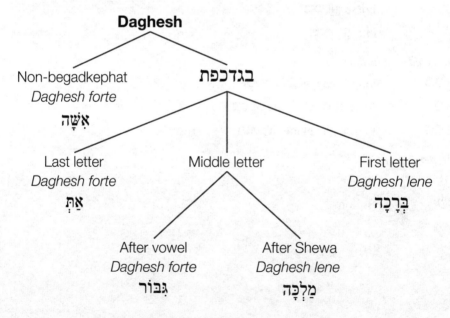

(1) Daghesh Lene occurs only in the begadkephat letters. If a Daghesh is in any other letter, it is a Daghesh Forte (e.g., אִשָּׁה, "woman").

(2) If a Daghesh is found in one of the begadkephat letters:

    (a) At the beginning of a word, it is Daghesh Lene (e.g., בְּרָכָה, "blessing").

(b) At the end of a word, it is Daghesh Forte (אַתְּ, "you").

(c) In the middle of a word,

    (i) after a vowel, it is Daghesh Forte (e.g., גִּבּוֹר, "hero");

    (ii) after a Shewa, it is Daghesh Lene (e.g., מַלְכָּה, "queen"). In such a situation, the Shewa will always be silent and be on the end of a closed syllable (CVC). In effect, if a begadkephat letter with a Daghesh in it is preceded by a Shewa, it is actually preceded by a consonant (the Shewa being silent).

Whenever a begadkephat letter has a Daghesh Forte, it is the hardened form that is doubled. That is, a begadkephat letter with a Daghesh Forte is, in effect, two of that letter, each with Daghesh Lene.

2. Syllable Division with Daghesh Forte

A letter with a Daghesh Forte is two letters. There is always a syllable division between the two letters of a Daghesh Forte (except in the special case where a letter with a Daghesh Forte is at the end of a word). Thus, a letter with a Daghesh Forte closes the syllable in front of it and begins the next syllable.

Therefore, words with Daghesh Forte are divided as follows:

חַטָּאת   →   חַט / טָאת

אִשָּׁה   →   אִשׁ / שָׁה

In cases where a Daghesh Forte is in a begadkephat letter, you can write the letter twice, each time with a Daghesh Lene, to show that it is the hardened form of the letter that is doubled. Of course, you would never see actual Hebrew written this way.

גִּבּוֹר   →   גִּבּ / בּוֹר

B. Rules for the Gutturals and Resh

Four special rules apply for the gutturals א, ה, ח, and ע:

(1) *They cannot be doubled*; that is, they do not take the Daghesh Forte. The letter ר, like the gutturals, never doubles. For example, for reasons that need not be discussed here, the middle letter in the word בֵּרֶךְ, "he blessed," would be doubled if it were a letter that allowed doubling. The ר, however, rejects doubling.

(2) *They cannot take a vocal Shewa*. Where one would expect a vocal Shewa, they will take one of the composite Shewas (אֲ or אֱ or אֳ). The word אֲדָמָה takes a Hateph Pathach under the א instead of the vocal Shewa that it would have with a non-guttural. Gutturals and Resh can take a silent Shewa, but where one would expect this, the composite Shewa will sometimes occur (as described for יַעֲקֹב, "Jacob," in chapter 2).

(3) *They tend to prefer a-class vowels*. Compare the nouns מֶלֶךְ and שַׁעַר. These two nouns are of the same grammatical type. But מֶלֶךְ has two Seghol vowels where the noun שַׁעַר has two Pathach vowels. This illustrates the guttural tendency to prefer a-class vowels.

(4) *Where a syllable has Hireq* (◌ִ) *with non-guttural letters, an analogous syllable that has a guttural may have Seghol* (◌ֶ). The words יִקְטֹל and אֶקְטֹל and יֶחֱטָא are grammatically similar. However, יִקְטֹל has Hireq where אֶקְטֹל has Seghol because of the guttural א, and יֶחֱטָא has a Seghol before the guttural ח.

Blackboard 3.1. The Guttural's Preference for Seghol

C. **Furtive Pathach**

We have already seen that when a vowel point is under a consonant, it is pronounced after the consonant. There is one exception to this: If the vowel Pathach is under a guttural that is the last letter of the word, the Pathach is pronounced before the guttural. This is a **furtive Pathach**. Still, this does not violate our rule that a syllable never begins with vowel, because a furtive Pathach does not constitute a separate syllable. For example, רוּחַ has a furtive Pathach, but it is a monosyllable; the sound of the Shureq glides into the Pathach.

Blackboard 3.2. The Furtive Pathach

D. **Mappiq**

The letter ה occasionally appears with a dot in it that looks exactly like a Daghesh (הּ). It is not a Daghesh; recall that only a begadkephat letter can take a Daghesh Lene and that a guttural never takes the Daghesh Forte. The dot in the ה is a **Mappiq**. It is placed in a ה at the end of a word when that ה is a true consonant and not a vowel letter. An example is סוּסָהּ, "her horse" (this is not the same as סוּסָה, "mare"). Another example is גָּבֹהַּ, "high." Note that the ה in גָּבֹהַּ also has a furtive Pathach.

E. Recognizing Qamets Hatuph and the Use of the Metheg

1. Qamets Hatuph

A closed, unaccented syllable is always short. Any time the ambiguous vowel sign (◌ָ) appears in a closed, unaccented syllable, it must be short and thus must be a Qamets Hatuph. In חָכְמָה, "wisdom," the syllable division is חָכְ/מָה, and the accent is on the last syllable (מָה). The first syllable (חָכְ) is closed and unaccented, and its vowel is Qamets Hatuph. The word is pronounced like *hok̲/mâ* and never as *hā/k̆e/mâ*. As a practical rule, when you see a combination in a word like ◌ָ◌ְ (without an accent), assume that you have a Qamets Hatuph with silent Shewa and not a Qamets followed by a vocal Shewa.

Blackboard 3.3. Recognizing Qamets Hatuph

2. Metheg

Sometimes a Qamets is followed by a vocal Shewa. For example, you could easily (and wrongly) take כָּתְבָה to be a two syllable word (כָּתְ/בָה) pronounced *kot/bâ*. However, it is pronounced as *kā/t̆e/bâ*. The syllabification of the word is כָּ/תְ/בָה. The syllable תְ has a vocal Shewa (not a silent Shewa), and the syllable כָּ has a Qamets (not a Qamets Hatuph). To help the reader in cases like this, the Hebrew Bible often inserts a small, vertical line called a **Metheg** ("bridle") to indicate that there is a short pause after the vowel and that the following consonant does not close the syllable. The presence of the Metheg marks the vowel as Qamets and not Qamets Hatuph. The Metheg is sometimes called a "Gaya."

↑
Metheg

F. The Basic Idea of the Verbless/Nominal Clause

Although Hebrew has a verb that can be translated as "is" or "are" or "am," this verb is not really necessary in a sentence such as the Hebrew equivalent to "David is a king," and it is often left out. When the "to be" verb is left out, the resulting sentence is called a **verbless** or **nominal** clause. Thus, מֶלֶךְ דָּוִד by itself means "David is a king."

(1) The general rule is that the more defined noun is the subject whereas the less defined noun is the predicate. In מֶלֶךְ דָּוִד, the word דָּוִד, being a proper name, is definite, while מֶלֶךְ is indefinite. Therefore, דָּוִד is the subject.

(2) In our example, מֶלֶךְ דָּוִד, the predicate is first, and the subject follows. But the words could be reversed; דָּוִד מֶלֶךְ would also mean "David is a king."

(3) The predicate can also be an adjective ("David is wise"), a prepositional phrase ("David is in Bethlehem"), or an adverb ("David is there").

G. Vocabulary

1. Core Vocabulary

אֲדָמָה	ground, land F |אַדְמַת|
אוֹ	or
אִשָּׁה	woman, wife F |אֵשֶׁת| (plural = נָשִׁים)
בְּרָכָה	blessing F |בִּרְכַּת|
גִּבּוֹר	mighty, strong (adjective); strong man, hero (noun) M |גִּבּוֹר|
חַטָּאת	sin, sin offering F |חַטַּאת|
חָכְמָה	wisdom (חָכְ/מָה with Qamets Hatuph in חָכְ) F |חָכְמַת|
כֹּהֵן	priest M |כֹּהֵן|
עַם	people M |עַם|
רוּחַ	wind, breath, spirit, (divine) Spirit F |רוּחַ|
שָׂדֶה	field M |שְׂדֵה|
שַׁעַר	gate M |שַׁעַר|

2. Proper Names

גֶּזֶר	Gezer
דָּוִד	David
דָּן	Dan (with preposition בְּ, בְּדָן)
יְהוֹשֻׁעַ	Joshua
יַעֲקֹב	Jacob
מֹשֶׁה	Moses
רִבְקָה	Rebekah
רָחֵל	Rachel
תִּמְנָה	Timnah

CHAPTER 4
ACCENT SHIFT AND VOWEL CHANGES

In order to understand the frequent changes in the vowels of biblical Hebrew, you must understand the principles of vowel reduction and lengthening.

A. Definitions

(1) **Open syllable**: A syllable that begins with a consonant but ends with a vowel. In דָּבָר, /דְּ/ is open.

(2) **Closed syllable**: A syllable that is consonant-vowel-consonant. In דָּבָר, /בָר/ is closed.

(3) **Ultima**: The last syllable of a word. In דָּבָר, /בָר/ is the ultima.

(4) **Penult**: The second-to-last syllable. In דָּבָר, /דְּ/ is the penult. In a three-syllable word, it is the second syllable.

(5) **Antepenult**: The third-from-last syllable. In a three-syllable word, it is the first syllable. In אֱלֹהִים, /אֱ/ is the antepenult.

(6) **Tone syllable**: The accented syllable. In דָּבָר, /בָר/ is the tone syllable.

(7) **Pretonic**: The syllable immediately in front of the tone syllable. In דָּבָר, /דְּ/ is pretonic.

(8) **Propretonic**: The syllable immediately in front of the pretonic. Also, any syllable before the pretonic is called a **distant** syllable; it may be the propretonic or be in front of the propretonic. Thus, both the propretonic syllable and any syllable in front of it is "distant." In אֱלֹהִים, /אֱ/ is distant (propretonic also).

(9) **Full vowel**: A long or short vowel such as Qamets or Pathach, but not a vocal Shewa or Hateph vowel (i.e., a composite Shewa).

(10) **Reduced vowel**: A Shewa or Hateph vowel (composite Shewa); not a long or short vowel.

Blackboard 4.1. Syllable Definitions with בְּרָכָה and מִצְרַיִם

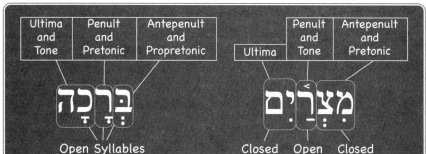

B. General Rules of Vowel Transformation

The rules that follow apply to changeable (full/simple and reduced) vowels. It is important to realize that these rules typically do not apply to the vowels with vowel letters. Remember that "distant" refers to the propretonic and to any syllable in front of the propretonic.

(1) An accented syllable must have a full vowel (i.e., long or short but not reduced). An accented syllable is never reduced. This is true whether the syllable is open or closed. Monosyllable words may be either long or short but will never have just a Shewa.

 ◦ עַם, and עֶֽבֶד, דָּבָר

 ◦ In each example, the accented syllable is long or short but never reduced.

  • The noun דָּבָר has a closed, accented syllable which is long (בָר).

  • The first syllable of עֶֽבֶד (עֶ) is open and accented, and it has a short vowel.

  • The monosyllable עַם is short. In this case, a closed, accented syllable is short.

(2) An open, unaccented syllable is never short. It will be long or reduced.

 ◦ (אֲ/דָ/מָה) אֲדָמָה and (דָּ/בָר) דָּבָר

  • In דָּבָר, /דָּ/ is open, unaccented, and long.

  • In אֲדָמָה, /דָ/ is open, unaccented and long, and /אֲ/ is open, unaccented, and reduced.

(3) A closed, unaccented syllable is short.

 ◦ מַלְכָּה

 ◦ The first syllable (מַל) is closed and unaccented and therefore short.

(4) An open, pretonic is generally long.

 ◦ (אֲ/דָ/מָה) אֲדָמָה and (דָּ/בָר) דָּבָר

 ◦ In both words, the penult (דָ and דָּ) is an open pretonic.

(5) An open, distant syllable generally reduces to Shewa or to a composite Shewa.

 ◦ (אֲ/דָ/מָה) אֲדָמָה and (דְּ/בָ/רִים) דְּבָרִים

 ◦ In both examples, the accent is on the ultima with the result that the antepenults are open and distant. This has caused vowel reduction.

  • In דְּבָרִים, /דְּ/ is reduced.

  • In אֲדָמָה, /אֲ/ is reduced. A composite Shewa is used because א is a guttural.

(6) An open, distant syllable with an unchangeable long vowel will not reduce.

 ◦ שׁוֹפְטִים (remember that this is often written defectively as שֹׁפְטִים)

 ◦ The syllable division is שׁוֹ/פְ/טִים (or שֹׁ/פְ/טִים), and the ultima is accented. The antepenult /שׁוֹ/ is thus open and distant, but the Holem here is unchangeably long and does not reduce.

(7) If the distant syllable will not reduce, an open, pretonic may reduce. This is often seen if the vowel in the pretonic is i-class or u-class, but it sometimes occurs with a-class vowels as well.

 ◦ שׁוֹפְטִים

- The word שׁוֹפְטִים is the plural of the singular noun שׁוֹפֵט. Note the presence of the Tsere (i-class) in the ultima of שׁוֹפֵט.
  - In the plural form שׁוֹפְטִים (שׁוֹ/פְ/טִים), the accent shifts to the new syllable /טִים/ so that /שׁוֹ/ is now an open propretonic (distant). But the Holem-Waw will not reduce, as described in rule 6.
  - Instead, the Tsere of the singular form (שׁוֹ/פֵט) reduces to Shewa in /פְ/ of the plural form. Thus, there is open pretonic reduction in שׁוֹפְטִים.

The rules of accent shift and vowel length are set forth in the tree diagram below.

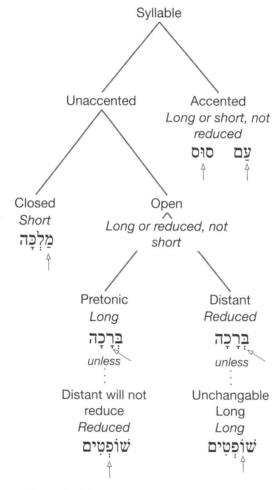

(8) Gutturals and ר will not double. When a guttural or ר ought to be doubled, the preceding vowel is often lengthened to compensate for the lost doubling. This is called **compensatory lengthening**. A vowel made long by compensatory lengthening will not change; it remains long.

- מֵאֲשֶׁר compared to מֵאֲשֶׁר

- For reasons that need not be fully explained here, מִשַּׁעַר means "from a gate." Notice that שַׁעַר, "gate," has מִ in front of it and that the שׁ of שַׁעַר is doubled with a Daghesh Forte.

- The word מֵאָשֵׁר means "from Asher." In this word, the א ought to be doubled (like the שׁ of שַׁעַר) but cannot because it is a guttural. The Tsere under the מ is long by compensatory lengthening (normally, it would have a Hireq, as in מִשַּׁעַר). Therefore it remains long and does not reduce even though it is an open propretonic.

  ○ Compensatory lengthening most often occurs with א, ע, and ר. Often the letters ה and ח do not cause compensatory lengthening even though they do not double.

(9) Sometimes the letter א will "quiesce": the א will have no vowel (not even a silent Shewa), and the preceding vowel will be lengthened. The vowel before a quiescent א is long and does not reduce.

  ○ חַטָּאת

  ○ The ט has a long vowel (Qamets), and the א is quiescent (with no vowel at all).

(10) Hebrew has two vowel combinations that readily contract to single vowels. Contraction occurs when they lose their accents. These two are ַיְ as in עַיִן, "eye," and ָוְ as in מָוֶת, "death." If either ַיְ or ָוְ loses its accent, it contracts to a single long vowel.

  ○ ַיְ becomes ֵי

  ○ ָוְ becomes ֹו

    • עַיִן without its accent becomes עֵין.

    • מָוֶת without its accent becomes מוֹת.

    • We will soon learn why these words would lose their accents.

C. Vocabulary

1. Core Vocabulary

אֹיֵב	enemy (also spelled אוֹיֵב) M	אֹיֵב
זָהָב	gold M	זְהַב
חוֹמָה	wall F	חוֹמַת
כֶּסֶף	silver M	כֶּסֶף
מָוֶת	death M	מוֹת
מַיִם	water M	מֵי
נָבִיא	prophet M	נְבִיא
עַיִן	eye, spring (of water) F	עֵין
צָבָא	army, host, service in war M F	צְבָא
רֹאשׁ	head, top, leader M	רֹאשׁ

שְׁנַיִם   two (with masculine nouns as in שְׁנַיִם מְלָכִים, "two kings," but often seen as שְׁנֵי as in שְׁנֵי מְלָכִים; with feminine nouns שְׁתַּיִם or שְׁתֵּי as in שְׁתֵּי נָשִׁים, "two women")

שָׁמַיִם   heaven(s), sky Ⓜ |שְׁמֵי

2. Proper Names

יְרוּשָׁלַיִם   Jerusalem (often as יְרוּשָׁלַם)

יִשְׂרָאֵל   Israel

מִצְרִי   Egyptian(s)

מִצְרַיִם   Egypt

3. Inflected Vocabulary

נָשִׁים   women (plural of אִשָּׁה)

CHAPTER 5
GENDER AND NUMBER IN NOUNS

A. Gender and Number: An Overview

Hebrew nouns have singular and plural **number**, analogous to the English "horse" and "horses." Hebrew nouns also have masculine and feminine **gender**, analogous to the English "rooster" and "hen." Hebrew has no neuter nouns; *every noun is considered to be either masculine or feminine*, at least grammatically. Using the words סוּס ("[male] horse") and סוּסָה ("mare"), we see the basic pattern for the Hebrew noun.

Table 5.1. The Basic Noun Pattern

	Singular	Plural
Masculine	סוּס horse	סוּסִים horses
Feminine	סוּסָה mare	סוּסוֹת mares

Note:

(1) There is no ending associated with the masculine singular. סוּס means "horse."

(2) The feminine singular often ends in ◌ָה (but it sometimes ends in ◌ַת or ◌ֶת and often has no ending). סוּסָה means "mare."

(3) The masculine plural typically has the ◌ִים ending. סוּסִים means "horses."

(4) The feminine plural typically has the וֹת ending. סוּסוֹת means "mares."

Hebrew also has a **dual** form ◌ַיִם. The dual form indicates that there are two of something, and it is only seen with a few specific nouns. For example, the dual of עַיִן is עֵינַיִם, "two eyes." This is a feminine noun; the ending ◌ַיִם is the same for both masculine and feminine dual nouns. Also, some nouns are dual in *form* but not in *meaning*; an example is מַיִם, "water," and שָׁמַיִם, "heaven."

Table 5.2. Noun Endings

	Singular	Plural	Dual
Masculine	(none)	◌ִים	◌ַיִם
Feminine	◌ָה or ◌ַת or ◌ֶת or none	וֹת	

Table 5.3. Examples of Nouns

Masculine (no ending)	Feminine with ending	Feminine with no ending	Dual
אִישׁ man	אִשָּׁה woman	אֶרֶץ land	שָׁמַיִם heaven
אָב father	תּוֹרָה law	עִיר city	יוֹמַיִם two days
יוֹם day	דַּעַת knowledge	עַיִן eye	עֵינַיִם two eyes

יוֹם, "day," is masculine, but אֶרֶץ, "land," is feminine. Thus in Hebrew one would always refer to יוֹם as a "he" and אֶרֶץ as a "she." There is no "it," although when translating we often must use "it" for the sake of English grammar. As an interpreter, you must distinguish natural gender (living things that are actually male or female) from grammatical gender (gender as part of a grammatical system and applied to nouns that are not intrinsically male or female). Grammatical gender is a way of organizing a language. With a few exceptions, English recognizes only natural gender (everything else is neuter). Hebrew has no neuter, and every noun is masculine or feminine as a grammatical category. The fact that a noun is classed as masculine or feminine in Hebrew does not imply that the noun is metaphorically male or female. You should not suppose that the Hebrew speakers thought of "day" (יוֹם) as ideally masculine.

B. How Plural Nouns are Formed

With the addition of the plural endings, most nouns show changes in their vowels; however, a few do not. When changes occur, they normally follow the rules of accent shift and vowel transformation specified in chapter 4. Many nouns form their plurals according to one of the following patterns.

1. Plurals that Do Not Change the Noun Vowels

a. Monosyllabic nouns with an unchangeable long vowel

The unchangeable vowel, as one would expect, does not change.

סוּס	→	סוּסִים	horse / horses
אוֹת	→	אוֹתוֹת	sign / signs

b. Polysyllabic nouns with Shewa or composite Shewa in the first syllable

יְשׁוּעָה	→	יְשׁוּעוֹת	salvation / acts of salvation

2. Plurals with Propretonic Reduction

The word דָּבָר, "word, thing," is a two-syllable noun. In the singular, it is stressed on the final syllable (the ultima). With the addition of the plural ending, a transformation to דְּבָרִים occurs due to the fact that the accent moves back to the new syllable formed by the plural ending (remember that an open propretonic reduces to Shewa).

Blackboard 5.1. From Singular to Plural with דָּבָר

The following nouns have the same pattern:

| נָבִיא | → | נְבִיאִים | prophet / prophets |
| זָקֵן | → | זְקֵנִים | elder / elders |

3. Plurals with Pretonic Reduction

If for some reason the propretonic cannot reduce, an open pretonic that had contained Tsere will reduce when a plural ending is added. This happens in two types of nouns:

a. Two-syllable nouns with a closed first syllable

An example is מִזְבֵּחַ, "altar." When a plural ending is added, the accent moves back. Because a closed, unaccented syllable is always short, the syllable /מִ/ cannot reduce to Shewa. Thus, the Tsere reduces when the plural ending is added. Recall that if a propretonic cannot reduce, an i- or u-class open pretonic often will reduce.

Blackboard 5.2. From Singular to Plural with מִזְבֵּחַ

b. Two-syllable nouns with an unchangeable long vowel in the first syllable

An example is שׁוֹפֵט, "judge." Because /שׁוֹ/ has an unchangeably long vowel and cannot reduce to Shewa, the Tsere reduces when the plural ending is added. Again, if a propretonic cannot reduce, an i- or u-class open pretonic often will reduce.

Blackboard 5.3. From Singular to Plural with שׁוֹפֵט

By contrast, a two-syllable noun with Qamets in the second syllable will often not have vowel reduction in the same circumstances, as the example below illustrates.

מִשְׁפָּטִים ← מִשְׁפָּט

Remember: when the propretonic will not reduce, an open pretonic often will reduce, but this most often occurs when the pretonic vowel is i-class or u-class. In the case of מִשְׁפָּט → מִשְׁפָּטִים, the open pretonic is a-class and here does not reduce.

C. Irregular Plurals

Many nouns are irregular and unpredictable in their plural forms. Some of the most common are given in the list below. Where the gender of a noun does not match its ending, its gender is mentioned in brackets. Thus, with אָב → אָבוֹת (meaning "fathers"), the word "masculine" in brackets refers to the fact that, although it looks like a feminine plural noun, it is masculine. Here are some examples:

אָב → אָבוֹת father / fathers [masculine]

אִישׁ → אֲנָשִׁים man / men

אִשָּׁה → נָשִׁים woman / women [feminine]

בַּיִת → בָּתִּים house / houses

בֵּן → בָּנִים son / sons

יוֹם → יָמִים day / days

מִזְבֵּחַ → מִזְבְּחוֹת altar / altars [masculine]

עִיר → עָרִים city / cities [feminine]

D. Additional Notes on Feminine Plurals

(1) When the plural ending וֹת is added, the singular ending הָ disappears.

(2) A two-syllable word with an initial closed syllable may become a three-syllable word when it becomes plural.

מַלְכָה → מְלָכוֹת queen / queens

E. Vocabulary

1. Core Vocabulary

אָב father Ⓜ |אֲבִי| (irregular plural אָבוֹת)

אוֹת sign ⓂⒻ |אוֹת|

בַּיִת house Ⓜ |בֵּית| (irregular plural בָּתִּים)

בֵּן son Ⓜ |בֶּן| (irregular plural בָּנִים)

דָּם   blood Ⓜ |דָּם|

יוֹם   day Ⓜ |יוֹם| (irregular plural יָמִים)

יְשׁוּעָה   salvation (also seen as יְשׁוּעָתָה) Ⓕ |יְשׁוּעַת|

כְּ   as, like (attached directly to a noun, as in כְּדָוִד, "like David")

מִזְבֵּחַ   altar Ⓜ |מִזְבַּח|

מִצְוָה   command Ⓕ |מִצְוַת| (plural מִצְוֹת with consonantal ו)

עוֹלָה   whole burnt offering (also spelled עֹלָה) Ⓕ |עֹלַת|

תּוֹרָה   instruction, teaching, law Ⓕ |תּוֹרַת|

2. Inflected Vocabulary

וַיְהִי   "and there was" (for now, treat this as a past tense form of יֵשׁ [used
             with a masculine singular noun; it can also mean "and (he) was" as
             in וַיְהִי מֹשֶׁה, "and Moses was"])

CHAPTER 6
HEBREW VERBS

A. Inflected Verbs

1. Using Inflected Verbs

Consider the following:

(1) יִפֹּל by itself can be translated "he will fall," but the subject is always masculine and singular. This verb is **inflected**, meaning that it is in a specific form that indicates, among other things, gender (masculine) and number (singular).

(2) As you know, מֶלֶךְ means "(a) king" and is a masculine, singular noun.

(3) Thus, what does מֶלֶךְ יִפֹּל mean? "A king will fall."

It is not necessary to comprehend fully the complexities of Hebrew grammar in order to begin to read sentences with verbs. One can begin by using a small set of inflected verbs.

2. Glosses and Alternative Translations

Look at יִפֹּל in the box below and see that it has several possible meanings, including, "(he) will fall," "(he) should fall," "(he) is going to fall," and "(he) used to fall."

Meaning	Verb	Gloss	Alternative Translations
fall	יִפֹּל	(he) will fall	(he) should fall / used to fall / is falling

(1) The first translation given after each form in the chart (such as "[he] will fall" for יִפֹּל) is the **gloss**. This is a simplified, basic translation that you can give in the absence of any context.

(2) The **alternative translations** represent other conceivable translations that you may use, depending on context.

(3) Notice that יִפֹּל can refer to the future ("he will fall"), to the past ("he used to fall"), to the subjunctive ("he should fall"), or to the present durative ("he is falling")

(4) All the translations of יִפֹּל basically mean to "fall," and all have an implied subject "he." יִפֹּל is never translated simply as "fall" but as "*he* will fall" or in a way similar to the other listed translations. תִּפֹּל (a feminine form of the same verb) is used if you mean to say "*She* will fall."

(5) Even other meanings are also possible! יִפֹּל could mean "May he fall." The reasons that one verb form can have so many meanings are given below.

It is important to understand that an inflected verb like יִפֹּל can be translated differently in different contexts. If you learn only the meaning "(he) will fall" for יִפֹּל, you may find yourself bewildered by texts where a future tense makes no sense. It it is hard to "unlearn" misconceptions.

Table 6.1. Some Inflected Verbs

Meaning	Verb	Gloss	Alternative Translations
arise	קָם	(he) arose	(he) arises; (he) has / had arisen
	יָקוּמוּ	(they) will arise	(they) should arise / used to arise / are arising
encircle	וַיָּסָב	and (he) encircled, went about	and (he) encircles, goes about
fall	יִפֹּל	(he) will fall	(he) should fall / used to fall / is falling
	תִּפֹּל	(she) will fall	(she) should fall / used to fall / is falling
give	אֶתֵּן	(I) will give	(I) should give / used to give / am giving

How can you deal with all these possible meanings?

(1) *First, memorize the gloss translations*. Memorize that יִפֹּל means "(he) will fall," just as you memorized that מֶלֶךְ means "king."

(2) Then, take into account that every verb with "will (do)" in its gloss can also mean "should (do)" or "used to (do)" or "is (doing)."

(3) Similarly, first learn that קָם means "(he) arose." But take into account that it could also mean "arises" or "has arisen."

If it seems astonishing that a single verb form like קָם could be both past and present, remember that English has many verbs that are similar. Compare the following two examples: "I *hit* the ball yesterday" (past); "I *hit* a punching bag every day" (present). We use this verb and others like it without confusion or ambiguity.

B. Names for Hebrew Verb Types

If you look at the **gloss** translations in the above list, you will see three verb types:

(1) Several have the future as their gloss, such as יִפֹּל, "(he) will fall." These are traditionally called **imperfect** verbs, but today they are commonly called *yiqtol* verbs.

(2) One verb has the simple past as its gloss: קָם, "(he) arose." This kind of verb form is traditionally called the **perfect** tense, but it is now often called the *qatal* verb.

(3) One verb has the simple past meaning with the word "and" in its gloss: וַיָּסָב, "and (he) encircled." This kind of verb typically begins with ו followed directly by a letter with Daghesh Forte, as you see in וַיָּסָב. We will call these the *wayyiqtol* verbs.

C. Gender, Number, and Person in Verbs

The **gender**, **number**, and **person** of the subject is implied in the form of the Hebrew verb.

(1) Hebrew verbs are inflected for **gender**.

    (a) If a verb is **masculine** in gender, it takes a masculine subject.

    (b) If a verb is **feminine** in gender, it takes a feminine subject.

(c) Some verb forms are **common** in gender, meaning that the subject can be either masculine or feminine.

(2) Hebrew verbs are also inflected for **number**, indicating whether the subject is singular or plural.

(3) Hebrew verbs are also inflected for **person**, including first person ("I, we"), second person ("you"), and third person ("he, she, they").

To better understand gender, number, and person, observe the following:

(1) יִפֹּל means "(he) will fall," but תִּפֹּל means "(she) will fall." Both are singular and both are third person, but the former is masculine while the latter is feminine.

(2) Of course, you can use a noun as the subject of the verb, as in מֶלֶךְ יִפֹּל, "a king will fall." The **gender** and **number** of the verb should agree with the noun; both מֶלֶךְ and יִפֹּל are masculine and singular. If you wanted to say "A woman will fall," it would be a mistake to use יִפֹּל since that is the masculine form of the verb. Since תִּפֹּל is the feminine form, you would say אִשָּׁה תִּפֹּל.

(3) The verb יָקוּמוּ is a *yiqtol* that is both masculine and plural. It means "(they) will arise." This verb must have a plural subject, as in the phrase מְלָכִים יָקוּמוּ, "kings will arise." You cannot use the singular noun מֶלֶךְ as the subject of the plural verb יָקוּמוּ. Notice also that in מְלָכִים יָקוּמוּ the subject (מְלָכִים), like the verb, is masculine.

(4) Notice that אֶתֵּן means "I will give." It is first person singular. It is also **common** in **gender**, meaning that the speaker could be a male or a female.

D. Verb Tense, Mood, Aspect, and Voice

1. Defining Terms

English speakers have been taught to think of verbs first in terms of **tense** and then in terms of **mood** (or **modality**) and **voice**. We also need to be aware of **aspect**.

(1) **Tense** tells us whether the situation expressed by the verb is past, present, or future. English uses, for example, simple past ("he *ate* it") and future ("he *will eat* it").

(2) **Mood** or **modality** tells us whether the action or state expressed in a verb is actual ("was," "is," "will") or merely possible ("may," "would," "could").

(a) For actual situations, we have the **indicative** mood ("he *eats* vegetables").

(b) For possible situations, we have the **subjunctive** mood ("he *should eat* vegetables"). A subjunctive verb can be described as **non-indicative** or as a **modal**.

(i) Modals can express what is possible but not certain ("He *could die*").

(ii) Some modals are classed as **volitives**, because they express the volition or desire of the speaker, as in "he *should go*."

(iii) Modals can also express purpose ("he stood by the road so that he *would see* her go by").

(3) **Aspect** relates to how a speaker portrays an action, whether it is presented as a whole event ("it happened") or as a process ("it was happening"). There are two aspects we are concerned with: **perfective** and **imperfective**.

(a) **Perfective** aspect portrays an action as a whole. Its focus is on *the fact that* an action took place, as opposed to viewing an activity *in process* as it happens or happened. English examples of perfectives would be as follows:

  (i) *The professor ate the apple*. This is a past action viewed as a whole, stated as a simple act that took place in the past.

  (ii) *He has eaten the apple*. This is completed action.

  (iii) *He eats apples*. Here, although the tense is present, the action is portrayed as a whole rather than as ongoing. It could answer the question, "Should I give him an apple to eat?" and imply, "Yes, give him one; he likes them." This is not the same as "He *is eating* apples," which indicates ongoing activity in the present. Notice also that *He eats apples* is perfective but does not imply a completed action; it merely states that such an action takes place.

(b) **Imperfective** aspect portrays an action *in process* rather than as a whole. It is sometimes open-ended as to the outcome, and it may be habitual or repeated.

  (i) *He was walking home after work*. Focus is on the process of walking home. It is open-ended because we don't know if he made it home or not. Contrast "He walked home after work," which is perfective in that it portrays the action as a whole and implies the outcome: he arrived at his home.

  (ii) *I used to walk home*. This describes an action that habitually took place in the past.

(4) **Voice** tells us whether the subject of a verb acts or is acted upon. For voice, English has the **active** ("Bill *hit* the ball") and the **passive** ("The ball *was hit* by Bill").

2. An Overview of Tense, Mood, Aspect and Voice in Biblical Hebrew

Many western languages, such as French, Latin, and Greek, have elaborate inflection systems that explicitly mark their verbs with such things as past and present tense or indicative and subjunctive mood. In contrast, biblical Hebrew finite verbs do not inflect verbs specifically for tense or mood. No Hebrew verb form is solely used for the "future tense" or the "indicative mood," but for the *yiqtol*, *qatal*, and *wayyiqtol*, these general rules apply:

(1) **Tense**: The *yiqtol* is more likely to be future, and the *qatal* and *wayyiqtol* are more likely to be past. Any of them can be present tense in certain contexts.

(2) **Mood**: The *qatal* and *wayyiqtol* are much more likely to be indicative (a real situation), whereas the the *yiqtol* may be either indicative or non-indicative (a possible or desirable situation).

(3) **Aspect**: The *qatal* and *wayyiqtol* are generally perfective. A speaker who wishes to indicate imperfective action is more likely to use the *yiqtol*. But this does not mean that every *yiqtol* implies continuous or repeated action. The *yiqtol* is likely to be imperfective if it is in the past or present tense (not future) and is indicative (not modal).

(4) **Voice**: Hebrew has a way of marking the passive voice independently of whether the verb is *yiqtol*, *qatal*, or *wayyiqtol*. We will deal with the passive later in our study. For now, all the verbs we are looking at are active.

E. Tense in the Hebrew Verb

Although the various Hebrew conjugations are not by nature specific about tense, certain verb types more naturally align with past or non-past contexts.

1. The Uses of Yiqtol, Qatal, and Wayyiqtol for Tense

(1) **Yiqtol** verbs are often **future** tense. This is why the gloss for יִפֹּל is "he *will fall*." However, the *yiqtol* can mark ongoing present activity or recurrent past action. A *yiqtol* is rarely translated as a simple past, such as "he fell." Here are two places where one might use יִפֹּל as the verb:

   (a) Future tense: "Within a year that evil man *will fall*." The *yiqtol* here marks a simple act (not repeated action or action in process) in the future.

   (b) Past imperfect: "The old man *would fall* when he tried to walk." Notice that this is imperfective and not a simple past tense as in, "He fell when he tried to walk."

(2) **Qatal** verbs most commonly represent the **past** tense, and thus the gloss for קָם is "he *arose*." Yet *qatal* does not equal past tense, as it can also mark present or typical events. Also, the *qatal* may or may not describe completed action.

   (a) Simple past tense: "He *rose* to power at a young age." The simple past is the default translation (the gloss).

   (b) A past tense indicating completed action: "He *has arisen*."

   (c) Not past tense or completed action, but a timeless fact: "The people *rise* when the king enters the room."

(3) **Wayyiqtol** verbs often express **simple past** action (and also have the conjunction "and"), and thus the gloss for וַיָּסָב is "*and* he *encircled*." This is the default. There are other uses for the *wayyiqtol*, but we will not encounter these for some time.

2. How do You Tell the Difference?

We have seen that יִפֹּל might mean "he will fall" or "he used to fall." Both meanings are indicative (not subjunctive/modal). But how do you tell whether יִפֹּל is future or is past in meaning?

(1) The basic answer is **context**. This describes the situation in which a statement is made. If יִפֹּל is in a narrative about the past, it is a past imperfective ("he used to fall"). If יִפֹּל is in a future context, it has a future meaning. The future meaning of the *yiqtol* is far more common than the past imperfect.

(2) Context will also determine the tense of a *qatal* or *wayyiqtol* verb. The *qatal* in verbs describing what one thinks or feels is often present tense. For example, "They *know* (this is a *qatal* verb) the way of YHWH" (Jer 5:5); "I *love* (this is a *qatal* verb) the habitation of your house" (Ps 26:8). But usually *qatal* and *wayyiqtol* are past tense.

(3) In the absence of context (as in the exercise sentences), use the default translation.

F. Mood in the Hebrew Verb: The *Yiqtol*

As explained, a speaker can describe a situation as actual (indicative mood) or as merely desirable or possible (non-indicative or modal). For non-indicative statements, Hebrew is far more likely to use a *yiqtol* than a *qatal* or *wayyiqtol*. There are patterns in which Hebrew uses a *qatal* for a non-indicative, such as in **contrary-to-fact** statements (a *qatal* is used in, "we *would have been* like Sodom" [Isa 1:9]), but these are not common. We will focus here on non-indicative statements that employ the *yiqtol*.

The basic question is this: How do you tell whether a *yiqtol* such as יִפֹּל is a future indicative, "He *will fall*," or a modal, "He *should fall*"? Once again, you need to be aware of **context**, but you also need to look at **syntax**. Context is the situation in which a statement is made, and syntax is how a sentence is put together (its word order and its use of certain modifiers such as "perhaps" or "in order that").

1. Context and Mood

First, you should not be surprised that context is important for understanding *yiqtol* verbs. Context is important in many languages. For example, in English we say that "will (do)" is future tense, but it is actually more complex than that. Consider the following:

(1) An investment counselor tells a client, "Don't worry, you *will* make money this year." The counselor is making a prediction (future tense).

(2) A sergeant tells his troops, "You *will* stay together and you *will* not talk!" He is not making a prediction; he is giving a command.

(3) An employee tells a co-worker, "I *will* ask the boss for a raise!" He is not really making a prediction; he is expressing determination to do something.

There is nothing that distinguishes these three sentences grammatically, but in each case the meaning of "will (do)" is different. The important point is this: *Context often plays a key role in determining the mood of a verb.*

For now, the sentences you see in the exercises will have little if any context. Most of these *yiqtol* verbs can be translated with the gloss: you can render יִפֹּל as "(he) will fall" and not worry about other meanings. As you progress, however, pay attention to context and don't automatically translate every *yiqtol* as future indicative.

2. Syntax and Mood

There is one general rule of Hebrew **syntax** that can help you refine your translation: pay attention to where the *yiqtol* verb is placed in the sentence. This will help you determine whether the verb is indicative or non-indicative (modal).

(1) *If the* yiqtol *is the first word in the sentence, it is probably modal.* Thus, when it is the first word in a sentence, a *yiqtol* verb usually means "he *should do*" or "*may he* do," or it expresses possibility or determination to do something.

(2) *If the* yiqtol *is not the first word in the sentence, it is probably indicative.* Remember: depending on **context**, it could be a future ("he will do") or a past imperfect ("he used to do"). Most often, it will be future, and this should be your default translation.

There are exceptions to the above rules. For example:

(1) *A* yiqtol *in a question may be modal regardless of its position in a sentence.* As a question, אִשָּׁה תִּפֹּל בַּצָּבָא could mean "*Should* a woman *fall* in battle?"

(2) *Occasionally a* yiqtol *is modal even when it is not first*. This is often the case when God is the subject. Therefore, while a sentence like אֱלֹהִים יִתֵּן אוֹת might mean "God will give a sign," it could mean "May God give a sign!"

(3) *If the* yiqtol *is in a conditional statement, the question of indicative or non-indicative is determined by context.*

    (a) A conditional statement is an "If... then..." sentence. The "if" clause is called a **protasis**, and the "then" clause is called an **apodosis**, as in the following:

        (i) **Protasis**: "If you worship other gods,"

        (ii) **Apodosis**: "then you will die."

    (b) Similar patterns are found where the conditional sentence is **temporal** ("When... then...") or **causal** ("Because... therefore...").

    (c) In such cases, word position does not indicate whether a *yiqtol* is indicative or non-indicative; it is simply **conditional**, and the translation you apply will depend on context.

G. Aspect and the Hebrew Verb: The *Yiqtol*

For the imperfective aspect, the *yiqtol* is much more likely to be used than the *qatal* and *wayyiqtol*. In many cases, however, even the *yiqtol* does not describe repeated or habitual action, and there is no reason to think of it as describing a process. This is especially so if the *yiqtol* is either future tense or non-indicative, as in these two examples:

(1) Future: "He who is near *will fall* (יִפֹּל) by the sword" (Ezek 6:12).

(2) Non-indicative: "A thousand *may fall* (יִפֹּל) at your feet" (Ps 91:7).

An imperfective aspect for a *yiqtol* is more likely if the sentence is either past or present tense and in the indicative mood, as in these two examples:

(1) Present imperfective: "Why do you *keep looking* (this is a *yiqtol* verb) at each other?" (Gen 42:1).

(2) Past imperfective: "Whenever the cloud was taken up... the Israelites *would move out* (this is a *yiqtol* verb) on each stage of their journey" (Exod 40:36).

H. Summary of Important Points

Here are the main points of this chapter:

(1) Hebrew verbs are inflected for **gender** (male or female), **number** (singular or plural), and **person** (first, second, or third person). A verb and its subject should agree in gender, number, and person. For example, one does not use a masculine subject with a feminine verb or use the pronoun "I" as the subject of a third person verb.

(2) Hebrew verbs are not strictly inflected for tense (such as past or future) or mood (such as indicative or subjunctive), but Hebrew can express tense, mood, and aspect through *qatal*, *yiqtol*, and *wayyiqtol* verbs in specific contexts.

(3) Hebrew has a way of showing the passive voice, but we have not yet studied it.

(4) At this point, you have learned about three types or conjugations of verbs:

(a) *Qatal* (traditionally, the **perfect**): This verb has the past tense, indicative mood, and perfective aspect as its default but may be present or present perfect in tense.

(b) *Wayyiqtol*: This verb has the past tense, indicative mood, and perfective aspect as its default, and it has "and" in front of it (as in "*and* he *did*").

(c) *Yiqtol* (traditionally, the **imperfect**): This verb has the future indicative as its default, but context and syntax are important for determining its function.

   (i) If it is the first word in a sentence, a *yiqtol* verb is often modal (non-indicative), as in "he *should do*."

   (ii) If it is not in the first position, a *yiqtol* is usually indicative. There are exceptions to this (see the table below). Depending on context, the *yiqtol* may be used for future action ("he *will do*") or for past action ("he *used to do*"). The future is far more common.

   (iii) If it is in a past or present tense indicative statement, the *yiqtol* is probably imperfective in aspect.

The following chart will give you some basic guidelines about determining the tense, mood, and aspect of *yiqtol* verbs.

For the new vocabulary used in this chart, see the table of verbs on the next page.

Table 6.2. General Rules for the *Yiqtol* (Imperfect) Verb

*The **default** is **future indicative**.*	מֶלֶךְ יִפֹּל	A king *will fall*.	
*In the **first position**,* *the* yiqtol *usually is **modal**.*	יִתֵּן אֱלֹהִים אוֹת	*May* God *give* a sign!	
*Not in the **first position**,* *the* yiqtol *usually is **indicative**.*	כֹּהֵן יִתֵּן בְּרָכָה	A priest *will give* a blessing!	
*In a **question**, a* yiqtol ***not in the first** position* *may be **modal**.*	אִשָּׁה תִּפֹּל בְּצָבָא	*Should* a woman *fall* in battle?	
If God is the subject, a yiqtol ***not in** the first position* *may be **modal**.*	אֱלֹהִים יִתֵּן אוֹת	*May* God *give* a sign!	
If the yiqtol *is **indicative**,* *the **context** determines its **tense**.*	... יִפֹּל ...	Tomorrow *he will fall*	In his childhood, *he used to fall*
If the yiqtol *is **indicative** and **past** or **present**, it is probably **imperfective**.*	... יִפֹּל ...	He *used to fall* a lot when he skied, but he is better now.	
*A **conditional** sentence: **Protasis*** ***Apodosis***	אִם יֶחֱטָא אִישׁ יִפֹּל	If a man *should sin*, he *will fall*.	

I. Vocabulary

1. Inflected Vocabulary

Qatal and *wayyiqtol* verbs are in gray boxes; *yiqtol* verbs are in white.

Meaning	Verb	Gloss	Alternative Translations
arise	קָם	(he) arose	(he) arises / has arisen
	יָקֹ֫ומוּ	(they) will arise	(they) should arise / used to arise / are arising
choose	יִבְחַר	(he) will choose	(he) should choose / used to choose / is choosing
encircle	יָסֹב	(he) will encircle, go about	(he) should encircle, go about / used to encircle, go about / is encircling, going about
	וַיָּ֫סָב	and (he) encircled	and (he) encircles
fall	יִפֹּל	(he) will fall	(he) should fall / used to fall / is falling
	תִּפֹּל	(she) will fall	(she) should fall / used to fall / is falling
find	יִמְצָא	(he) will find	(he) should find / used to find / is finding
give	יִתֵּן	(he) will give	(he) should give / used to give / is giving
	אֶתֵּן	(I) will give	(I) should give / used to give / am giving
give birth	יָלְדָה	(she) bore	(she) bears / has borne
hear	יִשְׁמַע	(he) will hear	(he) should hear / used to hear / is hearing
	תִּשְׁמַע	(she) will hear	(she) should hear / used to hear / is hearing
kill	קָטַל	(he) killed	(he) kills / has killed
sin	יֶחֱטָא	(he) will sin	(he) should sin / used to sin / is sinning

2. Core Vocabulary

אִם   if

לְ   to, for (directly attached to a noun, as in לְדָוִד, "for David")

לְמַ֫עַן   "for the sake of" (with a following noun, as in לְמַ֫עַן דָּוִד, "for the sake of David"); "in order that, so that" (with a following *yiqtol*, as in לְמַ֫עַן יִתֵּן, "so that he may give")

CHAPTER 7
THE DIRECTIVE הָ, NEGATIVE לֹא, AND INTERROGATIVE הַ

A. Directive הָ

If a noun or pronoun that refers to a place (e.g., מִצְרַיִם, "Egypt") has an unaccented ending הָ attached to it (e.g., מִצְרַיְמָה), the word describes motion toward that place ("to Egypt"). If the word already has the feminine ending הָ, the ending with directive הָ added becomes תָה. For example, תִּמְנָה, "Timnah," with directive הָ becomes תִּמְנָתָה, "to Timnah."

Table 7.1. Examples of the Directive הָ

יְרוּשָׁלַיִם	Jerusalem	יְרוּשָׁלַיְמָה	to Jerusalem
אֶרֶץ	land	אַרְצָה	to the land
שָׁם	there	שָׁמָּה	to there
תִּמְנָה	Timnah	תִּמְנָתָה	to Timnah

The directive הָ can also mean "in" a place. Thus, תִּמְנָתָה could mean "in Timnah."

B. The Negative לֹא

The word לֹא means "no" or "not," and it is usually put at the beginning of a clause. If there is a verb, לֹא is generally directly in front of the verb. לֹא יִשְׁמַע אִישׁ means "A man will not hear." When a verb has the negative לֹא, the subject is almost always immediately after the verb, as in the above example.

C. The Interrogative הַ

1. Function

A question is often introduced by the particle הַ prefixed to the first word of a sentence. An example is הֲמֶלֶךְ יִפֹּל ("Will a king fall?"). This is the interrogative הַ. It tells you that the sentence is a question and not an assertion.

(1) It can be attached to any kind of word, be it verb, noun, or particle. It is always at the beginning of the sentence.

(2) Use of the interrogative הַ is optional; some questions do not use it. If it is not used and if one of the other interrogatives (whether adverb or pronoun) is not explicit, one can determine only by context whether a sentence is interrogative.

(3) Sometimes the interrogative הַ is prefixed to the negative לֹא to introduce a rhetorical question: "Is it not (the case that)…?" For example, הֲלֹא יָלְדָה בֵן means "Is it not the case that she bore a son?" (or more simply, "Didn't she bear a son?").

2. Form

(1) The interrogative הַ is usually pointed with Hateph Pathach (הֲ), as in הֲמֶלֶךְ.

(2) When attached to a word beginning with a guttural or to a word having Shewa as its first vowel, the interrogative ה is usually vocalized as הַ.

    (a) For example, עוֹד means "still" and הַעוֹד means "Is it still (the case that)…?" Thus, הַעוֹד דָּוִד שָׁם would mean "Is it still (the case that) David (is) there?" (in other words, "Is David still there?"). Note that this is a verbless/nominal clause.

    (b) Similarly, "Is there not a horse?" would be written as הַאֵין סוּס.

(3) When attached to a guttural pointed with Qamets or Hateph Qamets, the interrogative ה is pointed with a Seghol (הֶ), as in הֶאָב שָׁם, "Is father there?"

D. The Verb וַיֹּאמֶר

One of the most common verbs in the Hebrew Bible is וַיֹּאמֶר, meaning "and he said." It is a verb of the *wayyiqtol* type and like many such verbs is accented on the penult. Learn this verb well and pronounce it with the accentuation in the proper syllable.

Blackboard 7.1. The Syllable Division and Accentuation of וַיֹּאמֶר

E. Vocabulary

1. Inflected Vocabulary

Table 7.2. More Inflected Verbs

Meaning	Verb	Gloss	Alternative Translations
love	יֶאֱהַב	(he) will love	(he) should love / used to love / is loving
possess	יִירַשׁ	(he) will possess	(he) should possess / used to possess / is possessing
	תִּירַשׁ	(she) will possess	(she) should possess / used to possess / is possessing
return	שָׁב	(he) returned	(he) returns / has returned
	שָׁבָה	(she) returned	(she) returns / has returned
	שָׁבוּ	(they) returned	(they) return / have returned
	יָשׁוּב	(he) will return	(he) should return / used to return / is returning
	וַיָּשָׁב	and (he) returned	and (he) returns

say	יֹאמַר	(he) will say	(he) should say / used to say / is saying
	וַיֹּאמֶר	and (he) said	and (he) says
sit	יֵשֵׁב	(he) will sit, dwell	(he) should sit, dwell / used to sit, dwell / is sitting, dwelling
	תֵּשֵׁב	(she) will sit, dwell	(she) should sit, dwell / used to sit, dwell / is sitting, dwelling
	וַיֵּשֶׁב	and (he) sat, dwelt	and (he) sits, dwells
	וַתֵּשֶׁב	and (she) sat, dwelt	and (she) sits, dwells
stand	יַעֲמֹד	(he) will stand	(he) should stand / used to stand / is standing
	תַּעֲמֹד	(she) will stand	(she) should stand / used to stand / is standing

2. Core Vocabulary

אֶל   to, toward (often with Maqqeph ["joiner"], a hyphen-like mark [־], as in אֶל־תִּמְנָה, "to Timnah")

הֲ   (interrogative particle)

לֹא   no, not, never

עוֹד   still, yet

שָׁם   there

3. Proper Names

יוֹסֵף   Joseph

שְׁלֹמֹה   Solomon

CHAPTER 8 ·
THE DEFINITE ARTICLE

A. Rules for the Definite Article

The Hebrew word for "horse" or "a horse" is סוּס. There is no indefinite article ("a") in Hebrew. The definite article in Hebrew is the counterpart to "the" in English. In Hebrew, "the horse" is הַסּוּס.

Blackboard 8.1. The Definite Article

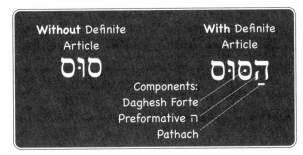

(1) A noun is made definite by prefixing the definite article, which consists of הַ plus Daghesh Forte in the first consonant of the noun. Therefore, סוּס with the definite article is הַסּוּס.

(2) When prefixing a definite article to a noun with an initial "begadkephat" consonant, the initial Daghesh Lene becomes a Daghesh Forte. For example, בַּיִת with the definite article is הַבַּיִת with a doubled letter בּ.

(3) A guttural or ר cannot be doubled.

   (a) With א, ר, and often with ע, Hebrew compensates by lengthening the vowel of the article from Pathach (◌ַ) to Qamets (◌ָ). For example, אִישׁ with the definite article is הָאִישׁ with "compensatory lengthening."

   (b) With nouns that begin with gutturals ח or ה, "virtual doubling" applies. This simply means that the vowel remains short, as though the guttural had been doubled. For example, חוּמָה with the definite article is הַחוּמָה with virtual doubling. Because of virtual doubling, the definite article is treated as if it were a closed, unaccented syllable, and therefore it is short.

(4) Before nouns that begin with unaccented עָ or הָ, and always before חָ (the vowel in each case is Qamets, not Qamets Hatuph), the article is הֶ without Daghesh Forte. For example:

   (a) חָכָם with the definite article is הֶחָכָם.

   (b) עָפָר with the definite article is הֶעָפָר.

(5) A few nouns change a vowel of the noun when the definite article is added.

   (a) אֶרֶץ with the definite article is הָאָרֶץ.

(b) הַר with the definite article is הָהָר.

(c) עַם with the definite article is הָעָם.

(6) With some exceptions, words that begin with the syllables יְ or מְ lose the Daghesh Forte with the article. For example, יְשָׁרִים with the definite article is הַיְשָׁרִים.

(7) The definite article should not be confused with the interrogative ה. Contrast the interrogative in הֲמֶלֶךְ ("is a king…?") with the article in הַמֶּלֶךְ ("the king").

   (a) In case you are wondering: the interrogative ה is never affixed to a definite article, so you will never see the two together.

   (b) The definite article will never occur on a verb, whereas the interrogative ה frequently does.

Table 8.1. Nouns with the Definite Article

Patterns	Without Article	With Article
Basic Pattern	מֶלֶךְ a king	הַמֶּלֶךְ the king
	זָקֵן elder	הַזָּקֵן the elder
With begadkephat Letter	בַּיִת house	הַבַּיִת the house
	דֶּרֶךְ road	הַדֶּרֶךְ the road
Before א, ע, or ר	אִישׁ man	הָאִישׁ the man
	רֹאשׁ head	הָרֹאשׁ the head
	עִיר city	הָעִיר the city
Before ה or ח	חוֹמָה wall	הַחוֹמָה the wall
Before *unaccented* עָ or הָ, and always before חָ	חָכָם a wise man	הֶחָכָם the wise man
	עָפָר dust	הֶעָפָר the dust
Irregular vowel changes in the article or noun	אֶרֶץ earth, land	הָאָרֶץ the earth
	הַר mountain	הָהָר the mountain
	עַם people	הָעָם the people
Before יְ	יְשָׁרִים upright ones	הַיְשָׁרִים the upright ones

B. The Definite Article with an Inseparable Preposition

If a preposition such as בְּ is added to a word with a definite article, the preposition displaces the ה of the article, but the vowel and Daghesh Forte of the definite article remain in place.

Blackboard 8.2. Preposition Added to a Noun with the Article

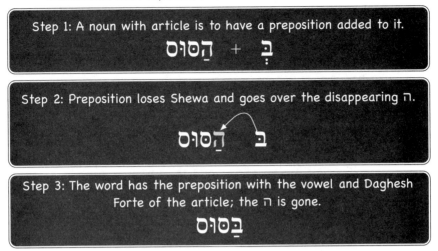

Similarly, הָעִיר with בְּ is בָּעִיר, "in the city," and הֶעָפָר with בְּ is בֶּעָפָר, "in the dust."

The same rule works with כְּ, "like, as," and לְ, "to, for." That is, when כְּ is added to הַסּוּס, it becomes כַּסּוּס. When לְ is added to הַסּוּס, it becomes לַסּוּס.

C. Additional Note on Shewa and the Daghesh Forte

Often a Daghesh Forte will be "lost" in a consonant that has a Shewa (e.g., וַיְהִי where we would expect וַיְּהִי as with other *wayyiqtol* verbs). This occurs with sibilants (שׁ, שׂ, צ, ס, ז) and with the consonants ק, נ, מ, ל, ו, י. Some remember these consonants through the artificial memory words *SQiNeM-LeVI* (סקנם לוי), the ס standing for all sibilants.

D. The Direct Object Marker

In Hebrew, definite direct objects are usually marked with אֶת־. It may appear as אֵת or אֶת (without Maqqeph). This word has no English translation and can be regarded as a grammatical tag.

הַנָּבִיא יִתֵּן אֶת־הַסֵּפֶר	The prophet will give the book.
הַגִּבּוֹר יִשְׁמַע אֶת־הַמֶּלֶךְ	The hero will hear the king.

(1) In each of the above cases, the direct object is definite because it has a definite article. If any of the nouns had not been definite (or had not been the direct object), it would not have had the object marker אֶת־.

(2) Proper nouns are by nature definite. A proper noun that is a direct object can be marked with אֶת־, as in:

הָעָם יִשְׁמַע אֶת־שְׁמוּאֵל	The people will hear Samuel.

(3) In a construction that has several definite direct objects, one or all nouns may be marked with אֶת־.

(4) On the other hand, the direct object marker is not necessary and may be omitted.

(5) Indefinite direct objects are not marked with אֶת־.

E. Construct Nouns and the Definite Article

There are two important rules regarding construct nouns and the definite article.

(1) A noun in the construct form never takes the definite article.

(2) In a construct chain, however, if the noun in the absolute has the definite article, the construct is regarded as definite.

Blackboard 8.3. The Definite Article in a Construct Chain

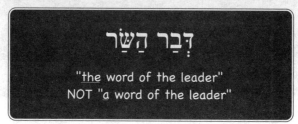

דְּבַר הַשַּׂר

"the word of the leader"
NOT "a word of the leader"

F. Vocabulary

1. Core Vocabulary

אֶבֶן	stone [F] |אֶבֶן|
אוֹר	light [F] |אוֹר|
אֲשֶׁר	who, which, that
דֶּרֶךְ	road, way, path [M] [F] |דֶּרֶךְ|
הַר	hill, mountain [M] |הַר|
חָכָם	wise (adjective), wise man/woman (noun) [M] [F] |חָכָם|
יָשָׁר	upright (adjective), upright man/woman (noun) [M] [F] |יָשָׁר|
לֵב	heart (an alternative form of this word is לֵבָב) [M] |לֵב *or* לֵבָב|
לֶחֶם	bread [M] |לֶחֶם|
עָפָר	dust [M] |עָפָר|

2. Reading Vocabulary

אַשְׁרֵי	"blessings of" (from a hypothetical noun אֶשֶׁר); used idiomatically in אַשְׁרֵי־הָאִישׁ to mean "Blessed is the man" or "Happy is the man"

G. Guided Reading from Psalm 1

By means of the guided readings you will now begin to work with actual biblical Hebrew. The explanations that go with the readings are complete enough to allow you to understand the text, but they do not go into all the grammatical details. The readings serve as previews of grammar that is to come and also as reinforcement for grammar and vocabulary already studied. Read the text with the notes and work through the text until you can read all the way through with understanding. Then, read through the text as many times as possible for practice and learning. As a rule, you should read every biblical text fifteen times. These readings will give you a sense of the look and feel of actual Hebrew text.

אַשְׁרֵי־הָאִישׁ אֲשֶׁר

(1) You should now recognize the word אִישׁ with the definite article.

(2) With אַשְׁרֵי, the two together mean "Happy is the man."

(3) אֲשֶׁר is the relative pronoun "who," so that the whole line means "Happy is the man who…" Obviously, this is only the beginning of a verse. It is continued in the next chapter's reading.

(4) Notice the poetic use of *assonance* (words that sound alike) in the words אַשְׁרֵי־הָאִישׁ אֲשֶׁר.

CHAPTER 9
ROOTS, STEMS, AND THE QAL *QATAL*

A. Hebrew Roots

1. An Overview

In English, using the basic word *walk*, we can create various inflections such as *walks*, *walked*, or *walking*. In Hebrew, you can see many examples of verbs inflected from a single root. In the vocabulary you have studied, the words יָקוּמוּ and קָם both come from a root that means to "arise." יִפֹּל and תִּפֹּל both come from a root that means to "fall."

The root of a Hebrew verb is usually made up of three letters known as radicals. Both יִשְׁמַע and תִּשְׁמַע are from the root שׁמע. קָטַל comes from the root קטל. Do not concern yourself with the fact that you cannot yet determine what is the common root behind יִפֹּל and תִּפֹּל or behind יָקוּמוּ and קָם. We will soon learn how to identify these roots.

2. Strong and Weak Roots

Hebrew roots come in two varieties:

(1) **The Strong Root.** This is a root in which none of the three root letters has any peculiarities. That is, all three letters are stable, and they do not have distinctive traits. The paradigm Hebrew verb is קָטַל, "he killed," from the root קטל. It is used as the paradigm because it has a very simple and basic inflection. קטל is a strong root.

(2) **The Weak Root.** This is a root in which at least one of the three letters has distinctive traits that affect how the word is formed.

    (a) For example, יִשְׁמַע, "he will hear," is from the root שׁמע, which has ע as its third letter. This letter is a guttural, a "weak" letter, and it will cause the verb to behave in ways that are normal for a guttural. You know, for example, that gutturals tend to prefer a-class vowels, and you can see that the vowel before the ע is Pathach, an a-class vowel. In other words, a root with a guttural will have certain "guttural traits" that a strong root will not have (by definition, a strong root never has a guttural letter).

    (b) There are other kinds of weak roots besides those with gutturals. For example, קָם is a verb from a different kind of weak root. It has no guttural, but it is weak for reasons we will soon learn.

    (c) Comparison of a strong to a weak verb shows how different they can be. קָטַל is a strong verb that means "he killed." קָם is a weak verb that means "he arose." Grammatically, these two are identical except that the former is from a strong root and the latter from a weak root. But you can see that the one has three consonants where the other has only two.

You must not think of the "strong" verb as normal and of all others as aberrant or unusual. "Weak" roots are very consistent in following the rules that govern their patterns; *they are not irregular.* Most of the Hebrew verbs in the Bible are in fact "weak." The Hebrew Bible has 25 verbs that occur over 500 times each; of these, only one is from a "strong" root.

Most of the verbs you see in the Hebrew Bible are Qal stem verbs from weak roots. *The student who masters the "strong verb" but who has only cursory knowledge of the weak verb will not be able to read biblical Hebrew.* Therefore, we must become familiar with weak root verbs right away. All of the verbs listed in the inflected verb charts in chapters 6 and 7 are weak (except for קָטַל). We will not, however, worry about understanding their full inflections until later.

B. Verbal Stems

Hebrew verbs are also said to have "stems." The most basic and by far the most common is called the **Qal** stem. All of the verbs that you have learned so far are Qal verbs. Other stems tend to have distinctive usage and meaning. For example:

(1) A stem called the Niphal is generally passive (as in "it was done"). This and other stems give us the passive voice in Hebrew.

(2) A stem called the Hiphil is said to be "causal," meaning that you cause something (to happen). An English analogy for the Hiphil is in verbs that end with "-ize." We have "sanitize," meaning to make something sanitary, and "maximize," meaning to make something as large as possible. English verbs ending in "-fy" (such as "sanctify") are similar. In the same way, the Hiphil verb often implies causing something to change in some way.

(3) There are other stems as well, and we will study them all in due time.

At present, however, we will focus primarily on the Qal stem. There are over 50,000 occurrences of Qal verbs in the Hebrew Bible; all other stems *combined* make up about 22,000 occurrences.

C. The Qal *Qatal* (Perfect)

The first conjugation we will learn is the Qal *qatal*. This is the "did/does/has done" verb that we have already looked at. It is sometimes called the "suffixed" verb but is traditionally called the "perfect." *Be sure that you understand that* qatal = *"perfect," since lexicons use the traditional terminology.*

(1) As already described, the strong verb is not really normative for the Hebrew verb system, and it is by no means the most common verb type. At the same time, it is valuable as a foundation for learning Hebrew verbs.

(2) In addition, however, we will learn basic conjugations with the III-ה verb, using the verb בָּנָה, "build." It is called III-ה because its third consonant is ה. This is one of the most common weak verb types, and by learning it now, you will save yourself from the unwitting assumption that the strong verb pattern should be regarded as the "correct" pattern.

1. The Strong Verb

The root קטל in the Qal stem means "kill." As mentioned above, it is the strong verb paradigm verb. The *qatal* gains its name from the 3ms form קָטַל.

Table 9.1. The Qal *Qatal* (Perfect)

	Singular	Plural
Third Masculine (3m)	קָטַל	קָטְלוּ
Third Feminine (3f)	קָטְלָה	קָטְלוּ
Second Masculine (2m)	קָטַֿלְתָּ	קְטַלְתֶּם
Second Feminine (2f)	קָטַלְתְּ	קְטַלְתֶּן
First Common (1c)	קָטַֿלְתִּי	קָטַֿלְנוּ

(1) The *qatal* is generally perfective in aspect and is thus often termed the **perfect** conjugation. Some scholars, however, believe the *qatal* is basically "unmarked" with respect to tense, mood, and aspect, thus allowing its meaning to be coordinated to its context. (See the discussion of *weqatal* in chapter 10.) When used without a conjunction, the *qatal* bears a default meaning of past tense, indicative mood, and perfective aspect. As such, it normally portrays action in a straitforward manner, as a complete whole with no focus on process. The *qatal* may, but does not necessarily, indicate "completed action," as does the English "he has done it." When giving a **gloss**, a translation without context, we typically use a simple past tense.

(2) The title **suffixed** verb comes from the fact that inflection is marked by different word endings called **sufformatives**. That is, the ending for the first singular form is different from the ending for the first plural form. The third masculine singular has no ending, and thus it is the basic form.

(3) The gender, number, and person of the verb helps determine the appropriate translation. Thus, the *glosses* would be as follows (but remember the alternative translations!):

  (a) The third masculine singular (3ms) קָטַל means "he killed."

  (b) The third feminine singular (3fs) קָטְלָה means "she killed."

  (c) The second masculine singular (2ms) קָטַֿלְתָּ means "you killed," where the subject is one male.

  (d) The 2fs (קָטַלְתְּ) means "you killed," where the subject is one female.

  (e) The 2mp (קְטַלְתֶּם) means "you killed," where the subject is a group of males or a mixed group of males and females.

  (f) The 2fp (קְטַלְתֶּן) means "you killed," where the subject is a group of females.

  (g) The third masculine and third feminine plurals are the same in the *qatal*. The form קָטְלוּ, "they killed," is called the "third common plural" (3cp).

(h) First person forms are common in gender. The 1cs (קָטַ֫לְתִּי) means "I killed," and the subject may be female or male. Also, the 1cp (קָטַ֫לְנוּ) means "we killed," and the subjects may be female or male.

(4) Observe that the 2ms, 1cs, and 1cp are accented on the penult. Accent position helps to determine vowel length in accordance with the rules of vowel changes. The 2ms and the 2mp illustrate how verbs follow the rules of accent shift and vowel length.

(a) In קָ/טַ֫ל/תָּ, the antepenult is an open pretonic and lengthens to Qamets.

(b) In קְ/טַל/תֶּם, the syllable קְ is a distant, open syllable and reduces to Shewa.

Blackboard 9.1. Vowel Shift and Accent Change in the Qal *Qatal* (Perfect)

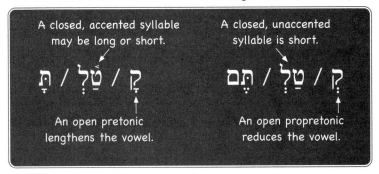

(c) The 2fs (קָטַלְתְּ) is only two syllables (*qa/taltt*). It is unusual on two counts: it has a Daghesh Forte and a silent Shewa at the end of a word.

(5) The 3fs (קָטְלָה) and 3cp (קָטְלוּ) forms have the Metheg under the ק (קָ), indicating that the vowel with the ק is Qamets in an open syllable, and that the Shewa with ט is a vocal Shewa. Without the Metheg, both verbs would appear to have Qamets Hatuph in a closed syllable. The Metheg sometimes is left out, yet the word is pronounced as though it were there.

Blackboard 9.2. Metheg and Syllable Divisions in קָטְלוּ

2. The Qal Qatal (Perfect) with begadkephat Letters

Many strong verbs have begadkephat letters. Their inflections are identical to קטל except that we must deal with the problem of the Daghesh Lene. כָּתַב begins with כ, which has the Daghesh Lene throughout the declension. The middle radical ת and the final ב are also begadkephat, but here they are always preceded by a vowel or vocal Shewa and so never have the Daghesh Lene.

Table 9.2. The Qal *Qatal* (Perfect) of כתב

	Singular	Plural
3m	כָּתַב	כָּתְבוּ
3f	כָּתְבָה	
2m	כָּתַבְתָּ	כְּתַבְתֶּם
2f	כָּתַבְתְּ	כְּתַבְתֶּן
1c	כָּתַבְתִּי	כָּתַבְנוּ

3. The III-ה Verb

The III-ה verb is extremely common. You should learn it with the strong verb.

Table 9.3. The Qal *Qatal* (Perfect) of the III-ה Verb בנה

	III-ה	Strong
3ms	בָּנָה	קָטַל
3fs	בָּנְתָה	קָטְלָה
2ms	בָּנִיתָ	קָטַלְתָּ
2fs	בָּנִית	קָטַלְתְּ
1cs	בָּנִיתִי	קָטַלְתִּי
3cp	בָּנוּ	קָטְלוּ
2mp	בְּנִיתֶם	קְטַלְתֶּם
2fp	בְּנִיתֶן	קְטַלְתֶּן
1cp	בָּנִינוּ	קָטַלְנוּ

The ה of בנה is a vowel letter, not a consonant, and it has no guttural traits.

(1) In the *qatal* 3ms, the ה is present as a vowel Qamets-Hey (בָּנָה).

(2) With a sufformative that begins with a consonant (e.g., the 2ms תָּ), the ה is replaced by a pointed vowel letter י, as in the 2ms בָּנִיתָ. Contrast קָטַלְתָּ.

(3) With a vowel sufformative, the ה drops off (e.g., the 3cp בָּנוּ). Contrast קָטְלוּ.

(4) The *qatal* 3fs drops the ה and adds תָה, as in בָּנְתָה.

Blackboard 9.3. Suformatives on the III-ה Verb

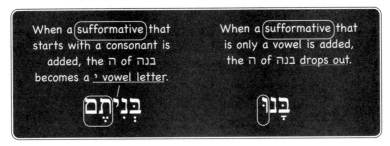

4. The Qatal *(Perfect) Sufformatives*

From the above conjugations, you can see that the sufformative endings for the *qatal* remain the same for all roots. The Daghesh Lene will drop out of the sufformative ת, however, if it follows a vowel, as is the case in the III-ה verbs.

Table 9.4. The *Qatal* (Perfect) Sufformatives

	Singular	Plural
3m	(none)	◌וּ◌◌◌
3f	◌ָה◌◌◌	
2m	◌ָֿת◌◌◌	◌ֶם◌◌◌
2f	◌ְת◌◌◌	◌ֶן◌◌◌
1c	◌ְתִּי◌◌◌	◌נוּ◌◌◌

5. *Observing Other* Qatal *(Perfect) Verbs with Weak Roots*

When you memorized inflected verbs in chapters 6 and 7, you learned several weak verb *qatal* forms. Compare the words you learned to their counterparts in the strong verb and pay particular attention to the consistency of the personal sufformatives.

Table 9.5. Comparing Sufformatives on Inflected Weak Verbs to the Strong Verb

Weak Verb	Strong Verb	Comment
שָׁב	קָטַל	3ms has no sufformative
שָׁבָה	קָטְלָה	3fs sufformative is Qamets-Hey
שָׁבוּ	קָטְלוּ	3cp sufformative is Shureq

6. Summary of *Qal* Qatal *(Perfect) Verb*

The following table summarizes the Qal *qatal* verb to date.

Table 9.6. Summary of the Qal *Qatal* (Perfect)

	Sufformatives	*Strong*	*begadkephat*	*III-ה*
3ms	(none)	קָטַל	כָּתַב	בָּנָה
3fs	◌ָה◌◌◌	קָטְלָה	כָּתְבָה	בָּנְתָה
2ms	תָּ◌◌◌	קָטַלְתָּ	כָּתַבְתָּ	בָּנִיתָ
2fs	תְּ◌◌◌	קָטַלְתְּ	כָּתַבְתְּ	בָּנִית
1cs	תִּי◌◌◌	קָטַלְתִּי	כָּתַבְתִּי	בָּנִיתִי
3cp	וּ◌◌◌	קָטְלוּ	כָּתְבוּ	בָּנוּ
2mp	תֶּם◌◌◌	קְטַלְתֶּם	כְּתַבְתֶּם	בְּנִיתֶם
2fp	תֶּן◌◌◌	קְטַלְתֶּן	כְּתַבְתֶּן	בְּנִיתֶן
1cp	נוּ◌◌◌	קָטַלְנוּ	כָּתַבְנוּ	בָּנִינוּ

D. Vocabulary

With verbs, vocabulary is listed by the three consonants of the root (these letters are called the **radicals**, from the Latin *radix* ["root"]). With each root and stem, we give the *qatal* 3ms form, or another form if that form is not extant. For example, in the list below, בנה is a three-letter root. The Qal *qatal* 3ms of that verb is listed as בָּנָה. Also, when pronouncing a root, it is common to pronounce the Qal *qatal* 3ms form.

1. Core Vocabulary

a. Verbs

בנה	Qal: בָּנָה build
הלך	Qal: הָלַךְ walk, go
כתב	Qal: כָּתַב write
מלך	Qal: מָלַךְ be king, rule
עשׂה	Qal: עָשָׂה do, make, build, bring about
ראה	Qal: רָאָה see, inspect
שׁפט	Qal: שָׁפַט judge, rule

b. Other Words

גְּבוּל	territory, border Ⓜ |גְּבוּל|
מִדְבָּר	desert, wilderness Ⓜ |מִדְבַּר|
עַל	upon, over, against (this word can stand by itself, but it is often attached to a noun with a *Maqqeph*, as in עַל־הָאָרֶץ, "upon the earth")
עֵצָה	advice Ⓕ |עֲצַת|
רָשָׁע	wicked (adjective)

2. Proper Names

אַבְרָם	Abram
בַּת־שֶׁבַע	Bathsheba
גִּדְעוֹן	Gideon
נֶגֶב	Negev, often with article as in "the Negev"
קַיִן	Cain

E. Guided Reading from Psalm 1

לֹא הָלַךְ בַּעֲצַת רְשָׁעִים

(1) The phrase לֹא הָלַךְ means "(he) does not walk." לֹא precedes the verb it negates. Notice that הָלַךְ is translated here as a present tense. It is *not* to be translated, "he did not walk."

(2) You recognize the בּ on בַּעֲצַת as being בְּ, "in" (it has Pathach instead of Shewa because of the guttural in עֲצַת, which prefers an a-class vowel). עֲצַת is the construct of עֵצָה and means "advice of." The Pathach in בּ is *not* from a definite article. Remember that a noun in construct never has the definite article.

(3) The masculine plural adjective רְשָׁעִים means "wicked (people)." Therefore, בַּעֲצַת רְשָׁעִים means "in (the) advice of (the) wicked (people)."

(4) The whole clause means "(he) does not walk in the advice of the wicked."

(5) You recall that the reading from Ps 1 in chapter 8 was אַשְׁרֵי־הָאִישׁ אֲשֶׁר, "Happy is the man who...." Those words are followed by the line you see here, לֹא הָלַךְ בַּעֲצַת רְשָׁעִים, which forms part of the relative clause introduced by אֲשֶׁר. The whole would be translated, "Happy is the man *who does not walk* in the advice of the wicked." In other words, because of the presence of the relative pronoun "who" (אֲשֶׁר), we drop "he" from our translation, "(he) does not walk in the advice of the wicked."

CHAPTER 10
THE CONJUNCTION AND THE QAL *YIQTOL* AND *WEQATAL*

A. The Conjunction

1. The Meaning and Function of the Conjunction וְ

The conjunction וְ, "and, but," is the most common word in the OT, occuring over 50,000 times. It is also one of the most important words for understanding literary structure, for it provides the interpreter with clues about the author's flow of thought. Specifically, the conjunction links nouns to nouns, phrases to phrases, clauses to clauses, etc., creating chains of text units that are to be read together.

The conjunction can be translated as "and," "but," and sometimes as "even."

- (1) Context determines which translation is most appropriate, but it should generally be translated "and."

- (2) On the other hand, "but" is often appropriate if the conjunction is on a noun that precedes the main verb of the clause.

If two or more nouns connected by the conjunction are the subjects of a single verb and the first noun is singular, the verb often is in the singular rather than the plural, as in רָאָה דָוִד וְשָׁאוּל אֶת־הָאִישׁ, "David and Saul saw the man."

2. The Form of the Conjunction וְ

The conjunction וְ has several different spelling possibilities depending on the type of syllable to which it is prefixed.

- (1) The most common spelling of the conjunction will be וְ. It will have this spelling before most consonants with full vowels (i.e., not Shewa). Note the loss of the Daghesh Lene in the ד when the conjunction is prefixed. A begadkephat letter normally loses its Daghesh Lene if it is preceded by a vowel, even if that vowel is only a vocal Shewa.

  דָּבָר a word   וְדָבָר and a word

- (2) When the conjunction is added to a word that begins with a labial (פ, מ, בּ), it is vocalized as a Shureq (וּ). Again, observe the loss of the Daghesh Lene in the בּ when the conjunction is prefixed.

  בַּיִת a house   וּבַיִת and a house

- (3) The וְ is also vocalized as Shureq (וּ) when it is prefixed to a word beginning with any consonant (except י) followed by vocal Shewa.

  דְּבָרִים words   וּדְבָרִים and words

(4) When the conjunction is וְ prefixed to consonant י followed by vocal Shewa, the two syllables contract to become וִי. In the case below, the י of יְהוּדָה has become a vowel letter Hireq-Yod.

יְהוּדָה Judah   וִיהוּדָה and Judah

NOTE: The Shureq (וּ) as a conjunction at the beginning of a word is an exception to the rule that a word in Hebrew never begins with a vowel. On the other hand, it is possible that this was pronounced something like *wū*, in which case the form of the conjunction would not violate the rule.

(5) When prefixed to a guttural followed by a composite Shewa, the conjunction takes the short vowel that corresponds to the class of the composite Shewa.

אֲנִי I   וַאֲנִי and I

אֱדֹום Edom   וֶאֱדֹום and Edom

חֳלִי illness   וְחֳלִי and illness

(6) When the וְ is prefixed to אֱלֹהִים, the initial א quiesces. With the loss of א in pronunciation, the vowel of the conjunction becomes the long vowel Tsere.

אֱלֹהִים God   וֵאלֹהִים and God

(7) Sometimes before a monosyllable or before a word accented on the penult, the conjunction is written as וָ. For example, the word for "night" is לַיְלָה; with the conjunction, it is וָלַיְלָה. Remember, however, that this rule is often not applied.

לַיְלָה night   וָלַיְלָה and night

Table 10.1. The Conjunction

	Form	Example
Most common form	וְ	וְדָבָר
Before labial	וּ	וּבַיִת
Before letter with vocal Shewa	וּ	וּדְבָרִים
Before Yod with vocal Shewa	וִי	וִיהוּדָה
Before guttural with composite Shewa	וַ / וֶ / וָ	וַאֲנִי
Before accented syllable (sometimes)	וָ	וָלַיְלָה
Before אֱלֹהִים	וֵ	וֵאלֹהִים

B. The Qal *Yiqtol* (Imperfect)

In contrast to the suffixed *qatal* form, the **yiqtol** is sometimes called the **prefixed** form because it is marked primarily by preformatives in front of the root. The *yiqtol* is traditionally called the **imperfect**, and the form generally expresses imperfective aspect. *Be sure that you understand that* yiqtol = **imperfect**, *since lexicons use the traditional terminology.*

1. The Strong Verb

The *yiqtol* gets its name from the 3ms form יִקְטֹל.

Table 10.2. The Qal *Yiqtol* (Imperfect)

	Singular	Plural
3m	יִקְטֹל	יִקְטְלוּ
3f	תִּקְטֹל	תִּקְטֹלְנָה
2m	תִּקְטֹל	תִּקְטְלוּ
2f	תִּקְטְלִי	תִּקְטֹלְנָה
1c	אֶקְטֹל	נִקְטֹל

(1) As a conjugation commonly expressing imperfective aspect, the Hebrew *yiqtol* often portrays an action as open-ended, ongoing, or in process. It includes many *subjunctive* type modal actions and *repeated* actions and also most *future* actions. As such, the *yiqtol* can be translated as the future ("he will do"), the subjunctive ("he should / would / could do"), or as an English imperfect ("he used to do"). When giving a gloss for a *yiqtol*, we typically use the simple future. Thus, the gloss for the *yiqtol* 1cp נִקְטֹל is "we will kill."

(2) A number of observations are noteworthy from the above paradigm.

(a) Notice that the 3fs and 2ms have the same form: תִּקְטֹל. Context determines which of the two it is in a text. If the verb has a feminine subject, it is the 3fs.

(b) Similarly, the 2fp and 3fp are identical in form; meaning is determined by context.

(c) Only the first person forms are common in gender.

(d) The guttural א takes Seghol instead of the Hireq in the 1cs. Frequently where a strong letter takes Hireq, the guttural will take a Seghol.

(e) In the syllables of the 3mp (יִק/טְ/לוּ) and 2mp (תִּק/טְ/לוּ), an open pretonic (טְ) follows a closed, unaccented syllable (which must remain short). In this situation, the open pretonic often reduces to Shewa, as we see here.

(f) *Yiqtol* forms have preformatives on all forms and inflectional suffformatives on the 2fs and on all second and third person plural forms.

(3) The inflected *yiqtol* verbs that you memorized for chapters 6 and 7 have the same preformative *letters* and *personal suffformatives* as found in strong verbs. However,

the *vowel patterns* of the weak *yiqtol* verbs can be very different from the strong verb *yiqtol*.

Table 10.3. A Comparison of Strong and Weak *Yiqtols* (Imperfects)

Weak Yiqtol	Strong counterpart	Weak Yiqtol	Strong counterpart
יָקוּמוּ	יִקְטְלוּ	תִּירַשׁ	תִּקְטֹל
יִמְצָא	יִקְטֹל	יֵשֵׁב	יִקְטֹל
תִּשְׁמַע	תִּקְטֹל	יָשׁוּב	יִקְטֹל

2. The Yiqtol *(Imperfect) Preformatives and Sufformatives*

Preformatives and endings of the Qal *yiqtol* are below. Except for sufformatives, vowels are not included because, as you have seen, the Qal *yiqtol* can have a wide range of vowels.

Table 10.4. Preformatives and Sufformatives of the *Yiqtol* (Imperfect)

	Singular	Plural
3m	יOOO	יOOOוּ
3f	תOOO	תֶּOOOֽנָה
2m	תOOO	תOOOוּ
2f	תOOOִי	תOOOֽנָה
1c	אOOO	נOOO

3. The Yiqtol *(Imperfect) in Verbs with begadkephat Letters*

The verb כתב has no weak letters, but every letter is begadkephat. The full conjugation of the verb illustrates how the Daghesh Lene will be added or dropped from a letter as circumstances demand. Observe how begadkephat letters function in this inflection in the chart below. Remember that as a general rule, a begadkephat letter preceded by a vowel (including vocal Shewa) will not have a Daghesh Lene. With כתב in the Qal *yiqtol*:

(1) The כ is always preceded by a vowel and so never has the Daghesh Lene. Remember that a begadkephat letter preceded by a vowel will generally not have a Daghesh Lene.

(2) The middle radical ת is always preceded by silent Shewa (i.e., by a closed syllable) and so always has the Daghesh Lene.

(3) The ב in the Qal *yiqtol* is always preceded by a vowel or vocal Shewa, and so it never has the Daghesh Lene.

Table 10.5. The Qal *Yiqtol* (Imperfect) of כתב

	Singular	Plural
3m	יִכְתֹּב	יִכְתְּבוּ
3f	תִּכְתֹּב	תִּכְתֹּבְנָה
2m	תִּכְתֹּב	תִּכְתְּבוּ
2f	תִּכְתְּבִי	תִּכְתֹּבְנָה
1c	אֶכְתֹּב	נִכְתֹּב

4. The III-ה Verb

Table 10.6. The Qal *Yiqtol* (Imperfect) of בנה

	III-ה	Strong
3ms	יִבְנֶה	יִקְטֹל
3fs	תִּבְנֶה	תִּקְטֹל
2ms	תִּבְנֶה	תִּקְטֹל
2fs	תִּבְנִי	תִּקְטְלִי
1cs	אֶבְנֶה	אֶקְטֹל
3mp	יִבְנוּ	יִקְטְלוּ
3fp	תִּבְנֶינָה	תִּקְטֹלְנָה
2mp	תִּבְנוּ	תִּקְטְלוּ
2fp	תִּבְנֶינָה	תִּקְטֹלְנָה
1cp	נִבְנֶה	נִקְטֹל

The III-ה *yiqtol* has certain features in common with the III-ה *qatal*.

(1) *With no ending, the ה is present.* In the *yiqtol*, it is the vowel letter Seghol-Hey (e.g., יִבְנֶה). Compare the *qatal* 3ms, which has Qamets-Hey: בָּנָה.

(2) *With a sufformative that begins with a consonant, the ה is replaced by a pointed vowel letter with י.* In the *yiqtol*, it appears in the 3fp תִּבְנֶינָה as Seghol-Yod (the sufformative is נָה). Compare the *qatal* 2ms בָּנִיתָ.

(3) *With a sufformative that is only a vowel, the ה drops off.* In the *yiqtol*, we see the 3mp יִבְנוּ. Compare the *qatal* 3cp בָּנוּ.

5. *Summary of Qal* Yiqtol *(Imperfect) Verb*

The following table summarizes the Qal *yiqtol* verb to date:

Table 10.7. Summary of the Qal *Yiqtol* (Imperfect)

	Affixes	*Strong*	*begadkephat*	*III-ה*
3ms	יְ‏ООО	יִקְטֹל	יִכְתֹּב	יִבְנֶה
3fs	תְ‏ООО	תִּקְטֹל	תִּכְתֹּב	תִּבְנֶה
2ms	תְ‏ООО	תִּקְטֹל	תִּכְתֹּב	תִּבְנֶה
2fs	יОООתִ	תִּקְטְלִי	תִּכְתְּבִי	תִּבְנִי
1cs	ООО‏א	אֶקְטֹל	אֶכְתֹּב	אֶבְנֶה
3mp	וּООО‏יְ	יִקְטְלוּ	יִכְתְּבוּ	יִבְנוּ
3fp	תООО‏נָה	תִּקְטֹלְנָה	תִּכְתֹּבְנָה	תִּבְנֶינָה
2mp	וּООО‏תִ	תִּקְטְלוּ	תִּכְתְּבוּ	תִּבְנוּ
2fp	תООО‏נָה	תִּקְטֹלְנָה	תִּכְתֹּבְנָה	תִּבְנֶינָה
1cp	ООО‏נְ	נִקְטֹל	נִכְתֹּב	נִבְנֶה

C. The Verb היה

Table 10.8. The *Qatal* (Perfect) and *Yiqtol* (Imperfect) of היה

	Qatal		Yiqtol	
	Singular	*Plural*	*Singular*	*Plural*
3m	הָיָה	הָיוּ	יִהְיֶה	יִהְיוּ
3f	הָיְתָה		תִּהְיֶה	תִּהְיֶינָה
2m	הָיִיתָ	הֱיִיתֶם	תִּהְיֶה	תִּהְיוּ
2f	הָיִית	הֱיִיתֶן	תִּהְיִי	תִּהְיֶינָה
1c	הָיִיתִי	הָיִינוּ	אֶהְיֶה	נִהְיֶה

You have already seen the form וַיְהִי, and you have read it as a past tense for יֵשׁ to be translated "and there was." It is actually the 3ms form of the verb היה, "be," in the *wayyiqtol* pattern. וַיְהִי could be translated as "and there was," "and he was," or "and it happened." The verb היה is a normal III-ה verb, and it has regular *qatal* and *yiqtol* forms. The above table shows both. The forms may look a little odd, but actually they are like the forms you have seen for בנה.

D. The *Weqatal*

1. The Form of the Weqatal: Basic Pattern and Accent Shift

In form, the *weqatal* is nothing more than a *qatal* with a simple וְ conjunction in front of it (וְקָטַל). Because of this, scholars have at times called it the conjoined perfect. While not always the case, the accent on the *weqatal* generally shifts to the ultima in the 2ms and 1cs (וְקָטַלְתִּי and וְקָטַלְתָּ; contrast the simple *qatals* קָטַלְתָּ and קָטַלְתִּי). Accent shift does not affect the vowels of the *weqatal*; the vowels are the same as in the regular *qatal*. Today, just as Hebrew grammarians often refer to the perfect as the *qatal* and the imperfect as the *yiqtol*, so also they refer to this form as the *weqatal*.

2. The Function of the Weqatal

The *weqatal* works in a way that most students of Hebrew find surprising. Consider the following sentence:

הַמֶּלֶךְ יֵשֵׁב בֶּחָצֵר וְשָׁפַט אֶת־הָעָם

The king would sit in the courtyard and judge the people.

Depending on context, you can translate the sentence either as a past imperfect (as is done above) or as a future ("The king *will* sit in the courtyard and judge the people"). Notice that וְשָׁפַט is a *weqatal* and that it appears to have similar if not the same significance as the *yiqtol* verb יֵשֵׁב. Depending on the translation, both verbs refer to actions done repeatedly in the past or both verbs refer to future actions.

Now look at another example.

יִשְׁמַע הַמֶּלֶךְ אֶת־הַתּוֹרָה וְשָׁפַט אֶת־הָעָם

The king should hear the Law and judge the people.

In this case, יִשְׁמַע is clearly modal (note that it is in first position) and describes what ought" to be done. But notice that וְשָׁפַט in this sentence appears to have a similar if not the same function. It, too, is modal, expressing either a further desire of the speaker or the ultimate purpose for which he should "hear."

Now look at this example.

אִם יָשׁוּב הַמֶּלֶךְ וְשָׁפַט אֶת־הָעָם

If the king returns, then he will judge the people.

Here, we have a conditional statement with the *yiqtol* יָשׁוּב as the protasis and the *weqatal* וְשָׁפַט marking the apodosis. That is why וְשָׁפַט is translated "*then* he will judge."

Finally, look at this example.

לֵךְ וְשָׁפַטְתָּ אֶת־הָעָם

Go and judge the people!

or Go, so that you may judge the people!

לֵךְ is an **imperative**, a word used to make a command, and it means "go!" The *weqatal* is second person (וְשָׁפַטְתָּ) because a command is by nature a second person statement. וְשָׁפַטְתָּ might simply have the force of another command (first translation), or it might express purpose (second translation). Either way, its meaning is closely tied to the imperative לֵךְ ("Go!").

How can the *weqatal* have all these meanings, and why is it so different from the normal *qatal* without conjunction, which frequently just expresses simple past tense, indicative mood, and perfective aspect? Why is וְשָׁפַט not translated "and he judged" in any of the above sentences? Scholars have long debated this, and there is no certain explanation. Several explanations are proposed.

(1) A traditional view is that the conjunction "converts" the *qatal* so that it simply has the same significance as the verb in front of it. Thus, if a future tense *yiqtol* is followed by a *weqatal*, the *weqatal* is also future. If an imperative is followed by a *weqatal*, the *weqatal* is also a command. As a rule of thumb, this often works, but often the force of the *weqatal* is not precisely the same as that of the preceding verb. Furthermore, scholars today no longer believe the conjunction carries "converting" power.

(2) Some scholars believe that the *weqatal* is also a type of modal, marked by virtue of always being the first word in its clause and signalled by its ability to express potential, telic, resultative, or imperatival force.

(3) Some believe that the *qatal* should be considered basically an "unmarked" form in terms of tense, mood, *and* aspect. When a *qatal* is by itself (with no conjunction), it usually has a default meaning of past tense, indicative mood, and perfective aspect. However, when the *qatal* has a conjunction, its meaning is coordinated to its context. Thus, *weqatal* can be a future, a past imperfect, an apodosis, a purpose clause, or a command, depending on its placement in a text.

It is important to realize that *you don't have to determine the correct theory about the weqatal* in order to understand it. It is sufficient to understand how to read it. Also, in English we have a similar pattern that we use all the time. Look at the examples below.

Table 10.9. Common Uses of the Conjoined Verb in English

1. As an Apodosis	Keep this law, and *live*; don't keep it, *and die.*
2. As a Subjunctive	He should learn this law, *and keep* it *and teach* it to his children.
3. In a Series of Commands	Go, *and stay* in your homes *and watch over* your families.
4. As a Prediction	The king of Nineveh will come here *and destroy* this city *and take away* the people.

(1) The first example is really two conditional sentences; the phrases "and live… and die" form the apodosis parts of each conditional statement. In effect, what is being

said is, "*If* you keep this law, *then* you will live; *if* you don't keep it, *then* you will die."

(2) In the second example, "he should learn" is subjunctive, implying moral obligation, and the phrases "and keep… and teach" have a similar force. The latter verbs could be understood to express the ultimate purpose of the first action.

(3) In the third example, "and stay… and watch" follow the command "go" and are also in effect commands growing out of the initial order.

(4) In the last example, "and destroy… and take away" are in effect future tense and continue the prediction begun with "The king of Nineveh will come."

By itself, the significance of a phrase like "and live" or "and teach" is unclear. It is, in effect, unmarked. Within a context, however, the meaning of each verb with "and" is fairly obvious. The Hebrew *weqatal* is similar to English in this way. Keep this in mind, and you should have no problem with the *weqatal*.

E. Vocabulary

1. Core Vocabulary

a. Verbs

אמר	Qal: אָמַר say
היה	Qal: הָיָה be, become
ישׁב	Qal: יָשַׁב sit, dwell
נתן	Qal: נָתַן give, place
שׁמע	Qal: שָׁמַע hear, listen
שׁמר	Qal: שָׁמַר keep, guard, observe

b. Other Words

אָז	then
אֲנִי / אָנֹכִי	I (pronoun; either form may be used)
בָּשָׂר	meat, flesh, skin Ⓜ |בְּשַׂר|
וְ	and, but
כִּי	because, although, indeed, that, rather, instead
לַיְלָה	night (plural = לֵילוֹת) Ⓜ |לֵילֵי|

2. Reading Vocabulary

יֶהְגֶּה	"he will meditate" (Qal *yiqtol* 3ms of הגה)

3. Proper Names

אַבְרָהָם	Abraham

אֵלִיָּהוּ	Elijah
דָּגוֹן	Dagon (Canaanite and later Philistine god)
יְהוּדָה	Judah
לוֹט	Lot

F. Guided Reading from Psalm 1

וּבְתוֹרָתוֹ יֶהְגֶּה יוֹמָם וָלָיְלָה

(1) You know that תּוֹרָה means "law." וּבְתוֹרָתוֹ is a form of this word that means "and in his law." You can see the preposition בְּ meaning "in" (the Daghesh Lene is lost because it follows a vowel). You know that the וּ means "and." The וֹ on the end is a pronoun suffix meaning "his."

(2) You have just learned about the Qal *yiqtol*, which follows the pattern יִקְטֹל for the strong verb. יֶהְגֶּה is also a Qal *yiqtol* 3ms, but it is from a III-ה root (הגה) and thus is similar to יִבְנֶה. In יֶהְגֶּה, however, the vowel under the preformative י is Seghol and not Hireq (as in יִבְנֶה) because הגה also has a guttural ה in the first position. Why is there a Daghesh in the ג?

(3) יוֹמָם is a form of יוֹם that means "by day."

(4) The form וָלָיְלָה means "and night." We would expect to see וְלַיְלָה, with Pathach under the first Lamed, but this word has its accented vowel lengthened because of its position in the verse. It is called a "pausal" form.

(5) The whole means "And in his law he will meditate by day and night."

Chapter 11
The Qal Infinitive Construct and *Wayyiqtol*

A. The Rule of Shewa

Hebrew does not allow a word to begin either with two contiguous (side-by-side) vocal Shewas or with a vocal Shewa and a composite Shewa. When such a construction would occur,
the rule of Shewa must be applied.

1. Two Vocal Shewas

If a prefix containing a vocal Shewa is joined to a word beginning with a vocal Shewa, the
first vocal Shewa becomes Hireq, and the second becomes a silent Shewa.

שְׁמוּאֵל + כְּ → כִּשְׁמוּאֵל   like Samuel

The same rule applies when vowel change due to accent shift creates the potential for two
contiguous Shewas at the front of a word. In such instances, however, the initial Shewa may become a vowel other than Hireq (you will see this in chapter 26).

2. Vocal Shewa Plus Composite Shewa

If a prefix containing a vocal Shewa is set before a composite Shewa, the vocal Shewa is replaced by the short vowel that corresponds to the composite Shewa, and the composite Shewa becomes silent.

חֲלוֹם + כְּ → כַּחֲלוֹם   like a dream

אֱנוֹשׁ + כְּ → כֶּאֱנוֹשׁ   like a man

חֳלָיִים + בְּ → בָּחֳלָיִים   in sicknesses

Note that in בָּחֳלָיִים the syllable בָּ has a Qamets Hatuph (not a Qamets).

3. Vocal Shewa Plus יְ

If a word begins with יְ and has a prefix containing a vocal Shewa set in front of it, the combination becomes Hireq-Yod (i.e., the vocal Shewa becomes Hireq, and the Shewa in the
original יְ is lost).

יְהוּדָה + בְּ → בִּיהוּדָה   in Judah

Blackboard 11.1. The Rule of Shewa

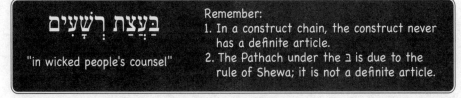

בַּעֲצַת רְשָׁעִים

"in wicked people's counsel"

Remember:
1. In a construct chain, the construct never
   has a definite article.
2. The Pathach under the בַּ is due to the
   rule of Shewa; it is not a definite article.

B. The Qal Infinitive Construct

1. General Concept

In English, infinitives are commonly used to express the purpose of a given action ("He came *to study*"). Hebrew regularly uses its infinitive construct in the same way, but as we shall see, Hebrew also uses its infinitives in ways quite foreign to English usage.

While not a finite verb form, the **infinitive construct** is in effect a verb used as a noun. Like a noun, it can serve as a verb's subject ("*Forgiving* is divine") or object ("I like *to eat*"). In the latter instances, the infinitive construct completes the main verbal idea and is thus called the **verbal complement**. The infinitive construct can also describe the purpose or intent of another action ("He went *to read*"). Here the infinitive, identified in this instance as a **verbal adjunct**, does not complete the original action but adds a new action that grows directly out of the first. Finally, the infinitive construct can operate in an adverbial phrase modifying a following clause ("*When he left* [lit. in his leaving], he was rejoicing").

  (1) The infinitive construct does not inflect for gender, person, or number.

  (2) The infinitive construct has no tense, mood, or aspect. Such features are signalled by a clause's finite verbs within their given contexts.

2. Form

Having neither gender, number, person, or tense, the infinitive construct is very simple.

  (1) The Qal infinitive construct has the form קְטֹל, as in כְּתֹב, "the act of writing."

  (2) It is often found with an inseparable preposition attached, frequently לְ, "to." English, similarly, tends to use "to" with its infinitive. In this circumstance, following the rule of Shewa, we have the pattern לִקְטֹל, as in לִכְתֹּב.

$$ \text{כְּתֹב} \quad + \quad \text{לְ} \quad \rightarrow \quad \text{לִכְתֹּב} \qquad \text{to write} $$

  (3) The addition of a preposition causes begadkephat letters to lose or gain a Daghesh Lene, such as is seen in comparing the letters כ and ת in כְּתֹב and לִכְתֹּב.

  (4) The infinitive construct of the III-ה verb has a fixed rule: it always ends in וֹת (the ה of the root is dropped).

    (a) Thus, the infinitive construct of בנה is בְּנוֹת (sometimes written בְּנֹת).

    (b) With לְ, we see לִבְנוֹת.

Table 11.1. The Qal Infinitive Construct

Root	Inf. Con.	Inf. Con. with לְ
קטל	קְטֹל	לִקְטֹל
כתב	כְּתֹב	לִכְתֹּב
בנה	בְּנוֹת	לִבְנוֹת
ראה	רְאוֹת	לִרְאוֹת

C. The *Wayyiqtol*

The *wayyiqtol* is the primary conjugation biblical Hebrew uses for telling a story, which by nature is a chain of temporally consecutive past events. This narrative function has led some to call the *wayyiqtol* the **waw (vav) consecutive**, while others prefer the term **preterite**, because the form most commonly expresses simple past time. As would be expected, *wayyiqtol* dominates historical narrative texts such as Genesis, 1 Kings, and Ruth.

In form, the *wayyiqtol* looks like a *yiqtol* that has וֹ at the beginning and a Daghesh Forte in the preformative of the *yiqtol*. The similarity between the forms, however, is only superficial, for there is no true relationship between them.

Table 11.2. The *Yiqtol* (Imperfect) and *Wayyiqtol*

Qal Yiqtol 3ms	Qal Wayyiqtol 3ms
יִקְטֹל	וַיִּקְטֹל

1. The Strong Verb

The conjunction וֹ is part of this form; thus, it is often translated "and" as in "and he saw." It generally means something like "and he did," although occasionally it can be pluperfect in meaning ("and he had done"). It can also at times be epexegetical (explanatory) in function, as in 2 Sam 14:5: "I am a widow—my husband *has died*" (אִשָּׁה־אַלְמָנָה אָנִי *וַיָּמָת אִישִׁי*) [*wayyiqtol* at italicized words]).

Table 11.3. The Qal *Wayyiqtol*

	Singular	Plural
3m	וַיִּקְטֹל	וַיִּקְטְלוּ
3f	וַתִּקְטֹל	וַתִּקְטֹלְנָה
2m	וַתִּקְטֹל	וַתִּקְטְלוּ
2f	וַתִּקְטְלִי	וַתִּקְטֹלְנָה
1c	וָאֶקְטֹל	וַנִּקְטֹל

(1) *The* wayyiqtol *is not a modified* yiqtol *and should not be parsed as a* yiqtol. It is a distinctive form, and its similarity to the *yiqtol* is accidental. The formal similarity between conjugations did cause older grammarians to think that the וֹ converted a future tense into a past tense. In reality, the simple *yiqtol* and *wayyiqtol* come from two different earlier verb forms. For memorization and recognition sake, however, this resemblance is a happy development. If you know the *yiqtol*, you know the *wayyiqtol*.

(2) The name *wayyiqtol* is derived from the 3ms form in the paradigm (וַיִּקְטֹל). It is pronounced *vayyiqtol* by those who follow modern, Israeli pronunciation.

(3) The *wayyiqtol* is usually a simple past tense (like the *qatal* but unlike the *yiqtol*), and due to the conjunction it is generally linked to a previous statement. The distinct events in the chained clauses are usually temporally sequential ("He arose and [then] he departed"), but the *wayyiqtol* can also be pluperfect or explanatory.

(4) The ַו and the Daghesh Forte in the preformative are the distinctive marks of the *wayyiqtol*; this makes it easy to recognize. In the 1cs, the preformative letter is the guttural א, which does not double, and therefore through compensatory lengthening we see וָ instead of וַ.

2. The III-ה Verb

You already know וַיְהִי ("and there was / and he was"), the *wayyiqtol* 3ms of היה. Notice that the final ה of the root has dropped out. This is called "apocopation" (or "shortening"), and it is a feature of the III-ה *wayyiqtol* in the 3ms, 3fs, and 2ms. When this happens, the final ה of the root is dropped, and the accent shifts forward, which causes vowel changes.

The III-ה *wayyiqtol* is very common, and thus one sees many examples of apocopation.

Blackboard 11.2. Vowel Change in the Apocopated III-ה *Wayyiqtol*

The Yiqtol	The Wayyiqtol	Syllables of Wayyiqtol
יִבְנֶה	וַיִּ֫בֶן	וַ יִּ בֶן

A closed, unaccented syllable is short

The loss of the final ה and accent shift causes a change in the vowels. Compare also the *yiqtol* 3ms of היה (יִהְיֶה) to the *wayyiqtol* 3ms (וַיְהִי). In this case, the consonant Yod of היה becomes the vowel letter Hireq-Yod in וַיְהִי.

Table 11.4. The *Wayyiqtol* and *Yiqtol* (Imperfect) in the III-ה

	Wayyiqtol III-ה		Yiqtol III-ה	
3ms/p	וַיִּ֫בֶן	וַיִּבְנוּ	יִבְנֶה	יִבְנוּ
3fs/p	וַתִּ֫בֶן	וַתִּבְנֶ֫ינָה	תִּבְנֶה	תִּבְנֶ֫ינָה
2ms/p	וַתִּ֫בֶן	וַתִּבְנוּ	תִּבְנֶה	תִּבְנוּ
2fs/p	וַתִּבְנִי	וַתִּבְנֶ֫ינָה	תִּבְנִי	תִּבְנֶ֫ינָה
1cs/p	וָאֶבְנֶה	וַנִּבְנֶה	אֶבְנֶה	נִבְנֶה

Most roots do not have an "apocopated" form for the *wayyiqtol,* and even those roots that do typically have it only in the 3ms, 3fs, and 2ms.

D. Vocabulary

1. Core Vocabulary

a. Verbs

חפץ   Qal: חָפֵץ desire, enjoy, want (the *qatal* 3ms is חָפֵץ, but other forms are normal, e.g., *qatal* 2ms is חָפַצְתָּ)

נפל   Qal: נָפַל fall

b. Other Words

אֶחָד   one (masculine; feminine = אַחַת; can follow a noun, as in עַם אֶחָד, "one people")

בַּת   daughter [F] |בַּת| (plural = בָּנוֹת)

גַּם   also, even

גּוֹי   nation [M] |גּוֹי| (plural = גּוֹיִם)

כֵּן   thus

מִלְחָמָה   war, battle [F] |מִלְחֶמֶת|

מִשְׁפָּחָה   family [F] |מִשְׁפַּחַת|

עֵדָה   congregation [F] |עֲדַת|

צַדִּיק   righteous (adjective)

שָׁלֹשׁ   three (with feminine noun like שָׁלֹשׁ נָשִׁים; with masculine noun like שְׁלֹשָׁה אֲנָשִׁים)

2. Reading Vocabulary

בַּעֲדַת   "in the congregation of"; a form of עֵדָה; it also has the preposition בְּ

חַטָּאִים   "sinners"

3. Proper Names

אוּרִיָּה   Uriah

E. Guided Reading from Psalm 1

עַל־כֵּן לֹא־יָקֻמוּ רְשָׁעִים בַּמִּשְׁפָּט

וְחַטָּאִים בַּעֲדַת צַדִּיקִים

(1) עַל־כֵּן is a combination of עַל and כֵּן (lit., "upon thus") that means "therefore."

(2) יָקֻמוּ is an alternative form of a verb you know, יָקוּמוּ. Usually it is seen with the Shureq but sometimes with the Qibbuts. Remember that an accented syllable can be long or short.

(3) In בַּעֲדַת, you see עֲדַת, the construct of עֵדָה. Thus, עֲדַת צַדִּיקִים means "(the) congregation of (the) righteous." We will study the construct in the next chapter. Notice that
we have to supply the definite article in the English translation because of English
style.

(4) In בַּעֲדַת, you also see an example of the rule of Shewa. In this case, the preposition בְּ
has been added to עֲדַת. By the rules of Shewa, hypothetical בְּעֲדַת becomes בַּעֲדַת.

(5) לֹא־יָקֻמוּ does "double-duty" in that it governs both lines; it is understood to be the
verb for the second line. The phenomenon of a single verb governing two separate
lines, sometimes called "gapping," is common in poetry.

(6) The two lines together mean "Therefore, wicked (people) will not rise in the judgment, / and sinners (will not rise) in (the) congregation of (the) righteous."

CHAPTER 12
THE CONSTRUCT CHAIN

A. Introduction and Terminology

You have already learned to deal with **construct chains**, as in the following example:

קוֹל אִישׁ a voice of a man (a man's voice)

Remember that there is no word for *of* in Hebrew but that *of* is implied simply in having these two nouns stand side by side. In this case, the first noun (קוֹל) is in the **construct** state and is translated "(a) voice of." The second noun (אִישׁ) is in the **absolute** state and is translated "(a) man." Similarly, we have קוֹל in the construct state and אִשָּׁה in the absolute in the following example:

קוֹל אִשָּׁה a voice of a woman (a woman's voice)

B. Definiteness and Indefiniteness

In the above examples, both the construct and absolute nouns are indefinite, and thus we have the meanings "a man's voice" and "a woman's voice." In order to make the construct chain definite, the definite article is added *only to the absolute noun* and never to the noun in construct. For example,

קוֹל הָאִישׁ the voice of the man (the man's voice)

If the absolute noun in a construct chain is definite, the whole chain is definite. Put another way, the construct noun never has a definite article but is regarded as definite if the absolute noun is definite.

קוֹל נָבִיא a voice of a prophet

קוֹל הַנָּבִיא the voice of the prophet

A noun is considered to be definite under the following three circumstances:

 (1) if it has the definite article, as in הַמַּלְכָּה, "the queen";
 (2) if it is a proper noun, as in שְׁמוּאֵל, "Samuel";
 (3) if it is defined as belonging to someone, as in "his horse." (We will soon study how Hebrew does this.)

Thus, the following construct chains are definite:

קוֹל־דָּוִד the voice of David

עֶבֶד הַמֶּלֶךְ the servant of the king

רוּחַ שְׁמוּאֵל the spirit of Samuel

C. Construct Nouns with an Inseparable Preposition

Although a construct noun does not take a definite article, it may appear with one of the in-separable prepositions (כְּ, לְ, בְּ) as in לְקוֹל דָּוִד, "to the voice of David." The chain is defi-nite because the absolute noun is a proper name.

D. The Formation of Construct Nouns

In all the above examples, the construct noun looks no different from its ordinary form. For example, קוֹל means "voice" and is *not a construct noun* in this sentence:

דָּוִד יִשְׁמַע קוֹל   David will hear a voice

But קוֹל is in the construct in this phrase:

קוֹל־דָּוִד   the voice of David

In קוֹל־דָּוִד, the construct קוֹל is identical in spelling to the absolute (קוֹל). This is true of many nouns.

Many construct nouns, however, are spelled differently than their absolute forms, whether singular or plural. Most commonly, construct form can differ from the absolute in two features:

(1) the noun's sufformative (ending), and

(2) changes in the vowels of the noun due to accent shift.

1. Normal Patterns

a. Changes in Noun Sufformatives

Consider the following chart and pay special attention to the sufformatives of the nouns when going from absolute to construct.

Table 12.1. Construct Sufformatives

	Absolute	*Construct*
ms	סוּס	סוּס
fs	סוּסָה	סוּסַת
mp	סוּסִים	סוּסֵי
fp	סוּסוֹת	סוּסוֹת

From the above you can make the following observations:

(1) There is no special ending for the masculine singular construct.

סוּס horse	סוּס horse of
דָּבָר word	דְּבַר word of

(2) In the feminine singular, the absolute ending הָ◌ becomes תַ◌ in the construct. Thus, מַלְכַּת יִשְׂרָאֵל means "the queen of Israel."

סוּסָה mare	סוּסַת mare of
תּוֹרָה law	תּוֹרַת law of
מַלְכָּה queen	מַלְכַּת queen of

(3) In the masculine plural, the absolute ending ◌ִים becomes ◌ֵי in the construct. The same is true of feminine nouns that have the plural ending ◌ִים, such as עָרִים ("cities")

סוּסִים horses	סוּסֵי horses of
עָרִים cities	עָרֵי cities of

(4) The feminine plural ending וֹת remains the same for both the absolute and construct forms.

סוּסוֹת mares	סוּסוֹת mares of

(5) In the case of a feminine noun without the ending הָ◌, such as עִיר, "city," the construct also has no special ending. Thus, עִיר דָּוִד means "the city of David."

(6) Nouns with the dual ending ◌ַיִם become ◌ֵי in the construct. Thus, the construct of מַיִם is מֵי.

b. Vowel Changes Due to Accent Shift

The principal rule for the vowel pattern of a construct is as follows: *for purposes of vowel lengthening, shortening, or reduction, a construct chain is treated like a single word with the accent in the absolute noun.* It is as though the only accent were the accent in the absolute word (although in reality the construct often has a minor accent). With that understanding, the normal rules for changing vowel length apply. For example, the construct of דָּבָר is דְּבַר.

Blackboard 12.1. Absolute and Construct of דָּבָר Compared

The rules of accent shift and vowel change explain why the construct looks as it does.

Blackboard 12.2. Accent Shift in the Construct Noun

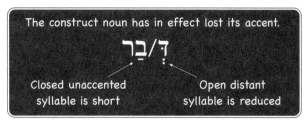

We see a similar process with the formation of the construct of the plural noun דְּבָרִים.

Blackboard 12.3. Vowel Change in the Formation of a Construct Plural Noun

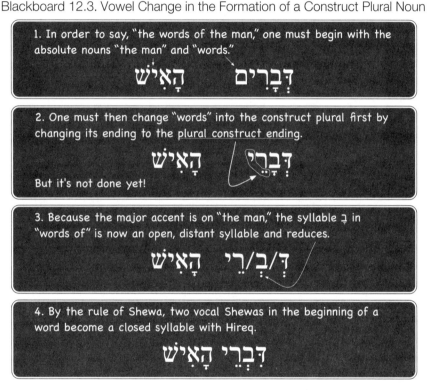

Remember:

(1) A construct chain is treated as though it were a single word with one accent (in the absolute noun); *the construct noun is in effect an unaccented proclitic.* A proclitic is a small word that, when joined to a following word, has no accent of its own but gets its accentuation from the following word.

(2) Normal rules of accent shift and vowel change then apply in the construct noun.

The next table shows how this loss of accent changes a vowel pattern.

Table 12.2. Accent Shift and Vowel Changes in the Construct Chain

הֵיכַל יְהוָה	the temple of YHWH	Syllables of הֵיכַל are הֵי/כַל, in which כַל is closed and unaccented and therefore short. הֵי is unchangeably long. The absolute of הֵיכַל is הֵיכָל.
דְּבַר הָאִישׁ	the word of the man	Syllables of דְּבַר are דְּ/בַר. בַר is closed and unaccented and therefore short. דְּ is distant and open and so reduced. The absolute of דְּבַר is דָּבָר.
יַד הַמֶּלֶךְ	the hand of the king	יַד is closed and unaccented and therefore short. The absolute of יַד is יָד.
בֵּית דָּוִד	the house of David	The absolute of בֵּית is בַּיִת. The construct is בֵּית because ־ַי becomes ־ֵ with loss of accent.
מוֹת דָּוִד	the death of David	The absolute of מוֹת is מָוֶת. The construct is מוֹת because ־ָו becomes וֹ with loss of accent.
עָרֵי הַמֶּלֶךְ	the cities of the king	The Qamets in עָרֵי is long, due to compensatory lengthening (the root is ערר). Vowels made long by compensatory lengthening do not shorten or reduce. The absolute of עָרֵי is עָרִים.
בֶּן־דָּוִד	the son of David	בֶּן is closed and unaccented and therefore short; the construct usually has the Maqqeph. The absolute of בֶּן־ is בֵּן.
בְּנֵי דָן	the sons of Dan	In בְּנֵי, בְּ is distant and open and therefore reduced. The ending ־ֵי is normal for a masculine plural construct. The absolute of בְּנֵי is בָּנִים.
אַנְשֵׁי־יִשְׂרָאֵל	the men of Israel	The absolute plural of אִישׁ is אֲנָשִׁים. As is normal, the plural construct has ־ֵי as its ending. This leads to the form אֲנָשֵׁי but /נָ/ is now a distant, open syllable and so reduces, giving us אֲנְשֵׁי. Under the rule of Shewa, however, this changes to אַנְשֵׁי.

c. Special Rule for the Absolute Singular Ending Seghol-Hey

The absolute singular ending ־ֶה becomes ־ֵה in the construct. This pattern illustrates the principle that pointed vowel letters follow specific rules and do not come under the general rules of vowel transformation (chapter 4).

מַחֲנֶה camp	מַחֲנֵה camp of

2. Irregular Construct Nouns

There are construct forms that are unpredictable in their formation.

Table 12.3. Irregular Construct Nouns

Absolute	Construct
אָב father	אֲבִי father of
אָח brother	אֲחִי brother of
אִשָּׁה woman	אֵשֶׁת woman of
מִלְחָמָה war	מִלְחֶמֶת war of
מִשְׁפָּחָה family	מִשְׁפַּחַת family of
פֶּה mouth	פִּי mouth of

For these irregular patterns, one must memorize the construct nouns since there is no rule to follow. Examples of usage are as follows.

אֲבִי יִרְמְיָהוּ The father of Jeremiah

אֲחִי יוֹנָה The brother of Jonah

פִּי יְהוָה The mouth of YHWH

3. Constructs Based on Irregular Plurals

Remember that some construct nouns are not themselves irregular but are based on irregular plural nouns. That is, they follow the normal rules for forming a construct noun but use an irregular absolute plural as their starting point.

Table 12.4. Construct Nouns Based on Irregular Plural Nouns

Absolute	Construct
אֲנָשִׁים men	אַנְשֵׁי men of
נָשִׁים women	נְשֵׁי women of
בָּנִים sons	בְּנֵי sons of
אָבוֹת fathers	אֲבוֹת fathers of
יָמִים days	יְמֵי days of
עָרִים cities	עָרֵי cities of
בָּתִּים houses	בָּתֵּי houses of

נְשֵׁי מִצְרַיִם The women of Egypt

בְּנֵי יִשְׂרָאֵל The sons of Israel

יְמֵי דָוִד הַמֶּ֫לֶךְ   The days of King David

4. Identical Absolute Singular and Construct Singular Forms

You have already seen that sometimes the absolute and construct singular forms of a noun are the same. For example, the absolute singular forms of קוֹל and of מֶ֫לֶךְ are the same as their construct singular forms.

הַקּוֹל הָיָה קוֹל־דָוִד   The voice was the voice of David.

הַמֶּ֫לֶךְ בִּירוּשָׁלַ֫יִם הָיָה מֶ֫לֶךְ יִשְׂרָאֵל   The king in Jerusalem was the king of Israel.

In general, there are two types of nouns in which the absolute and construct forms are the same in the singular.

(1) Nouns that are monosyllables with unchangeable long vowels, such as קוֹל and סוּס. These nouns have no endings to change, and their vowels, being unchangeable, do not change.

(2) All nouns that are of the מֶ֫לֶךְ class (with accent on the penult). These nouns are called "segholates." We will learn more about them in chapter 16.

Table 12.5. Some Nouns that are the Same in the Absolute and Construct Singular

Absolute	Construct
קוֹל voice	קוֹל voice of
סוּס horse	סוּס horse of
מֶ֫לֶךְ king	מֶ֫לֶךְ king of
עֶ֫בֶד servant	עֶ֫בֶד servant of

E. Vocabulary

1. Special Vocabulary Word: יהוה

יהוה   This is the proper name of Israel's God. English Bibles routinely translate it as "the LORD," but it was supposedly pronounced "Yahweh" (יַהְוֶה) in biblical times. Out of reverence for the divine name, it is occassionally rendered *haššēm* ("the name" in Hebrew) or *šĕmā'* ("the name" in Aramaic), but more often, it is pronounced *'ădōnay* ("my/the lord"). The Masoretes signaled this pronunciation by using the vowel pattern of אֲדֹנָי, while retaining the consonants of Yahweh (= יְהֹוָה or simply יְהוָה). The Germanized *Jehovah* resulted from a misunderstanding of this Masoretic signal.

2. Core Vocabulary

a. Verbs

יָרַד	Qal: יָרַד go down, descend
עָמַד	Qal: עָמַד stand

b. Other Words

אָח	brother Ⓜ |אֲחִי| (plural = אַחִים)
הֵיכָל	temple, palace Ⓜ |הֵיכַל|
יָד	hand Ⓕ |יַד|
מֵאָה	hundred Ⓕ |מְאַת| (usually precedes a *singular* noun, as in מֵאָה שָׁנָה ["100 years"], sometimes written מְאַת שָׁנָה)
מַחֲנֶה	camp, army ⓂⒻ |מַחֲנֵה|
מַלְאָךְ	messenger, angel Ⓜ |מַלְאַךְ|
פֶּה	mouth Ⓜ |פִּי|
קוֹל	voice Ⓜ |קוֹל|
שָׁנָה	year Ⓕ |שְׁנַת| (plural = שָׁנִים)
תַּחַת	under, instead of

3. Reading Vocabulary

לֵץ	mocker, scorner
חַטָּא	sinful, sinner
חֶפְצוֹ	"his delight"
מוֹשַׁב	seat

4. Proper Names

בָּרוּךְ	Baruch
יוֹנָה	Jonah
יִרְמְיָהוּ	Jeremiah
נִינְוֵה	Nineveh
קֹרַח	Korah

F. Guided Reading from Psalm 1

וּבְדֶרֶךְ חַטָּאִים לֹא עָמָד

וּבְמוֹשַׁב לֵצִים לֹא יָשָׁב

כִּי אִם בְּתוֹרַת יְהוָה חֶפְצוֹ

(1) וּבְדֶרֶךְ חַטָּאִים has the conjunction and the preposition בְּ, and it is a construct chain. It means "and in (the) way of sinners."

(2) וּבְמוֹשַׁב לֵצִים is also a construct chain with the conjunction and the preposition בְּ.

(3) These two lines mean "And in the way of sinners he does not stand, / and in the seat of mockers he does not sit."

(4) The words כִּי אִם look like they would mean "for if," and indeed sometimes they have that meaning. Often, however, they function idiomatically to mean "rather," "except," or "to the contrary."

(5) You can recognize בְּתוֹרַת as the construct of תוֹרָה with the preposition בְּ.

(6) חֶפְצוֹ, "his delight," is the noun חֵפֶץ with a pronoun suffix וֹ that means "his."

(7) The last line means "To the contrary, his delight is in the law of YHWH."

CHAPTER 13
PREPOSITIONS

There are several types of prepositions in Hebrew. You are already very familiar with many of them.

A. Inseparable Prepositions

1. Review of Basic Rules

(1) **Inseparable** prepositions are prefixed directly to words. They do not occur independently as separate words:

בְּ   in, by, with

לְ   to, for; sometimes it means "of"

כְּ   like, as, according to

(2) In nouns without the article, the inseparable prepositions are simply prefixed as בְּ, לְ or כְּ.

שָׂדֶה	+ בְּ	→	בְּשָׂדֶה	in a field
יֶלֶד	+ לְ	→	לְיֶלֶד	to *or* for a boy
מֶלֶךְ	+ כְּ	→	כְּמֶלֶךְ	like a king

(3) Remember that with the definite article present, the הַ of the article disappears and is replaced by the consonant of the preposition:

הַשָּׂדֶה	+ בְּ	→	בַּשָּׂדֶה	in the field
הַיֶּלֶד	+ לְ	→	לַיֶּלֶד	to *or* for the boy
הַמֶּלֶךְ	+ כְּ	→	כַּמֶּלֶךְ	like the king

2. Additional Note: The Disappearing הַ in Biblical Hebrew

Frequently a הַ at the beginning of a word, especially if it is a preformative, will be lost when another, stronger letter is superimposed over it. This occurs especially with certain verb forms. For now, you will see the disappearing הַ in the form of a preposition superimposed on a definite article.

B. Independent Prepositions

Independent prepositions are those that stand as separate words before the nouns they govern, such as תַּחַת ("under, beneath, instead of"), אַחַר ("after, behind"), or לִפְנֵי ("before, in front of, in the presence of").

| לִפְנֵי הַמֶּלֶךְ | before the king |
| תַּחַת הַבַּיִת | under the house |

C. Maqqeph Prepositions

Some prepositions are prefixed to a word with a Maqqeph. A Maqqeph (⁻), like a hyphen, joins two words together. Words joined with Maqqeph are treated as though they were a single word with one accent. Among the most common prepositions of this type are the following.

Table 13.1. Maqqeph Prepositions

עַל	on, upon, concerning	עַל־הַהֵיכָל	upon the temple
אֶל	to, toward	אֶל־הַהֵיכָל	to the temple
אֶת	with	אֶת־הַמֶּלֶךְ	with the king
עַד	until, as far as	עַד־הַהֵיכָל	as far as the temple
מִן	from	מִן־הַהֵיכָל	from the temple

Distinguish אֶת meaning "with" from the sign of the direct object. Also, אֶת is sometimes written without the Maqqeph as אֵת.

D. The Preposition מִן

1. The Morphology of מִן

The preposition מִן appears in several forms.

(1) Frequently, מִן will be prefixed to a word with Maqqeph as above. For example, מִן־הַבַּיִת, "from the house."

(2) The preposition can also occur with assimilation of the נ. **Assimilation** refers to one letter being absorbed by and doubling the following letter. In Hebrew, the letter נ frequently assimilates to a following letter. In English, by analogy, "in" + "legal" yields "illegal," with an assimilated "n" and a doubled "l." Similarly, the נ of the preposition מִן will assimilate into the following consonant and be represented as a Daghesh Forte.

מִן + מֶלֶךְ → מִמֶּלֶךְ from a king

The Daghesh Forte in the second מ represents the assimilated נ of the preposition.

(3) The gutturals and ר cannot be doubled. If a preposition is affixed to a word that begins with a guttural or ר, either compensatory lengthening or virtual doubling occurs, as in מֵאִישׁ, "from a man," or מֵחוּץ, "from outside." You learned about compensatory lengthening in chapter 4. In "virtual doubling," a guttural is treated as though it had doubled, and the vowel in front of it will be short, exactly as though it were in a

closed, unaccented syllable. In מֵחוּץ, because of virtual doubling, the Hireq under the מ does not lengthen even though it appears to be in an open pretonic.

מִן + אִישׁ → מֵאִישׁ from a man

(compensatory lengthening)

מִן + חוּץ → מֵחוּץ from outside

(virtual doubling)

(4) Before י the Shewa is lost. Therefore, יְרוּשָׁלַם with מִן becomes מִירוּשָׁלַם, "from Jerusalem."

(5) If the noun has a definite article, the ה of the article is not supplanted. Instead,

   (a) either the Maqqeph is used (מִן־הַמֶּלֶךְ)

   (b) or compensatory lengthening occurs (מֵהַמֶּלֶךְ).

2. Meaning and usage of מִן

(1) As in the previous examples, מִן often means "from," as in מִן־הַבַּיִת, "*from* the house."

(2) Used with an adjective, מִן often means "than," and the adjective has a comparative sense.

Blackboard 13.1. The Comparative Use of מִן

צַדִּיק הַנָּבִיא

By itself, this simply means "The prophet is righteous."

מֵהַמֶּלֶךְ

By itself, this could be taken to mean "from the king" or "than the king."

צַדִּיק הַנָּבִיא מֵהַמֶּלֶךְ

Together, these words mean "The prophet is more righteous than the king."

(3) A variant usage of מִן with a comparative sense is where it implies that something is "too much for " someone or something to deal with. For example:

קָשָׁה הָעֲבוֹדָה מֵהָאֲנָשִׁים The work (הָעֲבוֹדָה) is *too* difficult (קָשָׁה) *for* the men.

(4) Sometimes מִן has a "partitive" meaning with the sense of "some of," as in:

מֵהָאֲנָשִׁים *some of* the men

E. The Preposition בֵּין

The preposition בֵּין means "between." It is actually the construct of בַּיִן, meaning "interval." It is usually used without a Maqqeph, as in בֵּין הַחוֹמֹת ("between the walls"). However, with two different objects or groups, Hebrew often either repeats בֵּין or has בֵּין followed by לְ, as in the following:

בֵּין הַהֵיכָל וּבֵין הַמִּזְבֵּחַ　 between the temple and the altar

בֵּין הַהֵיכָל וְלַמִּזְבֵּחַ　 between the temple and the altar

An expression such as בֵּין מַיִם לְמָיִם would not mean simply "between water" but would indicate distinguishing one body of water from another body of water.

F. Additional Remarks on Prepositions

1. Compounding of Prepositions

Hebrew frequently compounds or "stacks" prepositions as in the following examples.

(1) מֵעַל　　　　"from upon"
　　　　　　　(מִן is prefixed to עַל)

(2) מִתַּחַת　　　"from under"
　　　　　　　(מִן is prefixed to תַּחַת)

(3) מֵאֵת　　　　"from with"
　　　　　　　(מִן is prefixed to אֵת)

In translating, any one of the above three examples might be is rendered simply as "from."

2. The Noun פָּנִים as a Preposition

The noun פָּנִים means "face." It is only found in the plural form although it often has a singular meaning. פְּנֵי is the construct form of פָּנִים and means "face of." פְּנֵי lies behind a number of common prepositions. For example, פְּנֵי combined with the preposition לְ yields לִפְנֵי, meaning "to the face of." In ordinary usage, לִפְנֵי has the meaning "before" or "in the presence of."

Common examples of this kind include:

(1) לִפְנֵי　　　　before, in the presence of

(2) מִפְּנֵי　　　　away from, out from, from the presence of, from before, on account of, because of

(3) מִלִּפְנֵי　　　away from, from the presence of, on account of

(4) עַל־פְּנֵי　　　in the face of, in the sight of, in front of, before, up against, opposite to

3. The Noun תָּוֶךְ as a Preposition

The noun תָּוֶךְ means "middle," and it is used in the construct to form a preposition such as מִתּוֹךְ, "from the middle of."

Common examples include:

(1)	בְּתוֹךְ	in the middle of
(2)	מִתּוֹךְ	from the middle of

G. Vocabulary

1. Core Vocabulary

a. Verbs

ענה	Qal: עָנָה answer
פקד	Qal: פָּקַד inspect, attend to, urge, muster, call to account, visit, punish

b. Other Words

אֵת	with (distinguish this from the direct object particle אֵת)
בֵּין	between (this is actually the construct of בַּיִן, "interval")
חָמֵשׁ	five (with a feminine noun, as in חָמֵשׁ נָשִׁים, "five women"; חֲמִשָּׁה with a masculine noun, as in חֲמִשָּׁה אֲנָשִׁים, "five men")
יָם	sea Ⓜ |יַם| (plural = יַמִּים)
לִפְנֵי	before, in the presence of
מִן	from, than
עַד	until, as far as, unto
עִם	with
פָּנִים	face, front (plural in form but often singular in meaning) Ⓜ Ⓕ |פְּנֵי|
תָּוֶךְ	middle, midst Ⓜ |תוֹךְ|

2. Reading Vocabulary

מֹץ	chaff
תִּדְּפֶנּוּ	"she will drive away him"; a Qal *yiqtol* 3fs (תִּדֹּף, "she will drive away") with a suffix that means "him"

3. Proper Names

סְדֹם	Sodom

H. Guided Reading from Psalm 1

כִּי אִם־כַּמֹּץ אֲשֶׁר־תִּדְּפֶנּוּ רוּחַ

(1) You have already seen כִּי אִם.

(2) The subject and verb "he is" are not explicitly stated but are implied.

(3) In כַּמֹּץ, you see מֹץ with the definite article and the preposition כְּ. Notice how the preposition has displaced the ה of the definite article.

(4) Thus, כִּי אִם־כַּמֹּץ means "Rather, (he is) like the chaff."

(5) אֲשֶׁר is the relative pronoun "which."

(6) In תִּדְּפֶנּוּ, you see a Qal *yiqtol* 3fs, but it also has a suffix.

  (a) The *yiqtol* 3fs used here is תִּדֹף. Notice that in form it is similar to תִּפֹּל, "she will fall." תִּדֹף means "She will drive away."

  (b) The verb is feminine because the subject, רוּחַ, is feminine. תִּדֹף רוּחַ would mean "the wind will drive away."

  (c) It has a suffix נּוּ that means "him." When נּוּ is added to תִּדֹף, the result is תִּדְּפֶנּוּ. Thus, תִּדְּפֶנּוּ רוּחַ means "the wind will drive away him."

  (d) The suffix "him" refers to the masculine noun "chaff" (מֹץ). In English, since the word refers to chaff, we would say "it" instead of "him." Thus, תִּדְּפֶנּוּ רוּחַ would mean "the wind will drive away it."

  (e) אֲשֶׁר־תִּדְּפֶנּוּ רוּחַ is therefore literally, "which the wind will drive away it." That is, both אֲשֶׁר, "which," and the נּוּ suffix ("it") refer back to the chaff. In normal English, we would simply translate the words as "which the wind will drive away" without using the word "it."

  (f) What we see in this Hebrew phrase is called a "resumptive pronoun." Contrast the two following sentences.

   (i) "The man whom you see is my brother." This is a normal English sentence.

   (ii) "The man who you see him is my brother." This is an artificial English sentence that imitates the style of the Hebrew resumptive pronoun. It means the same thing as the first sentence.

   (iii) Thus, "who" + (verb + subject) + "him" = "whom" + (verb + subject)

(7) The whole line means "Rather, (he is) like the chaff that the wind drives away."

CHAPTER 14
PRONOMINAL SUFFIXES ON NOUNS AND PREPOSITIONS

A. An Introduction to Pronominal Suffixes

A **pronominal suffix**, as its name implies, is a suffix that represents a pronoun. You have already seen this in Ps 1, where וּבְתוֹרָתוֹ means "and in *his* law." Here, the suffix וֹ represents the 3ms pronoun "his." In the same way, סוּסוֹ means "*his* horse."

Pronominal suffixes come in two forms, which we refer to as Type-1 and Type-2 suffixes. When attached to a noun, pronoun suffixes mark possession (e.g., *his, my, their*). Similar suffixes occur on prepositions and verbs, where they commonly mark an object (e.g., *him, me, them*). Type-2 suffixes are distinguished by the presence of י in every form, whether as a true consonant or as a vowel letter.

Table 14.1. Type-1 and Type-2 Pronoun Suffixes

	Type-1 Suffixes	Type-1 Alternate	Type-2 Suffixes	Translation: Possessive/ Objective
3ms	◌וֹ	◌ֹהוּ	◌ָיו	his/him
3fs	◌ָהּ	◌ֹהָ	◌ֶיהָ	her/she
2ms	◌ְךָ[1]		◌ֶיךָ	your / you (ms)
2fs	◌ֵךְ		◌ַיִךְ	your / you (fs)
1cs	◌ִי	נִי	◌ַי	my / me
3mp	◌ָם	הֶם	◌ֵיהֶם	their / them (mp)
3fp	◌ָן	הֶן	◌ֵיהֶן	their / them (fp)
2mp	◌ְכֶם[2]		◌ֵיכֶם	your / you (mp)
2fp	◌ְכֶן[2]		◌ֵיכֶן	your / you (fp)
1cp	◌ֵנוּ		◌ֵינוּ	our / us

B. Pronominal Suffixes on Nouns

Regardless of whether a noun is singular or plural, it can take a singular or plural suffix. For example, the masculine singular noun סוּס could appear as סוּסָהּ, "her horse," or סוּסָן, "their

---

1. Vocal shewa.
2. Silent shewa.

(fp) horse." (Note the Mappiq in the ה of the 3fs Type-1 suffix, marking the ה as a true consonant and not a vowel letter.) Similarly, the feminine plural noun שְׁפָחוֹת can take a singular suffix (e.g., שְׁפָחוֹתַי, "my maids") or a plural suffix (e.g., שְׁפָחוֹתֵינוּ, "our maids"). What is intriguing is that Type-1 suffixes are always applied to singular nouns, whereas Type-2 suffixes are consistently restricted to plural nouns.

1. Pronominal Suffixes on Masculine Nouns

a. Type-1 Pronominal Suffixes with Masculine Singular Nouns

The full paradigm of the masculine singular noun סוּס, "horse," with pronoun suffixes is as follows.

Table 14.2. סוּס with Type-1 Suffixes

	Singular Suffix	Plural Suffix
3m	סוּסוֹ his horse	סוּסָם their (mp) horse
3f	סוּסָהּ her horse	סוּסָן their (fp) horse
2m	סוּסְךָ your (ms) horse	סוּסְכֶם your (mp) horse
2f	סוּסֵךְ your (fs) horse	סוּסְכֶן your (fp) horse
1c	סוּסִי my horse	סוּסֵנוּ our horse

Notice first how the singular noun סוּס can take both singular and plural suffixes. Since סוּס is a single syllable with the unchangeable long vowel Shureq, it is a particularly simple paradigm. The vowel וּ in סוּס does not change regardless of what suffixes are added to the word.

Most nouns are more complex because, when a suffix is added, the addition of a new syllable causes the accent to shift. This in turn causes some vowels to shorten, lengthen, or reduce. For example, when the suffix וֹ is added to the noun דָּבָר, the new word is דְּבָרוֹ, "his word."

These changes are usually quite easy to deal with as long as you remember the guidelines for accent shift and vowel transformation (chapter 4). Remember, for example, that an open propretonic or distant syllable generally reduces to Shewa, whereas an open pretonic syllable is generally long. The following examples with דָּבָר illustrate this:

Table 14.3. Examples of דָּבָר with Type-1 Suffixes

Form	Meaning	Syllables	Comments
דְּבָרוֹ	his word	דְּ/בָ/רוֹ	/דְּ/ is distant open and thus reduced. /בָ/ is an open pretonic syllable and long.

דְּבָרָהּ	her word	דְּ/בָ/רָהּ	/דְ/ is distant open and thus reduced. /בָ/ is an open pretonic syllable and long.
דְּבַרְכֶם	your (mp) word	דְּ/בַרְ/כֶם	/דְ/ is distant open and thus reduced. /בַרְ/ is a closed, unaccented syllable and short.

There are some alternative forms of the pronouns. In the reading from Ps 1 with this chapter, we see a word with the alternative 3ms pronoun suffix נֵהוּ. It means "his," just as the suffix וֹ on סוּסוֹ does. For now, however, focus on learning the standard suffixes in the above table. Also, alternative suffixes appear on verbs. You have seen the suffix with נ and meaning "him" in the word תִדְּפֶנּוּ, "she drives away him."

b. Type-2 Pronominal Suffixes with Masculine Plural Nouns

The Type-2 pronominal suffixes that Hebrew adds to a plural noun are similar to but not the same as the Type-1 suffixes that it adds to singular nouns. Note the distinctive ׳ throughout the Type-2 suffix paradigm. When adding a suffix to a masculine plural noun,

(1) the plural ending ִים is dropped and

(2) the distinctive Type-2 pronominal suffix is added in its place.

For example, the first singular pronoun suffix ("my") for plurals is ַי, and thus the noun סוּסִים with this suffix is סוּסַי, "my horses." In this case, the noun is plural, but the suffix is singular.

Table 14.4. סוּסִים with Type-2 Suffixes

	Singular Suffix	*Plural Suffix*
3m	סוּסָיו his horses	סוּסֵיהֶם their (mp) horses
3f	סוּסֶיהָ her horses	סוּסֵיהֶן their (fp) horses
2m	סוּסֶיךָ your (ms) horses	סוּסֵיכֶם your (mp) horses
2f	סוּסַיִךְ your (fs) horses	סוּסֵיכֶן your (fp) horses
1c	סוּסַי my horses	סוּסֵינוּ our horses

Once again, many nouns will undergo vowel transformation due to accent shift, but the normal rules of vowel transformation still apply (such as that an open pretonic tends to lengthen the vowel). The following examples of דְּבָרִים with pronominal suffixes illustrate how the rules are applied.

Table 14.5. Examples of דְּבָרִים with Type-2 Suffixes

Form	Meaning	Syllabification	Comments
דְּבָרַי	my words	דְּ/בָ/רַי	/דְ/ is distant open and thus reduced. /בָ/ is an open pretonic syllable and thus long.

דְּבָרֶיהָ	her words	דְּ/בָ/רֶ/יהָ	/דְּ/ is distant open and thus reduced. /בָ/ is an open pretonic syllable and thus long.
דִּבְרֵיכֶם	your (mp) words	דִּבְ/רֵי/כֶם	Hypothetically it was דְּ/בָ/רֵי/כֶם, in which both /בָ/ and /דְּ/ were distant open syllables and so reduced, but through the rule of Shewa, the two combined to form the single closed syllable /דִּבְ/.
דִּבְרֵיהֶן	their (fp) words	דִּבְ/רֵי/הֶן	Hypothetically it was דְּ/בָ/רֵי/הֶן, in which both /בָ/ and /דְּ/ were distant open syllables and so reduced, but through the rule of Shewa, the two combined to form the single closed syllable /דִּבְ/.

2. Pronominal Suffixes on Feminine Nouns

a. Type-1 Pronominal Suffixes with Feminine Singular Nouns

Feminine singular nouns with the ending הָ replace that ending with either תַ or תָ; normal rules of vowel transformation determine whether Qamets or Pathach is used. Other than that, feminine singular nouns have the normal Type-1 pronominal suffixes that are used with singular nouns. This can be illustrated with suffixes added to שִׁפְחָה, "maidservant."

(1) The syllabification of שִׁפְחָתִי, "my maidservant," is שִׁפְ/חָ/תִי. The syllable /חָ/ is open pretonic and therefore is long (Qamets).

(2) The syllabification of שִׁפְחַתְכֶם, "your (mp) maidservant," is שִׁפְ/חַתְ/כֶם. The syllable /חַתְ/ is closed and unaccented and therefore short. We would expect to see a Daghesh Lene in the כ of שִׁפְחַתְכֶם, but it almost never has one.

(3) The Qamets in /חָתְ/ of שִׁפְחָתְךָ, "your (ms) maidservant," appears odd, but there is probably a minor accent over the Qamets.

The paradigm below applies to feminine singular nouns ending with הָ. Feminine nouns without special endings and those with the ending ת behave like masculine singular nouns. For example, with עִיר, we see עִירָם, "their city," and עִירוֹ, "his city." With בְּרִית, we see בְּרִיתִי, "my covenant," and בְּרִיתוֹ, "his covenant."

Table 14.6. שִׁפְחָה with Type-1 Suffixes

	Singular Suffix	*Plural Suffix*
3m	שִׁפְחָתוֹ his maid	שִׁפְחָתָם their (mp) maid
3f	שִׁפְחָתָה her maid	שִׁפְחָתָן their (fp) maid
2m	שִׁפְחָתְךָ your (ms) maid	שִׁפְחַתְכֶם your (mp) maid
2f	שִׁפְחָתֵךְ your (fs) maid	שִׁפְחַתְכֶן your (fp) maid
1c	שִׁפְחָתִי my maid	שִׁפְחָתֵנוּ our maid

Blackboard 14.1. Suffixed Masculine and Feminine Nouns Compared

Masculine noun: אִישׁ	Feminine noun: תּוֹרָה	Feminine noun without feminine ending: עִיר
אִישָׁהּ	**תּוֹרָתִי**	**עִירָם**
"her husband"	"my law"	"their city"

b. Type-2 Pronominal Suffixes with Feminine Plural Nouns

Feminine plural nouns with the ending וֹת retain the וֹת ending and add the pronominal suffix directly after that ending. Feminine plurals with suffixes of this kind are easy to recognize because there is little if any vowel transformation. Type-2 suffixes with the plural of שִׁפְחָה, "maid," are as follows:

Table 14.7. שְׁפָחוֹת with Type-2 Suffixes

	Singular Suffix	*Plural Suffix*
3m	שִׁפְחוֹתָיו his maids	שִׁפְחוֹתָם their (mp) maids
3f	שִׁפְחוֹתֶיהָ her maids	שִׁפְחוֹתָן their (fp) maids
2m	שִׁפְחוֹתֶיךָ your (ms) maids	שִׁפְחוֹתֵיכֶם your (mp) maids
2f	שִׁפְחוֹתַיִךְ your (fs) maids	שִׁפְחוֹתֵיכֶן your (fp) maids
1c	שִׁפְחוֹתַי my maids	שִׁפְחוֹתֵינוּ our maids

(1) The feminine plural ending וֹת is often written defectively, with a simple Holem instead of Holem-Waw. We thus frequently see forms like שִׁפְחֹתַי instead of שִׁפְחוֹתַי.

(2) The third plural suffixes on feminine nouns are usually ◌ָם and ◌ָן rather than ◌ֵיהֶם and ◌ֵיהֶן (e.g., חֻקּוֹתָם, "their statutes").

(3) Adding a suffix sometimes causes vowel changes in a feminine noun.

  (a) When the suffix is added to שְׁפָחוֹת, the resultant form is first a hypothetical form: שְׁ/פְ/חוֹ/תָיו (both /שְׁ/ and /פְ/ are distant open syllables and reduced).

  (b) By the rule of Shewa, this becomes שִׁפְחוֹתָיו.

(4) If a feminine plural noun has the ending ◌ִים instead of the normal וֹת, it follows the rules for masculine plural nouns. With the feminine plural עָרִים, "cities," therefore, we see forms like עָרֵיהֶם, "their cities," and עָרָיו, "his cities."

3. Pronominal Suffixes in Construct Chains

A construct noun will never have a pronominal suffix, but an absolute can take such a suffix. A pronoun suffix makes a noun definite. Thus, in a construct chain, the construct noun is also definite by reason of the definiteness of the absolute. Therefore, רֶגֶל סוּסוֹ means "*the* foot of *his* horse" or "his horse's foot."

4. Irregularities in Nouns with Pronominal Suffixes

Some nouns behave in an irregular manner with pronoun suffixes. For example, שֵׁם ("name") is irregular: "his name" is שְׁמוֹ; "her name" is שְׁמָהּ; and "your (ms) name" is שִׁמְךָ.

C. Pronominal Suffixes on Prepositions

Prepositions can also take pronoun suffixes. While some use Type-1 suffixes, others take Type-2. Regardless of which pattern is used, the translation value is the same for both types. Usually the formation of a preposition with a suffix is easy to recognize. In some cases, however, prepositions with suffixes follow patterns that are peculiar.

1. Prepositions with Type-1 Suffixes

a. The Prepositions לְ and בְּ

The inseparable prepositions לְ, "to, for," and בְּ, "in, with," take Type-1 pronoun suffixes (like those found with סוּס).

Table 14.8. The Preposition לְ with Type-1 Suffixes

לוֹ to him	לָהֶם to them (mp)
לָהּ to her	לָהֶן to them (fp)
לְךָ to you (ms)	לָכֶם to you (mp)
לָךְ to you (fs)	לָכֶן to you (fp)
לִי to me	לָנוּ to us

Table 14.9. The Preposition בְּ with Type-1 Suffixes

בּוֹ in him	בָּהֶם or בָּם in them (mp)
בָּהּ in her	בָּן or בָּהֶן in them (fp)
בְּךָ in you (ms)	בָּכֶם in you (mp)
בָּךְ in you (fs)	בָּכֶן in you (fp)
בִּי in me	בָּנוּ in us

(1) If the suffix begins with a consonant, it will have Qamets as the "linking vowel" with the preposition (except with the 2ms suffix).

(2) Note that the 3mp and 3fp have the alternate Type-1 suffixes הֶם and הֶן.

b. Prepositions from Geminate Roots

Some prepositions come from "geminate" roots. A geminate root is one in which the last two of the three root letters are the same. For example, עַם, "with," is from the root עמם. The repeated letter (in this case, מ) is called the "geminate" letter.

(1) When the preposition stands by itself, the final letter of the root עמם is lost so that the word appears as עַם.

(2) When a Type-1 suffix is added, the original doubling of the geminate letter appears in the form of a Daghesh Forte. Thus, "with him" is עִמּוֹ.

(3) If the suffix begins with a consonant, the linking vowel between the preposition and the suffix is Qamets (except with the 2ms suffix).

Table 14.10. The Preposition עַם with Type-1 Suffixes

עִמּוֹ with him	עִמָּם with them (mp)
עִמָּהּ with her	עִמָּן with them (fp)
עִמְּךָ with you (ms)	עִמָּכֶם with you (mp)
עִמָּךְ with you (fs)	עִמָּכֶן with you (fp)
עִמִּי with me	עִמָּנוּ with us

The preposition אֵת (also meaning "with") is also geminate, from the root אתת. Its pattern is very similar to that of עַם with suffixes.

(1) When the preposition stands by itself, the final letter of the root אתת is lost, so that the word appears as אֵת.

(2) When a suffix is added, the original doubling of the geminate letter appears in the form of a Daghesh Forte. Thus, "with him" is אִתּוֹ.

(3) If the suffix begins with a consonant, the linking vowel between the preposition and the suffix is vocal Shewa or Qamets.

Table 14.11. The Preposition אֵת with Type-1 Suffixes

אִתּוֹ with him	אִתָּם with them (mp)
אִתָּהּ with her	אִתָּן with them (fp)
אִתְּךָ with you (ms)	אִתְּכֶם with you (mp)
אִתָּךְ with you (fs)	אִתְּכֶן with you (fp)
אִתִּי with me	אִתָּנוּ with us

c. The Prepositions כְּ and מִן

With pronominal suffixes, the prepositions כְּ, "as, like," and מִן, "from," only look as we would expect in the *third and second person plural forms*. For example:

(1) "From you" (mp) is מִכֶּם; it is similar to לָכֶם (remember that the ן of מִן assimilates).

(2) "Like them" (mp) is כָּהֶם; it is similar to לָהֶם.

As is clear in the paradigms below, when the suffix is *singular or first plural*, the patterns are quite different.

(1) With כְּ, these forms are actually based on an alternative preposition that also means "like," כְּמוֹ. When the Type-1 suffix is added, the vowel lengthens to Qamets in accordance with the normal rule that an open pretonic lengthens (e.g., כָּמוֹנוּ).

(2) With מִן, the forms are based on a reduplicated form of the preposition, מִן + מִן, which gives us a form something like מִמֶּן, to which the suffix is added. The exact forms the words take, however, are not easily predicted and must be learned; see the table below.

(3) The 3ms suffix with these prepositions is הוּ◌.

   (a) Added to כְּמוֹ, this gives us כָּמוֹהוּ.

   (b) Added to מִן, it gives us מִמֶּנּוּ, which can be confusing since it is also the form of מִן with a 1cs suffix. Observe the full declensions of the two patterns below.

Table 14.12. The Preposition כְּ with Type-1 Suffixes

כָּמוֹהוּ like him	כָּהֶם like them (mp)
כָּמוֹהָ like her	כָּהֵן like them (fp)
כָּמוֹךָ like you (ms)	כָּכֶם like you (mp)
כָּמוֹךְ like you (fs)	כָּכֵן like you (fp)
כָּמוֹנִי like me	כָּמוֹנוּ like us

Table 14.13. The Preposition מִן with Type-1 Suffixes

מִמֶּנּוּ from him	מֵהֶם from them (mp)
מִמֶּנָּה from her	מֵהֶן from them (fp)
מִמְּךָ from you (ms)	מִכֶּם from you (mp)
מִמֵּךְ from you (fs)	מִכֵּן from you (fp)
מִמֶּנִּי from me	מִמֶּנּוּ from us

Remember, מִמֶּנּוּ can mean either "from him" or "from us."

2. Prepositions with Type-2 Suffixes

Several prepositions take Type-2 suffixes (like those found on plural nouns such as סוּסָיו, "his horses"). This is strictly a matter of morphology (that is, of the form the word takes). The preposition is not understood to be somehow a plural.

(1) The word לִי, "to me," has the preposition לְ with the Type-1 pronoun suffix, as in סוּסִי, "my horse."

(2) By contrast, עָלַי, "on me," has the preposition עַל, "upon, over," with the Type-2 suffix, as in סוּסַי, "my horses."

(3) The normal Hebrew tendencies for vowel lengthening and reduction are apparent, as in עָלַי (the Qamets is in an open pretonic syllable and thus is lengthened) and עֲלֵיכֶם (the Hateph Pathach is in a distant open syllable and thus is reduced).

(4) The endings on אֶל, "to, toward," תַּחַת, "under, instead of," and אַחֲרֵי, "after, behind," are like those on עַל as presented here.

Table 14.14. The Preposition עַל with Type-2 Suffixes

עָלָיו	on him	עֲלֵיהֶם	on them (mp)
עָלֶיהָ	on her	עֲלֵיהֶן	on them (fp)
עָלֶיךָ	on you (ms)	עֲלֵיכֶם	on you (mp)
עָלַיִךְ	on you (fs)	עֲלֵיכֶן	on you (fp)
עָלַי	on me	עָלֵינוּ	on us

The preposition לִפְנֵי naturally takes Type-2 suffixes because the preposition is actually based on the noun פָּנִים, "face," which is plural in form though usually singular in meaning. Thus, we see examples such as לְפָנָיו, "before him," לְפָנֶיךָ, "before you," and לִפְנֵיהֶם, "before them."

D. Alternate Pronominal Suffixes

Learn the pronominal suffixes by memorizing either the initial table of Type-1 and Type-2 suffixes or the singular and plural forms of סוּס and שִׁפְחָה. However, remember that sometimes the pronominal suffixes take alternate forms. In כָּמוֹהוּ, "like him," you saw that the 3ms suffix is sometimes הוּ◌. In Ps 1, you saw the 3ms suffix נּוּ◌ in the verb תִּדְּפֶנּוּ. Suffixes like this are common on verbs, but for now, we will concentrate on the suffixes that are common with nouns and prepositions.

E. Vocabulary

1. Core Vocabulary

a. Verbs

כרת	Qal: כָּרַת cut, cut off (when used with בְּרִית, it means "make a covenant")
קרב	Qal: קָרַב draw near, approach
שכב	Qal: שָׁכַב lie (down), have sexual intercourse

b. Other Words

אַחֲרֵי   after, behind (also found as the singular אַחַר)

כֹּה   thus

כֹּל   all, whole, every (in construct with Maqqeph כָּל־)

עֵת   time, season F |עֵת|

פְּרִי   fruit M |פְּרִי|

קֹדֶשׁ   holiness, holy thing M |קֹדֶשׁ|

רֶגֶל   foot F |רֶגֶל|

שֶׁבַע   seven (used with a feminine noun; the feminine form שִׁבְעָה is used
                  with a masculine noun)

שֵׁם   name M |שֵׁם|

2. Reading Vocabulary

וְעָלֵהוּ   "and his leaf"

יִבּוֹל   "it will wither"

3. Proper Names

אֲבִימֶלֶךְ   Abimelech

נָחוֹר   Nahor

שָׂרָה   Sarah

F. Guided Reading from Psalm 1

אֲשֶׁר פִּרְיוֹ יִתֵּן בְּעִתּוֹ
וְעָלֵהוּ לֹא־יִבּוֹל

(1) You already know אֲשֶׁר.

(2) You can see that פִּרְיוֹ is פְּרִי with the 3ms suffix. פִּרְיוֹ is divided into syllables as /פִּר
     יוֹ. The syllable /פִּר/ is now closed and unaccented, and it must be short (not reduced,
     as in the lexical form, פְּרִי).

(3) You know יִתֵּן.

(4) בְּעִתּוֹ is the preposition בְּ and the 3ms suffix on עֵת.

(5) וְעָלֵהוּ is the noun עָלֶה, "leaf," with the conjunction and an alternative 3ms suffix,
     ֵהוּ. It means "and his leaf"; in English we say, "and its leaf."

(6) יִבּוֹל is a Qal *yiqtol* 3ms of the verb נבל, "wither."

(7) The whole means "Which gives its fruit in its season. And its leaf does not wither."

CHAPTER 15
ADJECTIVES AND THE QAL PARTICIPLES

A. Adjectives

1. The Inflection of Adjectives

a. Adjective Endings

The conjugation of טוֹב, "good," illustrates basic adjective inflection.

Table 15.1. The Adjective טוֹב

	Singular	Plural
Masculine	טוֹב	טוֹבִים
Feminine	טוֹבָה	טוֹבוֹת

Thus, the endings for the adjective are as in the table below.

Table 15.2. Adjective Endings

	Singular	Plural
Masculine	(none)	◌ִים
Feminine	◌ָה	וֹת

b. Adjectives with Propretonic Reduction

Two-syllable adjectives with Qamets (◌ָ) in the first syllable undergo vowel reduction to Shewa (◌ְ) when a feminine or plural inflectional ending is added. The adjective גָּדוֹל, "great," illustrates this.

Table 15.3. The Adjective גָּדוֹל

	Singular	Plural
Masculine	גָּדוֹל	גְּדוֹלִים
Feminine	גְּדוֹלָה	גְּדוֹלוֹת

Sometimes adjectives are irregular, as is קָטֹן, "small." Note that here, the נ is doubled in the feminine singular and the masculine and feminine plurals, and there is a vowel change. Remember that although there are reasons that irregular words have certain patterns, there is no rule to be derived from an irregular pattern.

Table 15.4. The Adjective קָטֹן

	Singular	Plural
Masculine	קָטֹן	קְטַנִּים
Feminine	קְטַנָּה	קְטַנּוֹת

2. The Use of Adjectives

An adjective is a word that limits or qualifies a noun or other substantive. Adjectival usage falls into three categories: (1) attributive, (2) predicative, (3) substantive.

a. Attributive Usage

An attributive adjective modifies a noun but is not a predicate (that is, it does not form a complete clause). An example is "A big dog." In Hebrew attributive usage, the adjective follows the noun and agrees in gender, number, and "definiteness." The term "definiteness" means that if the noun is definite, then the following adjective must have a definite article. If the noun is indefinite, the adjective will appear without the definite article.

Table 15.5. The Attributive Adjective

הָאִישׁ הַטּוֹב the good man
Noun and adjective are masculine, singular, and definite
הָאִשָּׁה הַטּוֹבָה the good woman
Noun and adjective are feminine, singular, and definite
אִשָּׁה טוֹבָה (a) good woman
Noun and adjective are feminine, singular, and indefinite
הָאֲנָשִׁים הַטּוֹבִים the good men
Noun and adjective are masculine, plural, and definite
אֲנָשִׁים טוֹבִים good men
Noun and adjective are masculine, plural, and indefinite

b. Predicative Usage

A predicate adjective is in a predicate relationship to a noun, the combination of which forms a complete thought. That is, a predicate adjective forms a complete clause with the noun, as in "The dog is *big*."

(1) A verb is not needed in Hebrew. The verb "to be" is understood.

(2) As a predicate, the Hebrew adjective usually precedes the noun.

(3) The adjective agrees with the noun in gender and number but never takes the definite article.

Blackboard 15.1. The Predicate Adjective Sentence

טוֹב הָאִישׁ means "The man is good." Of course, a feminine singular subject will have a feminine singular adjective, but the predicate remains indefinite. The following examples further illustrate usage.

Table 15.6. Predicate Adjective Examples

טוֹבָה הָאִשָּׁה	The woman is good.
טוֹבוֹת הַנָּשִׁים	The women are good.

Given that the predicate adjective never takes the definite article, certain constructions may be ambiguous, as in אִישׁ טוֹב, meaning either "a good man" or "a man is good." Context usually makes clear the adjectival function.

c. Substantive Usage

An adjective may also be used as a noun (i.e., a substantive). You have already seen that הָרָשָׁע can mean "the wicked (man)." As a substantive, a noun may refer to a person who has the quality of the adjective. Also, the singular forms of a few adjectives may be used as abstract nouns.

Table 15.7. The Substantive Adjective

חָכָם a wise man
an indefinite adjective is used to refer to a person who is חָכָם
הֶחָכָם the wise man
a definite adjective is used to refer to a person who is חָכָם
הָרָע evil *or* the evil man
רַע with definite article either for evil as an abstraction or for a man who is evil
הָרָעָה evil *or* the evil woman
רַע with definite article either for evil as an abstraction or for a woman who is evil

3. The Construct Chain with Attributive Adjectives

An adjective that modifies a noun in a construct chain must follow the entire chain, even if the adjective modifies the construct noun (the first noun). The chain is almost never broken by a word inserted between the construct and absolute. As always, a modifying adjective will agree with its noun in gender, number, and definiteness. Remember that the construct noun never has a definite article, but it is still definite if the absolute noun is definite.

Table 15.8. The Construct Chain with Adjectives

קוֹל הַמַּלְכָּה הַטּוֹב   the good voice of the queen
masculine singular adjective modifies the construct noun
קוֹל הַמַּלְכָּה הַטּוֹבָה   the voice of the good queen
feminine singular adjective modifies the absolute noun
קוֹל הַנְּבִיאִים הַטּוֹב   the good voice of the prophets
masculine singular adjective modifies the construct noun
קוֹל הַנְּבִיאִים הַטּוֹבִים   the voice of the good prophets
masculine plural adjective modifies the absolute noun

The meaning of a construct chain can be ambiguous if the absolute and construct nouns have the same gender and number.

קוֹל הַמֶּלֶךְ הַטּוֹב   the good voice of the king *or* the voice of the good king

B. The Qal Active Participle

A **participle** is an adjectival verbal form. Like adjectives, Hebrew participles are declined by gender and number.

1. The Strong Verb

Table 15.9. The Qal Active Participle in the Strong Verb

	Singular	Plural
Masculine	קֹטֵל	קֹטְלִים
Feminine	קֹטֶלֶת	קֹטְלוֹת

(1)   The key diagnostic for the Qal active participle is the Holem after the first radical (◌ֹ◌◌). It is a reliable indicator that the form is a Qal active participle.

(2)   The Holem in this pattern is unchangeably long. It does not normally have the Holem-Waw, but we sometimes do see it written like קוֹטֵל. An unchangeably long

Holem without the ו is said to be written "defectively." Taking this into account, the vowel reductions in the plural follow the normal rule that if an open, distant syllable will not reduce, the open pretonic normally reduces instead. Thus we see the reduction to Shewa in the mp קֹ/טְ/לִים, as well as in the fp קֹ/טְ/לוֹת.

(3) Note that the fs has the pattern קֹטֶלֶת. We also occasionally see the fs participle with the הָ ending (קֹטְלָה), the pattern that is normal for adjectives, but this is quite rare except in certain weak roots.

(4) In English, active participles end in *-ing* in words like *running*, *eating*, and *sleeping*. A participle has the following functions:

    (a) A predicate adjective (אֱלֹהִים כֹּרֵת בְּרִית = "God [is] making a covenant"), where אֱלֹהִים is the subject and כֹּרֵת is the predicate.

    (b) An attributive adjective (טוֹב הָאִישׁ הַכֹּרֵת בְּרִית = "The man making a covenant is good"), where הַכֹּרֵת qualifies the noun הָאִישׁ.

    (c) Hebrew can also use a participle as a noun (הַשֹּׁמֵר "the guarding one" or "the guard").

(5) An ambiguity in English is that it can also use the *-ing* ending for a gerund ("I like running" = "I like to run"). This ambiguity does not exist in Hebrew; participles in Hebrew never have this function.

2. The III-ה Verb

Using בנה, we see that the pattern for the III-ה Qal active participle is as follows.

Table 15.10. The Qal Active Participle of the III-ה

	Singular	*Plural*
Masculine	בֹּנֶה	בֹּנִים
Feminine	בֹּנָה	בֹּנוֹת

Observe the following about the III-ה.

(1) If no sufformative is added (that is, in the ms), the ה of the root is present as a Seghol-Hey (הֶ). The construct form has Tsere-Hey (הֵ).

(2) If there is a sufformative, it replaces the ה of the root.

(3) The fs sufformative is הָ, unlike what we see in the strong verb, קֹטֶלֶת.

C. The Qal Passive Participle

In addition to the Qal active participle, Hebrew has a Qal passive participle. The passive participle is a verb used as an adjective but with a passive, not active, meaning. Thus, if the active participle is "killing," the passive participle is "killed." The passive participle can be used as an attributive or predicate adjective. For example, 1 Sam 5:4 says that the god Dagon fell over and his hands were "cut off" (the passive participle of כרת) on the threshold of the temple.

1. The Strong Verb

Table 15.11. The Qal Passive Participle in the Strong Verb

	Singular	Plural
Masculine	קָטוּל	קְטוּלִים
Feminine	קְטוּלָה	קְטוּלוֹת

A common word in this pattern is ברך, "bless," giving us phrases such as found in Ps 119:12: בָּרוּךְ אַתָּה יְהוָה, "Blessed are you, YHWH!" The Qal passive participle functions as an adjective and can be either attributive ("Our blessed Hebrew professor has said…") or predicative ("Whoever masters the Qal passive participle shall be blessed").

2. The III-ה Verb

Throughout the III-ה Qal passive participle, the final ה is gone and we see י instead. This demonstrates an important fact about the III-ה: the root is in fact originally III-י. Throughout its conjugations, the III-ה does not behave like a normal guttural, and this is because it originally was not a guttural; it was a י. This is why the III-ה must be learned as a distinctive weak root and not treated as one of the guttural roots.

Table 15.12. The Qal Passive Participle in the III-ה

	Singular	Plural
Masculine	בָּנוּי	בְּנוּיִם
Feminine	בְּנוּיָה	בְּנוּיוֹת

D. Introduction to Pausal Forms

Often, a vowel is lengthened at the end of a verse or at a point where one pauses at the middle of a verse (analogous to a place where English would put a period or semi-colon). This is a **pausal form**. For example, מַיִם, "water," in a pausal form is מָיִם. For now, we will note pausal forms as needed.

E. Vocabulary

1. Core Vocabulary

a. Verbs

אהב	Qal: אָהַב love
ברך	Qal: בָּרוּךְ (passive participle) blessed
זכר	Qal: זָכַר remember

b. Other Words

אַחֵר	other, another

גָּדוֹל	great, big
חַי	alive (חַיִּים [mp] = "life")
טָהוֹר	clean (ritually)
טוֹב	good
עֵץ	tree, wood
קָדוֹשׁ	holy
קָטֹן	small
רַע	evil, bad, wicked, trouble (adjective or noun; also רָע; feminine is רָעָה)

2. Reading Vocabulary

שׁתל	Qal: שָׁתוּל (passive participle) planted
פֶּלֶג	channel, canal

3. Proper Names

בִּנְיָמִן	Benjamin
בֶּן־יְמִינִי	Benjaminite(s)
יִצְחָק	Isaac
לֵאָה	Leah
לָבָן	Laban
עֶזְרָא	Ezra

F. Guided Reading from Psalm 1

וְהָיָה כְּעֵץ שָׁתוּל עַל־פַּלְגֵי מָיִם

(1) You should recognize וְהָיָה as the Qal *weqatal* 3ms of היה.

(2) You can see that שָׁתוּל is a Qal passive participle.

(3) פַּלְגֵי is the construct plural of the noun פֶּלֶג, and so means "channels of." We will study this kind of noun, called a **segholate**, in the next chapter.

(4) You are familiar with מָיִם as מַיִם, "water." This illustrates the pausal form. The meaning is not changed.

(5) The whole means "and he will be like a tree planted close by channels of water."

CHAPTER 16
GEMINATE AND SEGHOLATE NOUNS

A. Geminate Nouns

1. Basic Concept

The term **geminate** comes from the Latin *gemini*, meaning "twins." As already noted in our discussion of the prepositions עִם ("with" = root עמם) and אֶת ("with" = root אתת) with pronominal suffixes (chapter 14), words of this type were originally composed of three consonants in which the second and third consonants were identical. The doubled letter is the "geminate letter." The root of the noun עַם, "people," is עמם. The plural of עַם is עַמִּים, "peoples."

> (1) Hebrew generally does not end a word with two of the same consonants, and, apart from a few exceptions, it almost never ends a word with a Daghesh Forte in the final letter. Thus, the singular of a geminate noun only has the geminate letter written once (no Daghesh Forte).

> (2) If a geminate noun has an ending attached (such as a plural ending), the original gemination (doubling) reappears as a Daghesh Forte in the geminate letter.

Blackboard 16.1. The Pattern of the Geminate Noun

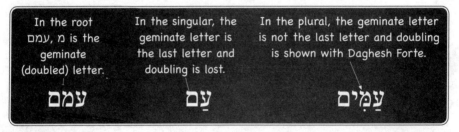

There are some geminate nouns that have preserved both geminate consonants in the singular, such as לְבָב, "heart."

2. Vowel Classes in Geminates

There are three classes of geminate nouns, depending on which short vowel appears in the initial syllable of the plural form: Pathach (ַ), Hireq (ִ) or Qibbuts (ֻ).

a. A-Class Geminate Nouns

Table 16.1. The A-Class Geminates

Singular	Plural	Root	Translation
עַם	עַמִּים	עמם	people
הַר	הָרִים	הרר	mountain

The plural nouns have the short vowel Pathach (◌ַ) in the initial syllable because a closed, unaccented syllable must be short. If the geminate consonant is a guttural or ר, as in הָרִים, compensatory lengthening occurs.

Blackboard 16.2. The Geminate Noun הַר

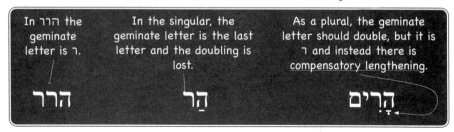

b. I-Class Geminate Nouns

These have Tsere (◌ֵ) in the singular but Hireq (◌ִ) in the first syllable of the plural.

Table 16.2. The I-Class Geminates

Singular	Plural	Root	Translation
חֵץ	חִצִּים	חצץ	arrow
אֵם	אִמּוֹת	אמם	mother

When the plural syllable is added and the geminate letter is doubled, a closed, unaccented syllable is the result (e.g., in חִצִּים [חִצ/צִים] the syllable חִצ is closed and unaccented). Again, a closed, unaccented syllable is always short. The same occurs in the feminine plural אִמּוֹת (אִמ/מוֹת), from אֵם, "mother."

Blackboard 16.3. The Feminine Geminate אֵם

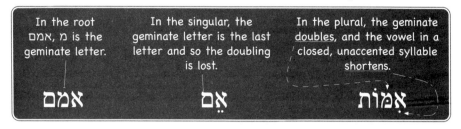

c. U-Class Geminate Nouns

Nouns of this type often have Holem in the singular form. Observe how the Holem shortens to Qibbuts with the noun חֹק. In the plural, the ק has Daghesh Forte, and thus the syllabification is as follows: חֻק/קִים. The closed, unaccented syllable /חֻק/ is short.

Table 16.3. The U-Class Geminate

Singular	Plural	Root	Translation
חֹק	חֻקִּים	חקק	statute

d. Feminine Singular Geminates

A feminine singular geminate without a feminine ending behaves like a masculine singular geminate. אֵם, "mother," is an example of this. A feminine geminate noun with the ◌ָה ending, like אַמָּה, "cubit," shows gemination in the singular as well as the plural.

Table 16.4. The Feminine Geminate

Singular	Plural	Root	Translation
אַמָּה	אַמּוֹת	אמם	cubit

3. Geminate Adjectives

Adjectives can also have geminate roots. The adjective רַב, "much, many," is derived from the root רבב. The doubled (or "geminate") letter reappears as a Daghesh Forte when an ending is added.

Table 16.5. The Adjective רַב

	Singular	Plural
Masculine	רַב	רַבִּים
Feminine	רַבָּה	רַבּוֹת

4. Geminate Construct Forms

(1) The geminate singular construct typically looks the same as the absolute. The construct of עַם, "people," is עַם.

(2) However, a geminate that has a long vowel in the absolute singular may shorten the vowel in the construct, particularly if the construct is joined by Maqqeph to the following noun. For example, with the noun חֹק, "rule," we see the expression חָק־עוֹלָם, "rule of eternity" (i.e., "perpetual statute"). The vowel in חָק is Qamets Hatuph.

(3) If the geminate has the feminine ending ◌ָה, the construct singular is like the normal feminine singular construct. Thus, the construct of אַמָּה, "cubit," is אַמַּת.

(4) Geminate construct plurals generally look as one would expect. The construct plural of חֵץ, "arrow," is חִצֵּי, with shortening of the I-class vowel in a closed, unaccented syllable.

5. Geminates with Pronominal Suffixes

With a pronominal suffix, the geminate letter usually is doubled with a Daghesh Forte. This often causes the vowel to shorten since what had been a closed, *accented* syllable becomes a closed, *unaccented* syllable due to the pronoun suffix. For example, from אֵם, "mother," we get אִמָּה (אִמְ/מָה), "her mother," in which the syllable /אִמ/ has lost its accent due to the addition of the suffix and thus has shortened.

Table 16.6. Geminates with Pronominal Suffixes

With Suffix	Lexical Form	Root	Translation
עַמִּי	עַם	עמם	my people
שִׁנָּיו	שֵׁן	שׁנן	his teeth
חֻקּוֹ	חֹק	חקק	his statute
אִמָּהּ	אֵם	אמם	her mother

B. The Segholates

1. Introduction to Segholate Nouns

Certain nouns are called **segholates**. You have already seen a number of such nouns. Examples include אֶרֶץ, "earth," נַעַר, "young man," and מֶלֶךְ, "king." Each of these nouns has two syllables with the accent on the penult. This is the defining characteristic of a segholate. The name **segholate**, however, comes from the fact that a large number of these nouns have the vowel Seghol in one or both syllables, as does מֶלֶךְ. Bear in mind, however, that a segholate may have only one Seghol or no Seghol at all, as is the case with נַעַר.

2. Plural Segholate Nouns

Regardless of the vowels in the singular form, every segholate noun uses the same vowel pattern to form a plural. They always have

(1) a vocal Shewa (ְ) in the first syllable (composite Shewa if under a guttural),

(2) a Qamets (ָ) in the second syllable,

(3) and either the masculine or feminine plural ending as the final syllable.

Table 16.7. Segholate Singular and Plural Nouns

מֶלֶךְ	king	מְלָכִים	kings
נֶפֶשׁ	soul	נְפָשׁוֹת	souls
עֶבֶד	servant	עֲבָדִים	servants
נַעַר	boy	נְעָרִים	boys
אֶרֶץ	land	אֲרָצוֹת	lands

3. Segholate Nouns in the Construct Singular

With segholate nouns, the absolute and construct forms are identical in the singular. Only context tells you whether it is absolute or construct.

Table 16.8. Segholate Construct Singular Nouns

מֶ֫לֶךְ	king	מֶ֫לֶךְ	king of
עֶ֫בֶד	servant	עֶ֫בֶד	servant of
סֵ֫פֶר	book	סֵ֫פֶר	book of

4. Segholate Nouns in the Construct Plural

Segholates have a peculiarity that reflects the historical development of this form.

(1) Originally, segholates had a single vowel (a-, i-, or u-class) between the first and second consonant, and there was no vowel between the second and third consonant (originally these words probably also had case endings, but this is not relevant to our discussion).

    (a) The word מֶ֫לֶךְ, "king," was originally *malk* (a-class).

    (b) But סֵ֫פֶר, "book," was *sipr* (i-class).

    (c) More obviously, אֹ֫זֶן, "ear," was *ʾozn* (u-class).

(2) Eventually, Hebrew began to avoid a consonant cluster at the end of a word by inserting a Seghol as a "helping" vowel between the second and third consonants. For example, *malk* (or *malku*) became *málek*, which in turn became *mélek* (מֶ֫לֶךְ).

(3) The habit of pronouncing the word with the accent on the penult and not the ultima (as in מֶ֫לֶךְ) persisted because originally the only vowel was behind the first consonant.

Blackboard 16.4. Evolution of מֶ֫לֶךְ

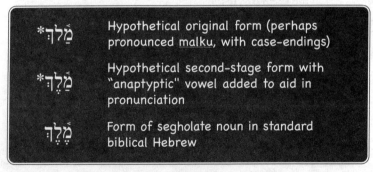

*מַ֫לְךְ	Hypothetical original form (perhaps pronounced malku, with case-endings)
*מַ֫לֶךְ	Hypothetical second-stage form with "anaptyptic" vowel added to aid in pronunciation
מֶ֫לֶךְ	Form of segholate noun in standard biblical Hebrew

(4) However, when מְלָכִים, the plural of מֶ֫לֶךְ, is put into the construct with the primary accent shifting to the absolute noun, the original a-class vowel reappears (מַלְכֵי) due to the application of the rule of Shewa. The following Blackboard walks step-by-step through the process:

Blackboard 16.5. The Formation of Segholate Nouns in the Construct Plural

מְלָכִים	We begin with the absolute form.
מְלָכֵי*	We then add the construct ending.
מְֽלָכֵי*	The shift in accent to the absolute noun creates the potential for two contiguous, initial vocal Shewas because open distant syllables generally reduce.
מַלְכֵי	The rule of Shewa necessitates that the first vocal Shewa become a full short vowel, which in this instance is the original a-class vowel of the Segholate.

(a) Similarly, the construct plural of the i-class segholate סֵ֫פֶר is סִפְרֵי.

(b) The construct plural of the u-class segholate אֹ֫זֶן is אָזְנֵי (note: Qamets Hatuph in אָזְנֵי).

(5) Construct plurals of segholates begin with a closed, unaccented syllable and thus have a short vowel. This vowel will reflect the vowel class of the word, whether a, i, or u. The following table illustrates the three noun classes in the construct plural and how their original vowel classes show themselves. Notice that in many segholates, the original vowel class cannot be determined by looking at the lexical form (the singular absolute).

Table 16.9. The Segholate Construct Plural

Class	Abs./Const. Singular	Absolute Plural	Construct Plural
A	מֶ֫לֶךְ	מְלָכִים	מַלְכֵי
A	עֶ֫בֶד	עֲבָדִים	עַבְדֵי
A	נֶ֫פֶשׁ	נְפָשׁוֹת	נַפְשׁוֹת
I	סֵ֫פֶר	סְפָרִים	סִפְרֵי
U	אֹ֫זֶן	אֲזָנִים	אָזְנֵי

נַפְשׁוֹת illustrates the pattern of the feminine plural construct in segholates.

5. Singular Segholate Nouns with Pronominal Suffixes

When a singular segholate noun has a pronominal suffix, the original vowel class is evident, as in the following examples.

Table 16.10. Singular Segholate Nouns with Pronominal Suffixes

Class	Singular	Singular with 1cs Suffix	Translation
A	מֶ֫לֶךְ	מַלְכִּי	my king
A	עֶ֫בֶד	עַבְדִּי	my servant
I	סֵ֫פֶר	סִפְרִי	my book
U	קֹ֫דֶשׁ	קָדְשִׁי	my holiness

Usually, the singular absolute of a segholate will not show what its vowel class is. But there are a few general rules:

(1) Segholate nouns with Seghol in the absolute singular penult are usually a-class, but they may be i-class.

(2) Segholate nouns with Tsere in the absolute singular penult are usually i-class.

(3) Segholate nouns with Holem in the absolute singular penult are u-class.

6. Plural Segholate Nouns with Pronominal Suffixes

a. Masculine Plural Nouns

The plural noun מְלָכִים, "kings," with a selection of pronominal suffixes illustrates how pronoun suffixes are added to a plural segholate. Note that there are two distinct types.

Table 16.11. Examples of Masculine Plural Segholate Nouns with Suffixes

מְלָכַי	my kings	1cs suffix
מְלָכֶ֫יהָ	her kings	3fs suffix
מַלְכֵיכֶם	your kings	2mp suffix
מַלְכֵיהֶם	their kings	3mp suffix

In the first two forms, the vowels of the absolute plural (מְלָכִים) are preserved. The third and fourth examples have the vowels of the construct plural (מַלְכֵי). The patterns are:

(1) Segholate masculine plural nouns with singular suffixes or the 1cp suffix preserve the vowel pattern of the absolute plural.

(2) Segholate masculine plural nouns with the third person and second person plural suffixes have in the first syllable the short vowel that is found in construct plurals.

Table 16.12. Patterns of Masculine Plural Segholate Nouns with Suffixes

Like the plural absolute מְלָכִים	Like the plural construct מַלְכֵי
All singular suffixes and the first common plural suffix	The second and third plural suffixes
מְלָכַי	מַלְכֵיכֶם

The two different spellings appear to result from the normal rules of vowel transformation when accent shift occurs. In the first group, the open pretonic is long and is reduced to a vocal Shewa. In the second group, the shift in accent results in what would be two open, distant syllables, causing two Shewas. But the rule of Shewa forces the first vocal Shewa to become the short, original-vowel of the Segholate, resulting in an initial closed syllable.

$$ מְלָכִים \quad + \quad \begin{array}{c}\text{2ms suffix}\\ (\text{ֶיכֶם}) \end{array} \quad → \quad → \quad *מְלָכֵיכֶם \quad → \quad *מְלָכֵיכֶם \quad → \quad מַלְכֵיכֶם $$

(1) In מְלָכֶיהָ (מְ/לָ/כֶי/הָ), the syllable לָ is an open pretonic and therefore long, but מְ is an open propretonic syllable and thus reduced.

(2) In מַלְכֵיכֶם (מַלְ/כֵי/כֶם), the syllable מַלְ is closed and unaccented and therefore short.

Table 16.13. Masculine Plural Segholate Nouns with Suffixes

	Singular Suffix	*Plural Suffix*
3m	מְלָכָיו his kings	מַלְכֵיהֶם their (mp) kings
3f	מְלָכֶיהָ her kings	מַלְכֵיהֶן their (fp) kings
2m	מְלָכֶיךָ your (ms) kings	מַלְכֵיכֶם your (mp) kings
2f	מְלָכַיִךְ your (fs) kings	מַלְכֵיכֶן your (fp) kings
1c	מְלָכַי my kings	מְלָכֵינוּ our kings

b. Feminine Plural Nouns

Segholate feminine plural nouns (that have the וֹת ending) typically have the pattern of the construct plural for all forms with pronominal suffixes.

Table 16.14. Feminine Plural Segholate Nouns with Suffixes

Singular	*Plural Construct*	*Plural with Suffix*	*Suffix*	*Translation*
אֶרֶץ	אֲרָצוֹת	אַרְצֹתָם	3mp	"their lands"
חֶרֶב	חֲרָבוֹת	חַרְבוֹתָיו	3ms	"his swords"
נֶפֶשׁ	נְפָשׁוֹת	נַפְשֹׁתֵינוּ	1cp	"our souls"
נֶפֶשׁ	נְפָשׁוֹת	נַפְשׁוֹתֵיכֶם	2mp	"your souls"

7. Additional Remark: The Mysterious Disappearing Daghesh

The attentive reader will note that in a number of cases the Daghesh Lene is missing where we would expect to see it. Normally, whenever a begadkephat letter follows a closed syllable (that is, when it follows a silent Shewa), the begadkephat letter has a Daghesh Lene. An example of this is with מַלְכִּי, "my king." On the other hand, a word such as מַלְכֵיהֶם has a closed syllable מַל with no Daghesh Lene in the next letter (כ). What is happening here? Two observations help explain this.

(1) The Masoretes pointed the text as they heard it. If they did not hear a hardened כ, they did not insert a Daghesh Lene even if the rules seemed to call for it.

(2) The pronunciation of מַלְכֵיהֶם seems to follow the analogy of the plural מְלָכִים in respect to not giving the כ a Daghesh Lene. Omission of the Daghesh in words such as מַלְכֵיהֶם is common in Hebrew but not always followed. The Hebrew text is not consistent.

C. Vocabulary

1. Core Vocabulary

a. Verbs

אבד	Qal: אָבַד die, be lost
ידע	Qal: יָדַע know
עבר	Qal: עָבַר pass over, through, by; cross; transgress
שתה	Qal: שָׁתָה drink

b. Other Words

אֵם	mother F |אֵם|
אַמָּה	cubit F |אַמַּת|
חֹק	rule, statute, law M |חָק־|
חֶרֶב	sword F |חֶרֶב|
חֹשֶׁךְ	darkness M |חֹשֶׁךְ|
נַעַר	boy, youth M |נַעַר|
נֶפֶשׁ	life, self, person, soul F |נֶפֶשׁ|
סֵפֶר	scroll, book M |סֵפֶר|
רַב	much, many (adjective)

2. Proper Names

אֲרָם	Aram, Syria
אֲרַמִּי	Aramean(s), Syrian(s)
יַרְדֵּן	Jordan
כְּנַעַן	Canaan
כְּנַעֲנִי	Canaanite(s)
מוֹאָב	Moab
מוֹאָבִי	Moabite(s)

D. Guided Reading from Psalm 1

כִּי־יוֹדֵעַ יְהוָה דֶּרֶךְ צַדִּיקִים

וְדֶרֶךְ רְשָׁעִים תֹּאבֵד

(1) You can see that יוֹדֵעַ is a Qal active participle from ידע. It has a guttural (ע) in the third radical position, and that is why it has furtive Pathach. Remember that a guttural prefers an a-class vowel. Otherwise, it is a normal Qal active participle ms.

(2) תֹּאבֵד is a Qal *yiqtol* 3fs from אבד. This is a distinctive kind of weak root with א in the first position, and its *yiqtol* follows the pattern you have seen in יֹאמַר. The verb תֹּאבֵד is feminine because דֶּרֶךְ is here treated as feminine (although it is sometimes treated as a masculine noun).

(3) The whole means "For YHWH knows (the) way of (the) righteous, / but (the) way of (the) wicked will perish."

CHAPTER 17
PRONOUNS

A. The Demonstratives

1. Nomenclature and Inflection of Demonstratives

There are four **demonstratives** in English (this, that, these, those), and each may be used as an **determiner** (*this* man) or as a pronoun (*this* is the man). **Determinative demonstratives** in Hebrew are used in the same way, except that they are also inflected for gender.

Table 17.1. The Demonstrative Pronouns

	Singular	Plural
Masculine	זֶה this	אֵלֶּה these
Feminine	זֹאת this	
Masculine	הוּא that	הֵם those
Feminine	הִיא that	הֵנָּה those

(1) אֵלֶּה, "these," is a common form (not inflected for gender).

(2) The demonstratives הוּא and הִיא are also used as independent personal pronouns ("he" and "she" respectively).

2. Usage of Demonstratives

a. Determinative Demonstratives

A determinative demonstrative is like an attributive adjective in that it follows the noun and agrees in gender, number, and definiteness. The noun is always definite (since one cannot say "this girl" in reference to any but a specific girl).

Table 17.2. Determinative Demonstratives

הַסֵּפֶר הַזֶּה this book		הַבָּנִים הָאֵלֶּה these sons	
הַיַּלְדָּה הַזֹּאת this girl		הָאִמּוֹת הָאֵלֶּה these mothers	
הַיֶּלֶד הַהוּא that boy		הָאֲנָשִׁים הָהֵם those men	
הָאִשָּׁה הַהִיא that woman		הַנָּשִׁים הָהֵנָּה those women	

An adjective, if present, will go between the noun and the demonstrative. The noun, adjective, and demonstrative agree in gender and number, and all have the definite article. "This small boy" (הַנַּעַר הַקָּטֹן הַזֶּה) is literally "the boy, the small, the this."

Table 17.3. Nouns with Both Adjectives and Determinative Demonstratives

הַנַּעַר הַקָּטֹן הַזֶּה	this small boy
הָאָרֶץ הַטּוֹבָה הַזֹּאת	this good land
הָעִיר הַגְּדוֹלָה הַהִיא	that great city
הָאֲנָשִׁים הַטּוֹבִים הָהֵם	those good men

A determinative demonstrative will behave like an attributive adjective. If it is connected to a construct chain, it is important to take note of the gender and number of the demonstrative so that you will know whether it goes with the absolute or the construct noun.

Table 17.4. Demonstratives with Construct Chains

אֵשֶׁת הָאִישׁ הַזֶּה	the wife of this man
אֵשֶׁת הָאִישׁ הַטּוֹב הַזֶּה	the wife of this good man
דִּבְרֵי הַנָּבִיא הָאֵלֶּה	these words of the prophet
דִּבְרֵי הַנָּבִיא הַזֶּה	the words of this prophet

b. Demonstrative Pronouns Used as Clause Subjects

Demonstratives can stand in the place of a noun and function as the subject in verbless/nominal clauses. As a subject, the demonstrative pronoun precedes the predicate noun and agrees in gender and number only.

Table 17.5. The Use of Demonstrative Pronouns

זֶה הָאִישׁ	this is the man
זֹאת הָעִיר	this is the city
הוּא הַנַּעַר	that is the boy
אֵלֶּה הַנָּשִׁים	these are the women
הֵם הַשֹּׁפְטִים	those are the judges
הֵנָּה הֶעָרִים	those are the cities
אֵלֶּה הָאֲנָשִׁים הַטּוֹבִים	these are the good men
הִיא הָאִשָּׁה הַטּוֹבָה	that is the good woman

B. Personal Pronouns

1. Subject Pronouns

Like English, Hebrew has independent personal pronouns (I, you, he, she, we, they). Unlike English, Hebrew distinguishes gender for all personal pronouns except for those in the first person. (English distinguishes gender only in the third singular forms "he" and "she.")

Table 17.6. The Subject Pronouns

	Singular	Plural
3m	הוּא he	הֵם / הֵ֫מָּה they
3f	הִיא she	הֵ֫נָּה they
2m	אַתָּה you	אַתֶּם you
2f	אַתְּ you	אַתֵּ֫נָה / אַתֵּן you
1c	אֲנִי / אָנֹכִי I	אֲנַ֫חְנוּ we

(1) Hebrew distinguishes number in all persons. In contemporary English, the second person is "you" regardless of whether one is speaking to one man or many women. Hebrew, in this respect, is more precise. The independent personal pronouns are only used as subjects and almost never have prefixes or suffixes.

(2) The 1cs, 2fp, and 3mp pronouns have alternative forms. Thus, for example, one may say אֲנִי or אָנֹכִי ("I") without any difference in meaning.

(3) Although the independent personal pronouns may be used in several different ways, two usages are common:

   (a) They are used as the subject of a sentence especially when the sentence is a verb-less/nominal clause.

   (i) In these four examples, the pronouns precede the predicate noun.

   הוּא הַמֶּ֫לֶךְ He is the king.

   אַתָּה נָבִיא You (ms) are a prophet.

   הֵם הַזְּקֵנִים They (m) are the elders.

   אֲנַ֫חְנוּ הַנָּשִׁים We are the women.

   (ii) It is also possible for the pronoun to follow the noun, although this happens less frequently.

   נָבִיא הוּא He is a prophet.

   יְשָׁרָה אַתְּ You (fs) are upright.

(b) The other main usage of the independent personal pronoun is to mark "emphasis" or some other discourse function.

    (i) The pronoun הוּא may appear as the subject of a clause after a preceding pendent element (i.e., a word or phrase outside a clause that "hangs" before a clause to draw special attention to itself). In such contexts הוּא is sometimes regarded as a kind of linking verb.

$$\text{יְהוָה הוּא הָאֱלֹהִים} \quad \text{YHWH is God (YHWH, He is the God)}$$

    (ii) The pronoun may appear before a finite verb to give focus to the subject or to signal a shift in the discourse. In the following example, the verb form מָלַכְתִּי is preceded by the 1cs independent personal pronoun. It is important to note that the finite verbal form itself indicates the person, so, in effect, the 1cs pronominal element appears twice (in the verb form and in the pronoun). This construction makes the 1cs pronoun the focus of the sentence.

$$\text{אָנֹכִי מָלַכְתִּי} \quad \text{I reigned}$$

2. Object Pronouns

In addition to the personal pronouns that serve as subjects of sentences (such as אֲנִי, "I"), Hebrew has pronouns that serve as direct objects. These correspond to English pronouns such as *me* and *her*. Once again, Hebrew often distinguishes gender where English does not.

Table 17.7. The Direct Object Pronouns

	Singular	*Plural*
3m	אֹתוֹ him	אֹתָם / אֶתְהֶם them
3f	אֹתָהּ her	אֹתָן / אֶתְהֶן them
2m	אֹתְךָ you	אֶתְכֶם you
2f	אֹתָךְ you	(not extant) you
1c	אֹתִי me	אֹתָנוּ us

A simple example of usage is אָהֵב הוּא אֹתָהּ ("he loves her").

C. Interrogative Pronouns

An **interrogative pronoun** introduces a question. The Hebrew equivalent to "Who?" is מִי. Hebrew commonly distinguishes the interrogative from the relative pronoun, whereas English uses *who* for both pronouns. In Hebrew, אֲשֶׁר is never used as an interrogative.

The Hebrew interrogative מַה means "What?" and it is pointed as follows:

(1) Before all normal consonants (i.e., except the gutturals and ר), the form is מַה, and the following consonant is doubled with Daghesh Forte. For example, מַה־זֹּאת means "What is this?"

(2) Before א, ע, or ר, it is normally מָה. For example, מָה אָנִי ("What am I?").

(3) Before ח or ה, it is usually מַה although it can be מָה before ה (e.g., it is מָה before the article). For example, מַה־הוּא ("What is that?") but מָה־הַדָּבָר הַזֶּה ("What is this thing?").

(4) Before a guttural with Qamets, the form is generally מֶה. For example, מֶה־עָשָׂה לְךָ ("What did he do to you?").

The interrogatives can take prepositions (as in לְמִי, "for whom?"). The most common word for "why" is לָמָּה (lit. "for what?"). But מָה by itself at times also means "Why?"

D. Vocabulary

1. Core Vocabulary

אֵלֶּה	these (common gender)
אֲנַחְנוּ	we
אַף	also, even
אַתָּה	you (2ms, subject pronoun; the 2fs subject pronoun is אַתְּ)
אַתֶּם	you (2mp, subject pronoun; the 2fp subject pronoun is אַתֵּנָה or אַתֵּן)
הוּא	he, that
הִיא	she, that
הֵם / הֵמָּה	they, those (3mp, subject pronoun; the 3fp subject pronoun is הֵנָּה)
זֹאת	this (f)
זֶה	this (m)
מָה	what? why?
מִי	who?

2. Reading Vocabulary

יַצְלִיחַ	"he will succeed" (Hiphil *yiqtol* 3ms of צלח)

3. Proper Names

אָסָא	Asa
הֶבֶל	Abel
נָתָן	Nathan
עֵשָׂו	Esau

רוּת   Ruth

E. Guided Reading from Psalm 1

וְכֹל אֲשֶׁר־יַעֲשֶׂה יַצְלִיחַ

לֹא־כֵן הָרְשָׁעִים

(1) יַעֲשֶׂה is the Qal *yiqtol* 3ms of עשׂה, "do." You can see that it is a III-ה verb like יִבְנֶה, but it also has a guttural in the first position. That is why the vowel under the *yiqtol* preformative is Pathach.

(2) "And all that he will do" (וְכֹל אֲשֶׁר־יַעֲשֶׂה) can be rendered "and whatever he does."

(3) The whole can be rendered, "And whatever he does succeeds. / The wicked (are) not like that."

CHAPTER 18
MORE ABOUT יֵשׁ AND אֵין AND THE QAL IMPERATIVE

A. More About יֵשׁ and אֵין

You know that the Hebrew particles יֵשׁ and אֵין respectively describe the existence or non-existence of something. Thus, יֵשׁ סוּס means "there is a horse" or "a horse exists" and אֵין סוּס means "there is not a horse" or "no horse exists." To form a more complete sentence, one might say something like יֵשׁ סוּס בַּשָּׂדֶה, "there is a horse in the field," or אֵין סוּס בַּשָּׂדֶה, "there is no horse in the field."

These **existential particles** can also describe possession of something by using the pattern "There is (יֵשׁ) X to (לְ) Y," meaning "Y has X." For example, יֵשׁ סוּס לַמֶּלֶךְ means "The king has a horse" (lit., "there is a horse to the king"). Negated, this sentence becomes אֵין סוּס לַמֶּלֶךְ, "there is no horse to the king" or "the king has no horse." A similar example with a pronoun suffix is יֵשׁ סוּס לִי, "there is a horse to me" or "I have a horse."

יֵשׁ sometimes is joined to the following word with a Maqqeph, in which case it is written יֶשׁ־. The word אֵין is actually a construct form; the absolute form is אַיִן, but the absolute is much less common than the construct.

B. The Qal Imperative

1. The Strong Verb

The **imperative** is a grammatical form that expresses a command, as in "When I die, *bury* me with my Hebrew textbook." Because imperatives express a speaker's will (or volition), these second person forms are often called volitives. In form, the imperative is simply a second person *yiqtol* with the preformative removed. Observe, however, that the removal of the *yiqtol* preformative can lead to vowel changes. When the preformative תִּ is removed from תִּקְטְלִי, the resulting form would begin with two vocal Shewas (קְטְלִי). Instead, by the rule of Shewa, it becomes קִטְלִי.

Table 18.1. The Qal Imperative

	Singular	Plural
Masculine	קְטֹל	קִטְלוּ
Feminine	קִטְלִי	קְטֹלְנָה

Removal of the *yiqtol* preformative can cause certain changes with begadkephat letters, as we see with כתב. With the preformative present, the כ follows a vowel and has no Daghesh Lene. When the preformative is gone and the כ becomes the first letter in the word, it receives a Daghesh Lene.

Table 18.2. The Qal Imperative and *Yiqtol* (Imperfect) Second Person of כתב

	Imperative	Yiqtol	
ms	כְּתֹב	תִּכְתֹּב	2ms
fs	כִּתְבִי	תִּכְתְּבִי	2fs
mp	כִּתְבוּ	תִּכְתְּבוּ	2mp
fp	כְּתֹבְנָה	תִּכְתֹּבְנָה	2fp

All four imperative forms of כתב listed above would be properly translated as "write!" Hebrew distinguishes gender and number in places where English does not.

We see that when the *yiqtol* preformative is removed,

(1) כ is now the first letter of the word and so has the Daghesh Lene.

(2) The rule of Shewa has applied in the vocalization of the first syllable in the fs and mp forms (two initial vocal Shewas become a closed syllable with Hireq and silent Shewa).

(3) The radical ת in the root כתב now follows a vocal Shewa or Hireq and so loses the Daghesh Lene.

Blackboard 18.1. Formation of the Qal Imperative mp of כתב

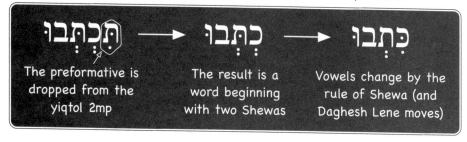

The preformative is dropped from the yiqtol 2mp	The result is a word beginning with two Shewas	Vowels change by the rule of Shewa (and Daghesh Lene moves)

2. The III-ה Verb

The III-ה imperative looks just like the *yiqtol* with the initial ת dropped except in the ms imperative, where you see Tsere instead of Seghol.

Table 18.3. The Qal Imperative and *Yiqtol* (Imperfect) Second Person of בנה

	Imperative	Yiqtol	
ms	בְּנֵה	תִּבְנֶה	2ms
fs	בְּנִי	תִּבְנִי	2fs
mp	בְּנוּ	תִּבְנוּ	2mp
fp	בְּנֶינָה	תִּבְנֶינָה	2fp

3. Paragogic ה

Often, the masculine singular imperative will appear with an הָ ending. This is the **paragogic ה** (paragogic means "added"). It should be regarded as an alternative masculine singular form. *It is not a feminine ending!*

(1) Regular imperative ms: זְכֹר, "remember!"

(2) Imperative ms with paragogic ה: זָכְרָה, "remember!" (Qamets Hatuph in penult)

The הָ ending does not change the meaning of the imperative, so the translation value is the same whether or not it is present.

The paragogic ה is also found on other forms discussed later. Because it most commonly occurs in volitional contexts (i.e., those in which the desire or volition of a speaker is expressed), some term it the **volitional ה**. Its presence, however, does not appear to be tied to modal meaning.

The form of the imperative with paragogic ה is perhaps surprising. We would have expected to see the paragogic ה simply added to the imperative, so that זְכֹר with paragogic ה would be *זְכֹרָה. In fact, however, the Israelites seem to have preferred not to pronounce it in this way. It is possible that it may have begun as a word with three open syllables, which, over the course of time, gave way to pronouncing it with just two syllables. Pronouncing the first syllable as a closed, unaccented syllable required a short vowel, usually Qamets Hatuph (as in זָכְרָה), but sometimes Hireq, as in שִׁלְחָה, "send!"

Blackboard 18.2. The Imperative with Paragogic ה

4. Negative Commands

A negative command (**prohibition**) in Hebrew is not created by negating an imperative form. Instead, negative commands are formulated with a negative particle (either לֹא or אַל) before a second person *yiqtol* form. As a general rule, immediate commands that apply to specific situations (e.g., "Don't close that door!") are made with אַל before a *yiqtol*. Permanent prohibitions (e.g., "Never steal!") have לֹא before a *yiqtol*. Which pattern do you think is found repeated in the Ten Commandments?

אַל־תִּירָא אֹתוֹ Do not fear him (ירא = "to fear")

לֹא תִגְנֹב Do not steal (גנב = "to steal")

5. The Particle נָא

Frequently, imperatives will be followed by the particle נָא. It is best left untranslated. Some suggest that it makes a command more formal or polite (e.g., "please").

The נָא may be connected to the imperative with Maqqeph (⁻). If a Maqqeph is present, the words are joined and, for accentuation, they are treated as a single word. This means that the imperative loses its primary stress, and this brings about a vowel change. (Remember that words joined by Maqqeph are, in accentuation, treated as one word.) For example, in the phrase כְּתֹב נָא without Maqqeph, the syllable /תֹב/ is accented and can be long. But in כְּתָב־נָא with Maqqeph (the vowel in /תָב/ is Qamets Hatuph), the syllable /תָב/ is closed and unaccented and therefore must be short.

Blackboard 18.3. Maqqeph Causing Accent Shift and Vowel Shortening

C. Vocabulary

1. Core Vocabulary

a. Verbs

אכל	Qal: אָכַל eat
אסף	Qal: אָסַף gather, take in, retract
עלה	Qal: עָלָה go up
קרא	Qal: קָרָא call, summon, proclaim
שלח	Qal: שָׁלַח send, stretch out

b. Other Words

אַל	not
כֶּרֶם	vineyard M |כֶּרֶם|
מָקוֹם	place M |מְקוֹם|
נַחֲלָה	possession, inheritance F |נַחֲלַת|
עוֹלָם	remote time; eternity, forever M (construct not extant)
שְׁמֹנֶה	eight

תֵּ֫שַׁע	nine

2. Proper Names

אַשּׁוּר	Assyria, Assyrian(s)
בִּלְעָם	Balaam
בָּלָק	Balak
יוֹאָב	Joab
יוֹנָתָן	Jonathan
לֵוִי	Levi, Levite(s)
שָׁאוּל	Saul

D. Reading—Psalm 1

אַשְׁרֵי־הָאִישׁ אֲשֶׁר

לֹא הָלַךְ בַּעֲצַת רְשָׁעִים

וּבְדֶ֫רֶךְ חַטָּאִים לֹא עָמָד

וּבְמוֹשַׁב לֵצִים לֹא יָשָׁב

כִּי אִם בְּתוֹרַת יְהוָה חֶפְצוֹ

וּבְתוֹרָתוֹ יֶהְגֶּה יוֹמָם וָלָ֫יְלָה

וְהָיָה כְּעֵץ שָׁתוּל עַל־פַּלְגֵי מָ֫יִם

אֲשֶׁר פִּרְיוֹ יִתֵּן בְּעִתּוֹ

וְעָלֵ֫הוּ לֹא־יִבּוֹל

וְכֹל אֲשֶׁר־יַעֲשֶׂה יַצְלִיחַ

לֹא־כֵן הָרְשָׁעִים

כִּי אִם־כַּמֹּץ אֲשֶׁר־תִּדְּפֶ֫נּוּ רוּחַ

עַל־כֵּן לֹא־יָקֻ֫מוּ רְשָׁעִים בַּמִּשְׁפָּט

וְחַטָּאִים בַּעֲדַת צַדִּיקִים

כִּי־יוֹדֵעַ יְהוָה דֶּ֫רֶךְ צַדִּיקִים

וְדֶ֫רֶךְ רְשָׁעִים תֹּאבֵד

CHAPTER 19

NUMBERS

A. Cardinal Numbers

1. Mastering the Numbers

The Hebrew number system is very complex. But dealing with Hebrew numbers need not be painful. For numbers, you should learn the forms listed in the chart below and familiarize yourself with the other forms as described in this section. Recognition of numbers then will pose no problem.

Table 19.1. Essential Hebrew Numbers

אֶחָד	1	אַחַד עָשָׂר	11
שְׁנַיִם	2	שְׁנֵים עָשָׂר	12
שָׁלֹשׁ	3	שְׁלֹשָׁה עָשָׂר	13
אַרְבַּע	4	אַרְבָּעָה עָשָׂר	14
חָמֵשׁ	5	עֶשְׂרִים	20
שֵׁשׁ	6	שְׁלֹשִׁים	30
שֶׁבַע	7	אַרְבָּעִים	40
שְׁמֹנֶה	8	מֵאָה	100
תֵּשַׁע	9	אֶלֶף	1,000
עֶשֶׂר	10	רְבָבָה	10,000

2. The Number One

The number one is אֶחָד in the masculine absolute and אַחַת in the feminine absolute. It functions like an attributive adjective. That is, it stands after the noun it modifies and agrees with it in gender, number, and definiteness. For example, אִשָּׁה אַחַת = "one woman," הָאִשָּׁה הָאַחַת = "the one woman," and אִישׁ אֶחָד = "one man." The construct forms (masculine = אַחַד; feminine = אַחַת) are used as substantives in phrases like אַחַד מֵהַנְּעָרִים, "one of the boys" (lit., "one from the boys"). A plural form (אֲחָדִים) meaning "few" is occasionally found.

3. The Number Two

The number two stands before the word it modifies, is used as a substantive (not as an adjective), and agrees in gender and number. It may be either absolute or construct in form. The forms of the number two are as follows:

Table 19.2. The Number Two

Masc. Absolute	Masc. Construct	Fem. Absolute	Fem. Construct
שְׁנַיִם	שְׁנֵי	שְׁתַּיִם	שְׁתֵּי

Examples of usage are as follows:

שְׁנַיִם חֳדָשִׁים   two months

שְׁנֵי־אֲנָשִׁים   two men

שְׁנֵי נְעָרִים   two boys

שְׁתַּיִם נָשִׁים   two women

4. The Numbers Three through Ten

An unusual feature is that the masculine forms of these numbers go with feminine nouns, and the feminine forms go with masculine nouns.

Table 19.3. The Numbers Three through Ten

	Masc. Absolute	Masc. Construct	Fem. Absolute	Fem. Construct
3	שָׁלֹשׁ	שְׁלֹשׁ	שְׁלֹשָׁה	שְׁלֹשֶׁת
4	אַרְבַּע	אַרְבַּע	אַרְבָּעָה	אַרְבַּעַת
5	חָמֵשׁ	חֲמֵשׁ	חֲמִשָּׁה	חֲמֵשֶׁת
6	שֵׁשׁ	שֵׁשׁ	שִׁשָּׁה	שֵׁשֶׁת
7	שֶׁבַע	שְׁבַע	שִׁבְעָה	שִׁבְעַת
8	שְׁמֹנֶה	שְׁמֹנֶה	שְׁמֹנָה	שְׁמֹנַת
9	תֵּשַׁע	תְּשַׁע	תִּשְׁעָה	תִּשְׁעַת
10	עֶשֶׂר	עֶשֶׂר	עֲשָׂרָה	עֲשֶׂרֶת

Examples of usage are as follows:

שְׁלֹשֶׁת יָמִים   three days (יָמִים is masculine)

שָׁלֹשׁ עָרִים   three cities (עָרִים is feminine)

אַרְבַּע חַיּוֹת   four animals (חַיּוֹת is feminine)

חָמֵשׁ שָׁנִים   five years (שָׁנִים is feminine)

5. *The Teens*

The numbers eleven and twelve agree with the noun they modify in gender. There are alternative forms for each.

Table 19.4. Eleven and Twelve

	Masculine		Feminine	
11	אַחַד עָשָׂר	עַשְׁתֵּי עָשָׂר	אַחַת עֶשְׂרֵה	עַשְׁתֵּי עֶשְׂרֵה
12	שְׁנֵים עָשָׂר	שְׁנֵי עָשָׂר	שְׁתֵּים עֶשְׂרֵה	שְׁתֵּי עֶשְׂרֵה

In thirteen through nineteen, masculine numbers go with feminine nouns and feminine numbers with masculine nouns. Note, however, עָשָׂר with masculine nouns and עֶשְׂרֵה with feminine nouns.

Table 19.5. Thirteen through Nineteen

	With Masc. Noun	With Fem. Noun
13	שְׁלֹשָׁה עָשָׂר	שְׁלֹשׁ עֶשְׂרֵה
14	אַרְבָּעָה עָשָׂר	אַרְבַּע עֶשְׂרֵה
15	חֲמִשָּׁה עָשָׂר	חֲמֵשׁ עֶשְׂרֵה
16	שִׁשָּׁה עָשָׂר	שֵׁשׁ עֶשְׂרֵה
17	שִׁבְעָה עָשָׂר	שְׁבַע עֶשְׂרֵה
18	שְׁמֹנָה עָשָׂר	שְׁמֹנֶה עֶשְׂרֵה
19	תִּשְׁעָה עָשָׂר	תְּשַׁע עֶשְׂרֵה

Hebrew often uses a singular form of the noun with numbers in the teens, but the plural form is generally found if the numbered item precedes the number. Examples of usage are as follows:

שְׁתֵּים עֶשְׂרֵה שָׁנָה twelve years

חֲמִשָּׁה עָשָׂר שֶׁקֶל fifteen shekels

נָשִׁים שְׁמוֹנֶה־עֶשְׂרֵה eighteen women

6. *The Tens*

The tens are formed by adding the plural ending ים◌ to the root of the single digit number. An unusual case is the number twenty, which is formed by adding ים◌ to the root עֶשֶׂר of the number ten.

Table 19.6. The Tens

עֶשְׂרִים 20	שִׁשִּׁים 60
שְׁלֹשִׁים 30	שִׁבְעִים 70
אַרְבָּעִים 40	שְׁמֹנִים 80
חֲמִשִּׁים 50	תִּשְׁעִים 90

Hebrew often uses a singular form of the noun with numbers above twenty, but the plural form is frequently used if the numbered item precedes the number. Numbers such as "twenty-three" may be given in Hebrew as "three and twenty" or "twenty and three." The rules for gender agreement for the numbers one through ten apply here also. Examples of usage are as follows:

שְׁלֹשִׁים יוֹם thirty days

שְׁלֹשִׁים וְאַחַת שָׁנָה thirty-one years

אַרְבָּעִים וּשְׁתַּיִם עִיר forty-two cities

תֵּשַׁע וְאַרְבָּעִים שָׁנָה forty-nine years

חֲמִשִּׁים וְחָמֵשׁ שָׁנָה fifty-five years

7. The Hundreds and Thousands

Examples with hundreds and thousands are listed below.

Table 19.7. The Hundreds and Thousands

מֵאָה 100	שְׁלֹשֶׁת אֲלָפִים 3,000
מָאתַיִם 200	אַרְבַּעַת אֲלָפִים 4,000
שְׁלֹשׁ מֵאוֹת 300	רְבָבָה 10,000
אַרְבַּע מֵאוֹת 400	רִבּוֹתַיִם 20,000
אֶלֶף 1,000	שְׁלֹשׁ רִבּוֹת 30,000
אַלְפַּיִם 2,000	אַרְבַּע רִבּוֹת 40,000

The hundreds and thousands utilize the dual form for 200, 2,000, and 20,000. Also, note that multiples of 100 use מֵאוֹת, the plural form of מֵאָה, and that for a number such as 300, the normal rule is followed that the seemingly masculine form of the number 3 is written with the feminine noun מֵאוֹת. Thus, we see 300 as שְׁלֹשׁ מֵאוֹת. Also, multiples of 1,000 use the plural אֲלָפִים. The plural of אֶלֶף is אֲלָפִים. The plural of רְבָבָה is רִבּוֹת. An alternative way to describe multiple thousands is using אֶלֶף, as in שִׁבְעִים אֶלֶף (70,000). Examples of usage are as follows:

שְׁלֹשָׁה וַחֲמִשִּׁים אֶלֶף וְאַרְבַּע מֵאוֹת 53,400

וְאֶלֶף וּשְׁבַע מֵאוֹת וַחֲמִשָּׁה וְשִׁבְעִים שָׁקֶל and 1,775 shekels

B. Ordinal Numbers

Hebrew has a distinct set of ordinal numbers for the "first" through the "tenth" ordinal, although the relationship to the cardinals is obvious. Beyond the tenth ordinal, Hebrew simply uses cardinal numbers for ordinals. The ordinals are as follows.

Table 19.8. The Ordinal Numbers

Meaning	Masculine	Feminine
First	רִאשׁוֹן	רִאשׁוֹנָה
Second	שֵׁנִי	שֵׁנִית
Third	שְׁלִישִׁי	שְׁלִישִׁית
Fourth	רְבִיעִי	רְבִיעִית
Fifth	חֲמִישִׁי	חֲמִישִׁית
Sixth	שִׁשִּׁי	שִׁשִּׁית
Seventh	שְׁבִיעִי	שְׁבִיעִית
Eighth	שְׁמִינִי	שְׁמִינִית
Ninth	תְּשִׁיעִי	תְּשִׁיעִית
Tenth	עֲשִׂירִי	עֲשִׂירִית

אֶחָד, "one," is often used for "first." Like other attributive adjectives, the ordinal numbers follow the nouns they modify and agree in gender, number, and definiteness. Sometimes, however, an indefinite noun in the construct will be qualified by a definite ordinal number.

Examples include יוֹם שְׁלִישִׁי, "a third day," בֵּן חֲמִישִׁי, "a fifth son," and, found with the definite article, וּבַשָּׁנָה הַחֲמִישִׁית, "and in the fifth year," and בַּחֹדֶשׁ הַתְּשִׁיעִי, "in the ninth month."

An example of a date formula is בָּרִאשׁוֹן בְּאֶחָד לַחֹדֶשׁ, "in the first month (בָּרִאשׁוֹן) on the first day (בְּאֶחָד) of the month (לַחֹדֶשׁ)." Another is בִּשְׁנַת הַתְּשִׁיעִית לְהוֹשֵׁעַ, "in the ninth year of Hosea" (lit., "in the year of the ninth to Hosea").

C. Vocabulary

1. Core Vocabulary

a. Verbs

יָלַד	Qal: יָלַד give birth, beget
יָצָא	Qal: יָצָא go out

b. Other Words

אֶלֶף	thousand, clan, troop M |אֱלֶף|
אַרְבַּע	four
בֹּקֶר	morning, sunrise
מַטֶּה	tribe, rod, staff M |מַטֶּה|
מִסְפָּר	number M |מִסְפָּר|
מַעַל	above; מַעְלָה = "upwards"
עֶרֶב	evening, sunset
עֶשֶׂר	ten; in numbers eleven through nineteen, עָשָׂר as in אַחַד עָשָׂר, "eleven"
רִאשׁוֹן	first
שֵׁשׁ	six

2. Special Vocabulary

תּוֹלְדוֹת	official records of descendants from an ancestor, often translated "generations" or "account"

3. Proper Names

אֶפְרַיִם	Ephraim
גָּד	Gad
זְבוּלֻן	Zebulun
יְהוֹיָקִים	Jehoiakim
יִשָּׂשכָר	Issachar
מְנַשֶּׁה	Manasseh
נֹחַ	Noah

D. Reading—Numbers 1:24–35

24 לִבְנֵי גָד תּוֹלְדֹתָם לְמִשְׁפְּחֹתָם לְבֵית אֲבֹתָם בְּמִסְפַּר שֵׁמוֹת מִבֶּן עֶשְׂרִים
שָׁנָה וָמַעְלָה כֹּל יֹצֵא צָבָא

25 פְּקֻדֵיהֶם² לְמַטֵּה גָד חֲמִשָּׁה וְאַרְבָּעִים אֶלֶף וְשֵׁשׁ מֵאוֹת וַחֲמִשִּׁים

26 לִבְנֵי יְהוּדָה תּוֹלְדֹתָם לְמִשְׁפְּחֹתָם לְבֵית אֲבֹתָם בְּמִסְפַּר שֵׁמֹת מִבֶּן עֶשְׂרִים
שָׁנָה וָמַעְלָה כֹּל יֹצֵא צָבָא

27 פְּקֻדֵיהֶם לְמַטֵּה יְהוּדָה אַרְבָּעָה וְשִׁבְעִים אֶלֶף וְשֵׁשׁ מֵאוֹת

28 לִבְנֵי יִשָּׂשכָר תּוֹלְדֹתָם לְמִשְׁפְּחֹתָם לְבֵית אֲבֹתָם בְּמִסְפַּר שֵׁמֹת מִבֶּן
עֶשְׂרִים שָׁנָה וָמַעְלָה כֹּל יֹצֵא צָבָא

29 פְּקֻדֵיהֶם לְמַטֵּה יִשָּׂשכָר אַרְבָּעָה וַחֲמִשִּׁים אֶלֶף וְאַרְבַּע מֵאוֹת

30 לִבְנֵי זְבוּלֻן תּוֹלְדֹתָם לְמִשְׁפְּחֹתָם לְבֵית אֲבֹתָם בְּמִסְפַּר שֵׁמֹת מִבֶּן עֶשְׂרִים
שָׁנָה וָמַעְלָה כֹּל יֹצֵא צָבָא

31 פְּקֻדֵיהֶם לְמַטֵּה זְבוּלֻן שִׁבְעָה וַחֲמִשִּׁים אֶלֶף וְאַרְבַּע מֵאוֹת

32 לִבְנֵי יוֹסֵף לִבְנֵי אֶפְרַיִם תּוֹלְדֹתָם לְמִשְׁפְּחֹתָם לְבֵית אֲבֹתָם בְּמִסְפַּר שֵׁמֹת
מִבֶּן עֶשְׂרִים שָׁנָה וָמַעְלָה כֹּל יֹצֵא צָבָא

33 פְּקֻדֵיהֶם לְמַטֵּה אֶפְרַיִם אַרְבָּעִים אֶלֶף וַחֲמֵשׁ מֵאוֹת

34 לִבְנֵי מְנַשֶּׁה תּוֹלְדֹתָם לְמִשְׁפְּחֹתָם לְבֵית אֲבֹתָם בְּמִסְפַּר שֵׁמוֹת מִבֶּן עֶשְׂרִים
שָׁנָה וָמַעְלָה כֹּל יֹצֵא צָבָא

35 פְּקֻדֵיהֶם לְמַטֵּה מְנַשֶּׁה שְׁנַיִם וּשְׁלֹשִׁים אֶלֶף וּמָאתָיִם

---

1. Literally "from a son of twenty years," מִבֶּן עֶשְׂרִים שָׁנָה, is a Hebrew idiom for describing age. Hence, it means "from twenty years old." Observe that שָׁנָה is in the singular with the number עֶשְׂרִים, "twenty."

2. פְּקֻדֵיהֶם is the Qal passive participle mp of פקד with the 3mp suffix. Literally, "their mustered (men)," it is the men assembled for the army. In effect, it means "their militia."

CHAPTER 20
STEMS, ROOTS, AND PRINCIPAL PARTS OF WEAK ROOTS WITH GUTTURALS IN THE QAL STEM

A. Vowel Position in Verbs

The following terms describe the positions for vowels with verbs:

(1) **Preformative vowel**: The vowel with a preformative, such as the vowel in a *yiqtol* preformative.

(2) **First-radical vowel**: The vowel after the first consonant of the root.

(3) **Stem vowel**: The vowel after the second consonant of the root.

(4) **Linking vowel**: a vowel inserted between the final consonant of the root and a sufformative or suffix.

B. The Seven Major Stems

There are seven main stems for the verb (there are a few other unusual stems). The Qal is the basic stem. The other six, called **derived stems**, are **Niphal**, **Piel**, **Pual**, **Hiphil**, **Hophal**, and **Hithpael**. These names are all *qatal* 3ms forms of the verb פָעַל, "do." Today, even though most scholars continue to use the terms Niphal, Piel, and so forth, קטל is used as the paradigm verb. The reason פעל is no longer used as a paradigm is that it has a guttural letter in the middle position (as you know, gutturals are subject to special rules). To master these stems, begin by learning the *qatal* 3ms forms of קטל along with the names of the stems.

Table 20.1. The Stem Names and Patterns with Roots פעל and קטל

	פעל	קטל
Qal	פָּעַל	קָטַל
Niphal	נִפְעַל	נִקְטַל
Piel	פִּעֵל	קִטֵּל
Pual	פֻּעַל	קֻטַּל
Hithpael	הִתְפַּעֵל	הִתְקַטֵּל
Hiphil	הִפְעִיל	הִקְטִיל
Hophal	הָפְעַל	הָקְטַל

As a tree grows, its branches go off in different directions, but you could follow any branch back to the trunk and down to the root. Analogously, a derived stem takes the root meaning of a word and moves it in a specific semantic direction with a specific meaning. In the following diagram, we see that the Qal, like the trunk of a tree, carries the root meaning of a word. It may be regarded as "unmarked" in the sense that it does not have a distinctive semantic nuance. The other stems take the root meaning in various directions.

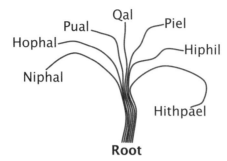

(1) The three stems on the left side of the tree are essentially passive.

(2) The Piel and Hiphil are active and have explicit or implied direct objects.

   (a) An explicit direct object would be "him" in, "He struck him."

   (b) An implied object would be something like "a word" or "a sentence" in the statement, "He spoke."

(3) The Hithpael is primarily reflexive, meaning that the subject acts upon itself. (The Niphal is sometimes reflexive as well.)

The root בקע, which in the Qal means "split," is one of the few roots that appears in all seven stems in the Hebrew Bible. The Qal may be **transitive** (taking a direct object) or **intransitive** (active but not taking a direct object). The Niphal of בקע is a middle voice; it means to "split open," as when the ground split open in Num 16:31. The Piel is transitive and means "tear (something) to pieces," and the Pual, the passive of the Piel, means to be "torn" or "ripped up." The reflexive Hithpael means to "burst open." The Hiphil means to "breach" the defenses of a city, and the Hophal, as the passive of the Hiphil, means "be breached." The following illustrates how one root has different meanings in its various stems.

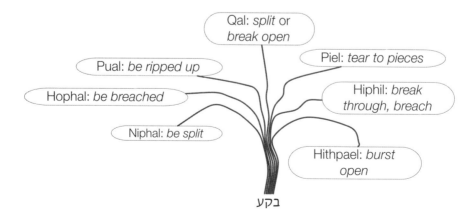

You should be aware that the stems do not always neatly follow these patterns. Some Niphal verbs, for example, are active in meaning.

1. The Meaning of Verbs in the Qal

The Qal is the basic stem. It is also called the **G** stem (from German *Grund*, meaning "ground" or "basic"). It has the following functions:

(1) **Transitive**. A transitive verb is active and takes a direct object, as in "He forgot the Daghesh Forte!"

(2) **Intransitive**. An intransitive verb is active but will not take a direct object, as in "He sleeps in Hebrew class."

(3) **Stative**. Not really active or passive, a stative verb describes the status of its subject. English does not use stative verbs, but uses a form of "to be" with an adjective, as in "This is confusing, and we are weary." Hebrew often uses Qal stative verbs where English uses adjectives.

2. The Meaning of Verbs in the Niphal

Verbs in the Niphal stem (also called the **N** stem) usually have one of the following meanings:

(1) **Passive**. The Niphal is frequently passive in meaning, as in "The food was eaten by Abraham." Verbs that are active in the Qal are often passive in the Niphal. The root אכל means to "eat" in the Qal and to "be eaten" in the Niphal.

(2) **Reflexive**. When a verb is reflexive, the action of the verb comes back upon the subject, or the subject acts upon himself. For example, "He hid himself from the Hebrew professor."

3. The Meaning of Verbs in the Piel

The Piel (also called the **D** or "doubled" stem) is active (not passive). In this respect, the Piel is similar to the Qal, except that the Piel is not used for stative verbs. Many Piel forms have a simple active meaning. For example, הלל in the Piel means to "praise." Other uses are as follows:

(1) **Factitive**. A verb that is intransitive in the Qal may become transitive in the Piel. A transitive verb can take a direct object; an intransitive verb cannot. Hebrew can use the root אבד to mean "die" in the Qal but "kill" in the Piel, as in "Either he will die (אבד, Qal) in battle or he will kill (אבד, Piel) his enemy." Similarly, גלה ("be naked" in the Qal) is to "expose" in the Piel.

(2) **Frequentive**. A simple action (as indicated by the Qal) can become a frequent or repeated action in the Piel. For example, the root הלך means "go" in the Qal but "go about" in the Piel.

(3) **Denominative**. A verb that is derived from a noun or adjective is often inflected in the Piel. The root דבר is used for the noun "word" and the Piel verb "speak," as in "I don't understand that word (דבר, noun); please speak (דבר, Piel verb) in plain Hebrew!"

(4) **Causative**. The root למד means to "learn" in the Qal stem but to "cause to learn," that is, to "teach," in the Piel stem.

4. The Meaning of Verbs in the Pual

The Pual is the passive of the Piel. For example, the root דבר means "speak" in the Piel but "be spoken" in the Pual, as in "Hebrew is spoken here." The Pual is also called the **Dp** or "doubled passive" stem.

5. The Meaning of Verbs in the Hithpael

The Hithpael is often reflexive or reciprocal. It is also called the **HtD** stem because it has a preformative הת and doubles the middle radical.

(1) **Reflexive**. Like the Niphal, a Hithpael verb can be reflexive. As a reflexive, the action of the verb comes back upon the subject. The root קדש means to "sanctify" in the Piel but to "sanctify oneself" in the Hithpael, as in "You must sanctify yourself before entering the temple."

(2) **Reciprocal**. Hithpael verbs can also be translated with the notion of reciprocity: ראה means to "see" in the Qal and to "look at each other" in the Hithpael, as in "The students saw (ראה, Qal) the Hebrew test and then looked at each other (ראה, Hithpael) in dismay."

(3) **Frequentive**. This nuance also appears in the Piel.

6. The Meaning of Verbs in the Hiphil

The Hiphil is also called the **H** stem. It often has one of the following functions:

(1) **Causative**. This implies that someone is causing someone else (or something else) to do something. Verbs that are active in the Qal are often causal in the Hiphil. For example, the root אכל means "eat" in the Qal but "make someone eat" (i.e., "feed") in the Hiphil, as in "Sarah fed Isaac raisins and dates." The Hiphil is causative more often than is the Piel.

(2) **Factitive**. As in the Piel, sometimes verbs that are intransitive or stative in the Qal become transitive in the Hiphil.

7. The Meaning of Verbs in the Hophal

The Hophal is the passive of the Hiphil and is therefore sometimes called the **Hp** stem. The root שמד means to "destroy" in the Hiphil and to "be destroyed" in the Hophal, as in the ancient curse, "He who destroys (שמד, Hiphil) this Hebrew textbook, his house shall be destroyed (שמד, Hophal) before dawn!"

8. Verbs in Other Stems

Other stems, far less frequent than the six principal derived stems, are also attested in biblical Hebrew. Some of these are so infrequent that it is impossible to generate complete paradigms, but some are important and will be described in chapter 35.

C. Types of Weak Roots

Most Hebrew roots have three consonants. Hebrew consonants that do not cause changes in conjugations are called **strong** letters. A root made up of all strong letters is a **strong root**. קטל is a strong root because it follows a simple, basic inflection pattern, without any peculiarities. In contrast, a **weak** letter often changes the form a verb will take. A vowel may be lengthened, a consonant may be lost, or the like. Any root with at least one weak letter is weak. For now, we will focus on how weak roots work in the Qal stem.

(1) The principal weak letters are the gutturals (א, ע, ה and ח) and י, נ, and ר (like a guttural, ר will not double).

(2) A weak root is classified according to where in the root the weak letter falls.

  (a) For example, if the weak letter is a נ and it is the first of the three root letters, the root is called a "first Nun" (I-נ) root.

  (b) If the weak letter is א and it falls in the third position, it is called a "III-א" root.

(3) Two weak roots are distinctive.

  (a) The **hollow** root has only two consonants with a pointed vowel letter between the two. It is sometimes called **biconsonantal**. The consonants may not be weak, but the root is weak because it has this distinct pattern.

  (b) The **geminate** root is one in which the second and third letters are repeated. Again, the consonants may not be weak, but the root is weak because it has this unusual pattern.

(4) Some grammars and lexicons describe weak letters in a scheme that uses the root פעל as the paradigm. In this scheme, consonant position corresponds to the letters of this root פעל. The first consonant position is called the "פ position," the second is the "ע position," and the third is the "ל position." When referring to these grammars, you must understand this terminology.

  (a) What this grammar calls a I-נ root would be in some grammars called "Pe-Nun" (it is written as פ״נ), meaning that there was a נ in the first or פ position.

  (b) Similarly, what in this grammar is called a III-ה root would be called "Lamed-Hey" (ל״ה) in a grammar using this terminology.

(5) The I-א and I-י roots have two patterns each, as given below.

Table 20.2. Common Weak Root Types

Type	Root and Example		Comments
I-ע or ח	עמד	יַעֲמֹד	The first letter has the normal traits of a guttural, such as preferring an a-class vowel.
I-א	אמר	יֹאמַר	In the Qal *yiqtol*, it takes a Holem with the preformative and a Pathach as the stem vowel.

I-א	אהב	יֶאֱהַב	In the Qal *yiqtol*, it takes a Seghol with the preformative and a Pathach as the stem vowel.
II-Guttural	בחר	יִבְחַר	The second letter has the normal traits of a guttural, such as preferring an a-class vowel.
III-ח or ע	שמע	יִשְׁמַע	The guttural will especially influence the verb's form by its preference for the a-class vowel.
III-א	מצא	יִמְצָא	The א will often quiesce and cause the vowel in front of it to lengthen.
I-נ	נפל	יִפֹּל	The I-נ generally assimilates to the following letter when a preformative is added.
I-י	ישב	תֵּשֵׁב	The first letter of the root (the י) drops out if a preformative is added.
I-י	ירש	יִירַשׁ	The first letter of the root (the י) becomes a vowel letter י if a preformative is added.
Hollow	שוב	שָׁב יָשׁוּב	The vowel between the two consonants does not reduce and is usually long.
Geminate	סבב	יָסֹב	The geminate verb tends to mimic other patterns. In this case, it is similar to the *yiqtol* of the hollow verb.
III-ה	בנה	בָּנִיתָ	The III-ה has a fixed set of rules that it follows with great consistency.

Some roots are doubly-weak; that is, two of the root letters are weak (these are not listed in the chart above). For example, עשׂה is both a I-Guttural and a III-ה root. Doubly-weak roots will combine the peculiarities of both weak roots and can be difficult to recognize.

D. Introduction to Principal Parts

Having mastered the full paradigms for the Qal strong and III-ה verbs in the various conjugations, you are now ready to tackle the weak roots noted above. Rather than beginning with numerous full paradigms, we will approach weak roots through their **principal parts**. These are the most basic forms of a given verbal root in the primary conjugations, and their memorization provides a manageable and helpful way to identify weak forms in all stems.

(1) The charts below only give the principal parts of weak verbs.

    (a) For the *qatal* and *yiqtol*, we usually have only the 3ms forms.

    (b) For the infinitive construct, we have the simple form without the ל preposition.

    (c) For the participle, we have only the ms forms.

(2) We will study the complete paradigms later. At the same time, with the knowledge of the principal parts and the patterns of the conjugations in the Qal strong verb, you should have no trouble recognizing the other inflections of these verbs. For example, since the Qal *yiqtol* 3ms of עמד is יַעֲמֹד, its 3fs would be תַּעֲמֹד. If you know that the ms Qal active participle of בחר is בֹּחֵר, you should recognize בֹּחֲרִים as the mp Qal active participle.

(3) The principal parts of the strong root קטל are provided for the sake of comparison.

(4) When we say that a pattern is "Like strong," we mean that as a general rule its inflection is similar to that of the strong verb קטל. This does not mean that there are no differences whatsoever, but it does mean that differences are minimal. For example, the Qal *qatal* 3cp of בחר is בָּחֲרוּ, which differs from קָטְלוּ in that it has a Hateph Pathach where the strong verb has a vocal Shewa. But this is a very minor difference, and in most cases the vowel patterns of the Qal *qatal* of קטל and בחר are identical.

E. Qal Weak Verbs with Gutturals

Gutturals pose no real difficulty with the Qal stem. Remember that gutturals prefer a-class vowels, take composite Shewas instead of vocal Shewas, and will not double.

Table 20.3. The Qal Verb with Gutturals

	Qatal	Yiqtol	Inf. Con.	Participle
Strong	קָטַל	יִקְטֹל	קְטֹל	קֹטֵל
I-ח/ע עמד *stand*	Like strong עָמַד	A-class preformative יַעֲמֹד	Composite Shewa עֲמֹד	Like strong עֹמֵד
II-Guttural בחר *choose*	Like strong בָּחַר	A-class stem vowel יִבְחַר	Like strong בְּחֹר	Like strong בֹּחֵר
III-ח/ע שמע *hear*	Like strong שָׁמַע	A-class stem vowel יִשְׁמַע	Like strong; furtive Pathach שְׁמֹעַ	Like strong; furtive Pathach שֹׁמֵעַ
III-א מצא *find*	Quiescent א מָצָא	Quiescent א; A-class stem vowel יִמְצָא	Like strong מְצֹא	Like strong מֹצֵא
I-ח + III-א חטא *sin*	Quiescent א חָטָא	Seghol preformative; quiescent א יֶחֱטָא	Composite Shewa חֲטֹא	Like strong חוֹטֵא

The vowels of the strong verb *yiqtol* are not normative. Note the following:

(1) The vowel pattern of the Qal *yiqtol* is highly variable.

   (a) A first-position guttural (I-guttural) in the Qal *yiqtol* will often have Pathach pre-formative and Hateph Pathach under the first radical. Sometimes, however, it will have Seghol in the preformative position, as with יֶחֱטָא.

   (b) In *yiqtol* verbs with gutturals in the second and third positions, Qal verbs have a-class stem vowels.

(2) The III-א verb מצא shows quiescence of the א in the *qatal* (contrast מָצָא with קָטַל) and shows both quiescence and preference for the a-class vowel in the *yiqtol* (contrast יִמְצָא with יִשְׁמַע and יִקְטֹל).

(3) A III-guttural will at times have a furtive Pathach.

(4) In all the above roots, the infinitive construct has a Holem stem vowel. In some roots, however, this is not the case.

(5) For the most part, imperatives look like *yiqtol* verbs with the preformative dropped. Thus, the ms imperative of שמע is שְׁמַע. In many cases, the form of the imperative ms is the same as that of the infinitive construct (important exceptions are in the II- and III-guttural and the I-י roots). Thus, if you know the principal parts, you can often use the infinitive to figure out the imperative.

(6) The root חטא is doubly-weak, being I-ח and III-א.

   (a) The *yiqtol* has a preformative with Seghol, illustrating the fact that some I-ח roots will take Seghol (contrast יַעֲמֹד).

   (b) The III-א has the normal quiescence.

F. Vocabulary

1. Core Vocabulary

a. Verbs

בחר	Qal: בָּחַר choose
חטא	Qal: חָטָא miss (a mark), sin
ירא	Qal: יָרֵא fear, be afraid
	Niphal: נוֹרָא (= participle) be feared
ירש	Qal: יָרַשׁ possess, inherit, dispossess
	Hiphil: הוֹרִישׁ take possession of, dispossess, drive out
מצא	Qal: מָצָא find, seek
	Niphal: נִמְצָא be found
נשא	Qal: נָשָׂא carry, lift up
	Niphal: נִשָׂא be carried

b. Other Words

אָדוֹן	lord, master Ⓜ |אָדֹן|; אֲדֹנָי = "my/the Lord"
דּוֹר	generation Ⓜ |דּוֹר|
חֶסֶד	loyalty, steadfast love, devotion, faithfulness Ⓜ |חֶסֶד|
מְאֹד	very much, very
עָנִי	poor, wretched Ⓜ |עָנִי|
פַּחַד	dread, trembling, deep fear Ⓜ |פַּחַד|

2. Reading Vocabulary

לַמְנַצֵּחַ	precise meaning unknown; often rendered, "for the director of music"
נָבָל	fool, arrogant person Ⓜ
פחד	Qal: פָּחַד fear, be in dread

3. Previously Learned Verbs in Derived Stems

כתב	Qal: chapter 9
	Niphal: יִכָּתֵב (*yiqtol* 3ms) be written
מלך	Qal: chapter 9
	Hiphil: הִמְלִיךְ install someone as king
שמר	Qal: chapter 10
	Niphal: נִשְׁמַר be kept, be guarded

4. Proper Names

פְּלֶשֶׁת	Philistia
פְּלִשְׁתִּי	Philistine(s)
צִיּוֹן	Zion

G. Reading from Psalm 14

לַמְנַצֵּחַ לְדָוִד[1]

אָמַר נָבָל בְּלִבּוֹ

אֵין אֱלֹהִים

---

1.   This could be translated "by David," "of David," or "to David."

שָׁם פָּחֲדוּ פָֿחַד¹

כִּי־אֱלֹהִים בְּדוֹר צַדִּיק

מִי יִתֵּן² מִצִּיּוֹן יְשׁוּעַת יִשְׂרָאֵל

---

1. This looks like it means something like, "There they are in dread of dread." It is actually a "cognate accusative," in which the verb and its direct object are both from the same root. It can be translated simply as "There they are in deep dread."
2. You can easily recognize that מִי יִתֵּן means "Who will give?" This is an idiom that expresses strong desire for something. It could be translated "If only (X would happen)." Thus, this line means "If only the salvation of Israel (would come) from Zion!"

CHAPTER 21
PRINCIPAL PARTS OF OTHER WEAK ROOTS IN THE QAL STEM

A. I-נ, Hollow, and Geminate Verbs

These roots can be quite different from their strong verb counterparts, as the chart below illustrates. Not only will vowel patterns change, but radicals (consonants that are part of the root) may drop off or change as well. The I-נ and hollow roots are especially likely to show significant change.

Table 21.1. The Qal Verb with I-נ, Hollow, and Geminate Roots

	Qatal	Yiqtol	Inf. Con.	Participle
Strong	קָטַל	יִקְטֹל	קְטֹל	קֹטֵל
I-נ נָפַל *fall*	Like strong נָפַל	נ assimilates יִפֹּל	Like strong נְפֹל	Like strong נֹפֵל
Hollow שׁוּב *return*	Hollow vowel lost; a-class stem vowel שָׁב	Hollow vowel present, Qamets preformative יָשׁוּב	Hollow vowel present שׁוּב	Hollow vowel lost; a-class stem vowel שָׁב
Geminate סבב *go around*	Like strong סָבַב	Qamets in preformative יָסֹב	Like strong סָבַב	Like strong סֹבֵב

Observe the following:

(1) Again, you should not have great difficulty in identifying various forms if you know these principal parts. Since the Qal *qatal* 3ms of שׁוּב is שָׁב, it is not hard to recognize שַׁבְתָּ as the *qatal* 2ms, notwithstanding the short vowel.

(2) The I-נ is like the strong verb except in the *yiqtol*, where the נ assimilates. Thus the *yiqtol* 3fs is תִּפֹּל. The I-נ infinitive construct is often just like the strong verb, but in a number of verbs it is different, as we shall study later.

(3) The hollow verb in the table above uses שׁוּב, a verb you already know from forms such as שָׁב.

(4) The geminate verb is actually more complicated than the principal parts imply. The geminate *qatal*, *yiqtol*, and infinitive construct often look as they do in the chart above, but there are alternative patterns for all of these. Even so, these principal parts make a good starting point for learning the geminate root.

B. I-י Verbs

The *yiqtol* verbs יֵשֵׁב and יִירַשׁ are already familiar to you. Therefore, these principal parts should be easy to learn, but take note of the infinitive constructs.

Table 21.2. The Qal Verbs with I-י Roots

	Qatal	Yiqtol	Inf. Con.	Participle
Strong	קָטַל	יִקְטֹל	קְטֹל	קֹטֵל
I-י יָשַׁב *dwell*	Like strong יָשַׁב	י dropped; Tsere preformative תֵּשֵׁב | יֵשֵׁב (3ms and 3fs)	י dropped; ת added as ending שֶׁבֶת	Like strong יֹשֵׁב
I-י יָרַשׁ *possess*	Like strong יָרַשׁ	י vowel letter; a-class stem vowel יִירַשׁ	י dropped; ת added as ending רֶשֶׁת	Like strong יוֹרֵשׁ

Observe the following:

(1) The I-י of the יָשַׁב type is the most common type of I-י root and should be considered normative. It can be called "Original I-ו" since it originally did have ו in the first position. This original ו will reappear in certain other stems.

(2) The I-י of the יָשַׁב type is like the strong verb in the *qatal* and participle, but in the *yiqtol* and infinitive construct, the י of the root יָשַׁב drops off. In the *yiqtol* 3ms (יֵשֵׁב), the י is the *yiqtol* preformative; *it is not part of the root*. תֵּשֵׁב is the *yiqtol* 3fs; it shows that the י of the root is gone. The vowel under the *yiqtol* preformative is a Tsere; the stem vowel is also a Tsere, but it can shorten or reduce.

(3) The I-י infinitive construct loses its initial י but adds a ת to the end and has a vowel pattern like a segholate noun, as in the form שֶׁבֶת. In the Qal I-י, the infinitive construct and imperative are different.

(4) The I-י of the יָרַשׁ type could be called Original I-י in that it did not have ו originally in the first position. A consistent Original I-י will have י (or a vowel letter with י) in the first root position in all stems. The root יטב, "be good," is an example of this, but it is not used for principal parts since it has no extant Qal infinitive construct. The root יָרַשׁ is actually of a mixed type; it has the pattern of Original I-י in the Qal but the pattern of Original I-ו in the Hiphil.

(5) The I-י of the יָרַשׁ type is like the strong verb in its *qatal* and participle. It is like יָשַׁב in its infinitive construct; you have already learned the *yiqtol* יִירַשׁ.

C. I-א Verbs

There are two basic patterns for the I-א root, as illustrated in these two verbs. The *yiqtol* verbs יֹאמַר and יֶאֱהַב are already familiar to you. The Holem with the preformative of אמר is also very familiar to you because of the *wayyiqtol* form וַיֹּאמֶר. Another very common form of אמר is the infinitive construct with לְ, which appears as לֵאמֹר.

Table 21.3. The Roots אמר and אהב

	Qatal	Yiqtol	Inf. Con.	Participle
Strong	קָטַל	יִקְטֹל	קְטֹל	קֹטֵל
I-א אמר *say*	Like strong אָמַר	Holem with preformative; Pathach stem vowel יֹאמַר	Like strong לֵאמֹר / אֱמֹר	Like strong אֹמֵר
I-א אהב *love*	Like strong אָהַב	Seghol with preformative; Pathach stem vowel יֶאֱהַב	ת ending added אַהֲבַת / לְאַהֲבָה	Like strong אֹהֵב

Observe the following:

(1) Both patterns are like the strong verb in *qatal* and participle.

(2) אמר is like the strong verb in the infinitive construct but is almost always seen with the preposition לְ as לֵאמֹר (over 900 occurrences in the Hebrew Bible). The א quiesces and the Shewa with לְ lengthens to Tsere.

(3) You already know the two *yiqtol* forms.

(4) The infinitive construct of אהב is fairly rare in the form אַהֲבַת. With the לְ preposition, it has the form לְאַהֲבָה, "to love," which is very common.

D. The III-ה Verbs

You are already familiar with the III-ה verb and recognize that its principal parts are as follows:

בָּנָה	יִבְנֶה	בְּנוֹת	בּוֹנֶה

Mastering all the paradigms of the III-ה is fairly simple if you keep in mind the following rules for this root:

(1) With no ending, the ה is present (e.g., בָּנָה and יִבְנֶה).

   (a) In the *qatal* 3ms, the ה is pointed with Qamets.

   (b) In the *yiqtol* and participle, the ה is pointed with Seghol.

(2) The *qatal* 3fs ending is תָה, as in בָּנְתָה.

(3) With an ending that has a consonant, the ה is replaced by a pointed vowel letter with
י, as in the *qatal* 2ms בָּנִיתָ. Contrast קָטַלְתָּ.

(4) With a vowel ending, the ה drops off (e.g., the *qatal* 3cp בָּנוּ). Contrast קָטְלוּ.

(5) The infinitive construct always ends with וֹת, as in the Qal infinitive construct בְּנוֹת.

E. Vocabulary

1. Core Vocabulary

a. Verbs

חזק	Qal: חָזַק be strong, have courage
	Piel: חִזַּק make firm, strengthen, harden (the heart)
	Hiphil: הֶחֱזִיק seize, grasp, feel strengthened
יכל	Qal: יָכֹל be able to, be capable of (*yiqtol* 3ms is יוּכַל, and the rest of the Qal *yiqtol* has a similar pattern)
לקח	Qal: לָקַח take, grasp, capture (*yiqtol* 3ms is יִקַּח, and the rest of the Qal *yiqtol* has a similar pattern)
מלא	Qal: מָלֵא be full, fill up
	Niphal: יִמָּלֵא (= *yiqtol*) be filled
	Piel: מִלֵּא fill, endow, devote, fulfill
נטה	Qal: נָטָה reach out, spread out, stretch out, turn aside
	Hiphil: הִטָּה stretch out, extend, guide away
פעל	Qal: פָּעַל do
רדף	Qal: רָדַף pursue

b. Other Words

אָוֶן	iniquity, evil, disaster Ⓜ |אוֹן|
אֵל	God, god; Mighty One; El Ⓜ |אֵל|
כָּבוֹד	heaviness, honor, glory Ⓕ |כְּבוֹד|
מִנְחָה	gift, present; offering
נְאֻם	utterance, declaration Ⓕ |נְאֻם|

2. Previously Learned Verbs in Derived Stems

כרת	Qal: chapter 14
	Niphal: נִכְרַת be cut off, eliminated
	Hiphil: הִכְרִית exterminate

פקד	Qal: chapter 13
	Niphal: נִפְקַד be missed, be punished
	Hiphil: הִפְקִיד appoint
קרב	Qal: chapter 14
	Hiphil: הִקְרִיב bring (near), take, offer

3. Proper Names

אַהֲרֹן	Aaron
בָּבֶל	Babylon
בַּבְלִי	Babylonian(s)
חִזְקִיָּה	Hezekiah; also seen as חִזְקִיָּהוּ
שְׁמוּאֵל	Samuel

F. Reading from Psalm 14

הֲלֹא יָדְעוּ כָּל־פֹּעֲלֵי אָוֶן

אֹכְלֵי עַמִּי

אָכְלוּ לֶחֶם

יְהוָה לֹא קָרָאוּ[1]

G. Unified Chart of Qal Stem Principal Parts

The table on the following page lays out all the principal parts of the strong and weak Hebrew roots for the Qal stem. It is imperative that the student learn this table, as full understanding of the Qal verbs follows naturally from mastery of these forms.

---

1.   We should probably understand הֲלֹא יָדְעוּ כָּל־ to govern the second line (אֹכְלֵי עַמִּי) as well as for the first. Notice that אֹכְלֵי עַמִּי grammatically parallels פֹּעֲלֵי אָוֶן. So interpreted, it means "Do not all doers of iniquity know? / (Do not all) eaters of my people (know)? / They eat food; / they do not call on YHWH." The traditional translation is "Eaters of my people eat bread" (usually modified to something like "They eat my people as they eat bread").

Table 21.4. Qal Stem Principal Parts

	Qatal	Yiqtol	Inf. Con.	Participle
Strong	קָטַל	יִקְטֹל	קְטֹל	קֹטֵל
III-ה בנה	בָּנָה	יִבְנֶה	בְּנוֹת	בּוֹנֶה
I-ע/ח עמד	עָמַד	יַעֲמֹד	עֲמֹד	עֹמֵד
II-Guttural בחר	בָּחַר	יִבְחַר	בְּחֹר	בֹּחֵר
III-ע/ח שמע	שָׁמַע	יִשְׁמַע	שְׁמֹעַ	שֹׁמֵעַ
III-א מצא	מָצָא	יִמְצָא	מְצֹא	מֹצֵא
III-א + I-ח חטא	חָטָא	יֶחֱטָא	חֲטֹא	חוֹטֵא
I-נ נפל	נָפַל	יִפֹּל	נְפֹל	נֹפֵל
Hollow שוב	שָׁב	יָשׁוּב	שׁוּב	שָׁב
Geminate סבב	סָבַב	יָסֹב	סְבֹב	סֹבֵב
I-י ישב	יָשַׁב	תֵּשֵׁב | יֵשֵׁב[1]	שֶׁבֶת	יֹשֵׁב
I-י ירש	יָרַשׁ	יִירַשׁ	רֶשֶׁת	יוֹרֵשׁ
I-א אמר	אָמַר	יֹאמַר	לֵאמֹר[2]	אֹמֵר
I-א אהב	אָהַב	יֶאֱהַב	אַהֲבַת	אֹהֵב

---

1. The 3fs is included to make clear that the י in the *yiqtol* 3ms is not part of the root.
2. This is the form with the לְ preposition. The simple infinitive אֱמֹר is very rare, but the form with לְ preposition, לֵאמֹר, is extremely common.

CHAPTER 22
CHARACTERISTICS OF THE NIPHAL, PIEL, AND HIPHIL

A. Depictions of the Derived Stems Using Graphics

The following discussion makes use of both symbolic "Romanized Patterns" and Hebrew examples to explain the patterns of the derived stems. For example, for the Niphal *qatal*, we see the following:

Romanized Pattern	Example
◻◻◻ℙ (a i)	נִקְטַל

In the "Romanized Pattern" diagram, the following conventions are followed:

(1) ◻ represents a *root radical* (i.e., the three consonants of the root).

   (a) There are normally three boxes for the radicals, like ◻◻◻.

   (b) A box with a dot in it (◻̇) is a radical doubled with a Daghesh Forte.

(2) The small Roman letter under a box represents the vowel class of the vowel that goes in that position.

   (a) ◻ (a) is a radical with an a-class vowel.

   (b) ◻ (i) is a radical with an i-class vowel.

   (c) ◻ (u) is a radical with a u-class vowel.

(3) ℙ represents a preformative.

   (a) It may be a characteristic of a stem, such as the characteristic נ preformative of the Niphal *qatal* or הִת preformative of the Hithpael.

   (b) If the ℙ is in gray, it means that there is no characteristic stem preformative, but there are *yiqtol* and participle preformatives (Piel and Pual).

(4) An upside down e (ə) is a Shewa.

   (a) ℙ (ə) is thus a preformative with a Shewa.

   (b) This happens with the Piel and Pual preformatives.

B. The Niphal

1. The Principal Parts

The principal parts of the Niphal stem are as follows.

Table 22.1. Principal Parts of the Niphal

Qatal	Yiqtol	Inf. Con.	Participle
נִקְטַל	יִקָּטֵל	הִקָּטֵל	נִקְטָל

(1) Both the *qatal* and participle have the נ preformative. The vowel pattern is i-class (with the preformative נ) followed by a-class (as the "stem vowel," the vowel that is with the middle root letter).

(2) The *yiqtol* and the *infinitive construct* have the following features:

   (a) Both have an "a-class followed by i-class" vowel pattern. They have Qamets (a-class) under the first radical and Tsere (i-class) as the stem vowel.

   (b) Both seem to have had a preformative הִן. The Hireq in הִן is part of the preformative; it is not part of the "a-class followed by i-class" vowel pattern.

   (i) The נ of הִן has doubled the ק.

   (ii) The infinitive construct is thus הִקָּטֵל.

   (iii) In the *yiqtol* יִקָּטֵל, the *yiqtol* preformative י has displaced the ה of הִן.

   (c) The imperative ms is הִקָּטֵל, comparable to the *yiqtol* 2ms תִּקָּטֵל. When the ת of the *yiqtol* drops off in order to form the imperative, the original ה of the הִן reappears. Similarly, the *yiqtol* 2fs is תִּקָּטְלִי, and the imperative fs is הִקָּטְלִי.

(3) Thus, we see that there are two distinct patterns for the Niphal stem.

2. The Two Patterns of the Niphal

a. Qatal *and Participle*

The Niphal *qatal* and participle patterns have three main features:

(1) The preformative is נ.

(2) The preformative has an i-class vowel.

(3) The stem vowel is a-class.

Blackboard 22.1. The Patterns of the Niphal *Qatal* (Perfect) and Participle

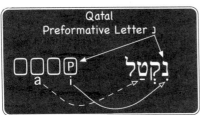

Sometimes, as in the *qatal* 3cp נִקְטְלוּ, the stem vowel will reduce according to the normal rules of vowel change. Also, remember that a participle always has a long stem vowel; thus, the Niphal participle is נִקְטָל.

b. Other Patterns

The other patterns of the Niphal appear to have a preformative הִן, as described above. Notice that the vowel pattern for these forms is a-class followed by i-class.

As in the *qatal*, the stem vowel of the *yiqtol* can reduce to Shewa according to normal rules of vowel reduction. An example of such reduction is the Niphal *yiqtol* 2fs תִּקָּטְלִי.

Blackboard 22.2. The Pattern of the Niphal Infinitive Construct

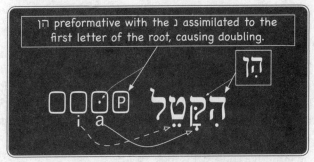

Recognizing the displacement of the ה in the הַן preformative by the *yiqtol* preformative letter helps us understand why the Niphal *yiqtol* looks as it does. Notice that in the *yiqtol* 3ms יִקָּטֵל, the *yiqtol* preformative י has replaced the ה that we see in the Niphal infinitive construct הִקָּטֵל.

Blackboard 22.3. The Formation of the Niphal *Yiqtol* (Imperfect)

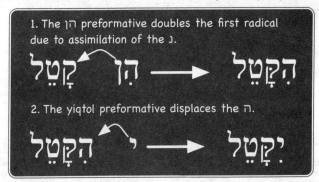

This also helps us to understand the form of the Niphal imperative. Remember that an imperative is usually simply a second person *yiqtol* with the ת preformative dropped off. When this happens in the Niphal, the original ה of the הַן preformative reappears.

Blackboard 22.4. The Niphal Imperative

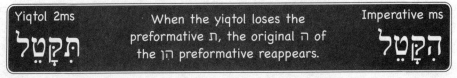

Table 22.2. Patterns and Examples of the Niphal Stem

Qatal and Participle	All Other Inflections
Preformative is נ	Preformative is הִנ with נ assimilated
"i-a" pattern	*"a-i" pattern*
☐☐☐Ⓟ (a/i)	☐☐☐·Ⓟ (i/a)
Qatal נִקְטַל (3ms)	Yiqtol יִקָּטֵל (3ms)
נִקְטְלוּ (3cp)	תִּקָּטְלִי (2fs)
Participle נִקְטָל (ms)	Imperative הִקָּטֵל (ms)
	הִקָּטְלִי (fs)
	Infinitive Construct הִקָּטֵל

The נ preformative has no vowel and so takes the "i" vowel of the "i-a" pattern in the *qatal*/participle. The הִנ preformative has a vowel and is not considered part of the "a-i" vowel pattern.

C. The Piel

1. The Principal Parts

The principal parts of the Piel stem are as follows.

Table 22.3. Principal Parts of the Piel

Qatal 3ms	Qatal 2ms	Yiqtol	Inf. Con.	Participle
קִטֵּל	קִטַּלְתָּ	יְקַטֵּל	קַטֵּל	מְקַטֵּל

(1) The Piel always doubles the middle radical of the root.

(2) There is no Piel preformative. However, the participle has a preformative מ, and of course the *yiqtol* has its preformatives.

2. The Three Patterns of the Piel

(1) The *qatal* always has the i-class vowel under the first radical. The *qatal* stem vowel consistently is as follows:

   (a) For the 3ms, there is an i-class stem vowel (קִטֵּל), which reduces in the 3fs and 3cp (קִטְּלוּ).

   (b) In the second and first person, the stem vowel is a-class (קִטַּלְתָּ).

   Some forms deviate slightly from the norm; for example, the *qatal* 3ms of קדשׁ is קִדַּשׁ.

Blackboard 22.5. Characteristics of the Piel *Qatal* (Perfect) 3ms

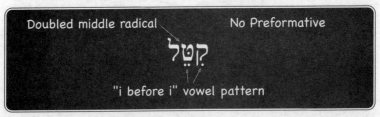

Blackboard 22.6. Characteristics of the Piel *Qatal* (Perfect) 2ms

(2) In the *yiqtol*, the infinitive construct, and the participle (that is, in all non-*qatal* forms), we have the following pattern.

(a) The vowel pattern is a-class with the first radical followed by i-class with the stem vowel.

(b) Following normal rules of vowel change, the stem vowel may reduce to Shewa, as in the *yiqtol* 3mp (יְקַטְּלוּ). You should be able to break יְקַטְּלוּ into its syllables and see why there is a Shewa in the open pretonic position under the ט.

(c) If there is a preformative (*yiqtol* and participle), it always has a Shewa.

Blackboard 22.7. Characteristics of the Piel *Yiqtol* (Imperfect)

Blackboard 22.8. Characteristics of the Piel Infinitive Construct

Blackboard 22.9. Characteristics of the Piel Participle

Table 22.4. Patterns and Examples of the Piel Stem

Qatal		All Other Inflections
3rd person	2nd and 1st person	Preformative with *yiqtol* and participle
"i-i" pattern	*"i-a" pattern*	*"a-i" pattern*
☐·☐☐ i i	☐·☐☐ a i	☐·☐☐[P] i a ə
קִטֵּל (3ms)	קִטַּלְתָּ (2ms)	*Yiqtol* יְקַטֵּל (3ms)
קִטְּלוּ (3cp)	קִטַּלְתִּי (1cs)	יְקַטְּלוּ (3mp)
The Piel has no preformative, and thus the vowel patterns relate only to the root letters. A *yiqtol* or participle preformative has only a Shewa.		*Participle* מְקַטֵּל (ms)
		מְקַטְּלִים (mp)
		Imperative קַטֵּל (ms)
		קַטְּלִי (fs)
		Infinitive Construct קַטֵּל

D. The Hiphil

1. The Principal Parts

The principal parts of the Hiphil stem are as follows.

Table 22.5. Principal Parts of the Hiphil

Qatal 3ms	Qatal 2ms	Yiqtol	Inf. Con.	Participle
הִקְטִיל	הִקְטַלְתָּ	יַקְטִיל	הַקְטִיל	מַקְטִיל

2. The Three Patterns of the Hiphil

Like the Piel, the Hiphil has three basic patterns, and these three patterns are very similar to those of the Piel.

(1) The *qatal* always has the i-class vowel under the diagnostic preformative ה. The stem vowel is as follows:

    (a) In the third person forms, the stem vowel is typically Hireq-Yod (i-class).

    (b) In the second person forms, the stem vowel is typically Pathach (a-class).

Blackboard 22.10. The Patterns of the Hiphil *Qatal* (Perfect)

(2) In all other forms (*yiqtol*, participle, imperative, and infinitive construct), the vowel pattern is typically Pathach followed by Hireq-Yod ("a-class followed by i-class"). The i-class stem vowel is Tsere or Seghol in various forms, such as the imperative ms (הַקְטֵל).

The following further observations are also noteworthy:

(1) The stem vowel of the Hiphil may shorten but typically will not reduce.

(2) The Hiphil has a preformative with ה in all forms except where the ה is displaced by another preformative. This happens

    (a) in the participle (which has the preformative מ),

    (b) and in the *yiqtol* (which has the normal preformatives י, ת, א, and נ).

The following Blackboards illustrate this displacement through contrasting the formation of the Hiphil infinitive construct with that of the *yiqtol* 3ms and participle.

Blackboard 22.11. The Pattern of the Hiphil Infinitive Construct

Blackboard 22.12. The Displacement of the ה in the Hiphil *Yiqtol* (Imperfect)

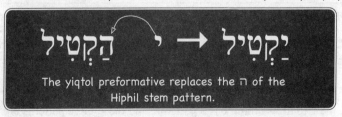

Blackboard 22.13. The Displacement of the ה in the Hiphil Participle

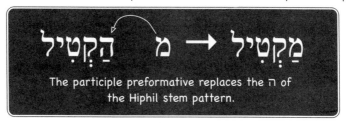

מַקְטִיל ← מ הַקְטִיל

The participle preformative replaces the ה of
the Hiphil stem pattern.

Table 22.6. Patterns and Examples of the Hiphil Stem

Qatal		All Other Inflections
3rd person	2nd and 1st person	Preformative ה displaced by *yiqtol* or participle preformative
"i-i" pattern	"i-a" pattern	"a-i" pattern
⬜⬜⬜Ⓟ i i	⬜⬜⬜Ⓟ a i	⬜⬜⬜Ⓟ i a
הִקְטִיל (3ms)	הִקְטַלְתָּ (2ms)	Yiqtol יַקְטִיל (3ms)
הִקְטִילוּ (3cp)	הִקְטַלְנוּ (1cp)	יַקְטִילוּ (3mp)
In the Hiphil, the ה preformative has no vowel; thus, the first vowel of the "i-a" or "a-i" vowel patterns goes with the ה.		תַּקְטֵלְנָה (3/2fp)
		Participle מַקְטִיל (ms)
		Imperative הַקְטֵל (ms)
		הַקְטִילוּ (mp)
		Infinitive Construct הַקְטִיל

E. Comparison of the Niphal, Piel, and Hiphil

From the above presentation, it is evident that these three stems have important features in common.

Table 22.7. Representative Examples of the Niphal, Piel, and Hiphil Stems

"I before A" Vowel Pattern	"A before I" Vowel Pattern
נִקְטַל (Niphal *qatal* 3ms)	הִקָּטֵל (Niphal infinitive construct)
קִטַּלְתָּ (Piel *qatal* 2ms)	קַטֵּל (Piel infinitive construct)
הִקְטַלְתָּ (Hiphil *qatal* 2ms)	הַקְטִיל (Hiphil infinitive construct)

(1) Each stem has two patterns, and these patterns have analogous vowel patterns.

    (a) The Niphal has one for the *qatal* and participle, with the vowel pattern "i before a," and one for everything else, with the vowel pattern "a before i."

    (b) The Piel has one for the *qatal*, with the vowel pattern "i before i or a," and one for everything else, with the pattern "a before i."

    (c) The Hiphil has one for the *qatal*, with the vowel pattern "i before i or a," and one for everything else, with the vowel pattern "a before i."

(2) Both the Niphal and Piel will reduce the stem vowel, but the Hiphil will not.

(3) Both the Piel and the Hiphil have i-class stem vowels in the *qatal* third person, and a-class stem vowels in the *qatal* second and first person. The Niphal *qatal* has an a-class stem vowel throughout.

(4) Both the Hiphil and Piel have a מ preformative for the participle.

(5) In general, the Hiphil and Piel are more like each other than either is like the Niphal. The table below shows how similar the two are.

Table 22.8. Comparison of the Piel and Hiphil Patterns

	Qatal Vowel Pattern is "I-I" or "I-A"		All Other Forms Vowel Pattern is "A-I"		
	3rd	*2nd & 1st*	*Yiqtol*	*Inf. Con.*	*Participle*
Piel	קִטֵּל	קִטַּלְתָּ	יְקַטֵּל	קַטֵּל	מְקַטֵּל
Hiphil	הִקְטִיל	הִקְטַלְתָּ	יַקְטִיל	הַקְטִיל	מַקְטִיל

F. Vocabulary

1. Core Vocabulary

a. Verbs

בוא	Qal: בָּא enter, come, go in
	Hiphil: הֵבִיא bring, lead in
דבר	Piel: דִּבֶּר speak
דרש	Qal: דָּרַשׁ seek
סור	Qal: סָר turn away, turn aside
	Hiphil: הֵסִיר remove
קדשׁ	Piel: קִדַּשׁ sanctify
	Hiphil: הִקְדִּישׁ make or treat as holy
שׂכל	Hiphil: הִשְׂכִּיל understand, have insight, behave wisely, achieve success

שׁוּב	Qal: שָׁב return
	Hiphil: הֵשִׁיב bring back
שׁחת	Piel: שִׁחֵת ruin, destroy
	Hiphil: הִשְׁחִית ruin, destroy, corrupt
שׁפך	Qal: שָׁפַךְ pour out
	Niphal: נִשְׁפַּךְ be poured out

b. Other Words

אַף	nose, nostrils; anger Ⓜ אַף|
חֹדֶשׁ	new moon Ⓜ חֹדֶשׁ|
עַתָּה	now

2. Previously Learned Verbs in Derived Stems

בּרך	Qal: chapter 15
	Piel: בֵּרַךְ bless, praise
זכר	Qal: chapter 15
	Niphal: נִזְכַּרְתֶּם (*qatal* 2mp) be remembered
	Hiphil: הִזְכִּיר make known, report
שׁלח	Qal: chapter 18
	Piel: שִׁלַּח stretch out, let go, expel

3. Reading Vocabulary

אלח	Niphal: נֶאֱלָחוּ (*qatal* 3cp) be corrupt
יַחְדָּו	together
עֲלִילָה	deed, behavior
שׁקף	Hiphil: הִשְׁקִיף look down
תעב	Piel: יְתָעֵב (*yiqtol* 3ms) abhor
	Hiphil: הִתְעִיבוּ (*qatal* 3cp) make abominable

G. Reading from Psalm 14

הִשְׁחִיתוּ הִתְעִיבוּ עֲלִילָה¹

אֵין עֹשֵׂה־טוֹב

יְהוָה מִשָּׁמַיִם הִשְׁקִיף עַל־בְּנֵי־אָדָם

---

1. Literally, "they ruin, they make abominable deed"; this means "They make their deeds corrupt and abominable."

לִרְאוֹת הֲיֵשׁ' מַשְׂכִּיל

דֹּרֵשׁ אֶת־אֱלֹהִים

הַכֹּל² סָר

יַחְדָּו נֶאֱלָחוּ

אֵין עֹשֵׂה־טוֹב

אֵין גַּם־אֶחָד

---

1. יֵשׁ with the ה interrogative, this means "if there is…"
2. "The all" = "everyone."

CHAPTER 23
CHARACTERISTICS OF THE PUAL, HOPHAL, AND HITHPAEL

A. The Pual

Like the Piel, the Pual has a diagnostic doubled middle radical. The principal parts of the Pual stem are as follows:

Table 23.1. Principal Parts of the Pual

"u-a" pattern ◯◯̇◯Ⓟ a u ə			
Qatal	*Yiqtol*	*Inf. Con.*	*Participle*
קֻטַּל	יְקֻטַּל	קֻטַּל	מְקֻטָּל

(1) Unlike the Niphal, Piel, and Hiphil, the Pual has only one pattern. The vowel pattern is "u-class followed by a-class."

(2) When a sufformative is added to a form, the stem vowel may shorten in accordance with normal rules. Thus, the *qatal* 3fs is קֻטְּלָה.

(3) The Pual is the passive of the Piel. Since יְבַקֵּשׁ (Piel) means "he will seek," יְבֻקַּשׁ (Pual) means "he will be sought." In form, it is very similar to the Piel.

  (a) There is no distinctive Pual preformative.

  (b) If there is a *yiqtol* or participle preformative, it has a Shewa.

  (c) The participle preformative is מ.

  (d) The middle radical of the root is doubled with a Daghesh Forte.

Blackboard 23.1. The Pattern of the Pual Stem

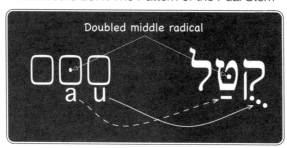

B. The Hophal

Like the Hiphil, the Hophal has a ה preformative. Like the Pual, the Hophal has only one pattern. The vowel pattern has a u-class vowel followed by an a-class vowel. The principal parts of the Hophal stem are as follows:

Table 23.2. Principal Parts of the Hophal

"u-a" pattern			
Qatal	Yiqtol	Inf. Con.	Participle
הָקְטַל	יָקְטַל	הָקְטַל	מָקְטָל

Note that the vowel under the ה in הָקְטַל is Qamets Hatuph.

(1) When a sufformative is added to a form, the stem vowel may shorten in accordance with normal rules. Thus, the *qatal* 3fs is הָקְטְלָה.

(2) The Hophal is the passive of the Hiphil. For example, you know that the noun מָוֶת means "death," and thus that the root מות relates to death. The Hiphil of that root, הֵמִית, therefore means "he caused (someone) to die" (that is, he killed someone). Similarly, the Hophal הוּמַת is passive and means "he was put to death." Morphologically, the Hophal is similar to the Hiphil.

 (a) The distinctive Hophal preformative is ה.

 (b) If there is a *yiqtol* or participle preformative, that preformative replaces the Hophal preformative ה.

 (c) The participle preformative is מ.

Blackboard 23.2. The Pattern of the Hophal Stem

C. The Pual and Hophal Compared

It is evident from the above that the two passive stems, Pual and Hophal, are both marked by a "u-class followed by a-class" vowel pattern.

Table 23.3. Comparison of the Pual and Hophal Principal Parts

	Qatal	Yiqtol	Inf. Con.	Participle
Pual	קֻטַל	יְקֻטַל	קֻטַל	מְקֻטָל
Hophal	הָקְטַל	יָקְטַל	הָקְטַל	מָקְטָל

Looking at the above and remembering the comparison between the Piel and Hiphil stems, we can see how these four stems are related. The following table attempts to capture the similarities. We use only the *qatal* 3ms, 2ms, and infinitive construct forms to illustrate the patterns that these stems follow. Here, we can see that there is one vowel pattern for the active Piel and Hiphil and one pattern for the passive Pual and Hophal stems.

Table 23.4. Piel, Hiphil, Pual, and Hophal Compared

	Active			Passive
	"i before i"	"i before a"	"a before i"	"u before a"
***Piel* and *Pual*:** Doubled Middle Radical	Piel *Qatal* 3ms קֻטֵּל	Piel *Qatal* 2ms קִטַּ֫לְתָּ	Piel Inf. Con. קַטֵּל	Pual Inf. Con. קֻטַּל
***Hiphil* and *Hophal*:** ה Preformative	Hiphil *Qatal* 3ms הִקְטִיל	Hiphil *Qatal* 2ms הִקְטַ֫לְתָּ	Hiphil Inf. Con. הַקְטִיל	Hophal Inf. Con. הָקְטַל

D. The Hithpael

The Hithpael stem has a preformative הִת and a doubled middle radical. Its vowel pattern is similar to that of the Piel *yiqtol*, infinitive construct, and participle.

Table 23.5. Principal Parts of the Hithpael

"a-i" pattern *(except qatal 2ⁿᵈ and 1ˢᵗ person, which is "a-a")* ☐ · ☐ P i a				
Qatal 3ms	Qatal 2ms	Yiqtol	Inf. Con.	Participle
הִתְקַטֵּל	הִתְקַטַּ֫לְתָּ	יִתְקַטֵּל	הִתְקַטֵּל	מִתְקַטֵּל

(1) The stem has a preformative הִת. If there is a *yiqtol* or participle preformative, that preformative will replace the ה in הִת. Thus, the *yiqtol* 3ms is יִתְקַטֵּל. The participle adds מ to the preformative הִת but displaces the ה, forming מִת.

(2) Like the Pual and Hophal, the Hithpael has only one pattern. The vowel pattern is "a-class followed by i-class."

(3) When a sufformative is added to a form, the stem vowel may shorten in accordance with normal rules. Thus, the *qatal* 3fs is הִתְקַטְּלָה.

(4) The Hithpael is similar to the Piel.

     (a) The middle radical of the root is doubled with a Daghesh Forte.

(b) The "a-class followed by i-class" vowel pattern is similar to what we see in all forms of the Piel except the *qatal*.

(c) In the second and first person of the Hithpael *qatal*, the stem vowel changes from i-class to a-class. Thus, the *qatal* 2ms is הִתְקַטַּ֫לְתָּ. This is analogous to what we see in the Piel and Hiphil.

Blackboard 23.3. The Pattern of the Hithpael Stem

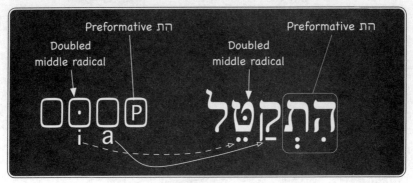

E. The Principal Parts of the Six Derived Stems

Learning the Hebrew derived stems will be far easier if you memorize the principal parts of each in the strong verb.

Table 23.6. Principal Parts of the Six Derived Stems in the Strong Verb

	Qatal		Yiqtol	Inf. Con.	Participle
Niphal	נִקְטַל		יִקָּטֵל	הִקָּטֵל	נִקְטָל
Piel	קִטֵּל	קִטַּ֫לְתָּ	יְקַטֵּל	קַטֵּל	מְקַטֵּל
Hiphil	הִקְטִיל	הִקְטַ֫לְתָּ	יַקְטִיל	הַקְטִיל	מַקְטִיל
Hithpael	הִתְקַטֵּל	הִתְקַטַּ֫לְתָּ	יִתְקַטֵּל	הִתְקַטֵּל	מִתְקַטֵּל
Pual	קֻטַּל		יְקֻטַּל	קֻטַּל	מְקֻטָּל
Hophal	הָקְטַל		יָקְטַל	הָקְטַל	מָקְטָל

Notice that the participles all have a preformative מ (with the exception of the Niphal). Also notice that in the participle, the stem vowel is always long. Although we do not elsewhere memorize the *qatal* 2ms as one of the principal parts, it is worth doing so for the Piel, Hiphil, and Hithpael.

F. Vocabulary

1. Core Vocabulary

a. Verbs

בוש	Qal: בּוֹשׁ be ashamed
	Hiphil: הֵבִישׁ put to shame
בקש	Piel: בִּקֵּשׁ seek, search for; discover, find
הרג	Qal: הָרַג kill, slay
חלל	Piel: חִלֵּל defile, profane
טמא	Qal: טָמֵא be unclean
	Piel: טִמֵּא defile, declare unclean
כלה	Qal: כָּלָה stop, be finished; perish
	Piel: כִּלָּה complete, finish; destroy
עזב	Qal: עָזַב leave, abandon
	Niphal: נֶעֱזַב be abandoned

b. Other Words

אָרוֹן	chest, Ark (of the Covenant) Ⓜ Ⓕ	אֲרוֹן	
בֶּגֶד	garment, covering Ⓜ	בֶּגֶד	
מַמְלָכָה	kingdom Ⓕ	מַמְלֶכֶת	
עָוֹן	sin, transgression; guilt caused by sin Ⓜ	עֲוֹן	
שָׁלוֹם	peace, well-being, wholeness Ⓜ	שְׁלוֹם	

2. Reading Vocabulary

גיל	Qal: יָגִיל (*yiqtol* 3ms) rejoice, celebrate; יָגֵל = apocopated modal *yiqtol* called a **jussive**, "let (him) rejoice" [see chapter 30]
מַחֲסֶה	refuge
שְׁבוּת	exile, captivity

G. Reading from Psalm 14

עֲצַת־עָנִי¹ תָבִֽישׁוּ²

כִּי³ יְהוָה מַחְסֵהוּ⁴

בְּשׁוּב יְהוָה שְׁבוּת עַמּוֹ⁵

יָגֵל⁶ יַעֲקֹב

יִשְׂמַח יִשְׂרָאֵל

In the above reading, the verb יָגֵל is a *yiqtol* of גִּיל, but it is **apocopated**. This simply means that the verb is written in a shorter form. In this case, the vowel letter י is dropped. Note, however, that its vowel is still long. This often occurs in a **jussive**, a verb form that generally means "Let him/her/them (do something)." We will give more attention to the jussive in chapter 30.

Blackboard 23.4. The Apocopated Hollow Verb

The hollow verb גיל means "to rejoice."

יָגִיל

יָגֵל

The yiqtol has the normal pattern for a hollow Qal yiqtol 3ms, like יָשׁוּב

The jussive, "let him rejoice," is like the long yiqtol except that it apocopates by replacing Hireq Yod with Tsere

---

1. The "counsel of the poor" means, in effect, the hope or consolation of the poor.
2. To "put to shame" in this line means to despise or to mock.
3. The word כִּי can be translated "because," "although," or "that." Here, "that" may be the best rendition, the point being that the poor man's consolation (עֲצַת־עָנִי) is the fact that YHWH is his refuge, and this is the very thing that the wicked revile.
4. When a noun ending in הֶ‍ such as מַחֲסֶה has a 3ms suffix, it is like מַחְסֵהוּ. Thus, this means "his refuge."
5. יְהוָה is bound to the infinitive construct בְּשׁוּב, and the construct chain שְׁבוּת עַמּוֹ is the direct object of the infinitive. Literally, it means "in YHWH's return of the captivity of his people." Translate it as a temporal clause: "When YHWH returns the captivity of his people."
6. The modal *yiqtol*, translated as "let him…," often has an apocopated form known as the jussive. See Blackboard 23.4 and the discussion in chapter 30.

CHAPTER 24
PRINCIPAL PARTS OF WEAK ROOTS IN THE DERIVED STEMS

A. Introduction

This is a selective, introductory presentation of derived stems in weak roots. Focus on bringing together two concepts: the characteristics of each stem and the tendencies of each weak root. Learn to recognize these principal parts.

B. The Niphal

Table 24.1. The Niphal Stem in Weak Roots

Root Type		Niphal Pattern →	☐☐☐Ⓟ a i	☐☐☐Ⓟ i a	☐☐☐Ⓟ a i	
		Gloss	Qatal	Yiqtol	Inf. Con.	Participle
Strong	קטל		נִקְטַל	יִקָּטֵל	הִקָּטֵל	נִקְטָל
III-ה	בנה	be built	נִבְנָה	יִבָּנֶה	הִבָּנוֹת	נִבְנֶה
I-Guttural	עבד	be served	נֶעֱבַד	יֵעָבֵד	הֵעָבֵד	נֶעֱבָד
I-נ	נצל	be rescued	נִצַּל	יִנָּצֵל	הִנָּצֵל	נִצָּל
Original I-ו	ישב	be inhabited	נוֹשַׁב	יִוָּשֵׁב	הִוָּשֵׁב	נוֹשָׁב
Hollow	כון	be firm	נָכוֹן	יִכּוֹן	הִכּוֹן	נָכוֹן

The following examples illustrate how the Niphal pattern and weak root tendencies combine in a verb.

(1) In the III-ה, we see the characteristic infinitive construct ending. Remember that the infinitive construct of the III-ה verb always has the ending וֹת.

Blackboard 24.1. The Niphal Infinitive Construct in the III-ה Verb

וֹת ending of III-ה infinitive construct — הִבָּנוֹת — הִן preformative (with assimilated נ) of Niphal infinitive construct

A-class vowel of Niphal vowel pattern

(2) In the I-guttural Niphal *yiqtol*, we see an example of compensatory lengthening. The הִן preformative has assimilated to the guttural; the guttural rejects doubling and thus there is compensatory lengthening. However, the preformative for the *yiqtol* displaces the ה of the הִן preformative, as follows.

Blackboard 24.2. Formation of the Niphal *Yiqtol* (Imperfect) in the I-Guttural

(3) In the Niphal, the fact that some I-י verbs were originally I-ו is very evident because the original I-ו shows up either as a consonant or vowel in all conjugations. For example, in the Niphal *yiqtol* 3ms יִוָּשֵׁב ("it was inhabited"), the consonant ו has replaced the expected י and is doubled, as is normal in the first radical of the Niphal *yiqtol* (this is not a Shureq!). Once this alteration is recognized, יִוָּשֵׁב is exactly like the strong Niphal *yiqtol* יִקָּטֵל.

C. The Piel

The Piel forms in weak roots are shown below.

Table 24.2. The Piel Stem in Weak Roots

	Piel Pattern →	▢ַ▢ִ▢	▢ְ▢ַ▢Ⓟ		
Root Type		Gloss	Qatal	Yiqtol	Inf. Con.	Participle
Strong	קטל		קִטֵּל	יְקַטֵּל	קַטֵּל	מְקַטֵּל
III-ה	כסה	*cover*	כִּסָּה	יְכַסֶּה	כַּסּוֹת	מְכַסֶּה
II-Guttural or ר	ברך	*bless*	בֵּרַךְ	יְבָרֵךְ	בָּרֵךְ	מְבָרֵךְ

(1) Most Piel forms are easy to recognize and hardly need explanation.

    (a) For example, the original I-ו Piel is for the most part like the strong root Piel and therefore requires no special attention.

    (b) Roots with a first or third guttural cause little or no change in the Piel.

    (c) The Piel preformative for *yiqtol* or participle always has a reduced vowel.

(2) The normal pattern of the Piel is evident even in most weak roots.

    (a) The middle radical is doubled.

    (b) The vowel patterns are the same as in the strong verb.

    (c) If there is a preformative, it has a Shewa.

(3) The III-ה shows its features in all stems. This can alter the vowel patterns in the Piel.

    (a) The *qatal* has its normal Qamets-Hey ending (כִּסָּה). Contrast the strong verb קִטֵּל.

    (b) The infinitive construct ends with וֹת, as in כַּסּוֹת. Contrast the strong verb קַטֵּל.

    (c) The *yiqtol* has the normal Seghol-Hey ending, as in the Qal יִבְנֶה.

    (d) Other rules of the III-ה are normal. For example, if a finite verb has a personal sufformative that is only a vowel, as in the 3mp, the ה is replaced by the vowel, as in יְכַסּוּ, the Piel *yiqtol* 3mp of כסה.

(4) The II-guttural / ר needs special attention because the middle letter will not double. Thus, there is often compensatory lengthening, as in the forms with ברך.

(5) The hollow verb and geminate are not mentioned here because they are rarely found in the Piel; those roots use other stems in place of the Piel.

Blackboard 24.3. Piel *Yiqtol* (Imperfect) in the III-ה and II-Guttural Roots

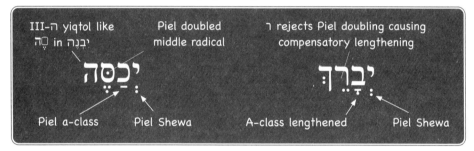

D. The Pual

The Pual patterns are, of course, very similar to those of the Piel.

Table 24.3. The Pual Stem in Weak Roots

Pual Pattern →		$\square\square\overset{a}{\square}\overset{u}{\square}\overset{\partial}{\square}^{\text{P}}$			
Root Type		Gloss	Qatal	Yiqtol	Inf. Con.	Participle
Strong	קטל		קֻטַּל	יְקֻטַּל	קֻטַּל	מְקֻטָּל
III-ה	כסה	covered	כֻּסָּה	יְכֻסֶּה	n/a*	מְכֻסֶּה
II-Guttural or ר	ברך	blessed	בֹּרַךְ	יְבֹרַךְ	בֹּרַךְ	מְבֹרָךְ

*The III-ה Hophal infinitive construct is not extant in the Bible.

(1) Again, in a II-guttural / ר root, the middle letter will not double, and thus there is compensatory lengthening (e.g., the *qatal* 3ms בֹּרַךְ). However, even in a II-guttural / ר root, the pattern of a u-class vowel followed by an a-class vowel is maintained.

(2) The original I-ו root is like the strong root in the Pual and needs no special attention.

(3) Other weak roots (e.g., the III-guttural or the III-א) require only minor changes in the inflections and are easy to recognize. The hollow and geminate verbs use alternative stems to replace the Pual, just as they do for the Piel.

Blackboard 24.4. The Pual III-ה Infinitive Construct

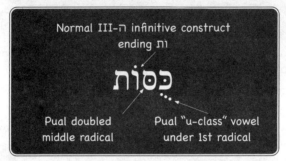

E. The Hithpael

The Hithpael weak roots show up in the same places as in the Piel and Pual, and the patterns are common except in one surprising weak root.

Table 24.4. The Hithpael Stem in Weak Roots

	Hithpael Pattern →	☐ִ☐ַ☐℗ i a			
Root Type		Gloss	Qatal	Yiqtol	Inf. Con.	Participle
Strong	קטל		הִתְקַטֵּל	יִתְקַטֵּל	הִתְקַטֵּל	מִתְקַטֵּל
III-ה	כסה	cover oneself	הִתְכַּסָּה	יִתְכַּסֶּה	הִתְכַּסּוֹת	מִתְכַּסֶּה
II-Guttural or ר	ברך	bless oneself	הִתְבָּרֵךְ	יִתְבָּרֵךְ	הִתְבָּרֵךְ	מִתְבָּרֵךְ
I-S	שׁמר	be careful	הִשְׁתַּמֵּר	יִשְׁתַּמֵּר	הִשְׁתַּמֵּר	מִשְׁתַּמֵּר

(1) Again, the III-ה root shows its normal patterns.

(2) A middle guttural or ר will reject the doubling of the middle radical and often shows compensatory lengthening of the a-class vowel.

The examples below with participles illustrate how the patterns are followed.

Blackboard 24.5. Hithpael Participle in III-ה and in II-Guttural or ר

(3) The one weakness that is unique to this stem is illustrated in the Hithpael *qatal* 3ms of שׁמר. Whenever a root beginning with a sibilant (s-type letter) appears in the Hithpael stem, metathesis occurs: the ת of the הת preformative changes places with the sibilant. Apparently the ancient Israelites found something like the hypothetical *הִתְשַׁמֵּר hard to pronounce, and so they simply switched the letters to form הִשְׁתַּמֵּר.

Blackboard 24.6. Metathesis in the I-Sibilant Hithpael

(4) Other similar peculiarities with the Hithpael are discussed in chapter 34.

F. **The Hiphil**

The Hiphil stem in weak roots is quite different from the strong verb Hiphil.

Table 24.5. The Hiphil Stem in Weak Roots

Root Type		Gloss	Qatal	Yiqtol	Inf. Con.	Participle
Strong	קטל		הִקְטִיל	יַקְטִיל	הַקְטִיל	מַקְטִיל
III-ה	רבה	*multiply*	הִרְבָּה	יַרְבֶּה	הַרְבּוֹת	מַרְבֶּה
I-Guttural	עבד	*enslave*	הֶעֱבִיד	יַעֲבִיד	הַעֲבִיד	מַעֲבִיד
I-נ	נפל	*make fall*	הִפִּיל	יַפִּיל	הַפִּיל	מַפִּיל
Original I-ו	ישב	*make dwell*	הוֹשִׁיב	יוֹשִׁיב	הוֹשִׁיב	מוֹשִׁיב
Hollow	שׁוב	*bring back*	הֵשִׁיב	יָשִׁיב	הָשִׁיב	מֵשִׁיב

(1) The III-ה follows all the normal patterns for this root, as is illustrated by the Hiphil infinitive construct of רבה, which has the וֹת ending characteristic of every III-ה infinitive construct.

Blackboard 24.7. The Hiphil Infinitive Construct of רבה

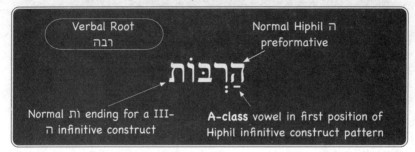

(2) The I-guttural (e.g., עבד) prefers a composite Shewa to a Shewa, and thus the *qatal* has the pattern הֶעֱבִיד instead of הִקְטִיל.

(3) The I-נ will assimilate in all Hiphil principal parts because all have a preformative, as is illustrated by the Hiphil *qatal* 3ms of נפל.

Blackboard 24.8. The Hiphil *Qatal* (Perfect) 3ms in the I-נ

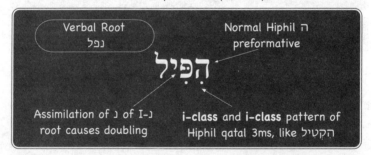

(4) The original I-ו in the Hiphil always has a preformative and so always loses the י of the root. Surprisingly, the vowel of the preformative is consistently וֹ, which appears to be a hold-over from the original I-ו root.

Blackboard 24.9. The Hiphil *Qatal* (Perfect) 3ms in the original I-ו

(5) The hollow root has Tsere as the preformative vowel in the *qatal* 3ms and participle

ms but Qamets in the *yiqtol* 3ms and infinitive construct. The preformative is an open pretonic and long. The i-class vowel with the participle preformative is surprising.

Blackboard 24.10. The Hiphil *Qatal* (Perfect) 3ms in the Hollow Root

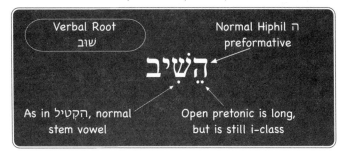

G. The Hophal

The Hophal is similar to the Hiphil, and most patterns do as one would expect.

(1) As is common, the I-נ verb shows assimilation of the נ in all forms since there is always a preformative before the root.

(2) Roots with gutturals do not cause unusual problems.

(3) The u-class vowel of the Hophal "u-class followed by a-class" pattern may appear as a Shureq or a Qibbuts. In the original I-ו root ירד, the u-class vowel is Shureq. Similarly, in the Hophal *qatal* 3ms form שוב, we see that the u-class vowel is a Shureq.

Blackboard 24.11. The Hophal *Qatal* (Perfect) 3ms from שוּב

Table 24.6. The Hophal Stem in Weak Roots

	Hophal Pattern →		◻◻◻℗ a u		
Root Type		Gloss	Qatal	Yiqtol	Inf. Con.	Participle
Strong	קטל		הָקְטַל	יָקְטַל	הָקְטַל	מָקְטָל
I-נ	נגד	be told	הֻגַּד	יֻגַּד	הֻגַּד	מֻגָּד
Original I-ו	ירד	be taken down	הוּרַד	יוּרַד	הוּרַד	מוּרָד
Hollow	שׁוּב	be returned	הוּשַׁב	יוּשַׁב	הוּשַׁב	מוּשָׁב

H. The Consistency of the III-ה Roots

You have already devoted time and attention to learning the III-ה root patterns. The value of doing this can be appreciated from the table below. Observe how consistently the rules for the III-ה root are followed in these stems.

Table 24.7. The III-ה Principal Parts in Various Stems

	Root	Qatal	Yiqtol	Inf. Con.	Participle
Qal	בנה	בָּנָה	יִבְנֶה	בְּנוֹת	בּוֹנֶה
Niphal	בנה	נִבְנָה	יִבָּנֶה	הִבָּנוֹת	נִבְנֶה
Piel	כסה	כִּסָּה	יְכַסֶּה	כַּסּוֹת	מְכַסֶּה
Hiphil	רבה	הִרְבָּה	יַרְבֶּה	הַרְבּוֹת	מַרְבֶּה
Hithpael	כסה	הִתְכַּסָּה	יִתְכַּסֶּה	הִתְכַּסּוֹת	מִתְכַּסֶּה
Pual	כסה	כֻּסָּה	יְכֻסֶּה	כֻּסּוֹת	מְכֻסֶּה

I. Vocabulary

1. Core Vocabulary

a. Verbs

יסף
> Qal: יָסַף add, continue to do
> Hiphil: הֹסִיף or הוֹסִיף add, increase, do again

כון
> Niphal: נָכוֹן be firm, be established, be fixed
> Polel[1]: כּוֹנֵן establish, set up, fix solidly
> Hiphil: הֵכִין prepare, set up, make firm

כסה
> Piel: כִּסָּה cover, conceal

נגד
> Hiphil: הִגִּיד tell
> Hophal: הֻגַּד be told

נכה
> Hiphil: הִכָּה strike, smite, injure

נצל
> Niphal: נִצַּל be rescued
> Hiphil: הִצִּיל snatch away, deliver

קום
> Qal: קָם rise, get up
> Hiphil: הֵקִים raise up, confirm, erect, raise up, keep, confirm

רבה
> Hiphil: הִרְבָּה make numerous, multiply

---

1. A stem related to the Piel. We will study it in chapter 35.

b. Other Words

אֹזֶן	ear F |אֹזֶן|
חַיִל	strength, power; wealth; army M |חֵיל|
מַעֲשֶׂה	work, labor, accomplishment M |מַעֲשֵׂה|
סָבִיב	surrounding(s), circuit M |סְבִיב|
פֶּן	lest

2. Previously Learned Verbs in Derived Stems

בנה	Qal: chapter 9
	Niphal: נִבְנָה be built
עשׂה	Qal: chapter 9
	Niphal: נַעֲשָׂה be done, be prepared
ראה	Qal: chapter 9
	Niphal: נִרְאָה appear, present oneself
	Hiphil: הֶרְאָה show someone, cause to experience
שׁמע	Qal: chapter 10
	Niphal: נִשְׁמַע be heard
	Hiphil: הִשְׁמִיעַ cause to hear, summon

J. Reading—Psalm 14

1 לַמְנַצֵּחַ לְדָוִד

אָמַר נָבָל בְּלִבּוֹ

אֵין אֱלֹהִים

הִשְׁחִיתוּ הִתְעִיבוּ עֲלִילָה

אֵין עֹשֵׂה־טוֹב

2 יְהוָה מִשָּׁמַיִם הִשְׁקִיף עַל־בְּנֵי־אָדָם

לִרְאוֹת הֲיֵשׁ מַשְׂכִּיל

דֹּרֵשׁ אֶת־אֱלֹהִים

3 הַכֹּל סָר

יַחְדָּו נֶאֱלָחוּ

אֵין עֹשֵׂה־טוֹב

אֵין גַּם־אֶחָד

4   הֲלֹא יָדְעוּ כָּל־פֹּעֲלֵי אָוֶן

אֹכְלֵי עַמִּי

אָכְלוּ לֶחֶם

יְהוָה לֹא קָרָאוּ

5   שָׁם פָּחֲדוּ פָּחַד

כִּי־אֱלֹהִים בְּדוֹר צַדִּיק

6   עֲצַת־עָנִי תָבִישׁוּ

כִּי יְהוָה מַחְסֵהוּ

7   מִי יִתֵּן מִצִּיּוֹן יְשׁוּעַת יִשְׂרָאֵל

בְּשׁוּב יְהוָה שְׁבוּת עַמּוֹ

יָגֵל יַעֲקֹב

יִשְׂמַח¹ יִשְׂרָאֵל

---

1.   שׂמח Qal yiqtol 3ms, "rejoice."

Table 24.8. The Principal Parts of the Derived Stems with Weak Roots

	Qatal		Yiqtol	Inf. Con.	Participle
Niphal	נִקְטַל		יִקָּטֵל	הִקָּטֵל	נִקְטָל
עבד	נֶעֱבַד		יֵעָבֵד	הֵעָבֵד	נֶעֱבָד
בנה	נִבְנָה		יִבָּנֶה	הִבָּנוֹת	נִבְנֶה
נצל	נִצַּל		יִנָּצֵל	הִנָּצֵל	נִצָּל
ישב	נוֹשַׁב		יִוָּשֵׁב	הִוָּשֵׁב	נוֹשָׁב
כון	נָכוֹן		יִכּוֹן	הִכּוֹן	נָכוֹן
Piel	קִטֵּל	קִטַּלְתָּ	יְקַטֵּל	קַטֵּל	מְקַטֵּל
כסה	כִּסָּה	כִּסִּיתָ	יְכַסֶּה	כַּסּוֹת	מְכַסֶּה
ברך	בֵּרֵךְ	בֵּרַכְתָּ	יְבָרֵךְ	בָּרֵךְ	מְבָרֵךְ
Hiphil	הִקְטִיל	הִקְטַלְתָּ	יַקְטִיל	הַקְטִיל	מַקְטִיל
רבה	הִרְבָּה	הִרְבִּיתָ	יַרְבֶּה	הַרְבּוֹת	מַרְבֶּה
עבד	הֶעֱבִיד	הֶעֱבַדְתָּ	יַעֲבִיד	הַעֲבִיד	מַעֲבִיד
נפל	הִפִּיל	הִפַּלְתָּ	יַפִּיל	הַפִּיל	מַפִּיל
ישב	הוֹשִׁיב	הוֹשַׁבְתָּ	יוֹשִׁיב	הוֹשִׁיב	מוֹשִׁיב
שוב	הֵשִׁיב	הֲשִׁיבוֹת	יָשִׁיב	הָשִׁיב	מֵשִׁיב
Hithpael	הִתְקַטֵּל	הִתְקַטַּלְתָּ	יִתְקַטֵּל	הִתְקַטֵּל	מִתְקַטֵּל
כסה	הִתְכַּסָּה	הִתְכַּסִּיתָ	יִתְכַּסֶּה	הִתְכַּסּוֹת	מִתְכַּסֶּה
ברך	הִתְבָּרֵךְ	הִתְבָּרַכְתָּ	יִתְבָּרֵךְ	הִתְבָּרֵךְ	מִתְבָּרֵךְ
שמר	הִשְׁתַּמֵּר	הִשְׁתַּמַּרְתָּ	יִשְׁתַּמֵּר	הִשְׁתַּמֵּר	מִשְׁתַּמֵּר
Pual	קֻטַּל		יְקֻטַּל	קֻטַּל	מְקֻטָּל
כסה	כֻּסָּה		יְכֻסֶּה	כֻּסּוֹת	מְכֻסֶּה
ברך	בֹּרַךְ		יְבֹרַךְ	בֹּרַךְ	מְבֹרָךְ
Hophal	הָקְטַל		יָקְטַל	הָקְטַל	מָקְטָל
ירד	הוּרַד		יוּרַד	הוּרַד	מוּרָד
שוב	הוּשַׁב		יוּשַׁב	הוּשַׁב	מוּשָׁב
נגד	הֻגַּד		יֻגַּד	הֻגַּד	מֻגָּד

CHAPTER 25
PRONOMINAL SUFFIXES ON VERBS

A. Introduction to Pronominal Suffixes on Verbs

You are already familiar with the fact that suffixes can appear on prepositions and nouns, as in סוּסוֹ, "his horse." Suffixes can also be added to verbs. When this happens with a finite verb, the suffix is usually the direct object of the verb. For example, קְטָלוּהוּ would mean "they killed him." קְטָלוּהוּ is the Qal *qatal* 3mp (קָטְלוּ) with the 3ms suffix הוּ. Notice that the vowels have changed. On an infinitive construct, as you have seen, the suffix is often the subject of the verbal action.

The following chart lists some of the common forms that suffixes on verbs will take in comparison to how they generally appear on nouns.

Table 25.1. The *Qatal* (Perfect) of שׁמר with Pronominal Suffixes

PGN of Suffix	With Noun	Common Verb Suffixes	With Verb	Meaning
3ms	סוּסוֹ	ֹהוּ / הוּ / וֹ	שְׁמָרֹהוּ	He kept him
3fs	סוּסָהּ	ָהּ / הָ	שְׁמָרָהּ	He kept her
2ms	סוּסְךָ	ְךָ / ָךְ	שְׁמָרְךָ	He kept you (ms)
2fs	סוּסֵךְ	ֵךְ/ָךְ / ךְ	שְׁמָרֵךְ	He kept you (fs)
1cs	סוּסִי	ַנִי / נִי	שְׁמָרַנִי	He kept me
3mp	סוּסָם	ָם / הֶם / ם	שְׁמָרָם	He kept them (mp)
3fp	סוּסָן	ָן / ן	שְׁמָרָן	He kept them (fp)
2mp	סוּסְכֶם	ְכֶם / כֶם	שְׁמַרְתִּיכֶם	I kept you (mp)
2fp	סוּסְכֶן	(not extant)		
1cp	סוּסֵנוּ	ָנוּ / נוּ	שְׁמָרָנוּ	He kept us

The fourth column ("With Verb") gives a verb with a pronominal suffix. The verb is the Qal *qatal* 3ms of שׁמר, except for the form with the 2mp suffix. Thus we have the 1cs *qatal* שְׁמַרְתִּיכֶם, "I kept you." (It so happens that there is no extant Qal *qatal* 3ms with a 2mp suffix.)

In שְׁמָרָם, "he kept them," the 3mp suffix moves the accent back. As a result, the syllables are as follows: שְׁ/מָ/רָם. In this word, /מָ/ is an open pretonic and therefore lengthens. /שְׁ/ is an open, distant syllable and thus reduces to Shewa.

Blackboard 25.1. Qal *Qatal* (Perfect) 3ms without and with a Pronominal Suffix

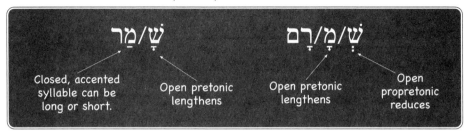

B. Pronominal Suffixes on *Qatal* (Perfect)-Type Verbs

1. Suffix Patterns

There are two types of suffixes for *qatal*-type verbs: suffixes for *qatals* that end in a vowel and suffixes for *qatals* that end in a consonant.

Table 25.2. Suffixes on *Qatal* (Perfect)-Type Forms

	When Form Ends with a Vowel	*When Form Ends with a Consonant*
3ms	הוּ / וֹ	הֻוֹ / וֹ
3fs	הָ	הָ
2ms	ךָ	ךָ
2fs	ךְ	ךְ / ךֻ
1s	נִי	נִי
3mp	הֶם / ם	ם
3fp	ן	ן
2mp	כֶם	כֶם
2fp	(not extant)	(not extant)
1p	נוּ	נוּ

2. Changes to the Personal Endings of Qatal (Perfect)-Type Verbs

In four cases, the endings on the *qatal*-type verbs are slightly altered when a pronominal suffix is added.

(1) The normal 3fs ending is הָ (e.g., שָׁמְרָה "she kept"), but with a pronominal suffix the 3fs ending is תַ or תָ (e.g., שְׁמָרַתְנוּ, "she kept us").

(2) The normal 2ms ending is תָ (e.g., שָׁמַרְתָ, "you [ms] kept"), but with a pronominal suffix the 2ms ending is sometimes תַ (e.g., שְׁמַרְתַּנִי, "you kept me;" the Pathach under the תַ is part of the נִי suffix).

(3) The normal 2fs ending is תְ (e.g., שָׁמַרְתְ, "you [fs] kept"), but with a pronominal suffix the 2fs ending is תִי (e.g., שְׁמַרְתִּים, "you kept them").

(4) The normal 2mp ending is תֶם (e.g., שְׁמַרְתֶּם, "you kept"), but with a pronominal suffix the 2mp ending is תוּ. This occurs only three times; one example is Num 20:5: הֶעֱלִיתֻנוּ, "You (2mp) brought us up" (the others are in Num 21:5 and Josh 1:15).

3. Accent Shift and Vowel Changes

You are already familiar with the principles of accent shift and subsequent vowel changes. When analyzing vowel changes due to the addition of pronominal suffixes to verbs, you must bear these rules in mind. If you take these rules into account, vowel changes in *qatal*-type verbs with pronominal suffixes will pose little problem.

Table 25.3. Examples of Accent Shift and Vowel Change in *Qatal* (Perfect) Verbs with Pronominal Suffixes

W/o Suffix	With Suffix	Remarks on Changes Due to Suffix
שָׁלַח	שְׁלָחַנִי	"He sent me." Note open pretonic lengthening and open propretonic reduction.
עָזַב	עֲזָבְךָ	"He abandoned you." Vowel reduction follows the normal I-guttural pattern.
שִׁלַּח	שִׁלְּחוֹ	"He sent him": שֶׁל / לְ / חוֹ. Piel stem; the propretonic is closed and does not reduce (it is short), and therefore the open pretonic reduces.
וְשִׁלַּחְתִּי	וְשִׁלַּחְתִּיךָ	"And I send you." Piel stem; both the pretonic and propretonic are closed, and no vowel changes occur.
הִמְלַכְתָּ	הִמְלַכְתַּנִי	"You made me king." Hiphil stem; the 2ms ending is תַ as described above. Pretonic and propretonic are both closed and therefore short.

C. Pronominal Suffixes on *Yiqtol* (Imperfect)-Type Verbs

1. Suffix Patterns

There are two types of suffixes for *yiqtol*-type verbs: suffixes for *yiqtol* verbs that end in a vowel and suffixes for *yiqtol* verbs that end in a consonant.

Table 25.4. Suffixes on *Yiqtol* (Imperfect)-Type Forms

	When Form Ends with a Vowel	When Form Ends with a Consonant
3ms	הוּ / וֹ	ֵהוּ
3fs	הָ	ֶ֫הָ / ֶ֫הָ
2ms	ךָ	ֶ֫ךָ
2fs	ךְ	ֵךְ
1s	נִי	ֵ֫נִי
3mp	ם	ֵם
3fp	ן	ֵן
2mp	כֶם	ְכֶם
2fp	(not extant)	(not extant)
1p	נוּ	ֵ֫נוּ

2. The Energic Nun

Biblical Hebrew often inserts a נ between the *yiqtol*-type verb and the pronominal suffix. This is called an "energic Nun." Assimilation causes the doubling of letters. Compare, for example, the following:

(1) יִמְצָאֵ֫הוּ, "he will find him" (Qal *yiqtol* 3ms of מצא with 3ms suffix)

(2) יִדְרְשֶׁ֫נּוּ, "he will seek him" (Qal *yiqtol* 3ms of דרש with 3ms suffix and energic Nun).

Extant forms are below (asterisked forms are hypothetical). You can see that with the energic Nun, the 3ms and the 1cp forms are the same.

Table 25.5. Pronoun Suffixes with the Energic Nun

3ms	ֶ֫נּוּ	from	ֶ֫נְהוּ*
3fs	ֶ֫נָּה	from	ֶ֫נְהָ*

2ms	קֶּ֫ךָ	from	*קֶ֫נְךָ
1cs	קֶ֫נִי	from	*קֶ֫נְנִי
1cp	קֶּ֫נּוּ	from	*קֶ֫נְנוּ

3. Vowel Changes Due to Accent Shift with Yiqtol *(Imperfect)-Type Verbs*

(1) With *yiqtol*, *wayyiqtol*, and *weyiqtol* verbs (on the latter, see chapter 30), vowel changes follow the general rules for reduction and lengthening due to accent shift. A distinction, however, is that in a Qal stem *yiqtol* with a pronominal suffix, an open pretonic i-class or u-class vowel will tend to reduce if the propretonic will not reduce, but an open pretonic a-class vowel will tend to lengthen even if the propretonic will not reduce.

Blackboard 25.2. The Suffixed Finite Verb

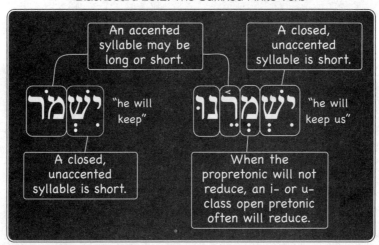

(2) Imperatives with pronominal suffixes generally follow these same rules, except that

(a) in the Qal ms imperative, the normal pattern (שְׁמֹר) becomes שָׁמְר with a pronominal suffix (e.g., שָׁמְרֵם, "keep them"), and

(b) in an imperative, any Tsere that loses its accent will tend to reduce, even if it becomes pretonic.

In the notes that follow, the abbreviation "x" stands for "suffix," as in "3fsx" (third feminine singular suffix).

Table 25.6. Vowel Change in *Yiqtol* (Imperfect) or Imperative Verbs with Suffixes

W/o Suffix	With Suffix	Remarks on Changes Due to Suffix
יִשְׁמֹר	יִשְׁמְרֵנִי	"He will keep me." Qal *yiqtol* 3ms with 1csx. Open pretonic reduces (מְ) because the propretonic is closed.
יִשְׁמֹר	יִשְׁמָרְךָ	"He will keep you." Qal *yiqtol* 3ms with 2msx. The pretonic (מָר) is closed and shortens to Qamets Hatuph.
שְׁמֹר	שָׁמְרֵנִי	"Keep me!" Qal Imperative ms with 1csx. The imperative goes through the vowel change described above.
תֵּן	תְּנֶנָּה	"Give her!" Qal Imperative ms with 3fsx. The imperative with a Tsere reduces. Observe the energic Nun in the suffix.

D. More on Pausal Forms and Accent Marks

You have already seen pausal forms of words, wherein the vowel of the accented syllable is lengthened. Pausal forms often appear when the word is the last in a major clause or verse. In the Hebrew Bible, such words are often marked with special accents called **Silluq** (used on the last word of a verse) or **Athnach** (used only once within a verse and usually at a major break, such as the end of a clause). The Silluq looks like a Metheg, but remember that it only comes in the last word of the verse. The Athnach looks something like an upside-down "v." A word with Silluq or Athnach is often said to be "in pause." Note the following pausal forms of מֶלֶךְ.

 (1) With Silluq: מֶלֶךְ
 (2) With Athnach: מֶלֶךְ

Two other significant accents, neither of which identify pausal forms, are **Zaqeph Qaton** (used to subdivide a Silluq or Athnach portion of a verse) and **Munaḥ** (used to mark the joining of one word to the next word, often as part of the same phrase). The Zaqeph Qaton looks like a small colon (:) above the accented syllable, whereas the Munaḥ looks like a backwards "L" underneath the accented syllable. Observe the following examples with מֶלֶךְ.

 (1) With Zaqeph Qaton: מֶלֶךְ
 (2) With Munaḥ: מֶלֶךְ

From this point forward, your readings and translation exercises will include all instances of Silluq, Athnach, Zaqeph Qaton, and Munaḥ. Keep your eye out for the pausal forms, and note how Silluq and Athnach almost always occur at major clausal breaks. Use the accent marks to assist your reading, for their purpose is either to signal disjunction, much like a comma, semi-colon, or period would in English (so Silluq, Athnach, and Zaqeph Qaton), or to mark conjunction, as is present in the linking of elements in a construct chain or prepositional phrase (so Munaḥ). We will study the other common accent marks and pausal forms in chapter 36.

E. Vocabulary

1. Core Vocabulary

a. Verbs

From this point forward, some of the verbs will not have an extant *qatal* 3ms in the Hebrew Bible. In that case, for the core vocabulary verbs a reconstructed *qatal* 3ms will appear with an asterisk and will be followed by a form that is actually extant, as in the Polel of רוּם below.

גלה	Qal: גָּלָה uncover, leave, go into exile
	Niphal: נִגְלָה expose, announce, reveal oneself
	Piel: גִּלָּה uncover, disclose, sleep with
	Hiphil: הִגְלָה deport
זבח	Qal: זָבַח slaughter, sacrifice
	Piel: זִבַּח sacrifice
ישׁע	Niphal: נוֹשַׁע receive help, be victorious, be rescued
	Hiphil: הוֹשִׁיעַ help, save
רום	Qal: רָם be high above, be exalted, rise, go up, be haughty
	Polel: *רוֹמֵם; רוֹמַמְתִּי (*qatal* 1cs) bring up, exalt
	Hiphil: הֵרִים raise up, lift up, erect
שׂים	Qal: שָׂם set, put, place
שׂמח	Qal: שָׂמַח rejoice, be merry
	Piel: שִׂמַּח gladden, make (someone) merry, cause to rejoice

b. Other Words

אָמָה	(female) slave, handmaid [F]	אַמַת	
בְּהֵמָה	animals (in general), beasts, cattle (domesticated animals) [F]	בֶּהֱמַת	
בַּעַל	owner, husband; Baal [M]	בַּעַל	
טָמֵא	(ceremonially) unclean
לָכֵן	therefore
מוֹעֵד	appointed place or time, season [M]	מוֹעֵד	
שֵׁבֶט	rod, staff, scepter; tribe [M]	שֵׁבֶט	

2. Reading Vocabulary

אַוָּה	desire, longing
אַיָּל	deer
מַעֲשֵׂר	tithe

מִשְׁלָח   undertaking

צְבִי   gazelle

רַק   only, nevertheless

3. Previously Learned Verbs in Derived Stems

הלך   Qal: chapter 9

         Hiphil: הוֹלִיךְ bring, lead

         Hithpael: הִתְהַלֵּךְ walk about, go about, disperse

ישׁב   Qal: chapter 10

         Hiphil: הוֹשִׁיב set, inhabit, cause to dwell

נפל   Qal: chapter 11

         Hiphil: הִפִּיל drop, throw down

נתן   Qal: chapter 10

         Niphal: נִתַּן be given

עלה   Qal: chapter 18

         Hiphil: הֶעֱלָה lead up, cause to rise, offer (sacrifice)

F. Reading—Deuteronomy 12:13–16

13   הִשָּׁמֶר¹ לְךָ פֶּן־תַּעֲלֶה² עֹלֹתֶיךָ בְּכָל־מָקוֹם אֲשֶׁר תִּרְאֶה

14   כִּי אִם־בַּמָּקוֹם אֲשֶׁר־יִבְחַר יְהוָה בְּאַחַד³ שְׁבָטֶיךָ שָׁם תַּעֲלֶה עֹלֹתֶיךָ וְשָׁם

      תַּעֲשֶׂה כֹּל אֲשֶׁר אָנֹכִי מְצַוֶּךָ⁴

15   רַק בְּכָל־אַוַּת נַפְשְׁךָ תִּזְבַּח וְאָכַלְתָּ בָשָׂר כְּבִרְכַּת יְהוָה אֱלֹהֶיךָ אֲשֶׁר

      נָתַן־לְךָ בְּכָל־שְׁעָרֶיךָ הַטָּמֵא וְהַטָּהוֹר יֹאכְלֶנּוּ⁵ כַּצְּבִי וְכָאַיָּל

16   רַק הַדָּם לֹא תֹאכֵלוּ עַל־הָאָרֶץ תִּשְׁפְּכֶנּוּ כַּמָּיִם

---

1.   Niphal imperative ms of שָׁמַר, "be careful."
2.   This is the Hiphil *yiqtol* of עלה.
3.   The construct of אֶחָד, "one."
4.   Piel participle of צוה ("command") with a 2ms suffix.
5.   This is the 3ms suffix with energic נ; it is not a 1cp suffix (note the Daghesh Forte).

CHAPTER 26

THE QAL INFINITIVE CONSTRUCT WITH SUFFIXES, THE QAL INFINITIVE ABSOLUTE, AND הִנֵּה

A. More on the Qal Infinitive Construct

1. Pronominal Suffixes on the Infinitive Construct

The Hebrew infinitive construct can take pronominal suffixes, but this causes significant vowel changes. For example, when the 3ms suffix וֹ is added to קְטֹל, the following occurs:

(1)   Adding וֹ to קְטֹל changes the syllabification from קְ/טֹל to קָטְ/לוֹ.

(2)   The first syllable (קָטְ) is a closed, unaccented syllable (which is always short). Thus, the vowel is Qamets Hatuph (not Qamets).

Table 26.1. The Infinitive Construct of כתב with Pronominal Suffixes

Suffix	Singular	Plural
3m	כָּתְבוֹ	כָּתְבָם
3f	כָּתְבָהּ	כָּתְבָן
2m	כָּתְבְךָ	כָּתְבְכֶם
2f	כָּתְבֵךְ	כָּתְבְכֶן
1c	כָּתְבִי	כָּתְבֵנוּ

If the third radical is "begadkephat," it may or may not have Daghesh Lene, as you can see in the tables above and below. With the weak verb, the Qal infinitive construct with suffix has patterns consistent with the above.

Table 26.2. The Weak Root Qal Infinitive Construct with Suffixes

Root	Inf. Con.	Inf. Con. with Suffix	
עזב	עֲזֹב	עָזְבֵךְ	(2fs suffix)
שמע	שְׁמֹעַ	שָׁמְעִי	(1cs suffix)
עלה	עֲלוֹת	עֲלוֹתוֹ	(3ms suffix)
בנה	בְּנוֹת	בְּנוֹתַיִךְ	(2fs suffix)
ירש	רֶשֶׁת	רִשְׁתּוֹ	(3ms suffix)
ישב	שֶׁבֶת	שִׁבְתִּי	(1cs suffix)
נשא	שְׂאֵת	שְׂאֵתִי	(1cs suffix)

קוֹם	קוֹם	קוּמְךָ	(2ms suffix)
בּוֹא	בּוֹא	בּוֹאוֹ	(3ms suffix)
שִׂים	שׂוֹם	שׂוֹמִי	(1cs suffix)

2. Meaning and Usage

English has no equivalent to this pattern.

(1) The suffix on an infinitive construct can be either the subject or the object of the infinitive. Thus, קָטְלוֹ could mean either "his (act of) killing [something]" or "the (act of) killing him."

(2) The suffixed infinitive construct very often has a preposition in front of it, and the three elements—the preposition, the infinitive, and the suffix—form a single phrase. For example, when the preposition בְּ and the 3ms pronominal suffix are attached to the infinitive construct of the root שׁמע, we see בְּשָׁמְעוֹ, meaning "when (בְּ) he (וֹ) heard (infinitive construct of שׁמע)" (lit., "in his act-of-hearing").

Blackboard 26.1. The Preposition and Pronominal Suffix on an Infinitive Construct

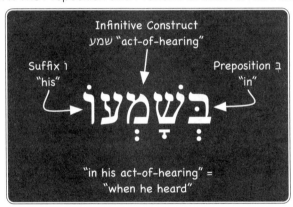

(3) The suffix is regularly the object when the infinitive construct has the preposition לְ (e.g., לְעָבְדוֹ, "to serve him"); otherwise, the suffix is almost always the subject. With the prepositions בְּ and כְּ, the infinitive construct commonly forms a temporal phrase, and the suffix is the subject of the phrase.

(4) The suffix sometimes refers to an impersonal noun. If so, it is translated as "it" rather than "he" or "she." For example, in Josh 4:7, בְּעָבְרוֹ means "when (בְּ) it (וֹ) crossed over (infinitive construct of עבר)." In this case, the suffix is 3ms but is translated "it" because it refers to the Ark of the Covenant.

(5) לְבִלְתִּי "that ... not" is the normal particle for negating an infinitive construct.

3. More on Prepositions with the Infinitive Construct

In general, the infinitive construct with pronominal suffixes follows one of two patterns that are distinguished by the type of preposition used.

(1) When the infinitive construct has the preposition לְ, a pronominal suffix is usually the *direct object* of the verbal action.

   (a) An example is in לְרִשְׁתָּהּ, "to possess (ירשׁ) it." Translating woodenly, this is "to possess her" ("her" refers to אֶרֶץ, "land," a feminine noun).

   (b) This usage is similar to English, which uses "to" in order to express purpose ("He came to kill him!"), to mark a verb complement ("He is able to kill him!"), or to refer to impending events ("He is about to kill him!").

(2) When the infinitive construct has any preposition other than לְ, a pronominal suffix is normally the *subject* of the verbal action. An infinitive construct can take a wide variety of prepositions.

   (a) בְּ "when" or "while," as in בְּנָסְעָם, "when they set out" (נסע in the infinitive construct with the 3mp suffix). Translating woodenly, this is "in their setting out." The use of the infinitive construct with בְּ is very common and is typically equivalent to an English temporal clause.

   (b) כְּ "when, as soon as," as in וּכְשָׁמְעוֹ אֶת־דִּבְרֵי רִבְקָה, "and as soon as he heard (שׁמע) the words of Rebekah." Translating woodenly, this is "and as his hearing the words of Rebekah." The preposition כְּ with the infinitive construct also typically introduces a temporal expression, but it tends to have more the nuance of "as soon as" instead of simply "when."

   (c) עַד "until," as in עַד שׁוּבְךָ, "until you return" (שׁוּב). Translating woodenly, this is "until your returning."

   (d) מִן "from, than, because," as in וּמִשָּׁמְרוֹ אֶת־הַשְּׁבֻעָה, "and because he kept (שׁמר) the oath." Translating woodenly, this is "and from his keeping the oath."

   (e) לְבִלְתִּי "that...not," as in לְבִלְתִּי הָפְכִּי אֶת־הָעִיר, "that I not overthrow (הפך) the city." Translating woodenly, this is "that not my overthrowing the city"; the suffix is the subject. לְבִלְתִּי is the normal particle for negating an infinitive.

Like a pronoun suffix, a noun can follow an infinitive construct to act as its subject. Thus, כְּבוֹא אַבְרָם מִצְרָיְמָה means "as soon as Abram came to Egypt."

B. The Infinitive Absolute

1. Forms

a. The Infinitive Absolute in the Qal Stem

Whereas the infinitive construct with לְ is roughly analogous to the English infinitive, the **infinitive absolute** has no close English analogy. The two infinitives should be regarded as two distinct forms with distinctive functions.

The basic vowel pattern for the Qal infinitive absolute is קָטוֹל. In the chart below, note that almost every root type follows the same pattern. Only the hollow verb is significantly different.

Table 26.3. The Qal Infinitive Absolute with Various Root Types

Root Type	Root	Form
Strong	כתב	כָּתוֹב
I-Guttural	עבר	עָבוֹר
III-ה	בכה	בָּכֹה
I-א	אכל	אָכוֹל
II-Guttural	גאל	גָּאוֹל
II-Guttural	בחר	בָּחוֹר
III-ח	שכח	שָׁכוֹחַ
III-ע	שמע	שָׁמוֹעַ
III-א	יצא	יָצוֹא
I-נ	נפל	נָפוֹל
Original I-ו	ילד	יָלוֹד
Hollow	מות	מוֹת
Hollow	שׁוּב	שׁוֹב
Geminate	סבב	סָבוֹב

Like the infinitive construct, the infinitive absolute is not inflected for person, gender, or number. Unlike the infinitive construct, it does not take pronoun suffixes or prepositions.

b. The Infinitive Absolute in the Derived Stems

The infinitive absolute forms in other stems are not dramatically different from the infinitive construct forms of those stems, and they can easily be recognized. Sometimes there are alternative forms of the infinitive absolute.

Some infinitive absolutes in derived stems are fairly common and have taken on idiomatic meanings. For example, הַרְבֵּה, the Hiphil infinitive absolute of רבה ("be numerous") is often used as an adverb or adjective meaning "many," "much," or "very."

Infinitive absolute forms in derived stems are not often encountered; biblical Hebrew prefers to use the Qal infinitive absolute. For example, in the Hebrew Bible there are 84 Piel infinite absolute words and only one Pual infinitive absolute. There are over 500 occurrences of the Qal infinitive absolute.

Table 26.4. The Infinitive Absolute in the Derived Stems

	Inf. Con.	Inf. Abs.	Alternative Inf. Abs.
Niphal	הִקָּטֵל	הִקָּטֹל	נִקְטֹל
Piel	קַטֵּל	קַטֵּל	קַטֹּל
Pual	קֻטַּל	קֻטֹּל	
Hithpael	הִתְקַטֵּל	הִתְקַטֵּל	
Hiphil	הַקְטִיל	הַקְטֵל	
Hophal	הָקְטַל	הָקְטֵל	

2. Usage

The infinitive absolute has three primary functions: (1) as a kind of adverb, (2) as an infinitive or gerund, and (3) as a kind of surrogate for other forms.

a. As an Adverb

The infinitive absolute has an adverbial function that has no English analogy.

(1) An infinitive absolute may be a simple adverb. An example is הַרְבֵּה, "much," the Hiphil infinitive absolute of רבה.

אַחְאָב עָבַד אֶת־הַבַּעַל מְעָט   "Ahab served Baal a little;
יֵהוּא יַעַבְדֶנּוּ הַרְבֵּה   Jehu will serve him *much.*"

(2) Hebrew tends to put an infinitive absolute in front of a finite verb from the same root to imply that something is certain or to assert something more emphatically.

זָכוֹר תִּזְכְּרוּ   "You will *surely* remember!"
(Qal inf. abs. and Qal *yiqtol* 2mp זכר)

שָׁמוֹר תִּשְׁמְרוּ   "You *definitely* must observe"
(Qal inf. abs. and Qal *yiqtol* 2mp שמר)

(3) Sometimes the order is reversed.

בֵּרַכְתָּ בָרֵךְ   "You have *actually* blessed!"
(Piel *qatal* 2ms and Piel inf. abs. ברך)

(4) Sometimes the infinitive absolute is written after an imperative or participle of the same root. Some kind of intensification is usually implied.

בְּכוּ בָכֹו   "Weep *bitterly!*"
(Qal impv. mp and Qal inf. abs. בכה)

שִׁמְעוּ שָׁמוֹעַ   "Listen *carefully*!"

(Qal impv. mp and Qal inf. abs. שׁמע)

b. As an Infinitive or Gerund

Sometimes the infinitive absolute is used as an English gerund or in a way that is not very different from the infinitive construct.

(1) Used like an infinitive construct phrase:

לֹא־יִתְּנֵנִי הָשֵׁב רוּחִי   "He will not allow me (lit., give me) *to catch* (Hiphil inf. abs. שׁוּב) my breath"

(2) Used as a gerund, it can:

(a) be the subject of a clause,

אָכֹל דְּבַשׁ הַרְבּוֹת לֹא טוֹב   "*Eating* (Qal inf. abs. אכל) honey in abundance is not good"

(b) be the object of a verb,

לִמְדוּ הֵיטֵב   "Learn *to do right*" (Hiphil inf. abs. יטב)

(c) function like an absolute noun in a construct chain,

בְּרוּחַ מִשְׁפָּט וּבְרוּחַ בָּעֵר   "With a spirit of justice and with a spirit *of burning*" (Piel inf. abs. בער)

(d) or take a noun as its direct object.

הָרֹג בָּקָר וְשָׁחֹט צֹאן אָכֹל בָּשָׂר וְשָׁתוֹת יַיִן   "*Killing* cattle and *slaughtering* sheep, *eating* meat and *drinking* wine" (Four inf. abs. forms with direct object nouns)

For an example with the direct object marker, see Exod 8:11.

(e) Two infinitive absolutes may be used in association with a finite verb to indicate that two actions are happening simultaneously. This is an adverbial function: the infinitive absolute forms tell how the subject went about doing something.

וַיֵּלֶךְ הָלוֹךְ וְאָכֹל   "And he walked, *walking* and *eating*" (Two Qal inf. absolutes).

c. As a Surrogate for Other Forms

The infinitive absolute sometimes seems to be used as an imperative. In these cases, the command is often especially dramatic or significant, and the form might be regarded as a kind of "heavy imperative," as in the Ten Words at Exod 20:8.

זָכוֹר אֶת־יוֹם הַשַּׁבָּת "*Remember* (Qal inf. abs. זכר) the Sabbath day"

In some cases, many scholars believe, the infinitive absolute is used for other finite verb forms, such as for the *qatal* or *yiqtol*. But this is debatable; it may be that these infinitive absolute forms actually have a gerund function. For examples, see Hag 1:6.

C. הִנֵּה

The particle הִנֵּה is traditionally translated as "Behold!" but this is not very satisfactory since no one speaking modern English uses the word "behold" except when being deliberately archaic. The word הִנֵּה is essentially a **speech-act**. It performs the function of focusing attention on a person, thing, fact, situation, or activity. It can be used in a wide range of circumstances and can have either a positive or negative sense. The glosses with the examples below are somewhat exaggerated paraphrases but point out a few of the varied uses of הִנֵּה.

(1) To draw attention to the fact that one is making a bestowal, pronouncement, or decree (Gen 1:29):

הִנֵּה נָתַתִּי לָכֶם אֶת־כָּל־עֵשֶׂב "I *hereby* give you every plant"

(2) Negatively, to draw attention to something that is presented or given in anger (Gen 12:19):

וְעַתָּה הִנֵּה אִשְׁתְּךָ קַח וָלֵךְ "So now, *here's* your wife! Take (her) and go!"

(3) To draw attention to how a character perceived something (Gen 6:12):

וַיַּרְא אֱלֹהִים אֶת־הָאָרֶץ וְהִנֵּה נִשְׁחָתָה "And God saw the earth—*specifically, he saw that it was* corrupt"

(4) To draw attention to something significant, surprising, or exciting (Gen 8:11):

וַתָּבֹא אֵלָיו הַיּוֹנָה לְעֵת עֶרֶב וְהִנֵּה עֲלֵה־זָיִת "And the dove came to him at evening time and—*how about this*—an olive leaf!"

(5) Negatively, to draw attention to something that is a problem or disappointment (Gen 15:3):

וְהִנֵּה בֶן־בֵּיתִי יוֹרֵשׁ אֹתִי "*And do you know what?* A household slave will be my heir!"

(6) To draw attention to a critical point or item in a discussion (Gen 22:7):

הִנֵּה הָאֵשׁ וְהָעֵצִים וְאַיֵּה הַשֶּׂה לְעֹלָה "*Well, here is* the fire and the wood, but where is the lamb for the whole offering?"

(7) The word הִנֵּנִי (the particle הִנֵּה with a 1cs suffix) is used for responding to a call, indicating to the one calling that you have heard the call and are giving that person your attention; this may be used in responding to a subordinate or to a superior (Gen 22:7, 11):

וַיֹּאמֶר אָבִי וַיֹּאמֶר הִנֶּנִּי בְנִי

"And he said, 'My father!' And he said, 'Yes, my son?'"

וַיִּקְרָא אֵלָיו מַלְאַךְ יְהוָה מִן־הַשָּׁמַיִם
וַיֹּאמֶר אַבְרָהָם אַבְרָהָם וַיֹּאמֶר הִנֵּנִי

"And the Angel of YHWH called from heaven, and he said, 'Abraham! Abraham!' And he said, 'Yes?'"

(8) The particle הִנֵּה with a suffix is often used with a participle, and the suffix on הִנֵּה serves as the subject of the participle. The actual translation of הִנֵּה can vary according to context, as in the above examples. Here, הִנֵּה is used for a solemn bestowal (Num 25:12):

הִנְנִי נֹתֵן לוֹ אֶת־בְּרִיתִי

"I am *hereby* giving to him my covenant."

D. Vocabulary

1. Core Vocabulary

a. Verbs

גוּר	Qal: גָּר sojourn, live as an alien
חיה	Qal: חַי live (*qatal* 3ms; the root was originally חיי, a geminate)
	Piel: חִיָּה let live
יטב	Qal: *יִטַב; יְטַב (*yiqtol* 3ms) go well, do well
	Hiphil: הֵיטִיב treat well
שבע	Niphal: נִשְׁבַּע swear (an oath)
	Hiphil: הִשְׁבִּיעַ make (someone) swear (an oath), implore

b. Other Words

אָחוֹת	sister F |אֲחוֹת|
בִּלְתִּי	not (preposition); except, lest (adverb used to negate the infinitive construct); always found with לְ as לְבִלְתִּי
הֵן	behold! look! (interjection); if (conjunction); also found as הֶן־ and הֵן־
הִנֵּה	traditionally "behold"; translation varies according to context: perhaps "well now" or "look here"
כַּאֲשֶׁר	as, just as, because, when (lit. "like which," כְּ with אֲשֶׁר)

כָּבֵד	heavy, severe
מַרְאֶה	appearance, sight, visage Ⓜ |מַרְאֶה|
נָא	(a particle often used with commands or requests; do not translate)
רָעָב	famine, hunger Ⓜ |*construct not extant*|

2. Previously Learned Verbs in Derived Stems

אבד	Qal: chapter 16
	Piel: אִבֵּד cause to perish, destroy
	Hiphil: הֶאֱבִיד exterminate
אסף	Qal: chapter 18
	Niphal: נֶאֱסַף be gathered, be assembled
עבר	Qal: chapter 16
	Hiphil: הֶעֱבִיר allow to pass over, overlook
עמד	Qal: chapter 12
	Hiphil: הֶעֱמִיד set in position, erect, cause to stand

3. Reading Vocabulary

בַּעֲבוּר	on account of
בִּגְלַל	on account of
יָפֶה	beautiful

4. Proper Names

| פַּרְעֹה | Pharaoh |
| שָׂרַי | Sarai |

E. Reading—Genesis 12:10–14

10 וַיְהִי רָעָב בָּאָרֶץ וַיֵּרֶד אַבְרָם מִצְרַיְמָה לָגוּר שָׁם כִּי־כָבֵד הָרָעָב בָּאָרֶץ

11 וַיְהִי כַּאֲשֶׁר הִקְרִיב¹ לָבוֹא מִצְרָיְמָה וַיֹּאמֶר אֶל־שָׂרַי אִשְׁתּוֹ² הִנֵּה־נָא יָדַעְתִּי
כִּי אִשָּׁה יְפַת³־מַרְאֶה אָתְּ

12 וְהָיָה כִּי־יִרְאוּ אֹתָךְ הַמִּצְרִים וְאָמְרוּ אִשְׁתּוֹ זֹאת וְהָרְגוּ אֹתִי וְאֹתָךְ יְחַיּוּ

---

1. Hiphil *qatal* 3ms of קרב. It normally means to "bring near" or "offer." However, here it may mean simply "come near," or it may mean "as soon as he had brought (his family) near to entering Egypt."
2. אִשָּׁה with 3msx.
3. Feminine singular construct of יָפֶה.

13 אִמְרִי־נָא אֲחֹתִי אָתְּ לְמַ֫עַן יִֽיטַב־לִי בַעֲבוּרֵ֑ךְ וְחָיְתָה נַפְשִׁי בִּגְלָלֵךְ

14 וַיְהִי כְּבוֹא אַבְרָם מִצְרָ֑יְמָה וַיִּרְאוּ הַמִּצְרִים אֶת־הָ֣אִשָּׁה כִּֽי־יָפָה הִוא֙ מְאֹֽד

_____

1.   The feminine pronoun הִוא usually has this form in the Pentateuch.

CHAPTER 27
THE QAL *YIQTOL* AND *WAYYIQTOL* WITH WEAK ROOTS

A. The Qal *Yiqtol* (Imperfect) with Weak Roots

Yiqtol verbs from weak roots can be very different from the strong verb paradigm with קָטַל. The vowels in the strong verb Qal *yiqtol* (יִקְטֹל) are often not seen with weak roots. Learn the Qal *yiqtol* preformatives simply as consonants and not with the vowels of the strong root. The vowels simply change too much to be considered part of the regular pattern. The stem vowel (the vowel under the middle radical) is also subject to numerous changes in the Qal stem.

Table 27.1. The Qal *Yiqtol* (Imperfect) of I-Guttural, II-Guttural, III-ח/ע, and III-א Verbs

	I-Guttural עמד	II-Guttural בחר	III-ע/ח שמע	III-א מצא	Strong קטל
3ms	יַעֲמֹד	יִבְחַר	יִשְׁמַע	יִמְצָא	יִקְטֹל
3fs	תַּעֲמֹד	תִּבְחַר	תִּשְׁמַע	תִּמְצָא	תִּקְטֹל
2ms	תַּעֲמֹד	תִּבְחַר	תִּשְׁמַע	תִּמְצָא	תִּקְטֹל
2fs	תַּעַמְדִי	תִּבְחֲרִי	תִּשְׁמְעִי	תִּמְצְאִי	תִּקְטְלִי
1cs	אֶעֱמֹד	אֶבְחַר	אֶשְׁמַע	אֶמְצָא	אֶקְטֹל
3mp	יַעַמְדוּ	יִבְחֲרוּ	יִשְׁמְעוּ	יִמְצְאוּ	יִקְטְלוּ
3fp	תַּעֲמֹדְנָה	תִּבְחַרְנָה	תִּשְׁמַעְנָה	תִּמְצֶאנָה	תִּקְטֹלְנָה
2mp	תַּעַמְדוּ	תִּבְחֲרוּ	תִּשְׁמְעוּ	תִּמְצְאוּ	תִּקְטְלוּ
2fp	תַּעֲמֹדְנָה	תִּבְחַרְנָה	תִּשְׁמַעְנָה	תִּמְצֶאנָה	תִּקְטֹלְנָה
1cp	נַעֲמֹד	נִבְחַר	נִשְׁמַע	נִמְצָא	נִקְטֹל

1. The I-Guttural

Observe the following:

(1) A guttural in the first radical position takes Hateph Pathach instead of vocal Shewa. Under the influence of the guttural, the preformative takes Pathach.

(2) In the forms with a vowel sufformative (2fs, 3mp, 2mp), the first radical of the root has a Pathach because a closed, unaccented syllable is always short (e.g., /עַמ/ in the 3mp יַ/עַמ/דוּ).

(3) The 1cs form has Seghol and Hateph Seghol where the others have Pathach and Hateph Pathach.

2. The II-Guttural

The root בחר follows the normal tendencies of a guttural to prefer a-class vowels and reject the vocal Shewa (taking, in this case, Hateph Pathach).

3. The III-ע/ח

With ע or ח, the Qal *yiqtol* shows in its stem vowel the preference for a-class vowels.

4. The III-א

The III-א also prefers the a-class vowel, but it tends to lengthen the stem vowel to Qamets (recall that א quiesces). Contrast the Pathach of the III-ח form יִשְׁלַח. The feminine plural forms are distinctive for having the Seghol as the stem vowel.

Table 27.2. The Qal *Yiqtol* (Imperfect) of I-נ, Original I-ו, and True I-י Verbs

	I-נ נפל	Original I-ו ישב	True I-י ירש	Strong קטל
3ms	יִפֹּל	יֵשֵׁב	יִירַשׁ	יִקְטֹל
3fs	תִּפֹּל	תֵּשֵׁב	תִּירַשׁ	תִּקְטֹל
2ms	תִּפֹּל	תֵּשֵׁב	תִּירַשׁ	תִּקְטֹל
2fs	תִּפְּלִי	תֵּשְׁבִי	תִּירְשִׁי	תִּקְטְלִי
1cs	אֶפֹּל	אֵשֵׁב	אִירַשׁ	אֶקְטֹל
3mp	יִפְּלוּ	יֵשְׁבוּ	יִירְשׁוּ	יִקְטְלוּ
3fp	תִּפֹּלְנָה	תֵּשַׁבְנָה	תִּירַשְׁנָה	תִּקְטֹלְנָה
2mp	תִּפְּלוּ	תֵּשְׁבוּ	תִּירְשׁוּ	תִּקְטְלוּ
2fp	תִּפֹּלְנָה	תֵּשַׁבְנָה	תִּירַשְׁנָה	תִּקְטֹלְנָה
1cp	נִפֹּל	נֵשֵׁב	נִירַשׁ	נִקְטֹל

5. The I-נ

The tendency of the I-נ to assimilate is apparent in the Qal *yiqtol*. In the above examples from נפל, the נ assimilates to the פ and doubles it. The reason for the assimilation is not hard to imagine. It is difficult to pronounce יִנְפֹל, and therefore the נ assimilates and gives us יִפֹּל. Except for the assimilation of the נ, the pattern for the Qal *yiqtol* of נפל is exactly like the strong *yiqtol*.

A noteworthy phenomenon is that the root לקח, "take," acts like a I-נ verb in the Qal *yiqtol* and *wayyiqtol*. For example, the Qal *yiqtol* 3ms and 3fs forms are יִקַּח and תִּקַּח. Also, note that לקח has a guttural ח in the third position, and thus takes the a-class stem vowel.

6. The Original I-ו

Recall that roots with י as the first radical are often originally I-ו (some are true I-י roots). An example of an original I-ו is יָשַׁב, "sit" or "dwell." An original I-ו root loses the first root radical י whenever a preformative is added. Since the *yiqtol* always has a preformative, the י of the root is missing from every example. You already know the Qal *yiqtol* 3ms and 3fs forms יֵשֵׁב and תֵּשֵׁב. This root displays the following Qal *yiqtol* inflection:

(1) The י of the root has dropped in every form of the paradigm.

(2) The preformative vowel is Tsere throughout.

(3) The stem vowel is Tsere if there is no inflectional ending, Shewa if there is a vowel ending, and Pathach if the ending begins with a consonant.

Interestingly, the very common root הלך, "walk," acts like an original I-ו verb in the Qal *yiqtol*, *wayyiqtol*, and imperative. For example, the Qal *yiqtol* 3ms and 3fs forms are יֵלֵךְ and תֵּלֵךְ, and the Qal *wayyiqtol* 3mp and 3fp are וַיֵּלְכוּ and וַתֵּלַכְנָה. (A similar situation occurs with הלך in all conjugations of the Hiphil—recall the form הוֹלִיךְ in the "Previously Learned Verbs" section of chapter 25 vocabulary.)

7. The True I-י

Some verbs that are true original I-י verbs; these do not drop the י in the Qal *yiqtol*. An example is ירש, "possess," with the *yiqtol* 3ms form יִירַשׁ.

(1) This verb shows both the *yiqtol* preformative letter and the י in the first position of the root, but the י of the root has become a vowel letter Hireq-Yod.

(2) It does not have the vowel pattern of the original I-ו *yiqtol*.

(3) Unlike the strong root, the original I-י root has a vowel pattern of "i-class followed by a-class."

(4) Notice that the stem vowel (the vowel under the middle radical of the root) is Pathach, not the Holem you see in the strong verb (יִקְטֹל).

(5) Other verbs of this type are יטב (Qal *yiqtol* 3ms is יִיטַב) and ירא (Qal *yiqtol* 3ms is יִירָא; the א quiesces and lengthens the stem vowel).

8. The I-א

Verbs I-א are of two types: those that have Seghol as the preformative vowel and those that have Holem as the preformative vowel. Both usually have Pathach as the stem vowel.

(1) אהב has the Seghol preformative. Notice that this conforms to the rule that where a strong root has a Hireq, a root with a guttural often takes Seghol.

(2) Several important verbs, such as אמר, have the pattern with Holem in the preformative. Common verbs of this type include אכל, "eat"; אבד, "die"; אבה, "be willing"; אפה, "bake"; and most commonly, אמר, "say." We should note that, because of the normal quiescence of the א, one does not not see an א with a vowel followed by another א. For that reason, the *yiqtol* 1cs of אמר is אֹמַר and not *אאֹמַר.

Table 27.3. The Qal *Yiqtol* (Imperfect) of I-א Verbs

	אהב	אמר	Strong
3ms	יֶאֱהַב	יֹאמַר	יִקְטֹל
3fs	תֶּאֱהַב	תֹּאמַר	תִּקְטֹל
2ms	תֶּאֱהַב	תֹּאמַר	תִּקְטֹל
2fs	תֶּאֱהֲבִי	תֹּאמְרִי	תִּקְטְלִי
1cs	אֹהַב	אֹמַר	אֶקְטֹל
3mp	יֶאֱהֲבוּ	יֹאמְרוּ	יִקְטְלוּ
3fp	תֶּאֱהַֿבְנָה	תֹּאמַֿרְנָה	תִּקְטֹֿלְנָה
2mp	תֶּאֱהֲבוּ	תֹּאמְרוּ	תִּקְטְלוּ
2fp	תֶּאֱהַֿבְנָה	תֹּאמַֿרְנָה	תִּקְטֹֿלְנָה
1cp	נֶאֱהַב	נֹאמַר	נִקְטֹל

9. The Hollow Roots

Table 27.4. The Qal *Yiqtol* (Imperfect) forms of the Hollow Verb

	שׁוּב	שִׂים	בּוֹא	Strong
3ms	יָשׁוּב	יָשִׂים	יָבוֹא	יִקְטֹל
3fs	תָּשׁוּב	תָּשִׂים	תָּבוֹא	תִּקְטֹל
2ms	תָּשׁוּב	תָּשִׂים	תָּבוֹא	תִּקְטֹל
2fs	תָּשֹׁוּבִי	תָּשִֹׂימִי	תָּבֹואִי	תִּקְטְלִי
1cs	אָשׁוּב	אָשִׂים	אָבוֹא	אֶקְטֹל
3mp	יָשֹׁוּבוּ	יָשִֹׂימוּ	יָבוֹאוּ	יִקְטְלוּ
3fp	תְּשׁוּבֶֿינָה	תְּשִׂימֶֿינָה	תָּבֹאנָה	תִּקְטֹֿלְנָה
2mp	תָּשֹׁוּבוּ	תָּשִֹׂימוּ	תָּבוֹאוּ	תִּקְטְלוּ
2fp	תְּשׁוּבֶֿינָה	תְּשִׂימֶֿינָה	תָּבֹאנָה	תִּקְטֹֿלְנָה
1cp	נָשׁוּב	נָשִׂים	נָבוֹא	נִקְטֹל

The hollow roots are easy to recognize in the Qal *yiqtol* (you already know יָשׁוּב). Recall that they tend

(1) to retain the pointed vowel letter of the lexical form and

(2) to have Qamets with the preformative.

The examples with שׁוּב, שִׂים, and בּוֹא all follow this pattern. The feminine plural forms use Seghol-Yod as a linking vowel before the sufformative נָה.

10. The Geminate

The geminates are the most difficult inflection of the Qal *yiqtol*. Just as they do in the Qal *qatal*, geminates distinguish the transitive (can take a direct object) from the stative (never takes a direct object; describes state-of-being) in the Qal *yiqtol*.

Table 27.5. The Qal *Yiqtol* (Imperfect) of Transitive and Stative Geminate Verbs

	Transitive Quasi-Hollow סבב	*Stative* Quasi-נ סבב	*Strong* קטל
3ms	יָסֹב	יִסֹּב	יִקְטֹל
3fs	תָּסֹב	תִּסֹּב	תִּקְטֹל
2ms	תָּסֹב	תִּסֹּב	תִּקְטֹל
2fs	תָּסֹּבִי	תִּסֹּבִי	תִּקְטְלִי
1cs	אָסֹב	אֶסֹּב	אֶקְטֹל
3mp	יָסֹבּוּ	יִסֹּבּוּ	יִקְטְלוּ
3fp	תְּסֻבֶּינָה	תִּסֹּבְנָה	תִּקְטֹלְנָה
2mp	תָּסֹבּוּ	תִּסֹּבּוּ	תִּקְטְלוּ
2fp	תְּסֻבֶּינָה	תִּסֹּבְנָה	תִּקְטֹלְנָה
1cp	נָסֹב	נִסֹּב	נִקְטֹל

(1) The transitive pattern, which might be called the "quasi-hollow" type (meaning that it looks like the hollow verb), is characterized with Qamets as the preformative vowel. But the geminate lacks the pointed vowel letter of the hollow (e.g., יָקוּם from קוּם). Also, if there is a sufformative with a geminate root, the geminate letter is doubled with a Daghesh Forte (e.g., the 3mp יָסֹבּוּ). An example of this type is found in Josh 6:4: "And on the seventh day, *you shall go around* the city" (תָּסֹבּוּ אֶת־הָעִיר).

(2) The stative pattern might be called the "quasi-I-נ" type. That is, it looks like the I-נ verb. It is characterized by the preformative with Hireq and the doubled first consonant. There is no good reason for the first letter to double; it seems to be a case of analogy (this is when a word is inflected according to the pattern of another word's

inflection, as when someone uses "thunk" as the past tense of "think" on the analogy of "sink /sunk"). But if a geminate root has a vowel suffformative, the geminate letter is doubled with a Daghesh Forte (e.g., the 3mp יָסֹבּוּ). An example of this pattern is found in Num 36:9: "*And* an inheritance to the Israelites *shall not go around* (וְלֹא־תִסֹּב) from tribe to tribe."

11. The Doubly-Weak Yiqtol *(Imperfect)*

Many Qal *yiqtol* verbs are formed from doubly-weak roots.

(1) For example, נסע is both I-נ and III-ע. In the 2fs, 3mp, and 2mp, the ס has lost its Daghesh because it is pointed with a Shewa. Often a letter that ought to double, if pointed with a Shewa, will not have a Daghesh Forte.

(2) The root נתן can be peculiar: it can have assimilation of the נ on both ends. In the 3fp, for example, the final נ of the root has assimilated to the ending נָה. Also, it has Tsere as its stem vowel rather than the normal Holem. Thus, in contrast to the strong verb Qal *yiqtol* 2ms תִּקְטֹל, we see תִּתֵּן with נתן.

Table 27.6. The Qal *Yiqtol* (Imperfect) of the Doubly-Weak Roots נסע and נתן

	נסע	נתן	*Strong*
3ms	יִסַּע	יִתֵּן	יִקְטֹל
3fs	תִּסַּע	תִּתֵּן	תִּקְטֹל
2ms	תִּסַּע	תִּתֵּן	תִּקְטֹל
2fs	תִּסְעִי	תִּתְּנִי	תִּקְטְלִי
1cs	אֶסַּע	אֶתֵּן	אֶקְטֹל
3mp	יִסְעוּ	יִתְּנוּ	יִקְטְלוּ
3fp	תִּסַּעְנָה	תִּתֵּנָּה	תִּקְטֹלְנָה
2mp	תִּסְעוּ	תִּתְּנוּ	תִּקְטְלוּ
2fp	תִּסַּעְנָה	תִּתֵּנָּה	תִּקְטֹלְנָה
1cp	נִסַּע	נִתֵּן	נִקְטֹל

B. The Apocopated *Wayyiqtol*

Many Qal *wayyiqtols* look just like their *yiqtol* counterparts except that they have the characteristic וַ and Daghesh Forte at the beginning of the word. This holds true for verbs from most roots. However, *wayyiqtols* that are different from the *yiqtol* appear with roots that are I-א of the אמר type, and with III-ה, original I-ו, hollow, and geminate roots. Two tendencies mark these forms:

(1) The accent moves away from the ultima toward the penult.

(2) The form tends to **apocopate** or shorten. A III-ה root will drop the ה ending from all singular forms except the 1cs. A hollow root will have the short vowel Qamets Hatuph instead of Shureq.

Table 27.7. The Qal Apocopated *Wayyiqtol* in אמר-Type, Original I-ו, and Hollow Verbs

	אמר-Type אָמַר	Original I-ו יָשַׁב	Hollow שׁוּב	Strong קָטַל
3ms	וַיֹּאמֶר	וַיֵּשֶׁב	וַיָּשָׁב	וַיִּקְטֹל
3fs	וַתֹּאמֶר	וַתֵּשֶׁב	וַתָּשָׁב	וַתִּקְטֹל
2ms	וַתֹּאמֶר	וַתֵּשֶׁב	וַתָּשָׁב	וַתִּקְטֹל
2fs	וַתֹּאמְרִי	וַתֵּשְׁבִי	וַתָּשֻׁבִי	וַתִּקְטְלִי
1cs	וָאֹמַר	וָאֵשֵׁב	וָאָשׁוּב	וָאֶקְטֹל
3mp	וַיֹּאמְרוּ	וַיֵּשְׁבוּ	וַיָּשֻׁבוּ	וַיִּקְטְלוּ
3fp	וַתֹּאמַרְנָה	וַתֵּשַׁבְנָה	וַתָּשֹׁבְנָה	וַתִּקְטֹלְנָה
2mp	וַתֹּאמְרוּ	וַתֵּשְׁבוּ	וַתָּשֻׁבוּ	וַתִּקְטְלוּ
2fp	וַתֹּאמַרְנָה	וַתֵּשַׁבְנָה	וַתָּשֹׁבְנָה	וַתִּקְטֹלְנָה
1cp	וַנֹּאמֶר	וַנֵּשֶׁב	וַנָּשָׁב	וַנִּקְטֹל

1. The אמר Type

Two features characterize the אמר type pattern:

(1) Where possible, the accent moves to the penult. This occurs in all singular forms (except the 1cs) and in the 1cp. When accent shift occurs, the vowel Pathach is replaced by Seghol. Compare the *yiqtol* 3ms יֹאמַר to the *wayyiqtol* 3ms וַיֹּאמֶר.

(2) In the 1cs, the preformative א will not double and, by compensatory lengthening, there is a Qamets under the ו instead of Pathach. Note also that the א of the root and the א of the preformative have assimilated.

2. The Original I-ו

The original I-ו *wayyiqtol* is identical in form to the Qal *yiqtol* (after adding ו and Daghesh Forte) except that in the apocopated 3ms, 3fs, 2ms, and 1cp the accent has shifted to the penult. This makes the ultima a closed, unaccented syllable, and thus it is short (וַיֵּשֶׁב). The root here is ישׁב; the Qal *yiqtol* 3ms is יֵשֵׁב.

3. The Hollow Roots

The Qal *yiqtol* 3ms of שׁוּב is יָשׁוּב, and the Qal *wayyiqtol* 3ms is וַיָּשָׁב. Observe what has happened to the vowels.

(1) The syllable /שָׁבּ/ in the 3ms, 3fs, and 2ms *wayyiqtol* forms is closed and unaccented, and thus the vowel is Qamets Hatuph. These are apocopated forms.

(2) But for the 3mp and 2mp forms, we often see וַתָּשׁוּבוּ and וַיָּשׁוּבוּ. Also, וַנָּשָׁב only appears in one text (Neh 4:9), and an alternative reading is וַנָּשׁוּב.

Distinguish the pattern of שׁוּב from the inflection of ישׁב by paying close attention to the preformative vowel (Qamets with שׁוּב and Tsere with ישׁב). Compare וַיָּשָׁב from שׁוּב to וַיֵּשֶׁב from ישׁב.

4. The Geminate

Table 27.8. The Qal *Wayyiqtol* of Transitive and Stative Geminate Verbs

	Transitive Quasi-Hollow סבב	*Stative* Quasi-I-נ סבב	*Strong* קטל
3ms	וַיָּסָב	וַיִּסֹב	וַיִּקְטֹל
3fs	וַתָּסָב	וַתִּסֹב	וַתִּקְטֹל
2ms	וַתָּסָב	וַתִּסֹב	וַתִּקְטֹל
2fs	וַתָּסֹבִּי	וַתִּסֹבִּי	וַתִּקְטְלִי
1cs	וָאָסֹב	וָאֶסֹב	וָאֶקְטֹל
3mp	וַיָּסֹבּוּ	וַיִּסֹבּוּ	וַיִּקְטְלוּ
3fp	וַתְּסֻבֶּינָה	וַתִּסֹבְנָה	וַתִּקְטֹלְנָה
2mp	וַתָּסֹבּוּ	וַתִּסֹבּוּ	וַתִּקְטְלוּ
2fp	וַתְּסֻבֶּינָה	וַתִּסֹבְנָה	וַתִּקְטֹלְנָה
1cp	וַנָּסָב	וַנִּסֹב	וַנִּקְטֹל

Geminates of the *wayyiqtol* patterns are similar to *yiqtol* patterns except where the *wayyiqtols* are apocopated, as in וַיָּסָב (note the Qamets Hatuph in a closed, unaccented syllable). As with the *yiqtol*, there are two patterns: one that is more like the normal hollow verb pattern and one that seems to mimic the I-נ pattern (the latter does not apocopate).

Blackboard 27.1. The *Yiqtol* (Imperfect) and *Wayyiqtol* of the Geminate סבב

C. Vocabulary

1. Core Vocabulary

a. Verbs

הלל[1] Piel: הַלֵּל praise
Hithpael: הִתְהַלֵּל*; יִתְהַלֵּל (*yiqtol* 3ms) boast

נגע Qal: נָגַע touch, strike
Piel: נִגַּע*; וַיְנַגַּע (*wayyiqtol* 3ms) afflict
Hiphil: הִגִּיעַ touch, happen, hurl

פתח Qal: פָּתַח open
Piel: פִּתַּח break open, let loose

רעה Qal: רָעָה feed, graze, nourish, protect as a shepherd; (often as a substantive in the participle: רֹעֶה) shepherd

b. Other Words

בָּקָר cattle Ⓜ |בְּקַר|

חֲמוֹר donkey Ⓜ |חֲמֹר|

גָּמָל camel Ⓜ |*construct not extant*|

יֶלֶד boy Ⓜ |וְיֶלֶד|; יַלְדָּה = girl Ⓕ |*construct not extant*|

כְּמוֹ like, as

נֶגַע blow, wound, plague Ⓜ |נֶגַע|

פֶּתַח opening, entrance, gateway Ⓜ |פֶּתַח|

שִׁפְחָה slave-girl, handmaid, maidservant Ⓕ |שִׁפְחַת|

2. Previously Learned Verbs in Derived Stems

אכל Qal: chapter 18
Niphal: נֶאֱכַל be eaten
Hiphil: הֶאֱכַלְתִּי (*qatal* 1cs) feed

ילד Qal: chapter 19
Niphal: נוֹלַד be born
Pual: יֻלַּד / יוֹלַד be born (sometimes considered a Qal passive)
Hiphil: הוֹלִיד beget

---

1. This is the second of three different homonymous roots הלל. Root #1 is to "shine" and root #3 is "to treat as a fool." The others have the same root letters but different meanings.

יָרַד	Qal: chapter 12
	Hiphil: הוֹרִד[1] bring down, cause to fall
קרא	Qal: chapter 18
	Niphal: נִקְרָא be summoned, be proclaimed

3. Reading Vocabulary

אָתוֹן	female donkey

D. Reading—Genesis 12:15–17

15 וַיִּרְאוּ אֹתָהּ שָׂרֵי פַרְעֹה וַיְהַלְלוּ אֹתָהּ אֶל־פַּרְעֹה וַתֻּקַּח[2] הָאִשָּׁה בֵּית פַּרְעֹה

16 וּלְאַבְרָם הֵיטִיב בַּעֲבוּרָהּ וַיְהִי־לוֹ צֹאן־וּבָקָר וַחֲמֹרִים וַעֲבָדִים וּשְׁפָחֹת וַאֲתֹנֹת וּגְמַלִּים

17 וַיְנַגַּע[3] יְהוָה אֶת־פַּרְעֹה נְגָעִים גְּדֹלִים וְאֶת־בֵּיתוֹ עַל־דְּבַר[4] שָׂרַי אֵשֶׁת[5] אַבְרָם

---

1. One would expect to see הוֹרִיד, but in fact the *qatal* 3ms appears written defectively as הוֹרִד.
2. Pual *wayyiqtol* 3fs לקח. With this root, the ל will assimilate as though it were a root with I-נ.
3. Notice that this root has a final guttural and compare it to the paradigm Piel *wayyiqtol* וַיְקַטֵּל. How has the final guttural affected the vowels?
4. עַל־דְּבַר "upon the word of" means "on account of."
5. The construct form of אִשָּׁה.

CHAPTER 28
THE QAL IMPERATIVE AND PARTICIPLE WITH WEAK ROOTS

A. The Qal Imperative

Although the imperative in form is generally a second person *yiqtol* with the preformative removed, you should learn the imperative as a separate paradigm.

1. The III-ע/ה

Since the imperative is derived from the *yiqtol*, in most weak verbs the imperative has the same characteristics as its counterpart in the *yiqtol*, as in שְׁמַע, "listen."

Table 28.1. The Qal *Yiqtol* (Imperfect) Second Person and Imperative of שמע

	Yiqtol	Imperative		
	שמע	שמע	Strong	
2ms	תִּשְׁמַע	שְׁמַע	קְטֹל	ms
2fs	תִּשְׁמְעִי	שִׁמְעִי	קִטְלִי	fs
2mp	תִּשְׁמְעוּ	שִׁמְעוּ	קִטְלוּ	mp
2fp	תִּשְׁמַעְנָה	שְׁמַעְנָה	קְטֹלְנָה	fp

2. The I-א

I-א verbs of the אמר type are like the strong verb except for having Hateph Seghol. Therefore, the imperative (e.g., אֱמֹר) has different vowels from the *yiqtol* (e.g., תֹּאמַר).

Table 28.2. The Qal *Yiqtol* (Imperfect) Second Person and Imperative of אמר

	Yiqtol	Imperative		
	אמר	אמר	Strong	
2ms	תֹּאמַר	אֱמֹר	קְטֹל	ms
2fs	תֹּאמְרִי	אִמְרִי	קִטְלִי	fs
2mp	תֹּאמְרוּ	אִמְרוּ	קִטְלוּ	mp
2fp	תֹּאמַרְנָה	אֱמֹרְנָה	קְטֹלְנָה	fp

3. The I-נ

There are two types of I-נ imperatives: (1) those that drop the נ of the root and (2) those that preserve the first נ.

Table 28.3. The Qal Imperative of the Two Types of I-נ Verbs

	נסע	נפל	*Strong*
ms	סַע	נְפֹל	קְטֹל
fs	סְעִי	נִפְלִי	קִטְלִי
mp	סְעוּ	נִפְלוּ	קִטְלוּ
fp	סַעְנָה	נְפֹלְנָה	קְטֹלְנָה

(1) The first type of imperative is illustrated by נסע ("set out" or "travel"), where the נ of the root is lost. This is the most common type of I-נ imperative, and you should regard it as the norm. Note that נסע is also III-guttural. Other examples of I-נ roots that drop the initial נ in the imperative forms include דַּע ("know!"), from ידע, and תֵּן ("give!"), from נתן. There is also an alternative masculine singular form with paragogic Hey: תְּנָה ("Give!" — Qal impv. ms of נתן with paragogic Hey).

(2) The second type of imperative is illustrated by נפל, "fall," where the נ is not dropped. This pattern is like the strong verb. In this case, the נ of the root comes back from assimilation when the *yiqtol* preformative ת is dropped.

4. The Original I-ו

Except in the feminine plural, the Original I-ו imperative is simply a *yiqtol* with the preformative dropped. Notice that the י of the root ישב does not come back when the ת of the *yiqtol* is dropped.

Table 28.4. The Qal *Yiqtol* (Imperfect) Second Person and Imperative of ישב

	Yiqtol	*Imperative*		
	ישב	ישב	*Strong*	
2ms	תֵּשֵׁב	שֵׁב	קְטֹל	*ms*
2fs	תֵּשְׁבִי	שְׁבִי	קִטְלִי	*fs*
2mp	תֵּשְׁבוּ	שְׁבוּ	קִטְלוּ	*mp*
2fp	תֵּשַׁבְנָה	שֵׁבְנָה	קְטֹלְנָה	*fp*

5. The Hollow

Except in the feminine plural, the Hollow imperative is simply a *yiqtol* with the preformative dropped. The feminine plural drops the linking vowel and changes the stem vowel. Distinguish the imperative of שׁוּב from the imperative of ישׁב.

Table 28.5. The Qal Imperative and *Yiqtol* (Imperfect) Second Person of the Hollow Verb

שׁוּב		קוּם	
Yiqtol	*Imperative*	*Yiqtol*	*Imperative*
תָּשׁוּב	שׁוּב	תָּקוּם	קוּם
תָּשׁוּבִי	שׁוּבִי	תָּקוּמִי	קוּמִי
תָּשׁוּבוּ	שׁוּבוּ	תָּקוּמוּ	קוּמוּ
תְּשֻׁבֶּינָה	שֹׁבְנָה	תְּקוּמֶּינָה	קֹמְנָה

6. The Geminate

Once more, except in the feminine plural, the Hollow imperative is simply a *yiqtol* with the preformative dropped. It makes no difference whether the "quasi-Hollow" or "quasi-I-נ" pattern is considered the starting point; except for the feminine plural (which is built on the I-נ pattern), the imperative pattern is the same.

Table 28.6. The Qal Imperative and *Yiqtol* (Imperfect) Second Person Patterns of the Geminate Verb סבב

	Yiqtol		Imperative	
	Transitive Quasi-Hollow	*Stative Quasi-I-נ*		
ms	תָּסֹב	תִּסֹּב	סֹב	2ms
fs	תָּסֹבִּי	תִּסֹּבִי	סֹבִּי	2fs
mp	תָּסֹבּוּ	תִּסֹּבוּ	סֹבּוּ	2mp
fp	תְּסֻבֶּינָה	תְּסֻבְּנָה	סֹבְנָה	2fp

7. Other Common Imperatives

These three imperatives are very common in the Hebrew Bible.

Table 28.7. Imperatives for הלך and לקח and נתן

	Yiqtol 2ms	Imperative ms	Comments	Meaning
הלך	תֵּלֵךְ	לֵךְ	הלך in its *yiqtol* follows the pattern of ישׁב (2ms = תֵּשֵׁב).	Go!
לקח	תִּקַּח	קַח	לקח in its *yiqtol* follows the pattern of נסע (2ms = תִּסַּע).	Take!
נתן	תִּתֵּן	תֵּן	Often with paragogic ה as תְּנָה.	Give!

B. The Qal Participle

1. Weak Active Participle Forms Similar to the Strong Pattern

Many weak verbs show little variation from the strong verb active participles. The mp of the root עמד is עֹמְדִים. The mp of שאל is שֹׁאֲלִים. The fs from the root אמר is אֹמֶרֶת. The mp of ישׁב is יֹשְׁבִים. You should have no difficulties with these patterns.

Table 28.8. The Qal Active Participle of III-ה/ע, III-א, Hollow, and III-ה Verbs

	III-ה/ע שׁמע	III-א מצא	Hollow שׁוב	III-ה בנה	Strong קטל
ms	שֹׁמֵעַ	מֹצֵא	שָׁב	בֹּנֶה	קֹטֵל
fs	שֹׁמַעַת	מֹצֵאת	שָׁבָה	בֹּנָה	קֹטֶלֶת
mp	שֹׁמְעִים	מֹצְאִים	שָׁבִים	בֹּנִים	קֹטְלִים
fp	שֹׁמְעוֹת	מֹצְאוֹת	שָׁבוֹת	בֹּנוֹת	קֹטְלוֹת

2. The III-ה/ע

The guttural preference for a-class vowels appears (in the feminine singular). The furtive Pathach is on the ms form, שֹׁמֵעַ. The root שׁמע, "hear," illustrates this.

3. The III-א

The tendency of the א to quiesce is evident in the fs here. In מֹצֵאת, the fs of מצא, "find," note that the א has lost its vowel and that the vowel in front of it is lengthened (contrast the paradigm קֹטֶלֶת).

4. The Hollow

You already know that the ms participle is שָׁב. The fs is שָׁבָה (contrast קֹטֶלֶת); it is distinguished from the *qatal* 3fs (שָׁבָה) by its accent.

5. The III-ה

In the declension of בנה ("build"), we see the following characteristics:

(1) The masculine singular absolute participle in the III-ה verb always ends in Seghol-Hey (בֹּנֶה).

(2) For the fs, instead of the normal pattern קֹטֶלֶת, we see a pattern like בֹּנָה.

(3) As is normal in III-ה forms, the final ה drops off when a vowel inflectional ending is added. This is evident in the plural forms.

C. Vocabulary

1. Core Vocabulary

a. Verbs

נוּס   Qal: נָס flee

סבב   Qal: סָבַב turn around, go around, surround
                           Hiphil: הֵסֵב make to go around, bring around, turn away

צוה   Piel: צִוָּה command, instruct

שאל   Qal: שָׁאַל ask, consult, demand

שכן   Qal: שָׁכַן reside, dwell, settle

b. Other Words

אַךְ   surely, only, however

זֶבַח   (communal) sacrifice, offering Ⓜ |זֶבַח|

כֶּבֶשׂ   young ram Ⓜ |כֶּבֶשׂ| (כִּבְשָׂה ewe-lamb Ⓕ |כִּבְשַׂת|)

לְבַד   alone (adverb); besides (preposition)

לָמָה   why? (also seen as לָמֶה or לָמָה or לְמֶה)

מִשְׁכָּן   dwelling place, abode (often of the abode of YHWH = tabernacle, central sanctuary)

פַּר   steer, young bull Ⓜ |פַּר| (פָּרָה cow Ⓕ |*construct not extant*|)

2. Previously Learned Verbs in Derived Stems

ידע   Qal: chapter 16
                        Niphal: נוֹדַע reveal, become known
                        Hiphil: הוֹדִיעַ make known, inform

3. Proper Names

אֱדוֹם   Edom

אֱדוֹמִי   Edomite(s)

עַמּוֹן   Ammon

עַמּוֹנִי   Ammonite(s)

שֹׁמְרוֹן   Samaria

D. Reading—Genesis 12:18–20

18 וַיִּקְרָא פַרְעֹה לְאַבְרָם וַיֹּאמֶר מַה־זֹּאת עָשִׂיתָ לִּי לָמָה לֹא־הִגַּדְתָּ לִּי כִּי
אִשְׁתְּךָ הִוא

19 לָמָה אָמַרְתָּ אֲחֹתִי הִוא וָאֶקַּח¹ אֹתָהּ לִי לְאִשָּׁה וְעַתָּה הִנֵּה אִשְׁתְּךָ קַח וָלֵךְ

20 וַיְצַו² עָלָיו פַּרְעֹה אֲנָשִׁים וַיְשַׁלְּחוּ אֹתוֹ וְאֶת־אִשְׁתּוֹ וְאֶת־כָּל־אֲשֶׁר־לוֹ

---

1. Qal *wayyiqtol* 1cs לקח. Remember that with this root, the ל will assimilate as though it were a root with I-נ.
2. An apocopated *wayyiqtol* from צוה.

CHAPTER 29
THE QAL *QATAL* WITH WEAK ROOTS, QAL STATIVES, AND THE
QAL PASSIVE PARTICIPLE

A. The Qal *Qatal* (Perfect) with Weak Roots

Table 29.1. The Qal *Qatal* (Perfect) of I-Guttural, II-Guttural, and III-ח/ע Verbs

	I-Guttural עמד	II-Guttural בחר	III-ח/ע שמע	Strong קטל
3ms	עָמַד	בָּחַר	שָׁמַע	קָטַל
3fs	עָמְדָה	בָּחֲרָה	שָׁמְעָה	קָטְלָה
2ms	עָמַ֫דְתָּ	בָּחַ֫רְתָּ	שָׁמַ֫עְתָּ	קָטַ֫לְתָּ
2fs	עָמַדְתְּ	בָּחַרְתְּ	שָׁמַעַתְּ	קָטַלְתְּ
1cs	עָמַ֫דְתִּי	בָּחַ֫רְתִּי	שָׁמַ֫עְתִּי	קָטַ֫לְתִּי
3cp	עָמְדוּ	בָּחֲרוּ	שָׁמְעוּ	קָטְלוּ
2mp	עֲמַדְתֶּם	בְּחַרְתֶּם	שְׁמַעְתֶּם	קְטַלְתֶּם
2fp	עֲמַדְתֶּן	בְּחַרְתֶּן	שְׁמַעְתֶּן	קְטַלְתֶּן
1cp	עָמַ֫דְנוּ	בָּחַ֫רְנוּ	שָׁמַ֫עְנוּ	קָטַ֫לְנוּ

1. The I-Guttural

The I-guttural roots pose no real problem in the Qal *qatal*. There is Hateph Pathach where the strong verb has a vocal Shewa (2mp and 2fp). Gutturals do not take vocal Shewa, and they prefer a-class vowels. The conjugation for עמד, "stand," is shown above.

2. The II-Guttural

The Hateph Pathach appears where the strong verb has a vocal Shewa (3fs and 3cp). The various inflections of בחר, "choose," represent this pattern.

3. The III-ח/ע

With these gutturals, the Qal *qatal* is inflected like the strong verb, except at the 2fs, where the guttural preference for a-class vowels is evident. Note the conjugation of שמע, "hear," in the above table.

Table 29.2. The Qal *Qatal* (Perfect) of III-א and Hollow Verbs

	III-א מצא	Hollow שׁוּב	Strong קטל
3ms	מָצָא	שָׁב	קָטַל
3fs	מָצְאָה	שָׁבָה	קָטְלָה
2ms	מָצָאתָ	שַׁבְתָּ	קָטַלְתָּ
2fs	מָצָאת	שַׁבְתְּ	קָטַלְתְּ
1cs	מָצָאתִי	שַׁבְתִּי	קָטַלְתִּי
3cp	מָצְאוּ	שָׁבוּ	קָטְלוּ
2mp	מְצָאתֶם	שַׁבְתֶּם	קְטַלְתֶּם
2fp	מְצָאתֶן	שַׁבְתֶּן	קְטַלְתֶּן
1cp	מָצָאנוּ	שַׁבְנוּ	קָטַלְנוּ

4. The III-א

As seen with the verb מצא, "find," the א quiesces here. When the א quiesces,

(1) the א has no vowel,

(2) the vowel before it lengthens, and

(3) any begadkephat letter that follows it loses its Daghesh Lene.

The 3fs and 3cp forms are regular.

5. The Hollow Verb

In their lexical forms, hollow verbs are written with a pointed vowel letter as the middle letter (e.g., קוּם). They have consonants only in the first and third positions; the middle position is occupied by a vowel. You already know the principal parts for the hollow Qal *qatal* with שָׂם and שָׁב. In the Qal *qatal*, the pointed vowel letter drops out altogether and is replaced by either Qamets (third person forms) or Pathach (second and first person forms). A number of features of this conjugation are unusual.

(1) The 3fs (קָמָה) and 3cp (קָמוּ) forms are not accented on the ultima but the penult. Compare the strong verb קָטְלָה.

(2) The 2fs (קַמְתְּ) is a monosyllable with a large consonant cluster at the end; it can be transliterated as *qamtt*. Also, note that it has two silent Shewas side-by-side, which is odd. Outside of the 2fs, such patterns are rare in Hebrew.

(3) In hollow verbs with Holem-Waw as the vowel (e.g., בּוֹשׁ, "be ashamed"), we often see Holem as the stem vowel (e.g., בֹּשׁוּ, "they are ashamed").

6. The Geminate

As with the *yiqtol*, the *qatal* forms of geminate verbs vary according to whether the verb is transitive (can take a direct object) or stative (never takes a direct object; describes state-of-being).

Table 29.3. The Qal *Qatal* (Perfect) of Transitive and Stative Geminate Verbs

	Transitive סבב	*Stative* קלל	*Strong* קטל
3ms	סָבַב	קַל	קָטַל
3fs	סָבְבָה	קַלָּה	קָטְלָה
2ms	סַבּוֹתָ	קַלּוֹתָ	קָטַלְתָּ
2fs	סַבּוֹת	קַלּוֹת	קָטַלְתְּ
1cs	סַבּוֹתִי	קַלּוֹתִי	קָטַלְתִּי
3cp	סָבְבוּ	קַלּוּ	קָטְלוּ
2mp	סַבּוֹתֶם	קַלּוֹתֶם	קְטַלְתֶּם
2fp	סַבּוֹתֶן	קַלּוֹתֶן	קְטַלְתֶּן
1cp	סַבּוֹנוּ	קַלּוֹנוּ	קָטַלְנוּ

a. Transitive Geminates

In the *yiqtol*, we saw that the root סבב, "surround," carries both transitive and stative forms. In contrast, the root in the *qatal* always follows the transitive pattern (although at times it still bears intransitive meaning, "go around").

   (1) The third person forms are like the strong verb. A Metheg is implied under the first radical but not always present in the text (as in קָטְלָה).

   (2) Second and first person forms double the geminate letter (in this case, ב) with a Daghesh Forte and insert ו as a linking vowel between the root and the ending.

b. Stative Geminates

The root קלל is of the stative type; it means "be slight" or "swift."

   (1) The gemination (doubling) is not evident at all in the 3ms. In this, the stative geminate verb is like the geminate adjective (e.g., דַּל, "poor," from דלל). This similarity is useful for remembering that it is the adjective-like stative geminate that does not write out all three letters in the 3ms, while the transitive does.

   (2) Similarly, the stative uses the Daghesh Forte for the 3fs and 3cp. Compare the adjective forms דַּלָּה (fs) and דַּלִּים (mp).

(3) The second and first person forms are like the transitive forms.

(4) Sometimes we see geminate stative forms that lack the linking vowel, as in תַּמְנוּ, "we come to an end," from תמם.

7. Doubly-Weak Verbs

Many roots are **doubly-weak**, meaning that they are roots that have two weak letters. For example, a verb may be I-Guttural and III-ה (עשׂה, "do"). It may be both hollow and III-א (בוֹא, "come"), or it may be II-Guttural and III-ה (ראה, "see").

For the most part, doubly-weak verbs simply combine features of the two types. For example, the 2mp of עשׂה is עֲשִׂיתֶם, with the Hateph Pathach under the ע (like a I-Guttural) and the Hireq-Yod replacing the ה (as is normal for a III-ה). The paradigm of ראה is exactly like the normal III-ה verb except that the 3fs is רָאֲתָה (compare בָּנְתָה).

The inflection of בוֹא is a normal hollow except that it also has the quiescence of the א. The full declension is as follows (cf. Table 29.2).

Table 29.4. The Qal *Qatal* (Perfect) of בוֹא

	בוֹא	*Strong*
3ms	בָּא	קָטַל
3fs	בָּאָה	קָטְלָה
2ms	בָּאתָ	קָטַלְתָּ
2fs	בָּאת	קָטַלְתְּ
1cs	בָּאתִי	קָטַלְתִּי
3cp	בָּאוּ	קָטְלוּ
2mp	בָּאתֶם	קְטַלְתֶּם
2fp	בָּאתֶן	קְטַלְתֶּן
1cp	בָּאנוּ	קָטַלְנוּ

B. The Qal Statives

1. Qatal *and* Yiqtol

Stative verbs are those that describe a state-of-being; they are descriptive and not active. Stative verbs often have distinctive vowel patterns. The most common vowel patterns for strong *qatal* and *yiqtol* verbs are קָטַל and יִקְטֹל. In contrast, the most common stative patterns for the strong verb are כָּבֵד (*qatal*) and יִכְבַּד (*yiqtol*).

Table 29.5. The Basic *Qatal* (Perfect) and *Yiqtol* (Imperfect) Stative Vowel Patterns

	Qatal	Yiqtol	Meaning
כבד	כָּבֵד	יִכְבַּד	be heavy
צדק	צָדֵק	יִצְדַּק	be righteous

The כָּבֵד vowel pattern of the stative *qatal* class only shows up in the 3ms form. Otherwise, the vowel pattern is identical to the normal Qal *qatal* (e.g., the *qatal* 3fs of כבד is כָּבְדָה; the *qatal* 1cs of צדק is צָדַקְתִּי). In the *yiqtol*, the only significant difference is that the stative pattern takes the Pathach as its stem vowel rather than the Holem of the strong Qal *yiqtol*.

Table 29.6. *Qatal* (Perfect) and *Yiqtol* (Imperfect) Paradigms for the Qal Stative

	Qatal		Yiqtol	
	Stative	Strong	Stative	Strong
3ms	כָּבֵד	קָטַל	יִכְבַּד	יִקְטֹל
3fs	כָּבְדָה	קָטְלָה	תִּכְבַּד	תִּקְטֹל
2ms	כָּבַדְתָּ	קָטַֽלְתָּ	תִּכְבַּד	תִּקְטֹל
2fs	כָּבַדְתְּ	קָטַלְתְּ	תִּכְבְּדִי	תִּקְטְלִי
1cs	כָּבַֽדְתִּי	קָטַֽלְתִּי	אֶכְבַּד	אֶקְטֹל
3mp	כָּבְדוּ	קָטְלוּ	יִכְבְּדוּ	יִקְטְלוּ
3fp			תִּכְבַּֽדְנָה	תִּקְטֹֽלְנָה
2mp	כְּבַדְתֶּם	קְטַלְתֶּם	תִּכְבְּדוּ	תִּקְטְלוּ
2fp	כְּבַדְתֶּן	קְטַלְתֶּן	תִּכְבַּֽדְנָה	תִּקְטֹֽלְנָה
1cp	כָּבַֽדְנוּ	קָטַֽלְנוּ	נִכְבַּד	נִקְטֹל

In addition, you should remember the following points:

(1) Not all "normal" verbs are transitive, and not all verbs that are stative in form are actually stative in meaning.

(2) There are other Qal stative vowel patterns and mixing of patterns besides those described here, but they are confined to a few specific verbs and are not especially difficult.

2. Infinitive Construct and Participle

The Qal infinitive construct of the stative typically has Pathach as its stem vowel (כְּבַד). The Qal stative participle ms typically has the same vowel pattern as the *qatal* 3ms. Thus, from the root ירא, the form יָרֵא could be a *qatal* 3ms or a participle ms. In Gen 22:12, the phrase יְרֵא אֱלֹהִים means "a fearer of God" (note the construct form). Qal stative participles function as nouns or adjectives and are declined like adjectives (e.g., the masculine plural participle / adjective of כבד is כְּבֵדִים).

C. More on the Qal Passive Participle

1. Form and Usage

In biblical Hebrew, the Niphal has for the most part taken the role of being the passive form of the Qal. But the language also retains the remnants of an older Qal passive system. The only part of this that is still significant for biblical Hebrew is a Qal passive participle. It is not uncommon to see the Qal passive participle written defectively as בְּרֻכִים (instead of בְּרוּכִים, from ברך). The Qal passive participle can be in the construct state, as in Exod 38:25 פְּקוּדֵי הָעֵדָה ("the registered [ones] of the congregation"; Qal passive participle mp construct of פקד).

2. The Qal Passive Participle in Weak Verbs

Qal passive participles with weak roots have familiar traits and are easy to recognize.

Table 29.7. Select Weak Roots in the Qal Passive Participle Masculine Singular

	Passive Participle	Meaning
שלח	שָׁלוּחַ	sent
אהב	אָהוּב	loved
גאל	גָּאוּל	redeemed
ידע	יָדוּעַ	known
שנא	שָׂנוּא	hated

III-ה verbs are the most peculiar of the Qal passive participles. The following paradigm with בנה shows that the III-ה verb was originally III-י.

Table 29.8. The Qal Passive Participle of בנה

	III-ה	Strong
ms	בָּנוּי	קָטוּל
fs	בְּנוּיָה	קְטוּלָה
mp	בְּנוּיִם	קְטוּלִים
fp	בְּנוּיוֹת	קְטוּלוֹת

The Qal passive participles of hollow or geminate roots are very rare. The ms of the verb מוּל, "circumcise," is מוּל. The geminate ארר appears as אָרוּר, "accursed."

D. Vocabulary

1. Core Vocabulary

a. Verbs

גדל   Qal: גָּדַל be(come) great, be(come) strong
                       Piel: גִּדֵּל/גִּדַּל bring up, let grow, praise
                       Hiphil: הִגְדִּיל enlarge, show to be great, magnify oneself

זרע   Qal: זָרַע sow (of seed)

כבד   Qal: כָּבֵד be heavy, weighty, honored
                       Niphal: נִכְבַּד be honored, enjoy honor, appear in one's glory
                       Piel: *כִּבֵּד; כִּבְּדוּ (*qatal* 3cp) honor

לחם   Niphal: נִלְחַם fight

שמם   Qal: שָׁמֵם be desolate, deserted; be astonished, shudder
                       Niphal: נָשַׁמָּה (*qatal* 3fs) be uninhabited, tremble
                       Hiphil: הֲשִׁמּוֹתָ (*qatal* 2ms) make deserted, make desolated

b. Other Words

זֶרַע   seed, offspring (s or pl collective) Ⓜ |זֶרַע|

כַּף   palm of hand or sole of foot Ⓕ |כַּף|

מָגֵן   shield Ⓜ |מָגֵן|

מְלָאכָה   work, service, fruit of labor Ⓕ |מְלֶאכֶת|

צֶדֶק   righteousness: what is right, just, accurate, normal Ⓜ |צֶדֶק|

צְדָקָה   righteousness, justness, justice, communal loyalty Ⓕ |צִדְקַת|

שֶׁ   who, which, that (attached to a word, as the definite article does, with daghesh in following consonant); also found as שַׁ, שֶׁ, or שָׁ

2. Reading Vocabulary

מַחֲזֶה   vision, appearance

מֵעֶה   entrails, intestines, loins, genitals, inner being, emotions

מֶשֶׁק   meaning unknown; perhaps "possession"

עֲרִירִי   childless

שָׂכָר   wages (for work/deeds done), reward

3. Proper Names

אֱלִיעֶ֫זֶר	Eliezer
דַּמֶּ֫שֶׂק	Damascus

E. Reading—Genesis 15:1–4

1   אַחַ֣ר הַדְּבָרִ֣ים הָאֵ֗לֶּה הָיָ֤ה דְבַר־יְהוָה֙ אֶל־אַבְרָ֔ם בַּמַּחֲזֶ֖ה לֵאמֹ֑ר

    אַל־תִּירָ֣א אַבְרָ֗ם אָנֹכִי֙ מָגֵ֣ן לָ֔ךְ שְׂכָרְךָ֖ הַרְבֵּ֥ה מְאֹֽד

2   וַיֹּ֣אמֶר אַבְרָ֗ם אֲדֹנָ֤י יֱהוִה֙ מַה־תִּתֶּן־לִ֔י וְאָנֹכִ֖י הוֹלֵ֣ךְ עֲרִירִ֑י וּבֶן־מֶ֣שֶׁק בֵּיתִ֗י[1]

    ה֖וּא דַּמֶּ֥שֶׂק אֱלִיעֶֽזֶר

3   וַיֹּ֣אמֶר אַבְרָ֔ם הֵ֣ן לִ֔י לֹ֥א נָתַ֖תָּה[2] זָ֑רַע וְהִנֵּ֥ה בֶן־בֵּיתִ֖י יוֹרֵ֥שׁ אֹתִֽי

4   וְהִנֵּ֨ה דְבַר־יְהוָ֤ה אֵלָיו֙ לֵאמֹ֔ר לֹ֥א יִֽירָשְׁךָ֖ זֶ֑ה כִּי־אִם֙ אֲשֶׁ֣ר יֵצֵ֣א מִמֵּעֶ֔יךָ ה֖וּא

    יִֽירָשֶֽׁךָ

---

1.   "And the son of possession of my house" = "and the heir of my house." The phrase is likely functioning as a pendent element before the actual clause: "And as for the heir of my house, he is ...."

2.   Remember that the *qatal* 2ms sufformative often has the vowel Qamets-Hey. The root is נתן.

CHAPTER 30
THE QAL COHORTATIVE, JUSSIVE, AND *WEYIQTOL*

A. The Qal Cohortative and Jussive

In addition to the imperative, one can express a desire that someone do something with the **cohortative** ("Let's do this!") or the **jussive** ("May he do this!"). The cohortative is first person, and the jussive is third person. The cohortative, imperative, and jussive are called "volitives" because they all convey a speaker's will (i.e., volition). In Hebrew, all are formally variants of the *yiqtol*.

1. The Cohortative

The Qal cohortative is formed by adding a paragogic Hey (הָ֫) to the form of a first person *yiqtol*.

(1) The accent shifts to the הָ֫ ending except in hollow verbs.

(2) Weak roots follow the normal rules for *yiqtol* verbs. The accent shift caused by the added syllable הָ֫ makes the stem vowel of the *yiqtol* form reduce in all forms (except the hollow). Remember: With verbs, if the propretonic cannot reduce, an open pretonic with i-class or u-class vowel will reduce.

(3) The III-ה cohortative does not take the paragogic ה; it is identical in form to the *yiqtol* III-ה.

Blackboard 30.1. The Formation of the Qal Cohortative of שׁלח

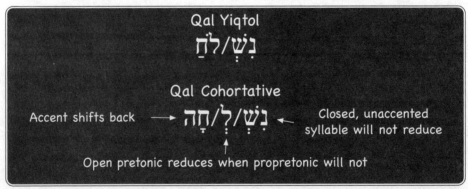

Table 30.1. Examples of the Qal Cohortative

	Yiqtol	*Cohortative*	*Meaning*
קטל	נִקְטֹל	נִקְטְלָה	Let us kill
שׁלח	נִשְׁלַח	נִשְׁלְחָה	Let us send
שׁוּב	אָשׁוּב	אָשׁוּבָה	Let me return

יֵשֵׁב	אֵשֵׁב	אֵשְׁבָה	"Let me stay"
יָרַד	נֵרֵד	נֵרְדָה	"Let us go down"

2. The Jussive

In most verbs, the Qal jussive is formed in exactly the same way as the simple *yiqtol*. יִקְטֹל can mean "he will kill" or "may he kill." Three kinds of roots, however, use an "apocopated" or shortened form of the jussive *yiqtol*. These are the hollow, the original I-ו, and the III-ה.

(1) In the shortened form, the accent is on the penult.

(2) In the original I-ו and the hollow, the stem vowel is changed.

(3) In the III-ה, the final ה drops off, and the vowels will be modified.

The process of forming the jussive of עשה (יַעַשׂ) from the simple ("long") *yiqtol* (יַעֲשֶׂה) illustrates the formation of the jussive.

Blackboard 30.2. Steps in the Formation of the Qal Jussive in a III-ה Verb

1. The process begins with a normal III-ה yiqtol	יַעֲ/שֶׂה
2. The III-ה ending drops off and accent shifts forward	יַ/עַשׂ
3. The final closed, unaccented syllable must be short	יַ/עַשׂ

Table 30.2. Examples of the Qal Jussive

	Yiqtol	*Jussive*	*Meaning*
קטל	יִקְטֹל	יִקְטֹל	Let him kill
עשה	יַעֲשֶׂה	יַעַשׂ	Let him make
שׁוּב	יָשׁוּב	יָשֹׁב	Let him return
ירד	תֵּרֵד	תֵּרֵד	Let her go down

3. The Cohortative and Jussive vs. the Modal (Long) Yiqtol

You remember that the *yiqtol* when in the first position has a modal or jussive function (such as, "May he do"). Most Qal *yiqtol* verbs, even when jussive in meaning, do not appear in a shortened or apocopated form. Only the hollow, original I-ו, and III-ה roots typically have an apocopated jussive. Some cohortatives, specifically those with a III-ה root, do not take paragogic ה and are formally identical to the simple first-person *yiqtol*. All of these forms, including apocopated jussives and cohortatives with paragogic ה, usually occur in first position within a clause. Consequently, in parsing it is best simply to identify a form as a *yiqtol* and then note whether it includes a paragogic ה or is apocopated.

4. Negative Commands

We noted earlier that a negative command (prohibition) in Hebrew is created by adjoining a negative particle (either לֹא or אַל) before a second person *yiqtol* form.

  (1) לֹא is usually used with simple ("long") *yiqtols* and generally expresses permanent prohibitions (e.g., "Never commit adultery").

  (2) אַל may occur with short or long *yiqtols* and most commonly expresses immediate commands that apply to specific situations (e.g., "Don't close that door").

B. The *Weyiqtol*

Adding וְ to a simple *yiqtol*, jussive, or cohortative generally does more than simply add the word *and*. Often it has distinctive usage and meaning. We may call this form the *weyiqtol*.

1. Form

In form, it is often a *yiqtol* with a simple conjunction וְ added. Frequently, however, the conjoined *yiqtol* has a cohortative or jussive form. That is, it may have the paragogic ה (in the first person) or be apocopated (in the third person). The next two tables illustrate forms of the *weyiqtol*.

Table 30.3. The Qal *Weyiqtol* of the Strong Verb

	Singular	*Plural*
3m	וְיִקְטֹל	וְיִקְטְלוּ
3f	וְתִקְטֹל	וְתִקְטֹלְנָה
2m	וְתִקְטֹל	וְתִקְטְלוּ
2f	וְתִקְטְלִי	וְתִקְטֹלְנָה
1c	וְאֶקְטְלָה	וְנִקְטְלָה

Often, as seen below, the *weyiqtol* tends to take the paragogic ה normally associated with the cohortative, or the apocopated (shortened) form normally associated with the jussive.

Table 30.4. Examples of Simple Qal *Yiqtols* (Imperfects) Compared to *Weyiqtols*

	Yiqtol	*Weyiqtol*
שׁוּב	אָשׁוּב	וְאָשׁוּבָה
שׁוּב	יָשׁוּב	וְיָשֵׁב
הלך	אֵלֵךְ	וְאֵלְכָה
היה	יִהְיֶה	וִיהִי
ידע	אֵדַע	וְאֵדְעָה

In the first person, the *weyiqtol* normally has the cohortative form with paragogic ה (except in III-ה verbs, which almost never take the paragogic ה). In the third person, the *weyiqtol* with hollow and III-ה roots often has the shortened jussive form.

The *weyiqtol* is different in form from the *wayyiqtol*, which has ו with Daghesh Forte in the preformative. Never confuse these two!

Table 30.5. The Qal *Wayyiqtol* Compared to *Weyiqtol*

Wayyiqtol	Weyiqtol
וַיִּקְטֹל	וְיִקְטֹל

2. Usage

The *weyiqtol*'s form and placement (always in first position) suggest that it is a modal rather than an indicative *yiqtol*. *Weyiqtols* often appear in volitional contexts to express purpose or intent, regardless of whether the forms are apocopated. For example, 1 Kgs 22:20 has, "Who will entice Ahab, so that he will go up…" (using the apocopated form וְיַעַל). However, 1 Kgs 15:19 has, "break your covenant with King Baasha of Israel, so that he will go up…" (using the simple וְיַעֲלֶה). The *weyiqtol* is used in the following ways:

(1) The *weyiqtol* frequently appears in the context of a volitive. When following an imperative, cohortative, jussive, or simple modal *yiqtol*, it often indicates purpose or result, as in "so that he may do." Gen 1:6 can be translated "And God said, 'Let there be an expanse in the middle of the waters, *so that there may be* (וִיהִי) a divider between the [two] waters.'"

(2) *Weyiqtols* that continue a jussive series have high thematic prominence (they are important). This contrasts with *weqatals* that continue a jussive series; they typically do not have high thematic prominence.

(3) The *weyiqtol* is rarely just a simple future. It usually connotes purpose or, if referring to the future, makes a more dramatic, prominent proclamation than a simple *yiqtol* or *weqatal* would. Gen 12:2 has three *weyiqtols*, which may either express purpose or prominent future: "*And I will make* of you a great nation, *and I will bless* you, *and I will make great* your name."

(4) Occassionally, *weyiqtol* conveys *and* plus a jussive or cohortative meaning to the verb, as in "and let him do." Gen 9:27 is an example:

וִיהִי כְנַעַן עֶבֶד לָמוֹ   and may Canaan be his servant.

וְיִשְׁכֹּן בְּאָהֳלֵי־שֵׁם   and may he dwell in the tents of Shem,

C. Vocabulary

1. Core Vocabulary

a. Verbs

אמן   Niphal: נֶאֱמַן / נֶאֱמָן be faithful, reliable, permanent

                 Hiphil: הֶאֱמִין believe, trust, think

חשב   Qal: חָשַׁב regard, assume, plan

                 Niphal: נֶחֱשַׁב be regarded

נבט   Hiphil: הִבִּיט look, look at, behold; (by extension) accept favorably

נוח   Qal: *נָח; נָחָה (*qatal* 3fs) rest, settle down

                 Hiphil (2 forms): הֵנִיחַ cause to rest, secure, repose, pacify; הִנִּיחַ place, set, leave (untouched)

ספר   Qal: סָפַר count, number, write

                 Piel: *סִפֵּר; סִפַּרְתִּי (*qatal* 1cs) count up, announce, report

b. Other Words

אַיִל   ram; (metaphorically) ruler Ⓜ |אֵיל|

אֱמֶת   trustworthiness, constancy, faithfulness, truth Ⓕ |אֲמֶת|

חוּץ   a place outside the house, street Ⓜ |חוּץ|; outside, without (preposition, adverb)

יָמִין   right side, south Ⓕ |יְמִין|

עֵז   goat, goat hair Ⓕ |*construct not extant*|

צָפוֹן   north; mountain of the gods (in the north) Ⓕ |צְפוֹן|

תָּמִים   complete, without blemish, honest, impeccable (adjective); honesty, blamelessness (noun) Ⓜ

2. Previously Learned Verbs in Derived Stems

יצא   Qal: chapter 19

                 Hiphil: הוֹצִיא lead, cause to go out

3. Proper Names

אוּר   Ur

אֱלִישָׁע   Elisha

בֵּית־אֵל   Bethel

כַּשְׂדִּים   Chaldeans

4. Reading Vocabulary

שָׁלֵשׁ	Piel: שִׁלֵּשְׁתָּ (*qatal* 2ms) divide into three, do (something) on the third day, do (something) for a third time Pual: מְשֻׁלָּשׁ (ms participle) three years old
גּוֹזָל	young bird, pigeon, turtle-dove
כּוֹכָב	star
עֶגְלָה	heifer, young cow
תּוֹר	turtle-dove

D. Reading—Genesis 15:5–9

5 וַיּוֹצֵא¹ אֹתוֹ הַחוּצָה וַיֹּאמֶר הַבֶּט²־נָא הַשָּׁמַיְמָה וּסְפֹר הַכּוֹכָבִים אִם־תּוּכַל לִסְפֹּר אֹתָם וַיֹּאמֶר לוֹ כֹּה יִהְיֶה זַרְעֶךָ

6 וְהֶאֱמִן³ בַּיהוָה וַיַּחְשְׁבֶהָ לּוֹ צְדָקָה

7 וַיֹּאמֶר אֵלָיו אֲנִי יְהוָה אֲשֶׁר הוֹצֵאתִיךָ⁴ מֵאוּר כַּשְׂדִּים לָתֶת⁵ לְךָ אֶת־הָאָרֶץ הַזֹּאת לְרִשְׁתָּהּ⁶

8 וַיֹּאמַר אֲדֹנָי יְהוִה בַּמָּה⁷ אֵדַע כִּי אִירָשֶׁנָּה⁸

9 וַיֹּאמֶר אֵלָיו קְחָה⁹ לִי עֶגְלָה מְשֻׁלֶּשֶׁת וְעֵז מְשֻׁלֶּשֶׁת וְאַיִל מְשֻׁלָּשׁ וְתֹר וְגוֹזָל

---

1. Hiphil *wayyiqtol* 3ms of יצא.
2. Hiphil imperative ms of נבט.
3. Hiphil *weqatal* 3ms of אמן. The use of the *weqatal* in a past tense narrative is somewhat unusual, and it suggests that v 6 is parenthetical and thematically important.
4. Hiphil *qatal* 1cs of יצא with 2ms suffix. Compare the Hiphil *wayyiqtol* וַיּוֹצֵא in v 5.
5. The Qal infinitive construct of נתן is תֵּת.
6. Qal infinitive construct of ירשׁ with ל and 3fs suffix. The infinitive construct is רֶשֶׁת.
7. Literally "in what," this means "How?"
8. Qal *yiqtol* 1cs of ירשׁ with 3fs suffix. The suffix has an energic נ.
9. Imperative of לקח with paragogic ה.

CHAPTER 31
THE NIPHAL

A. The Niphal Pattern

When studying the derived stems:

(1) Review the vowel patterns and strong verb principal parts.

(2) Then learn the full paradigms of the strong verb.

(3) Then learn charts describing the principal parts with weak roots.

In the chart below, you can see the two basic patterns of the Niphal with their principal parts. You already know the principal parts of the Niphal stem. Review its pattern and characteristics.

Table 31.1. The Basic Pattern of the Niphal

	Qatal and Participle		All Other Inflections	
Pattern	"i-a" pattern ☐☐☐P̲ a i		"a-i" pattern ☐☐˙☐P̲ i a	
Principal Parts	Qatal נִקְטַל	Participle נִקְטָל	Yiqtol יִקָּטֵל	Inf. Con. הִקָּטֵל
Preformative	I-class vowel with preformative נ		Preformative הִן with נ assimilated	
First Radical	(No change)		Doubled by assimilation of נ (Daghesh Forte)	
First Radical Vowel	Silent Shewa		A-class vowel (Qamets)	
Stem Vowel	A-class vowel or Shewa		I-class vowel (often Tsere) or Shewa	

B. The Niphal *Qatal* (Perfect)

The Niphal strong *qatal* follows its vowel pattern in a straightforward manner. <u>Notice how the stem vowel reduces when it is an open pretonic</u> (this is because the propretonic—a closed, unaccented syllable—cannot reduce).

Table 31.2. The Niphal *Qatal* (Perfect) of נקטל

	Singular	Plural
3m	נִקְטַל	נִקְטְלוּ
3f	נִקְטְלָה	
2m	נִקְטַׄלְתָּ	נִקְטַלְתֶּם
2f	נִקְטַלְתְּ	נִקְטַלְתֶּן
1c	נִקְטַׄלְתִּי	נִקְטַׄלְנוּ

1. The I-Guttural

With the Niphal *qatal*, the I-guttural does not pose a particular problem. The trait of the guttural that comes into play is its use of semi-vowels. From עזר, for example, we have נֶעֱזַׄרְתִּי, "I was helped," where under the influence of the guttural, the vowel with the נ is Seghol rather than Hireq (still i-class). We often see the Seghol with the נ in the I-guttural Niphal *qatal*. Other examples are נֶחְשַׄבְנוּ, "we are regarded as" (from חשב) and נֶאֶמְנוּ, "they were trustworthy" (from אמן).

2. The III-א

The א quiesces here, as is usual. Thus we see נִקְרָא (3ms) with Qamets instead of נִקְטַל and נִקְרֵׄאתִי (1cs) instead of נִקְטַׄלְתִּי.

3. The III-ה

The Niphal *qatal* III-ה has all the normal characteristics of the *qatal* III-ה.

(1) The 3ms ends in הָ.

(2) The 3fs ends in תָה.

(3) Consonant endings cause the final ה to become a י pointed vowel letter. When this happens, the Niphal does not have an a-class stem vowel (it is i-class).

(4) Vowel endings cause the final ה to drop off.

From בנה ("build"), therefore, we have the forms נִבְנוּ (3mp), נִבְנָה (3ms), and נִבְנֵית (2fs; the stem vowel is a י vowel letter, as is typical for a III-ה with a consonant sufformative).

4. The I-נ

Because of the נ *preformative* that every Niphal has, the נ *of the root* assimilates to the second radical. Thus, the Niphal *qatal* 3ms of נתן, "give," is נִתַּן (compare נִקְטַל). Since נתן also ends in נ, the final נ will also assimilate to a consonant suffix, as in the 2mp נִתַּתֶּם. The Niphal of נחם, "regret," is quite common; an example is נָחַׄמְתִּי (1cs). The נ of this form is the Niphal preformative; the נ of the root has assimilated, but the guttural ח rejects the Daghesh Forte and employs virtual doubling.

Blackboard 31.1. Formation of the Niphal *Qatal* (Perfect) 1cs from נחם

> Hypothetical form; assimilation shown by arrow
>
> נִנְחַ֫מְתִּי
>
> Actual form after assimilation of נ and virtual doubling
>
> נִחַ֫מְתִּי

5. The Geminate

The geminate Niphal *qatal* is rare but appears in forms such as the 3cp of גלל, "be rolled": נָגֹ֫לּוּ. The preformative has the Qamets (similar to the hollow verb), and the ל is doubled with a Daghesh Forte.

6. The Original I-ו

In an original I-ו root like ילד, the first radical becomes either וֹ or וּ in the Niphal *qatal* rather than following the norm of having an i-class vowel. Examples are נוֹלַד (3ms) and נוֹלְדוּ (3cp).

7. The Hollow

The Niphal *qatal* 3cp of כון, "be established," is נָכֹ֫נוּ. The preformative has Qamets instead of an i-class vowel. First and second person forms use a Holem-Waw linking vowel between the root and the personal ending. The 1cs is נְכוּנ֫וֹתִי.

8. Understanding the Original I-ו and Hollow Niphal Qatals

To understand why the hollow and original I-ו do not follow the normal vowel pattern in the *qatal* (and participle), we need a somewhat more sophisticated understanding of Hebrew vowels.

(1) Although it is generally true that vowels change within their vowel classes, in certain cases an a-class vowel shifted to an i-class vowel when a syllable became closed and unaccented. This is called **attenuation**.

(2) Although it is correct to say that the Niphal *qatal* and participle have an i-class vowel under the preformative נ, originally this was an a-class vowel. It became i-class through attenuation in a closed, unaccented syllable.

(3) In the hollow *qatal* נָכוֹן, the penult (נָ) is not closed and unaccented but an open pretonic. It did not attenuate but became a long a-class vowel in accordance with normal rules.

(4) Although it is generally true that Holem-Waw is a u-class vowel, the combination of *a* and *w* in an unaccented syllable yields Holem-Waw (וֹ). You already know that when מָ֫וֶת loses its accent it becomes מוֹת. In the original I-ו, the Niphal combination נָו produced נוֹ. Thus, the Niphal *qatal* 3mp of ישב (originally ושב) is נוֹשָׁ֫בוּ.

C. The Niphal *Yiqtol* (Imperfect)

In the Niphal *yiqtol*, the נ of the הִנ preformative assimilates to the first radical of the root, and the first radical also has a Qamets under it. The *yiqtol* preformative has a Hireq and the stem vowel is Tsere, although it can shorten or reduce to Shewa (2fs and masculine plurals). The Niphal *yiqtol* pattern is easily recognizable.

Table 31.3. The Niphal *Yiqtol* (Imperfect) of קטל

	Singular	Plural
3m	יִקָּטֵל	יִקָּטְלוּ
3f	תִּקָּטֵל	תִּקָּטַׄלְנָה
2m	תִּקָּטֵל	תִּקָּטְלוּ
2f	תִּקָּטְלִי	תִּקָּטַׄלְנָה
1c	אֶקָּטֵל	נִקָּטֵל

1. The I-Guttural

With the Niphal *yiqtol*, the I-guttural (or I-ר) rejects the doubling that is normal with the assimilation of the נ. This generally causes compensatory lengthening. From חשׁב, we have יֵחָשֵׁב, "it shall be reckoned."

2. The III-ה/ע

The III-guttural has little effect on the Niphal *yiqtol* beyond its preference for the a-class vowel and the occasional furtive Pathach. Thus we see יִשָּׁמַע (3ms) with Pathach instead of the Tsere of יִקָּטֵל.

3. The III-ה

The Niphal *yiqtol* III-ה has all the normal characteristics of the *yiqtol* III-ה.

(1) If there is no personal ending, the *yiqtol* will end with ֶה.

(2) Consonant personal endings (the feminine plurals with נָה) cause the final ה to become a י pointed vowel letter.

(3) Vowel personal endings (e.g., the masculine plural וּ) cause the final ה to drop.

From בנה, "build," therefore, we have the forms יִבָּנֶה (3ms), תִּבָּנֶה (3fs), and תִּבָּנֶׄינָה (3fp). The doubly-weak verb ראה gives us יֵרָאֶה (where we see compensatory lengthening because the ר rejects doubling).

4. The I-נ

In the Niphal *yiqtol*, the I-נ root looks like the strong verb. The 3ms of נתן, "give," is יִנָּתֵן (compare יִקָּטֵל). The root נזר gives us the *yiqtol* 3mp יִנָּזְרוּ, "they will be consecrated"; the root נצל gives us the *yiqtol* 2ms תִּנָּצֵל, "you will be delivered."

5. The Original I-ו

In the original I-ו root ילד, the fact that the first radical was originally ו is very clear. An example is the Niphal *yiqtol* 3ms יִוָּלֵד, "he will be born." Note that the וָ in this word is the doubled consonant ו with the vowel Qamets; it is not the vowel Shureq. Taking this into account, יִוָּלֵד is exactly like the strong Niphal *yiqtol* יִקָּטֵל.

6. The Hollow

In the Niphal *yiqtol*, the hollow tends to have ו as its stem vowel. The נ of the Niphal assimilates, and thus we have יִכּוֹן as the 3ms of כון, "be established."

7. The Geminate

The geminate Niphal *yiqtol* retains the i-a vowel pattern but loses the stem vowel. If there is no personal ending, the gemination is lost, as in יִמַּס, the 3ms from מסס, "melt" (compare יִקָּטֵל). In יִקַּלּוּ, the 3mp of קלל, "be swift," the ק has doubled from assimilation of the Niphal נ, and the ל is doubled because of the geminate root.

D. The Niphal Volitives

1. The Niphal Imperative

Like all imperatives, the Niphal imperative looks like a *yiqtol* with the preformative dropped off. The Niphal imperative adds a wrinkle, however, in that it has the preformative ה in front of the root. This can cause the reader to confuse this stem with the Hiphil. Remember: the Niphal imperative has the doubled first radical with Qamets.

Table 31.4. The Niphal Imperative of קטל

	Singular	Plural
Masculine	הִקָּטֵל	הִקָּטְלוּ
Feminine	הִקָּטְלִי	הִקָּטַלְנָה

2. The Niphal Cohortative

When the paragogic ה is added to the Niphal *yiqtol*, the stem vowel reduces to Shewa. Thus we see אֶכָּבְדָה, "let me be glorified" (from כבד), where the *yiqtol* is אֶכָּבֵד.

3. The Niphal Jussive

The jussive has the shortened form in the III-ה root, as in the 3fs תִּגָּל, "let it be exposed" (from גלה). Otherwise, the jussive is generally like the simple *yiqtol*.

E. The Niphal Conjoined Finite Verbs

1. The Niphal Wayyiqtol

The Niphal *wayyiqtol* has the normal pattern, as in וַיִּוָּלֵד, "and he was born" (from the original I-ו root ילד). With the III-ה root, we see the shortened form, as in וַיֵּרָא, "and he appeared" (from ראה).

2. *The Niphal* Weqatal

In form, the *weqatal* is again simply the *qatal* with וְ added, as in וְנִבְרְכוּ, "and they will be blessed" (from בֿרֿךְ). Usually the accent is on the ultima in the 1cs and 2ms.

3. *The Niphal* Weyiqtol

As is normal, we often see the וְ added to a cohortative or jussive form, as in וְאִכָּבְדָה, "so that I shall be honored," or וְיֵּרָא, "that he may be seen" (from ראה). Otherwise, the conjunction is simply added to the normal *yiqtol* form, as in וְיִקָּרֵא, "that it may be called" (from קרא).

F. The Niphal Infinitives

1. *The Niphal Infinitive Construct*

The strong infinitive construct is הִקָּטֵל. This is also the pattern of the ms imperative, but the infinitive construct often has a preposition (לְהִקָּטֵל) or a pronominal suffix. The Niphal imperative never has a preposition and almost never has a pronominal suffix. The stem vowel reduces if the infinitive construct has a pronominal suffix (e.g., with 3mp suffix, הִקָּטְלָם).

The Niphal infinitive construct tends to respond to weak roots in the same ways that the Niphal *yiqtol* does. Thus, we have יֵעָמֵד (*yiqtol* 3ms) and הֵעָמֵד (inf. con.), as well as יִשָּׁלַח (*yiqtol* 3ms) and הִשָּׁלַח (inf. con.), and יִבָּנֶה (*yiqtol* 3ms) and הִבָּנוֹת (inf. con.). The last example, a III-ה, shows that as in all other stems, the III-ה Niphal infinitive construct ends in וֹת.

2. *The Niphal Infinitive Absolute*

The Niphal Infinitive Absolute has two alternative forms: נִקְטֹל and הִקָּטֹל.

G. The Niphal Participle

The Niphal participle ms is very consistent about looking like the *qatal* 3ms, except that its stem vowel is long (*qatal*: נִקְטַל; participle: נִקְטָל). An example of a participle is נִכְבָּד; the *qatal* is נִכְבַּד.

Table 31.5. The Niphal Participle of קטל

	Singular	Plural
Masculine	נִקְטָל	נִקְטָלִים
Feminine	נִקְטֶלֶת	נִקְטָלוֹת

The Niphal fs participle is often written with the נִקְטָלָה pattern instead of the נִקְטֶלֶת pattern. Also, we sometimes see the plurals in the forms נִקְטָלִים and נִקְטָלוֹת. The Niphal participle responds to weak roots in exactly the same way as the Niphal *qatal*, as the comparisons below illustrate.

Table 31.6. Niphal *Qatal* (Perfect) and Participle Forms with Weak Roots

	Qatal	Participle
לחם	נִלְחָם	נִלְחָם
אמן	נֶאֱמָן	נֶאֱמָן
כון	נָכוֹן	נָכוֹן
נצב	נִצָּב	נִצָּב
ירא	נוֹרָא	נוֹרָא

H. Summary of the Niphal Principal Parts

Table 31.7. The Niphal in Weak Roots

	Gloss	Qatal	Yiqtol	Inf. Con.	Participle
קטל		נִקְטַל	יִקָּטֵל	הִקָּטֵל	נִקְטָל
עבד	be served	נֶעֱבַד	יֵעָבֵד	הֵעָבֵד	נֶעֱבָד
בנה	be built	נִבְנָה	יִבָּנֶה	הִבָּנוֹת	נִבְנֶה
נצל	be rescued	נִצַּל	יִנָּצֵל	הִנָּצֵל	נִצָּל
ישב	be inhabited	נוֹשַׁב	יִוָּשֵׁב	הִוָּשֵׁב	נוֹשָׁב
כון	be firm	נָכוֹן	יִכּוֹן	הִכּוֹן	נָכוֹן

I. Vocabulary

1. Core Vocabulary

a. Verbs

לכד   Qal: לָכַד seize, capture
           Niphal: נִלְכַּד get trapped, be overpowered, be selected

נבא   Niphal: נִבָּא prophesy, behave like a prophet

עבד   Qal: עָבַד serve, work, accomplish

ענה   Piel: עִנָּה afflict, oppress

קבץ   Qal: קָבַץ collect, assemble, gather
           Niphal: *נִקְבְּצוּ ;נִקְבַּץ (*qatal* 3cp) assemble, be assembled
           Piel: *קִבְּצָה ;קִבֵּץ (*qatal* 3fs) gather together

קרא   Qal: *קָרָא; קָרָאת (*qatal* 3fs) meet, encounter, happen; לִקְרַאת (infinitive construct) "to meet," but it can be used used as a preposition: "over against, opposite"

b. Other Words

גֵּר   sojourner Ⓜ |*construct not extant*|

יַיִן   wine Ⓜ |יֵין|

עֲבֹדָה   service, work, labor Ⓕ |*construct not extant*|

קָהָל   contingent, assembly, congregation Ⓜ |קְהַל|

רֵעַ   counterpart, companion, friend Ⓜ |*construct not extant*|

שֶׁמֶשׁ   sun ⓂⒻ |שֶׁמֶשׁ|

2. Reading Vocabulary

בתר   Qal: בָּתַר split
                 Piel: וַיְבַתֵּר (*wayyiqtol* 3ms) split

דין   Qal: דָּן judge

נשב   Hiphil: וַיַּשֵּׁב (*wayyiqtol* 3ms) drive away

אֵימָה   horror, dread

בֶּתֶר   part, piece

חֲשֵׁכָה   darkness

עַיִט   bird of prey

פֶּגֶר   carcass

צִפּוֹר   bird, fowl

רְכוּשׁ   possession, property

תַּרְדֵּמָה   deep sleep

J. Reading—Genesis 15:10–14

10 וַיִּקַּֽח־לֹ֣ו אֶת־כָּל־אֵ֗לֶּה וַיְבַתֵּ֤ר אֹתָם֙ בַּתָּ֔וֶךְ וַיִּתֵּ֥ן אִישׁ־בִּתְרֹ֖ו² לִקְרַ֣את רֵעֵ֑הוּ³ וְאֶת־הַצִפֹּ֖ר לֹ֥א בָתָֽר

11 וַיֵּ֥רֶד הָעַ֖יִט עַל־הַפְּגָרִ֑ים וַיַּשֵּׁ֥ב אֹתָ֖ם אַבְרָֽם

12 וַיְהִ֤י הַשֶּׁ֙מֶשׁ֙ לָבֹ֔וא וְתַרְדֵּמָ֖ה נָפְלָ֣ה עַל־אַבְרָ֑ם וְהִנֵּ֥ה אֵימָ֛ה חֲשֵׁכָ֥ה גְדֹלָ֖ה נֹפֶ֥לֶת עָלָֽיו

13 וַיֹּ֣אמֶר לְאַבְרָ֗ם יָדֹ֨עַ תֵּדַ֜ע כִּי־גֵ֣ר ׀ יִהְיֶ֣ה זַרְעֲךָ֗ בְּאֶ֙רֶץ֙ לֹ֣א לָהֶ֔ם וַעֲבָד֖וּם וְעִנּ֣וּ אֹתָ֑ם אַרְבַּ֥ע מֵאֹ֖ות שָׁנָֽה

14 וְגַ֧ם אֶת־הַגֹּ֛וי אֲשֶׁ֥ר יַעֲבֹ֖דוּ דָּ֣ן⁴ אָנֹ֑כִי וְאַחֲרֵי־כֵ֥ן יֵצְא֖וּ בִּרְכֻ֥שׁ גָּדֹֽול

---

1. Remember that לקח behaves like a I-נ verb so that the ל assimilates as though it were a נ in a *yiqtol*-type construction. Also, it is a III-guttural and so prefers an a-class stem vowel.
2. "Each his part" = "each part."
3. "His counterpart" = the opposite half of the carcass
4. Context will tell you whether this hollow verb has to be a *qatal* or a participle.

CHAPTER 32
THE PIEL AND PUAL

A. The Piel Pattern

Today the Piel stem is sometimes called the D stem (i.e., "Doubled Stem") because its most pronounced characteristic is the doubling of the middle radical with a Daghesh Forte. The doubling of the middle radical is a reliable indicator of the Piel, Pual, and Hithpael. These three stems can all be regarded as related to each other because of this tendency. The Piel has one vowel pattern for the *qatal* and one for all others.

Table 32.1. The Basic Pattern of the Piel

	Qatal		All Other Inflections		
Patterns	3rd person "i-i" pattern ◯·◯◯ i i	2nd and 1st person "i-a" pattern ◯·◯◯ a i	Preformative is only with *yiqtol* and participle "a-i" pattern ◯·◯◯Ⓟ i a ə		
Principal Parts	קִטֵּל	קִטַּֽלְתָּ	*Yiqtol* יְקַטֵּל	Inf. Con. קַטֵּל	Participle מְקַטֵּל
Middle Radical	Doubled with Daghesh Forte				

1. The Piel Qatal (Perfect)

Remember the two vowel patterns for the Piel *qatal*. Remember also that the stem vowel reduces in the 3fs and 3cp.

Table 32.2. The Piel *Qatal* (Perfect) of קטל

	Singular	Plural
3m	קִטֵּל	קִטְּלוּ
3f	קִטְּלָה	
2m	קִטַּֽלְתָּ	קִטַּלְתֶּם
2f	קִטַּלְתְּ	קִטַּלְתֶּן
1c	קִטַּֽלְתִּי	קִטַּֽלְנוּ

a. The II-Guttural (and II-ר)

With the Piel *qatal*, a II-guttural or ר rejects the doubling that is characteristic of the Piel stem. There are two kinds of Piel II-guttural inflections:

(1) Those that employ virtual doubling. The initial Hireq is unchanged, but in the 3ms, the Tsere becomes Pathach under the influence of the guttural. From טהר, "cleanse" in the Piel, we have טִהַר (3ms) and טִהַרְתָּ (2ms).

(2) Those that employ compensatory lengthening. The initial Hireq becomes Tsere. From מאן, "refuse" in the Piel, we have מֵאֵן (3ms) and מֵאַנְתֶּם (2mp).

Table 32.3. The Piel *Qatal* (Perfect) of ברך

	Singular	Plural
3m	בֵּרַךְ	בֵּרְכוּ
3f	(not extant)	
2m	בֵּרַכְתָּ	בֵּרַכְתֶּם
2f	(not extant)	(not extant)
1c	בֵּרַ֫כְתִּי	בֵּרַ֫כְנוּ

b. The III-ח/ע

A III-guttural (ע or ח) causes the 3ms to have Pathach instead of Tsere. Thus we see שִׁלַּח, "he sent away."

c. The III-א

The quiescence of the א causes this inflection to have Tsere as its stem vowel rather than Pathach, and, as usual, it causes the inflectional ending to go without a Daghesh Lene. From מלא, "fill" in the Piel, we have the 2ms מִלֵּאתָ and the 1cs מִלֵּ֫אתִי.

d. The III-ה

The Piel *qatal* III-ה also has all characteristics that any *qatal* III-ה has.

(1) The 3ms ends in ﬥ‎ה.
(2) The 3fs ends in תָה.
(3) Consonant endings cause the final ה to become a pointed vowel letter י.
(4) Vowel endings cause the final ה to drop off.

From כלה ("finish"), we have the forms כִּלָּה (3ms), כִּלּוּ (3cp), וְכִלִּיתָ (*weqatal* 2ms) and כִּלִּיתֶם (2mp).

2. The Piel Yiqtol *(Imperfect)*

Bear in mind the following:

(1) Like every Piel, the *yiqtol* doubles the middle radical.
(2) The Piel *yiqtol* has a vocal Shewa with the preformative (Hateph Pathach in the 1cs).

(3) The vowel pattern is then a-class followed by i-class.

(4) The stem vowel Tsere reduces to vocal Shewa if there is a vowel ending. Recall that if the propretonic will not reduce, an open pretonic with an i-class vowel will reduce. In this case, the propretonic is closed (קַטְ in יְקַטְּלוּ) and so cannot reduce. Thus, the pretonic reduces.

Table 32.4. The Piel *Yiqtol* (Imperfect) of קטל

	Singular	Plural
3m	יְקַטֵּל	יְקַטְּלוּ
3f	תְּקַטֵּל	תְּקַטֵּלְנָה
2m	תְּקַטֵּל	תְּקַטְּלוּ
2f	תְּקַטְּלִי	תְּקַטֵּלְנָה
1c	אֲקַטֵּל	נְקַטֵּל

a. The II-Guttural

In the Piel *yiqtol*, the II-guttural (or II-ר) rejects the doubling that is characteristic of the Piel stem. Again, there are two kinds of Piel II-guttural inflections:

(1) Those that employ virtual doubling. The initial Pathach is unchanged. From טהר, "cleanse," in the Piel, we have אֲטַהֵר (1cs).

(2) Those that employ compensatory lengthening. The initial Pathach becomes Qamets. From מאן, "refuse" in the Piel, we have יְמָאֵן (3ms) and תְּמָאֲנוּ (2mp).

b. The III-ח/ע

The guttural causes the Piel *yiqtol* to have Pathach instead of Tsere as the stem vowel. Thus we see יְשַׁלַּח (3ms) from the root שלח, "send away."

c. The III-ה

The Piel *yiqtol* III-ה also has all characteristics that any *yiqtol* III-ה has.

(1) The 3ms ends in הֶ.

(2) Personal endings that begin with a consonant (in the *yiqtol*: feminine plurals) cause the final ה to become a pointed vowel letter י, as in תְּחַיֶּינָה (the 2fp of חיה, "keep alive").

(3) Vowel endings cause the final ה to drop off.

From כלה, "finish," therefore, we have אֲכַלֶּה, תְּכַלֶּה, and יְכַלּוּ (2ms, 1cs, and 3mp). From צוה, "command," we have the 3ms form יְצַוֶּה (the ו is a doubled ו).

3. The Piel Volitives

a. The Piel Cohortative

The cohortative takes the paragogic ה, with the result that the stem vowel will reduce (e.g., אֲדַבְּרָה, "let me speak"; contrast the *yiqtol* אֲדַבֵּר).

b. The Piel Imperative

The Piel imperative is extremely simple.

Table 32.5. The Piel Imperative of קטל

	Singular	Plural
Masculine	קַטֵּל	קַטְּלוּ
Feminine	קַטְּלִי	קַטֵּלְנָה

Like most imperatives, it is formed by removing the preformative from the *yiqtol*. The ms imperative also looks like the infinitive construct. The fs, mp, and fp have the normal endings.

Weak roots in the Piel imperative show the same traits as their counterparts in the Piel *yiqtol*. From the III-guttural שׁלח, we get the ms שַׁלַּח with the typical preference for the a-class vowel. From the II-guttural, we see the ms Piel imperative מַהֵר ("Hasten!") with virtual doubling. We see compensatory lengthening in בָּרֵךְ, the imperative ms of ברך, "bless." In all stems, the ms imperative of a III-ה verb has the Tsere-Hey, and so we see כַּלֵּה from the root כלה.

c. The Piel Jussive

The Piel jussive looks like the simple *yiqtol*, but in the III-ה verb it takes the shortened form. For example, for צוה, we have the 3ms jussive יְצַו, "let him command." The final ה has dropped off, and this has made the middle letter ו become the final letter. Since Hebrew does not like to end a word with a doubled letter, the ו loses its Daghesh Forte. The normal 3ms *yiqtol* is יְצַוֶּה.

4. The Piel Conjoined Finite Verbs

a. The Piel Wayyiqtol

(1) The *wayyiqtol* adds the normal וַ to a *yiqtol*, but the fact that the Piel *yiqtol* preformative has a Shewa under it often causes the Daghesh Forte to drop out of the preformative letter. Thus from the root דבר, we see וַיְדַבֵּר, "and he spoke" (with no Daghesh Forte in the י).

(2) The *wayyiqtol* in the III-ה verb takes the shortened form of the *yiqtol*. In this form, the final ה drops off, and this makes what was the middle letter become the final letter. Therefore, it loses its Daghesh Forte. וַיְכַל, "and he finished," is an example from כלה (contrast the *yiqtol* יְכַלֶּה).

b. The Piel Weqatal

This is again simply the *qatal* with וְ added, as in וּבֵרַכְתֶּם, "and you (mp) will bless" (from בֵרֵךְ). As is usual for the *weqatal*, the 2ms and 1cs tend to be accented on the ultima, as in וְדִבַּרְתָּ (contrast דִּבַּרְתָּ).

c. The Piel Weyiqtol

The *weyiqtol* adds the conjunction to a form of the *yiqtol* (often the cohortative or jussive form), but the fact that the Piel preformative has vocal Shewa under the *yiqtol* preformative causes the rules of the conjunction to come into play. Thus we see וִיבָרֵךְ, "that he may bless" (from בֵרֵךְ), and וּתְדַבֵּר, "that you (ms) may speak" (דִּבֵּר). Also, with the III-ה we may see the shortened form of the verb, as in וּתְכַל, "and you (ms) will finish" (כִּלָּה).

5. The Piel Infinitives

a. The Piel Infinitive Construct

As stated above, the infinitive construct has the basic pattern קַטֵּל (with לְ, לְקַטֵּל). Weak roots follow normal patterns, such as לְבָרֵךְ (compensatory lengthening) and לְשַׁלַּח (preference of guttural for a-class vowel). The III-ה infinitive construct, as always, ends in וֹת (e.g., כַּלּוֹת [from כִּלָּה] and לְצַוּוֹת [from צִוָּה]).

b. The Piel Infinitive Absolute

The Piel infinitive absolute usually looks just like the infinitive construct and ms imperative (קַטֵּל). Rarely, however, we see the pattern קַטֹּל.

6. The Piel Participle

The Piel participle has the distinctive feature of the preformative מְ:

Table 32.6. The Piel Participle of קַטֵּל

	Singular	*Plural*
Masculine	מְקַטֵּל	מְקַטְּלִים
Feminine	מְקַטֶּלֶת	מְקַטְּלוֹת

(1) For the fs participle, we sometimes see the alternative form מְקַטְּלָה. The fs participle of the III-ה always has this pattern, as in מְצַוָּה, "commanding."

(2) Weak roots behave in typical ways. For example, we see compensatory lengthening in מְבָרֵךְ, "blessing" (ms).

7. Summary of the Piel Principal Parts

Most Piel verbs are easy to spot in weak roots. Be sure, however, to remember the principal parts of the III-ה verb and the II-guttural / ר verb, as listed below. The III-ה Piel has the features common to all verbs of this root. The II-guttural / ר verb is different from the normal Piel because the guttural or ר will not double. Hollow verbs and geminates are generally not found in the Piel. They usually follow the alternative stems described in Chapter 35.

Table 32.7. The Piel in Weak Roots

	Gloss	Qatal	Yiqtol	Inf. Con.	Participle
קטל		קִטֵּל	יְקַטֵּל	קַטֵּל	מְקַטֵּל
כסה	cover	כִּסָּה	יְכַסֶּה	כַּסּוֹת	מְכַסֶּה
ברך	bless	בֵּרַךְ	יְבָרֵךְ	בָּרֵךְ	מְבָרֵךְ

B. The Pual Pattern

The Pual is quite rare—so much so that no verbal root appears more than a few times. It is sometimes called the Dp stem because it is the passive of the "Doubled" or Piel stem. Like the Piel, it has the characteristic doubling of the middle radical with a Daghesh Forte. In all forms, its vowel pattern is u-class under the first radical, doubled second radical, and a-class (or Shewa) as the stem vowel.

Table 32.8. The Basic Pattern of the Pual

Pattern	*"u-a" pattern* ☐ ˙ ◡ Ⓟ a u			
Principal Parts	Qatal קֻטַּל	Yiqtol יְקֻטַּל	Inf. Con. קֻטַּל	Participle מְקֻטָּל
Middle Radical	Doubled with Daghesh Forte			
Preformative	No Pual preformative; *yiqtol* and participle preformatives have Shewa			

1. The Pual Qatal (Perfect)

The inflections of the strong verb are as follows:

Table 32.9. The Pual *Qatal* (Perfect) of קטל

	Singular	Plural
3m	קֻטַּל	קֻטְּלוּ
3f	קֻטְּלָה	
2m	קֻטַּלְתָּ	קֻטַּלְתֶּם
2f	קֻטַּלְתְּ	קֻטַּלְתֶּן
1c	קֻטַּלְתִּי	קֻטַּלְנוּ

a. The II-Guttural

In the Pual *qatal*, the II-guttural (or II-ר) rejects the doubling that is characteristic of the Pual stem. There are two kinds of Pual II-guttural inflections:

(1) Those that employ virtual doubling. The initial Qibbuts is unchanged. From רחם, "be pitied" in the Pual, we have רֻחֲמָה (3fs) and רֻחַמְתְּ (2fs).

(2) Those that employ compensatory lengthening. The initial Qibbuts becomes Holem. From גרש, "be driven out" in the Pual, we have גֹּרְשׁוּ (3cp).

b. The III-א

The quiescence of the א causes the *qatal* to have Qamets as its stem vowel rather than Pathach although, as usual, the stem vowel reduces when the verb has a vowel sufformative. From חבא, "be hidden" in the Pual, we have the 3cp חֻבְּאוּ, and from קרא, "be called" in the Pual, we have קֹרָא (3ms; note that this form is also II-ר).

c. The III-ה

The Pual *qatal* III-ה also has all characteristics that any *qatal* III-ה has.

(1) The 3ms ends in ָה.

(2) The 3fs ends in תָה.

(3) Consonant endings cause the final ה to become י as a pointed vowel letter.

(4) Vowel endings cause the final ה to drop off.

From נכה, "be struck" in the Pual, therefore, we have the forms נֻכְּתָה (3fs) and נֻכּוּ (3cp). Similarly, from צוה, "be commanded" in the Pual, we have צֻוֵּיתִי (1cs).

2. The Pual Yiqtol (Imperfect)

The Pual *yiqtol*, like the Piel, has a Shewa under the preformative.

Table 32.10. The Pual *Yiqtol* (Imperfect) of קטל

	Singular	Plural
3m	יְקֻטַּל	יְקֻטְּלוּ
3f	תְּקֻטַּל	תְּקֻטַּלְנָה
2m	תְּקֻטַּל	תְּקֻטְּלוּ
2f	תְּקֻטְּלִי	תְּקֻטַּלְנָה
1c	אֲקֻטַּל	נְקֻטַּל

a. The II-Guttural

In the Pual *yiqtol*, the II-guttural (or II-ר) rejects the doubling of the middle radical.

(1) Those with middle ה or ח use virtual doubling. The initial Qibbuts is unchanged. From נחם, "be comforted" in the Pual, we have תְּנֻחֲמוּ (2mp). From רחם, "be pitied" in the Pual, we have יְרֻחַם (3ms).

(2) Those with middle א, ע, or ר use compensatory lengthening. The initial Qibbuts becomes Holem. From בְרך, "be blessed," we have יְבֹרַךְ (3ms) and תְּבֹרַךְ (3fs).

b. The III-א

The א causes the stem vowel Pathach to lengthen to Qamets. Thus we see יְדֻכָּא (*yiqtol* 3ms) from the root דכא, "be crushed" in the Pual.

c. The III-ה

The Pual *yiqtol* III-ה has the characteristics that all *yiqtol* III-ה verbs have. For example, if there is no inflectional ending, the word ends in ֶה. From כסה, "be covered" in the Pual, we have יְכֻסֶּה (3ms). From צוה, "be commanded" in the Pual, we have the 3ms form יְצֻוֶּה.

3. The Pual Volitives

There are no Pual volitives in the Hebrew Bible.

4. The Pual Conjoined Finite Verbs

a. The Pual Wayyiqtol

As is normal, the *wayyiqtol* adds וַ to a *yiqtol*, but the fact that the Pual *yiqtol* preformative has a Shewa under it often causes the Dagesh Forte to drop out of the preformative letter. Thus, from the root בקש, we see the 3ms וַיְבֻקַּשׁ, "and he was investigated" (with no Dagesh Forte in the י). The III-ה verb has the normal characteristics of that root. This gives us וַיְכֻלּוּ, "and they were finished" (from כלה).

b. The Pual Weqatal and Weyiqtol

These add the conjunction to the normal form of the *qatal* or *yiqtol*, as in וְכֻפַּר (3ms *weqatal* from כפר) and וּתְבֻקְשִׁי (2fs *weyiqtol* from בקש).

5. The Pual Infinitives

There is one Pual infinitive construct in the Hebrew Bible (עֻנּוֹת, from ענה, "be afflicted"). Note that it is III-ה. There is also one Pual infinitive absolute in the Hebrew Bible (גֻּנֹּב, from גנב, "stolen").

6. The Pual Participle

The Pual participle has the normal u-class followed by a-class vowel pattern, but like the Piel participle, the Pual participle has a preformative מְ. Along with the following inflections, an alternative fs participle is מְקֻטָּלָה.

Table 32.11. The Pual Participle of קטל

	Singular	Plural
Masculine	מְקֻטָּל	מְקֻטָּלִים
Feminine	מְקֻטֶּלֶת	מְקֻטָּלוֹת

The Pual participle has the normal patterns with weak verbs. For example, we see compensatory lengthening with ברך in the form מְבֹרָךְ, "blessed" (ms). The III-ה root drops the ה if there is an ending that starts with a vowel, as in מְכֻסּוֹת, "covered" (fp, from כסה). The III-guttural fs participle of צרע ("leprous") is מְצֹרַעַת, showing preference for a-class vowels.

7. Summary of the Pual Principal Parts

Puals are rather rare and, because of their distinctive pattern, are easy to recognize even in most weak roots. It is, however, useful to know the principal parts of the Pual III-ה verb and II-guttural or ר verb. If you master the following principal parts you should have no difficulty with Pual verbs.

Table 32.12. The Pual in Weak Roots

	Gloss	Qatal	Yiqtol	Inf. Con.	Participle
קטל		קֻטַּל	יְקֻטַּל	קֻטַּל	מְקֻטָּל
כסה	be covered	כֻּסָּה	יְכֻסֶּה	כֻּסּוֹת	מְכֻסֶּה
ברך	be blessed	בֹּרַךְ	יְבֹרַךְ	בֹּרַךְ	מְבֹרָךְ

C. Vocabulary

1. Core Vocabulary

a. Verbs

כפר   Piel: כִּפֶּר cover, appease, (by extension) make atonement

נחם   Niphal: נָחַם/נִחַם regret, be sorry

        Piel: נִחַם comfort

קבר   Qal: קָבַר bury

        Niphal: *נִקְבַּר; יִקָּבֵר (yiqtol 3ms) be buried

קטר   Piel: *קִטֵּר; קִטְּרוּ (qatal 3cp) send (an offering) up in smoke

        Hiphil: הִקְטִיר cause (a sacrifice) to go up in smoke

שבר   Qal: שָׁבַר shatter, smash, break (of things broken in a single action—e.g., sticks, pottery, bones)

        Niphal: נִשְׁבַּר be smashed, be broken, be destroyed

        Piel: שִׁבֵּר smash (into fragments) (of things not easily broken in a single action—e.g., stone, metal, trees)

שלם   Piel: שִׁלֵּם make complete, make restitution

b. Other Words

בְּכוֹר   firstborn M |בְּכֹר|

חֻקָּה   statute, regulation F |חֻקַּת|

נָהָר	river, stream M |נְהַר|
נַחַל	river valley, wadi, stream, trench M |נַחַל|
רְבִיעִי	fourth, one-fourth F |רְבִיעִית|
שְׁבִיעִי	seventh F

2. Proper Names

אֱמֹרִי	Amorite(s)
גִּרְגָּשִׁי	Girgashite
חֵת	Heth
חִתִּי	Hittite
יְבוּסִי	Jebusite
יִשְׁמָעֵאל	Ishmael
פְּרִזִּי	Perizzite
פְּרָת	Euphrates
קַדְמֹנִי	Kadmonite
קֵינִי	Kenite
קְנִזִּי	Kenizzite
רְפָאִים	Rephaim

3. Reading Vocabulary

גֶּזֶר	piece
הֵנָּה	here
לַפִּיד	torch, lightning
עֲלָטָה	darkness
עָשָׁן	smoke
שֵׂיבָה	gray hair, old age
שָׁלֵם	complete, untouched, whole
תַּנּוּר	oven, furnace

D. Reading—Genesis 15:15–21

15 וְאַתָּ֛ה תָּב֥וֹא אֶל־אֲבֹתֶ֖יךָ בְּשָׁל֑וֹם תִּקָּבֵ֖ר בְּשֵׂיבָ֥ה טוֹבָֽה

16 וְד֥וֹר רְבִיעִ֖י יָשׁ֣וּבוּ הֵ֑נָּה כִּ֧י לֹא־שָׁלֵ֛ם עֲוֺ֥ן הָאֱמֹרִ֖י עַד־הֵֽנָּה¹

17 וַיְהִ֤י הַשֶּׁ֙מֶשׁ֙ בָּ֔אָה וַעֲלָטָ֖ה הָיָ֑ה וְהִנֵּ֨ה תַנּ֤וּר עָשָׁן֙ וְלַפִּ֣יד אֵ֔שׁ אֲשֶׁ֣ר עָבַ֔ר בֵּ֖ין הַגְּזָרִ֥ים הָאֵֽלֶּה

18 בַּיּ֣וֹם הַה֗וּא כָּרַ֧ת יְהֹוָ֛ה אֶת־אַבְרָ֖ם בְּרִ֣ית לֵאמֹ֑ר לְזַרְעֲךָ֗ נָתַ֙תִּי֙ אֶת־הָאָ֣רֶץ הַזֹּ֔את מִנְּהַ֣ר מִצְרַ֔יִם עַד־הַנָּהָ֥ר הַגָּדֹ֖ל נְהַר־פְּרָֽת

19 אֶת־הַקֵּינִ֥י וְאֶת־הַקְּנִזִּ֖י וְאֵ֥ת הַקַּדְמֹנִֽי

20 וְאֶת־הַחִתִּ֥י וְאֶת־הַפְּרִזִּ֖י וְאֶת־הָרְפָאִֽים

21 וְאֶת־הָֽאֱמֹרִי֙ וְאֶת־הַֽכְּנַעֲנִ֔י וְאֶת־הַגִּרְגָּשִׁ֖י וְאֶת־הַיְבוּסִֽי ס

---

1.   עַד־הֵנָּה = "as far as here" (of place) or "until now" (of time).

CHAPTER 33
THE HIPHIL AND HOPHAL

A. The Hiphil Pattern

The Hiphil is characterized first of all by the preformative letter ה attached to the root. It is thus often called the H stem. Like the Piel, it has one vowel pattern for the *qatal* and another for all other inflections.

Table 33.1. The Basic Pattern of the Hiphil

Patterns	Qatal		All Other Inflections		
	3rd person	2nd and 1st person	Hiphil preformative ה will be displaced by *yiqtol* or participle preformative		
	"i-i" pattern	*"i-a" pattern*	*"a-i" pattern*		
	⬜⬜⬜Ⓟ i i	⬜⬜⬜Ⓟ a i	⬜⬜⬜Ⓟ i a		
Principal Parts	הִקְטִיל	הִקְטַלְתָּ	*Yiqtol* יַקְטִיל	*Inf. Con.* הַקְטִיל	*Participle* מַקְטִיל
Preformative Letter	ה (will be displaced by preformative in *yiqtol* and participle)				

1. The Hiphil Qatal *(Perfect)*

The basic patterns of the Hiphil *qatal* are הִקְטִיל (third person) and הִקְטַלְתָּ (second and first person).

Table 33.2. The Hiphil *Qatal* (Perfect) of קטל

	Singular	Plural
3m	הִקְטִיל	הִקְטִילוּ
3f	הִקְטִילָה	
2m	הִקְטַלְתָּ	הִקְטַלְתֶּם
2f	הִקְטַלְתְּ	הִקְטַלְתֶּן
1c	הִקְטַלְתִּי	הִקְטַלְנוּ

Note that it has:

(1) A preformative ה (with i-class vowel)

(2) Hireq-Yod as its stem vowel (i-class) in the third person

(3) Pathach as its stem vowel (a-class) in the second and first person.

a. The I-נ

As is typical, the I-נ will assimilate to the following letter. Thus, from נגד, "tell" in the Hiphil, we get הִגִּיד (3ms) and הִגַּדְתָּ (2ms).

b. I-Guttural

Under the influence of the I-guttural, the i-class vowel with the preformative ה is Seghol in-instead of Hireq; the guttural has Hateph Seghol instead of a Shewa. Thus we see from עמד the form הֶעֱמִיד, "he set up." We also see forms such as הֶעֱשַׁרְתִּי, "I have enriched" (a 1cs from עשׁר).

c. The III-ח/ע

This root pattern has a furtive Pathach in the 3ms *qatal*, as in הִשְׁמִיעַ, "he announced" (from שׁמע). Otherwise, it is like the strong verb.

d. The III-ה

The III-ה root in the Hiphil *qatal* has all the normal qualities of a III-ה. Thus we see הִשְׁקְתָה, "she gave a drink" (from שׁקה), and הִרְבֵּיתִי, "I multiplied" (from רבה). The double weak root נכה gives us הִכֵּיתִי, "I struck down."

Table 33.3. The Hiphil *Qatal* (Perfect) of נכה

	Singular	Plural
3m	הִכָּה	הִכּוּ
3f	(not extant)	
2m	הִכִּיתָ	הִכִּיתֶם
2f	(not extant)	(not extant)
1c	הִכֵּיתִי	(not extant)

e. The Original I-ו

The original I-ו of roots such as ירד, "take down" in the Hiphil, reappears as Holem-Waw in the *qatal*. Thus we see forms such as הוֹרִיד (3ms), הוֹרַדְתָּ (2ms), and הוֹרִידוּ (3cp). Note that the stem vowel is the same as in the strong verb.

f. The True I-י

From the root יטב, "treat well," we see the Hiphil *qatals* הֵיטִיב (3ms), הֵיטִיבוּ (3cp), and הֵיטַבְתָּ (2ms). The Tsere-Yod with the preformative ה will not change.

g. The Hollow

These roots have a complex although easy-to-recognize form in the Hiphil *qatal*. The basic pattern is like הֵשִׁיב (the 3ms from שׁוּב), but note the following:

(1) The preformative ה has Tsere as its vowel if it is pretonic (only in third person forms); otherwise it reduces to Hateph Pathach or Hateph Seghol.

(2) The stem vowel is Hireq-Yod.

(3) If there is a consonant ending, a linking vowel Holem-Waw stands between the root and the ending (e.g., the 2ms הֲשִׁיבֹוֹת, from שׁוּב). This is also called an "anaptyptic vowel."

(4) Frequently, one or both of the pointed vowel letters is written defectively.

Using the roots קוּם, "raise up" in the Hiphil, and שׁוּב, "bring back" in the Hiphil, we see forms such as the following:

(1) From קוּם: הֵקִים (3ms), הֲקִמֹתִי (1cs; note defective writing), and הֵקִימוּ (3cp);

(2) From שׁוּב: הֵשִׁיב (3ms), הֵשִׁיבוּ (3cp), הֲשִׁיבֹוֹת (2ms), and הֲשֵׁבֹתֶם (2mp; note defective writing).

h. The Geminate

Geminates are also somewhat complex in their formation.

(1) The preformative ה has Tsere as its vowel if it is pretonic (only in third person forms); otherwise the vowel reduces to Hateph Pathach.

(2) The stem vowel is Tsere in the 3ms, Pathach in the 3mp, and otherwise is generally Hireq.

(3) If there is a personal sufformative that begins with a consonant, a linking vowel Holem-Waw stands between the root and the ending.

(4) Unless there is no inflectional ending (i.e., the 3ms), the geminate letter will be written with Daghesh Forte.

Using the roots סבב, "turn (something)" in the Hiphil, and שמם, "obliterate (something)" in the Hiphil, we see forms such as the following:

(1) From סבב: הֵסֵב (3ms), הֲסִבֹּתָ (2ms), and הֵסֵבּוּ (3cp).

(2) From שמם: הֵשַׁמּוּ (3cp) and הֲשִׁמֹּוֹת (2ms).

i. The III-א

The III-א root in the Hiphil as elsewhere is distinguished by the quiescence of the א, but a simple III-א root is rare in the Hiphil *qatal*. Instead, doubly-weak roots with III-א are much more common. In particular, we regularly see forms from בוֹא, "bring" in the Hiphil, and יצא, "bring out" in the Hiphil. Because of the quiescent א, the stem vowel remains long. With these roots, we see forms such as the following:

(1) From בוֹא: הֵבִיא (3ms), הֵבֵאתָ (2ms), הֵבֵאתִי (1cs), and הֵבִיאוּ (3cp).

(2) From יצא: הוֹצִיא (3ms), הוֹצִיאוּ (3cp), and הוֹצֵאתָ (2ms).

2. The Hiphil Yiqtol *(Imperfect)*

The basic pattern is יַקְטִיל. The strong Hiphil *yiqtol* has the following characteristics:

(1) A *yiqtol* preformative with Pathach (the *yiqtol* preformative has replaced the ה of the Hiphil);

(2) The pointed vowel letter Hireq-Yod as its stem vowel in all forms except the 3fp and 2fp;

(3) Tsere as its stem vowel in the 3fp and 2fp.

Table 33.4. The Hiphil *Yiqtol* (Imperfect) of קטל

	Singular	*Plural*
3m	יַקְטִיל	יַקְטִ֫ילוּ
3f	תַּקְטִיל	תַּקְטֵ֫לְנָה
2m	תַּקְטִיל	תַּקְטִ֫ילוּ
2f	תַּקְטִ֫ילִי	תַּקְטֵ֫לְנָה
1c	אַקְטִיל	נַקְטִיל

a. The I-נ

As usual, the I-נ will assimilate to the following letter. Thus, from נגד, "tell" in the Hiphil, we get אַגִּיד (1cs), יַגִּיד (3ms), and יַגִּ֫ידוּ (3mp).

b. The I-Guttural

The preformative vowel of the Hiphil *yiqtol* is already Pathach; the guttural has no significant effect other than taking Hateph Pathach instead of a Shewa. Thus we see from עמד the form יַעֲמִיד, "he will set up." We also see forms such as אַעֲבִיר, "I will take across" (from עבר).

c. The III-ח/ע

This root pattern has a furtive Pathach when there is no *yiqtol* inflectional ending, as in יַשְׁמִיעַ, "he will announce" (from שמע). Otherwise, it is like the strong verb.

d. The III-ה

The III-ה root in the Hiphil *yiqtol* has all the normal qualities of a III-ה, such as an ending הֶ◌ when there is no sufformative and the dropping of the ה when there is a vowel sufformative. Thus we see from שקה forms such as נַשְׁקֶה, "we will give a drink"; יַשְׁקוּ, "they (3mp) will give a drink"; and תַּשְׁקֶה, "you (2ms) will give a drink." The doubly-weak root נכה gives us יַכֶּה, "he will strike down."

e. The Original I-ו

As in the Hiphil *qatal*, the original I-ו of roots such as ירד, "take down" in the Hiphil, reappears as Holem-Waw in the *yiqtol*. Thus we see forms such as אוֹרִיד (1cs) and יוֹרִ֫ידוּ (3mp). We also see defective writing, such as יְרִדוּ. The fact that we have a Holem-Waw here where normally there is an a-class vowel may seem surprising, but recall that an a-class vowel with ו can become Holem-Waw, as when מָוֶת loses its accent (as in the construct) and becomes מוֹת. Thus, something like *yawrîdû* became *yōrîdû* (יֹרִדוּ).

f. The True I-י

From the root יטב, "treat well," we see the Hiphil *yiqtol* verbs יֵיטִיב (3ms), תֵּיטִ֫יבוּ (2mp), and תֵּיטִ֫יבִי (2fs). The Tsere-Yod in the preformative will not change.

g. The Hollow

As with the Hiphil *qatal*, these roots have an easy-to-recognize pattern in the Hiphil *yiqtol*. The basic pattern is יָשִׁיב. Observe the following.

(1) The *yiqtol* preformative has Qamets as its vowel. This long a-class vowel (יָשִׁיב in contrast to the Pathach in יַקְטִיל) is accounted for by the fact that in יָשִׁיב it is in an open pretonic rather than a closed, unaccented syllable.

(2) The stem vowel is Hireq-Yod, as is normal for the Hiphil *yiqtol*.

From קוּם, "raise up" in the Hiphil, we have אָקִים (1cs) and תְּקִימֶנָה (3fp). We occasionally see a feminine plural like תְּהִימֶנָה, "they will make noise" (from הוּם). From רוּם, "hold up" in the Hiphil, we see forms such as יָרִים (3ms).

h. The Geminate

Geminates in the Hiphil *yiqtol* are (like most geminates) rather confusing. There are two basic patterns: יָחֵל (quasi-hollow from חלל) and יָשִׁים (quasi-I-נ from שׁמם; this form will have the Daghesh Forte in the first radical).

(1) The *yiqtol* preformative has Qamets or Pathach as its vowel.

(2) The stem vowel is Tsere (if the preformative has Qamets) or Hireq-Yod (if the preformative has Pathach).

(3) With an inflectional ending, the geminate letter has a Daghesh Forte.

From the root חלל, "begin" in the Hiphil, we see the pattern of the "quasi-hollow" form. Examples include תָּחֵל (2ms), אָחֵל (1cs), and תָּחֵלּוּ (2mp). A similar example is תָּפֵר, "you (ms) will annul" (from פרר). The root שׁמם, "obliterate (something)" in the Hiphil, illustrates the "quasi-I-נ" pattern. An example is יָשִׁים (3ms).

i. The III-א

Again, the III-א root in the Hiphil has the quiescence of the א, but examples of a simple III-א root are sparse in the Hiphil *yiqtol*. Using the doubly-weak forms from the hollow בוא, "bring" in the Hiphil, and the original I-ו root יצא, "bring out" in the Hiphil, we see the following examples:

(1) From בוא: תָּבִיא (2ms) and יָבִיאוּ (3mp).

(2) From יצא: יוֹצִיא (3ms), תּוֹצִיא (3fs), אוֹצִיא (1cs), and תּוֹצִיאוּ (2mp).

3. The Hiphil Volitives

a. The Hiphil Cohortative

The Hiphil cohortative adds paragogic ה to the first person *yiqtol* forms. Examples of cohortatives include נַשְׁלִיכָה, "let us throw" (from שׁלך); נַשְׁכִּימָה, "let us rise early" (from שׁכם); אוֹדִיעָה, "let me make known" (from ידע); אָשִׁיבָה, "let me bring back" (from שׁוב); אַגִּידָה, "let me tell" (from נגד); and אוֹצִיאָה, "let me bring out" (from יצא).

b. The Hiphil Imperative

The Hiphil imperative is again essentially a second person *yiqtol* with the ת preformative dropped off. When this happens, the ה of the Hiphil stem reappears. Therefore, in effect, the imperative replaces the *yiqtol* תַ preformative with הַ. Note that the masculine singular, however, has an apocopated form with Tsere instead of the pointed vowel letter (contrast the *yiqtol* 2ms תַּקְטִיל).

Table 33.5. The Hiphil Imperative of קטל

	Singular	Plural
Masculine	הַקְטֵל	הַקְטִילוּ
Feminine	הַקְטִילִי	הַקְטֵלְנָה

Because the imperative form is essentially the *yiqtol* with the preformative removed, weak patterns are very similar to their strong counterparts in the *yiqtol*.

i. The I-נ

As is normal, the I-נ will assimilate to the following letter. Thus, from נגד, "tell" in the Hiphil, we get הַגֵּד (ms), הַגִּידָה (ms with paragogic ה), הַגִּידוּ (mp), and הַגִּידִי (fs).

ii. The I-Guttural

The guttural has no significant effect other than taking Hateph Pathach instead of a Shewa. Thus, we see from עמד the form הַעֲמֵד (ms).

iii. The III-ע/ח

This root has a furtive Pathach when there is no inflectional ending (i.e., in the ms). Otherwise, it is like the strong verb. From שמע, we get הַשְׁמִיעִי (fs) and הַשְׁמִיעוּ (mp).

iv. The III-ה

The III-ה root in the Hiphil imperative has all the normal qualities of a III-ה. Thus we see from שקה the ms form הַשְׁקֵה. Other forms are הַשְׁקִי (fs) and הַשְׁקוּ (mp). Observe that the fs or mp vowel personal ending has caused the ה to drop off, as is normal.

v. The Original I-ו

As in the Hiphil *yiqtol*, the original I-ו of roots such as ירד, "take down" in the Hiphil, reappears as Holem-Waw in the imperative. Thus we see the ms form הוֹרֵד and the mp form הוֹרִידוּ.

vi. The True I-י

From the root יטב, "treat well," we see the Hiphil imperatives הֵיטִיבָה (ms with paragogic ה) and הֵיטִיבוּ (mp).

vii. The Hollow

As with the Hiphil *yiqtol*, these roots have Qamets with the preformative in the Hiphil imperative. Observe the following.

(1) The imperative preformative ה has Qamets as its vowel (pretonic lengthening).

(2) The stem vowel is Tsere or Hireq-Yod, as is normal for the Hiphil.

From קום, "raise up" in the Hiphil, we have הָקֵם (ms) and הָקִימוּ (mp).

viii. The Geminate

Geminates in the Hiphil imperative follow the "quasi-hollow" verb pattern.

(1) The imperative preformative has Qamets as its vowel but can reduce.

(2) The stem vowel is Tsere, but it can shorten.

(3) If there is an inflectional ending or suffix, the geminate letter will be written with Daghesh Forte.

From the root חלל, "begin" in the Hiphil, we see הָחֵל (ms). The root סבב, "make (something) go around" in the Hiphil, gives us הָסֵב (ms). From שׁמם, "obliterate (something)" in the Hiphil, we get הָשַׁמּוּ (mp).

ix. The III-א

The III-א root in the Hiphil has the quiescence of the א, but examples of a simple III-א root are few in the Hiphil imperative. Much more common is the hollow בוא, "bring" in the Hiphil, which gives us הָבִיאָה (ms with paragogic ה) and הָבִיאוּ (mp).

c. The Hiphil Jussive

We have already seen many examples of "apocopation" with Hebrew verbs in the 3ms, 3fs, and 2ms.

(1) For example, the normal Qal *wayyiqtol* pattern is וַיִּקְטֹל, a pattern that shows no apocopation. But in the hollow, the original I-ו, and the III-ה roots, the Qal *wayyiqtol* has the apocopated or shortened form. An example is וַיָּשָׁב in contrast to the Qal *yiqtol* יָשׁוּב.

(2) We also see apocopation in the Qal jussives of these roots, as in the Qal jussive 3ms יָשֹׁב (from שׁוּב; again contrast to the Qal *yiqtol* יָשׁוּב).

It turns out that in the Hiphil jussive we have apocopation not just in a few but in *all* roots.

Table 33.6. Hiphil Jussive Patterns

Root Type	Root	Jussive	Yiqtol
Strong	שׁלך	יַשְׁלֵךְ	יַשְׁלִיךְ
I-Guttural	חזק	יַחֲזֵק	יַחֲזִיק
II-Guttural or ר	כרת	יַכְרֵת	יַכְרִית
III-Guttural	שׁמע	תַּשְׁמַע	תַּשְׁמִיעַ
III-ה	רבה	יֶרֶב	יַרְבֶּה
I-נ	נגד	יַגֵּד	יַגִּיד
Original I-ו	ירד	יוֹרֵד	יוֹרִיד
Hollow	קוּם	יָקֵם	יָקִים

You will see some Hiphil jussives without apocopation, especially when a pronoun suffix is present. The important point here is that where apocopation in the Qal is limited to the אמר type, III-ה, hollow, original I-ו, and geminate roots, a Hiphil from any kind of root, including the strong root, can apocopate.

4. The Hiphil Conjoined Finite Verbs

a. The Hiphil Wayyiqtol

The *wayyiqtol* preformative וֹ with Daghesh Forte attaches to the shortened or apocopated form of the *yiqtol*. Thus, all the apocopated forms for the Hiphil jussive (see above) will also appear in the Hiphil *wayyiqtol* in the 3ms, 3fs, and 2ms.

(1) In most roots, this is not especially troubling because the apocopated form is not radically different from the regular form.

(2) In the III-ה, however, the changes can be dramatic. For example, we see וַיַּשְׁקְ ("and he gave a drink," from שקה), where the *yiqtol* is יַשְׁקֶה.

(3) The doubly-weak root נכה gives us וַיַּךְ, "and he struck," in the Hiphil *wayyiqtol* 3ms; the נ has assimilated and the III-ה has dropped off due to apocopation.

(4) Also, the hollow שׁוּב gives us וַיָּשֶׁב, "and he brought back"; the Hiphil *yiqtol* is יָשִׁיב.

Apocopation does not always occur. It rarely occurs, for example, if there is a pronoun suffix.

b. The Hiphil Weqatal

This is again the simple conjunction on the form of the *qatal*. Usually in the 2ms and 1cs the ultima has the accent, as in וַהֲקִמֹתִי, "and I will establish" (from קוּם).

c. The Hiphil Weyiqtol

The conjunction in the *weyiqtol* is more likely to be attached to a cohortative or jussive form than to a simple *yiqtol*, and thus we see many examples of the apocopated form with the Hiphil *weyiqtol*. A good example of this is וְיַפְקֵד, "that he should appoint" (from פקד).

5. The Hiphil Infinitives

a. The Hiphil Infinitive Construct

The Hiphil infinitive construct, like all forms except the *qatal*, follows the basic pattern הַקְטִיל. Its forms in weak verbs are predictable and very similar to the weak verb *yiqtol* patterns described above.

(1) The III-guttural שמע, for example, has furtive Pathach (לְהַשְׁמִיעַ, here with preposition לְ).

(2) The original I-ו verb ירד has וֹ as its preformative vowel (לְהוֹרִיד, with preposition לְ).

(3) The hollow קוּם has the Qamets with the preformative (הָקִים).

(4) The III-ה infinitive construct from שקה has the normal ending וֹת (לְהַשְׁקוֹת, with preposition לְ).

(5) The geminate חלל has the "quasi-hollow" pattern (מֵהָחֵל, with preposition מִן).

b. The Hiphil Infinitive Absolute

The infinitive absolute (הַקְטֵל) looks like the infinitive construct except that it has Tsere as its stem vowel rather than Hireq-Yod.

6. The Hiphil Participle

The strong Hiphil participle has the pattern מַקְטִיל.

Table 33.7. The Hiphil Participle of קטל

	Singular	Plural
Masculine	מַקְטִיל	מַקְטִילִים
Feminine	מַקְטֶלֶת	מַקְטִילוֹת

Weak roots all have the participle preformative מ, but its vowel is not always Pathach. We occasionally see the fs participle with the pattern מַקְטִילָה.

a. The I-נ

As expected, the I-נ will assimilate to the following letter. Thus, from נגד, "tell" in Hiphil, we get מַגִּיד (ms).

b. The I-Guttural

The preformative vowel of the Hiphil participle is already Pathach; the guttural has no significant effect other than taking Hateph Pathach instead of a Shewa. Thus we see from עמד the form מַעֲמִיד (ms).

c. The III-ח/ע

This root takes a furtive Pathach when there is no participle ending (i.e., in the ms), as in מַשְׁמִיעַ, "he will announce" (from שמע). Otherwise, it is like the strong verb.

d. The III-ה

The III-ה root in the Hiphil participle has all the normal qualities of a III-ה. Thus, we see from שקה, "give water," the ms participle מַשְׁקֶה. The root רבה gives us the fs participle מַרְבָּה, "multiplying." (Remember that the III-ה feminine participle normally takes the הָ ending.)

e. The Original I-ו

As in the Hiphil *qatal* and *yiqtol*, the original I-ו of roots such as ירד, "take down" in the Hiphil, reappears as Holem-Waw in the participle (e.g., מוֹרִיד).

f. The True I-י

From the root יטב, "treat well," we see the Hiphil participles מֵיטִיב (ms) and מֵיטִיבִים (mp).

g. The Hollow

As with the Hiphil *qatal*, these roots have Tsere with the preformative in the Hiphil participle, but it can reduce to Shewa.

(1) The participle preformative מ has Tsere as its vowel unless it reduces due to accent position.

(2) The stem vowel is Hireq-Yod, as is normal for the Hiphil.

From קוּם ("raise up" in the Hiphil), we have מֵקִים (ms). From שׁוּב, "bring back" in the Hiphil, we see forms such as מֵשִׁיב (ms) and מְשִׁיבִים (mp).

h. The Geminate

Geminates in the Hiphil participle follow the pattern of מֵסֵב (from סבב), but both vowels can shorten or reduce due to accent shift.

(1) The participle preformative has Tsere as its vowel, but it can reduce.

(2) The stem vowel is Tsere, but it can shorten to Hireq.

(3) If there is a personal ending / suffix, the geminate letter takes a Daghesh Forte.

From the root חלל, "begin" in the Hiphil, we see מֵחֵל (ms). The root סבב, "surround (something)" in the Hiphil, gives us מֵסֵב (ms) and מְסִבַּי (mp with 1cs suffix).

i. The III-א

Again, the III-א root in the Hiphil has the quiescence of the א, but examples of a simple III-א root are sparse in the Hiphil participle. From מצא, "cause to encounter" in the Hiphil, we have the example of מַמְצִיא (ms). Much more common is the hollow בוא, "bring" in the Hiphil, which gives us מֵבִיא (ms). The original I-י root יצא, "bring out" in the Hiphil, provides מוֹצִיא (ms).

7. Vowels in the Hiphil Hollow and Original I-ו Verbs

We have seen the reasons for the vowels of the Niphal *qatal* and participle of the hollow and original I-ו verbs. Changes in the Hiphil are similar.

8. Summary of the Hiphil Principal Parts

Table 33.8. The Hiphil Stem in Weak Roots

	Gloss	*Qatal*	*Yiqtol*	*Inf. Con.*	*Participle*
קטל		הִקְטִיל	יַקְטִיל	הַקְטִיל	מַקְטִיל
נפל	make fall	הִפִּיל	יַפִּיל	הַפִּיל	מַפִּיל
ישב	make dwell	הוֹשִׁיב	יוֹשִׁיב	הוֹשִׁיב	מוֹשִׁיב
שׁוּב	bring back	הֵשִׁיב	יָשִׁיב	הָשִׁיב	מֵשִׁיב
עבד	enslave	הֶעֱבִיד	יַעֲבִיד	הַעֲבִיד	מַעֲבִיד
רבה	make numerous	הִרְבָּה	יַרְבֶּה	הַרְבּוֹת	מַרְבֶּה

(1) The Hiphil *qatal* originally had an a-class vowel in its preformative, but it usually became an i-class vowel through attenuation.

(2) Through the rule that *a+w* in an unaccented syllable becomes *ō*, the original I-ו Hiphil *qatal* of ירד is הוֹרִיד; *hawrîd* became *hôrîd*. All forms of the original I-ו Hiphil have Holem-Waw (Holem if defective) in the preformative.

(3) The a-class vowel in the hollow *yiqtol* and infinitive (יָקִים and הָקִים) is open pretonic and thus lengthens to Qamets.

(4) The formation of the hollow *qatal* and participle, הֵקִים and מֵקִים, with Tsere in the preformatives, may be due to analogy to the true I-י verb יטב, which has the Hiphil *qatal* הֵיטִיב and participle מֵיטִיב.

B. The Hophal Pattern

The Hophal is the passive of the Hiphil. It is quite simple in that it has a single vowel pattern. Hophal verbs typically have the pattern of a u-class vowel in the preformative followed by an a-class (or reduced) stem vowel.

Table 33.9. The Basic Pattern of the Hophal

Pattern	"u-a" pattern ◻◻◻Ⓟ a u			
Principal Parts	Qatal הָקְטַל	Yiqtol יָקְטַל	Inf. Con. הָקְטַל	Participle מָקְטָל
Preformative Letter	ה (will be displaced by preformative in *yiqtol* and participle)			

1. The Hophal Qatal (Perfect) and Weqatal

Table 33.10. The Hophal *Qatal* (Perfect) of קטל

	Singular	Plural
3m	הָקְטַל	הָקְטְלוּ
3f	הָקְטְלָה	
2m	הָקְטַֽלְתָּ	הָקְטַלְתֶּם
2f	הָקְטַלְתְּ	הָקְטַלְתֶּן
1c	הָקְטַֽלְתִּי	הָקְטַֽלְנוּ

The above paradigm is somewhat hypothetical; actual Hophal *qatals* of this pattern are fairly rare. Sometimes the u-class vowel is Qibbuts rather than Qamets Hatuph, as in הֻשְׁלְכוּ, "they have been cast" (from שׁלך).

(1) The doubly-weak root נכה gives us הֻכֵּיתִי, "I was wounded." The first נ has assimilated, and the third ה has become a pointed vowel letter י because of the suffix.

(2) Roots with gutturals do not pose a particular problem in the Hophal.

(3) Three weak roots tend to have Shureq (וּ) as the u-class vowel throughout the Hophal. These are original I-וֹ, hollow, and geminate roots.

2. The Hophal Yiqtol *(Imperfect) and* Weyiqtol

An example of a strong root Hophal *yiqtol* is תֻּקְטַר, "it (fs) shall be burned up" (קטר).

Table 33.11. The Hophal *Yiqtol* (Imperfect) of קטל

	Singular	*Plural*
3m	יָקְטַל	יָקְטְלוּ
3f	תָּקְטַל	תֻּקְטַלְנָה
2m	תָּקְטַל	תָּקְטְלוּ
2f	תָּקְטְלִי	תֻּקְטַלְנָה
1c	אָקְטַל	נָקְטַל

The weak root Hophal *yiqtol* has the same traits as the *qatal*. For example, from the geminate סבב סבב we get יוּסַּב, "it gets driven about." Note that this form has the same peculiar mimicry of the I-נ that we see in the Qal geminate. The hollow מות is very common in the Hophal *yiqtol* as יוּמַת, "he shall be put to death."

Weyiqtols simply add וְ to their respective forms. Note that Hophal verbs with original I-וֹ, hollow, and geminate roots again have Shureq as the u-class vowel.

Table 33.12. Hophal Finite Verbs with Original I-וֹ, Hollow, and Geminate Roots

Root Type	Root	Example	Form	Meaning
Orig. I-וֹ	ירד	הוּרַד	Qatal	he was taken down
Orig. I-וֹ	ירד	וְהוּרַדְתָּ	Weqatal	and you (ms) will be brought down
Hollow	כון	וְהוּכַן	Weqatal	and it will be established
Hollow	מות	יוּמַת	Yiqtol	he shall be put to death
Geminate	חדד	הוּחַדָּה	Qatal	she [a sword] has been sharpened

3. The Hophal Volitives

There are two Hophal imperatives in the Hebrew Bible. In Jer 49:8 we have הָפְנוּ ("Turn away!"; mp from פנה), and in Ezek 32:19 we have הָשְׁכְּבָה ("Lie down!"; ms with paragogic ה from שׁכב). There are no Hophal cohortatives in the Hebrew Bible, and Hophal jussives are formally the same as *yiqtol* verbs (there are no shortened forms).

4. The Hophal Wayyiqtol

The *wayyiqtol* simply adds the characteristic וַ with Daghesh Forte to the Hophal *yiqtol* form. A very common Hophal *wayyiqtol* is וַיֻּגַּד, "and it was told" (from נגד). True to type, the first נ of this root has assimilated.

5. The Hophal Infinitives

a. The Hophal Infinitive Construct

The Hophal infinitive construct is very rare. From the root ילד, we get הוּלֶּדֶת, "be born." This root is original I-ו, and it has its characteristic pattern for the infinitive construct (like the Qal infinitive construct לֶדֶת). But we also see הוּסַד, "be founded" (from יסד).

b. The Hophal Infinitive Absolute

The Hophal infinitive absolute is even less common than the infinitive construct. It differs from the normal Hophal pattern in that instead of an a-class vowel it has Tsere as its stem vowel. An example is הֻגֵּד, "be told" (from נגד).

6. The Hophal Participle

Like the Hophal *qatal* and *yiqtol*, the Hophal participle has the u-class and a-class vowel pattern. Like the Hiphil, it has a מ preformative. Weak verbs tend to behave the same here as in the *qatal* and *yiqtol*. For example, from the root שׁוּב we have the ms Hophal participle מוּשָׁב, "returned," showing the Shureq for the u-class vowel. From נכה, we have the mp form מֻכִּים, "being beaten," showing normal I-נ and III-ה behavior. The fs form of this participle is מֻכָּה; as is always the case with feminine singular participles from III-ה roots, it has the ending הֶ.

Table 33.13. The Hophal Participle of קטל

	Singular	Plural
Masculine	מָקְטָל	מָקְטָלִים
Feminine	מָקְטֶלֶת	מָקְטָלוֹת

7. Summary of the Hophal Principal Parts

This chart shows that Qamets Hatuph, Shureq, or Qibbuts can fill the Hophal u-class slot.

Table 33.14. The Hophal in Weak Roots

	Gloss	Qatal	Yiqtol	Inf. Con.	Participle
קטל		הָקְטַל	יָקְטַל	הָקְטַל	מָקְטָל
ירד	be taken down	הוּרַד	יוּרַד	הוּרַד	מוּרָד
שׁוּב	be returned	הוּשַׁב	יוּשַׁב	הוּשַׁב	מוּשָׁב
נגד	be told	הֻגַּד	יֻגַּד	הֻגַּד	מֻגָּד

C. Vocabulary

1. Core Vocabulary

a. Verbs

בקע	Qal: בָּקַע split, breach
	Piel: בִּקַּע split, rip up
חוה	Hishtaphel: הִשְׁתַּחֲוָה bow down (always found with הִשְׁתּ־ prefix)
יתר	Niphal: נוֹתַר be left, remain
	Hiphil: הוֹתִיר leave over/behind, have left over
שאר	Niphal: נִשְׁאַר/נִשְׁאָר remain, be left, survive
	Hiphil: הִשְׁאִיר leave over, allow to survive, preserve
שכם	Hiphil: הִשְׁכִּים do (something) early (e.g., rise early, set out early)
שלך	Hiphil: הִשְׁלִיךְ throw, hurl, cast

b. Other Words

יַחַד; יַחְדָּו	uniting, community (Ⓜ noun); together, at the same time (adverb)
יֶתֶר	remainder, the rest, what is left behind Ⓜ
כִּסֵּא	throne, chair Ⓜ |כִּסֵּא|
פֹּה; פּוֹ; פּוֹא	here, at this place
רָחוֹק	far, distant, remote (adjective); distance (noun)
שְׁלִישִׁי	third, one-third

2. Proper Names

חֶבְרוֹן	Hebron
מוֹרִיָּה	Moriah
שְׁכֶם	Shechem

3. Reading Vocabulary

חבש	Qal: וַיַּחֲבֹשׁ (*wayyiqtol*) bind, wrap, saddle
נסה	Piel: נִסָּה test, attempt
יָחִיד	only, solitary
מַאֲכֶלֶת	knife

D. Reading—Genesis 22:1–6

1 וַיְהִי אַחַר הַדְּבָרִים הָאֵלֶּה וְהָאֱלֹהִים נִסָּה אֶת־אַבְרָהָם וַיֹּאמֶר אֵלָיו
   אַבְרָהָם וַיֹּאמֶר הִנֵּנִי

2 וַיֹּאמֶר קַח־נָא אֶת־בִּנְךָ אֶת־יְחִידְךָ אֲשֶׁר־אָהַבְתָּ אֶת־יִצְחָק וְלֶךְ־לְךָ
   אֶל־אֶרֶץ הַמֹּרִיָּה וְהַעֲלֵהוּ שָׁם לְעֹלָה עַל אַחַד הֶהָרִים אֲשֶׁר אֹמַר אֵלֶיךָ

3 וַיַּשְׁכֵּם אַבְרָהָם בַּבֹּקֶר וַיַּחֲבֹשׁ אֶת־חֲמֹרוֹ וַיִּקַּח אֶת־שְׁנֵי נְעָרָיו אִתּוֹ וְאֵת
   יִצְחָק בְּנוֹ וַיְבַקַּע עֲצֵי עֹלָה וַיָּקָם וַיֵּלֶךְ אֶל־הַמָּקוֹם אֲשֶׁר־אָמַר־לוֹ הָאֱלֹהִים

4 בַּיּוֹם הַשְּׁלִישִׁי וַיִּשָּׂא אַבְרָהָם אֶת־עֵינָיו וַיַּרְא אֶת־הַמָּקוֹם מֵרָחֹק

5 וַיֹּאמֶר אַבְרָהָם אֶל־נְעָרָיו שְׁבוּ־לָכֶם פֹּה עִם־הַחֲמוֹר וַאֲנִי וְהַנַּעַר נֵלְכָה
   עַד־כֹּה וְנִשְׁתַּחֲוֶה וְנָשׁוּבָה אֲלֵיכֶם

6 וַיִּקַּח אַבְרָהָם אֶת־עֲצֵי הָעֹלָה וַיָּשֶׂם עַל־יִצְחָק בְּנוֹ וַיִּקַּח בְּיָדוֹ אֶת־הָאֵשׁ
   וְאֶת־הַמַּאֲכֶלֶת וַיֵּלְכוּ שְׁנֵיהֶם יַחְדָּו

CHAPTER 34
THE HITHPAEL

A. The Hithpael Pattern

The Hithpael is the third of the doubled (D) stems in Hebrew (the other two are the Piel and Pual). In addition to doubling the middle radical, it also has a preformative הִת attached to the root. Thus it is sometimes called the HtD stem. The essential pattern for the Hithpael includes the following:

(1) preformative הִת

(2) a-class vowel under first radical

(3) doubled middle radical

(4) i-class vowel under middle radical (a-class in *qatal* second and first person)

Table 34.1. The Basic Pattern of the Hithpael

Pattern	"a-i" pattern ☐ · ☐ ⓟ i a				
Principal Parts	*Qatal* 3ms הִתְקַטֵּל	*Qatal* 2ms הִתְקַטַּ֫לְתָּ	*Yiqtol* יִתְקַטֵּל	Inf. Con. הִתְקַטֵּל	Participle מִתְקַטֵּל
Preformative	הִת (ה will be displaced by preformative of *yiqtol* or participle)				

B. The Hithpael *Qatal* (Perfect)

Take note of the reduced stem vowels (3fs and 3cp) and the a-class stem vowels (second and first person forms).

Table 34.2. The Hithpael *Qatal* (Perfect) of קטל

	Singular	Plural
3m	הִתְקַטֵּל	הִתְקַטְּלוּ
3f	הִתְקַטְּלָה	
2m	הִתְקַטַּ֫לְתָּ	הִתְקַטַּלְתֶּם
2f	הִתְקַטַּלְתְּ	הִתְקַטַּלְתֶּן
1c	הִתְקַטַּ֫לְתִּי	הִתְקַטַּ֫לְנוּ

C. The Hithpael *Yiqtol* (Imperfect)

As is normal, the *yiqtol* preformative displaces the ה of the Hithpael הת.

Table 34.3. The Hithpael *Yiqtol* (Imperfect) of קטל

	Singular	Plural
3m	יִתְקַטֵּל	יִתְקַטְּלוּ
3f	תִּתְקַטֵּל	תִּתְקַטֵּלְנָה
2m	תִּתְקַטֵּל	תִּתְקַטְּלוּ
2f	תִּתְקַטְּלִי	תִּתְקַטֵּלְנָה
1c	אֶתְקַטֵּל	נִתְקַטֵּל

D. The Hithpael Volitives

1. The Hithpael Cohortative

The paragogic ה on the cohortative often causes the stem vowel to reduce, as in נִתְחַכְּמָה, "let us behave wisely" (from חכם); אֶתְהַלְּכָה, "let me go about" (from הלך); and נִתְחַזְּקָה, "let us show ourselves to be strong" (from חזק).

2. The Hithpael Imperative

As usual, the imperative is basically a *yiqtol* with the preformative dropped off. This means that the ה of the הת preformative comes back.

Table 34.4. The Hithpael Imperative of קטל

	Singular	Plural
Masculine	הִתְקַטֵּל	הִתְקַטְּלוּ
Feminine	הִתְקַטְּלִי	הִתְקַטֵּלְנָה

3. The Hithpael Jussive

The Hithpael jussive takes the shortened form in the III-ה verb, as in יִתְעַל, "let him go up" (from עלה). The III-ה has fallen off with the result that the ל, now the final letter, loses its doubling. Otherwise, a Hithpael jussive is like the simple *yiqtol*.

E. The Hithpael Conjoined Finite Verbs

1. The Hithpael Wayyiqtol

The *wayyiqtol* adds the normal וַ with Daghesh Forte to the *yiqtol* form, as in וַיִּתְחַבֵּא, "and he hid himself" (from חבא). The III-ה verb takes the shortened form, as in וַתִּתְכָּס, "and she covered herself" (from כסה), in which the ס has become the final letter and so lost its Daghesh Forte).

2. The Hithpael Weqatal *and* Weyiqtol

Again, these are simply their respective forms with the conjunction added. The *weyiqtol* will as usual tend to take the cohortative form (with paragogic ה) in the first person and the shortened form for the III-ה verb.

F. The Hithpael Infinitives

1. The Hithpael Infinitive Construct

The Hithpael infinitive construct is identical to the 3ms *qatal* or the ms imperative (הִתְקַטֵּל).

2. The Hithpael Infinitive Absolute

The Hithpael infinitive absolute is very rare, but where it exists it is identical in form to the infinitive construct. An example is הִתְחַפֵּשׂ, "disguising oneself" (from חפשׂ).

G. The Hithpael Participle

Like the Piel and the Pual, the Hithpael has a מ preformative with its participle. In this case, the מ preformative replaces the ה of the הִת preformative, giving us מִת.

Table 34.5. The Hithpael Participle of קטל

	Singular	Plural
Masculine	מִתְקַטֵּל	מִתְקַטְּלִים
Feminine	מִתְקַטֶּלֶת	מִתְקַטְּלוֹת

H. The Hithpael in Weak Roots

1. Normal Weak Patterns

Hithpael verbs follow the same patterns with weak roots that we have seen with the Piel and Pual. The principal patterns are as follows:

(1) II-guttural verbs have either compensatory lengthening or virtual doubling. An example of the latter is found in וְהִתְבָּרְכוּ, "and they will obtain a blessing," (*weqatal* 3cp from ברך, with compensatory lengthening).

(2) III-ה verbs follow the normal patterns. For example, the ה is dropped with personal ending that is only a vowel, as in תִּתְרָאוּ, "you look at each other" (*yiqtol* 2mp from ראה).

2. Metathesis and Other Consonant Changes

The ת of the Hithpael preformative הִת behaves strangely with a group of letters that normally are not considered weak: the sibilants (ז, ס, צ, שׂ, שׁ) and ט.

a. Simple metathesis (two letters changing places)

This occurs in roots that are I-שׂ, I-שׁ, or I-ס. An example is מִשְׂתַּכֵּר, "earning wages" (participle ms from שׂכר). Observe that the ת of the preformative הִת and the שׂ of the root שׂכר have changed places, giving us מִשְׂתַּכֵּר instead of what we might expect, the hypothetical

*מִתְשַׂכֵּר. Other examples are מִסְתַּתֵּר, "hiding oneself" (participle ms from סתר), and לְהִשְׁתַּבֵּחַ, "to worship" (infinitive construct from שבח).

Blackboard 34.1. Metathesis in מִשְׂתַּכֵּר, a Hithpael Participle ms from שׂכר

b. Assimilation of ת

The ת from the preformative הת is assimilated in a root that is I-ז or I-ט. An example is יִטַּמָּא, "he shall defile himself" (*yiqtol* 3ms from טמא). In this case, the ת of the הת preformative is assimilated to the first letter of the root and doubles it. Other examples are תִּטַּמְּאוּ, "you (mp) shall defile yourselves" (*yiqtol* 2mp from טמא), and הִזַּכּוּ, "purify yourselves" (imperative mp from זכה).

Blackboard 34.2. Assimilation of ת in יִטַּמָּא, the Hithpael *Yiqtol* (Imperfect) 3ms of טמא

c. Metathesis and ת *Transformed to* ט

There is metathesis and the ת becomes ט if the root is I-צ. An example is הִצְטַיַּדְנוּ, "we provided for ourselves" (*qatal* 1cp from ציד).

Blackboard 34.3. Metathesis in הִצְטַיַּדְנוּ, the Hithpael *Qatal* (Perfect) 1cp of ציד

I. Summary of the Hithpael Principal Parts

Learn the following Hithpael principal parts. The patterns for the III-ה and the II-guttural should be easy for you by now, but take special note of the forms of שׁמר, as this verb illustrates metathesis in the Hithpael.

Observe also that there are no hollow verbs or original I-ו verbs in the principal parts chart below. These roots typically occur with an alternative to the Hithpael and not with the Hithpael itself. We will deal with these alternative stems in chapter 35.

Table 34.6. The Hithpael in Weak Roots

	Gloss	*Qatal*	*Yiqtol*	*Inf. Con.*	*Participle*
קטל		הִתְקַטֵּל	יִתְקַטֵּל	הִתְקַטֵּל	מִתְקַטֵּל
כסה	cover oneself	הִתְכַּסָּה	יִתְכַּסֶּה	הִתְכַּסּוֹת	מִתְכַּסֶּה
ברך	bless oneself	הִתְבָּרֵךְ	יִתְבָּרֵךְ	הִתְבָּרֵךְ	מִתְבָּרֵךְ
שמר	be careful	הִשְׁתַּמֵּר	יִשְׁתַּמֵּר	הִשְׁתַּמֵּר	מִשְׁתַּמֵּר

J. Vocabulary

1. Core Vocabulary

a. Verbs

מלט — Niphal: נִמְלַט escape, flee to safety
Piel: מִלֵּט save, deliver, rescue

עֲרַךְ — Qal: עָרַךְ arrange, set in order, make ready

פלל — Hithpael: הִתְפַּלֵּל make intercession, pray

פנה — Qal: פָּנָה turn, turn about, turn aside

שחט — Qal: שָׁחַט slaughter, kill (usually of a cultic sacrifice)

שרת — Piel: שֵׁרֵת serve, minister

b. Other Words

מִגְרָשׁ — pastureland, outskirts Ⓜ |מִגְרְשׁ|

מְעַט — little, in small amount (adjective); a little (Ⓜ noun)

תּוֹעֵבָה — abomination, abhorrence Ⓕ |תּוֹעֲבַת|

קֶרֶב — inward part, midst Ⓜ |קֶרֶב|; בְּקֶרֶב in the midst of (preposition)

רַק — only, however, nevertheless

שֵׁנִי — second

2. Proper Names

אַבְשָׁלוֹם — Absalom

יְהוֹשָׁפָט — Jehoshaphat

יָרָבְעָם — Jeroboam

3. Reading Vocabulary

חָשַׂךְ	Qal: חָשַׂךְ keep back, spare
עָקַד	Qal: עָקַד bind
אַיֵּה	where?
יָחִיד	only, solitary
יָרֵא	afraid, fearing
מְאוּמָה	anything, something
מַאֲכֶלֶת	knife
שֶׂה	sheep or goat

K. Reading—Genesis 22:7–12

7 וַיֹּאמֶר יִצְחָק אֶל־אַבְרָהָם אָבִיו וַיֹּאמֶר אָבִי וַיֹּאמֶר הִנֶּנִּי בְנִי וַיֹּאמֶר הִנֵּה
   הָאֵשׁ וְהָעֵצִים וְאַיֵּה הַשֶּׂה לְעֹלָה

8 וַיֹּאמֶר אַבְרָהָם אֱלֹהִים יִרְאֶה־לּוֹ הַשֶּׂה לְעֹלָה בְּנִי וַיֵּלְכוּ שְׁנֵיהֶם יַחְדָּו

9 וַיָּבֹאוּ אֶל־הַמָּקוֹם אֲשֶׁר אָמַר־לוֹ הָאֱלֹהִים וַיִּבֶן שָׁם אַבְרָהָם אֶת־הַמִּזְבֵּחַ
   וַיַּעֲרֹךְ אֶת־הָעֵצִים וַיַּעֲקֹד אֶת־יִצְחָק בְּנוֹ וַיָּשֶׂם אֹתוֹ עַל־הַמִּזְבֵּחַ מִמַּעַל
   לָעֵצִים

10 וַיִּשְׁלַח אַבְרָהָם אֶת־יָדוֹ וַיִּקַּח אֶת־הַמַּאֲכֶלֶת לִשְׁחֹט אֶת־בְּנוֹ

11 וַיִּקְרָא אֵלָיו מַלְאַךְ יְהוָה מִן־הַשָּׁמַיִם וַיֹּאמֶר אַבְרָהָם אַבְרָהָם וַיֹּאמֶר הִנֵּנִי

12 וַיֹּאמֶר אַל־תִּשְׁלַח יָדְךָ אֶל־הַנַּעַר וְאַל־תַּעַשׂ לוֹ מְאוּמָה כִּי עַתָּה יָדַעְתִּי
   כִּי־יְרֵא אֱלֹהִים אַתָּה וְלֹא חָשַׂכְתָּ אֶת־בִּנְךָ אֶת־יְחִידְךָ מִמֶּנִּי

CHAPTER 35
THE ALTERNATIVE DOUBLED STEMS

A. Basic Concept

The normal doubled stems (Piel, Pual, and Hithpael) rarely occur with hollow or geminate roots. Sometimes, to be sure, one of these roots will behave like a normal strong root. An example is סַבֵּב, "change," the Piel infinitive construct of סבב. For the most part, however, the Piel, Pual, and Hithpael stems will not appear in the hollow or geminate verbs. The reason is not difficult to grasp. A distinctive feature of these stems is the doubled middle radical. The hollow verbs have no middle radical at all, and thus they have nothing to double. And although the geminates do have a middle radical, Hebrew does not normally like to see the same letter repeated three times in a row, as is the case if the second radical of a geminate is doubled.

B. Alternatives to the Piel

The alternatives to the Piel are the **Polel** and **Pilpel** stems. In the former, the last letter of the root is repeated; in the latter, the first and last letters are reduplicated.

Table 35.1. Polel Patterns

	Example	Explanation
Polel כון	כּוֹנֵן	"He established"; *qatal* 3ms. The last letter of the root (נ) is repeated. This shows us the distinctive vowel pattern of the Polel, ō followed by ē. Note that the stem vowel is the same as the Piel *qatal* 3ms קָטֵל.
	וְכֹנַנְתִּי	"And I will establish"; *weqatal* 1cs. The stem vowel is the same as the Piel *qatal* 1cs קָטַּלְתִּי.
	תְּכוֹנֵן	"You will establish"; *yiqtol* 2ms. The preformative has Shewa, as does the Piel *yiqtol* תְּקַטֵּל.
Polel קום	אֲקוֹמֵם	"I will raise up"; *yiqtol* 1cs.
Polel שיר	מְשׁוֹרֵר	"Singer"; participle ms. Like the Piel participle, it has a preformative מְ.
Polel שוב	לְשׁוֹבֵב	"To bring back"; infinitive construct with preposition לְ.
	וְשֹׁבַבְתִּי	"And I will bring back"; *weqatal* 1cs. Note the defective writing, with Holem instead of Holem-Waw.
	בְּשׁוֹבְבִי	"When I bring back"; infinitive construct with preposition בְּ and 1cs suffix.

| *Polel*
סבב | תְּסוֹבֵב | "She will encircle"; *yiqtol* 3fs. The preformative has Shewa, as does the Piel *yiqtol* תְּקַטֵּל. Since this is from the geminate root סבב, there is no need to repeat the final letter. Some call this a Poel pattern. The "Poel" is simply a Polel based on a geminate root. |

Table 35.2. Pilpel Patterns

	Example	*Explanation*
Pilpel כּוּל	וְכִלְכַּלְתִּי	"And I will provide"; *weqatal* 1cs. The first radical (כ) and last radical (ל) are reduplicated as כלכל. The vowel pattern is comparable to the strong verb equivalent וְקָטַלְתִּי.
	וַיְכַלְכֵּל	"And he provided"; *wayyiqtol* 3ms. The vowel pattern is comparable to the strong verb וַיְקַטֵּל.
Pilpel גלל	וְגִלְגַּלְתִּי	"And I will roll"; *weqatal* 1cs. The radicals ג and ל reduplicate as גלגל. The vowel pattern is like וְקָטַלְתִּי.

C. Alternatives to the Pual

The alternatives to the Pual are the **Polal** and **Polpal** stems (they are passive in meaning). These forms are rare. Again, in the former, the last letter of the root is repeated, and in the latter, the first and last letters are reduplicated. Notice that both the Polal and Polpal stems have the u-class followed by a-class vowel pattern that occurs in the Pual stem.

Table 35.3. Polal and Polpal Patterns

	Example	*Explanation*
Polal כּוּן	כּוֹנָנוּ	"They were prepared"; *qatal* 3mp. The last letter of the root (ן) is repeated.
Polal חִיל	חוֹלָלְתִּי	"I was born," *qatal* 1cs. The last letter of the root (ל) is repeated.
Polpal כּוּל	כָּלְכְּלוּ	"They were provisioned"; *qatal* 3cp. Note that the vowel in כָּל is Qamets Hatuph.

D. Alternatives to the Hithpael

The alternatives to the Hithpael are the **Hithpolel** and **Hithpalpel** stems. In the former, the last letter of the root is repeated, whereas in the latter, the first and last letters are reduplicated.

Table 35.4. Hithpolel Patterns

	Example	Explanation
Hithpolel עוּף	יִתְעוֹפֵף	"He will fly away"; *yiqtol* 3ms.
Hithpolel עוּר	הִתְעוֹרְרִי	"Wake up!"; imperative fs.
Hithpolel קוּם	מִתְקוֹמְמִים	"Raising up"; participle mp. The participle preformative מִתְ is the same as one sees on the Hithpael.
Hithpolel נוּד	מִתְנוֹדֵד	"Mourning"; participle ms.

Table 35.5. Hithpalpel Patterns

	Example	Explanation
Hithpalpel קלל	הִתְקַלְקָלוּ	"They moved to and fro"; *qatal* 3cp. The radicals ק and ל reduplicate as קלקל.
Hithpalpel שעע	הִשְׁתַּעֲשְׁעוּ	"Behave as though blinded!"; imperative mp. The radicals שׁ and ע reduplicate as שׁעשׁע. But since this root begins with שׁ, there is metathesis in the Hithpalpel just as in the normal Hithpael. That is, the pattern הת + שׁעשׁע becomes השׁתעשׁע.

E. Summary

From the above descriptions, it is obvious that there are two basic patterns:

(1) Those that repeat the final letter of the root and that have a vowel pattern *ō* before *ē* or *a*. From the old paradigm root פעל, this gives a pattern like פֹּלֵל, and hence the name "Polel." The main characteristic of this pattern is that the letter in the third position is repeated.

(2) Those that reduplicate the first and last letters of the root and tend to have the same vowel patterns as the Piel, Pual, or Hithpael patterns. From the old paradigm root פעל, this gives a pattern like פִּלְפֵּל, and hence the name "Pilpel." The main characteristic of this pattern is that the letters in the first and third position are reduplicated.

Table 35.6. Summary of Alternative Doubled Stem Patterns

	Piel Type	*Pual Type*	*Hithpael Type*
פלל *Pattern*	כּוֹנֵן	חוֹלָלְתִּי	יִתְעוֹפֵף
פלפל *Pattern*	כִּלְכַּלְתִּי	כָּלְכְּלוּ	הִתְקַלְקָלוּ

F. Vocabulary

1. Core Vocabulary

a. Verbs

אָחַז   Qal: אָחַז seize, grasp, hold fast
Niphal: נֶאֱחַז be held fast

בִּין   Qal: בִּין understand, perceive, consider
Niphal: *נָבוֹן; נְבוֹנֹתִי (qatal 1cs) be discerning, have understanding
Hiphil: הֵבִין have/get understanding, make understand
Hithpolel: הִתְבּוֹנָן behave intelligently, direct one's attention

חנה   Qal: חָנָה encamp, lay siege to

ידה   Hiphil: *הוֹדָה; הוֹדוּ (qatal 3cp) praise, thank

נגשׁ   Qal: נָגַשׁ approach, step forward, draw near
Hiphil: *הִגִּישׁ; הִגִּישׁוּ (qatal 3cp) bring near, present

שׁיר   Qal: שָׁר sing
Polel: *שׁוֹרֵר; שֹׁרְרוּ (qatal 3cp) burst into song, sing about; (participles of Qal שָׁרִים and Polel מְשֹׁרְרִים can be substantival) singers

b. Other Words

חֵמָה   heat, poison, rage, wrath [F] |חֲמַת|

יַעַן   because of, on account of (preposition); because (conjunction)

עַל־כֵּן   therefore

קֶרֶן   horn [F] |קַרְן|

רֹב   abundance, multitude [M] |רֹב|

שָׂפָה   lip; (by extension) edge, border [F] |שְׂפַת|

2. Proper Names

בְּאֵר שֶׁבַע   Beersheba

בּוּז   Buz

בְּתוּאֵל   Bethuel

גַּחַם   Gaham

חֲזוֹ   Hazo

טֶבַח   Tebah

יִדְלָף   Jidlaph

כֶּשֶׂד   Chesed

מִלְכָּה	Milcah
מַעֲכָה	Maacah
עוּץ	Uz
פִּלְדָּשׁ	Pildash
קְמוּאֵל	Kemuel
רְאוּמָה	Reumah
תַּחַשׁ	Tahash

3. Reading Vocabulary

חשׂך	Qal: חָשַׂךְ keep back, spare
חוֹל	sand, mud
כּוֹכָב	star
יָחִיד	only, solitary
סְבַךְ	thicket
עֵקֶב	on account of, because
פִּילֶגֶשׁ	concubine

G. Reading—Genesis 22:13–24

13 וַיִּשָּׂא אַבְרָהָם אֶת־עֵינָיו וַיַּרְא וְהִנֵּה־אַיִל אַחַר נֶאֱחַז בַּסְּבַךְ בְּקַרְנָיו וַיֵּלֶךְ אַבְרָהָם וַיִּקַּח אֶת־הָאַיִל וַיַּעֲלֵהוּ לְעֹלָה תַּחַת בְּנוֹ

14 וַיִּקְרָא אַבְרָהָם שֵׁם־הַמָּקוֹם הַהוּא יְהוָה יִרְאֶה אֲשֶׁר יֵאָמֵר הַיּוֹם[1] בְּהַר יְהוָה יֵרָאֶה

15 וַיִּקְרָא מַלְאַךְ יְהוָה אֶל־אַבְרָהָם שֵׁנִית מִן־הַשָּׁמָיִם

16 וַיֹּאמֶר בִּי נִשְׁבַּעְתִּי נְאֻם־יְהוָה כִּי יַעַן אֲשֶׁר עָשִׂיתָ אֶת־הַדָּבָר הַזֶּה וְלֹא חָשַׂכְתָּ אֶת־בִּנְךָ אֶת־יְחִידֶךָ

17 כִּי־בָרֵךְ אֲבָרֶכְךָ וְהַרְבָּה אַרְבֶּה אֶת־זַרְעֲךָ כְּכוֹכְבֵי הַשָּׁמַיִם וְכַחוֹל אֲשֶׁר עַל־שְׂפַת הַיָּם וְיִרַשׁ זַרְעֲךָ אֵת שַׁעַר אֹיְבָיו

18 וְהִתְבָּרֲכוּ בְזַרְעֲךָ כֹּל גּוֹיֵי הָאָרֶץ עֵקֶב אֲשֶׁר שָׁמַעְתָּ בְּקֹלִי

---

1. "The day" = "today."

19 וַיָּ֣שָׁב אַבְרָהָם אֶל־נְעָרָ֔יו וַיָּקֻ֥מוּ וַיֵּלְכ֛וּ יַחְדָּ֖ו אֶל־בְּאֵ֣ר שָׁ֑בַע וַיֵּ֥שֶׁב אַבְרָהָ֖ם בִּבְאֵ֥ר שָֽׁבַע

20 וַיְהִ֗י אַחֲרֵי֙ הַדְּבָרִ֣ים הָאֵ֔לֶּה וַיֻּגַּ֥ד לְאַבְרָהָ֖ם לֵאמֹ֑ר הִנֵּ֠ה יָלְדָ֨ה מִלְכָּ֥ה גַם־הִ֛וא בָּנִ֖ים לְנָח֥וֹר אָחִֽיךָ

21 אֶת־ע֥וּץ בְּכֹר֖וֹ וְאֶת־בּ֣וּז אָחִ֑יו וְאֶת־קְמוּאֵ֖ל אֲבִ֥י אֲרָֽם

22 וְאֶת־כֶּ֣שֶׂד וְאֶת־חֲז֔וֹ וְאֶת־פִּלְדָּ֖שׁ וְאֶת־יִדְלָ֑ף וְאֵ֖ת בְּתוּאֵֽל

23 וּבְתוּאֵ֖ל יָלַ֣ד אֶת־רִבְקָ֑ה שְׁמֹנָ֥ה אֵ֨לֶּה֙ יָלְדָ֣ה מִלְכָּ֔ה לְנָח֖וֹר אֲחִ֥י אַבְרָהָֽם

24 וּפִֽילַגְשׁ֖וֹ וּשְׁמָ֣הּ רְאוּמָ֑ה וַתֵּ֤לֶד גַּם־הִוא֙ אֶת־טֶ֣בַח וְאֶת־גַּ֔חַם וְאֶת־תַּ֖חַשׁ וְאֶת־מַעֲכָֽה

CHAPTER 36
THE CANTILLATION MARKS AND OTHER MASORETIC CONVENTIONS

A. Introduction to the Cantillation Marks

You are already familiar with Silluq and Athnach as signals of major pause in a verse. Along with these, Biblical Hebrew contains a bewildering array of other **cantillation marks**, which appear in the text as small markings similar to the vowel points. The standard Hebrew Bible is written with cantillation marks throughout, and henceforth the major Bible passages you read will contain them.

The cantillation marks are useful in at least four ways.

(1) They are a kind of musical notation meant to guide the cantors in synagogue as they chant the text. This is their primary function.

(2) They usually, but not always, fall on the accented syllable, and thus they are commonly called accents.

(3) They help to divide a verse into syntactical units. They often can clarify for the reader where there are divisions between phrases and clauses.

(4) They can help to distinguish lines of poetry, signalling where one poetic line ends and a new one begins.

Learning to chant or "cantillate" a text requires special training in a synagogue or Jewish seminary context. Even at that, there is no single standard for interpreting the musical value of the cantillation marks. Different Jewish traditions (Ashkenazic, Sephardic, Yemenite, and others) have different ways of chanting the text.

Using the cantillation marks to determine which word is accented is fairly straightforward. However, some marks are prepositive (placed in front of a word) and some are postpositive (placed after a word), and some words have two cantillation marks. Thus, not every cantillation mark will indicate the accented syllable.

1. Basic Principles

Cantillation marks are either "disjunctive" or "conjunctive," which is why they can be helpful for determining the syntax of a verse.

(1) A **disjunctive** cantillation mark shows that there is a break between two words.

    (a) Disjunctive marks can be weak, indicating a very minor or negligible break. A minor disjunctive might mark the end of a prepositional phrase or the end of a construct chain.

    (b) Strong disjunctive marks indicate the more significant division in the structure of the verse. The Silluq and Athnach are the strongest disjunctives.

    (c) Disjunctives can be graded in four tiers, from the strongest (level 1) to the weakest (level 4).

(2) A **conjunctive** cantillation mark indicates that two words are bound together as part of the same phrase, as in a construct chain. Conjunctive accents are sometimes called "servants" (Latin: *servus*; plural = *servi*). Thus, a construct noun will have a *servus* that binds it to the following noun. The *servi* are not stronger or weaker in the way that the disjunctive accents are. But various rules govern which *servus* is used in which circumstance.

(3) You can think of a verse as divided into two parts by a major disjunctive accent (usually the Athnach). Each part is then divided further by weaker disjunctive accents. Typically, the Silluq governs everything from after the Athnach to the end of the verse, and the Athnach governs everything from the beginning of the verse to itself.

(4) Other disjunctive accents, such as Zaqeph Qaton, Tifha, or Segholta, govern subdivisions of these two major parts. The *servi* are within the divisions and subdivisions governed by disjunctive accents.

Blackboard 36.1. The Cantillation Marks as Syntax Indicators

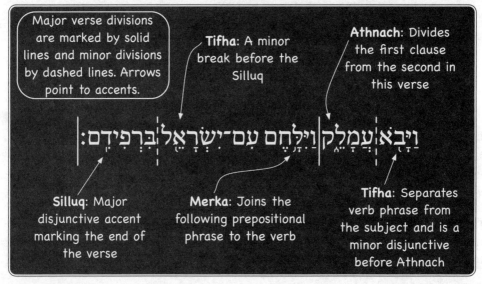

In the Blackboard above, the two major divisions of the verse are וַיָּבֹא עֲמָלֵק, "and Amalek came," and וַיִּלָּחֶם עִם־יִשְׂרָאֵל בִּרְפִידִם, "and he fought with Israel at Rephidim." Each of these is subdivided into two parts by the disjunctive Tifha.

The Athnach division (וַיָּבֹא עֲמָלֵק) has only two words. In such a case, the first word will often have a minor disjunctive accent and not a conjunctive accent. Otherwise, if a finite verb is followed by its subject, the finite verb has a conjunctive accent (by contrast, if the subject is before its verb, the subject usually has a disjunctive accent).

The words וַיִּלָּחֶם עִם־יִשְׂרָאֵל are governed by the Tifha. They form a subdivision of the clause וַיִּלָּחֶם עִם־יִשְׂרָאֵל בִּרְפִידִם (governed by Silluq). The Tifha unit has the *servus* Merka.

The following tables contain the most common disjunctive and conjunctive cantillation marks. Some less frequent cantillation marks are not listed.

Table 36.1. Disjunctive Cantillation Marks

Standard Disjunctive Cantillation Marks		
בֵּגֶד	Silluq	**Level 1.** Marks the end of a verse; found in the last word of a verse.
בֵּגֶד	Athnach	**Level 1.** Found in the semantic middle of a verse, at the main pause within a verse.
בֵּגֶד	Zaqeph Qaton	**Level 2.** The most common disjunctive accent, it subdivides a Silluq or Athnach portion of a verse. It usually has one or two *servi* in front of it.
בֵּגֶד	Zaqeph Gadol	**Level 2.** A variant of the Zaqeph Qaton, but much less common.
בֵּגֶד	Tifha	**Level 2.** The main pause of a short verse (if there is no Athnach) or a minor disjunctive in a small unit before Silluq or Athnach. It will have no *servi* or one, often the Merka.
בֵּגֶד	Segholta	**Level 2.** Postpositive. It is used in the first half of a verse and occurs after the Zarqa (see below).
בֵּגֶד	Shalshelet	**Level 2.** It is used when the Segholta should appear but there is no Zarqa. It is found 7 times in the Bible.
בֵּגֶד	Revia	**Level 3.** Used to divide sections governed by Zaqeph, Segholta, or Tifha. It can have up to three *servi*.
בֵּגֶד	Tevir	**Level 3.** A disjunctive; Not to be confused with the conjunctive Merka (see below), which lacks the dot.
בֵּגֶד	Pashta	**Level 3.** Postpositive. If the penult is the tone, a second Pashta will be written over the penult: הַמַּיִם. Distinguish Pashta from the conjunctive Azla (see below).
בֵּגֶד	Zarqa	**Level 3.** Postpositive. It occurs in the first half of a verse in a unit governed by Segholta.
בֵּגֶד	Geresh	**Level 4.** A minor disjunctive that is subordinate to Revia, Pashta, or Zarqa. Written doubled, it is called Gershayim.
בֵּגֶד	Pazer	**Level 4.** A minor disjunctive that is subordinate to Revia, Pashta, or Zarqa.
בֵּגֶד	Telisha Gedolah	**Level 4.** Prepositive disjunctive; does not mark tone. Contrast with the conjunctive Telisha Qetanna.
בֵּגֶד	Legarmeh	**Level 4.** A minor disjunctive that is usually subordinate to Revia. It has two parts; contrast the Munaḥ (see below).
A Special Disjunctive Accent Found in Psalms, Job, and Proverbs		
בֵּגֶד	Oleh weYored	**Level 1.** A major disjunctive accent made with two marks. If a verse has both Oleh weYored and Athnach, the Oleh weYored occurs before the Athnach.

Table 36.2. Some Common Conjunctive Cantillation Marks

בֶּגֶד	Munaḥ	A very common *servus*.
בֶּגֶד	Merka	This is a very common *servus*. Distinguish this from Tevir, which has a dot in it, as in יָדָ֖יו in Exod 17:12 in the Reading below.
בֶּגֶד	Mehuppak	Mehuppak is always followed by Pashta. A minor disjunctive accent that looks just like Mehuppak is the Yetiv. Yetiv is placed more to the right of its letter. But you should learn Mehuppak as part of the Mehuppak-Pashta combination, so that you will not get confused.
בֶּגֶד	Azla	The Azla is also called Qadma. Be careful about this one! It looks just like Pashta, but it is distinguished from Pashta by the fact that it is not postpositive. Azla is often followed by Geresh.
בֶּגֶד	Darga	A less common conjunctive; it looks something like the letter S.
בֶּגֶד	Telisha Qetanna	Telisha Qetanna is postpositive and so does not mark the tone syllable. It is followed by Telisha Gadol.

Complex rules govern the placement of cantillation marks. Nevertheless, it is useful to recognize the cantillation marks mentioned in the above charts. Knowing them will enable you to determine whether a word belongs more closely with the words in front of it or behind it. Of course, it is possible to disagree with the phrase division indicated by the cantillation marks. Still, the reading suggested by the cantillation marks represents a very old tradition and should not be discarded lightly. The accents are useful but not infallible guides to the syntax of the text.

2. Cantillation Marks in the Three

Psalms, Job, and Proverbs have a distinctive set of cantillation marks, although several are the same as in the standard set. These three books are called "the Three" in reference to the fact that they use this modified accent system. The most important disjunctive accent of the Three is the Oleh weYored.

In the example from Psalm 14:7 below, you can see some of the accents used in Psalms, Job, and Proverbs. Observe the following:

(1) Each of the poetic lines ends with one of the three major disjunctive accents: the Silluq, Athnach, or Oleh weYored.

(2) The Tifha in the second line is prepositive. This is true of Tifha in the Three, but in the other books the Tifha is not prepositive. Thus, the Tifha is not on the tone syllable in the Three.

(3) There is a two-part accent called Revia Mugrash in the third line in יַעֲקֹב. This is an accent found only in the Three. It is disjunctive, and it is a variation on the Revia (notice that its markings include the diamond-shaped Revia accent).

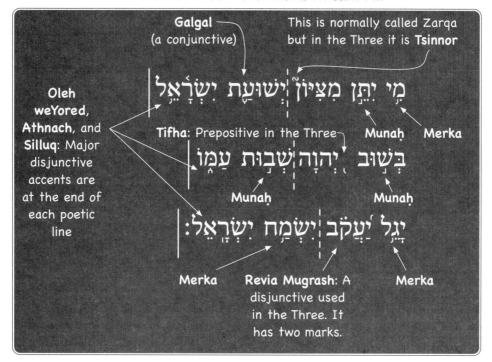

Blackboard 36.2. Cantillation Marks in Psalm 14:7

In poetry, Silluq, Athnach, Oleh weYored, and sometimes Zaqeph Qaton or Revia will come at the end of a line of poetry. This makes them useful for **colometry**, the process of dividing a poem into its lines (for more on this, see chapter 41). Again, however, the cantillation marks should be regarded as useful and important but not flawless guides. In some cases, the line division suggested by a cantillation mark is arguably not correct.

3. More on Words "in Pause"

You have already seen that the two major disjunctive cantillation marks, Silluq and Athnach, can lengthen a vowel. A word with a vowel made long by cantillations marks like Silluq or Athnach is the **pausal form** of that word. For example, the pausal form of חֶסֶד is חָסֶד (with Silluq) or חָסֶד (with Athnach). Note that חֶסֶד is an a-class segholate noun, and thus its pausal form is a-class.

Sometimes one sees pausal forms on words that do not have Silluq or Athnach. Rarely you may even see a pausal form with a conjunctive accent. In poetry, a pausal form often comes at the end of a poetic line.

4. Additional Comments on the Cantillation Marks

(1) The marks are most directly for cantillation, but they are often called "accents" because they usually fall on the tone syllable. In Hebrew, they are called טְעָמִים ("tastes").

(2) The Roman spellings given above for the accent names are simplified. There is no standard Roman spelling for the names of the cantillation marks.

(3) The cantillation marks appear to have entered the Hebrew text around A.D. 700. The Talmud (completed around A.D. 600) does not mention the accent signs by name, but one Talmudic text, commenting on Neh 8:8, does indicate that there was already a preferred or standard way of chanting the Torah. Some scholars find the oldest evidence for the cantillation system in the spacing of an early 2nd century B.C. Septuagint manuscript, along with various clues in Qumran materials. While no doubt the chanting of the text according to a set cantillation took place long before the elaborate system of marks was devised, we cannot be sure when it began. Rabbis first refer to the marks by name in the ninth century A.D.

(4) Distinguish the Silluq from the Metheg, as they both look the same. Remember that the Silluq only appears in the last word of a verse.

(5) Although we can describe a four-tier gradation from strongest to weakest in the disjunctive accents, this presentation is somewhat misleading. The strength of a disjunctive accent is relative to its context. In Exod 17:8 (Blackboard 36.1), the first Tifha has weak disjunctive value. In a longer verse a Tifha might have stronger force. In general, one can say that a disjunctive accent is stronger if it has a relatively weaker disjunctive within its domain.

(6) The basic principle of the disjunctive cantillation marks, as understood by most scholars, is that a verse is successively split into smaller and smaller halves (although the halves are not necessarily of equal length). Thus, a verse is first split into two parts by the Athnach, with the first part being the Athnach unit and the second part being the Silluq unit. Each of these two units is then split (e.g., by Zaqeph Qaton). The subdivisions can then be further subdivided.

(7) Although we say that the Athnach splits the verse, it certainly does not necessarily fall in the middle of the verse by word count. That is, in verses with ten words, the Athnach will only occasionally and coincidentally fall on the fifth word. Also, it is not always the case that the Athnach falls on the major syntactical division of a verse. Often, the Athnach will be placed at what the Masoretes evidently believed was a crucial point in the verse, even if that point was not a major syntactical break.

(8) Above all, remember that these marks are primarily guides to cantillation.

B. Other Important Masoretic Conventions

1. Kethiv and Qere

Kethiv (כְּתִיב), an Aramaic word, means "what is written"; **Qere** (קְרִי), also Aramaic, means "what is read." The basic idea is that the scribes received in the Hebrew text a word that they did not dare change (they would never deliberately alter the sacred text) but that they thought should not be read aloud as written. That is, a word was written in one way (the Kethiv), but it would be read differently. Instead of the received text a different word (the Qere) would be read.

In Hebrew Bibles, one often sees in the body of the text the *consonants* of the Kethiv written with the *vowels* of the Qere; the consonants of the Qere will be written in the margin. The reader is signaled to connect the vowel points in the body of the text to the Qere consonants written in the margin (see Blackboard 36.3). Not every printed Bible, however, follows this convention. Electronic texts often have the Kethiv written with Kethiv vowels in the text, followed in brackets by the Qere written with Qere vowels.

Blackboard 36.3. Kethiv and Qere

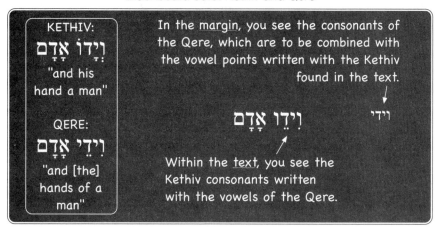

There are several reasons that a Kethiv / Qere situation might arise.

(1) *To correct an evident scribal error*. When the Masoretes were certain that an error had been made in copying the text (e.g., a letter might have been omitted or written wrongly), they would correct the error with a Qere. For example, in Ezek 1:8 (the example in Blackboard 36.3), the Kethiv is וְיָדוֹ אָדָם, "and his hand a man," but the Qere corrects this to וִידֵי אָדָם, "and (the) hands of a man."

(2) *Euphemism*. A word is thought to be offensive and is replaced by a euphemism.

(3) *Correcting unusual spellings*. A word in the text might be spelled in an unusual way. For example, a word might employ vowel letters in an unexpected manner, and the Qere will correct this.

(4) *Updating archaic forms*. In 2 Kgs 4:16, the pronoun אַתְּ has the archaic spelling אַתִּי (the Kethiv), and this is written as אַתְּ in the Qere.

(5) *The perpetual Qere*. The divine name יהוה is never pronounced in the Masoretic pointing of the text. Instead, one says either אֲדֹנָי (when it is pointed יְהֹוָה or, more commonly, יְהוָה) or אֱלֹהִים (when it is pointed יֱהוִה). The latter only occurs when אֲדֹנָי precedes the tetragrammaton. Significantly, the Masoretic vocalization of particles before the divine name presupposes the pronunciation אֲדֹנָי.

    (a) The preposition מִן becomes מֵ before a guttural (due to compensatory lengthening), and this is how it is spelled before the divine name: מֵאֲדֹנָי = מֵיְהוָה, "from the Lord" (e.g., Gen 18:14; Judg 14:4; 1 Kgs 2:15).

(b) The interrogative לָמָה becomes לָמֶה before the gutturals א, ה, and ע, and before the divine name we see: לָמָה יְהוָה = לָמָה אֲדֹנָי, "Why, O Lord?" (e.g., Exod 32:11; Judg 21:3; Ps 10:1; 88:14) or "Why is the Lord?" (e.g., Num 14:3).

2. Paragraph Markers

You will have noticed by now that some verses are followed by either ס or פ. The ס stands for **Sethumah** (סְתוּמָא = "closed") and the פ stands for **Pethuchah** (פְּתוּחָא = "opened"). Both indicate the beginning of a new paragraph (**Pisqot** [פסקות]). In a properly laid out liturgical text, a new paragraph break after Pethuchah must be written on a new line, but a new paragraph after Sethumah could be written on the same line as the previous paragraph but with a space between the end of the first paragraph and beginning of the second. It is not clear why some paragraphs were Sethumah and others Pethuchah, and there was a third type of paragraph division now lost to us.

The Masoretic paragraph markings are very old, reflecting a tradition that goes at least back to the third century A.D. You may find them helpful when you are attempting to work out the structure of a passage.

3. Sof Pasuq

You have seen that every verse ends with what appears to be two diamond shapes (׃). This is the **Sof Pasuq** (lit., "end of verse"). Importantly, while Sof Pasuq may designate the end of a verse, it may not mark the end of a sentence.

C. Vocabulary

1. Core Vocabulary

a. Verbs

מות	Qal: מֵת die
	Hiphil: הֵמִית cause to die, kill
	Hophal: הוּמַת be killed
נסע	Qal: נָסַע tear/pull out; journey, depart
נצב	Niphal: *נָצַב; נִצְּבָה (*qatal* 3fs) stand
	Hiphil: הִצִּיב place, set up
שׂנא	Qal: שָׂנֵא hate; (often as substantive in the participle: שֹׂנֵה) one who hates, enemy
שׂרף	Qal: שָׂרַף burn

b. Other Words

אֱמוּנָה	faithfulness, trustworthiness, steadfastness [F] |אֱמוּנַת
גִּבְעָה	hill [F] |גִּבְעַת
כֹּחַ	strength, power [M] |כֹּחַ

כָּנָף	wing, extremity, edge 𝐅 |כְּנַף|
מָחָר	tomorrow, next day
נְחֹשֶׁת	bronze, copper 𝐅 |נְחֹשֶׁת|
רֹחַב	breadth, expanse 𝐌 |רֹחַב|

2. Proper Names

בָּשָׁן	Bashan
חוּר	Hur
סֻכּוֹת	Succoth
עֲמָלֵק	Amalek
עֲמָלֵקִי	Amalekite(s)
רְפִידִים	Rephidim

3. Reading Vocabulary

גבר	Qal: גָּבַר be superior, increase
חלש	Qal: יַחֲלֹשׁ (*yiqtol* 3ms) defeat
מחה	Qal: מָחָה wipe out, annihilate
תמך	Qal: תָּמְכָה (3fs) תָּמְכוּ (3cp) take hold of, hold, grasp
זִכָּרוֹן	remembrance, memorial
זֵכֶר	mention
כָּבֵד	heavy, severe
כֵּס יָהּ	(short for כִּסֵּא־יְהוָה) throne of YHWH, but this may be a scribal error for נֵס יה, "standard of YHWH"
נֵס	standard, flag

D. Reading—Exodus 17:8–16

8 וַיָּבֹא עֲמָלֵק וַיִּלָּחֶם עִם־יִשְׂרָאֵל בִּרְפִידִם׃

9 וַיֹּאמֶר מֹשֶׁה אֶל־יְהוֹשֻׁעַ בְּחַר־לָנוּ אֲנָשִׁים וְצֵא הִלָּחֵם בַּעֲמָלֵק מָחָר אָנֹכִי נִצָּב עַל־רֹאשׁ הַגִּבְעָה וּמַטֵּה הָאֱלֹהִים בְּיָדִי׃

10 וַיַּעַשׂ יְהוֹשֻׁעַ כַּאֲשֶׁר אָמַר־לוֹ מֹשֶׁה לְהִלָּחֵם בַּעֲמָלֵק וּמֹשֶׁה אַהֲרֹן וְחוּר עָלוּ רֹאשׁ הַגִּבְעָה׃

11 וְהָיָה כַּאֲשֶׁר יָרִים מֹשֶׁה יָדוֹ וְגָבַר יִשְׂרָאֵל וְכַאֲשֶׁר יָנִיחַ יָדוֹ וְגָבַר עֲמָלֵק׃

12 וִידֵי מֹשֶׁה֙ כְּבֵדִ֔ים וַיִּקְחוּ־אֶ֙בֶן֙ וַיָּשִׂ֣ימוּ תַחְתָּ֔יו וַיֵּ֖שֶׁב עָלֶ֑יהָ וְאַהֲרֹ֨ן וְח֜וּר
    תָּֽמְכ֣וּ בְיָדָ֗יו מִזֶּ֤ה אֶחָד֙ וּמִזֶּ֣ה אֶחָ֔ד וַיְהִ֥י יָדָ֛יו אֱמוּנָ֖ה עַד־בֹּ֥א הַשָּֽׁמֶשׁ׃

13 וַיַּחֲלֹ֧שׁ יְהוֹשֻׁ֛עַ אֶת־עֲמָלֵ֥ק וְאֶת־עַמּ֖וֹ לְפִי־חָֽרֶב׃ פ

14 וַיֹּ֨אמֶר יְהוָ֜ה אֶל־מֹשֶׁ֗ה כְּתֹ֨ב זֹ֤את זִכָּרוֹן֙ בַּסֵּ֔פֶר וְשִׂ֖ים בְּאָזְנֵ֣י יְהוֹשֻׁ֑עַ כִּֽי־מָחֹ֤ה
    אֶמְחֶה֙ אֶת־זֵ֣כֶר עֲמָלֵ֔ק מִתַּ֖חַת הַשָּׁמָֽיִם׃

15 וַיִּ֥בֶן מֹשֶׁ֖ה מִזְבֵּ֑חַ וַיִּקְרָ֥א שְׁמ֖וֹ יְהוָ֥ה ׀ נִסִּֽי׃

16 וַיֹּ֗אמֶר כִּֽי־יָד֙ עַל־כֵּ֣ס יָ֔הּ מִלְחָמָ֥ה לַיהוָ֖ה בַּֽעֲמָלֵ֑ק מִדֹּ֖ר דֹּֽר׃ פ

E. Example of Disjunctive Domains in Exodus 17:11

This verse from the above reading gives us an example of how the cantillation marks have domains.

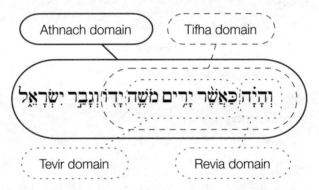

The above has the conjunctives Azla, Merka, and Munaḥ

The above has the conjunctive Merka twice

CHAPTER 37
AN OVERVIEW OF TEXT SYNTAX AND LITERARY STRUCTURE

A. Defining Syntax

Every language has its own system for communicating effectively. Hebrew uses a number of formal features to help the reader distinguish paragraph divisions, to lay out the logical relationship of clauses and larger text units, and to differentiate types of discourse. To this point, your study of Hebrew has focused on four areas:

(1) **Orthography** is the study of an alphabet and of how its letters combine to represent sounds and to form words.

(2) **Phonology** refers to the study of a language's system of sounds (phonemes).

(3) **Morphology** describes how the smallest grammatical units (morphemes) combine to form stems and words. It is the study of the formation of words.

(4) **Syntax** deals with how words combine to form clauses, sentences, and larger discourse structures.

In these final chapters, we will continue to wrestle with microsyntax (the shaping of clauses and sentences) and also consider further issues of macrosyntax (the shaping of texts), examining the way sentences join and relate to form meaningful discourse units.

B. Clauses and Sentences

The basic building block of text analysis is the **clause**, a grammatical construction that is made up of a subject and its predicate. For example, "he prayed" is a clause, with "he" being the subject and "prayed" being the predicate. By contrast, "in the house" is only a **phrase**.

(1) **Predication** refers to the state, process, or action associated with the subject.

    (a) The predicate may be a finite verb with all its complements (e.g., if the verb is transitive, its direct object). This creates a **verbal clause** (e.g., וַיִּקְרָא הַכֹּהֵן אֶת־הַסֵּפֶר, "And the priest *read the book*").

    (b) Sometimes, as you have already seen, the predicate can be another noun or an adjective without any explicit verb. This is called a **verbless** or **nominal clause** (e.g., קָדֹשׁ הַכֹּהֵן, "The priest [is] *holy*"). There is no finite verb in this clause (the verb "to be" is understood), yet the predication is marked by the adjective קָדֹשׁ ("holy").

(2) In both verbal and nominal clauses, the predicate can be the first word, or it can have some other part of the clause (e.g., subject, object, prepositional phrase) placed in front of it.

(3) The essential **nucleus** (Nuc) of a clause (Cl) is a subject and its predicate. Along with the clause nucleus can be various **modifiers** (Mod) and **connectors** (Con), such as conjunctions, exclamations, adverbs, and prepositional phrases.

Blackboard 37.1. Elements of a Clause

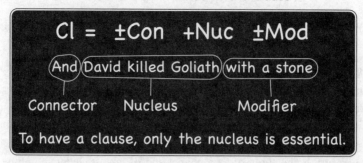

You can think of a clause as having **grammatical slots**: one slot for an optional connector, one slot for a mandatory nucleus (subject and predicate), and any number of slots for optional modifiers. The modifier slots may be filled by a word (such as an adverb), a phrase (such as a prepositional phrase), or even a whole clause (such as a relative clause). Here are examples of modifiers:

(1) A word: "*Yesterday* David slew Goliath." Here, "yesterday" is an adverbial modifier.

(2) A phrase: "David slew Goliath *in the afternoon*." A phrase is a group of words that fills a single modifier slot, as the adverbial prepositional phrase "in the afternoon" does here.

(3) A clause: "David, *who is but a boy,* slew Goliath." The words "who is but a boy" include a subject and predicate, but they form a relative clause and serve as a modifier of "David." They are in a subordinate position.

Thus, we can adopt the following definitions:

(1) **A phrase** is a group of words that fills a single slot in a clause.

(2) **A subordinate clause** is a clause that serves as a modifier and is embedded in a higher level clause, as in "who is but a boy" above.

(3) **A matrix** (Latin, "mother") **clause** is not grammatically subordinate to any other higher level clause. In the construction "David, who is but a boy, slew Goliath," the words "David… slew Goliath" form the matrix clause.

(4) **A sentence** is a matrix clause with all its subordinate clauses.

C. The Role of ו and Ø in Creating Discourse Blocks

Hebrew has a way of marking discrete units of discourse and of distinguishing primary from embedded material. Just as this chapter has an outline of primary and supporting points, so too Hebrew texts have discernible hierarchic structure. Two grammatical features are the primary guides in the literary shaping of texts.

(1) **The conjunction ו** ("and"). The conjunction links grammatical units of equal value (e.g., phrases to phrases, clauses to clauses), creating chains of discourse that are to be read together. The presence of ו assumes a preceding text; it generally does not signal an absolute beginning. That is, except for certain special patterns, a new discourse generally does not start with the conjunction ו, and if a discourse does begin

with that conjunction, there is usually a good reason. Sometimes, for example, biblical books or speeches do begin with the conjunction וְ, but even in these cases we should recognize that there is an implied prior discourse. Leviticus, Numbers, Joshua, Judges, Samuel, Ezekiel, Jonah, Ruth, and Esther begin with a *wayyiqtol* verb. Exodus, Kings, and Ezra-Nehemiah begin with a וְ + non-verb. In all of these cases, the authors are probably using the conjunction to set the books within the grand narrative of Israel's history. By contrast, Job, which is not part of that history, does not begin with a conjunction. Whenever we find a speech or a book that begins with a conjunction, we should ask why that conjunction is there.

(2) **Asyndeton.** This is the absence of a conjunction (grammarians use Ø, the symbol for an empty set, to indicate the absence). Asyndeton at the front of sentences most commonly signals either

(a) the start of a new unit of discourse or

(b) the restatement, clarification, or support of a previous text unit (such as a parenthetical comment).

In most instances, context alone clarifies for the reader whether asyndeton marks a fresh beginning or explication.

In summary, a discourse typically

(1) begins with a clause that does not start with a conjunction,

(2) is carried on by a chain of וְ clauses,

(3) but may include embedded units initiated by asyndetic clauses (i.e., those not fronted with a conjunction) that clarify or support the primary line of thought.

D. Reported Speech and Embedded Discourse

Often one block of discourse can be interrupted by another discourse. This is especially common with quotations, which we call **reported direct speech**. Consider the following:

> The night wore on, and John was bored. So he said, *"I am going to leave now."* And he got up, and he left the room.

In this illustration, the reported speech, "I am going to leave now," is set within a larger discourse. By itself, however, "I am going to leave now" is an independent discourse. We have the larger discourse by the narrator and, within that, we have the reported speech of John.

Sometimes, one discourse can be **embedded** in another discourse even when there is no reported speech. For example, there can be an embedded discourse that is by the narrator and not by a character in the story. For example, a narrator may give an **aside**, a brief narration that gives background information but is not actually part of the main narrative.

The following examples will clarify the special role of וְ and Ø in marking embedded units of texts. The diagrams below include the following features:

(1) The *coordination of phrases* is marked by a horizontal arrow (→).

(2) The *sequencing of clauses* is marked by a vertical arrow (↑).

(3) A *break in the flow of the discourse* with Ø is marked by a horizontal line (–).

Table 37.1. Reported Speech in Deuteronomy 5:30–31

אֱמֹר לָהֶם	–	Ø	30b
שׁוּבוּ לָכֶם לְאָהֳלֵיכֶם:	–	Ø	30c
וְאַתָּה פֹּה עֲמֹד עִמָּדִי	↑	וֹ	31a
וַאֲדַבְּרָה אֵלֶיךָ אֵת כָּל־הַמִּצְוָה (→) וְהַחֻקִּים (→) וְהַמִּשְׁפָּטִים	↑	וֹ	31b
30b	Say to them,
30c	*"Return to your tents."*
31a	But you, stand here with me,
31b	and I will tell you the whole commandment and the statutes and the rules…

In the above example, clauses 31a and 31b are within a continuous discourse initiated by 30b. This is marked by the fact that both 31a and 31b begin with the conjunction וֹ. But the clause in 30c is reported direct speech, and taken by itself is an independent discourse. It does not begin with a conjunction but is marked by Ø. After the reported speech, clause 31a resumes the prior discourse (30b) and thus begins with a conjunction.

It is possible, as stated above, to have one discourse embedded within another without reported speech. In such a case, the embedded discourse often explains or emphasizes something in the larger discourse.

Table 37.2. Embedded Discourse in 1 Kings 2:10–11

וַיִּשְׁכַּב דָּוִד עִם־אֲבֹתָיו	↑	וֹ	10a
וַיִּקָּבֵר בְּעִיר דָּוִד:	↑	וֹ	10b
וְהַיָּמִים אֲשֶׁר מָלַךְ דָּוִד עַל־יִשְׂרָאֵל אַרְבָּעִים שָׁנָה	↑	וֹ	11a
בְּחֶבְרוֹן מָלַךְ שֶׁבַע שָׁנִים	–	Ø	11b
וּבִירוּשָׁלַיִם מָלַךְ שְׁלֹשִׁים וְשָׁלֹשׁ שָׁנִים:	↑	וֹ	11c
10a	And David lay down with his fathers,
10b	and he was buried in the city of David.
11a	and the days that David reigned over Israel were forty years.
11b	*In Hebron he reigned seven years,*
11c	*and in Jerusalem he reigned thirty-three years.*

In the above example, the embedded discourse (11b-11c) explains the "forty years" mentioned in clause 11a. Note that the unit begins with asyndeton (Ø). There is also a relative clause in 11a, which for simplicity's sake has not been set on its own line. We will examine relative and other subordinate clauses in the next chapter.

Two final points are noteworthy here:

(1) Hebrew allows for sentence and paragraph embedding to occur recursively (i.e., embedding within embedding *ad infinitum*), so the interpreter must always be aware of the relationship of any given text block to the greater whole.

(2) The most important thematic material in a text is not necessarily to be found in the primary line of textual development. In other words, an embedded clause may be the main point of a discourse. Although the primary storyline in historical narrative is never embedded, the core message is often found not in the words of the narrator or in the actions of the characters but in a reported speech (e.g., God's words through a prophet), which is always embedded material.

E. Mainline and Offline Material

1. Mainline Material

In a discourse of several sentences or more, there is normally a structural backbone that moves the discourse forward in some kind of sequential manner. We call this structural backbone the **mainline** of the discourse. This is most obvious in historical narrative, which typically carries a story forward chronologically through a progression of events using *wayyiqtol* verbs to represent the mainline. Joshua 24:3 contains four mainline clauses, and it is here translated very literally for the sake of illustration.

Table 37.3. Mainline Clauses in Joshua 24:3

> *And I took* your father Abraham from beyond the River, *and I led* him through all the land of Canaan. *And I made numerous* his offspring, *and I gave* to him Isaac…
>
> וָאֶקַּח אֶת־אֲבִיכֶם אֶת־אַבְרָהָם מֵעֵבֶר הַנָּהָר וָאוֹלֵךְ אוֹתוֹ בְּכָל־אֶרֶץ כְּנָעַן וָאַרְבֶּה אֶת־זַרְעוֹ וָאֶתֶּן־לוֹ אֶת־יִצְחָק

In the above example, every italicized verb phrase represents a *wayyiqtol* verb; these verbs carry the historical narrative forward through a succession of events. One might think of a discourse as a journey, with each mainline verbal clause being one step in that journey.

But the *wayyiqtol* serves as the mainline only for historical discourse; other text types (such as a prediction or a series of commands) use other verb forms to set up the mainline of a text. In a predictive text, as below, the *weqatal* provides the mainline of the discourse.

Table 37.4. Mainline Clauses in Isaiah 2:2–3

> *and it shall be lifted up* above the hills; *and* all the nations *shall flow* to it, *and* many peoples *shall come, and they shall say*…
>
> וְנִשָּׂא מִגְּבָעוֹת וְנָהֲרוּ אֵלָיו כָּל־הַגּוֹיִם וְהָלְכוּ עַמִּים רַבִּים וְאָמְרוּ

In the above example, the mainline material is a series of *weqatal* clauses. Once again we have a sequence of temporally successive events, but now the events are in the future rather than the past.

2. Offline Material

In addition to the discourse mainline, there is also the discourse **offline**. To use the journey analogy again, each mainline clause is another step along the path of the narrative, but off-line clauses are a point in the journey where the traveller stops to look around, or where he temporarily steps off the main path to take a side trail for a while before getting back on the main path. Why might a discourse need offline text?

(1) *To give background information.* That is, offline material can describe the setting or the situation at the time of the main action.

(2) *To match multiple aspects of the same event.* That is, a single event may have two or more components or aspects, which may be contrasted or aligned.

   (a) **Contrastive matching:** A mainline and offline clause are together thought of as two contrasting parts of a single event or idea. This type of matching is often expressed when a mainline, verb-first clause (V[x]) is directly followed by an offline, non-verb-first clause ([x]V), resulting in the following pattern: V(x) + (x)V.

   (b) **Identical matching:** A series of offline statements that describe two or more examples of a single event. This type of matching occurs when multiple offline, non-verb-first clauses are aligned, resulting in the following pattern: (x)V + (x)V.

(3) *For an interruption or transition.* That is, this action breaks the main flow of thought, whether to mark dramatic pause, thematic division, or flashback. At times, such a clause is **thematically prominent**, meaning that its content sticks out from the main line of the text. Alternatively, it may signal a turning point in the discourse (called **hinge material**), whether by marking a mere paragraph division or by introducing an entirely new temporal, logical, or thematic point of departure. Such clauses can be very important.

(4) *For negated actions.* As a general rule, because a negative does not carry the action forward, it is by nature offline. There may be exceptions to this, but they would be rare. However, you must understand that "offline" does not mean "unimportant." An offline, negated clause can be the most thematically prominent and critical clause in a discourse.

Using historical narrative again, we can see examples of each of these types of offline texts. In the following, mainline verbs are in italics and the offline clauses are in bold typeface.

Table 37.5. Offline Background Information in 1 Kings 17:10

And he arose, and he went to Zarephath. *And he came* to the gate of the city, **and behold, a widow was there gathering wood**. *And he called* to her *and he said*…

וַיָּקָם וַיֵּלֶךְ צָרְפַתָה וַיָּבֹא אֶל־פֶּתַח הָעִיר וְהִנֵּה־שָׁם אִשָּׁה אַלְמָנָה מְקֹשֶׁשֶׁת עֵצִים
וַיִּקְרָא אֵלֶיהָ וַיֹּאמֶר

In this example, the offline material begins with וְהִנֵּה־שָׁם and includes a nominal participial clause. It represents the situation confronting Elijah when he arrived at the gate of the city.

By contrast, all the mainline verbs (in italics) are *wayyiqtol*. Each mainline *wayyiqtol* clause carries the historical account forward; the offline clause does not.

Table 37.6. Contrastive Matching in Genesis 1:4–5

And God saw that the light was good. *And God separated* the light from the darkness. *And God called* the light Day, **and the darkness he called Night.**

וַיַּ֧רְא אֱלֹהִ֛ים אֶת־הָא֖וֹר כִּי־ט֑וֹב וַיַּבְדֵּ֣ל אֱלֹהִ֗ים בֵּ֤ין הָאוֹר֙ וּבֵ֣ין הַחֹ֔שֶׁךְ וַיִּקְרָ֨א
אֱלֹהִ֤ים לָאוֹר֙ י֔וֹם וְלַחֹ֖שֶׁךְ קָ֣רָא לָ֑יְלָה

In the above example, the offline text (in bold) uses the conjunction וְ with a prepositional phrase followed by a *qatal* verb, and it represents the action of calling the darkness "night" as conceptually simultaneous with and contrasted with the calling of the light "day." The other actions are temporally successive and represented by *wayyiqtol* forms in italics. Conceptually, there are three (not four) events here: (1) God saw that it was good, (2) God separated light from darkness, and (3) God called the light "day" and the darkness "night."

Table 37.7. Identical Matching in 2 Kings 17:29–30

And nation after nation was making its gods. *And they placed them* in the shrine of the high places that the Samaritans had made—nation after nation in the cities in which they lived. **And the men of Babylon made Succoth-benoth, and the men of Cuth made Nergal, and the men of Hamath made Ashima.**

וַיִּהְי֣וּ עֹשִׂ֔ים גּ֥וֹי גּ֖וֹי אֱלֹהָ֑יו וַיַּנִּ֣יחוּ בְּבֵ֣ית הַבָּמ֗וֹת אֲשֶׁ֤ר עָשׂוּ֙ הַשֹּׁ֣מְרֹנִ֔ים גּ֥וֹי גּ֖וֹי בְּעָרֵיהֶ֔ם
אֲשֶׁ֛ר הֵ֥ם יֹשְׁבִ֖ים שָׁ֑ם **וְאַנְשֵׁ֣י בָבֶ֗ל עָשׂוּ֙ אֶת־סֻכּ֣וֹת בְּנ֔וֹת וְאַנְשֵׁי־כ֗וּת עָשׂ֤וּ
אֶת־נֵֽרְגַל֙ וְאַנְשֵׁ֣י חֲמָ֔ת עָשׂ֖וּ אֶת־אֲשִׁימָֽא**׃

In the above historical discourse, a series of offline, non-verb-first clauses (all in bold type face) together expound the earlier statements regarding the nations that crafted gods and placed them in the city shrines. Each nation's idolatrous actions are identical to that of all the others, and together they are here portrayed as a single event, each part clarifying the whole.

Table 37.8. Offline Prominent Action in Jonah 1:3–4

And Jonah rose to flee to Tarshish from the presence of YHWH. *And he went down* to Joppa *and he found* a ship going to Tarshish. *And he paid* its fare *and went down* on it to go with them to Tarshish away from the presence of YHWH. **But YHWH hurled a great wind upon the sea…**

וַיָּ֤קָם יוֹנָה֙ לִבְרֹ֣חַ תַּרְשִׁ֔ישָׁה מִלִּפְנֵ֖י יְהוָ֑ה וַיֵּ֨רֶד יָפ֜וֹ וַיִּמְצָ֥א אָנִיָּ֣ה ׀ בָּאָ֣ה תַרְשִׁ֗ישׁ וַיִּתֵּ֨ן
שְׂכָרָ֜הּ וַיֵּ֤רֶד בָּהּ֙ לָב֤וֹא עִמָּהֶם֙ תַּרְשִׁ֔ישָׁה מִלִּפְנֵ֖י יְהוָ֑ה **וַֽיהוָ֗ה הֵטִ֤יל רֽוּחַ־גְּדוֹלָה֙
אֶל־הַיָּ֔ם**

In the above example, the offline bold text uses the conjunction וְ with יְהוָה followed by a *qatal* verb, and it represents God's action of hurling a storm on the sea as a surprising interruption in the story flow. This action is more thematically prominent than the mainline clauses represented by *wayyiqtol* forms in italics. The offline pattern shows that the action is sudden, unexpected, and important.

Table 37.9. Discourse Initiation in Joshua 24:2–3

On the other side of the Euphrates lived your fathers long ago—Terah, the father of Abraham and the father of Nahor—*and they served* other gods. *And I took* your father Abraham from beyond the River...

> בְּעֵבֶר הַנָּהָר יָשְׁבוּ אֲבוֹתֵיכֶם מֵעוֹלָם תֶּרַח אֲבִי אַבְרָהָם וַאֲבִי נָחוֹר *וַיַּעַבְדוּ*
> אֱלֹהִים אֲחֵרִים *וָאֶקַּח* אֶת־אֲבִיכֶם אֶת־אַבְרָהָם מֵעֵבֶר הַנָּהָר

In the above, the first clause uses a prepositional phrase followed by a *qatal* verb to initiate a narrative. It is similar to other offline statements we have seen, except that it does not begin with the conjunction because it begins a discourse. The mainline clauses that carry the historical account forward are represented by *wayyiqtol* forms.

Table 37.10. Offline Negated Action in 2 Samuel 11:8–10

And Uriah went out of the king's house, *and a present went out* after him from the king. *And Uriah slept* at the door of the king's house with all the servants of his lord, **but he did not go down to his house**. *And they told* David...

> *וַיֵּצֵא אוּרִיָּה* מִבֵּית הַמֶּלֶךְ *וַתֵּצֵא* אַחֲרָיו מַשְׂאַת הַמֶּלֶךְ *וַיִּשְׁכַּב אוּרִיָּה* פֶּתַח בֵּית
> הַמֶּלֶךְ אֵת כָּל־עַבְדֵי אֲדֹנָיו **וְלֹא יָרַד אֶל־בֵּיתוֹ** *וַיַּגִּדוּ* לְדָוִד

In the above example, again in historical narrative, the offline text uses the conjunction וְ with לֹא followed by a *qatal* verb, and it indicates what did not happen. Here, the negated clause is more thematically prominent than the mainline clauses.

3. Important Points Related to Mainline and Offline Material

You should grasp three points at this juncture:

(1) Along with the use of context, Hebrew distinguishes mainline from offline material by using different kinds of predicates. In historical discourse, as in the above examples, *wayyiqtol* clauses mark the mainline, but offline material uses other patterns, such as a conjunction (וְ) with a noun followed by a *qatal* verb.

(2) Mainline and offline clauses have various functions in a discourse. Mainline clauses typically present the essential structure of a story or argument. Offline clauses have various functions. Some provide simple background material, such as a description of the setting of a story. Others could be an aside or a comment by the narrator. Still others may mark a decisive moment in the narrative. Do not think of mainline clauses as

important and offline clauses as unimportant. The importance of a clause is not a matter of being mainline or offline; it is a matter of the **prominence** of the clause.

(3) A clause that has prominence draws attention to itself. Mainline material carries the primary flow of thought; offline material impedes this flow for some reason. A clause that halts the flow of the text is often important. Therefore, the most important or **thematically prominent** information in a text is often not the mainline clause. Offline clauses can be thought of as on a **cline**, or continuum, with some having high prominence and others low prominence.The table below indicates the typical prominence of offline clause types. Remember that these are general rules only and do not cover every possible usage for the types of clauses indicated.

Table 37.11. Functions of Predicate Patterns in Historical Discourse[1]

Prominence	Function	Predicate Pattern
1: Offline	Primary marker of climax, or paragraph boundaries; can also be used with mainline *wayyiqtol* for identical or contrastive matching	*qatal* [x] + *qatal* וֹ + [x] + *qatal*
2: Offline	Backgrounded activities	Participial nominal clauses
3: Offline	Backgrounded description	Nominal clauses Existential clauses
4: Offline	Negative (*can shift to level 1 with "momentous negation")	לֹא or אַל + finite verb
Mainline	Primary storyline	*Wayyiqtol*

F. Text Types

We have seen that historical narrative (telling a story) is not the only kind of discourse. For example, one can also give commands (directive discourse) or describe events in the future (anticipatory discourse). We refer to the different kinds of discourse as **text types**.

We know also that the *wayyiqtol* serves as the mainline of historical narrative, and we have also seen some offline material in narrative. By contrast, we saw that the *weqatal* is used for the mainline in a prediction. Thus, each text type has its own preferred way of indicating which clauses are mainline and which are not. In addition, Hebrew uses different predicate patterns within various text types for offline clauses and to begin or end paragraphs. For

---

1. The following studies influenced the shape of the "clines" in this grammar: R. E. Longacre, *Joseph: A Story of Divine Providence—A Text Theoretical and Textlinguistic Analysis of Genesis 37 and 39–48*, 2nd ed. (Winona Lake, IN: Eisenbrauns, 2003), 79, 106, 121; R. L. Heller, *Narrative Structure and Discourse Constellations: An Analysis of Clause Function in Biblical Hebrew Prose*, HSS 55 (Winona Lake, IN: Eisenbrauns, 2004), 428–482; J. S. DeRouchie, *A Call to Covenant Love: Text Grammar and Literary Structure in Deuteronomy 5–11*, GD 30/BS 2 (Piscataway, NJ: Gorgias, 2007), 132–186.

example, in anticipatory discourse (as is found in predications and promises), a *yiqtol* may be used in a clause that begins a paragraph, or it may be used in an offline comment. You have seen that in historical discourse, a conjunction with a noun followed by a *qatal* can mark an offline comment. Thus, *we need to identify the various text types as well as the patterns that mark their mainline statements*, and then we can begin to spot and analyze various offline clauses.

The table below identifies the four main text types of the Hebrew Bible: Historical, Anticipatory, Descriptive, and Directive. Each discourse type is characterized by its own set of predicate patterns. The first three types are used to relay information, whereas the last one expresses a speaker's volition. Beneath the "Text Type" and "Function" columns you will see examples of the various discourse types from the Bible in English translation. Under the column "Formal Signals," you will see listed the standard predicate form used as the mainline for each text type (e.g., historical discourse uses the *wayyiqtol* as its mainline predicate pattern). You will also see some common forms of offline predication listed (usually to fall under "level 2") but remember that offline material can employ a wide variety of predicate patterns.

Table 37.12. Text Types: Their Function & the Forms that Signal Them

Text Type	Function	Formal Signals
Historical	Relays a succession of contingent events; usually past tense, with events having taken place prior to the report	Mainline = *wayyiqtol* clauses. [X] + *qatal* clauses often add offline events and/or mark the onset or termination of paragraphs.
Joshua 24:2–3: On the other side of the Euphrates lived your fathers long ago—Terah, the father of Abraham and the father of Nahor—and they served other gods. And I took your father Abraham from beyond the River, and I led him through all the land of Canaan.		
Anticipatory	Predicts or promises forthcoming events, at times in contingent succession; usually future tense, marking events that will occur after the speech	Mainline = *weqatal* clauses. [X] + *yiqtol* often marks offline predictions or promises and/or signals the onset or termination of paragraphs.
Isaiah 2:2–3: and it shall be lifted up above the hills; and all the nations shall flow to it, and many peoples shall come, and say...		
Isaiah 40:31: But they who wait for YHWH shall renew their strength; they shall mount up with wings like eagles; they shall run and not be weary; they shall walk and not faint.		

Descriptive	Static; explains a situation, state or activity that is occurring in the mainline timeframe of another discourse type or that is perpetually true	Clauses with הָיָה ("to be") Verbless/nominal clauses Existential clauses
	Ezekiel 40:21: Its side rooms (three on each side) and its jambs and its vestibule were of the same size as those of the first gate. Its length was fifty cubits, and its breadth twenty-five cubits.	
Directive	Commands or exhortations, at times in the form of progressive directions for a given task	Mainline = *weqatal* clauses, often after initial volitive(s). Modal *yiqtol* verbs and jussives mark offline instruction/exhortation or signal the onset or termination of paragraphs. לֹא + *yiqtol* or אַל + jussive express prohibitions
	Leviticus 3:2: And he shall lay his hand on the head of his offering and kill it at the entrance of the tent of meeting, and Aaron's sons the priests shall throw the blood against the sides of the altar.	
	Proverbs 3:5: Trust in YHWH with all your heart, and do not lean on your own understanding.	

G. Vocabulary

1. Core Vocabulary

a. Verbs

בטח	Qal: בָּטַח trust, be confident, feel secure
גאל	Qal: גָּאַל redeem, reclaim as one's own
יבש	Qal: יָבֵשׁ be(come) dry, wither
סתר	Niphal: נִסְתַּר hide oneself, be hidden Hiphil: הִסְתִּיר hide, conceal
קלל	Qal: *קַל; קַלּוֹתָ (*qatal* 2ms) be small, be insignificant; swift Piel: קִלֵּל belittle, curse, declare cursed

b. Other Words

אַחֲרוֹן	at the back (spatial), later on (temporal), last
אַלְמָנָה	widow F |construct not extant|
לָשׁוֹן	tongue (as part of the body, a language, or the shape) F M |לְשׁוֹן|
נָשִׂיא	prince M |נְשִׂיא|
קֵץ	end; boundary M |קֵץ|
קָצֶה	edge, end (spatial); end (temporal) M |קְצֵה|

שַׁבָּת	sabbath, rest ⓕ ⓜ	שַׁבָּת|
שֶׁמֶן	oil ⓜ	שֶׁמֶן|

2. Proper Names

אַחְאָב	Ahab
גִּלְעָד	Gilead
גִּלְעָדִי	Gileadite(s)
כְּרִית	Cherith
צִידוֹן	Sidon
צָרְפַת	Zarephath
תִּשְׁבִּי	Tishbite

3. Reading Vocabulary

כּוּל	Pilpel: כִּלְכַּל contain, sustain
קשׁשׁ	Polel: קֹשְׁשׁוּ (*qatal* 3cp) gather
גֶּשֶׁם	rain
טַל	dew, light rain
מָטָר	rain
עֹרֵב	raven
פַּת	scrap, piece
קֶדֶם	eastward, to the east
תּוֹשָׁב	sojourner, resident alien

H. Reading—1 Kings 17:1–11

1 וַיֹּאמֶר אֵלִיָּהוּ הַתִּשְׁבִּי מִתֹּשָׁבֵי גִלְעָד אֶל־אַחְאָב חַי־יְהוָֹה אֱלֹהֵי יִשְׂרָאֵל
אֲשֶׁר עָמַדְתִּי לְפָנָיו אִם־יִהְיֶה הַשָּׁנִים הָאֵלֶּה טַל וּמָטָר כִּי אִם־לְפִי דְבָרִי:
ס

2 וַיְהִי דְבַר־יְהוָה אֵלָיו לֵאמֹר:

3 לֵךְ מִזֶּה וּפָנִיתָ לְךָ קֵדְמָה וְנִסְתַּרְתָּ בְּנַחַל כְּרִית אֲשֶׁר עַל־פְּנֵי הַיַּרְדֵּן:

4 וְהָיָה מֵהַנַּחַל תִּשְׁתֶּה וְאֶת־הָעֹרְבִים צִוִּיתִי לְכַלְכֶּלְךָ שָׁם:

5 וַיֵּלֶךְ וַיַּעַשׂ כִּדְבַר יְהוָה וַיֵּלֶךְ וַיֵּשֶׁב בְּנַחַל כְּרִית אֲשֶׁר עַל־פְּנֵי הַיַּרְדֵּן:

6 וְהָעֹרְבִים מְבִיאִים לוֹ לֶחֶם וּבָשָׂר בַּבֹּקֶר וְלֶחֶם וּבָשָׂר בָּעָרֶב וּמִן־הַנַּחַל יִשְׁתֶּה׃

7 וַיְהִי מִקֵּץ יָמִים וַיִּיבַשׁ הַנָּחַל כִּי לֹא־הָיָה גֶשֶׁם בָּאָרֶץ׃ ס

8 וַיְהִי דְבַר־יְהוָה אֵלָיו לֵאמֹר׃

9 קוּם לֵךְ צָרְפַתָה אֲשֶׁר לְצִידוֹן וְיָשַׁבְתָּ שָׁם הִנֵּה צִוִּיתִי שָׁם אִשָּׁה אַלְמָנָה לְכַלְכְּלֶךָ׃

10 וַיָּקָם וַיֵּלֶךְ צָרְפַתָה וַיָּבֹא אֶל־פֶּתַח הָעִיר וְהִנֵּה־שָׁם אִשָּׁה אַלְמָנָה מְקֹשֶׁשֶׁת עֵצִים וַיִּקְרָא אֵלֶיהָ וַיֹּאמַר קְחִי־נָא לִי מְעַט־מַיִם בַּכְּלִי וְאֶשְׁתֶּה׃

11 וַתֵּלֶךְ לָקַחַת וַיִּקְרָא אֵלֶיהָ וַיֹּאמַר לִקְחִי־נָא לִי פַּת־לֶחֶם בְּיָדֵךְ׃

CHAPTER 38

MORE ON HISTORICAL DISCOURSE AND PARAGRAPHS,
CONNECTORS, AND SUBORDINATION

A. More on Historical Discourse and Paragraphs

Over 40 percent of the Hebrew Bible consists of stories, making it very important to understand how they work. Known also as historical narratives, stories relay a sequence of temporally successive events or actions, usually in simple past time.

1. Predicate Patterns and Paragraph Structure in Historical Discourse

Up to this point in our study of text syntax, we have been concerned only with whether *individual clauses* are mainline or offline and what role such clauses might play in a discourse. In historical texts, we have seen that the *wayyiqtol* verb form almost always expresses simple past time and stands as the principle marker of mainline in this text type. Common offline comments include:

(1) Single [x] + *qatal* clauses ("x" may be a noun, a prepositional phrase, an adverb, etc.)

(2) Copular clauses (nominal clauses and clauses with היה used as a linking verb)

(3) Single negated clauses

All of these constitute offline remarks *within a paragraph (= inner-paragraph comment) or at the boundaries of a paragraph*. In historical discourse, וַיְהִי, "and it came to pass that," also regularly marks the start of a new paragraph. The following table recalls the distinct role played by the various clause types in historical discourse.

Table 38.1. Functions of Predicate Patterns in Historical Discourse

Prominence	Function	Predicate Pattern
1: Offline	Primary marker of climax, or paragraph boundaries; can also be used with mainline *wayyiqtol* for identical or contrastive matching	*qatal* [x] + *qatal* וְ + [x] + *qatal*
2: Offline	Backgrounded activities	Participial nominal clauses
3: Offline	Backgrounded description	Nominal clauses Existential clauses
4: Offline	Negative (*can shift to level 1 with "momentous negation")	לֹא or אַל + finite verb
Mainline	Primary storyline	*Wayyiqtol*

But can an entire paragraph be made up of offline information? The answer, of course, is Yes. When telling a story, you can devote an entire paragraph to setting the stage for a narrative or to giving a flashback or some other kind of information.

2. Paragraph-Level Offline Material

A full paragraph can be offline within the structure of a larger narrative. Such a paragraph is directly related to the story line (as marked by the conjunction ו) but removed from any single element within the mainline. Paragraph-level offline material typically contains background information. That is, an offline paragraph often will not give a simple, successive narrative, but will refer to incidents or factors that help to explain the events of the larger main story line. An offline paragraph may include:

(1) Copular clauses,

(2) Multiple *qatal*, *weqatal*, and/or *yiqtol* clauses, or

(3) Single *wayyiqtol* clauses that are joined with offline clauses. A *wayyiqtol* marks mainline flow-of-thought in historical discourse only when it is sequenced to other mainline verbs. A text usually needs three mainline forms in a row to provide a structural backbone in a given text type. Thus, if a single *wayyiqtol* shows up in a predominantly offline context, the *wayyiqtol* is, in effect, offline. It may still provide some semblance of mainline development, but its role is restricted to the offline context.

3. A Case-Study in Historical Discourse

We will now evaluate the structure of the historical discourse in Gen 37:2–11. Mainline predicate patterns are italicized and offline predicate patterns are in bold. The essential Hebrew text (for observing clause types) is provided. For the sake of simplicity, subordinate clauses are not set apart.

Table 38.2. Historical Discourse in Genesis 37:2–11

Title. *This asyndetic (Ø) verbless clause marks the beginning of the last section of Genesis.*		*Predicate Pattern*	*Main*	*Off*
2a	**These are the generations of Jacob.**	אֵלֶּה תֹּלְדוֹת יַעֲקֹב	Ø+verbless		X

First Paragraph: Paragraph-Level Offline Material. *This unit provides a setting to the narrative that begins in 5a. 2b–4c is not a single, progressive narration but gives two examples of why Joseph's brothers hated him.*		*Predicate Pattern*	*Main*	*Off*
2b	**Joseph**, at seventeen years old, **was shepherding** the flock with his brothers.	יוֹסֵף ... הָיָה רֹעֶה	היה+[x]+Ø+ Participle		X
	Asyndeton (probably initiating a long explicatory development of 2a) and an offline descriptive clause begin the paragraph. The nominal participial clause (see chapter 39) portrays a background action running concurrent with the mainline action of 2d.				

2c	**And he was a youth,** with the sons of Bilhah and the sons of Zilpah, the wives of his father.	וְהוּא נַעַר...	וְ+verbless clause		X
	Epexegetical: further description of Joseph begun in 2b in order to provide a context for the action of 2d.				
2d	*And Joseph brought* a bad report of them to their father.	וַיָּבֵא יוֹסֵף...	WA	X	
	Temporally successive to 2bc; "mainline" to the context of this paragraph only.				
3a	**And Israel loved Joseph** more than all his (other) sons, because he was the son of his old age.	וְיִשְׂרָאֵל אָהַב אֶת־יוֹסֵף...	וְ+[x]+Q		X
	Offline inner-paragraph background comment.				
3b	**And he had made** for him a special tunic.	וְעָשָׂה...	WQ		X
	Further offline inner-paragraph comment on 3a, giving evidence for Jacob's preference for Joseph. Use of weqatal *rather than* wayyiqtol *indicates that this is not a simple succession of events; it is either pluperfect or resultative.*				
4a	*And his brothers saw* that their father loved him more than all his brothers.	וַיִּרְאוּ אֶחָיו...	WA	X	
	Temporally succesive to 3ab; "mainline" to the context of this paragraph only.				
4b	*And they hated him.*	וַיִּשְׂנְאוּ אֹתוֹ	WA	X	
	Temporally successive to the situation described in 2b–4a.				
4c	**And they were unable to speak** to him peacefully.	וְלֹא יָכְלוּ דַּבְּרוֹ...	וְלֹא+Q		X
	Offline statement closes the paragraph. The paragraph begins with Joseph working with his brothers and ends with their being unable to speak to him.				

Second Paragraph: The First Mainline Episode of the Narrative. Unlike vv 2–4, which give background information but do not constitute a simple, temporally successive narrative, vv 5–8 recount a single episode in a straightforward, step-by-step manner.			*Predicate Pattern*	*Main*	*Off*
5a	*And Joseph had a dream.*	וַיַּחֲלֹם יוֹסֵף חֲלוֹם	WA	X	
	Paragraph break is marked by offline clause in 4c; thus, a wayyiqtol is sufficient here.				
5b	*And he reported* (it) to his brothers.	וַיַּגֵּד...	WA	X	
5c	*And they increased* further their hatred of him.	וַיּוֹסִפוּ...	WA	X	
	5a–c report a simple sequence of temporally successive events.				
6a	*And he said* to them...	וַיֹּאמֶר...	WA	X	
	This wayyiqtol *is* **epexegetical** *of 5b, introducing the content of what Joseph reported to his brothers. It is not offline and is still giving information that is part of the mainline narrative; however, it* **does not temporally succeed** *the action of 5c. One mainline clause can be epexegetical of another mainline clause. Notice also that in 2c we saw an offline clause that was epexegetical of 2b, another offline clause.*				
6b-7e	[reported speech]				
8a	*And* his brothers *said* to him...	וַיֹּאמְרוּ...	WA	X	
	Temporally successive to 6a–7e.				
8b-c	[reported speech]				
8d	*And they increased* further their hatred of him on account of his dreams and on account of his words.	וַיּוֹסִפוּ...	WA	X	
	Temporally successive to 6a–8c; concludes paragraph. Notice that v 5 summarizes the whole paragraph, while vv 6–8 flesh out the details. 8d concludes paragraph by repeating and slightly expanding the summary conclusion in 5c.				

Third Paragraph: The Second Mainline Episode of the Narrative. Here, the paragraph break is not indicated by mainline or offline predicate patterns (notice that both 8d and 9a are *wayyiqtol*) but by the facts that vv 9–11 parallel vv 5–8 and that v 9 begins with "yet another dream." Thus, vv 9–11 are a second episode after vv 5–8. *Yet the narrator desired the two units to be read together for no formal markers are used to distinguish them.*			*Predicate Pattern*	*Main*	*Off*
9a	*And he dreamed* yet another dream.	וַיַּחֲלֹם...	WA	X	
9b	*And he relayed* it to his brothers.	וַיְסַפֵּר אֹתוֹ...	WA	X	
	The wayyiqtols *of 9ab are temporally successive and mainline.*				
9c	*And he said*...	וַיֹּאמֶר...	WA	X	
	*Introduces reported speech and is **epexegetical** of 9b, giving the content of what he relayed to his brothers.*				
9d-e	[reported speech]				
10a	*And he relayed* (it) to his father and to his brothers.	וַיְסַפֵּר...	WA	X	
	This event expressed by the wayyiqtol *does not follow 9d–e but resumes the story from 9b, taking up the story line again after the reported speech in 9c–e.*				
10b	*And his father rebuked him.*	וַיִּגְעַר־בּוֹ אָבִיו	WA	X	
	Temporally successive to 9a–10a.				
10c	*And he said* to him...	וַיֹּאמֶר...	WA	X	
	This wayyiqtol *is epexegetical of 10b, introducing the content of the father's rebuke.*				
10d-f	[reported speech]				
11a	*And his brothers were jealous of him.*	וַיְקַנְאוּ־בוֹ אֶחָיו	WA	X	
	Temporally successive to 9a–10a, and parallel to 10b.				
11b	**But his father kept the word** (in mind).	וְאָבִיו שָׁמַר אֶת־הַדָּבָר	ְו+[x]+Q		X
	Offline clause marks contrast and closes the paragraph.				

In the above chart, Gen 37:2–11 has been divided into a title and three paragraphs, though the last two units contains an unbroken chain of *wayyiqtols*. How do we determine where paragraphs begin and end? As you can readily see by comparing standard translations, scholars do not all agree about where paragraph breaks occur in the Hebrew Bible. From a formal perspective, a paragraph will often begin or end with a single offline clause. Where an offline clause terminates one paragraph, the next may begin with no explicit signal, as in a narrative paragraph beginning with a *wayyiqtol*. Rhetorically, paragraphs often have an **envelope structure**, in which the paragraph ending looks back to the paragraph beginning and in some manner echoes or concludes it. This is no different from what most of us were taught as children, that a paragraph should have a strong beginning and conclusion. Absolute certainty about where to place all paragraph breaks is impossible to achieve, but in most instances, the formal signals of the conjunction וֹ, asyndeton, and mainline and offline predicate patterns clearly align with the semantic divisions of the discourse, allowing the interpreter to make a strong case for how to divide the text.

B. More on Connectors and Subordination

Chapter 37 noted that the primary connector in Hebrew is the coordinating conjunction וֹ, "and." Any departure from וֹ marks a special discourse function. Among the other connectors are included:

(1) Coordinating (such as אוֹ, "or") and subordinating (such as אֲשֶׁר, "which, that"; אִם, "if") conjunctions and particles;

(2) The particle כִּי, which has a wide range of meanings;

(3) The negative subordinating adverb פֶּן, "lest";

(4) Emphatic adverbs (such as the coordinators אַף and גַּם, "also, even"; the logical markers כֵּן and כֹה, "thus"; the temporal markers אָז, "then" and עַתָּה, "now");

(5) Restrictive adverbs (such as כִּי אִם, "except"; רַק, "only").

Of these, three deserve further comment due to their high frequency in the Hebrew Bible: אֲשֶׁר, כִּי, אִם.

1. The Relative Particle אֲשֶׁר

אֲשֶׁר, "which, that," is the primary relative particle in Biblical Hebrew. Clauses beginning with אֲשֶׁר are usually one of two types:

(1) **Relative clauses**, modifying a previous element in the sentence, or

(2) **Complement clauses**, providing a clausal complement to the verb.

There are a few examples that do not easily fit into these categories, but we will concern ourselves with the most common usage.

a. Relative Clauses and Resumption

Relative clauses are descriptive and always follow their **head**—the noun, noun phrase, prepositional phrase, or clause they modify. You are already familiar with the use of אֲשֶׁר as a simple relative pronoun. In the following example, אֲשֶׁר modifies the head חַיַּת, which here means "animals."

Table 38.3. אֲשֶׁר as a Simple Relative Pronoun in Genesis 3:1

Now the serpent was more crafty than any of the animals of the field *that* YHWH God had made.
וְהַנָּחָשׁ הָיָה עָרוּם מִכֹּל חַיַּת הַשָּׂדֶה אֲשֶׁר עָשָׂה יְהוָה אֱלֹהִים

Many relative clauses have **resumption**, in which a pronoun or adverb later in the clause in some way recalls the head of the relative. Sometimes the resumptive pronoun or adverb is best left untranslated in English, and sometimes the text needs to be recast into English idiom, as in the example below from Gen 42:21. Here, "our brother" is the head of the relative pronoun, and the 3ms possessive pronoun "his" is the resumptive pronoun that looks back to "brother":

Table 38.4. Genesis 42:21: Resumption to Give אֲשֶׁר the Meaning "Whose"

... our brother, *who* we saw the distress of *his* soul (= the distress of *whose* soul we saw)
אָחִינוּ אֲשֶׁר רָאִינוּ צָרַת נַפְשׁוֹ

In the above example, the resumptive pronoun is necessary because without it, there would be no way to indicate that the relative pronoun אֲשֶׁר is to be understood as the possessor of the נֶפֶשׁ, "soul." In other words, Hebrew has no one-word equivalent for "whose" and must say "who... his soul" for "whose soul."

There are other situations in which a resumptive pronoun is needed in Hebrew. For example, consider this case taken from Gen 3:23, with אֲשֶׁר and מִן used to express "from which." In this example, Hebrew needs to include the resumptive adverb שָׁם, "there," which English can do without.

Table 38.5. Genesis 3:23: Resumption to Give אֲשֶׁר the Meaning "From Which"

to work the ground *which* he was taken *from there* (= to work the ground *from which* he was taken)
לַעֲבֹד אֶת־הָאֲדָמָה אֲשֶׁר לֻקַּח מִשָּׁם

Other instances of resumptive pronouns are optional and may be used for clarity. This is often the case when the relative pronoun is the direct object of a verb. For example, in the following excerpt from Jer 27:19–20, we have ambiguity in the words "and concerning the rest of the vessels, which remained in this city, which Nebuchadnezzar, king of Babylon, did not take." Does the second "which" refer to the vessels or to the city? Did Nebuchadnezzar not take the vessels or the city? In the Hebrew text, the resumptive pronoun helps the reader see that the head of אֲשֶׁר is the vessels and not the city.

Table 38.6. Resumption for Clarification in Jeremiah 27:19–20

... and concerning the rest of the vessels, which remained in this city, ***which*** Nebuchadnezzar, king of Babylon, did not take ***them*** (= the vessels, which remained in this city **and** which Nebuchadnezzar, king of Babylon, did not take)
וְעַל יֶתֶר הַכֵּלִים הַנּוֹתָרִים בָּעִיר הַזֹּאת אֲשֶׁר לֹא־לְקָחָם נְבוּכַדְנֶאצַּר מֶלֶךְ בָּבֶל

b. Complement Clauses

In English, we say, "He saw *that* the game was over" or "She said *that* she would not come." We use "that" after verbs of speaking and perception to mark a "complement clause." Hebrew does much the same. Usually כִּי will mark the complement clause, but occasionally אֲשֶׁר has this function. Compare the following excerpts from Esth 3:4 and Gen 29:12, respectively.

Table 38.7. Complement Clauses with אֲשֶׁר (Esther 3:4) and כִּי (Genesis 29:12)

For he had told them ***that*** he was a Jew.
כִּי־הִגִּיד לָהֶם אֲשֶׁר־הוּא יְהוּדִי
And Jacob announced to Rachel ***that*** he was the brother of her father.
וַיַּגֵּד יַעֲקֹב לְרָחֵל כִּי אֲחִי אָבִיהָ הוּא

2. The Emphatic and Restrictive Particle כִּי

The particle כִּי connects two clauses. It will have one of three functions: (1) logical subordination ("because, if"), (2) restrictive or emphatic coordination ("but, surely"), or (3) as a marker for a complement clause ("that"). In determining which function it has, the position of כִּי relative to the main clause is particularly important. Specifically, you need to take note of which of two positions כִּי occupies in the text:

(1)   כִּי before the main clause

(2)   כִּי after the main clause.

a. כִּי Clause before the Main Clause

When a כִּי clause *precedes* the main clause, the כִּי clause is always logically or temporally subordinate and will typically be translated with "because" or "if" (logical subordination) or with "when" (temporal subordination). Three related contexts exist, and at times it is difficult to discern which of the three is operative:

(1)   Occassionally, as in 2 Kgs 4:29 below, כִּי introduces the protasis of a two-element conditional construction ("if–then"). In such instances, it operates much like the particle אִם, "if."

Table 38.8. כִּי Introducing a Conditional Construction in 2 Kings 4:29

If you find a man, (then) you shall not bless him.
כִּי־תִמְצָא אִישׁ לֹא תְבָרֲכֶנּוּ

(2) כִּי also may introduce a temporal clause and is best translated "when."

Table 38.9. כִּי Introducing Temporal Clauses in Deuteronomy 6:10–12 and 7:1–2

And it shall be *when* YHWH your God brings you into the land ..., (then) take care to yourself lest you forget YHWH.
וְהָיָה כִּי יְבִיאֲךָ יְהוָה אֱלֹהֶיךָ אֶל־הָאָרֶץ ... הִשָּׁמֶר לְךָ פֶּן־תִּשְׁכַּח אֶת־יְהוָה
When YHWH your God brings you into the land ..., (then) you shall devote them to complete destruction.
כִּי יְבִיאֲךָ יְהוָה אֱלֹהֶיךָ אֶל־הָאָרֶץ ... תַּחֲרִים אֹתָם

(3) The particle often means "because"; it can introduce a causal clause that provides the logical ground for a following condition. This is the case in Gen 3:14.

Table 38.10. כִּי Introducing a Causal Clause in Genesis 3:14

Because you have done this, cursed are you more than all the beasts.
כִּי עָשִׂיתָ זֹּאת אָרוּר אַתָּה מִכָּל־הַבְּהֵמָה

b. כִּי *Clause after the Main Clause*

When כִּי *follows* the main clause, the כִּי clause may be subordinate, coordinate, or a complement to the main verb.

(1) Often in this position כִּי means "because," just as it sometimes means when it precedes the main clause. It indicates what is the logical reason for something, as in the following example from Num 21:34:

Table 38.11. כִּי Introducing a Causal Clause in Numbers 21:34

Do not fear him, *for* I have given him into your hand.
אַל־תִּירָא אֹתוֹ כִּי בְיָדְךָ נָתַתִּי אֹתוֹ

(2) In two contexts, כִּי marks a coordinating rather than a subordinating relationship. In other words, the כִּי clause is not subordinated to the main clause.

(a) At times it introduces a clause that stands as the positive counter-statement to a previous negative assertion ("but, except, unless, rather"), as in 1 Kgs 21:15. In such instances, כִּי is often substituted with כִּי אִם.

Table 38.12. כִּי as a Positive Counter-Statement in 1 Kings 21:15

For Naboth is not alive, *but* dead.	
	כִּי אֵין נָבוֹת חַי כִּי־מֵת

(b) כִּי can also stand as the equivalent of an exclamatory interjection, expressing confirmation to a previous statement ("surely, indeed, truly"). This has traditionally been called the "asseverative" use of כִּי, and it often shows up in contexts of oath taking, a feature apparent in 1 Sam 14:44.

Table 38.13. כִּי as an Exclamatory Interjection in 1 Samuel 14:44

Thus may God do (to me), and thus may he do again. *Surely* you will die!	
	כֹּה־יַעֲשֶׂה אֱלֹהִים וְכֹה יוֹסִף כִּי־מוֹת תָּמוּת

(3) As with אֲשֶׁר clauses but with much more frequency, כִּי clauses can serve as the object complement to verbs of perception (רָאה, "see"; שָׁמַע, "hear"), cognition (זכר, "remember"; יָדַע, "know"), or mental state (נחם, "be sorry"), as in Gen 12:11.

Table 38.14. כִּי as an Object Complement in Genesis 12:11

I know *that* you are a woman beautiful of appearance.	
	יָדַעְתִּי כִּי אִשָּׁה יְפַת־מַרְאֶה אַתְּ

3. The Conditional Particle אִם

The conditional particle אִם is commonly used to mark:

(1) Real conditions,

(2) Concessions,

(3) Alternatives, and

(4) Truncated oath formulas.

a. Real Conditions

The protasis of real conditions is most commonly introduced by the particle אִם ("if"). A positive apodosis, as is found in Gen 18:26, generally begins with a *weqatal*, whereas a negative apodosis, like the one found in Gen 43:5, is usually לֹא + *yiqtol*.

Table 38.15. אִם in Real Conditions with a Positive Apodosis in Genesis 18:26

If I find at Sodom fifty righteous (people) in the midst of the city, *(then) I will spare* the whole place on their account.	
	אִם־אֶמְצָא בִסְדֹם חֲמִשִּׁים צַדִּיקִם בְּתוֹךְ הָעִיר וְנָשָׂאתִי לְכָל־הַמָּקוֹם בַּעֲבוּרָם׃

Table 38.16. אִם in Real Conditions with a Negative Apodosis in Genesis 43:5

And if you are not sending, (then) *we will not go down.*
וְאִם־אֵינְךָ מְשַׁלֵּחַ לֹא נֵרֵד

Occasionally, as in Ps 81:8[9], the apodosis is not overt, resulting in the אִם clause express-ing the desire of the speaker. This is generally called the "disiderative" use and is best trans-lated by "if only."

Table 38.17. Disiderative Use of אִם in Psalm 81:8[9]

Israel, *if only* you would listen to me!
יִשְׂרָאֵל אִם־תִּשְׁמַע־לִי

b. Concessions

A related function of אִם is to mark concessions or contrary-to-fact statements. As in Num 22:18, אִם is best translated, "even if," "although," or "though."

Table 38.18. אִם Marking a Concession in Numbers 22:18

Even if Balak were to give me his whole house full of silver and gold, I would not be able to transgress the command (lit., the mouth) of YHWH my God.
אִם־יִתֶּן־לִי בָלָק מְלֹא בֵיתוֹ כֶּסֶף וְזָהָב לֹא אוּכַל לַעֲבֹר אֶת־פִּי יְהוָה אֱלֹהָי

c. Alternatives

In interrogative clauses, אִם can signal an alternative ("or"), as in Josh 5:13.

Table 38.19. אִם Marking an Alternative in Joshua 5:13

Are you for us *or* for our adversaries?
הֲלָנוּ אַתָּה אִם־לְצָרֵינוּ׃

d. Truncated Oath Formulas

A fully expressed oath might go something like this: "I tell you I did not steal that money. May YHWH strike me dead *if* I stole that money!" Or, one could say, "May God himself hold me accountable *if* I do not return by this time tomorrow!" In Hebrew, oaths are fre-quently abbreviated, resulting in comparable statements like, "If I stole that money!" or "If I do not return by this time tomorrow!" This is a **truncated oath formula**, in which the speaker gives only part of the oath, but the partial or truncated oath represents the full oath. Thus, "If I stole that money!" becomes an emphatic way of saying, "I did not steal that money!" Conversely, "If I do not return by this time tomorrow!" is an emphatic way of say-ing, "I will return by this time tomorrow!"

An example appears in 1 Kgs 17:1 (found in chapter 37's "Reading"), where Elijah the prophet proclaimed to Ahab, King of Israel, "As YHWH, the God of Israel lives, before whom I stand, if dew or rain happens these years!" By this statement, the prophet was declaring, "There will certainly be neither dew nor rain" or, more fully, "May YHWH punish me, if these years there is any moisture, except by my word."

Observe that when the speaker wants to make a strong *negative* statement, stressing that something is not true, he begins his oath with "if." Hebrew introduces such a clause with אִם ("if"). But when the speaker wants to stress that something is true, he begins it with "if not." Thus, strong *positive* assertions are introduced by אִם לֹא ("if not"). The following examples illustrate this.

Table 38.20. אִם Introducing a Negative Oath in Psalm 89:35[36]

One time I have sworn by my holiness: I will not lie (lit. *if* I lie) to David!
אַחַת נִשְׁבַּעְתִּי בְקָדְשִׁי אִם־לְדָוִד אֲכַזֵּב׃

Table 38.21. אִם לֹא Introducing a Positive Oath in Isaiah 5:9

In my hearing, YHWH of hosts (has sworn): Certainly (lit. *if not*) many houses will become for a desolation.
בְּאָזְנָי יְהוָה צְבָאוֹת אִם־לֹא בָּתִּים רַבִּים לְשַׁמָּה יִהְיוּ

4. A Series of Conjoined Clauses in a Subordinate Position

In Deut 7:3–4 we see an example of how וְ can connect several clauses that are all subordinated to a higher ranking clause. Clauses 3c–4d make up one sentence in Hebrew, with the *weqatal* clauses in 4b–d all building upon the initial כִּי clause in 4a. *The important thing to notice here is that clauses 4b–d are all on the same level of subordination as 4a.*

Although a subordinate connector always marks a subordinate clause, the coordinating connector וְ often does *not* signal a matrix clause, for strings of subordinate clauses are regularly coordinated together. One must, therefore, follow the trail of coordination to see if it begins with a matrix or subordinate clause.

The type of initial clause classifies the nature of all the clauses coordinated to it. Note also how the asyndetic (Ø) clause in 3b signals an embedded paragraph that clarifies the charge in 3a not to intermarry. The fact that long strings of coordinate clauses can themselves be embedded as subordinate clauses within a single matrix clause allows for single sentences in Hebrew to be made up of numerous clauses.

Table 38.22. A Series of Conjoined Subordinate Clauses in Deuteronomy 7:3–4

וְלֹא תִתְחַתֵּן בָּם	↑	וְ	3a
בִּתְּךָ לֹא־תִתֵּן לִבְנוֹ	–	∅	3b
וּבִתּוֹ לֹא־תִקַּח לִבְנֶךָ׃	↑	וְ	3c
כִּי־יָסִיר אֶת־בִּנְךָ מֵאַחֲרַי		כִּי	4a
וְעָבְדוּ אֱלֹהִים אֲחֵרִים	↑	וְ	4b
וְחָרָה אַף־יְהוָה בָּכֶם	↑	וְ	4c
וְהִשְׁמִידְךָ מַהֵר׃	↑	וְ	4d

3a	And you shall not intermarry with them.
3b	Your daughter you shall never give to his son.
3c	And his daughter you shall never take for your son,
4a	**because** it would turn aside your son from after me,
4b	**and** they would serve other gods,
4c	**and** the anger of YHWH would burn against you,
4d	**and** he would destroy you quickly.

C. Vocabulary

1. *Core Vocabulary*

a. Verbs

הפך	Qal: הָפַךְ overthrow, overturn, turn back to front
	Niphal: נֶהְפַּךְ/נֶהְפָּךְ be changed, be overthrown
לבש	Qal: לָבַשׁ put on, clothe
רוץ	Qal: רָץ run
שׂבע	Qal: שָׂבַע consume one's fill, satisfy oneself
שכח	Qal: שָׁכַח forget

b. Other Words

חָזָק	hard, strong, heavy, severe
חֲצִי	half, middle Ⓜ
עַמּוּד	pillar, upright support Ⓜ |עַמּוּד|
עֶצֶם	bone, skeleton Ⓕ |עֶצֶם|
פַּעַם	foot, step; time Ⓕ |פַּעַם|

רֶ֫כֶב   chariot, group of chariots (s or pl collective) Ⓜ |רֶ֫כֶב|

שֶׁ֫קֶר   lie, falsehood, deceit Ⓜ |שֶׁ֫קֶר|

2. Proper Names

אַבְנֵר   Abner

יְאֹר   (great) river (Nile, Euphrates)

יֵהוּא   Jehu

יוֹאָשׁ   Joash

צִדְקִיָּ֫הוּ   Zedekiah; also as צִדְקִיָּה

3. Reading Vocabulary

חסר   Qal: חָסֵר decrease, be devoid

מדד   Hithpolel: וַיִּתְמֹדֵד "and he stretched out"

בַּעֲלָה   mistress, female owner

גֶּ֫שֶׁם   rain

חֵיק   bosom, lap (i.e., lower, outer part of body where loved ones are pressed or hands kept)

חֳלִי   sickness, suffering

כַּד   jar

מְלֹא   that which fills, fullness

מִטָּה   couch, bed

מָעוֹג   feast, source of supply

נְשָׁמָה   movement of air, breath

עֻגָה   cake, round flat loaf

עֲלִיָּה   upper room

צַפַּ֫חַת   pitcher

קֶ֫מַח   flour

D. Reading—1 Kings 17:12-24

In this reading, a Kethiv text has a light gray background, and the Qere is in brackets.

12 וַתֹּאמֶר חַי־יְהוָה אֱלֹהֶיךָ אִם־יֶשׁ־לִי[1] מָעוֹג כִּי אִם־מְלֹא כַף־קֶמַח בַּכַּד
וּמְעַט־שֶׁמֶן בַּצַּפָּחַת וְהִנְנִי מְקֹשֶׁשֶׁת שְׁנַיִם עֵצִים וּבָאתִי וַעֲשִׂיתִהוּ לִי וְלִבְנִי
וַאֲכַלְנֻהוּ וָמָתְנוּ:

13 וַיֹּאמֶר אֵלֶיהָ אֵלִיָּהוּ אַל־תִּירְאִי בֹּאִי עֲשִׂי כִדְבָרֵךְ אַךְ עֲשִׂי־לִי מִשָּׁם עֻגָה
קְטַנָּה בָרִאשֹׁנָה וְהוֹצֵאת לִי וְלָךְ וְלִבְנֵךְ תַּעֲשִׂי בָּאַחֲרֹנָה: ס

14 כִּי כֹה אָמַר יְהוָה אֱלֹהֵי יִשְׂרָאֵל כַּד הַקֶּמַח לֹא תִכְלָה וְצַפַּחַת הַשֶּׁמֶן לֹא
תֶחְסָר עַד יוֹם תֵּתֶן תִּתֵּן [תֵּת][2]־יְהוָה גֶּשֶׁם עַל־פְּנֵי הָאֲדָמָה:

15 וַתֵּלֶךְ וַתַּעֲשֶׂה כִּדְבַר אֵלִיָּהוּ וַתֹּאכַל הוּא־וָהִיא [הִיא] [וָ][הוּא][3] וּבֵיתָהּ
יָמִים:

16 כַּד הַקֶּמַח לֹא כָלָתָה וְצַפַּחַת הַשֶּׁמֶן לֹא חָסֵר כִּדְבַר יְהוָה אֲשֶׁר דִּבֶּר בְּיַד
אֵלִיָּהוּ: פ

17 וַיְהִי אַחַר הַדְּבָרִים הָאֵלֶּה חָלָה בֶּן־הָאִשָּׁה בַּעֲלַת הַבָּיִת וַיְהִי חָלְיוֹ חָזָק
מְאֹד עַד אֲשֶׁר[4] לֹא־נוֹתְרָה־בּוֹ נְשָׁמָה:

18 וַתֹּאמֶר אֶל־אֵלִיָּהוּ מַה־לִּי וָלָךְ אִישׁ הָאֱלֹהִים בָּאתָ אֵלַי לְהַזְכִּיר אֶת־עֲוֹנִי
וּלְהָמִית אֶת־בְּנִי:

19 וַיֹּאמֶר אֵלֶיהָ תְּנִי־לִי אֶת־בְּנֵךְ וַיִּקָּחֵהוּ מֵחֵיקָהּ וַיַּעֲלֵהוּ אֶל־הָעֲלִיָּה
אֲשֶׁר־הוּא יֹשֵׁב שָׁם וַיַּשְׁכִּבֵהוּ עַל־מִטָּתוֹ:

20 וַיִּקְרָא אֶל־יְהוָה וַיֹּאמַר יְהוָה אֱלֹהָי הֲגַם עַל־הָאַלְמָנָה אֲשֶׁר־אֲנִי מִתְגּוֹרֵר[5]
עִמָּהּ הֲרֵעוֹתָ לְהָמִית אֶת־בְּנָהּ:

---

1. This אִם is part of a "truncated oath clause."

2. תִּתֵּן, a Qal *yiqtol* 3fs/2ms of נתן, is the Kethiv, and תֵּת, a Qal infinitive construct of נתן, is the Qere. The Qere is the correct reading here; ignore the Kethiv.

3. Notice that the Kethiv, הוּא־וָהִיא, is a 3ms pronoun followed by a conjunction and a 3fs pronoun, whereas the Qere, הִיא־וָהוּא, is a 3fs pronoun followed by a conjunction and a 3ms pronoun. What in context indicates that the Qere is preferable?

4. Sometimes the particle אֲשֶׁר follows prepositions, as in מֵאֲשֶׁר, "from where"; עִם אֲשֶׁר, "with whom"; עַד אֲשֶׁר, "until"; etc.

5. The Hithpolel of גּוּר means "stay as a stranger." You know the Qal.

21 וַיִּתְמֹדֵד עַל־הַיֶּלֶד שָׁלֹשׁ פְּעָמִים וַיִּקְרָא אֶל־יְהוָה וַיֹּאמַר יְהוָה אֱלֹהָי תָּשָׁב
נָא נֶפֶשׁ־הַיֶּלֶד הַזֶּה עַל־קִרְבּוֹ:

22 וַיִּשְׁמַע יְהוָה בְּקוֹל אֵלִיָּהוּ וַתָּשָׁב נֶפֶשׁ־הַיֶּלֶד עַל־קִרְבּוֹ וַיֶּחִי:

23 וַיִּקַּח אֵלִיָּהוּ אֶת־הַיֶּלֶד וַיֹּרִדֵהוּ מִן־הָעֲלִיָּה הַבַּיְתָה וַיִּתְּנֵהוּ לְאִמּוֹ וַיֹּאמֶר
אֵלִיָּהוּ רְאִי חַי בְּנֵךְ:

24 וַתֹּאמֶר הָאִשָּׁה אֶל־אֵלִיָּהוּ עַתָּה זֶה יָדַעְתִּי כִּי אִישׁ אֱלֹהִים אָתָּה
וּדְבַר־יְהוָה בְּפִיךָ אֱמֶת: פ

CHAPTER 39
MORE ON ANTICIPATORY AND DESCRIPTIVE DISCOURSE

A. More on Anticipatory Discourse

Anticipatory discourse is made up of predictions and promises that propose, plan, or depict events or actions that will occur in future time. All anticipatory discourse carries the same mainline and offline predicate patterns.

1. Predicate Patterns and Paragraph Structure in Anticipatory Discourse

Mainline predictions and promises are usually signaled by a sequence of *weqatal* clauses. The offline patterns are as follows:

(1) Paragraph boundaries are usually marked by a single [x] + *yiqtol* clause or some other independent offline clause. Paragraphs are also frequently introduced by וְהָיָה, "and it shall come about," which in anticipatory discourse stands as the future-oriented counterpart to וַיְהִי in historical texts.

(2) Single non-*weqatal* clauses or one or more linked copular ("to be") clauses regularly signal inner-paragraph comments.

(3) Multiple copular clauses or multiple non-*weqatal* clauses regularly mark paragraph-level offline material.

The table below summarizes the function of the various clause patterns.

Table 39.1. Functions of Predicate Patterns in Anticipatory Discourse

Prominence	Function	Predicate Pattern
1: Offline	Backgrounded predictions and promises. Can also mark climax, paragraph boundaries, identical or contrastive matching.	*yiqtol* [x] + *yiqtol* וְ + [x] + *yiqtol*
2: Offline	Backgrounded activities. Can also mark paragraph boundaries.	Participial nominal clauses
3: Offline	Backgrounded description. Can also mark paragraph boundaries.	Linking clauses Existential clauses
4: Offline	Negative (*can shift to level 1 with "momentous negation")	לֹא or אַל + finite verb
Mainline	Primary prediction or promise	*weqatal*

The mainline verb form, the *weqatal*, lays out the core predictions, promises, or threats around which the whole is structured. These mainline verbs do not, however, demand that events be in contingent temporal succession. At times we simply have a series of promises or threats with no contingent succession of events implied, and sometimes the contingency is more logical than temporal.

2. A Case-Study in Anticipatory Discourse

In the following, "Main" = Mainline; "Off" = Offline; "Sub" = Subordinate.

Table 39.2. Anticipatory Discourse in Deuteronomy 7:12–13

				Predicate Pattern	Main	Off	Sub
	12a	**And it shall be,**	וְהָיָה	WQ copula initiates protasis + apodosis construc-tion		X	
		The discourse marker וְהָיָה signals the start of a new paragraph that directly grows out of the preceding context. (See below for the offline role of copular constructions; for more on discourse markers, see chapter 40.)					
Protasis	12b	**because you will listen** to these rules	עֵקֶב תִּשְׁמְעוּן...	[x] + Y			X
		A causal subordinate clause used as a protasis.					
	12c	*and keep* (them)	וּשְׁמַרְתֶּם	WQ			X
		The weqatal is a development of the subordinate protasis begun in 12b.					
	12d	*and do* them,	וַעֲשִׂיתֶם...	WQ			X
		A further development and conclusion to the pro-tasis begun in 12b.					
Apodosis	12e	*that YHWH your God will keep* with you the covenant and the steadfast love that he swore to your fathers.	וְשָׁמַר יְהוָה אֱלֹהֶיךָ...	WQ	X		
		Weqatal used for an apodosis. The fact that this weqatal does not function the same as those in 12c and 12d is indicated by the change of subject from "you" to "YHWH."					
	13a	*And he will love you,*	וַאֲהֵבְךָ	WQ	X		
		A development of 12e.					
	13b	*and bless you,*	וּבֵרַכְךָ	WQ	X		
		A second development of 12e.					
	13c	*and multiply you....*	וְהִרְבֶּךָ	WQ	X		
		A third development of 12e.					

A number of points are noteworthy from the above example.

(1) Mainline verbs, along with the other syntax markers, give us the primary structure of the passage. In the above text, because Israel will heed the rules of God, God will in turn keep his covenant with the fathers, an act that is further defined as loving, blessing, and multiplying Israel.

(2) In these verses we see a mainline series of four promises that make up the apodosis of a protasis-apodosis construction. The latter three of these promises develop the initial promise that YHWH will keep the covenant that he swore to the fathers. Notice that *weqatal* clauses are used both in the subordinate protasis and the mainline apodosis. What indicates the change to the apodosis?

(3) One could argue that there is a degree of contingent temporal succession in the passage since doing the commands is subsequent to hearing them, and Israel's being multiplied is subsequent to being loved and blessed by YHWH.

B. Descriptive Discourse

1. Verbless/Nominal Clauses and the Special Nature of Copular Clauses

We have already noted the existence of nominal (or verbless) clauses, in which there is a complete clause with no finite verb. For example, an adjective can be used as a predicate in expressions such as טוֹבָה הָאִשָּׁה, "the woman is good." A participle can function similarly, as in מֹשֶׁה רֹעֶה אֶת־צֹאן אָבִיו, "Moses was shepherding the flock of his father." In such clauses, the predicate is made up of an understood copula or linking verb (= "to be"), which we supply in translation, plus a complement, which could be a noun, an adjective, a prepositional phrase, a participle, an infinitive construct, or some other nominal form or phrase. This complement is the predicate.

Copular clauses stand out in all languages, due to the special nature of the equative verb "to be." Its underlining meaning as "being, existence, or occurrence" distinguishes it from most other verbs, and its function is unique in that it serves to link a subject to its location, possession, identity, class, or status, among other things. In the first example above, "the woman" is classified or described as "good." In the second example, "Moses" is identified or characterized as "shepherding" the flock of Jethro.

2. Distinguishing S–P in Verbless/Nominal Clauses

A nominal (verbless) clause may have no more than two nominals (e.g., noun, pronoun, adjective, etc.) standing side-by-side. Because the predicate in nominal clauses is not identified by an explicit verb, there is difficulty at times distinguishing the subject (S) and the predicate (P). While the default word order in nominal clauses appears to be S–P, often the pattern is reversed, whether to help orient the audience to the greater context (= **contextualizing constituent**) or to highlight prominent information (= **focus**). In that situation, how does the reader know which noun is the subject and which is the predicate?

THE GUIDING PRINCIPLE: The subject is usually more defined or known in the communication situation than the predicate.

(1) Although certain kinds of definiteness are associated with specific forms like the definite article, all nominals have a relative level of definiteness in relation to one another. So, for example, a proper noun (e.g., Ruth) is more defined than an indefinite common noun (e.g., house), while the latter is itself more defined than an adjective (e.g., red).

(2) Generally, the more definite noun or noun phrase will be the subject.

    (a) In וְעַבְדִּי דָוִד מֶלֶךְ (Ezek 37:24), the subject is the definite noun phrase וְעַבְדִּי דָוִד and the predicate is the indefinite noun מֶלֶךְ. It means "and my servant David (will be) king."

    (b) In a clause like כִּי אֵל רַחוּם יְהוָה אֱלֹהֶיךָ (Deut 4:31), where we see an indefinite noun phrase (אֵל רַחוּם, "compassionate God") and a proper name (יְהוָה אֱלֹהֶיךָ, "YHWH your God") standing side-by-side, the proper name is more defined or specific and is therefore likely the subject: "for YHWH your God is a compassionate God" (rather than "for a compassionate God is YHWH your God").

(3) In a nominal clause that has an independent pronoun as one constituent and a noun or noun phrase as the other, the pronoun will be the subject. The pronoun either refers to an aforementioned item or it points ahead to new information.

    (a) In Ps 24:10, הוּא מֶלֶךְ הַכָּבוֹד, the pronoun is the subject because it refers back to an aforementioned item (in this case, the aforementioned item is יְהוָה from v. 8). הוּא is thus the subject: "He is the king of the glory!"

    (b) In Gen 9:12, זֹאת אוֹת־הַבְּרִית, "this is the sign of the covenant," the word זֹאת ("this") points ahead to an item not previously mentioned, that is, to new information ("the sign of the covenant").

(4) Sometimes both the subject and predicate in a nominal clause may be definite. In such a situation, it may be unclear or debatable which word is the subject and which word is the predicate. In Exod 9:27 we have יְהוָה הַצַּדִּיק, which could be translated either as "YHWH is in the right" or as "The one in the right is YHWH."

For more on distinguishing subject and predicate in nominal clauses, see Appendix 3.

3. Copular Clauses with and without Lexicalized היה

You have dealt with clauses that have the verb "to be" (e.g., "David is king"). This kind of clause is called a **copular clause**. These sentences may or may not include היה. The following concepts will help you understand the variety of such clauses.

(1) **Copula**: the verb "to be" (in Hebrew: היה).

(2) **Nominal clause**: a copular clause without an explicit copula. That is, היה is "understood" and not actually present. This is also called a **verbless** clause.

(3) **Lexicalized היה**: the verb היה is actually present in the clause.

(4) In a nominal clause, the **predicate** may be a noun ("David [is] *king*"), adjective ("David [is] *strong*"), participle ("David [is] *watching*"), prepositional phrase ("David [is] *in the house*"), or adverb ("David [is] *there*").

(5) In a copular clause with lexicalized היה, the predicate is actually היה plus the noun, adjective, participle, prepositional phrase, or adverb that goes with it. Thus, in דָּוִד הָיָה מֶלֶךְ, the verb הָיָה is the **predicate** and מֶלֶךְ is the **predicate complement**.

(6) Why might the author employ lexicalized היה instead of just using a nominal clause? The verb היה can be used to help mark tense, aspect, mood, or some other discourse function that would be missed if the verb was only understood and not actually present in the text.

(7) Otherwise, all copular clauses, whether nominal or with lexicalized היה, are essentially the same, as the examples below illustrate.

a. Copular Clause with Participle as Predicate or Predicate Complement

Table 39.3. Copular Clauses in Joshua 3:17 and 2 Chronicles 30:10

And all of Israel were *crossing* on dry ground.
וְכָל־יִשְׂרָאֵל עֹבְרִים בֶּחָרָבָה P   S
And the couriers *were passing* from city to city.
וַיִּהְיוּ הָרָצִים עֹבְרִים מֵעִיר לָעִיר P²   S   P¹

In these two examples, the participle עֹבְרִים is respectively the predicate and predicate complement (in the second example, P¹ is the predicate verb and P² is the predicate complement). As far as the action of the predicate participles is concerned, both of these clauses are essentially the same. This does not mean that the presence of וַיִּהְיוּ is completely irrelevant, but it relates to the macrosyntax of the discourse rather than to the microsyntax of the clause.

b. Copular Clause with Prepositional Phrase as Predicate or Predicate Complement

Table 39.4. Copular Clauses in Ezekiel 27:11 and Genesis 7:10

Sons of Arvad and Helech were *on your walls*.
בְּנֵי אַרְוַד וְחֵילֵךְ עַל־חוֹמוֹתַיִךְ P   S
And the waters of the flood were *on the earth*.
וּמֵי הַמַּבּוּל הָיוּ עַל־הָאָרֶץ P²   P¹   S

עַל־חוֹמוֹתַיִךְ, "on your walls," in Ezek 27:11 and עַל־הָאָרֶץ, "on the earth," in Gen 7:10 are respectively the predicate and predicate complement in these examples. Only the latter, however, operates with an explicit copula.

4. The Special Offline Role of Copular Clauses to Mark Descriptive Discourse

All copular clauses, with or without lexicalized היה (and clauses containing an existential particle [יֵשׁ, "there is," and אֵין, "there is not"]) have this in common: they provide static information by explaining a situation that is occurring alongside a mainline activity in another discourse type or that is perpetually true. This is due to the unique nature of the verb "to be." Except in texts that are purely descriptive (such as 1 Chron 1–8), copular clauses never develop the primary chain of events that shapes a text's skeleton. Since they point only to the existence, identity, or description of something, they lack any movement and, except for passages like the aforementioned 1 Chron 1–8, they are by nature offline.

We have termed such material descriptive discourse. However, viewing copular clauses as a distinct text type could be misleading if one expects to find a mainline predicate pattern like those found in other discourse types. While it may be possible to construe nominal clauses as mainline in a discourse that is purely description and has no action, it is debatable whether clauses that only express the existence of something would ever be perceived as structurally prominent. Most commonly, copular and existential clauses clarify setting, mark transition, or provide inner-paragraph comments within other discourse types.

While all copular clauses, whether nominal or with היה, function similarly in Hebrew, two groupings of copular clauses are apparent, depending on the type of predicate (complement) that is used.

(1) *If the predicate is a participle or infinitive construct*: Such clauses present an event, situation, or action that coincides with and clarifies the setting of more mainline events.

(2) *If the predicate is a non-verbal form*: These clauses are purely descriptive.

The text below from Deut 9:15–16b illustrates, first, a copulative clause with a participle describing concurrent action (וְהָהָר בֹּעֵר בָּאֵשׁ), and second, a copulative clause with a non-verbal predicate that is descriptive or static in nature (וּשְׁנֵי לֻחֹת הַבְּרִית עַל שְׁתֵּי יָדָי). Mainline predicate patterns are in italics, and offline clauses are in bold.

Table 39.5. The Backgrounding Role of Copular Clauses in Deuteronomy 9:15–16

And I turned and descended from the mountain. **And the mountain was blazing with fire, and the two tablets of the covenant were in my two hands.** *And I looked*, and indeed, you had sinned against YHWH your God.

וָאֵפֶן וָאֵרֵד מִן־הָהָר וְהָהָר בֹּעֵר בָּאֵשׁ וּשְׁנֵי לֻחֹת הַבְּרִית עַל שְׁתֵּי יָדָי וָאֵרֶא
וְהִנֵּה חֲטָאתֶם לַיהוָה אֱלֹהֵיכֶם

Moses recalls a chain of events he performed (all mainline *wayyiqtols*) in order to see the extent of Israel's misconduct: I turned > I descended > I looked. However, as if for dramatic pause, he makes two offline comments before recalling his overview of the people's situation. First, through a nominal participial clause, we are told that at the same time as Moses' descent "the mountain was blazing with fire (וְהָהָר בֹּעֵר בָּאֵשׁ)." A verbless clause then shows that Moses went down the mountain with the covenant documents (וּשְׁנֵי לֻחֹת הַבְּרִית עַל שְׁתֵּי יָדָי, "And the two tablets of the covenant were in my two hands"). While neither copular clause advances the storyline, both provide important background information.

C. Vocabulary

1. Core Vocabulary

a. Verbs

זנה	Qal: זָנָה commit fornication, be unfaithful
חרה	Qal: חָרָה be hot, burning, (by extension) be angry
טהר	Qal: טָהֵר be clean (usually ceremonially)
	Piel: טִהַר cleanse, purify, declare clean (ceremonially)
טוב	Qal: טוֹב be good
רעע	Qal: רַע / רָע be bad, wicked
	Hiphil: הֵרַע do evil, treat badly

b. Other Words

בָּמָה	high place (often cultic), grave F |*construct not extant*|
חָדָשׁ	new
חֵלֶב	fat, (by extension) choice part M |חֵלֶב|
חֶרְפָּה	disgrace, shame, taunt F |חֶרְפַּת|
נֶגֶד	opposite, in front of, corresponding to
עוֹר	skin (of a person or animal), leather M |עוֹר|
תָּמִיד	continuance M |*construct not extant*|; lasting, continually (adverb)

2. Proper Names

אֶסְתֵּר	Esther
דָּנִיֵּאל	Daniel
מָרְדֳּכַי	Mordecai
נְבוּכַדְנֶאצַּר	Nebuchadnezzar

3. Reading Vocabulary

זרק	Qal: זָרַק sprinkle
כלם	Niphal: נִכְלַמְתְּ (2fs) be(come) hurt, humiliated, ashamed

קוֹט	Niphal: נָקֹטָה feel disgust, loathe
טֻמְאָה	(state of) uncleanness
גִּלּוּל	idol (always pl.)
דָּגָן	grain
תְּנוּבָה	produce, yield
מַעֲלָל	deed

D. Reading—Ezekiel 36:22–32

22 לָכֵן אֱמֹר לְבֵית־יִשְׂרָאֵל כֹּה אָמַר אֲדֹנָי יְהוִֹה לֹא לְמַעַנְכֶם אֲנִי עֹשֶׂה בֵּית יִשְׂרָאֵל כִּי אִם־לְשֵׁם־קָדְשִׁי אֲשֶׁר חִלַּלְתֶּם בַּגּוֹיִם אֲשֶׁר־בָּאתֶם שָׁם:

23 וְקִדַּשְׁתִּי אֶת־שְׁמִי הַגָּדוֹל הַמְחֻלָּל בַּגּוֹיִם אֲשֶׁר חִלַּלְתֶּם בְּתוֹכָם וְיָדְעוּ הַגּוֹיִם כִּי־אֲנִי יְהוָֹה נְאֻם אֲדֹנָי יְהוִֹה בְּהִקָּדְשִׁי בָכֶם לְעֵינֵיהֶם:

24 וְלָקַחְתִּי אֶתְכֶם מִן־הַגּוֹיִם וְקִבַּצְתִּי אֶתְכֶם מִכָּל־הָאֲרָצוֹת וְהֵבֵאתִי אֶתְכֶם אֶל־אַדְמַתְכֶם:

25 וְזָרַקְתִּי עֲלֵיכֶם מַיִם טְהוֹרִים וּטְהַרְתֶּם מִכֹּל טֻמְאוֹתֵיכֶם וּמִכָּל־גִּלּוּלֵיכֶם אֲטַהֵר אֶתְכֶם:

26 וְנָתַתִּי לָכֶם לֵב חָדָשׁ וְרוּחַ חֲדָשָׁה אֶתֵּן בְּקִרְבְּכֶם וַהֲסִרֹתִי אֶת־לֵב הָאֶבֶן מִבְּשַׂרְכֶם וְנָתַתִּי לָכֶם לֵב בָּשָׂר:

27 וְאֶת־רוּחִי אֶתֵּן בְּקִרְבְּכֶם וְעָשִׂיתִי אֵת אֲשֶׁר־בְּחֻקַּי תֵּלֵכוּ[1] וּמִשְׁפָּטַי תִּשְׁמְרוּ וַעֲשִׂיתֶם:

28 וִישַׁבְתֶּם בָּאָרֶץ אֲשֶׁר נָתַתִּי לַאֲבֹתֵיכֶם וִהְיִיתֶם לִי לְעָם וְאָנֹכִי אֶהְיֶה לָכֶם לֵאלֹהִים:

29 וְהוֹשַׁעְתִּי אֶתְכֶם מִכֹּל טֻמְאוֹתֵיכֶם וְקָרָאתִי אֶל־הַדָּגָן וְהִרְבֵּיתִי אֹתוֹ וְלֹא־אֶתֵּן עֲלֵיכֶם רָעָב:

30 וְהִרְבֵּיתִי אֶת־פְּרִי הָעֵץ וּתְנוּבַת הַשָּׂדֶה לְמַעַן אֲשֶׁר לֹא תִקְחוּ עוֹד חֶרְפַּת רָעָב בַּגּוֹיִם:

---

1. וְעָשִׂיתִי אֵת אֲשֶׁר = "And I will make it so that…"

31 וּזְכַרְתֶּם֙ אֶת־דַּרְכֵיכֶ֣ם הָרָעִ֔ים וּמַעַלְלֵיכֶ֖ם אֲשֶׁ֣ר לֹֽא־טוֹבִ֑ים וּנְקֹֽטֹתֶם֙
    בִּפְנֵיכֶ֔ם עַ֚ל עֲוֺנֹ֣תֵיכֶ֔ם וְעַ֖ל תּוֹעֲבוֹתֵיכֶֽם׃

32 לֹ֧א לְמַעַנְכֶ֣ם אֲנִֽי־עֹשֶׂה֮ נְאֻם֙ אֲדֹנָ֣י יְהוִ֔ה יִוָּדַ֖ע לָכֶ֑ם בּ֣וֹשׁוּ וְהִכָּֽלְמ֛וּ מִדַּרְכֵיכֶ֖ם
    בֵּ֥ית יִשְׂרָאֵֽל׃ ס

CHAPTER 40
DISCOURSE MARKERS AND MORE ON DIRECTIVE DISCOURSE

A. Discourse Markers

In Hebrew there are words whose chief purpose is to signal structural features in a discourse rather than to convey semantic meaning. Indeed, sometimes you don't even translate them! You are already aware that, at the clause level, אֵת as a direct object marker is not to be translated. Similarly, there are words that operate at the text level in order to mark structure. Such words are macrosyntactic "sign-posts." They indicate subdivisions and the relationship of various parts of a text. English too has discourse structuring markers, as in the use of "well" or "now" in conversation or of "once upon a time" to begin a story.

1. הֵן/הִנֵּה: *Markers of Immediate Significance*

Often termed **presentative particles**, הִנֵּה and הֵן (with or without וְ) are clause modifiers that point forward in a discourse, focusing attention on the content of the clause that follows (see chapter 26). The particles always introduce an event or situation that has special relevance with respect to the actual moment of communication, whether to provide a basis for a forthcoming statement or command or to set a temporal connection, occasion, or condition for an ensuing clause. While traditionally translated with the archaic "Behold," they are perhaps best rendered "Look here," "Well now," or with some other modern idiom.

Table 40.1. הֵן Marking Immediate Significance in Deuteronomy 5:23–25

And all the heads of your tribes and your elders approached me [Moses] and said, *"Now look*, YHWH our God has shown us his glory and his greatness, and his voice we have heard out of the midst of the fire.... And now, why should we die, for this great fire will consume us?"
וַתִּקְרְבוּן אֵלַי כָּל־רָאשֵׁי שִׁבְטֵיכֶם וְזִקְנֵיכֶם וַתֹּאמְרוּ הֵן הֶרְאָנוּ יְהוָה אֱלֹהֵינוּ אֶת־כְּבֹדוֹ וְאֶת־גָּדְלוֹ וְאֶת־קֹלוֹ שָׁמַעְנוּ מִתּוֹךְ הָאֵשׁ ... וְעַתָּה לָמָּה נָמוּת כִּי תֹאכְלֵנוּ הָאֵשׁ הַגְּדֹלָה הַזֹּאת

In the above example, הֵן directs the audience's attention to the leaders' testimony of their recent encounter with YHWH and ties this past event with their present conversation with Moses. Specifically, their encounter with God is the basis for their question, "And now, why should we die?"

הִנֵּה can also mark the immediate significance of an event or situation by indicating how something looked through a character's eyes, as in the following example from Gen 18:2.

Table 40.2. הִנֵּה Marking Point-of-View in Genesis 18:2

And he lifted his eyes and looked, *and—get this—*three men were standing before him!
וַיִּשָּׂא עֵינָיו וַיַּרְא *וְהִנֵּה* שְׁלֹשָׁה אֲנָשִׁים נִצָּבִים עָלָיו

Here the narrator uses וְהִנֵּה to focus attention on what Abraham saw: שְׁלֹשָׁה אֲנָשִׁים נִצָּבִים עָלָיו. It is as if, for a brief moment, the reader is looking through Abraham's eyes, seeing what he is seeing.

הִנֵּה can also take pronominal suffixes. For example, when YHWH called to Samuel, he responded הִנֵּנִי, "Yes!" (lit., "Look, I am [here]") (1 Sam 3:4). Often the suffix serves as the subject of a following participle, as in Gen 41:17, הִנְנִי עֹמֵד, "Look, I (was) standing." The paradigm is as follows:

Table 40.3. הִנֵּה with Pronoun Suffixes

	Singular Suffix	*Plural Suffix*
3m	הִנּוֹ Look, he	הִנָּם Look, they
3f	(not extant)	(not extant)
2m	הִנְּךָ Look, you	הִנְּכֶם Look, you
2f	הִנָּךְ Look, you	(not extant)
1c	הִנְנִי/הִנֵּנִי Look, I	הִנְנוּ/הִנֶּנּוּ Look, we

2. *וְעַתָּה: An Inference Marker*

וְעַתָּה is a clause modifier that indicates that a given event or situation is the natural consequence or logical conclusion of an event or topic that directly precedes. We have already seen an example of this use in Deut 5:23–25 (Table 40.1), where a clause introduced by וְעַתָּה provided an **inference** from one begun with הֵן. A similar example is found in Exod 10:16–17.

Table 40.4. וְעַתָּה Marking an Inference in Exodus 10:16–17

And Pharaoh hastened to call Moses and Aaron and said, "I have sinned against YHWH your God and against you. *And now* (since I have realized and expressed my error), forgive my sin!"
וַיְמַהֵר פַּרְעֹה לִקְרֹא לְמֹשֶׁה וּלְאַהֲרֹן וַיֹּאמֶר חָטָאתִי לַיהוָה אֱלֹהֵיכֶם וְלָכֶם *וְעַתָּה* שָׂא נָא חַטָּאתִי

Usually the ground and its conclusion occur in the same paragraph, as in the above examples. At times, however, the ground can span several chapters before the conclusion is made. Such is the case in Deut 10:12, which builds an inference from the material begun in 9:1.

Table 40.5. וְעַתָּה Marking an Inference in Deuteronomy 10:12–13

And now, Israel, what is YHWH your God asking from you, but to fear YHWH your God by walking in all his ways?
וְעַתָּה יִשְׂרָאֵל מָה יְהוָה אֱלֹהֶיךָ שֹׁאֵל מֵעִמָּךְ כִּי אִם־לְיִרְאָה אֶת־יְהוָה אֱלֹהֶיךָ לָלֶכֶת בְּכָל־דְּרָכָיו

3. Primary and Secondary Citation Markers[1]

In the Hebrew Bible, almost every instance of reported direct speech is introduced by a form of אמר, "say." This particular verb plays a discourse structuring function in the context of speech citations. It is sometimes similar to quotation marks in English. Most importantly, אמר helps us to understand the nature of the reported speech.

a. Distinguishing Primary and Secondary Citations

Citations may be described as either *primary* or as *secondary*.

(1) A primary citation has the following features:

    (a) Reports a single event rather than many similar speeches reported as one;

    (b) Has its participants speak individually, rather than as groups speaking chorally;

    (c) Is not retold from a previous conversation;

    (d) Deals with full characters in the story, rather than agents or props;

    (e) Functions as the lively account of a direct conversation; it's how a storyteller would vividly recount a conversation in a narrative.

(2) A secondary citation, by contrast, has at least one of the following features:

    (a) Summarizes several similar speeches or one long speech;

    (b) Presents the statements of many people as one statement;

    (c) Has one character in the story cite a prior statement by another character in the story;

    (d) Comes through an agent or prop rather than a full character, or it is from someone who is not actually present and participating in the current conversation;

    (e) Functions as the official record of the principal points made by speakers and is

---

1. Much of the content in this section is drawn from Cynthia L. Miller, "Discourse Functions in Quotative Frames in Biblical Hebrew Narrative," in *Discourse Analysis of Biblical Literature: What It Is and What It Offers*, ed. Walter R. Bodine, SBLSS (Atlanta: Scholars, 1995), 155–82 and idem, *The Representation of Speech in Biblical Hebrew Narrative: A Linguistic Approach*, HSM 55 (Winona Lake, IN: Eisenbrauns, 1999). For our "primary citations," linguists may use the term "prototypical"; for our "secondary citations," linguists may use the term "non-prototypical."

thus less a vivid conversation than it is a documentation of the essential points made by the speakers.

In the Hebrew Bible, reported direct speeches are introduced in one of three ways:

Table 40.6. Forms of Direct Speech Frames

Category	Structure	Function	Example
Single-Verb Frames	Finite speech verb (usually אמר) + quotation	*Unmarked:* Either a primary or secondary citation	2 Sam 18:29 ... וַיֹּאמֶר הַמֶּלֶךְ "And the king said..."
Multiple-Verb Frames	Finite verb(s)* + finite speech verb (usually אמר) + quotation	*Marked:* A primary citation	Deut 9:26 ... וָאֶתְפַּלֵּל אֶל־יְהוָה וָאֹמַר "And I prayed to YHWH and I said..."
לֵאמֹר Frames	Finite verb(s)* (at times אמר) or no verb + לֵאמֹר + quotation	*Marked:* A secondary citation	Gen 1:22 ... וַיְבָרֶךְ אֹתָם אֱלֹהִים לֵאמֹר "And God blessed them saying..."

*At times, an infinitive construct stands in place of the initial finite verb.

A number of comments are noteworthy related to the above data.

(1) If only one finite verb (usually of the root אמר) introduces a citation, that citation may be primary or secondary. The citation is considered unmarked.

(2) If two or more finite verbs (usually one of them is of the root אמר) introduce a citation, that citation is marked as primary.

    (a) Examples of the verb used with אמר include:

        (i) ענה, as in Gen 18:27, וַיַּעַן אַבְרָהָם וַיֹּאמַר ("and Abraham answered and said");

        (ii) צוה, as in Gen 28:1, וַיְצַוֵּהוּ וַיֹּאמֶר לוֹ ("and he commanded him and said to him");

        (iii) קרא, as in Exod 32:5, וַיִּקְרָא אַהֲרֹן וַיֹּאמַר ("and Aaron called out and said");

        (iv) פלל, as in Deut 9:26 above.

    (b) The verbs that accompany אמר are commonly more specific in meaning than is אמר. They stand in the initial position (before the אמר verb), and they tell us what kind of speech act the speaker performed (she prayed, or commanded, or proclaimed, etc.).

    (c) The use of two or more verbs does not mean that the speaker spoke more than once. In Deut 9:26, the quotation that follows is the content of Moses' prayer.

The narrative does not suggest two actions on the part of the prophet, but one: the וָאֹמַר, "and I said," operates epexegetically to וָאֶתְפַּלֵּל, "and I prayed."

(3) When לֵאמֹר is present, the citation is marked as secondary. Examples are given below.

Table 40.7. לֵאמֹר in Genesis 21:22 Marking a Secondary Citation

And Abimelech and Phicol the commander of his forces *said* to Abraham *as follows*: "God is with you"
וַיֹּאמֶר אֲבִימֶלֶךְ וּפִיכֹל שַׂר־צְבָאוֹ אֶל־אַבְרָהָם לֵאמֹר אֱלֹהִים עִמְּךָ

In this case, the citation is secondary because it is not actually a quotation from one person. The words come from both Abimelech and Phicol but are presented as one speech.

Table 40.8. לֵאמֹר in Genesis 23:3 Marking a Secondary Citation

And he spoke to the Hittites, *as follows*:
וַיְדַבֵּר אֶל־בְּנֵי־חֵת לֵאמֹר

Abraham is purchasing a cave to serve as the burial place of Sarah. All of the citations here (vv. 3–16) are secondary, using לֵאמֹר. This makes the narrative more solemn and less lively, and it also serves as a record of the details of the purchase transaction.

Table 40.9. לֵאמֹר in Deuteronomy 9:23 Marking a Secondary Citation

And when YHWH *sent* you from Kadesh Barnea, *with the following words*...
וּבִשְׁלֹחַ יְהוָה אֶתְכֶם מִקָּדֵשׁ בַּרְנֵעַ לֵאמֹר ...

Here, Moses is secondarily recounting or retelling the essence of God's directive to Israel as he led them from Kadesh-barnea to Canaan. It is not a direct citation of a specific speech-act.

Table 40.10. לֵאמֹר in Deuteronomy 6:20 Marking a Secondary Citation

When your son *asks* you in the future, *saying*...
כִּי־יִשְׁאָלְךָ בִנְךָ מָחָר לֵאמֹר ...

This citation is secondary because it is not a quotation from an actual conversation but from a hypothetical, future conversation. The son is a "prop."

By contrast, consider the significance of the following primary citations.

Table 40.11. A Multiple-Verb Frame in Genesis 24:47 Marking a Primary Citation

And I asked her *and I said,* "Whose daughter are you?"
וָאֶשְׁאַל אֹתָהּ וָאֹמַר בַּת־מִי אַתְּ

Here, Abraham's servant is giving a lively account of his conversation with Rebekah, and a multiple-verb frame is used to mark the citation as primary.

Table 40.12. A Multiple-Verb Frame in Deuteronomy 5:1 Marking a Primary Citation

And Moses *called* to all Israel *and said* to them...
וַיִּקְרָא מֹשֶׁה אֶל־כָּל־יִשְׂרָאֵל וַיֹּאמֶר אֲלֵהֶם...

The above multiple-verb speech frame is made up of two verbs of saying—וַיִּקְרָא, "and he called" + וַיֹּאמֶר, "and he said." This quotation frame introduces the second major prophetic address in the book of Deuteronomy. What follows appears to be a single speech, recorded in the way it was given by the prophet. The primary speaker, Moses, is a full character in the narrative, begun in 4:44, and he speaks individually throughout the discourse. We thus have a primary citation.

b. Two Possible Misconceptions about Primary and Secondary Citations

One should not think that primary citations are more significant than secondary citations. If anything, the reverse is often the case. For example, in historical discourse, primary citations are simply spliced in among the mainline narrative of the *wayyiqtol* sequence. Secondary citations, however, are set off by the infinitive לֵאמֹר. As with offline statements generally, that which is set apart often has greater thematic prominence. The following artificial examples may help to illustrate this point.

> He spoke up and said, "I know who did this." And I turned to him and said, "Who did it?" And he said, "Nabal."

The above example is analogous to primary citations. Now consider the same conversation recounted with secondary citations, translating לֵאמֹר with "as follows" or "with the following."

> He spoke up, as follows: "I know who did this." And I turned to him with the following: "Who did it?" And he said, "Nabal."

The second example is less of a lively report of a conversation than it is an account of the giving of testimony. The quotations are set apart from the narrative by "as follows," making them less structurally integrated but more thematically prominent. In this latter version, *the content* of what was said is the focus; in the former, the primary citation version, *the narrative account* of the conversation is the focus.

Another misconception to avoid is that secondary citations only give the gist of a quotation, whereas primary citations give verbatim quotations. Although secondary citations often do summarize, that does not mean that they never give a verbatim citation of someone's words.

In the case of Abraham's negotiations over the cave of Machpelah (Gen 23), the use of לֵאמֹר does not necessarily mean that we do not have the verbatim comments of Abraham and Ephron the Hittite. Rather, by setting off with לֵאמֹר the words of the two parties from the narrative structure of the episode, the focus is on the specifics of their negotiations rather than on the fact that they had a conversation. The text serves as a record of the details of their transaction.

4. וַיְהִי *or* וְהָיָה *Marking a Turning Point or Climactic Event*

You know that Hebrew uses protasis–apodosis constructions to express relationships that are conditional ("if... then"), causal ("because... therefore"), and temporal ("when... then"). Hebrew also uses a protasis-apodosis construction with וַיְהִי (in historical narrative) or וְהָיָה (in anticipatory and directive discourse) to signal that something significant—a turning point or climactic event—took place or will take place.

a. Paragraph Initiation and Climax

In such a construction, the וַיְהִי or וְהָיָה will front the protasis and carry the respective meanings "And it came to pass that" or "And it will come to pass that." While these translations sound quaint and archaic, they nevertheless capture the way the discourse marker introduces the succeeding context. A more contemporary translation might be something like, "Now it happened that...."

(1) Following וַיְהִי or וְהָיָה, the protasis will often be made up of a temporal phrase or clause, though it could also be conditional or causal.

    (a) Past, with וַיְהִי: "And it came to pass *when he spoke* that...."

    (b) Future, with וְהָיָה: "And it will come to pass *in those days* that...."

(2) The apodosis will usually have one of the following patterns:

    (a) Past: after an initial וַיְהִי, the apodosis is often a *wayyiqtol* or (x) + *qatal*. For example: וַיְהִי כְּבֹא הַסֵּפֶר אֲלֵיהֶם וַיִּקְחוּ אֶת־בְּנֵי הַמֶּלֶךְ, "And it happened as soon as the scroll came to them that they took the king's sons."

    (b) Future: after an initial וְהָיָה, the apodosis is often a *weqatal* or (x) + *yiqtol*. For example: וְהָיָה בְּיוֹם זֶבַח יְהוָה וּפָקַדְתִּי עַל־הַשָּׂרִים, "And it shall happen on the day of YHWH's sacrifice that I will punish the officials."

(3) This construction often marks a new paragraph that grows directly out of some event, activity, or idea of the preceding context.

This discourse function is a distinctive usage for וַיְהִי or וְהָיָה. You already know that וַיְהִי can function as a full verb meaning "And there was" or "And he was," and that וְהָיָה can operate as a full verb meaning "And there will be" or "And he will be." But the use of וַיְהִי or וְהָיָה to mark a turning point and/or climax at the head of a protasis is different, as the examples below indicate.

Table 40.13. וַיְהִי as a Turning Point or Climax Marker in 1 Samuel 4:18

A New Paragraph with Climactic Stress			Predicate Pattern	Main	Off	Sub
18a	**And it came about that,**	וַיְהִי	WA copula initiates protasis + apodosis construction		X	
	The discourse marker וַיְהִי *signals the start of a new paragraph that directly grows out of and adds emphasis to the preceding report that the Philistines captured the ark of YHWH.*					
Protasis 18b	**as he mentioned** the ark of YHWH	כְּהַזְכִּירוֹ...				X
	A temporal subordinate phrase used as a protasis, which explicitly connects the paragraph to the preceding report.					
Apodosis 18c	*he [Eli] fell* off the seat backward beside the gate.	וַיִּפֹּל...	WA	X		
	The shift to a wayyiqtol *signals the start of the apodosis, which clarifies the gravity of the message.*					
18d	*and his neck was broken,*	וַתִּשָּׁבֵר...	WA	X		
	A further mainline event temporally successive to 18c.					
18e	*and he died....*	וַיָּמֹת...	WA	X		
	A further mainline event temporally successive to 18d.					

In order to highlight the gravity of the messenger's statement that "the ark of God was taken" (4:17), the narrator adds what we see in v. 18. It has וַיְהִי at its head, which brings out the dramatic response of Eli the priest to the terrible news.

Verse 18c, וַיִּפֹּל מֵעַל־הַכִּסֵּא אֲחֹרַנִּית, needs to be translated without "and" even though it has a *wayyiqtol* verb. The translation is simply, "he fell off the seat backward." Often when a *wayyiqtol*, *weqatal*, or *weyiqtol* clause marks an apodosis, the conjunction will be left untranslated. Genesis 11:12 (below) is similar; compare these to the וְהָיָה and *weqatal* in Gen 9:14–15.

Table 40.14. A *Wayyiqtol* Apodosis Translated without "And" in Genesis 12:11

> *And it happened* that as he came near to entering Egypt, *he said* to Sarai his wife…
>
> וַיְהִי כַּאֲשֶׁר הִקְרִיב לָבוֹא מִצְרָיְמָה וַיֹּאמֶר אֶל־שָׂרַי אִשְׁתּוֹ

Table 40.15. וְהָיָה as a Turning Point or Climax Marker in Genesis 9:14–15

		A New Paragraph with Climactic Stress		Predicate Pattern	Main	Off	Sub
	14a	**And it shall be**,	וְהָיָה	WQ copula initiates protasis + apodosis construction		X	
		The discourse marker וְהָיָה signals the start of a new paragraph that directly grows out of and adds clarification to the preceding statement regarding the rainbow as a sign of the covenant.					
Protasis	14b	**when I make** a cloud **appear** on the earth	...בְּעַנְנִי עָנָן				X
		A temporal subordinate phrase used as a protasis.					
	15a	**and** the bow **is seen** in a cloud,	...וְנִרְאֲתָה הַקֶּשֶׁת				X
		A development of the protasis begun in 14b.					
Apodosis	15b	*(then) I will remember* my covenant that is between me and you and every living creature among all flesh,	וְזָכַרְתִּי אֶת־בְּרִיתִי...	WQ	X		
		The shift to a weqatal *signals the start of the apodosis, which stresses the significance of the rainbow by describing how it will remind God of his covenant promise.*					
	15c	*and* the waters *will not* again *become* a flood to destroy all flesh.	...וְלֹא־יִהְיֶה	וְלֹא + *yiqtol*		X	
		In contrast to 15b, this negative + yiqtol *offline clause describes what will not happen (= contrastive matching: V[x] + [x]V).*					

The above context is the aftermath of the flood narrative. God has just established his covenant with creation. In order to clarify how the rainbow will stand as a "sign of the covenant" (9:12–13), God adds the above paragraph, marked by וְהָיָה at its head.

b. Determining whether וַיְהִי *as* וְהָיָה *are Discourse Markers or Full Verbs*

Sometimes, וַיְהִי and וְהָיָה function not as discourse markers but as a full verbs. This results in the translation of וַיְהִי as "And there was" or "And he was," and of וְהָיָה as "And there will be" or "And he will be." How do we determine which function is at work?

THE RULE: וַיְהִי *and* וְהָיָה *are operating as discourse markers when they introduce a protasis–apodosis construction and lack any clear subject (or antecedent) that agrees with it in number and gender.* Occasionally the forms function as discourse markers without introducing protasis–apodosis constructions (e.g., 1 Kgs 17:4). However, *usually* if there is no protasis–apodosis construction and *always* if you can identify a subject, you know you are looking at a full verb, as in Gen 4:2.

Table 40.16. וַיְהִי as a Full Verb in Genesis 4:2

And Abel *was* a shepherd of sheep, but Cain was a worker of ground.
וַיְהִי־הֶ֫בֶל רֹעֵה צֹאן וְקַ֫יִן הָיָה עֹבֵד אֲדָמָה

Compare the following examples:

Table 40.17. Contrasting Usage with וְהָיָה and וַיְהִי

	Protasis-Apodosis Construction: Discourse Marking Function	Non-Protasis-Apodosis Construction: Full Verb Function
וַיְהִי	וַיְהִי לְעֵת זִקְנַת שְׁלֹמֹה נָשָׁיו הִטּוּ אֶת־לְבָבוֹ אַחֲרֵי אֱלֹהִים אֲחֵרִים *And it came to pass at the time of Solomon's old age:* his wives turned his heart after other gods (1 Kgs 11:4)	וַיְהִי הַמֶּלֶךְ שְׁלֹמֹה מֶלֶךְ עַל־כָּל־יִשְׂרָאֵל *And* King Solomon *was* king over all Israel (1 Kgs 4:1)
וְהָיָה	וְהָיָה בְּאַחֲרִית הַיָּמִים נָכוֹן יִהְיֶה הַר בֵּית־יְהוָה בְּרֹאשׁ הֶהָרִים *And it shall come to pass in the last days:* the mountain of YHWH's house shall be established in the top of the mountains (Isa 2:2)	וְהָיָה בֵית־יַעֲקֹב אֵשׁ *And* the house of Jacob *shall be* a fire (Obad 18)

B. More on Directive Discourse

Directive discourse is address designed to change behavior or attitudes. By this text type, a speaker commands, exhorts, or advises an audience to do something; prohibits, admonishes, or discourages an audience from doing something; or provides instructions for a procedure.

1. Predicate Patterns and Paragraph Structure in Directive Discourse

(1) Mainline commands, exhortations, and instructions are usually signaled by a sequence of *weqatal* clauses, often following an initial imperative.

(2) The onset and termination of paragraph units are often marked by a single [x] + *yiqtol* clause, an imperative clause, a jussive clause, or some other independent [x] + non-*weqatal* clause. Paragraph initiation is also signalled by וְהָיָה ("and it shall come about that").

(3) Single non-*weqatal* clauses or one or more sequenced copular ("to be") clauses often signal offline comments. Single or multiple copular clauses, or multiple non-*weqatal* clauses, can mark paragraph-level offline material.

(4) לֹא + *yiqtol* or אַל + jussive expresses prohibition or admonition.

While directive discourse is regularly future-oriented, the mainline verb form, the *weqatal*, does not require that the commands or exhortations be in temporal succession. Naturally, while temporal progression is implied in a set of building instructions (e.g., for the tabernacle), the behavioral exhortations found in prophetic sermons are often driven more logically than temporally. Similarly, while commands and prohibitions, exhortations and admonitions, are almost always addressed to specific people, instructions for fulfilling a specific task could be stated either generally or to a specific audience. The following table describes the various predicate patterns in directive discourse.

Table 40.18. Functions of Predicate Patterns in Directive Discourse

Prominence	Function	Predicate Pattern
1: Offline	Secondary command or exhortation. It can mark climax or paragraph boundaries, and can be used for identical or contrastive matching.	Modal *yiqtol* [X] + modal *yiqtol*
2: Offline	Purpose, result, consequence. It is a secondary marker of paragraph boundaries.	*Weyiqtol* (after volitive or modal *yiqtol*) *Weqatal*
3: Offline	Backgrounded activities. It is a secondary marker of paragraph boundaries.	Participial nominal clauses
4: Offline	Backgrounded description. It is a secondary marker of paragraph boundaries.	Copulative clauses Existential clauses
Mainline	Initial command, exhortation, prohibition, or admonition. It is the primary marker of paragraph initiation.	Initial volitive לֹא + *yiqtol* or אַל + jussive
Mainline	Primary command, exhortation, or instruction.	*Weqatal* (usually after volitive)

2. A Case-Study in Directive Discourse

In the following two examples, mainline predicate patterns are italicized and offline predicate patterns are in bold. For the sake of simplicity subordinate clauses are not set apart. In these tables, "V" = imperative.

Table 40.19. Directive Discourse in Numbers 8:7

A Mainline Progression of Instructions. *This unit (only partially shown here) describes the procedure for cleansing the Levites. Note how the mainline is initiated by an imperative and carried on by a sequence of weqatal clauses.*		Predicate Pattern	Main	Off
7a	**And** thus **you shall do** to them to cleanse them:	וְכֹה־תַעֲשֶׂה לָהֶם...	Y		X
	Offline statement introducing the paragraph.				
7b	**Sprinkle** on them water of cleansing,	הַזֵּה עֲלֵיהֶם...	V	X	
	An asyndetic imperative clause introduces the mainline instructions for cleansing, all of which expound on 7a.				
7c	*and they shall pass* a razor over all their flesh,	וְהֶעֱבִירוּ תַעַר...	WQ	X	
	Probably temporally successive to 7b.				
7d	*and they shall wash* their clothes,	וְכִבְּסוּ בִגְדֵיהֶם	WQ	X	
	Probably temporally successive to 7c.				
7e	*And they shall wash themselves.*	וְהִטֶּהָרוּ	WQ	X	
	Probably temporally successive to 7d.				

Table 40.20. Directive Discourse in Deuteronomy 5:1

A Mainline Series of Exhortations. *This verse opens Moses' second sermon in Deuteronomy. The initial imperative is followed by a series of weqatals, the whole of which exhorts the reader to covenant loyalty.*		Predicate Pattern	Main	Off
1a	**Hear**, O Israel, the statutes and the judgments that I speak in your hearing today.	שְׁמַע יִשְׂרָאֵל...	V	X	
	An asyndetic imperative clause introduces the mainline of exhortations.				

1b	*And you shall learn* them,	וּלְמַדְתֶּם אֹתָם	WQ	X	
	Perhaps temporally but at least logically successive to 1a.				
1c	and you shall be careful to do them.	וּשְׁמַרְתֶּם לַעֲשֹׂתָם	WQ	X	
	Perhaps temporally but at least logically successive to 1b.				

In the above examples, *weqatal* clauses carry the primary instructions or commands to the reader. In each instance, an imperative signals the start of the directive discourse.

C. Vocabulary

1. Core Vocabulary

a. Verbs

למד	Qal: לָמַד learn
	Piel: לִמַּד teach
מהר	Piel: מִהַר hasten, hurry
נטע	Qal: נָטַע plant
סגר	Qal: סָגַר shut, close
	Hiphil: הִסְגִּיר surrender, deliver; separate
שׁית	Qal: שָׁת set, stand, place; ordain; direct towards
שׁמד	Niphal: נִשְׁמַד be destroyed, be exterminated, be rendered unusable
	Hiphil: הִשְׁמִיד exterminate

b. Other Words

בּוֹר	cistern Ⓜ |בּוֹר|
חַיָּה	animal(s) Ⓕ |חַיַּת|
חָלָל	pierced, slain, struck dead
מָלֵא	full (adjective); fullness (noun)
עֹז	strength, might Ⓜ |עָז / עֹז|; *as adjective* עַז strong, mighty
שִׂמְחָה	joy Ⓕ |שִׂמְחַת|

2. Proper Names

אִיּוֹב	Job
יְרִחוֹ	Jericho
לְבָנוֹן	Lebanon

3. Reading Vocabulary

אָרַךְ	Hiphil: הֶאֱרִיךְ	make long
זוּב	Qal: יָזוּב (*yiqtol* 3ms)	flow
חָצַב	Qal: חָצַב	hew, cut out
קָשַׁר	Qal: קָשַׁר	tie down, bind; conspire
שָׁנַן	Piel: וְשִׁנַּנְתָּם (*weqatal* 2ms with 2mpx)	repeat, recite(?)
זַיִת		olive, olive tree
חָלָב		milk
טוֹטָפֹת		phylacteries
מְזוּזָה		door-post
קַנָּא		jealous

D. Reading—Deuteronomy 6:1–15

1 וְזֹאת הַמִּצְוָה הַחֻקִּים וְהַמִּשְׁפָּטִים אֲשֶׁר צִוָּה יְהוָה אֱלֹהֵיכֶם לְלַמֵּד אֶתְכֶם
לַעֲשׂוֹת בָּאָרֶץ אֲשֶׁר אַתֶּם עֹבְרִים שָׁמָּה לְרִשְׁתָּהּ:

2 לְמַעַן תִּירָא אֶת־יְהוָה אֱלֹהֶיךָ לִשְׁמֹר אֶת־כָּל־חֻקֹּתָיו וּמִצְוֹתָיו אֲשֶׁר אָנֹכִי
מְצַוֶּךָ אַתָּה וּבִנְךָ וּבֶן־בִּנְךָ כֹּל יְמֵי חַיֶּיךָ וּלְמַעַן יַאֲרִכֻן יָמֶיךָ:

3 וְשָׁמַעְתָּ יִשְׂרָאֵל וְשָׁמַרְתָּ לַעֲשׂוֹת אֲשֶׁר יִיטַב לְךָ וַאֲשֶׁר תִּרְבּוּן מְאֹד כַּאֲשֶׁר
דִּבֶּר יְהוָה אֱלֹהֵי אֲבֹתֶיךָ לָךְ אֶרֶץ זָבַת חָלָב וּדְבָשׁ: פ

4 שְׁמַע יִשְׂרָאֵל יְהוָה אֱלֹהֵינוּ יְהוָה ׀ אֶחָד:

5 וְאָהַבְתָּ אֵת יְהוָה אֱלֹהֶיךָ בְּכָל־לְבָבְךָ וּבְכָל־נַפְשְׁךָ וּבְכָל־מְאֹדֶךָ:

6 וְהָיוּ הַדְּבָרִים הָאֵלֶּה אֲשֶׁר אָנֹכִי מְצַוְּךָ הַיּוֹם עַל־לְבָבֶךָ:

7 וְשִׁנַּנְתָּם לְבָנֶיךָ וְדִבַּרְתָּ בָּם בְּשִׁבְתְּךָ בְּבֵיתֶךָ וּבְלֶכְתְּךָ בַדֶּרֶךְ וּבְשָׁכְבְּךָ
וּבְקוּמֶךָ:

8 וּקְשַׁרְתָּם לְאוֹת עַל־יָדֶךָ וְהָיוּ לְטֹטָפֹת בֵּין עֵינֶיךָ:

9 וּכְתַבְתָּם עַל־מְזוּזֹת בֵּיתֶךָ וּבִשְׁעָרֶיךָ: ס

10 וְהָיָה כִּי יְבִיאֲךָ ׀ יְהוָה אֱלֹהֶיךָ אֶל־הָאָרֶץ אֲשֶׁר נִשְׁבַּע לַאֲבֹתֶיךָ לְאַבְרָהָם
לְיִצְחָק וּלְיַעֲקֹב לָתֶת לָךְ עָרִים גְּדֹלֹת וְטֹבֹת אֲשֶׁר לֹא־בָנִיתָ:

11 וּבָתִּים מְלֵאִים כָּל־טוּב אֲשֶׁר לֹא־מִלֵּאתָ וּבֹרֹת חֲצוּבִים אֲשֶׁר לֹא־חָצַבְתָּ כְּרָמִים וְזֵיתִים אֲשֶׁר לֹא־נָטָעְתָּ וְאָכַלְתָּ וְשָׂבָעְתָּ׃

12 הִשָּׁמֶר לְךָ פֶּן־תִּשְׁכַּח אֶת־יְהוָה אֲשֶׁר הוֹצִיאֲךָ מֵאֶרֶץ מִצְרַיִם מִבֵּית עֲבָדִים׃

13 אֶת־יְהוָה אֱלֹהֶיךָ תִּירָא וְאֹתוֹ תַעֲבֹד וּבִשְׁמוֹ תִּשָּׁבֵעַ׃

14 לֹא תֵלְכוּן אַחֲרֵי אֱלֹהִים אֲחֵרִים מֵאֱלֹהֵי הָעַמִּים אֲשֶׁר סְבִיבוֹתֵיכֶם׃

15 כִּי אֵל קַנָּא יְהוָה אֱלֹהֶיךָ בְּקִרְבֶּךָ פֶּן־יֶחֱרֶה אַף־יְהוָה אֱלֹהֶיךָ בָּךְ וְהִשְׁמִידְךָ מֵעַל פְּנֵי הָאֲדָמָה׃ ס

CHAPTER 41
AN OVERVIEW OF POETRY

A. The Cantillation Marks in the Three

The cantillation marks that are found in the Three (Psalms, Job, and Proverbs) are listed below. These are often called the **Poetic Accents**, but this term is misleading since there is an enormous amount of poetry outside of the Three that employs the standard cantillation marks and not the marks of the Three.

Table 41.1. Disjunctive Marks in the Three

בֶּגֶד	Silluq	Marks the end of a verse and is found in the last word of a verse.
בֶּגֶד	Athnach	If there is an Oleh weYored and an Athnach, the verse has at least 3 lines.
בֶּגֶד	Oleh weYored	A major disjunctive accent made with two marks. If a verse has both Oleh weYored and Athnach, the Oleh weYored occurs before the Athnach.
בֶּגֶד	Tifha	Also called Dehi. It is prepositive in the Three and does not mark the tone or the end of a poetic line.
בגד	Shalshelet Gedolah	It occurs in the second half of a verse, before Silluq, and does not indicate the end of a poetic line.
בֶּגֶד	Revia Gadol	It can mark the end of a poetic line. Distinguish it from Revia Qaton.
בֶּגֶד	Revia Qaton	Always comes immediately before Oleh weYored and does not mark the end of a poetic line.
בֶּגֶד	Revia Mugrash	It is made with two marks and does not indicate the end of a poetic line.
בגד	Tsinnor	Postpositive. Called Zarqa outside of the Three. In the Three, it occurs in a unit governed by Oleh weYored. It generally does not mark the end of a poetic line.
בֶּגֶד	Pazer	A minor disjunctive that generally does not mark the end of a poetic line.
בגד	Azla Legarmeh	Distinguish from conjunctive Azla. It does not mark the end of a poetic line.
בגד	Mehuppak Legarmeh	Distinguish from conjunctive Mehuppak. It does not mark the end of a poetic line.
בגד	Merka Legarmeh	Distinguish from conjunctive Merka. It does not mark the end of a poetic line.

Table 41.2. Conjunctive Marks in the Three

בַּגֵּד	Munah	A very common *servus*.
בַּגֵּד	Mehuppak	Distinguish this from the Mehuppak Legarmeh, which has a stroke after the word.
בַּגֵּד	Merka	Distinguish this from the Merka Legarmeh, which has a stroke after the word.
בַּגֵּד	Azla	Also called Qadma. It looks like Pashta, a disjunctive in the standard accents, but is not postpositive.
בַּגֵּד	Galgal	Also called Yerah.
בַּגֵּד	Illuy	Also called upper Munah.
בַּגֵּד	Tarha	It looks like a Tifha but is not prepositive. Outside of the Three, Tifha is disjunctive but not prepositive.
בַּגֵּד	Shalshelet Qetanna	An extremely rare *servus*. Unlike the Shalshelet Gedolah, it lacks the stroke after the word.
בַּגֵּד	Tsinnoreth	Placed over an open syllable before Mehuppak or Merka. It does not mark the tone. Unlike Tsinnor, it is not postpositive.

With the above disjunctive accents, you can see that some marks generally do or do not mark the end of a poetic line. The line breaks usually occur at the Silluq, the Athnach, the Oleh weYored, and the Revia Gadol. Be sure to distinguish Revia Gadol from Revia Qaton and Revia Mugrash, and remember that Revia Gadol is a stronger disjunctive when it has a minor disjunctive within its domain. But again, one should use the cantillation marks not as absolute authorities but as general guides. Other considerations may suggest ending a line at another point.

B. The Line and Other Divisions of the Poem

In the chart of disjunctive accents, we note that some accents are likely to come at the end of a poetic line. The **line** is the basic element of the Hebrew poem, and indeed of almost any poem. Psalm 126 in the text below has been divided into lines for you. A line is also called a **stich** (plural: **stichoi**) or **colon** (plural: **cola**). Determining where the line divisions are in a poem is called **colometry**.

Lines are grouped into verses, but the term **verse** is somewhat ambiguous in the Bible. The problem is that the entire Bible is now divided into numbered verses. Usually, the numbered verses correspond to the poetic verses of a Hebrew poem. At times, however, the numbered verse divisions arguably do not accurately reflect the actual versification of a poem. Thus, some people use the term **strophe** to refer to poetic verses and use the term "verse" strictly to refer to the numbered verses.

A poetic verse or strophe often has two lines and thus is called a "bicolon." It is wrong to think that the two-line verse or bicolon is an essential feature of Hebrew poetry, however, since many poetic verses have more lines than two.

(1) A one-line poetic verse is a **monocolon**.

(2) A two-line poetic verse is a **bicolon**.

(3) A three-line poetic verse is a **tricolon**.

(4) A four-line poetic verse is a **quatrain**.

In a larger poem, several poetic verses or strophes are grouped together in stanzas, which are something like paragraphs within a poem.

C. Meter in Hebrew Poetry

Poetry often has a kind of rhythm based on **meter**. In classical Greek poetry, meter is based on an arrangement of long and short syllables. For example, a line of iambic poetry is divided into units called **feet**, and each foot has a short syllable followed by a long syllable. In English poetry, meter is based on arranging stressed and unstressed syllables instead of long and short syllables. Shakespeare's Sonnet 1 illustrates iambic pentameter, with five feet of iambic meter.

> From *fairest* **creatures** *we* de*sire* in*crease*,
>
> That **thereby** **beauty**'s **rose** might **never** **die**,

It is important that a poem have some kind of regularity, and in western poetry this is commonly obtained through meter. Other poetry achieves regularity by different means. For example, the Japanese haiku poem must conform to an inflexible 5-7-5 pattern, in which the first line has five syllables, the second has seven, and the third has five.

Does biblical Hebrew poetry have meter? This is a debated matter. Today, among scholars who believe that it does, two different types of meter are often suggested.

1. Stress Counting

This model asserts that the meter of Hebrew poetry is based on the number of accents per line. The accents are not arranged in patterns like the iambus (although a small minority of scholars would argue for such patterns). Rather, it is simply a matter of how many accents there are on a given line. Meter is described for each verse with numbers like "3+3." This is a bicolon with three accents on each line. Similarly, "3+2" is a bicolon with three accents on the first line and two accents on the second line. This pattern is often called a **Qinah** or "lament" pattern since it is thought to be the standard form for poems of lamentation. In "3+3+3," one would have a tricolon with three accents on each line.

At one time, stress counting dominated scholars' understanding of how Hebrew poetry worked, and one can find many commentaries on the Psalms that lay out the supposed meter of all the psalms according to this model. It is probably safe to say that today a majority of Hebrew scholars are skeptical about stress counting for at least two reasons.

(1) The results are disappointing. The meter of a poem ought to be regular. For example, if Hebrew poetry really had stress meter, one should normally find poems in which

every verse has the same meter (e.g., 3+4/ /3+4/ /3+4). But when one simply counts the number of accents in lines of a poem, the results are often wildly inconsistent. The verses may be something like 3+2/ /5+3/ /3+2/ /5+4/ /2+2 (this is a real example produced by an advocate of stress-counting; it is not made-up). If there is no regularity, there is no meter. As a simple experiment, try counting the stress accents in the lines of Ps 126 below and grouping them by verse.

(2) There are no clear and consistent rules for knowing how to count the stresses in a line. Since the results from a simple counting of stresses are so bad, some scholars have sought to refine the model by asserting that some stresses count but that others do not. It is claimed, for example, that sometimes conjunctive accents in construct chains do not count when doing stress counting. But there is no agreement about the rules for stress counting, and the whole procedure is sometimes *ad hoc*. By claiming that stresses sometimes count and sometimes do not, one can manipulate the data to obtain a desirable result.

2. Syllable Counting

A few scholars believe that one should count the number of syllables per line in order to obtain its meter. In this model, neither stresses nor long and short vowels matter; one simply counts the number of syllables per line. Some special rules do apply. For example, a segholate such as מֶלֶךְ will typically be read as one syllable on the grounds that it was originally a monosyllabic word (*malk*). If this method were valid, it ought to show some kind of regularity in Hebrew poems (like the regularity of haiku). In fact, the results are often wildly irregular, with lines having apparently random length (for example, one line is 9 syllables, the next is 8, the next is 12, and so forth). For this reason, most scholars reject this model.

3. Conclusion Regarding Meter in Hebrew Poetry

Today, no one model for meter in Hebrew poetry is widely accepted as valid. Does this mean that Hebrew poetry had no meter? We do not know. We are at a huge disadvantage in that no one alive today has ever heard the ancient Israelites chant their poetry. Therefore, we simply cannot say with certainty whether it did or did not have meter. If it did, we do not know how that meter worked.

D. Parallelism

1. General Overview of the Approach

A large number of scholars and readers today consider *parallelism* to be the essential feature of Hebrew poetry. In its simplest form, this is a bicolon in which the second line in some way echoes the first. The most widely known description of parallelism was published by Robert Lowth in 1753. It asserts that there are three basic types of parallelism:

(1) **Synonymous parallelism**, as in Ps 3:2 ("YHWH, how many are my foes! / How many rise up against me!"). The second line essentially restates the first.

(2) **Antithetical parallelism**, as in Prov 3:33 ("YHWH's curse is on the house of the wicked, / but he blesses the home of the righteous"). In this, the second line echoes

the first using antithetical terms, as here with "curse" against "blesses" and "wicked" against "righteous."

(3) **Synthetic parallelism**, as in Prov 3:29 ("Do not plot evil against your neighbor, who lives trustfully near you"). Here, there is no true parallelism, but the verse is set up as a bicolon as if it had parallelism.

In recent years, scholars have sought to refine the definitions of parallelism by distinguishing more precisely different varieties of parallelism. For example, semantic parallelism is distinguished from syntactical parallelism. In **semantic parallelism**, the two lines have very nearly the same *meaning*, whereas in **syntactical parallelism**, two lines have the same *grammatical structure* (for example, both lines may have a *qatal* verb, followed by a subject and a prepositional phrase).

2. Challenges to Viewing Parallelism as Essential to Poetry

Parallelism is indeed very common in the Hebrew Bible, and many consider it to be the basic feature of the Hebrew poem. However, there are significant problems with this conclusion.

(1) Antithetical parallelism is really a feature of proverbs and wisdom poetry. Outside of the Book of Proverbs, one rarely sees antithetical parallelism. Thus, it is misleading to speak of this as a category of Hebrew poetry.

(2) Synthetic parallelism really has no parallelism at all, so it begs the question to call it parallelism. A bicolon with "synthetic parallelism" is really a bicolon with no parallelism.

(3) Some poetry that is arguably the best in the Bible uses parallelism sparingly, if at all. Parallelism is relatively rare, for example, in Song of Songs and Ps 23. If parallelism is the essence of Hebrew poetry, it is hard to understand why these texts do not use it more.

(4) Parallelism is also found in Hebrew *prose* (indeed, it is often found in well-written English prose, and it is also a feature of classical Greek rhetoric). There is nothing specifically *poetic* about parallelism.

E. The Poetic Constraints and Tropes

1. Summary of the Model

Michael O'Connor[1] and others have argued that the regularity of Hebrew poetry is found in neither meter nor parallelism but in conformity to certain **poetic constraints**. These are basic rules to which every Hebrew poetic line must conform. In addition, Hebrew poems make use of **tropes** that help unify and structure a poem. (A **trope** is a rhetorical or metaphorical use of language, but in O'Connor's presentation it refers to devices that Hebrew poets employed to link lines within a poem.)

---

1. Michael O'Connor, *Hebrew Verse Structure*, 2nd ed. (Winona Lake, IN: Eisenbrauns, 1997).

The constraints are as follows:

(1) *Every line has from 0 to 3 clause predicators*. A line may have no predicator, but it should have no more than three. A **clause predicator** may be

  (a) a finite verb (most common),

  (b) an infinitive absolute that functions as a finite verb (as opposed to when it is used adverbially, such as when it is bound to a cognate finite verb),

  (c) an infinitive construct phrase functioning verbally (for example, בְּשׁוּבוֹ, "when he returns," as opposed to something like, "he went home *to rest*," where the infinitive is only the object of the verb),

  (d) a participle that functions as a verb, as in "they are *watching* us" (as opposed to substantive participle, such as שׁוֹפֵט used as the noun "judge"),

  (e) a vocative,

  (f) a **pendent focus-marker** (a noun or phrase at the beginning of a clause that marks focus and that is referred to again in a pronoun), such as found in Isa 9:1, "*those dwelling in the land of darkness*—a light has shined on them," and

  (g) the particles אֵין and יֵשׁ.

(2) *Every line has from 1 to 4 constituents*. A **constituent** is a grammatical phrase such as a verb, a noun, a prepositional phrase, or a construct chain.

(3) *Every line has from 2 to 5 units*. A **unit** is basically a word, but small particles such as כִּי or אִם or prepositions such as אֶל do not count as units.

(4) *A constituent has no more than 4 units*.

(5) *If a line has three predicators, it will have nothing else; if a line has two predicators, only one may have a dependent nominal phrase (whether noun, adjective, etc.).*

(6) *A line must have syntactical integrity*. Similarly, a line will not end in the middle of a construct chain. These things stated, not every line is a complete clause.

As an example of the line constraints, we have in Ps 126:2 הִגְדִּיל יְהוָה לַעֲשׂוֹת עִם־אֵלֶּה (lit., "YHWH has made great to do with these").

(1) This line has one predicator, the verb הִגְדִּיל.

Blackboard 41.1. The Predicator

(2) This line has four constituents (verb, subject, infinitive construct, and prepositional phrase). The infinitive construct לַעֲשׂוֹת is a complement to the verb הִגְדִּיל and does not count as a predicator. The prepositional phrase עִם־אֵלֶּה is one constituent.

Blackboard 41.2. The Constituents

(3) This line has only four units since עַם does not count as a unit.

Blackboard 41.3. The Units

Some of the tropes of Hebrew poetry are as follows.

(1) **Gapping** or **ellipsis**, in which, for example, a word in one line is also implied in the next line. Psalm 126:2 ("Then our mouth *was filled* with laughter, / our tongue [was filled] with shouts") illustrates this, in that the verb יְמַלֵּא governs both lines.

(2) **Repetition** of a word, phrase, or line. This is seen in how the last line of Ps 126:2 is repeated almost verbatim in the first line of v 3. In v 6, the participle נֹשֵׂא is repeated at the beginning of lines 2 and 4.

(3) **Dependence**, when one line depends on another in order to make a complete thought. In Ps 126:4 ("Restore our fortunes, YHWH, / like streams in the Negev"), the second line depends on the first.

(4) **Matching** or syntactic parallelism; as described above, this is when the grammatical structure of one line is similar to that of another.

2. Critique

Two objections may be raised against this model.

(1) It seems to be a rather artificial and un-poetic way to create poetry. One could not hear the rhythm of the constraints in the way one could hear traditional meter, such as iambic pentameter.

(2) It is possible to find lines of biblical Hebrew poetry that cannot be forced into the constraints. That is, there are lines that violate the rules.

Having said that, in a large majority of cases it appears that the lines of Hebrew poetry do indeed conform to the constraints. In working on the colometry of a poem, one should take the constraints into account.

F. Summary of Biblical Poetry

(1) Although there may have been a kind of meter in biblical Hebrew poetry, we do not know what it was. It is probably best, at the present, to avoid analyzing poetry according to any theory of meter.

(2) Parallelism is very *common* in Hebrew poetry, but it should not be considered to be the *essence* of Hebrew poetry. It is not a necessary feature of a Hebrew poem.

(3) The cantillation marks are useful but not flawless guides to the colometry of a Hebrew poem.

    (a) In the Three, line breaks usually occur at the Silluq, the Athnach, the Oleh weYored, and also at the Revia Gadol when a minor disjunctive accent is within the domain governed by the Revia Gadol.

    (b) In the other books, a line break in poetry will most likely occur at the Silluq or the Athnach, and also at the Zaqeph Qaton or Revia when one of these has a minor disjunctive within its domain.

(4) Similarly, the constraints are useful and should be taken into account, but one should not consider them inviolable.

(5) Remember also that biblical Hebrew poems were really songs. Since we do not know how they were sung, much of the essence of Hebrew poetry is lost to us.

G. Poetry, Prose, and Biblical Prophecy

In recent days, scholars have noted that many biblical passages commonly considered prose contain features traditionally regarded as "poetic"—features like parellelism, the formation of lines, conciseness, gapping, etc. The presence of such features has suggested to many that the distinction between prose and poetry is more one of degree than kind and that we are better served to think of a continuum of elevated style. Biblical prophecy is usually regarded as falling somewhere in the middle of this cline. While much of the prophetic corpus is treated as poetry, large units (such as major blocks of Ezekiel) are treated as prose. Scholars debate whether some texts like Malachi are more on the prose or poetic side of the continuum. In approaching the debate, the following observations may be helpful.

(1) A basic means for distinguishing poetry from prose is to determine whether a text follows the constraints of a poetic line, having from 0 to 3 clause predicators, from 1 to 4 constituents, and from 2 to 5 units.

(2) Other syntactic features help distinguish the two:

    (a) Poetic texts are known to employ verb initial clauses at a rate equal to non-verb initial clauses. In contrast, the linear as opposed to segemented nature of prose gives rise to its being dominated by verb initial, mainline clauses.

    (b) Poetry regularly precedes a verb by two or more constitutents, whereas prose rarely does.

    (c) Comparatively infrequent in poetry, the definite article (הַ◌), the definite direct object marker (אֶת־), and the particle אֲשֶׁר occur in high concentrations in prose.

(3) Not all prose is plain and unadorned, and not all poetry is uniform.

   (a) The frequent shift between highly poetic and quite prosaic style in prophetic ad-
       dress is likely explained by its sermonic nature. In a pattern similar to traditional
       American preachers, and especially African-American preachers, the biblical
       prophets regularly use high rhetorical style, including literary features like alliter-
       ation, short parallel lines, and even rhyme. They could also use various types of
       speech. For example, they occasionally employed elevated prose in order to in-
       troduce short, self-contained songs (lyric poetry or psalms), as are found in Jon
       2:3–10; Hab 3, and perhaps Isa 5:1–7. Most often, however, their messages were
       fairly lengthy, complex discourses that employed poetic line constraints.

   (b) The Bible has some lengthy poems that follow rigid conventions, such as Ps 119
       and the book of Lamentations. It also has complex, lyric poetry such as Song of
       Songs. All are poems, but not all have the same makeup.

H. The Syntax and Structure of Biblical Proverbs

While the book of Proverbs does contain long exhortations (Chs. 1–9), the focus of this section is on the short, pithy aphorisms or proverbs from which the book gets its name (Chs.
10–30, esp. 10–22) and which can be found at other points throughout the Hebrew Bible.
What follows is an overview of the syntax and structure of individual proverbs.

(1) Proverbs are not specifically concerned with either the past or future but with typical
    behavior and its results. Therefore, the *qatal* and *yiqtol* generally describe customary
    actions with no focus on time, although the difference in aspect is occasionally sig-
    nificant. Consider the following English examples: "A wise man *will help* (analogous
    to the *yiqtol*) his friend" and "A wise man *helps* (analogous to the *qatal*) his friend."
    Both mean essentially the same thing, but the former is more open-ended ("you can
    expect this to happen"), whereas the latter is more straightforward ("this happens").

(2) Proverbs are usually composed of two lines (that is, a proverb is usually a bicolon) in
    which the second line complements the first. Often, each line will have at least one
    verb, with the actions of the two verbs being either successive or non-successive,
    complementary or contrasting.

   (a) In successive structures, the action of the second verb temporally or logically fol-
       lows that of the first. In non-successive structures, the actions of the two verbs
       are separate.

   (b) In complementary proverbs, the second reinforces the first or completes a
       thought. In contrasting proverbs, the two principle verbs are antonyms and typi-
       cally juxtapose the actions or fate of the wicked with that of the good. Such con-
       trasts have traditionally been called "antithetical parallelism."

(3) The pattern [x] + *yiqtol* followed by Waw + [x] + *yiqtol* can set up a proverb that is
    non-successive and contrasting.

Table 41.3. A Non-Successive, Contrasting Proverb in Proverbs 14:11

The house of the wicked will be destroyed / but the tent of the upright will flourish.
בֵּית רְשָׁעִים יִשָּׁמֵד וְאֹהֶל יְשָׁרִים יַפְרִיחַ

Observe that there is no succession between the two lines but that there is a clear contrast (cf. Prov 10:2, 8, 12, 21, 27, 31; 11:4, 5, 6, 7 etc.). An [x] + *yiqtol* followed by a Waw + verbless clause often has the same function (cf. Prov 10:1, 13, 14, 32; 12:27; 14:23).

(4) A *qatal* followed by a *wayyiqtol* can describe actions that are successive and complementary, as in Prov 21:22 (cf. 11:2, 8; 31:16).

Table 41.4. A Successive, Complementary Proverb in Proverbs 21:22

One wise man goes up against a city of warriors, / and he brings down the strength (that is their) confidence.
עִיר גִּבֹּרִים עָלָה חָכָם וַיֹּרֶד עֹז מִבְטֶחָה

This pattern can also describe actions that are simultaneous (18:22) or even contrastive (22:12). Note that both the *qatal* and the *wayyiqtol* are descriptive of typical actions rather than simple past events and so are translated in the present tense.

(5) An imperative followed by a *weyiqtol* can describe successive and complementary actions, as in Prov 22:10 (cf. 16:3; 20:22; 27:11; 29:17).

Table 41.5. A Successive, Complementary Proverb in Proverbs 22:10

Drive out a scoffer so that strife will disappear, / so that conflict and shameful behavior will stop.
גָּרֵשׁ לֵץ וְיֵצֵא מָדוֹן וְיִשְׁבֹּת דִּין וְקָלוֹן

(6) Proverbs 10–29 often appears as a rambling, unstructured collection of individual sayings with no direction whatsoever. This has led many interpreters to group individual proverbs according to topic (e.g., proverbs on laziness, proverbs on duty to parents, proverbs on the mocker, etc.), while others have attempted to rearrange them on historical and form-critical grounds (e.g., separating secular from religious proverbs). The obvious problem with such approaches is that they reorganize the book, acknowledging in effect that the book as it stands is in chaos.

In reality, we cannot help suspecting that there is some kind of order in Proverbs, for the book itself is the product of wisdom teachers, for whom order and structure in life was axiomatic. In at least some texts an underlying order is evident. For example, in Prov 14:8–15 there appears to be a chiastic structure.

(a) The outer verses (8, 15) both contrast the discerning person with the foolish and guillible, and both verses use the word עָרוּם.

(b) The second set of verses (9, 14) contrast the mocker and the apostate with the upright and good man.

(c) The third set of verses (10, 13) assert that the external expression of one's face may not reflect the true joy or sorrow that is in the heart, and both use the word שִׂמְחָה.

(d) The inner verses (11, 12) contrast the apparent but misleading security of the wicked ("the *house* of the wicked will perish") with the apparent but misleading vulnerability of the righteous ("but the *tent* of the righteous will flourish") and assert that the way that seems right can be totally wrong (12). The way that seems to lead to wealth and security in reality leads to disaster, whereas the marginal existence of the tent-dweller is absolutely secure if one lives rightly before God.

Taken together, Prov 14:8–15 contrast appearances with reality, and it makes the point that apparent success and happiness of the mocker is illusory. This truth will be obvious to the discerning, but gullible fools miss it entirely.

(7) The above discussion reminds us of the importance of paying attention to verb forms and syntax when reading biblical proverbs, as the relationship between the two lines of an aphorism and between their verb forms may be significant. This stated, the grammatical distinction between a *qatal* and *yiqtol* can at times be explained by factors totally unrelated to syntax. For example, **assonance** (the fact that two words in some way sound alike) can determine what specific words a proverb employs. Proverbs 22:3 begins, "A thoughtful man sees trouble (עָרוּם רָאָה רָעָה)." Here the employment of the *qatal* רָאָה over the *yiqtol* יִרְאֶה may have been driven more by רָאָה sounding like רָעָה than by grammatical concerns.

I. Vocabulary

1. Core Vocabulary

a. Verbs

בכה	Qal: בָּכָה weep
יעץ	Qal: יָעַץ advise, plan
	Niphal: נוֹעַץ consult, decide
מכר	Qal: מָכַר sell
משל	Qal: מָשַׁל rule
עזר	Qal: *עָזַר; עָזַרְתָּ (*qatal* 2ms) help, assist

b. Other Words

אֹרֶךְ	length Ⓜ |אֹרֶךְ|
זְרוֹעַ	arm, forearm, (by extension) power, force Ⓕ |זְרֹעַ|
כְּרוּב	cherub Ⓜ |כְּרוּב|

מַלְכוּת   kingdom; dominion Ⓕ |מַלְכוּת|

עֵבֶר   side, edge Ⓜ |עֵבֶר|

פֶּשַׁע   crime, rebellion, revolt, wrongdoing Ⓜ |פֶּשַׁע|

שִׁיר   song Ⓜ |שִׁיר| (also שִׁירָה Ⓕ |שִׁירַת|)

2. Proper Names

מִדְיָן   Midian

מִדְיָנִי   Midianite(s)

רְאוּבֵן   Reuben

רְאוּבֵנִי   Reubenite(s)

3. Reading Vocabulary

חלם   Qal: חָלַם dream

קצר   Qal: קָצְרוּ (*qatal* 3cp) gather in, harvest, reap

אֲלֻמָּה   sheaf

אָפִיק   stream bed

דִּמְעָה   tears

מַעֲלָה   ascent (the meaning of "psalm of ascent" is uncertain)

מֶשֶׁךְ   skin/leather (pouch)

רִנָּה   cry (of joy or lament, depending on the context)

שְׁבוּת   turning; (by extension) previous situation (also שְׁבִית)

שִׁיבָה   turning; (by extension) restoration

שְׂחוֹק   laughter, pleasure

שָׂמֵחַ   happy

J. Reading—Psalm 126

שִׁיר הַמַּעֲלוֹת   1
בְּשׁוּב יְהוָה אֶת־שִׁיבַת צִיּוֹן
הָיִינוּ כְּחֹלְמִים׃

2   אָז יִמָּלֵא שְׂחוֹק פִּינוּ[1]

וּלְשׁוֹנֵנוּ רִנָּה[2]

אָז יֹאמְרוּ בַגּוֹיִם

הִגְדִּיל יְהוָה לַעֲשׂוֹת עִם־אֵלֶּה[3]׃

3   הִגְדִּיל יְהוָה לַעֲשׂוֹת עִמָּנוּ

הָיִינוּ שְׂמֵחִים׃

4   שׁוּבָה יְהוָה אֶת־שְׁבוּתֵנוּ [שְׁבִיתֵנוּ][4]

כַּאֲפִיקִים בַּנֶּגֶב׃

5   הַזֹּרְעִים בְּדִמְעָה בְּרִנָּה יִקְצֹרוּ׃

6   הָלוֹךְ יֵלֵךְ וּבָכֹה[5]

נֹשֵׂא מֶשֶׁךְ־הַזָּרַע

בֹּא־יָבוֹא בְרִנָּה

נֹשֵׂא אֲלֻמֹּתָיו[6]׃

---

1. This line ends with a Tsinnor, which is unusual, but it is preceded by Pazer, which makes the Tsinnor a stronger disjunctive. The parallelism and "gapping" between this and the following line suggest that there should be a break here. Also, without this break, the line would have 5 constituents, which would violate the constraints.

2. This line has no predicator; there is gapping of אָז יִמָּלֵא from the previous line.

3. Literally, "YHWH has made great to do with them," this can be translated, "YHWH has done great things for them."

4. Notice here the Kethiv שְׁבוּתֵנוּ and the Qere שְׁבִיתֵנוּ. The distinction here appears to be a matter of spelling as there does not seem to be any difference in meaning between the two words.

5. Distinguish the Tsinnor from the Tsinnoreth in this line. The line break here is analogous to that in v. 2a, the Tsinnor having a disjunctive Azla Legarmeh in its domain.

6. Notice that נֹשֵׂא is repeated in v. 6b and v. 6d, while הָלוֹךְ יֵלֵךְ in v. 6a parallels בֹּא־יָבוֹא in v. 6c. In vv. 6a and 6c, וּבָכֹה contrasts with בְּרִנָּה; in vv. 6b and 6d, הַזָּרַע contrasts with אֲלֻמֹּתָיו.

APPENDIX 1
BASICS FOR USING YOUR HEBREW BIBLE

A. Introduction to the Masoretic Text, *BHS*, and *BHQ*

Until the sixth century A.D., the Hebrew text only contained consonants; the vowels were passed on orally but not written. Between A.D. 500 and 1000, however, a group of Jewish scholars known as the Masoretes (from מסר, "hand on, transmit," and מְסוֹרָה, "tradition") developed a system of vowel pointing, cantillation marks, notes, and various other conventions designed to guarantee a more accurate reading and transmission of the sacred text. Their work, known as the Masoretic Text (MT), was and still remains authoritative, and what we have termed biblical Hebrew grows out of the Masoretic tradition.[1]

Today the standard Hebrew text, known in successive editions as the *Biblia Hebraica Stuttgartensia* (*BHS*)[2] and the *Biblia Hebraica Quinta* (*BHQ*)[3], is a copy of the Leningrad Codex (A.D. 1008), the earliest complete Masoretic manuscript.[4] Since the completion of the *BHS* in 1977, new discoveries and advances in the science of textual criticism have justified the creation of the updated *BHQ*, which is being produced one fascicle (usually a single biblical book) at a time and will one day replace the *BHS*. While the beginning student should use the *BHS* until a single volume of the whole *BHQ* is complete, he or she should be acquainted with the structure and component parts of both editions. To this end, the following discussion includes images of the first page of Deuteronomy in both the *BHS* and *BHQ*, along with a description of the major features and distinctions of each of the volumes.

1. Book Titles and Arrangement in the Hebrew Bible

Open your *BHS* to the first page of Deuteronomy (p. 283). As you turn there, notice that in the *BHS* the biblical book titles are located at the top center of each page: the Hebrew title

---

1. Because the Masoretes principally lived and worked in the city of Tiberius on the western shores of the Sea of Galilee, some refer to their work as the Tiberian Masoretic text. Others term it the Ben Asher text in honor of Aaron ben Asher and his family who oversaw the text's final editing.
2. K. Elliger and W. Rudolph, eds., *Biblia Hebraica Stuttgartensia* (Stuttgart: German Bible Society, 1997; orig. 1967–77). Arguably the most important tool for studying the Hebrew Bible in the twentieth century, the *Biblia Hebraica* series was first published in 1906 under the oversight of Rudolph Kittel (*BHK*). The Leningrad Codex was not used as the basis until the third edition, completed in 1937. The *BHS* is the fourth revision, and the *BHQ*, the fifth. We thank the German Bible Society for allowing us to reproduce pages from both the *BHS* and *BHQ* in this grammar.
3. A. Schenker, ed., *Biblia Hebraica Quinta* (Stuttgart: German Bible Society, 2005–).
4. Another ancient Masoretic copy known as the Aleppo Codex (A.D. 925) is providing the basis for the forthcoming Hebrew University Bible Project (1965–), but because only about three-fourths of the Aleppo Codex has survived (most of the Torah is absent), it was not used in the *Biblia Hebraica* editions.

Appendix Table 1.1. Sample *BHS* Page

on even pages and the Latin title on odd pages. The same pattern is followed in the *BHQ*, except English has replaced the Latin. The first page of each book includes both the Hebrew title and the Latin (*BHS*) or English (*BHQ*) title together.

The Hebrew title is often the first word(s) of a biblical book. This is true in Deuteronomy, where the unvocalized title אלה הדברים corresponds to the book's first two words: אֵ֫לֶּה הַדְּבָרִים, "These are the words." In other instances, a book's title points to one of the book's main themes or characters. For example, Numbers is called במדבר, "in the wilderness" (בְּמִדְבַּר) (see the top of *BHS*, p. 282), and the book following Deuteronomy that records Israel's entrance into the Promised Land is titled יהושע, "Joshua" (יְהוֹשֻׁעַ) (see *BHS*, p. 354).

Appendix Table 1.2. Sample *BHQ* Page

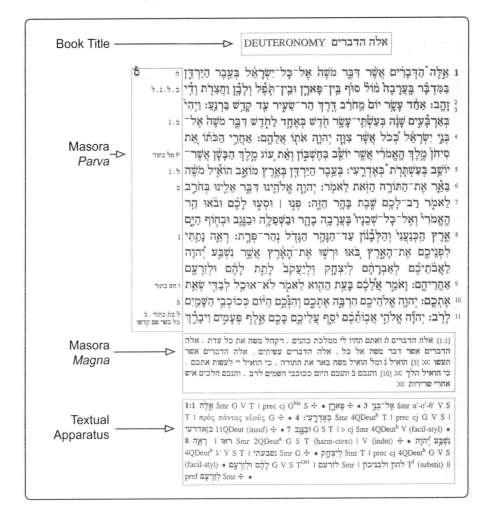

One feature of the Hebrew Bible that most English readers find surprising is that, while all the biblical books are the same, they are ordered differently and some are grouped as single books where our English Bibles distinguish them. Specifically, the Hebrew Bible is made up of twenty-four books (instead of thirty-nine!) beginning with Genesis and ending with Chronicles, and it is structured in three sections: the Law (תּוֹרָה), the Prophets (נְבִיאִים), and the Writings (כְּתוּבִים)—a pattern that appears to be echoed in Jesus' words in Luke 24:44. Because of this structure, the Hebrew Bible is commonly referred to as the TaNaK (or Tanach), an acronym derived from the first Hebrew letters of each of the three major section titles. Appendix Table 1.3 provides the groupings, arrangement, and titles for all the books as they appear in the *BHS* and *BHQ*.

Appendix Table 1.3. Book Order and Titles in the Hebrew Bible

		Titles		
		Latin (BHS)	*English (BHQ)*	*Hebrew (BHS & BHQ)* with *Translation*
Torah		Genesis	Genesis	בראשית "In the beginning"
		Exodus	Exodus	ואלה שמות "And these are the names of"
		Leviticus	Leviticus	ויקרא "And he called"
		Numeri	Numbers	במדבר "In the wilderness"
		Deuteronomium	Deuteronomy	אלה הדברים "These are the words"
Former Prophets		Josua	Joshua	יהושע "Joshua"
		Judices	Judges	שפתים "Judges"
		Samuel I II	1–2 Samuel	שמואל א ב "Samuel 1–2"
		Reges I II	1–2 Kings	מלכים א ב "Kings 1–2"
Latter Prophets		Jesaia	Isaiah	ישעיהו "Isaiah"
		Jeremia	Jeremiah	ירמיהו "Jeremiah"
		Ezechiel	Ezekiel	יחזקאל "Ezekiel"
	The Twelve	Hosea	Hosea	הושע "Hosea"
		Joel	Joel	יואל "Joel"
		Amos	Amos	עמוס "Amos"
		Obadia	Obadiah	עבדיה "Obadiah"
		Jona	Jonah	יונה "Jonah"
		Micha	Micah	מיכה "Micah"
		Nahum	Nahum	נחום "Nahum"
		Habakuk	Habakkuk	חבקוק "Habakkuk"
		Zephania	Zephaniah	צפניה "Zephaniah"
		Haggai	Haggai	חגי "Haggai"
		Sacharia	Zechariah	זכריה "Zechariah"
		Maleachi	Malachi	מלאכי "Malachi"
Writings		Psalmi	Psalms	תהלים "Songs of Praise"
		Iob	Job	איוב "Job"
		Proverbia	Proverbs	משלי "Proverbs of"
		Ruth	Ruth	רות "Ruth"
		Canticum	Canticles	שיר השירים "The Song of Songs"
		Ecclesiastes/Qohelet	Qoheleth	קהלת "Assembler/Preacher"
		Threni	Lamentations	איכה "How! / Alas!"
		Esther	Esther	אסתר "Esther"
		Daniel	Daniel	דניאל "Daniel"
		Esra–Nehemia	Ezra–Nehemiah	עזרא נחמיה "Ezra–Nehemiah"
		Chronica I II	1–2 Chronicles	דברי הימים א ב "The things of the days 1–2"

2. Paragraph, Lesson, Verse, and Chapter Divisions in the Hebrew Bible

The Hebrew Bible marks a number of divisions; all but the chapter divisions have been present in some form among the Jews for a long time. You should be aware of the following dividers.

(1) **Paragraphs.** The entire Hebrew Bible (except the Psalter) is divided into extended paragraphs. In a properly laid out liturgical text, an "open" paragraph, prefixed by a small פ and known as Pethuchah (פְּתוּחָא = "opened"), is one that starts a new line after an empty or incomplete line. In contrast, a "closed" paragraph, marked by a small ס and known as Sethumah (סְתוּמָא = "closed"), is separated from its preceding paragraph by a short space within the line. The excerpts from Deuteronomy 1 do not contain any paragraph marks, but a Pethuchah can be seen at Deut 5:1 (*BHS*, p. 294) and a host of Sethumah occur between each of the Ten Words in 5:6–22 (*BHS*, p. 295). While the *BHS* starts all Pethuchah on a new line, the *BHQ* patterns the spacing as if it were a Sethumah. The tendency to place spaces between paragraphs is evident as early as the Dead Sea Scrolls, and while no one today is certain why some paragraphs were Sethumah and others were Pethuchah, their presence can still at times aid in clarifying literary structure.

(2) **Lessons.** Throughout history, Jews have grouped certain texts to guide the reading of the Hebrew Bible. Jews in Palestine created a three-year lectionary cycle of 452 readings known as *Sedarim* (from סֵדֶר, "order, sequence"). The beginning of each Seder is marked in our Hebrew Bibles by what looks like a sideways Athnach over top of a large ס (not be confused with Sethumah). An example of this mark is found in the margin (inner for *BHS* and outer for *BHQ*) next to the first line of Deuteronomy 1. Similarly, Jews in Babylon, who read through the Torah each year, divided the first five books into fifty-four (or fifty-three) weekly lessons known as *Parashoth*, the beginning of which are marked by the characters פרש in the margin (inner for *BHS* and outer for *BHQ*). For an example of this marking, see Deut 3:23 in the *BHS* (p. 290).

(3) **Verses.** In biblical Hebrew, the Sof Pasuq (lit., "end of verse"), which looks similar to an English colon (:), signals the conclusion of a verse (though perhaps not the end of a sentence). The Jewish scribes probably began to separate verses during the age of the Talmud (ca. A.D. 135–500), but the actual numbering of verses did not occur until the sixteenth century. In the *BHS* and *BHQ*, the verse numbers are marked as superscripts at the inside margin. The *BHS* also includes the superscript numbers after each Sof Pasuq. Occasionally, especially in the Psalter, the Hebrew and English verse numbers do not align.

(4) **Chapters.** The Hebrew Bible did not include chapters until the early fourteenth century A.D. Intriguingly, the presence of these divisions derived from the Christian tradition of the Latin Vulgate. The Roman Church had adopted a system developed by Stephen Langton (1150–1228), and this scheme has been used in nearly all biblical texts and versions to the present day. In both the *BHS* and *BHQ*, large numbers at the inside margin signal the beginning of new chapters.

With the possible exception of the paragraph divisions, the principle purpose of the lessons, verses, and chapters has always been to make reading of and reference to the Hebrew Bible more manageable and easy. The purpose was never to guide interpretation. Interpreters should, therefore, use care in allowing the marked divisions to influence their understanding of the text's component boundaries and message.

3. The Masorah of the Hebrew Bible

One of the contributions the Masoretes made was a series of notes designed to assist a copyist in preserving an unaltered biblical text. Known as the Masorah, these notes are located in the manuscript margins and at the end of each book or section (e.g., at the end of the Torah). The marginal notes are known as the Masorah *parva* ("small Masorah") and the Masorah *magna* ("large Masorah"), respectively, and the concluding notes are called the Masorah *finalis* ("final Masorah"). While the Masorah is written in unpointed text (usually Aramaic), the *BHS* and *BHQ* assists the reader by including in the introduction a glossary of common terms. The glossary translations of the Aramaic/Hebrew are in Latin in the *BHS* but in English in the *BHQ*. Furthermore, in a separate section of each fascicle, the *BHQ* provides an English translation of and commentary on the Masorah *parva* and *magna*. (When the *BHQ* is complete, these latter elements will be included in a separate volume.)

(1) **Masorah *parva* (Mp).** The Masorah *parva* (or "small Masorah") is located in the outer page margins of the *BHS* and *BHQ*. It offers an array of statistical details regarding word counts, word placement (e.g., in the exact middle of the book), and spelling peculiarities, all designed to protect the text from scribal error. A small circle in the body of the text above a word or phrase (°) signals the reader to the marginal comment. For example, in Deut 1:1, a circle over the phrase אֵלֶּה הַדְּבָרִים ("these are the words") sends the reader to the margin where the letter ה with a dot over it (הֹ) informs the reader that the phrase shows up five total times in the Hebrew Bible (cf. Exod 19:6; 35:1; Isa 42:16; Zech 8:16). (The Medieval Jews editing the biblical text applied numerical values to all the alphabet, with א–ט representing the units [1–9]—e.g., א stands for *one* and ה for *five*).[1] With this information in hand, the copyist was charged to make sure the phrase only occurred this many times in his text.

While most notes in the Masorah *parva* are of little value to the interpreter, two should be given more care: Kethiv–Qere and unique forms known as *hapax legomena*.

(a) **Kethiv–Qere.** There were times when the scribes believed that a word *written* one way (the Kethiv) should be *read* another way (the Qere). In such instances,

---

1. While the practice of applying numeric values to letters of the alphabet dates back at least to the second century B.C., there are no traces of this system in the biblical text itself. The Medieval Jewish editors, however, employed the system in many of the their notes. The basic system is as follows: units, 1–9 = א–ט; tens, 10–90 = י–צ; hundreds: (a) 100–400 = ת–ק; (b) 500 = 400 + 100 = תק; (c) similarly for 600–800; (d) 900 = 400 + 400 + 100 = תתק; thousands, 1,000–9,000 = the letters for the units with two dots above—e.g., 1,000 = א̈.

they would leave the consonants of the Kethiv but point it with the vowels of the Qere; the consonants of the Qere would then be written in the Masorah *parva* and usually be marked by a ק with a dot over it (קׄ, short for the Aramaic קְרֵי). While there are no Kethiv–Qere issues in the Deuteronomy 1 samples, one is recorded in Deut 2:33 (*BHS*, p. 288). There we are told the word written בנו, "his son" (בְּנוֹ), should be read בָּנָיו, "his sons." For more on the Kethiv–Qere, see chapter 36.

(b) **Unique forms.** The Masorah *parva* uses the sigla ל (short for the Aramaic לֵיתָא, "There is no [other]") to mark when certain forms occur only once in the Hebrew Bible. This feature of *hapax legomenon* could mean the word is unique or that the spelling alone is unique. An example is found in Deut 1:1. After the Masorah *parva* notes that מוֹל, "opposite," occurs only twice (ב), we are informed that the form תֹּפֶל, "Tophel," a place name related to Israel's location during Moses' Deuteronomic sermons, shows up only here in the biblical text.

(2) **Masorah *magna* (Mm).** The Masorah *magna* (or "large Masorah") contains a more developed version of the information found in abbreviated form in the Masorah *parva*. The *BHS* does not actually include the Masorah *magna*, but it does retain a register just below the body of the biblical text that is accessed through footnotes in the Masorah *parva*. The register (e.g., Mm 617, etc.) sends the reader to another volume that contains the Masorah *magna*.[1] In contrast, the *BHQ* includes the full Masorah *magna* just underneath the biblical text, and it includes in the back of each fascicle (ultimately to be placed in a separate volume) both translation and commentary for the Masorah *parva* and Masorah *magna*.

(3) **Masorah *finalis* (Mf).** The Masoretic endnotes that conclude a book at the very least include a total verse count for the book. The Masorah *finalis* in Deuteronomy (*BHS*, p. 353) notes a total of 955 verses in the book, but it also identifies עַל־פִּי, "according to," in 17:10 as the book's middle point and that there are a total of thirty-one *Sedarim*. With this, as the final book in the Torah, it further clarifies that Genesis–Deuteronomy consists of 5,845 verses, 158 *Sedarim*, 79,856 words, and 400,945 letters! The Masoretes thus provided a level of quality control against which any new manuscript could be checked.

4. The Textual Apparatus

We noted above that the biblical text used in the *BHS* and *BHQ* is a copy of the Leningrad Codex (A.D. 1008). When a critical edition uses a single manuscript as its base, it is called a diplomatic text. All *Biblia Hebraica* editions to date follow this pattern, and they include in a textual apparatus at the bottom of each page the most important textual variants for translation and exegesis.[2] In a separate section of each fascicle, the *BHQ* also includes a minimal

---

1. Gérard E. Weil, ed., *Massorah Gedolah iuxta Codicem Leningradensem B19a*, vol. 1: *Catalogi* (Rome: Pontifical Biblical Institute Press, 1971).
2. For the *BHQ*, the United Bible Societies' Hebrew Old Testament Text Project (HOTTP)

commentary on the apparatus. (Once the *BHQ* is complete, this features will be located in a separate volume along with added commentary on the Masorah *parva* and Masorah *magna*.)

The contemporary scholar who edited the particular biblical book in either the *BHS* or *BHQ* is the one who prepared the apparatus. The textual notes included are of three sorts:

(1) Those that cite minor irregularities in the Leningrad Codex in distinction from other Masoretic manuscripts (e.g., accent or vocalization distinctions).

(2) Those that give the editor's suggestion for a textual emendation.

(3) Those that show alternate readings in other Hebrew texts or ancient translations. These notes are by far the most important.

(a) Challenges to Reading the Apparatus

The *BHQ* apparatus is relatively easy to understand, for it employs English abbreviations for both the textual witnesses and the notes. This is not the case, however, in the *BHS*, whose apparatus uses a mixture of symbols and Latin abbreviations.

(1) **Understanding the Sigla.** The various textual witnesses in the *BHS* are represented through a number of abbreviated symbols, known as "sigla." It also uses abbreviations for details about the nature of different variants. While a full list of sigla may be found in the introductions to both the *BHS* and *BHQ*, the following abbreviated list will help you become familiar with those that are most significant.

Appendix Table 1.4. The Most Common *BHS* and *BHQ* Sigla

BHS	BHQ	Title and Description
𝔪	M	**Masoretic Text (MT).** This is the received, standard text of the Hebrew Scriptures. It is called "Masoretic" because it is the text tradition of the Masoretes, a Jewish scribal school that worked from A.D. 500–1000.
L	M^L	**Leningrad Codex** (ca. A.D. 1008). This is the oldest complete copy of the Hebrew Bible and the basis for the *BHS* and *BHQ*.
א or A	M^A	**Aleppo Codex** (ca. A.D. 925). An important Masoretic manuscript dated earlier than the Leningrad Codex but only about three-fourths extant (most of the Torah is absent). It is the basis for the forthcoming Hebrew University Bible Project, but is not used in the *Biblia Hebraica*.

provided the guide for determining which variants would be addressed. For both the *BHS* and *BHQ*, the five-volume *Preliminary and Interim Report* (New York: United Biblical Societies, 1974–1980) is a handy, manageable reference to and through many of the variants discussed in the apparatus. In contrast to the structure of the *Biblia Hebraica* editions, the standard Greek New Testament (UBS[4] or NA[27]) is an eclectic text, not following only one manuscript in the body but rather presenting in the body a corrected text (according to general scholarly consensus) with variant readings noted in the apparatus.

C	M^C	**Cairo Codex of the Prophets**. Said to have been written by Moses ben Asher, it dates to about 895 A.D.
B	M^B	**Ben Chayyim Hebrew Bible** (ca. A.D. 1525). One of the first printed versions of the Hebrew Bible, this was once the standard rabbinic Bible. It is called the Bombergiana text. It contained not only the Hebrew Bible but also an Aramaic version and comments by renowned rabbis.
Ms(s)	ms(s)	**Other Hebrew Manuscripts**. The siglum Mss refers to various and sundry fragments and manuscripts of the Hebrew Scriptures, especially those found in the 1776–1780 edition of Benjamin Kennicott. This Oxford theologian and librarian collated more than 6,000 manuscripts with the aid of a staff and assistants and produced the *Vetus Testamentum Hebraicum cum variis lectionibus*.
Q	Q	**Qumran Texts (DSS)**. These are texts from the Dead Sea Scrolls. Because of their age and origin, they have taken on enormous importance in text critical studies. The most famous DSS text is the great Isaiah scroll (1QIsa^a), which contains the entire book of Isaiah.
C	Gnz	**Cairo Geniza Texts**. These are fragments of the Hebrew Scriptures found in the late nineteenth century in what had been the geniza of a Cairo synagogue. A geniza is a storage room used to house old, worn out copies of the Scriptures and other religious texts.
m	Smr	**Samaritan Pentateuch**. This is the Pentateuch of the Samaritan community, the semi-Jewish breakaway group that Jesus encountered several times in his ministry (John 4). They recognized only the Pentateuch as canonical. In some places the Samaritan Pentateuch seems to have been deliberately altered to support the theology of the Samaritans, but many differences between it and the MT are merely orthographic (i.e., spelling differences).
G	G	**Old Greek** or **Septuagint (LXX)**. This is the translation of the OT into Greek that became the Bible of the early church. Although its origins are debated, the process of translation probably began around the mid-third century B.C. in Alexandria, Egypt. It does not appear to be the work of a single translator or even of a single group of translators; it has been called a collection of translations. Some books in the LXX are translated fairly skillfully and accurately, but others, such as Job, are very free renditions. It is of great importance to textual criticism, but very few scholars would regard it as superior to the MT, even though some of its readings are supported in Qumran texts.
α'	α'	**Aquila** (ca. A.D. 150). A revision of the LXX into slavishly literal Greek, it survives today only in quotations, in fragments of the Hexapla (see Orig below), and in palimpsests (manuscripts erased and written over) from the Cairo geniza.

σ′	σ′	**Symmachus** (ca. A.D. 170). A more literary version of the Greek OT, it survives only in fragments of the Hexapla (see Orig below).
θ′	θ′	**Theodotian** (ca. A.D. 200). Another revision of the Greek OT. The so-called Theodotian text of Daniel replaced the inferior LXX Daniel, but the "Theodotian Daniel" may not actually be from Theodotian.
γ′	γ′	**The "Three."** Aquila, Symmachus, and Theodotian are all in agreement.
Orig	Hex	**Hexapla of Origen** (ca. A.D. 230). A polyglot (multi-lingual) work produced by Origen in Alexandria. It contained in six columns the Hebrew text, a transliteration of the Hebrew into Greek, Aquila, Symmachus, the LXX, and Theodotian. It survives only in fragments. Eusebius reports that Origen added three other Greek translations that are now called Quinta, Sexta, and Septima (i.e., "Fifth," "Sixth," and "Seventh").
𝕋	T	**Targums**. A Targum is an Aramaic translation of the Hebrew Scriptures made for postexilic Jews whose mother tongue was Aramaic. Targums tend to paraphrase freely—at times exceedingly so. Targum Onkelos is the official Targum for the Torah, and Targum Jonathan is the official Targum for the Prophets, but there are also a number of unofficial Targums.
𝕊	S	**Syriac**. Also called the Peshitta, this became the OT for the Syriac church. Syriac is a later dialect of Aramaic. Although the history of the Syriac text is complex and debated, it appears that its origin is in the Jewish rather than the Christian community and that it was translated from the Hebrew.
£	La	**Old Latin**. This is not the title of a single translation but is a collective term for various translations of the LXX OT into Latin. No complete text survives, but pieces of Old Latin texts survive in the church fathers, in old Latin liturgies, and in fragments.
𝔳	V	**Vulgate**. The standard Bible of the western church, the Vulgate OT is made up of Jerome's translation of the Hebrew text into Latin. It dates to the late fourth century.
𝕂	copt/ Sa, Akh, Bo	**Coptic Version**. This is the OT for Egyptian Coptic Christians and has different versions based on the Coptic dialect: Sahidic (upper Egyptian), Akhmimic, and Bohairic (lower Egyptian). Based on the LXX, it is especially useful for septuagintal studies.
Mp	Mp	**Masorah *parva***. Masoretic marginal notations that focus on word counts, word placement, and spelling peculiarities.
Mm	Mm	**Masorah *magna***. More developed descriptions of material found in the Masorah *parva*.

| K | ket | **Kethiv**. This siglum represents a given word in the MT as written, which the scribes reproduced without alteration but did not pronounce as written either because they believed the text had an error or because they thought it was irreverent to pronounce the word. |
| Q | qere | **Qere**. This is how the scribes pronounced a Kethiv word. |

(2) **Understanding the Latin abbreviations and phrases.** In contrast to the *BHQ*, which uses English for all notations, the *BHS* uses many Latin phrases and abbreviations in the textual apparatus. The *BHS* introduction has a Latin-English glossary for all forms encountered. Some of the most common are given below, listed alphabetically by column.

Appendix Table 1.5. Some Important Latin Abbreviations in the *BHS*

* *conjectural form*	de = *from*	nisi = *unless*	sed = *but*
+ *it adds*	dl = *delete*	nonnulli (nonn) = *several*	semper = *always*
> *it is missing*	e, ex = *from*	passim = *in various places*	si = *if*
a, ab = *from*	finis = *end*	pauci (pc) = *a few*	sic = *thus*
ac = *and, besides*	fortasse (frt) = *perhaps*	pf = *perfect*	sine = *without*
ad = *to*	gl = *gloss*	pl = *plural*	sq = *following*
aliter = *otherwise*	hic = *this, here*	post = *after*	sub = *under*
alius, alii = *other(s)*	ibi = *there*	potius = *preferably*	supra = *above*
an = *or*	ibidem = *in the same place*	praeter = *except*	tr = *transpose*
ante = *before*	id(em) = *the same*	prb = *probably*	tunc = *then*
at = *but*	in = *in*	pro = *for*	txt, textus = *text*
aut = *or*	iterum = *again*	propter = *because of*	ubi = *where*
bis = *twice*	l(ege) = *it ought to read*	prp = *it has been proposed*	ubique = *everywhere*
breve = *short*	lacuna = *lacuna, gap*	punct(um) = *point*	ut = *so that*
caput (cp) = *chapter*	lectio = *reading*	quam = *than*	v = *verse*
cet(eri) = *the rest*	locus = *place*	quasi = *as if*	vb = *verb*
contra = *against*	m = *masculine*	recte = *correctly*	vel = *or*
correctio =*correction*	melior = *better*	rectus = *correct*	verba = *words*
crrp = *corrupt*	metri causa (m cs) = *because of meter*	rursus = *again*	vide = *see*
cum = *with*	multa (mlt) = *many*	saepe = *often*	vv = *verses*

(b) Reading the Apparatus

The *BHS* and *BHQ* are distinct in the way they present the apparatus notations.

(1) **The *BHS* Apparatus.** The body of the *BHS* uses raised English letters to signal when words or phrases are addressed in the apparatus. When a single word is discussed, it is followed by a superscript lowercase English letter, as with ᵃאֵ֫לֶּה, "these," the first word of Deut 1:1. Two or more words that are addressed as a group are bracketed by the same raised lowercase letter, as in ᵇנִשְׁבַּ֥ע יְהוָ֖הᵇ, "YHWH swore," in 1:8. In the

first of these instances, the note tells us that two Hebrew manuscripts (Mss), one Greek manuscript ($\mathfrak{G}^A$), and one Syriac manuscript (S^W) add the conjunction before the word (= וְאֵלֶּה). In the example from 1:8, we see that the Samaritan Pentateuch (𝕸) and two Greek versions ($\mathfrak{G}^{-LO}$) have the verb in first person in accordance with the fact that YHWH is speaking in the context. As should be clear, the apparatus distinguishes chapter divisions by the abbreviation Cp, verses through the inclusion of verse numbers separated on each side by a space, and notes by two parallel vertical lines (‖).

(2) **The *BHQ* Apparatus.** In contrast to the pattern in the *BHS*, the *BHQ* offers no markings in the body of the text to signal comment in the apparatus. Each new entry in the *BHQ* apparatus, however, begins with a listing of the word or phrase in the Leningrad Codex that is being addressed. So, for example, אֵלֶּה is listed first after 1:1 in the apparatus, followed directly by those witnesses that agree with the Leningrad Codex: the Samaritan Pentateuch (Smr), the old Greek (G), the Vulgate (V), and the Targum (T). After a single vertical separator line, which marks that what follows disagrees with the reading of the Leningrad Codex, we read that a single Greek manuscript (G^{Ms}) and the Syriac (S) precede (prec) אֵלֶּה with the conjunction (cj). The cross symbol (✢) indicates that the apparatus commentary has a discussion of this case, and the black dot (●) concludes the note. Occasionally, before the note is concluded, two parallel vertical lines (‖) will signal the case conclusion, followed by a comment detailing the editor's preferred reading. For example, the last note in Deut 1:8 reveals that the editor believes the Samaritan Pentateuch retains the most original reading, one that does not include וְ לָהֶם, "to them and," before לְזַרְעָם, "to their offspring."

B. Introduction to Old Testament Textual Criticism

For all their care and attention to detail, the scribes who copied and recopied the Hebrew Bible were not perfect. Errors in copying did occur. For this reason, it is sometimes necessary to engage in textual criticism, suggesting a scribal error and proposing a more accurate, original reading for a passage.

A famous but debatable example of a commonly emended text is in Amos 6:12, where the prophet is speaking of things that are obviously absurd or impossible, and says, "Do horses run on stones, or does one plow with oxen (אִם־יַחֲרוֹשׁ בַּבְּקָרִים)? Yet you turn justice into poison...." The problem, of course, is that although horses do not run on rocks, people certainly do plow with oxen and therefore the whole comparison looks irrational. By emending the text to אִם־יַחֲרוֹשׁ בַּבָּקָר יָם, however, we can obtain the rendering, "Or does one plow the sea with an ox?" Many argue that this makes more sense. We will say more on this example later.

1. The Basic Tools of Textual Criticism

Because we no longer have the biblical authors' original documents (the "autographs"), ancient manuscripts and fragments of the Hebrew Scriptures (called "texts") and ancient translations of the Old Testament (called "versions") are the basic tools of textual criticism. These witnesses indicate different readings that have existed through the centuries.

Of course, there are problem passages for which the texts and versions give no real help, and in these cases a scholar must use context and analogy in order to proceed. The emendation of Amos 6:12 proposed above has no manuscript or versional support; it is a conjecture that the words בבקר ים were erroneously joined as one word, בבקרים.

Few students of the Hebrew Bible will have access to all the texts and versions that might have a bearing on the textual criticism of the OT. For the most part, however, the textual apparatus of the *BHS* or *BHQ* and the text-critical notes found in most major OT commentaries will suffice.[1]

2. Some Common Scribal Errors

In order to do textual criticism, you need to have some idea about the kinds of errors a scribe was likely to make. Errors of sight, understanding, sound, judgment, or memory often caused the best-intentioned scribes to omit, substitute, or repeat letters or entire words. While very few errors were likely ever brought about on purpose, scribes made both unintentional and intentional alterations to the text, which ultimately resulted in a departure from the original. Below are descriptions for some common scribal errors.[2]

(1) Accidental Changes: due to the physical deterioration of a manuscript

(2) Unintentional Changes

    (a) Errors related to the manuscript being copied

        (i) **Confusion of similar letters.** Hebrew students can understand this problem very well. Errors could occur at an early stage of textual transmission, when the archaic script was in use, as well as in a later stage, when the square script came into use.[3]

---

1. An added resource is the brief text critical commentary found in the five-volume *Preliminary and Interim Report* (New York: United Biblical Societies, 1974–1980), which presents the initial conclusions of the Hebrew Old Testament Text Project.

2. The structure and some of the content of this section is derived from Ellis R. Brotzman, *Old Testament Textual Criticism: A Practical Introduction* (Grand Rapids: Baker Books, 1994), 107–21. The beginning student will find this introductory guide a great first-step into the science and art of OT textual criticism.

3. Brotzman (109) notes the following examples where letters in the archaic script were easily confused: ב and ד (Gen 9:7); ב and ר (I Kgs 22:32); כ and מ (II Kgs 22:4); י and צ (Isa 11:15); מ and שׁ (Num 24:9); א and ד (II Chr 22:10); א and ת (Num 16:1); ל and ג (Job 15:35); and ג and פ (I Chr 11:37; cf. 2 Sam 23:35). In the later Aramaic script (which we have learned in this book and which is common in biblical manuscripts), the following pairs were easily confused: ב and כ (I Chr 17:20); י and ו (Isa 30:4); ה and ח

   (ii) **Incorrect joining or dividing of words.** A common example in English is the unseparated phrase GODISNOWHERE, which could be separated GOD IS NOW HERE or GOD IS NOWHERE. The proposed emendation of Amos 6:12 from בבקרים to בבקר ים is an example of this; scholars suggest that the words have been incorrectly joined.

   (iii) **Wrong assignment of vowels.** The incorrect placement of a vowel letter or a misreading of an ambiguous vowel letter could cause a scribe to misidentify or mistranslate a word.

   (iv) **Misunderstanding of abbreviations.** An earlier scribe may have used an abbreviation that a later scribe misunderstood.

   (v) **Omission by homoioteleuton.** Homoioteleuton means "similar ending," and it refers to an error of omission brought about by the similarity of the ending of neighboring words. For example, if two phrases end with the same word, the scribe's eye might jump from the end of the first phrase to the end of the second phrase without copying the words of the second phrase. If someone made this error while copying the previous sentence, it might read, "might jump from the end of the first phrase to the end of the second phrase" and skip "without copying the words of the second phrase."[1]

 (b) Errors of the scribe's fallibility

   (i) **Haplography.** This is writing a word or letter once where it should have been written twice.

   (ii) **Dittography.** This is writing a word or letter twice where it should have been written once.

   (iii) **Transposition of letters.** A scribe inadvertently switched the places of two letters, as when we type "teh" for "the."

 (c) Errors related to dictation or faulty hearing.

   (i) **Misunderstanding a spoken text.** It appears that sometimes the scribes wrote as another scribe read the text aloud. Some may have made mistakes based on words that sound alike. For example, at times we see לו in the text where we should see לא, or the reverse.

 (d) Errors of the scribe's judgment

   (i) **Faulty memory.** Sometimes scribes lapsed into copying from mistaken memory rather than from the manuscript(s) before them.

   (ii) **Improper conformity to parallels.** At other times scribes appear to have inadvertently made a text conform to a parallel reading.

   (iii) **Insertion of marginal note.** Some scholars suggest that occasionally a note in the margin of a text was accidentally inserted into the text itself.

    (Exod 34:19); and ח and ה (Ps 49:15).

1.   A less common error is omission by homoeoarkton, which means "similar beginning."

(3) Intentional Changes

      (i) **Deliberate alterations.** In comparing manuscripts of the Hebrew Bible, we occasionally see evidence that an early scribe engaged in a kind of textual emendation. For example, scribes may correct spelling or even grammatical peculiarities, update or clarify archaic or unclear words or phrases, adapt readings that were believed disrespectful to God or theologically question-able, conform divergent readings with parallel passages, or fix what were be-lieved to be historical or geographical problems. While these kinds of changes are quite rare and could in certain circumstances be justified, a mis-understanding could also distance the copied text from the original.

      (ii) **Deliberate omission of words or phrases.** From Jewish sources, we learn of seventeen instances in the whole OT where scribes felt certain words were out of place or improper in context.

      (iii) **Insertion of an explanatory gloss.** Some scholars suggest that occasionally a scribe added a clarifying note into the text.

Significantly, while textual changes resulting in error do exist among the biblical witnesses, most are quite small and have little impact on either the text's credibility or its message.[1] Just as an alert reader can understand a book or newspaper article that has typographical er-rors in it, so too the Bible is able to speak for itself in spite of the minor corruptions that may have arisen through scribal transmission. Most of the biblical text is certain, and where variations do occur among existing copies, the original wording can usually be determined with a good degree of certainty by a thorough acquaintance with the available manuscripts and the context.

3. Guidelines for Textual Criticism

The reader of the Hebrew Bible frequently encounters variant readings and must evaluate them to decide if a given emendation should be followed. This issue cannot be avoided. For

---

1. The student should be aware that certain OT books like Samuel and Jeremiah witness ma-jor differences between the Masoretic Text (MT) and other texts and versions. However, at least with Jeremiah the differences appear to point not to textual corruption but to there being two different editions of the book. Specifically, the Septuagint (LXX) is about one-eighth shorter than the MT and lacks approximately 2,700 words found in Hebrew text. It includes, however, nearly 100 words not present in the MT. Furthermore, the chapters in the LXX are arranged differently, the most striking distinction being that the oracles against foreign nations occur at the end of the MT edition (chs. 46–51) but in the middle of the LXX edition (between the MT 25:13 and 25:15 with v. 14 being omitted). With the discovery of the Dead Sea Scrolls, the conclusion that the differences found in LXX Jere-miah are not the result of scribal error but point to a totally different edition of the book has been made more plausible, in that the reading of Jer 9:22–10:18 found on one of the partial Jeremiah manuscripts found in the Dead Sea Scrolls in Cave 4 (4QJer[b]) appears to reflect the wording of the LXX over the MT.

the beginning reader, this is a bewildering enterprise, but the following guidelines may prove helpful.

THE GUIDING PRINCIPLE: The more original reading is the one that best explains the rise of all the others. The interpreter must assess which reading most likely came first and how other readings could have come about. In doing so, textual critics must evaluate both external and internal evidence. **External evidence** deals with the age and quality of the manuscripts. Older manuscripts may be closer to the original, but they could also contain old errors, so one must be cautious. Wrestling with **internal evidence** involves deciding what the author most likely wrote and which variant readings are best explained as unintentional or intentional changes made by copyists.

With these aspects in mind, at least one of the following should be true in order to justify emendation.

(1) The Hebrew of the received text is unintelligible or at least very strange. Sometimes the interpretation of a problematic line is so speculative in nature that it is difficult to have confidence in the text or in any translation allegedly based on that text.

(2) Support exists in Hebrew manuscripts for the proposed emendation.

(3) There is support in the versions for the proposed emendation, and we can offer a clear explanation of how the correct reading reflected in the version became corrupted to what we see in the MT.

(4) There is contextual support for emendation.

Having said all that, one would do well to heed a fundamental rule of OT textual criticism: *Emend with caution!* The reasons are as follows.

(1) The Masoretic scribes were very careful. They were not flawless, but the last 100 years of textual research has shown that they preserved the text remarkably well.

(2) Every argument for emending a text can be countered. For example, we may assert that the Hebrew is unclear. But Hebrew that appears to us to be unintelligible may simply be using an idiom that we do not know. We should bear in mind how little we know of ancient Israelite culture and dialect.

(3) The versions (LXX, etc.) have numerous problems of their own (inept or biased translators, corrupt manuscripts, use of paraphrase, etc.).

(4) Emendations are sometimes driven by theological considerations or some other agenda. A scholar may want to emend the text because the text contradicts a thesis that he or she is trying to push. Such emendations have little to commend them.

(5) Emendations tend to make a dynamic text pedestrian and flat. A heavily emended version of a Hebrew text often reads as generic Hebrew and lacks literary power. Moreover, a willingness to work with a text as it stands often yields a profound, or at least clear, sense of what the passage means.

(6) An excessively emended text is a new redaction! Someone who emends the text frequently has taken the position of being a redactor—one might say a co-author—of a biblical text. There is an inverse relationship between how much emending a scholar does and how much confidence people have in that scholar's results.

4. Final Reflections

We noted that Amos 6:12 is often emended to read, "Or does one plow the sea with an ox?" Is this conjectural emendation in fact necessary? Probably not, although many scholars hold to it. The Hebrew reads:

הַיְרֻצוּן בַּסֶּלַע סוּסִים אִם־יַחֲרוֹשׁ בַּבְּקָרִים

Rather than emend, we should probably assume that בַּסֶּלַע, "on stones," does "double-duty" (i.e., functions in both clauses). Taken this way, it means "Should horses run on stones, or should one plow (on stones) with oxen?" The image of someone trying to plow the sea with an ox is so far-fetched and implausible that it does not make for a good analogy, but this image works well: a foolish farmer trying to plow through a field that he has not taken the time to clear of stones.

APPENDIX 2

NOUN TYPES AND BASICS FOR USING YOUR HEBREW LEXICON

A. Introduction

What is known as a dictionary in the study of the English language is usually called a lexicon in Hebrew studies. Specifically, a lexicon is a book that lists the words of a language, usually in alphabetical order, and gives their range of meaning through equivalent words in a different language. In Hebrew lexicons, the various word glosses are usually accompanied by specific biblical verse references, allowing the lexicon to serve both as a dictionary and a sort of concordance.

The standard Hebrew–English lexicon is *The Hebrew and Aramaic Lexicon of the Old Testament* (often referred to by the acronym *HALOT*) by L. Koehler and W. Baumgartner.[1] While very valuable for all serious interpreters of the Hebrew Bible, its size and cost can be somewhat daunting for the beginning student. A very common alternative is W. L. Holladay's *A Concise Hebrew and Aramaic Lexicon of the Old Testament*[2] (often called simply "Holladay"), which itself is based on an earlier edition of Koehler and Baumgartner's work.

Some, however, still prefer the older standard, which is now commonly called *The Brown-Driver-Briggs Hebrew and English Lexicon* (normally abbreviated as *BDB*).[3] While *HALOT* and Holladay are strictly alphabetical, *BDB* is not, at least with respect to how it handles nouns. The following discussion is devoted to clarifying how noun types are distinguished in biblical Hebrew, how Holladay's lexicon and *BDB* differ in their approaches, and how to use a lexicon rightly.

B. Overview of Noun Types and Their Handling in Lexicons

Just as verbs can be categorized into various root types and stems, nouns also fall into various distinct patterns. We have already observed two different noun types (the geminates and the segholates). Many other noun types exist, and quite a few have some kind of preformative attached to the root. As with verbs, the three letters קטל are used when setting out noun types.

---

1. L. Koehler and W. Baumgartner, *The Hebrew and Aramaic Lexicon of the Old Testament*, rev. W. Baumgartner and J. J. Stamm, trans. by M. E. J. Richardson, 2 volume study edition (Leiden: Brill, 2000). Another very significant multi-volume lexicon in progress is D. J. A. Clines, ed., *The Dictionary of Classical Hebrew* (Sheffield: Sheffield Academic Press, 1993–).

2. W. L. Holladay, ed., *A Concise Hebrew and Aramaic Lexicon of the Old Testament* (Grand Rapids: Eerdmans, 1988).

3. F. Brown, S. R. Driver, C. A. Briggs, *The Brown-Driver-Briggs Hebrew and English Lexicon* (Peabody, MA: Hendrickson, 1996; originally published in 1907 as *The Hebrew and English Lexicon of the Old Testament*; reprinted with corrections 1951).

Sometimes a specific noun type is used to describe a category of persons or things.

(1) For example, the pattern קַטָּל (a Pathach under the first radical and a doubled second radical with Qamets under it) describes an *occupation or trade*. A טַבָּח is a "butcher" or a "guard," and a סַבָּל is a "porter" (i.e., a person hired to carry luggage or other large loads).

(2) Similarly, the noun type מַקְטֵל (a preformative מ and a Tsere under the second root radical) describes *tools or instruments*. מַסְמֵר means "nail," and a מַצְרֵף is a "crucible" (i.e., a container in which substances like metals can be subjected to high temperatures for purposes like melting).

While a noun type at times describes a single category of words, this is often not the case. Furthermore, sometimes the pool of biblical Hebrew words for a given type will be too small for meaningful generalizations.

Knowledge of noun types can be helpful in determining the root of a noun. For example, knowing that מ is a noun preformative helps one to recognize that the root of מַסְמֵר is סמר. For those who use *HALOT* or Holladay, knowledge of a noun's root is of little importance, since those lexicons list nouns alphabetically. Therefore, מַסְמֵר is found under the listings for the letter מ. On the other hand, to use the *Brown Driver-Briggs* Lexicon, the student must determine a noun's root in order to find the noun, since this lexicon lists nouns according to root. Therefore, in *BDB* the word מַסְמֵר is found under סמר, with the words beginning with ס and *not* with the words starting with מ.

While often inconvenient, there are some advantages to the way *BDB* lists nouns according to root.

(1) This format identifies at once all nouns and verbs that spring from a single root and shows how the various forms differ in usage from one another.

(2) Vocabulary memorization can be greatly helped by grouping words according to root. For example, the Hebrew verb זבח, which in Piel means "to sacrifice" (זִבַּח), is from the same root as מִזְבֵּחַ, "altar." Recognizing this connection can make vocabulary retention easier.

C. Principles for Determining Noun Types

In all, there are 199 Hebrew noun types, and most have at least some examples from biblical Hebrew (a few noun types occur only in post-biblical Hebrew). General principles for determining the type of a Hebrew noun are as follows:

(1) Many noun types simply have their three root radicals and some specific vowel pattern. Examples include the types קָטָל (e.g., דָּבָר, "word, thing") and קָטֵל (e.g., זָקֵן, "old man, elder").

(2) Many noun types have a feminine ending הָ or ת-. The ending ת may have a vowel letter, as in מַלְכוּת, "kingdom."

(3) Some nouns double the second radical on the analogy of the Piel stem. Examples include קַטָּל (e.g., אִכָּר, "farmer") and קַטָּל (e.g., סֻלָּם, "ladder").

(4) Some noun types have a suffformative וֹן- (e.g., יִתְרוֹן [root יתר], "advantage").

(5) Many noun types have an infixed vowel letter with י or ו (e.g., כְּסִיל [root כסל], "fool"; חַלּוֹן [root חלן], "dream.")

(6) Many noun types have a preformative consonant and vowel. The most common preformative letters are א, מ, and ת, but a few others are also found (e.g., אֶצְבָּע [root צבע], "finger"; מִסְפָּר [root ספר], "number"; תַּמְרוּק [root מרק], "cosmetics").

(7) Many noun types combine one or more of the above features. For example, גִּבּוֹר, "hero," has both a doubled second radical and an infixed Holem Waw; מַמְלָכָה, "kingdom," has both מ preformative and a feminine ending; בִּטָּחוֹן, "trust," has both a doubled second radical and the וֹן- sufformative.

(8) Some noun types are actually participles (e.g., הוֹרֵג [Qal ptc], "murderer"; מַשְׂכִּיל [Hiph ptc], "intelligent person").

(9) Noun types with weak roots will display the typical features of their roots. We have already seen geminate nouns. There are also nouns with I-נ roots, original I-ו roots, hollow roots, III-ה roots, and so forth. As with strong roots, nouns from weak roots may have preformatives, sufformatives, infixed vowel letters, and doubled middle radicals. Examples include מִבְנֶה, "building" (III-ה root with מ preformative); חֵיק, "lap" (hollow root); מַטֶּה, "staff" (I-נ and III-ה root with מ preformative and resulting assimilation of the נ); and מוֹעֵד, "appointed time" (original I-ו root with preformative מ).

D. Principles for Using Your Lexicon and Performing Word Studies

A lexicon is a remarkable tool when one uses it rightly. Far too often, however, errors occur because interpreters fail to heed a number of guiding principles.[1]

(1) The history and constituent parts of a word are not reliable guides to meaning:

    (a) *Past usage is not necessarily equivalent to current usage.* The original meaning (etymology) of a word is an unreliable guide to its current usage. "Awful" in English used to express reverence (i.e., full of awe), but today it most commonly means something that is very bad or unpleasant. Similarly, while זָקָן, "beard," was originally related to the idea of being old (cf. verb זָקֵן [Qal], "grow old"; adj. זָקֵן, "old"), this connection is not necessarily apparent in the Bible.

    (b) *Similar roots do not necessarily have similar meanings.*

        (i) Verbs and nouns that share the same root do not always share the same semantic meaning. An example in English is the verb "undertake" versus the noun "undertaker," the latter of which has a much more limited range of usage. In Hebrew, the noun מִדְבָּר, "wilderness," bears no connection in meaning to the Piel verb דִּבֶּר, "speak."

---

1. The following summary of principles and examples along with some of the wording is drawn from J. H. Walton, *Chronological and Background Charts of the Old Testament* (Grand Rapids: Zondervan, 1994), 94–95.

(ii) The various stems of a particular verbal root are not necessarily related in meaning. While English has no parallel in its use of verbs, the noun "adult" has no direct link with the noun "adultery." Similarly, in Hebrew, the Qal verb כָּפַר, "cover," may have no direct connection to the Piel כִּפֶּר, "atone."

(c) *Comparative languages are unreliable guides.* Similar (cognate) vocabulary from related languages is an unreliable guide to meaning. Just as one cannot determine the meaning of the English "dynamite" from the Greek cognate δύναμις (*dunamis*, "power"), so too the specific meaning of the Hebrew תְּשׁוּקָה, "desire," in Gen 3:16; 4:7 cannot be determined reliably from Arabic usage.

(2) Usage in context determines meaning:

(a) *Context is king.*

(i) Context is always determinative for meaning, most significantly when several different meanings exist for a given word. For example, in English, "minutes" can be parts of an hour or notes from a meeting, and context alone clarifies which meaning is in use. In Hebrew, רוּחַ can mean either "wind" or "spirit," depending on the context. *Interpreters are not at liberty to choose whichever meanings they want for a given word but must determine what the author intended.*

(ii) To understand the importance of a particular word usage in context, one must know what choices (synonyms) were available, and what is signified by the choice that was made. In English usage, the choice of "stallion" leads to certain conclusions, because the author did not use steed or charger. Similarly, in Hebrew, the nouns עַלְמָה, "young woman, girl of marriagable age"; בְּתוּלָה, "virgin"; and נַעֲרָה, "young (un)married girl," overlap in meaning, but each has its own semantic range. The interpreter must not only determine this range but clarify if there is significance to why a certain word was chosen over another (see עַלְמָה in Isa 7:14).

(iii) When a word has both a general and a technical sense, context alone must determine which was intended. For example, in English "reformed" can be a general adjective ("a reformed man"), but it can also be a technical term for a specific system of Christian doctrine ("Reformed Theology"). In Hebrew, שָׂטָן may refer generally to an "adversary, accuser," whether human (1 Kgs 11:23) or angelic (Num 22:22), or it may refer to the prince of demons himself: "Satan." Translating שָׂטָן as "Satan," however, must be defended from context; it is not necessarily the default meaning.

(b) *Look out for idioms.* One must consider whether verb + preposition combinations take on special meanings. In English, the idiomatic expression "just a minute" refers to an undefined period and could not be applied to, for example, the statement, "Class will be fifty minutes long." So too, in the Hebrew phrase "the day of YHWH," יוֹם does not refer to a twenty-four period, even though this is clearly the meaning in other contexts.

(c) *Assigned meanings must not be too limited.* While context is paramount for determining meaning, meaning must be construed broadly enough to fit all appropriate contexts (except in cases of idiomatic or technical usage). For example, the verb "swim" in English should not be defined by a particular arm stroke, for numerous arm strokes would qualify for "swimming." Accordingly, the Qal verb בָּרָא, "create," cannot mean "create out of nothing" for this meaning cannot apply to Gen 5:1, where God is said to have "created" man (cf. Gen 2:7).

Because intelligible communication is made up of clauses, which themselves are composed of words, word studies are a vital part of the interpretive enterprise. By use of a Hebrew concordance (never again use an English Bible concordance for a word study!),[1] interpreters must establish the range of usage for a given word. Once the various meanings are understood, the present context must then be evaluated to establish which of these meanings was intended by the author.

Lexicons can be valuable time savers in this process, for in a lexicon, scholars have already attempted to establish the semantic range of meanings for a given word. Furthermore, often lexicons have the particular uses already classified according to their various contexts.

Lexicons, however, are not infallible resources, and their purpose is principally to list the possible range of meanings. Therefore, interpreters must evaluate on their own to decide what meaning best fits the passage being studied.

Take the time to use your lexicon rightly, and study the biblical context thoroughly. With the above principles in hand, along with a cautious eye to varify the decisions suggested in your lexicon, you should be ready to establish accurately the meaning of words throughout the Hebrew Bible.

---

1.   For the purpose of concordance study, most interpreters today use computer search engines found in software like Bible Works for Windows (from Bible Works, LLC <www.bibleworks.com>) and Accordance for the Apple Macintosh (from Oak Tree Software, Inc. <www.accordancebible.com>). The standard printed Hebrew concordance is A. Even-Shoshan, *A New Concordance of the Old Testament Using the Hebrew and Aramaic Text*, 2nd ed. (Jerusalem: Kiryat Sefer, 1993). The challenge with this volume, however, is that all text except for the introduction is in biblical or modern Hebrew, making it difficult at times to navigate. A popular alternative, which uses NIV translations for easy access but is still structured according to Hebrew usage, is J. R. Kohlenberger III and J. A. Swanson, *The Hebrew-English Concordance ot the Old Testament* (Grand Rapids: Zondervan, 1998).

APPENDIX 3
DISTINGUISHING SUBJECT AND PREDICATE IN NOMINAL CLAUSES

In chapter 39, we noted that the *guiding principle* for distinguishing the subject and predicate in nominal clauses is that the subject is usually more defined or known in the communication situation than the predicate. For example, in דָּוִד אִישׁ ("David [was] a man") the word דָּוִד and not אִישׁ is the subject because the former is definite while the latter is indefinite. All nominals (whether noun, pronoun, adjective, participle, etc.) bear a relative level of definiteness in relation to one another. For example, a proper noun (e.g., Hebrew) is more defined than an indefinite common noun (e.g., book), while the latter is itself more defined than an adjective (e.g., easy).

The following list shows one proposal for the relative levels of definiteness expressed by the various phrase types found in nominal clauses.[1] You may use this hierarchy to distinguish subjects and predicates.

(1) Pronominal suffix on יֵשׁ, on אַיִן, on הִנֵּה, on עוֹד, or on a locative

(2) Demonstrative pronoun

(3) Personal pronoun

(4) Definite noun phrase or definite participle

(5) Proper noun or name

(6) Indefinite noun phrase or indefinite participle

(7) Interrogative pronoun or interrogative noun phrase

(8) Infinitive construct

(9) Adjective

(10) Prepositional phrase or locative

To use this with a nominal clause, find the two elements of your clause in the list. Whichever element has the lowest number is probably the subject. For example, we see in Exod 16:15 the following verbless clause (with a modifying relative clause):

הוּא הַלֶּחֶם אֲשֶׁר נָתַן יְהוָה לָכֶם לְאָכְלָה

That is the bread that YHWH your God gave to you for food.

In this case הוּא is the subject and הַלֶּחֶם is the predicate because הוּא is a demonstrative pronoun (level 2 on the list) and הַלֶּחֶם is a definite noun (level 4).

---

1. Adapted from Janet W. Dyk and Eep Talstra, "Paradigmatic and Syntagmatic Features in Nominal Clauses," in *The Verbless Clause in Biblical Hebrew: Linguistic Approaches*, ed. Cynthia L. Miller, Linguistic Studies in Ancient West Semitic, Volume 1 (Winona Lake, IN: Eisenbrauns, 1999), 152.

It is also worth noting that there are actually three ranges of definiteness in the above list:

(1) *Phrase types that are always the subject* (level 1: a pronominal suffix on יֵשׁ, on אַיִן, on הִנֵּה, on עוֹד, or on a locative). These suffixes will never be the predicate in a nominal clause.

(2) *Phrase types that may be either the subject or predicate* (levels 2–9: phrase types from a demonstrative pronoun to an adjective). Within this range, there may be some ambiguity or room for debate about a phrase type's level of definiteness. For example, one may argue that proper names should be ranked higher than definite nouns. On the other hand, an adjective almost never serves as a subject. An example of the latter would be an adjective that can function substantively, as in Ps 3:2, רַבִּים קָמִים עָלָי ("Many [are] rising against me").

(3) *Phrase types that are always the predicate* (level 10: a prepositional phrase or locative, such as שָׁם, "there").

We should also note that word order may play a role in nominal clauses. It appears that the default order is subject followed by predicate. If this order is reversed, the predicate is to be regarded as the focus of the sentence. It is possible that word order may disambiguate difficult clauses, where it is not certain which nominal is the subject. In such a case, the default interpretation would be that the first nominal is the subject.

Some scholars distinguish between clauses of identification (having the pattern of subject followed by predicate) and clauses of classification (having the pattern of predicate followed by subject). Following this line of thinking, the clause אֲנִי יהוה ("I am YHWH"; Exod 6:2) is a clause of identification, whereas טָמֵא הוּא ("he is unclean"; Lev 13:36) is a clause of classification.

The above discussion gives you general guidelines for interpreting nominal clauses, and understanding these issues helps you to analyze a text intelligently. But you should be aware that scholarly investigation of these matters is ongoing, and there is room for exceptions or even disagreement. Above all, you should be careful about interpreting a clause in a unusual way; such interpretations are often forced or unnatural.

APPENDIX 4
CONNECTION, OFFLINE CLAUSES, AND TEXT TYPE PREDICATE PATTERNS

A. The Role of וְ and Asyndeton in Creating Discourse Blocks (§37.C)

(1) **The conjunction וְ ("and"):** Links grammatical units of equal value, creating chains of discourse that are to be read together.

(2) **Asyndeton:** The absence of a conjunction at the front of a sentence, which signals:

    (a) *A fresh beginning*—i.e., the start of a new unit of discourse;

    (b) *Explication*—i.e., the restatement, clarification, or support of a previous text unit.

B. Offline Clause Functions (§37.E.2)

(1) **To give background information**, describing the setting or the situation at the time of the main action.

(2) **To match multiple aspects of the same event.**

    (a) *Contrastive matching:* V(x) + (x)V.

    (b) *Identical matching:* (x)V + (x)V.

(3) **For an interruption or transition**, whether to mark dramatic pause (climax), thematic division, or flashback.

    (a) *Marks thematically prominent material.*

    (b) *Signals hinge material* (i.e., a turning point in the discourse), such as paragraph divisions or new temporal, logical, or thematic points of departure.

(4) **For negated actions.**

C. Functions of Predicate Patterns in Text Types

Appendix Table 4.1. Historical Discourse

Prominence	Function	Predicate Pattern
1: Offline	Primary marker of climax, or paragraph boundaries; can also be used with mainline *wayyiqtol* for identical or contrastive matching	*qatal* [x] + *qatal* וְ + [x] + *qatal*
2: Offline	Backgrounded activities	Participial nominal clauses
3: Offline	Backgrounded description	Nominal clauses Existential clauses
4: Offline	Negative (*can shift to level 1 with "momentous negation")	לֹא or אַל + finite verb
Mainline	Primary storyline	*Wayyiqtol*

Appendix Table 4.2. Anticipatory Discourse

Prominence	Function	Predicate Pattern
1: Offline	Backgrounded predictions and promises. Can also mark climax, paragraph boundaries, identical or contrastive matching.	yiqtol [x] + yiqtol ו‍ + [x] + yiqtol
2: Offline	Backgrounded activities. Can also mark paragraph boundaries.	Participial nominal clauses
3: Offline	Backgrounded description. Can also mark paragraph boundaries.	Linking clauses Existential clauses
4: Offline	Negative (*can shift to level 1 with "momentous negation")	לֹא or אַל + finite verb
Mainline	Primary Prediction or Promise	weqatal

Appendix Table 4.3. Directive Discourse

Prominence	Function	Predicate Pattern
1: Offline	Secondary command or exhortation. It can mark climax or paragraph boundaries, and can be used for identical or contrastive matching.	Modal yiqtol [X] + modal yiqtol
2: Offline	Purpose, result, consequence. It is a secondary marker of paragraph boundaries.	Weyiqtol (after volitive or modal yiqtol) Weqatal
3: Offline	Backgrounded activities. It is a secondary marker of paragraph boundaries.	Participial nominal clauses
4: Offline	Backgrounded Description. It is a secondary marker of paragraph boundaries.	Copulative clauses Existential clauses
Mainline	Initial command, exhortation, prohibition, or admonition. It is the primary marker of paragraph initiation.	Initial volitive לֹא + yiqtol or אַל + jussive
Mainline	Primary command, exhortation, or instruction.	Weqatal (usually after volitive)

APPENDIX 5
GLOSSARY FOR THE STUDY OF HEBREW GRAMMAR

Absolute state: The simple form of a noun, in contrast to the construct. An absolute noun always falls at the end of a construct chain. In the phrase, "house of God," Hebrew would express "house of" as a construct noun and "God" as an absolute (= בֵּית אֱלֹהִים). Absolute nouns are also used as subjects, nominal predicate complements, and direct objects. In Hebrew lexicons, nouns are listed in the absolute state. §§1, 12

Active voice: The verbal voice that indicates that the subject of the verb acts rather than is acted upon, in contrast to the passive voice. An example of an active is "He hit the ball." §6

Anaptyptic vowel: A vowel that is inserted in a word to facilitate pronunciation; also called a "linking" vowel. Geminate verbs typically insert an anaptyptic vowel between the root and a *qatal* consonant sufformative. §§29, 33

Antepenult: The third from last syllable. In a three-syllable word, it is the first syllable. §4

Anticipatory discourse: The text type that predicts or promises forthcoming events, at times in contingent succession; usually future tense. The mainline is marked by *weqatal* clauses. §§37, 39

Apocopation: Shortening a word by dropping a letter or syllable from the end of the word. Apocopation occurs, for example, in the jussive and *Wayyiqtol* forms of III-ה verbs. §§11, 30

Aspect: How a speaker represents or portrays an action; the primary aspects in Hebrew are perfective and imperfective. §6

Aspirate: To follow a consonant or pronounce a vowel with an accompanying "h" sound. §1

Assimilation: The process of one consonant being absorbed into and doubling the following consonant. In Hebrew, נ frequently assimilates. §§13, 20

Asyndeton: The absence of any conjunction at the head of a clause. §37

Athnach: One of the two pausal accents in Hebrew. The Athnach looks something like an upside-down v (בָּגָד) and appears at the semantic middle of a verse, signaling the main pause. Compare Silluq. §§25, 36

Attenuation: A vowel change, when an a-class vowel in a closed, unaccented syllable becomes an i-class vowel, typically Hireq. §31

Attributive adjective: An adjective that modifies a noun without forming a complete sentence, as in "a brown dog." Contrast Predicate adjective. §15

Begadkephat letters: The letters בגדכפת. These are the only letters that take a Daghesh Lene. §1

Bicolon: A two-line poetic verse. §41

Biconsonantal root: See Hollow root.

BuMP letters: The labial letters (במפ). The conjunction appears as וּ rather than as וְ when attached to a labial. §10

Cardinal numbers: Numbers used in counting, as in 1, 2, 3, and so forth. Contrast Ordinal number. §19

Casus Pendens: See Pendent Element.

Clause: A grammatical construction that can stand on its own, expressing a complete thought, and that in its most basic form is made up of a subject and its predicate. Clauses may either be matrix or subordinate. §37

Closed syllable: A syllable that is consonant-vowel-consonant. Contrast Open syllable. §§2, 4

Cohortative: A first person volitive, as in "Let us go." Cohortatives also express determination. Cohortatives often have the הָ suffix (paragogic ה), which draws the accent to itself. §30

Collective noun: A noun that is singular in form but can refer to a plural group, such as the English "sheep." See vocabulary in §§1, 29, 38.

Colometry: Determining where the line divisions are in a poem. §41

Colon: See Line.

Comparative: The type of adjective used to express comparison. English uses patterns like "wiser" or "more wise." Hebrew uses the standard adjective with מִן attached to the noun to which comparison is made. §13

Compensatory lengthening: The lengthening of a vowel to compensate for a radical that ought to be doubled but cannot. This happens most frequently with א, ע, and ר and sometimes with ה and ח. See §4

Composite Shewa: A very short vowel sound used with gutturals; also called "Hateph vowels" or "Semi-vowels." The three composite Shewas are Hateph Pathach (◌ֲ), Hateph Qamets (◌ֳ), and Hateph Seghol (◌ֱ). §1

Conjoined Imperfect: See *Weyiqtol*.

Conjoined Perfect: See *Weqatal*.

Consonantal suffix (sufformative): A suffix or sufformative that begins with a consonant. §9

Construct chain: A noun phrase in which an absolute noun is preceded by at least one construct noun. A construct chain is analogous to an English noun phrase with "of," as in, "The man of God" (= אִישׁ הָאֱלֹהִים). For purposes of vowel lengthening, shortening, or reduction, a construct chain is treated like a single word with the accent in the absolute noun. §§1, 2, 8, 12

Construct state: A noun that is in a genitive relationship with a following noun. For simplicity's sake, one may think of the construct as adding the word "of" after a noun. Thus, אִישׁ in the absolute state means "man," but in the construct state means "man of." Nouns in the construct never take the definite article but receive their definiteness from the absolute noun. See Construct chain. §§1, 2, 8, 12

Copula: A form of "to be" used as a linking verb. See also Copular clause. §39

Copular clause: Clauses that use a form of the verb "to be," thus providing various levels of description without developing a text's mainline of discourse; the characteristic clause pattern in descriptive discourse. In Hebrew, while some copular clauses lexicalize a form of the verb הָיָה, most copular clauses are verbless/nominal, the copula being only understood and not explicit. §39

D stem: An alternative name of the Piel stem, derived from the stem's doubled (D) middle radical. §§20, 22, 24, 32

Daghesh: A dot placed in a consonant either as a Daghesh Forte or Daghesh Lene. §§1, 2, 3

Daghesh Forte: A Daghesh that doubles the letter in which it is inserted. §3

Daghesh Lene: A Daghesh that hardens the pronunciation of the letter in which it is inserted. It is used only with the Begadkephat letters. §§1, 2

Defective writing: Writing a word with only the simple Holem or Hireq where one might expect to see Holem-Waw (וֹ) or Hireq-Yod (יִ). See Full writing. §2

Definite direct object marker: The particle אֵת used to mark the next word as a direct object; it is only used if the direct object is a definite noun. §8, 17

Demonstrative pronoun: A pronoun that points to an implied thing, person, or idea. English examples are "this, that, these, those." §17

Denominative verb: A verb derived from a noun. In Hebrew, most denominatives are in the Piel or Hiphil stem. §2

Derived Stems: The six main stems other than Qal; these include the Niphal, Piel, Pual, Hiphil, Hophal, and Hithpael. Contrast G stem. §20, 22–24, 31–34

Descriptive discourse: The text type that explains a situation, state, or activity that is occurring in the mainline timeframe or that is perpetually true; characterized by copular clauses. §§37, 39

Diphthong: Two separate vowel sounds that are pronounced together as a single vowel.

Directive discourse: The text type of commands or exhortations, at times in the form of progressive directions for a given task. The mainline is marked by *weqatal* clauses, usually after an initial imperative(s). §37, 40

Discourse markers: Hebrew constructions whose chief purpose is to signal special structural features in a discourse rather than to convey semantic meaning; some are not translated. §40

Dp stem: An alternative name for the Pual stem, derived from this passive (p) stem's doubled (D) middle radical. §§20, 23, 24, 32

Energic נ: A נ added before a pronoun suffix. §25

Euphonic Daghesh: A Daghesh that is placed in the first consonant of a word. §2

Factitive: The function of transforming a stative verb into a transitive verb. For example, the root טהר in the Qal stem means "be clean" but in the Piel means "cleanse." §20

First-radical vowel: The vowel after the first consonant of the root. §20

Full vowel: A normal vowel, whether long or short but not reduced; any vowel other than the Shewa and the composite Shewas. Contrast Reduced vowel. §4

Full writing: Also called Plene; writing a word with the full Holem-Waw (וֹ) or Hireq-Yod (ִי) as opposed to using only the simple Holem or Hireq, as in defective writing. §2

G stem: An alternative name for the Qal stem, derived from the Qal's role as the "basic" or "ground" (Grund [G] in German) stem. Contrast Derived stems. §§9–11, 15, 18, 20–21, 27–30

Geminate: A root that doubles its second letter, as in סבב. Gemination can occur in both nouns and verbs. §§16, 21, 29

Gender: Classifying a word as masculine, feminine, or neuter. In Hebrew, all nouns are either masculine or feminine, and most finite verbs have gender. Grammatical gender is at times different than natural gender. §§5, 6

Gentilic: A marker that indicates that a word identifies a member of a nationality or racial group. The Hebrew masculine gentilic is a ִי sufformative, as in יִשְׂרְאֵלִי ("Israelite"). See vocabulary in, e.g., §16.

Guttural: The letters אעהח. Gutturals will not double (and thus do not take the Daghesh Forte), will not accept a vocal Shewa (and thus take a composite Shewa), and prefer a-class vowels. Like the gutturals, ר will not double. §1

Hateph vowels: See Composite Shewa.

H stem: An alternative name for the Hiphil stem, derived from the stem's ה preformative (H). §§20, 22, 24, 33

Hapax legomenon: A word that occurs only one time in the Hebrew Bible and thus is difficult to define. §Appendix 1

Hey directive: The ending הָ used to indicate movement toward something. For example, אַרְצָה means "to the land." §26

Hiphil stem: One of the major verbal stems in Hebrew; also called the H stem. It is often causal, indicating that the subject has caused someone or something to do something. §§20, 22, 24, 33

Historical discourse: The text type of OT narrative that conveys a succession of contingent events, usually in past tense. The mainline is marked by *wayyiqtol* clauses. §§37, 38

Hithpael stem: One of the major verbal stems in Hebrew; also called the HtD stem. It is often reflexive, indicating that the subject has done something to or for itself. §§20, 23, 24, 34

Hollow root: A verbal root that has only two radicals, and a vowel between the two, as in שׁוּב. Also called biconsonantal. §§20, 21

Hophal stem: One of the major verbal stems in Hebrew; also called the Hp stem. It is the passive of the Hiphil, indicating that a noun has been caused to do something. §§20, 23, 24, 33

Hp stem: An alternative name for the Hophal stem, derived from the stem's ה preformative (H) and passive (p) function. §§20, 23, 24, 33

HtD stem: An alternative name for the Hithpael stem, derived from the stem's הִתְ preformative (Ht) and doubled (D) middle radical. §§20, 23, 24, 34

Imperative: A verb used for giving a direct command. In Hebrew, it is always second person. §§18, 28

Imperfect: See *Yiqtol*.

Imperfective aspect: The portrayal of an action as a process, as in "He was eating the apple." Contrast Perfective aspect. §6

Interrogative Hey: A ה used at the beginning of a sentence to indicate that the sentence is a question. §7

Intransitive: A verb that is active but does not take a direct object, as in "He ran." Contrast Transitive. §20

Jussive: A third person volitive verb that expresses the desire of the speaker, as in "May he go"; it is also known as a short *yiqtol*. §30

Lengthening: The process of a short vowel becoming a long vowel. This typically happens when the accent shifts. Contrast Reduction. §4

Lexical form: The form a word takes in a lexicon; often it is the word's simplest form.

Line: The basic element of the Hebrew poem; usually a subdivision of a strophe; also called a stich (pl: stichoi) or colon (pl: cola). §41

Linking vowel: A vowel inserted between the final consonant (or radical) of the root and a sufformative or suffix. §20

Mainline: The structural backbone of a discourse, usually signalled by the sequencing

of certain predicate patterns. In Hebrew, every text type has its own mainline verb forms. §37

Mappiq: A dot in a final ה (הּ) showing that it is a true ה and not a vowel letter. §3

Masoretic text: The standard text of the Hebrew Bible as developed by the Masoretes around A.D. 1000.

Mater lectionis: "Mother of reading." The older term for vowel letter. §2

Matrix ("mother") clause: A clause that is not grammatically subordinate to any other higher level clause. In the construction, "David, who is but a boy, slew Goliath," the words "David ... slew Goliath," form the matrix clause. §37

Metathesis: The transposition of two letters for easier pronunciation. Metathesis occurs most commonly in the Hithpael stem when the הִת preformative is attached to a root beginning with a sibilant; for example, the hypothetical *הִתְשַׁמֵּר is spelled הִשְׁתַּמֵּר. See §§24, 34

Metheg: A small, vertical stroke under a radical that indicates a pause and helps a reader view a vowel as long rather than short. In the third feminine singular קָטְלָה the Metheg shows that the first syllable (קָ) has a Qamets (not Qamets Hatuph). §3

Middle voice: A verbal voice somewhere between the active and passive voices. An English analogy might be the expression, "The door opened," as opposed to the active "He opened the door" and the passive "The door was opened."

Mood: Also called "modality." Answers whether the action or state expressed in a verb is actual or only possible. The indicative mood ("He studies Hebrew") contrasts with the subjunctive ("He should study Hebrew"). Hebrew does not inflect for mood but marks it by word order and context. §6

Monocolon: A one-line poetic verse. §41

Morphology: The study of how the smallest grammatical units (morphemes) combine to form stems and words. §§1–4, 37

N stem: An alternative name for the Niphal stem, derived from the stem's נ preformative (N). §§20, 22, 24, 31

Niphal stem: One of the major verbal stems in Hebrew; also called the N stem. It is often passive in meaning. §§20, 22, 24, 31

Nominal clause: Also called "verbless clause"; a clause in which the predicate is made up of an understood copula along with a noun, adjective, prepositional phrase, or some other nominal form. Nominal clauses contain no explicit finite verb. §§3, 39

Nominal predicate (complement): In copular clauses, the predicate is made up of a lexicalized or unlexicalized copula plus a nominal complement, which could be a noun, an adjective, a prepositional phrase, a participle, an infinitive construct, or some other nominal phrase. In nominal clauses, where the complement alone is explicit in the context, the nominal complement by itself is called the predicate. §39

Offline: Material in a discourse off the mainline that regularly highlights background, transitional, or prominent information. §37

Open syllable: A syllable that begins with a consonant but ends with a vowel. Contrast Closed syllable. §§2, 4

Ordinal number: Numbers used in giving a sequence, as in "first, second, third," and so forth. Contrast Cardinal number. §19

Orthography: the study of an alphabet and of how its letters combine to represent sounds and to form words. §§1–4, 37

Paradigm: The standard declension of a given type of verb, noun, or pronoun. For example, in the paradigm of the Qal *qatal*, the strong root would include all its regular forms 3ms, 3fs, 2ms, etc.

Parse: To describe the grammatical components of a word (or clause). A given verb might be described as a Qal stem, *qatal*, third masculine singular of אהב with a third feminine singular suffix. A given noun might be described as masculine plural construct.

Passive voice: The verbal voice that indicates that the subject of the verb is acted upon (rather than acts as in the active voice). An example of a passive is "He was hit." §6

Pausal form: A word form usually occuring in last position of a major clause or verse in which the syllable accented with Silluq or Athnach is lengthened. For example, when in "pause," מֶ֫לֶךְ looks like מֶ֫לֶךְ with Silluq and מֶ֫לֶךְ with Athnach. §§25, 36.

Pendent element: A word or phrase that is not part of a clause but that "hangs" before a clause to draw attention to itself; also called *casus pendens*, "hanging case." §17

Penult: The second-to-last syllable. In a three-syllable word, it is the second syllable. §§1, 4

Perfect: See *Qatal*.

Perfective aspect: The portrayal of an action as a complete whole (but not necessarily "completed action"), as in "He ate the apple" or "He eats the apple." Contrast Imperfective aspect. §6

Phonology: The study of a system of sounds (called "phonemes") used in a given language. §§1–4, 37

Phrase: A group of words that fill a single slot in a clause. §37

Piel stem: One of the major verbal stems in Hebrew; also called the D stem. It is active and often transitive, and not passive or stative. §§20, 22, 24, 32

Plene: See Full writing.

Predicate adjective: An adjective that modifies a noun in such a way that it forms a complete sentence, as in "The dog is brown." Contrast Attributive adjective. §15

Predicate: The state, process, or action association with the subject. The predicate may be a finite verb, or it may be another noun or an adjective without any explicit verb, thus creating a verbless or nominal clause. See also Nominal predicate (complement). §37

Prefix: A morpheme added to the beginning of a word that is not essential to the word. The inseparable prepositions are prefixes in that they can be removed and still leave an intelligible word. Contrast Preformative.

Preformative: An inflectional morpheme added to the beginning of a word that is essential to the word. The *yiqtol* preformatives cannot be removed because they are essential to the *yiqtol* forms. Contrast Prefix.

Preformative vowel: The vowel with a preformative, such as a *yiqtol* preformative. §20

Preterite: Another name for the *wayyiqtol* (וַיִּקְטֹל). Also called Waw (vav) consecutive and, in the older terminology, the Waw (vav) conversive. §§11, 27

Pretonic: The syllable immediately in front of the tone syllable. §4

Primary citation: Direct reported speech that (1) reports a single event, (2) deals with full characters in a story, (3) has its characters speak individually, and/or (4) functions as a lively account of a direct conversation. Contrast Secondary citation. §40

Propretonic: The second syllable before the tone; it is immediately before the pretonic. §4

Pual stem: One of the major verbal stems in Hebrew; also called the Dp stem. It is the passive of the Piel stem. §§20, 23, 24, 32

Pure long vowel: Another term for an unchangeable long vowel. §1

Qal stem: One of the major verbal stems in Hebrew; also called the G stem. It is usually active rather than passive, but may be transitive, intransitive, or stative. It is the basic and most common Hebrew stem. §§9–11, 15, 18, 20–21, 27–30

Qatal: A finite verb form in biblical Hebrew; also called the perfect or the "suffixed form" by scholars. "Perfect" refers to perfective aspect, not tense. §9

Quatrain: A four-line poetic verse. §41

Quiescent א: When the consonant א becomes fully silent and stands only as a place holder in a word, having no vowel (not even silent Shewa). The vowel before a quiescent א is always long and does not reduce. §4

Radical: From the Latin radix ("root"); a consonant of the Hebrew alphabet used as one of the letters of a root. §9

Reduced vowel: A Shewa or composite Shewa; not a long or short vowel. Contrast Full vowel. §6

Reduction: The process of a full vowel reducing to a Shewa or composite Shewa. Also called volatilization. This typically happens when the accent shifts. Contrast Lengthening. §4

Rule of Shewa: When a word begins with two consecutive Shewas, the first becomes Hireq and the second becomes a silent Shewa. Special rules apply with gutturals. §11

Secondary citation: Direct reported speech that (1) reports multiple speeches as a single event, (2) deals with props rather than full characters in a story, (3) comes from someone who is not actually present and participating in the current conversation, and/or (4) functions as the official record of the principal points made by speakers. Contrast Primary citation. §40

Semi-vowels: See Composite Shewa.

Sentence: A matrix clause with all its subordinate clauses. §37

Sibilant: The S-type letters: ז, ס, צ, שׁ, שׂ. Such consonants often create metathesis in

the Hithpael stem. See §§1, 24.

Silluq: One of the two pausal accents in Hebrew. The Silluq looks like a Metheg (בֶּגֶד) and appears in the last word of a verse, signaling its end. Compare Athnach. §§25, 36

SQiNeM-LeVI (סקנם לוי): The artificial memory words used to remember those consonants that, when followed by a Shewa, lose a Daghesh Forte where the normal rules seem to require doubling. This phenomenon occurs with all the sibilants and with the consonants יְ, וְ, לְ, מְ, נְ, קְ. See §8

Stanza: A grouping of poetic verses, resulting in something like paragraphs within a poem. §41

Stative: A verb that describes the condition of its subject rather than an action. §29

Stem vowel: The vowel after the second consonant (or radical) of the root.

Stich: See Line.

Strong verb: A verbal root with no weak letters (e.g., gutturals) that would cause its paradigm to deviate from the standard form. קטל is the standard strong verb. Contrast Weak verb. §§9, 20

Strophe: A grouping of poetic lines; a subdivision of a stanza. Also called a verse but should not to be confused with the numbered verses found in our Bibles. §41

Subordinate Clause: A clause that serves as a modifier and is embedded in a higher level clause, as in "who is but a boy" in "David, who is but a boy, slew Goliath." Contrast Matrix clause. §37

Subjunctive: The mood of a finite verb that describes an action as possible ("he might do") or desired ("he should do"), in contrast to the indicative, that describes an action as real ("he does"). Also called "non-indicative" or "modal" §6

Suffix: A morpheme added to the end of a word that is not essential to the word. The pronominal suffixes are suffixes in that they can be removed and still leave an intelligible word. Contrast Sufformative.

Sufformative: A morpheme added to the end of a word that is essential to the word. The *qatal* sufformatives, as found in the 2ms form קָטַלְתָּ, cannot be removed because they are essential to the *qatal* verbs. Contrast Suffix.

Syntax: How words combine to form clauses and sentences (microsyntax) and larger text units (macrosyntax). §37

Tense: Time (e.g., past, present, future). For example, English uses simple past ("He ate it") and future ("he will eat it"). Biblical Hebrew does not inflect for tense, so the time of an action is always context determined. §6

Text types: The various kinds of Hebrew discourse (i.e., historical, anticipatory, descriptive, and directive), all of which utilize their own predicate patterns to distinguish mainline and offline material. §§37–40

Tone syllable: The accented syllable. §4

Transitive: An active verb that takes a direct object, as in "He saw the dog." Contrast Intransitive. §20

Tricolon: A three-line poetic verse. §41

Ultima: The last syllable of a word. §§1, 4

Unchangeable long vowel: A long vowel that remains long regardless of any change in the word's accent position. See Pure long vowel. §1

Verbal clause: A clause in which the predicate is a finite verb, as in "She studied Hebrew." §37

Verbal adjunct: The function of an infinitive construct when it describes the purpose or intent of another action ("He went to read"). Here the infinitive construct does not complete the original verbal action but adds a new action that grows directly out of the first. Contrast Verbal complement. §§11, 26

Verbal complement: The function of an infinitive construct when it is the object of a verb, completing the main verbal idea ("I like to eat"). Contrast Verbal adjunct. §§11, 26

Verbless clause: See Nominal clause.

Verse: See Strophe.

Voice: Expresses the relationship between the verb and its subject. Specifically, voice indicates whether the subject of the verb acts or is acted upon. For voice, English has, for example, the active ("Bill hit the ball") and the passive ("The ball was hit by Bill"). §6

Volatilization: See Reduction.

Volitive: A verb form used to express the desire of the speaker. Volitives include cohortatives, jussives, and imperatives. §§18, 28, 30

Vowel letter: One of the letters ה, ו, or י used as a vowel rather than as a consonant, as in the vowel וֹ. Also called matres lectionis. §2

Vowel suffix (sufformative): A suffix or sufformative that begins with a vowel. Also called "vocalic suffix."

Waw (vav) conjunction: Traditional name for the use of the ‎ו as a conjunction in the *weqatal* and *weyiqtol* forms. §§10, 30

Waw consecutive: Traditional name for the *wayyiqtol*; also called (conjoined) preterite or "Waw (vav) conversive." §§11, 27

Wayyiqtol: Also called a "Waw consecutive" or "preterite"; a finite verb form that is bound to a previous clause and perfective in aspect. It serves as the mainline predicate form in historical narrative, where it is almost always past tense. §§11, 27

Weak verb: A verbal root that contains one or more letters that in some way cause a deviation from the normal pattern of the strong verb. Common weak roots include I-, II-, or III-guttural, I-‎נ, original I-‎ו, III-‎ה, hollow, and geminate verbs. §§9, 20, 21, 24

Weqatal: Also called a conjoined perfect; a finite verb form that is bound to a previous clause in certain text types. It is used, for example, as the mainline predicate pattern in anticipatory discourse and, after an initial imperative, in directive discourse. In form, it is a simple conjunction attached to a *qatal* but often with accent shift to the ultima. §10

Weyiqtol: Also also called a conjoined imperfect; a finite verb form in certain text types. It is used, for example, to mark a purpose clause after a volitive. In form, it is a simple conjunction attached to a *yiqtol*. §30

Yiqtol: One of the forms of the Hebrew finite verb; also called the imperfect or "prefixed" form. "Imperfect" refers to imperfective aspect, not tense. See also Jussive and Cohortative. §§10, 27, 30

APPENDIX 6
HEBREW-ENGLISH VOCABULARY—BY CHAPTER

The following list includes only the core vocabulary and updates found in each chapter of the grammar; no inflected forms or proper names are incorporated. Each entry includes the Hebrew word, its basic definition, the chapter in which it is assigned, a note pointing to the chapter in which the definition is updated, and the number of times the word occurs in the Hebrew Bible. Some entries are also fronted by a number in parentheses, which indicates the lexicon entry that is included when two or more distinct (though perhaps related) words are spelled the same. For example, dependent on the context, the noun אָדָם can mean (1) "human," (2) "leather," (3) the man "Adam," (4) "ground," or (5) a place name.

Chapter 1

(1) אָדָם human, Adam – Ch. 1: 553

אֶרֶץ earth, land – Ch. 1: 2,498

(1) אֵשׁ fire – Ch. 1: 375

דָּבָר word, thing – Ch. 1: 1,426

דַּעַת knowledge – Ch. 1: 91

זָקֵן old (adj); elder, old man (noun) – Ch. 1: 178

חָצֵר courtyard, village – Ch. 1: 193

(1) מֶלֶךְ king – Ch. 1: 2,522

(1) עֶבֶד servant, slave – Ch. 1: 800

צֹאן flock (of sheep or goats) (s or pl collective) – Ch. 1: 275

שֹׁפֵט judge, leader – Ch. 1: 58

שַׂר ruler, leader, prince – Ch. 1: 412

Chapter 2

(1) אֹהֶל tent – Ch. 2: 342

(1) אַיִן there is no – Ch. 2: 773

(1) אִישׁ man, husband – Ch. 2: 2,149

(2) אֱלֹהִים God, gods – Ch. 2: 2,706

בְּ in, with, by, among – Ch. 2: 5,000+

בְּרִית covenant – Ch. 2: 287

יֵשׁ there is – Ch. 2: 139

כְּלִי vessel, tool, weapon, thing – Ch. 2: 324

מַלְכָּה queen – Ch. 2: 35

מִשְׁפָּט judgment, justice – Ch. 2: 425

(1) סוּס horse – Ch. 2: 139

(1) עִיר city – Ch. 2: 1,080

Chapter 3

(1) אֲדָמָה ground, land – Ch. 3: 225

אוֹ or – Ch. 3: 311

אִשָּׁה woman, wife – Ch. 3: 779

(1) בְּרָכָה blessing – Ch. 3: 71

גִּבּוֹר mighty, strong (adj); strong man, hero (noun) – Ch. 3: 161

חַטָּאת sin, sin offering – Ch. 3: 296

חָכְמָה wisdom – Ch. 3: 152

כֹּהֵן priest – Ch. 3: 749

(2) עַם people – Ch. 3: 1,827

רוּחַ wind, breath, spirit, (divine) Spirit – Ch. 3: 376

שָׂדֶה field – Ch. 3: 332

(1) שַׁעַר gate – Ch. 3: 368

Chapter 4

אֹיֵב enemy – Ch. 4: 281

זָהָב gold – Ch. 4: 383

חוֹמָה wall – Ch. 4: 133

כֶּסֶף silver – Ch. 4: 399

מָוֶת death – Ch. 4: 159

מַיִם water – Ch. 4: 574

נָבִיא prophet – Ch. 4: 313

עַיִן eye, spring (of water) – Ch. 4: 867

(1) צָבָא army, host; service in war – Ch. 4: 485

(1) רֹאשׁ head, top, leader – Ch. 4: 593

שָׁמַיִם heaven(s), sky – Ch. 4: 416

שְׁנַיִם ; שְׁתַּיִם two – Ch. 4: 739

Chapter 5

אָב father (irregular plural אָבוֹת) – Ch. 5: 1,568

(1) אוֹת sign – Ch. 5: 79

(1) בַּיִת house (irregular plural בָּתִּים) – Ch. 5: 2,039

(1) בֵּן son (irregular plural בָּנִים) – Ch. 5: 4,887

דָּם blood – Ch. 5: 356

(1) יוֹם day (irregular plural יָמִים) – Ch. 5: 2,241

יְשׁוּעָה salvation, also seen as יְשׁוּעָתָה – Ch. 5: 78

כְּ as, like (attached directly to a noun, as in כְּדָוִד ["like David"]) – Ch. 5: 5,000+

מִזְבֵּחַ altar – Ch. 5: 401

מִצְוָה command (plural מִצְוֹת with conso-nantal ו) – Ch. 5: 181

(1) עוֹלָה whole burnt offering – Ch. 5: 288

תּוֹרָה instruction, teaching, law – Ch. 5: 220

Chapter 6

אִם if – Ch. 6: 1,046

לְ to, for – Ch. 6: 5,000+

לְמַעַן for the sake of, in order that, so that – Ch. 6: 269

Chapter 7

אֶל to, toward – Ch. 7: 5,000+

הֲ (interrogative particle) – Ch. 7: 5,000+

לֹא no, not, never – Ch. 7: 4,973

עוֹד still, yet – Ch. 7: 481

שָׁם there – Ch. 7: 817

Chapter 8

אֶבֶן stone – Ch. 8: 268

אוֹר light – Ch. 8: 125

אֲשֶׁר who, which, that – Ch. 8: 5,000+

(1) אֵת (definite direct object marker) – Ch. 8: 5,000+

דֶּרֶךְ road, way, path – Ch. 8: 698

הַ (+ Daghesh in following consonant) the (definite article) – Ch. 8: 5,000+

הַר hill, mountain – Ch. 8: 554

חָכָם wise (adj), wise man (noun) – Ch. 8: 138

יָשָׁר upright (adj), upright man (noun) – Ch. 8: 119

לֵב heart (a "by-form" or alternative form of this word is לֵבָב) – Ch. 8: 844

לֶחֶם bread – Ch. 8: 296

עָפָר dust – Ch. 8: 110

Chapter 9

בנה Qal: בָּנָה build – Ch. 9-U24: 373

גְּבוּל territory, border – Ch. 9: 241

הלך Qal: הָלַךְ walk, go – Ch. 9: 1,504

כתב Qal: כָּתַב write – Ch. 9-U20: 222

(1) מִדְבָּר desert, wilderness – Ch. 9: 271

(1) מלך Qal: מָלַךְ be king, rule – Ch. 9-U20: 347

(2) עַל upon, over, against – Ch. 9: 4,898

(1) עֵצָה advice – Ch. 9: 89

עשה Qal: עָשָׂה do, make, build – Ch. 9-U24: 2,573

ראה Qal: רָאָה see, inspect – Ch. 9-U24: 1,294

רָשָׁע wicked – Ch. 9: 264

שפט Qal: שָׁפַט judge, rule – Ch. 9: 203

Chapter 10

אָז then – Ch. 10: 141

(1) אמר Qal: אָמַר say – Ch. 10: 5,000+

אֲנִי ; אָנֹכִי I – Ch. 10: 1,316

בָּשָׂר meat, flesh, skin – Ch. 10: 270

היה Qal: הָיָה be, become – Ch. 10: 3,514

וְ and, but – Ch. 10: 5,000+

ישׁב Qal: יָשַׁב sit, dwell – Ch. 10-U25: 1,078

(2) כִּי because, although, indeed, that, rather, instead – Ch. 10: 4,395

לַיְלָה night – Ch. 10: 231

נתן Qal: נָתַן give, place – Ch. 10-U25: 1,994

שׁמר Qal: שָׁמַר keep, guard, observe – Ch. 10-U20: 465

שׁמע Qal: שָׁמַע hear, listen – Ch. 10-U24: 1,136

Chapter 11

אֶחָד one masculine; feminine = אַחַת; can follow a noun, as in עַם אֶחָד, "one people" – Ch. 11: 959

(1) בַּת daughter (plural = בָּנוֹת) – Ch. 11: 582

גּוֹי nation (plural = גּוֹיִם) – Ch. 11: 545

גַּם also, even – Ch. 11: 812

(1) חפץ Qal: חָפֵץ desire, enjoy, want; the *qatal* 3ms is חָפֵץ, but other forms are normal, e.g., *qatal* 2ms is חָפַצְתָּ – Ch. 11: 86

כֵּן thus – Ch. 11: 707

מִלְחָמָה war, battle – Ch. 11: 319

מִשְׁפָּחָה family – Ch. 11: 300

נפל Qal: נָפַל fall – Ch. 11-U25: 433

(1) עֵדָה congregation – Ch. 11: 149

צַדִּיק righteous – Ch. 11: 206

שָׁלֹשׁ three; with feminine noun like שָׁלֹשׁ

סוּסוֹת; with masculine noun like שְׁלֹשָׁה סוּסִים – Ch. 11: 586

Chapter 12

(2) אָח brother construct = אֲחִי plural = אַחִים – Ch. 12: 626

הֵיכָל temple, palace – Ch. 12: 80

יָד hand – Ch. 12: 1,580

יהוה Yahweh, the LORD – Ch. 12: 5766

ירד Qal: יָרַד go down, descend – Ch. 12-U27: 380

(1) מֵאָה hundred – Ch. 12: 577

מַחֲנֶה camp, army – Ch. 12: 219

מַלְאָךְ messenger, angel – Ch. 12: 213

עמד Qal: עָמַד stand – Ch. 12-U26: 519

פֶּה mouth – Ch. 12: 492

קוֹל voice – Ch. 12: 499

שָׁנָה year – Ch. 12: 871

(1) תַּחַת under, instead of – Ch. 12: 490

Chapter 13

(2) אֵת with – Ch. 13: 5000+

בֵּין between – Ch. 13: 396

חָמֵשׁ five – Ch. 13: 478

יָם sea (plural = יַמִּים) – Ch. 13: 392

לִפְנֵי before, in the presence of – Ch. 13: 1,099

מִן from, than – Ch. 13: 1,279

(2) עַד until, as far as, unto – Ch. 13: 1,246

עִם with – Ch. 13: 1,076

(1) ענה Qal: עָנָה answer – Ch. 13: 314

פָּנִים face, front; (when linked with preps) before, away from (plural in form but usually singular in meaning) – Ch. 13: 2,120

פקד Qal: פָּקַד inspect, attend to, urge, muster, call to account, visit, punish – Ch. 13-U21: 301

תָּוֶךְ middle, midst – Ch. 13: 416

Chapter 14

אַחַר ; אַחֲרֵי after, behind – Ch. 14: 713

כֹּה thus – Ch. 14: 554

כֹּל all, whole, every (in construct with Maqqeph כָּל־) – Ch. 14: 5,000+

כרת Qal: כָּרַת cut, cut off (when used with בְּרִית, it means "make a covenant") – Ch. 14-U21: 287

עֵת time, season – Ch. 14: 282

פְּרִי fruit – Ch. 14: 119

קֹדֶשׁ holiness, holy thing – Ch. 14: 430

קרב Qal: קָרַב draw near, approach – Ch. 14-U21: 291

רֶגֶל foot – Ch. 14: 252

שֶׁבַע seven – Ch. 14: 492

שכב Qal: שָׁכַב lie (down), have sexual intercourse – Ch. 14: 211

(1) שֵׁם name – Ch. 14: 862

Chapter 15

אהב Qal: אָהַב love – Ch. 15: 205

(1) אַחֵר other, another – Ch. 15: 166

(2) ברך Qal: בָּרוּךְ (passive participle) blessed – Ch. 15-U22: 328

גָּדוֹל great, big – Ch. 15: 525

זכר Qal: זָכַר remember – Ch. 15-U22: 230

חַי alive (mp חַיִּים = life) – Ch. 15: 386

טָהוֹר clean (ritually) – Ch. 15: 95

(1) טוֹב good – Ch. 15: 612

עֵץ tree, wood – Ch. 15: 330

קָדוֹשׁ holy – Ch. 15: 115

קָטֹן small – Ch. 15: 54

רַע , רָע ; רָעָה evil, bad, wicked, trouble (adj, noun) – Ch. 15: 661

Chapter 16

אבד Qal: אָבַד die, be lost – Ch. 16-U26: 183

אֵם mother – Ch. 16: 219

(1) אַמָּה cubit – Ch. 16: 226

חֹשֶׁךְ darkness – Ch. 16: 82

חֶרֶב sword – Ch. 16: 407

חֹק rule, statute, law – Ch. 16: 128

ידע Qal: יָדַע know – Ch. 16-U28: 924

נֶפֶשׁ life, self, person, soul – Ch. 16: 753

נַעַר boy, youth – Ch. 16: 240

סֵפֶר scroll, book – Ch. 16: 185

(1) עבר Qal: עָבַר pass over/through/by, cross; transgress – Ch. 16-U26: 539

רַב much, many – Ch. 16: 475

(2) שתה Qal: שָׁתָה drink – Ch. 16: 217

Chapter 17

אֵלֶּה these (common gender) – Ch. 17: 738

אֲנַחְנוּ we – Ch. 17: 156

(1) אַף also, even – Ch. 17: 130

אַתָּה you (2ms, subject pronoun; the 2fs subject pronoun is אַתְּ) – Ch. 17: 893

אַתֶּם you (2mp, subject pronoun; the 2fp subject pronoun is אַתֵּן or אַתֵּנָה) – Ch. 17: 330

הוּא he, that – Ch. 17: 1,533

הִיא she, that – Ch. 17: 541

הֵם ; הֵמָּה they, those (3mp, subject pronoun; the 3fp subject pronoun is הֵנָּה) – Ch. 17: 1,553

זֹאת this (f) – Ch. 17: 605

זֶה this (m) – Ch. 17: 1,189

מָה what? why? – Ch. 17: 760

מִי who? – Ch. 17: 406

Chapter 18

אכל Qal: אָכַל eat – Ch. 18-U27: 795

(1) אַל not – Ch. 18: 738

אסף Qal: אָסַף gather, take in, retract – Ch. 18-U26: 203

(1) כֶּרֶם vineyard – Ch. 18: 93

מָקוֹם place – Ch. 18: 399

(1) נַחֲלָה inheritance, possession – Ch. 18: 223

עוֹלָם , עֹלָם remote time; eternity, forever – Ch. 18: 434

עלה Qal: עָלָה go up – Ch. 18-U25: 879

(1) קרא Qal: קָרָא call, summon, proclaim – Ch. 18-U27: 739

שלח Qal: שָׁלַח send, stretch out – Ch. 18-U22: 839

שְׁמֹנֶה eight – Ch. 18: 147

תֵּשַׁע nine – Ch. 18: 77

Chapter 19

אֶלֶף thousand, clan, troop – Ch. 19: 494

אַרְבַּע four – Ch. 19: 444

(2) בֹּקֶר morning, sunrise – Ch. 19: 200

ילד Qal: יָלַד give birth, beget – Ch. 19-U27: 488

יצא Qal: יָצָא go out – Ch. 19-U30: 1,055

מַטֶּה tribe; rod, staff – Ch. 19: 252

(1) מִסְפָּר number – Ch. 19: 134

(2) מַעַל above; מַעְלָה = "upwards" – Ch. 19: 138

(2) עֶרֶב evening, sunset – Ch. 19: 134

עֶשֶׂר ten; in numbers eleven through nineteen, עָשָׂר as in אַחַד עָשָׂר, "eleven" – Ch. 19: 173

רִאשׁוֹן first – Ch. 19: 182

שֵׁשׁ six – Ch. 19: 272

תּוֹלְדוֹת official records of descendants from an ancestor, often translated "generations" or "account" – Ch. 19: 39

Chapter 20

אָדוֹן , אֲדֹנָי lord, master; the Lord – Ch. 20: 770

(1) בחר Qal: בָּחַר choose – Ch. 20: 173

(2) דּוֹר generation – Ch. 20: 169

חטא Qal: חָטָא miss (a mark), sin – Ch. 20: 237

(2) חֶסֶד loyalty, steadfast love, devotion, faithfulness – Ch. 20: 250

(1) ירא Qal: יָרֵא fear, be afraid; Niphal: נוֹרָא (= ptc) be feared – Ch. 20: 377

ירש Qal: יָרַשׁ possess, inherit, dispossess; Hiphil: הוֹרִישׁ take possession of, dispossess, drive out – Ch. 20: 231

כתב Qal: Ch. 9; Niphal: יִכָּתֵב (*yiqtol* 3ms) be written – Ch. 20 Update

מְאֹד very, very much – Ch. 20: 287

מלך Qal: Ch. 9; Hiphil: הִמְלִיךְ install someone as king – Ch. 20 Update

מצא Qal: מָצָא find, seek; Niphal: נִמְצָא be found – Ch. 20: 451

נשא Qal: נָשָׂא carry, lift up; Niphal: נִשָּׂא be carried – Ch. 20: 651

עָנִי poor, wretched – Ch. 20: 76

(1) פַּחַד dread, trembling, deep fear – Ch. 20: 49

שמר Qal: Ch. 10; Niphal: נִשְׁמַר be kept, be guarded – Ch. 20 Update

Chapter 21

אָוֶן iniquity, evil, disaster – Ch. 21: 80

(5) אֵל God, god; Mighty One; El – Ch. 21: 236

חזק Qal: חָזַק be strong, have courage; Piel: חִזַּק make firm, strengthen, harden (the heart); Hiphil: הֶחֱזִיק seize, grasp, feel strengthened; Hithpael: הִתְחַזַּק show oneself courageous, feel strengthened, show oneself as strong – Ch. 21: 288

יכל Qal: יָכֹל be able to, be capable of (stative) – Ch. 21: 194

כָּבוֹד heaviness, honor, glory – Ch. 21: 200

כרת Qal: Ch. 14; Niphal: נִכְרַת be cut off,

eliminated; Hiphil: הִכְרִית exterminate – Ch. 21 Update

לקח Qal: לָקַח take, grasp, capture – Ch.
21: 964

מלא Qal: מָלֵא be full, fill up; Niphal: יִמָּלֵא
(= impf) be filled; Piel: מִלֵּא fill, endow, devote, fulfill – Ch. 21: 250

מִנְחָה gift, present; offering – Ch. 21: 211

נְאֻם utterance, declaration – Ch. 21: 378

נטה Qal: נָטָה reach out, spread out, stretch
out, turn aside; Hiphil: הִטָּה stretch
out, extend, guide away – Ch.
21: 215

פעל Qal: פָּעַל do – Ch. 21: 57

פקד Qal: Ch. 13; Niphal: נִפְקַד be missed,
be punished; Hiphil: הִפְקִיד appoint –
Ch. 21 Update

קרב Qal: Ch. 14; Hiphil: הִקְרִיב bring
(near), take, offer – Ch. 21 Update

רדף Qal: רָדַף pursue – Ch. 21: 143

Chapter 22

(2) אַף nose, nostrils; anger – Ch. 22: 279

בוא Qal: בָּא enter, come, go in; Hiphil:
הֵבִיא bring, lead in – Ch. 22: 2,530

(2) ברך Qal: Ch. 15; Piel: בֵּרֵךְ bless,
praise – Ch. 22 Update

דבר Qal: דָּבַר speak (intransitive); Piel:
דִּבֵּר speak (transitive) – Ch. 22: 1130

דרש Qal: דָּרַשׁ seek – Ch. 22: 163

זכר Qal: Ch. 15; Niphal: נִזְכַּרְתֶּם (*qatal*
2mp) be remembered; Hiphil: הִזְכִּיר
make known, report – Ch. 22 Update

(1) חֹדֶשׁ new moon – Ch. 22: 278

סור Qal: סָר turn away, turn aside; Hiphil:
הֵסִיר remove – Ch. 22: 298

עַתָּה now – Ch. 22: 432

קדש Piel: קִדַּשׁ sanctify, dedicate; Hiphil:
הִקְדִּישׁ mark or treat as holy – Ch.
22: 172

(1) שכל Hiphil: הִשְׂכִּיל understand, have
insight, behave wisely, achieve success – Ch. 22: 75

שוב Qal: שָׁב return; Hiphil: הֵשִׁיב bring
back – Ch. 22: 1,055

שחת Piel: שִׁחֵת ruin, destroy; Hiphil:
הִשְׁחִית ruin, destroy, corrupt – Ch.
22: 161

שפך Qal: שָׁפַךְ pour out; Niphal: נִשְׁפַּךְ be
poured out – Ch. 22: 116

שלח Qal: Ch. 18; Piel: שִׁלַּח stretch out, let
go, expel – Ch. 22 Update

Chapter 23

אָרוֹן chest, Ark (of the Covenant) – Ch.
23: 202

(2) בֶּגֶד garment, covering – Ch. 23: 214

(1) בוש Qal: בּוֹשׁ be ashamed; Hiphil:
תָּבִישׁוּ (*yiqtol* 2mp) put to shame –
Ch. 23: 126

בקש Piel: בִּקֵּשׁ seek, search for; discover,
find – Ch. 23: 225

הרג Qal: הָרַג kill, slay – Ch. 23: 168

(1) חלל Piel: חִלֵּל defile, profane – Ch.
23: 134

טמא Qal: טָמֵא be unclean; Piel: טִמֵּא defile,
declare unclean – Ch. 23: 161

(1) כלה Qal: כָּלָה stop, be finished; perish;
Piel: כִּלָּה complete, finish; destroy –
Ch. 23: 204

מַמְלָכָה kingdom – Ch. 23: 117

עָוֹן sin, transgression; guilt caused by sin –
Ch. 23: 231

(1) עזב Qal: עָזַב leave, abandon; Niphal:
נֶעֱזַב be abandoned – Ch. 23: 212

שָׁלוֹם peace, well-being, wholeness – Ch.
23: 242

Chapter 24

אֹזֶן ear – Ch. 24: 187

בנה Qal: Ch. 9; Niphal: נִבְנָה be built – Ch. 24 Update

חַיִל strength, power; wealth; army – Ch. 24: 246

יסף Qal: יָסַף add, continue to do; Hiphil: הֹ(ו)סִיף add, increase, do again – Ch. 24: 212

כון Niphal: נָכוֹן be firm, be established, be fixed; Polel: כּוֹנֵן establish, set up, fix solidly; Hiphil: הֵכִין prepare, set up, make firm – Ch. 24: 219

כסה Piel: כִּסָּה cover – Ch. 24: 157

מַעֲשֶׂה work, labor, accomplishment – Ch. 24: 235

נגד Hiphil: הִגִּיד tell; Hophal: הֻגַּד be told – Ch. 24: 369

נכה Hiphil: הִכָּה strike, smite, injure – Ch. 24: 504

נצל Niphal: נִצַּל be rescued; Hiphil: הִצִּיל snatch away, deliver – Ch. 24: 208

סָבִיב surrounding(s), circuit – Ch. 24: 309

עשה Qal: Ch. 9; Niphal: נֶעֱשָׂה be done, be prepared – Ch. 24 Update

פֶּן lest – Ch. 24: 133

קום Qal: קָם rise, get up; Hiphil: הֵקִים erect, raise up, keep, confirm – Ch. 24: 624

ראה Qal: Ch. 9; Niphal: נִרְאָה appear, present oneself; Hiphil: הֶרְאָה show someone, cause to experience – Ch. 24 Update

(1) רבה Hiphil: הִרְבָּה make numerous, multiply – Ch. 24: 226

שמע Qal: Ch. 10; Niphal: נִשְׁמַע be heard; Hiphil: הִשְׁמִיעַ cause to hear, summon – Ch. 24 Update

Chapter 25

אָמָה (female) slave, handmaid – Ch. 25: 56

בְּהֵמָה; בְּהֵמוֹת animals (in general), beasts, cattle (domesticated animals) – Ch. 25: 192

(1) בַּעַל owner, husband; Baal – Ch. 25: 198

גלה Qal: גָּלָה uncover, leave, go into exile; Niphal: נִגְלָה expose, announce, reveal oneself; Piel: גִּלָּה uncover, disclose, sleep with; Hiphil: הִגְלָה deport – Ch. 25: 187

הלך Qal: Ch. 9; Hiphil: הוֹלִיךְ bring, lead; Hithpael: הִתְהַלֵּךְ walk about, go about, disperse – Ch. 25 Update

זבח Qal: זָבַח slaughter, sacrifice; Piel: זִבַּח sacrifice – Ch. 25: 136

טָמֵא ; טָמְאָה (ceremonially) unclean – Ch. 25: 88

ישב Qal: Ch. 10; Hiphil: הוֹשִׁיב set, inhabit, cause to dwell – Ch. 25 Update

ישע Niphal: נוֹשַׁע receive help, be victorious, be rescued; Hiphil: הוֹשִׁיעַ help, save – Ch. 25: 205

לָכֵן therefore – Ch. 25: 196

מוֹעֵד appointed place or time, season – Ch. 25: 223

נפל Qal: Ch. 11; Hiphil: הִפִּיל drop, throw down – Ch. 25 Update

נתן Qal: Ch. 10; Niphal: נִתַּן be given – Ch. 25 Update

עלה Qal: Ch. 18; Hiphil: הֶעֱלָה lead up, cause to rise, offer (sacrifice) – Ch. 25 Update

רום Qal: רָם be high above, rise, go up, be haughty; Polel: רוֹמַמְתִּי (*qatal* 1cs) bring up, exalt; Hiphil: הֵרִים raise up, lift up, erect – Ch. 25: 195

(1) שׂים Qal: שָׂם set, put, place – Ch. 25: 584

שמח Qal: שָׂמַח rejoice, be merry; Piel: שִׂמַּח gladden, make (someone) merry, cause to rejoice – Ch. 25: 156

שֵׁבֶט rod, staff, scepter; tribe – Ch. 25: 190

Chapter 26

אבד Qal: Ch. 16; Piel: אִבַּד cause to perish, destroy; Hiphil: הֶאֱבִיד exterminate – Ch. 26 Update

אסף Qal: Ch. 18; Niphal: נֶאֱסַף be gathered, be assembled – Ch. 26 Update

אָחוֹת sister – Ch. 26: 114

בִּלְתִּי not (prep); except, lest (adv) (used to negate the infinitive construct) – Ch. 26: 111

(1) גור Qal: גָּר sojourn, live as an alien – Ch. 26: 81

(1) הֵן ; הֶן־ behold! (interjection); if (conjunction) – Ch. 26: 100

הִנֵּה traditionally "behold!"; translation varies according to context; perhaps "well now" or "look here" – Ch. 26: 1,037

חיה Qal: חַי live (the form of the *qatal* 3ms reflects the fact that the root was originally חיי, a geminate); Piel: חִיָּה let live – Ch. 26: 281

יטב Qal: יִיטַב (*yiqtol* 3ms) go well, do well; Hiphil: הֵיטִיב treat well – Ch. 26: 120

(כְּ+אֲשֶׁר) כַּאֲשֶׁר as, just as, because, when – Ch. 26: 504

מַרְאֶה appearance, sight, visage – Ch. 26: 103

נָא (particle used with commands or requests; do not translate) – Ch. 26: 401

עבר Qal: Ch. 16; Hiphil: הֶעֱבִיר allow to pass over, overlook – Ch. 26 Update

עמד Qal: Ch. 12; Hiphil: הֶעֱמִיד set in position, erect, cause to stand – Ch. 26 Update

רָעָב famine, hunger – Ch. 26: 103

שבע Niphal: נִשְׁבַּע swear (an oath); Hiphil:

הִשְׁבִּיעַ make (someone) swear (an oath), implore – Ch. 26: 186

Chapter 27

אכל Qal: Ch. 18; Niphal: נֶאֱכַל be eaten; Hiphil: הֶאֱכַלְתִּי (*qatal* 1cs) feed – Ch. 27 Update

בָּקָר cattle – Ch. 27: 183

גָּמָל camel – Ch. 27: 54

(2) הלל Piel: הַלְלֶהֶם (*qatal* 2mp) praise; Hithpael: יִתְהַלֵּל (*yiqtol* 3ms) boast – Ch. 27: 145

(1) חֲמוֹר donkey – Ch. 27: 97

ילד Qal: Ch. 19; Niphal: נוֹלַד be born; Pual: יוֹלַד be born; Hiphil: הוֹלִיד beget – Ch. 27 Update

יֶלֶד (ms) young male offspring, boy; יַלְדָּה (fs) young female offspring, girl – Ch. 27: 92

ירד Qal: Ch. 12; Hiphil: הוֹרִד bring down, cause to fall – Ch. 27 Update

כְּמוֹ like, as; it is a form of כְּ often found in poetry – Ch. 27: 139

נגע Qal: נָגַע touch, strike; Piel: וַיְנַגַּע (*wayyiqtol* 3ms) afflict; Hiphil: הִגִּיעַ touch, hurl, happen – Ch. 27: 150

נֶגַע blow, wound, plague (noun) – Ch. 27: 78

(1) פתח Qal: פָּתַח open; Piel: פִּתַּח break open, let loose – Ch. 27: 144

פֶּתַח opening, entrance, gateway – Ch. 27: 163

קרא Qal: Ch. 18; Niphal: נִקְרָא be summoned, be proclaimed – Ch. 27 Update

(1) רעה Qal: רָעָה feed, graze, nourish; (often as a substantive in the participle: רֹעֶה) shepherd – Ch. 27: 171

שִׁפְחָה slave-girl, handmaid, maidservant – Ch. 27: 63

Chapter 28

אַךְ surely, only, however – Ch. 28: 173

(1) זֶבַח (communal) sacrifice, offering – Ch. 28: 162

ידע Qal: Ch. 16; Niphal: נוֹדַע reveal, become known; Hiphil: הוֹדִיעַ make known, inform – Ch. 28 Update

כֶּבֶשׂ ; כִּבְשָׂה young ram; ewe-lamb – Ch. 28: 129

לְבַד alone (adv); besides (prep) – Ch. 28: 155

לָמָה ; לְמָה why? – Ch. 28: 173

מִשְׁכָּן dwelling place, abode (often of the abode of YHWH = tabernacle, central sanctuary) – Ch. 28: 139

נוס Qal: נָס flee – Ch. 28: 160

סבב Qal: סָבַב turn round, go around, surround; Hiphil: הֵסֵב make to go around, bring around, turn away – Ch. 28: 162

פַּר; פָּרָה steer, young bull (m), cow (f) – Ch. 28: 159

צוה Piel: צִוָּה command, instruct, send – Ch. 28: 494

שאל Qal: שָׁאַל ask, consult, demand – Ch. 28: 173

שכן Qal: שָׁכַן reside, dwell, settle – Ch. 28: 130

Chapter 29

גדל Qal: גָּדַל be(come) great, be(come) strong; Piel: גָּדַל/גִּדֵּל bring up, let grow, praise; Hiphil: הִגְדִּיל enlarge, show to be great, magnify oneself – Ch. 29: 122

זרע Qal: זָרַע sow (of seed) – Ch. 29: 56

זֶרַע seed, offspring (s or pl collective) – Ch. 29: 228

כבד Qal: כָּבֵד be heavy, weighty, honored; Niphal: נִכְבַּד be honored, enjoy honor, appear in one's glory; Piel: כִּבְּדוּ (*qatal* 3cp) honor (someone)– Ch. 29: 114

כַּף palm of hand *or* sole of foot – Ch. 29: 192

(1) לחם Niphal: נִלְחַם fight – Ch. 29: 171

(1) מָגֵן shield (as weapon, ornament, or protection) – Ch. 29: 59

מְלָאכָה work, service, fruit of labor – Ch. 29: 167

צֶדֶק righteousness: what is right, just, accurate, normal – Ch. 29: 116

צְדָקָה righteousness, justness, justice, communal loyalty – Ch. 29: 157

שֶׁ ; שַׁ (+ Daghesh in following consonant) who, which, that – Ch. 29: 139

שמם Qal: שָׁמֵם be desolate, deserted; be astonished, shudder; Niphal: נָשַׁמָּה (*qatal* 3fs) be uninhabited, tremble; Hiphil: הֲשִׁמּוֹתָ (*qatal* 2ms) cause to be deserted, cause to be desolated – Ch. 29: 95

Chapter 30

(1) אַיִל ram; (metaphorically) ruler – Ch. 30: 161

(1) אמן Niphal: נֶאֱמַן/נֶאֱמָן be faithful, reliable, permanent; Hiphil: הֶאֱמִין believe, trust, think – Ch. 30: 100

אֱמֶת trustworthiness, constancy, faithfulness, truth – Ch. 30: 127

חוץ a place outside the house, street (noun); outside, without (prep, adv) – Ch. 30: 165

חשב Qal: חָשַׁב regard, assume, plan; Niphal: נֶחְשַׁב be regarded – Ch. 30: 124

(1) יָמִין right side, south – Ch. 30: 139

יצא Qal: Ch. 19; Hiphil: הוֹצִיא lead, cause to go out – Ch. 30 Update

נבט Hiphil: הִבִּיט look, look at, behold; (by extension) accept favorably – Ch. 30: 70

(1) נוּחַ Qal: נָחָה (*qatal* 3fs) rest, settle down; Hiphil (2 forms): הֵנִיחַ cause to rest, secure repose, pacify; הִנִּיחַ place, set, leave (untouched) – Ch. 30: 143

ספר Qal: סָפַר count, number, write; Piel: סִפַּרְתִּי (*qatal* 1cs) count up, announce, report – Ch. 30: 162

עֵז goat, goat hair – Ch. 30: 74

(1) צָפוֹן north; mountain of the gods (in the north) – Ch. 30: 153

תָּמִים complete, without blemish, perfect, honest, impeccable (adj); honesty, blamelessness (noun) – Ch. 30: 91

Chapter 31

גֵּר sojourner – Ch. 31: 93

יַיִן wine – Ch. 31: 141

לכד Qal: לָכַד seize, capture; Niphal: נִלְכַּד get trapped, be overpowered, be selected – Ch. 31: 121

נבא Niphal: נִבָּא prophesy, behave like a prophet – Ch. 31: 115

עבד Qal: עָבַד serve, work, accomplish – Ch. 31: 289

עֲבֹדָה service, work, labor – Ch. 31: 143

(2) ענה Piel: עִנָּה afflict, oppress – Ch. 31: 79

קבץ Qal: קָבַץ collect, assemble, gather; Niphal: נִקְבְּצוּ (*qatal* 3cp) assemble, be assembled; Piel: קִבְּצָה (*qatal* 3fs) gather together – Ch. 31: 127

קָהָל contingent, assembly, congregation – Ch. 31: 123

(2) קרא Qal: קָרְאָת (*qatal* 3fs) meet, encounter, happen; לִקְרַאת over against, opposite (special use of the infinitive construct as a prep) – Ch. 31: 139

רֵעַ counterpart, companion, friend – Ch. 31: 195

שֶׁמֶשׁ sun – Ch. 31: 134

Chapter 32

בְּכֹר; בְּכוֹר firstborn – Ch. 32: 122

חֻקָּה statute, regulation – Ch. 32: 104

כפר Piel: כִּפֶּר cover, appease, (by extension) make atonement – Ch. 32: 102

נָהָר river, stream – Ch. 32: 117

(1) נַחַל river valley, wadi, stream, trench – Ch. 32: 138

נחם Niphal: נָחַם/נִחָם regret, be sorry; Piel: נִחַם comfort – Ch. 32: 108

קבר Qal: קָבַר bury; Niphal: יִקָּבֵר (*yiqtol* 3ms) be buried – Ch. 32: 132

(1) קטר Piel: קִטְּרוּ (*qatal* 3cp) send (an offering) up in smoke; Hiphil: הִקְטִיר cause (a sacrifice) to go up in smoke – Ch. 32: 116

רְבִיעִי fourth, one-fourth – Ch. 32: 55

שְׁבִיעִי seventh – Ch. 32: 96

(1) שבר Qal: שָׁבַר shatter, smash, break (of sticks, pottery, bones); Niphal: נִשְׁבַּר be smashed, be broken, be destroyed; Piel: שִׁבַּר smash (into fragments) (of things not easily broken in a single action—e.g., stone, metal, trees) – Ch. 32: 149

שלם Piel: שִׁלֵּם make complete, make restitution – Ch. 32: 117

Chapter 33

בקע Qal: בָּקַע split, breach; Piel: בִּקַּע split, rip up – Ch. 33: 51

(2) חוה Hishtaphel: הִשְׁתַּחֲוָה bow down (always found with הִשְׁתַּ- prefix) – Ch. 33: 174

יַחַד; יַחְדָּו uniting, community (noun); together, at the same time (adv) – Ch. 33: 142

יתר Niphal: נוֹתַר be left, remain; Hiphil: הוֹתִיר leave over/behind, have left over – Ch. 33: 106

(1) יֶתֶר remainder, the rest, what is left behind – Ch. 33: 93

כִּסֵּא throne, chair – Ch. 33: 136

פֹּה ; פּוֹ ; פֹּא here, at this place – Ch. 33: 68

רָחוֹק far, distant, remote (adj); distance (noun) – Ch. 33: 85

שאר Niphal: נִשְׁאַר/נִשְׁאָר remain, be left, survive; Hiphil: הִשְׁאִיר leave over, allow to survive, preserve – Ch. 33: 133

שכם Hiphil: הִשְׁכִּים do (something) early (e.g., rise early, set out early) – Ch. 33: 65

שְׁלִישִׁי third, one-third – Ch. 33: 106

שלך Hiphil: הִשְׁלִיךְ throw, hurl, cast – Ch. 33: 125

Chapter 34

מִגְרָשׁ pastureland, outskirts – Ch. 34: 115

(1) מלט Niphal: נִמְלַט escape, flee to safety; Piel: מִלֵּט save, deliver, rescue – Ch. 34: 95

מְעַט little, in small amount (adj); a little (noun) – Ch. 34: 96

ערך Qal: עָרַךְ arrange, set in order, make ready – Ch. 34: 75

(2) פלל Hithpael: הִתְפַּלֵּל make intercession, pray – Ch. 34: 80

פנה Qal: פָּנָה turn, turn about, turn aside – Ch. 34: 134

קֶרֶב inward part, midst; בְּקֶרֶב in the midst of (prep) – Ch. 34: 227

(2) רַק only, however, nevertheless – Ch. 34: 108

(1) שחט Qal: שָׁחַט slaughter, kill (usually of a cultic sacrifice) – Ch. 34: 85

שֵׁנִי second – Ch. 34: 156

שרת Piel: שֵׁרֵת serve, minister – Ch. 34: 98

תּוֹעֵבָה abomination, abhorrence – Ch. 34: 118

Chapter 35

(1) אחז Qal: אָחַז seize, grasp, hold fast; Niphal: נֶאֱחַז be held fast – Ch. 35: 63

בין Qal: בִּין understand, perceive, consider; Niphal: נְבֻנוֹתִי (*qatal* 1cs) be discerning, have understanding; Hiphil: הֵבִין have/get understanding, make understand; Hithpolel: הִתְבּוֹנֵן behave intelligently, direct one's attention – Ch. 35: 171

חֵמָה heat, poison, rage, wrath – Ch. 35: 126

(1) חנה Qal: חָנָה encamp, lay siege to – Ch. 35: 143

(2) ידה Hiphil: הוֹדוּ (*qatal* 3cp) praise, thank – Ch. 35: 115

יַעַן because of, on account of (prep); because (conjunction) – Ch. 35: 93

נגש Qal: נָגַשׁ approach, step forward, draw near; Hiphil: הִגִּישׁוּ (*qatal* 3cp) bring near, present – Ch. 35: 125

עַל־כֵּן therefore – Ch. 35: 149

קֶרֶן horn – Ch. 35: 76

רֹב abundance, multitude – Ch. 35: 153

שיר Qal: שָׁר sing; Polel: שֹׁרְרוּ (*qatal* 3cp) burst into song, sing about; (the participle forms of both the Qal שָׁרִים and Polel מְשֹׁרְרִים are often used as substantives) singers – Ch. 35: 88

שָׂפָה lip; (by extension) edge, border – Ch. 35: 178

Chapter 36

אֱמוּנָה faithfulness, trustworthiness, steadfastness – Ch. 36: 53

(1) גִּבְעָה hill – Ch. 36: 63

(1) כֹּחַ strength, power – Ch. 36: 125

כָּנָף wing, extremity, edge – Ch. 36: 110

מוּת Qal: מֵת die; Hiphil: הֵמִית cause to die, kill; Hophal: הוּמַת be killed – Ch. 36: 737

מָחָר tomorrow, next day – Ch. 36: 52

נְחֹשֶׁת bronze, copper – Ch. 36: 139

נסע Qal: נָסַע tear/pull out; journey, depart – Ch. 36: 146

(1) נצב Niphal: נִצְּבָה (*qatal* 3fs) stand; Hiphil: הִצִּיב place, set up – Ch. 36: 75

רֹחַב breadth, expanse – Ch. 36: 101

שׂנא Qal: שָׂנֵא hate; (often as substantive in the participle: שֹׂנֶה) one who hates, enemy – Ch. 36: 148

שׂרף Qal: שָׂרַף burn – Ch. 36: 117

Chapter 37

אַחֲרוֹן at the back (spatial), later on (temporal), last – Ch. 37: 50

אַלְמָנָה widow – Ch. 37: 55

(1) בטח Qal: בָּטַח trust, be confident, feel secure – Ch. 37: 119

(1) גאל Qal: גָּאַל redeem, reclaim as one's own – Ch. 37: 104

יבש Qal: יָבֵשׁ be(come) dry, wither – Ch. 37: 55

לָשׁוֹן tongue (as part of the body, a language, or the shape) – Ch. 37: 117

(1) נָשִׂיא prince – Ch. 37: 133

סתר Niphal: נִסְתַּר hide oneself, be hidden; Hiphil: הִסְתִּיר hide, conceal – Ch.

37: 83

קלל Qal: קַלּוֹתָ (*qatal* 2ms) be small, be insignificant; swift; Piel: קִלֵּל belittle, curse, declare cursed – Ch. 37: 82

קֵץ end; boundary – Ch. 37: 67

קָצֶה edge, end (spatial); end (temporal) – Ch. 37: 90

שַׁבָּת sabbath, rest – Ch. 37: 106

שֶׁמֶן oil – Ch. 37: 193

Chapter 38

הפך Qal: הָפַךְ overthrow, overturn, turn back to front; Niphal: נֶהְפַּךְ/נֶהְפַּךְ be changed, be overthrown – Ch. 38: 95

חָזָק hard, strong, heavy, severe – Ch. 38: 56

חֲצִי half, middle – Ch. 38: 123

לבש Qal: לָבֵשׁ put on, clothe – Ch. 38: 113

עַמּוּד pillar, upright support – Ch. 38: 111

(1) עֶצֶם bone, skeleton – Ch. 38: 123

פַּעַם foot, step; time – Ch. 38: 111

רוּץ Qal: רָץ run – Ch. 38: 103

רֶכֶב chariot, group of chariots (s or pl collective) – Ch. 38: 120

שבע Qal: שָׂבַע consume one's fill, satisfy oneself – Ch. 38: 97

(1) שכח Qal: שָׁכַח forget – Ch. 38: 102

שֶׁקֶר lie, falsehood, deceit – Ch. 38: 113

Chapter 39

בָּמָה high place (often cultic), grave – Ch. 39: 103

(1) זנה Qal: זָנָה commit fornication, be unfaithful – Ch. 39: 95

חָדָשׁ new – Ch. 39: 53

(1) חֵלֶב fat, (by extension) choice part – Ch. 39: 92

(1) חרה Qal: חָרָה be(come) hot, be(come) burning, (by extension) be(come) angry – Ch. 39: 94

חֶרְפָּה disgrace, shame, taunt – Ch. 39: 73

טהר Qal: טָהַר be clean (usually ceremonially); Piel: טִהַר cleanse, purify, declare clean (ceremonially) – Ch. 39: 94

טוב Qal: טוֹב be good – Ch. 39: 90

נֶגֶד opposite, in front of, corresponding to – Ch. 39: 151

עוֹר skin (of a person or animal), leather – Ch. 39: 99

(1) רעע Qal: רַע; רָע be bad, wicked; Hiphil: הֵרַע do evil, treat badly – Ch. 39: 99

תָּמִיד continuance (noun); lasting, continually (adv) – Ch. 39: 104

Chapter 40

בּוֹר cistern – Ch. 40: 69

(1) חַיָּה animal(s) (s or pl collective) – Ch. 40: 97

חָלָל pierced, slain, struck dead – Ch. 40: 94

למד Qal: לָמַדְתִּי (*qatal* 1cs) learn; Piel: לִמַּד teach – Ch. 40: 85

(1) מהר Piel: מִהַר hasten, hurry – Ch. 40: 83

מָלֵא full (adj); fullness (noun) – Ch. 40: 67

נטע Qal: נָטַע plant – Ch. 40: 57

סגר Qal: סָגַר shut, close; Hiphil: הִסְגִּיר surrender, deliver; separate – Ch. 40: 90

עֹז ; עַז strength, might (noun); strong, mighty (adj) – Ch. 40: 94

שִׂמְחָה joy (its feeling and display) – Ch. 40: 94

שית Qal: שָׁת set, stand, place; ordain; direct towards – Ch. 40: 87

שמד Niphal: נִשְׁמַד be destroyed, be exterminated, be rendered unusable; Hiphil: הִשְׁמִיד exterminate – Ch. 40: 90

Chapter 41

אֹרֶךְ length – Ch. 41: 95

בכה Qal: בָּכָה weep – Ch. 41: 114

זְרוֹעַ arm, forearm, (by extension) power, force – Ch. 41: 91

יעץ Qal: יָעַץ advise, plan; Niphal: נוֹעַץ consult, decide – Ch. 41: 82

(1) כְּרוּב cherub – Ch. 41: 92

(1) מכר Qal: מָכַר sell – Ch. 41: 81

מַלְכוּת kingdom; dominion – Ch. 41: 91

(2) משל Qal: מָשַׁל rule – Ch. 41: 82

(1) עֵבֶר side, edge – Ch. 41: 91

(1) עזר Qal: עָזַרְתָּ (*qatal* 2ms) help, assist – Ch. 41: 82

פֶּשַׁע crime, rebellion, revolt, wrongdoing – Ch. 41: 93

שִׁיר ; שִׁירָה song – Ch. 41: 91

APPENDIX 7
HEBREW-ENGLISH VOCABULARY—BY ALPHABET

The following list includes only the core vocabulary and updates found in each chapter of the grammar; no inflected forms or proper names are incorporated. Each entry includes the Hebrew word, its basic definition, the chapter in which it is assigned, a note pointing to the chapter in which the definition is updated, and the number of times the word occurs in the Hebrew Bible. Some entries are also fronted by a number in parentheses, which indicates the lexicon entry that is included when two or more distinct (though perhaps related) words are spelled the same. For example, dependent on the context, the noun אָדָם can mean (1) "human," (2) "leather," (3) the man "Adam," (4) "ground," or (5) a place name.

א

אָב father (irregular plural אָבוֹת) – Ch. 5: 1,568

אבד Qal: אָבַד die, be lost – Ch. 16; Piel: אִבֵּד cause to perish, destroy; Hiphil: הֶאֱבִיד exterminate – Ch. 26 Update 183

אֶבֶן stone – Ch. 8: 268

אָדוֹן ; אֲדֹנָי lord, master; the Lord – Ch. 20: 770

(1, 3) אָדָם human, Adam – Ch. 1: 553

(1) אֲדָמָה ground, land – Ch. 3: 225

אהב Qal: אָהַב love – Ch. 15: 205

(1) אֹהֶל tent – Ch. 2: 342

אוֹ or – Ch. 3: 311

אָוֶן iniquity, evil, disaster – Ch. 21: 80

אוֹר light – Ch. 8: 125

(1) אוֹת sign – Ch. 5: 79

אָז then – Ch. 10: 141

אֹזֶן ear – Ch. 24: 187

(2) אָח brother construct = אֲחִי plural = אַחִים – Ch. 12: 626

אֶחָד one masculine; feminine = אַחַת; can follow a noun, as in עַם אֶחָד, "one people" – Ch. 11: 959

אָחוֹת sister – Ch. 26: 114

(1) אחז Qal: אָחַז seize, grasp, hold fast; Niphal: נֶאֱחַז be held fast – Ch. 35: 63

(1) אַחֵר other, another – Ch. 15: 166

אַחַר ; אַחֲרֵי after, behind – Ch. 14: 713

אַחֲרוֹן at the back (spatial), later on (temporal), last – Ch. 37: 50

אֹיֵב enemy – Ch. 4: 281

(1) אַיִל ram; (metaphorically) ruler – Ch. 30: 161

(1) אַיִן there is no – Ch. 2: 773

(1) אִישׁ man, husband – Ch. 2: 2,149

אַךְ surely, only, however – Ch. 28: 173

אכל Qal: אָכַל eat – Ch. 18; Niphal: נֶאֱכַל be eaten; Hiphil: הֶאֱכַלְתִּי (qatal 1cs) feed – Ch. 27 Update 795

(1) אַל not – Ch. 18: 738

(5) אֵל God, god; Mighty One; El – Ch. 21: 236

אֶל to, toward – Ch. 7: 5,000+

אֵלֶּה these (common gender) – Ch. 17: 738

(2) אֱלֹהִים God, gods – Ch. 2: 2,706

אַלְמָנָה widow – Ch. 37: 55

אֶלֶף thousand, clan, troop – Ch. 19: 494

אִם if – Ch. 6: 1,046

אֵם mother – Ch. 16: 219

אָמָה (female) slave, handmaid – Ch. 25: 56

(1) אַמָּה cubit – Ch. 16: 226

(1) אמן Niphal: נֶאֱמָן/נֶאֱמַן be faithful, reliable, permanent; Hiphil: הֶאֱמִין believe, trust, think – Ch. 30: 100

(1) אמר Qal: אָמַר say – Ch. 10: 5,000+

אֱמֶת trustworthiness, constancy, faithfulness, truth – Ch. 30: 127

אֱמוּנָה faithfulness, trustworthiness, steadfastness – Ch. 36: 53

אֲנַחְנוּ we – Ch. 17: 156

אֲנִי ; אָנֹכִי I – Ch. 10: 1,316

אסף Qal: אָסַף gather, take in, retract – Ch. 18; Niphal: נֶאֱסַף be gathered, be assembled – Ch. 26 Update 203

(1) אַף also, even – Ch. 17: 130

(2) אַף nose, nostrils; anger – Ch. 22: 279

אַרְבַּע four – Ch. 19: 444

אֲרוֹן chest, Ark (of the Covenant) – Ch. 23: 202

אֶרֶץ earth, land – Ch. 1: 2,498

אֹרֶךְ length – Ch. 41: 95

(1) אֵשׁ fire – Ch. 1: 375

אִשָּׁה woman, wife – Ch. 3: 779

אֲשֶׁר who, which, that – Ch. 8: 5,000+

(1) אֵת־ (definite direct object marker) – Ch. 8: 5,000+

(2) אֵת with – Ch. 13: 5000+

אַתָּה you (2ms, subject pronoun; the 2fs subject pronoun is אַתְּ) – Ch. 17: 893

אַתֶּם you (2mp, subject pronoun; the 2fp subject pronoun is אַתֵּנָה or אַתֵּן) – Ch. 17: 330

ב

בְּ in, with, by, among – Ch. 2: 5,000+

(2) בֶּגֶד garment, covering – Ch. 23: 214

בְּהֵמָה; בְּהֵמוֹת animals (in general), beasts, cattle (domesticated animals) – Ch. 25: 192

בוא Qal: בָּא enter, come, go in; Hiphil: הֵבִיא bring, lead in – Ch. 22: 2,530

בּוֹר cistern – Ch. 40: 69

(1) בּוֹשׁ Qal: בּוֹשׁ be ashamed; Hiphil: תָּבִישׁוּ (*yiqtol* 2mp) put to shame – Ch. 23: 126

(1) בחר Qal: בָּחַר choose – Ch. 20: 173

(1) בטח Qal: בָּטַח trust, be confident, feel secure – Ch. 37: 119

בין Qal: בִּין understand, perceive, consider; Niphal: נְבוּנֹתִי (*qatal* 1cs) be discerning, have understanding; Hiphil: הֵבִין have/get understanding, make understand; Hithpolel: הִתְבּוֹנָן behave intelligently, direct one's attention – Ch. 35: 171

בֵּין between – Ch. 13: 396

(1) בַּיִת house (irregular plural בָּתִּים) – Ch. 5: 2,039

בכה Qal: בָּכָה weep – Ch. 41: 114

בְּכֹר; בְּכוֹר firstborn – Ch. 32: 122

בִּלְתִּי not (prep); except, lest (adv) (used to negate the infinitive construct) – Ch. 26: 111

בָּמָה high place (often cultic), grave – Ch. 39: 103

(1) בֵּן son (irregular plural בָּנִים) – Ch. 5: 4,887

בנה Qal: בָּנָה build – Ch. 9; Niphal: נִבְנָה be built – Ch. 24 Update 373

(1) בַּעַל owner, husband; Baal – Ch. 25: 198

בקע Qal: בָּקַע split, breach; Piel: בִּקַּע split, rip up – Ch. 33: 51

בָּקָר cattle – Ch. 27: 183

(2) בֹּקֶר morning, sunrise – Ch. 19: 200

בקש Piel: בִּקֵּשׁ seek, search for; discover, find – Ch. 23: 225

בְּרִית covenant – Ch. 2: 287

(2) ברך Qal: בָּרוּךְ (passive participle) blessed – Ch. 15; Piel: בֵּרַךְ bless, praise – Ch. 22 Update 328

(1) בְּרָכָה blessing – Ch. 3: 71

בָּשָׂר meat, flesh, skin – Ch. 10: 270

(1) בַּת daughter (plural = בָּנוֹת) – Ch. 11: 582

ג

(1) גאל Qal: גָּאַל redeem, reclaim as one's own – Ch. 37: 104

גְּבוּל territory, border – Ch. 9: 241

גִּבּוֹר mighty, strong (adj); strong man, hero (noun) – Ch. 3: 161

(1) גִּבְעָה hill – Ch. 36: 63

גָּדוֹל great, big – Ch. 15: 525

גדל Qal: גָּדַל be(come) great, be(come) strong; Piel: גִּדֵּל/גַּדֵּל bring up, let grow, praise; Hiphil: הִגְדִּיל enlarge, show to be great, magnify oneself – Ch. 29: 122

גּוֹי nation (plural = גּוֹיִם) – Ch. 11: 545

(1) גור Qal: גָּר sojourn, live as an alien – Ch. 26: 81

גלה Qal: גָּלָה uncover, leave, go into exile; Niphal: נִגְלָה expose, announce, reveal oneself; Piel: גִּלָּה uncover, disclose, sleep with; Hiphil: הִגְלָה deport – Ch. 25: 187

גַּם also, even – Ch. 11: 812

גָּמָל camel – Ch. 27: 54

גֵּר sojourner – Ch. 31: 93

ד

דבר Qal: דָּבַר speak (intransitive); Piel: דִּבֶּר to speak (transitive) – Ch. 22: 1130

דָּבָר word, thing – Ch. 1: 1,426

(2) דּוֹר generation – Ch. 20: 169

דָּם blood – Ch. 5: 356

דַּעַת knowledge – Ch. 1: 91

דֶּרֶךְ road, way, path – Ch. 8: 698

דרש Qal: דָּרַשׁ seek – Ch. 22: 163

ה

הַ (+ Daghesh in following consonant) the (definite article) – Ch. 8: 5,000+

הֲ (interrogative particle) – Ch. 7: 5,000+

הוּא he, that – Ch. 17: 1,533

הִיא she, that – Ch. 17: 541

היה Qal: הָיָה be, become – Ch. 10: 3,514

הֵיכָל temple, palace – Ch. 12: 80

הלך Qal: הָלַךְ walk, go – Ch. 9; Hiphil: הוֹלִיךְ bring, lead; Hithpael: הִתְהַלֵּךְ walk about, go about, disperse – Ch. 25 Update 1,504

(2) הלל Piel: הִלְלְתֶם (*qatal* 2mp) praise; Hithpael: יִתְהַלֵּל (*yiqtol* 3ms) boast – Ch. 27: 145

הֵמָּה ; הֵם they, those (3mp, subject pronoun; the 3fp subject pronoun is הֵנָּה) – Ch. 17: 1,553

(1) הֵן ; הֶן behold! (interjection); if (conjunction) – Ch. 26: 100

הִנֵּה traditionally "behold!"; translation varies according to context; perhaps "well now" or "look here" – Ch. 26: 1,037

הפך Qal: הָפַךְ overthrow, overturn, turn back to front; Niphal: נֶהְפַּךְ/נֶהֱפַךְ be changed, be overthrown – Ch. 38: 95

הַר hill, mountain – Ch. 8: 554

הרג Qal: הָרַג kill, slay – Ch. 23: 168

ו

וְ and, but – Ch. 10: 5,000+

ז

זֹאת this (f) – Ch. 17: 605

זבח Qal: זָבַח slaughter, sacrifice; Piel: זִבַּח sacrifice – Ch. 25: 136

(1) זֶבַח (communal) sacrifice, offering – Ch. 28: 162

זֶה this (m) – Ch. 17: 1,189

זָהָב gold – Ch. 4: 383

זכר Qal: זָכַר remember – Ch. 15; Niphal: נִזְכַּרְתֶּם (qatal 2mp) be remembered; Hiphil: הִזְכִּיר make known, report – Ch. 22 Update 230

(1) זנה Qal: זָנָה commit fornication, be unfaithful – Ch. 39: 95

זָקֵן old (adj); elder, old man (noun) – Ch. 1: 178

זְרֹועַ arm, forearm, (by extension) power, force – Ch. 41: 91

זרע Qal: זָרַע sow (of seed) – Ch. 29: 56

זֶרַע seed, offspring (s or pl collective) – Ch. 29: 228

ח

חָדָשׁ new – Ch. 39: 53

(1) חֹדֶשׁ new moon – Ch. 22: 278

(2) חוה Hishtaphel: הִשְׁתַּחֲוָה bow down (always found with הִשְׁתּ־ prefix) – Ch. 33: 174

חֹומָה wall – Ch. 4: 133

חוץ a place outside the house, street (noun); outside, without (prep, adv) – Ch. 30: 165

חזק Qal: חָזַק be strong, have courage; Piel: חִזַּק make firm, strengthen, harden (the heart); Hiphil: הֶחֱזִיק seize, grasp, feel strengthened; Hithpael: הִתְחַזַּק show oneself courageous, feel strengthened, show oneself as strong – Ch. 21: 288

חָזָק hard, strong, heavy, severe – Ch. 38: 56

חטא Qal: חָטָא miss (a mark), sin – Ch. 20: 237

חַטָּאת sin, sin offering – Ch. 3: 296

חַי alive (mp חַיִּים = life) – Ch. 15: 386

חיה Qal: חַי live (the form of the qatal 3ms reflects the fact that the root was originally חיי, a geminate); Piel: חִיָּה let live – Ch. 26: 281

(1) חַיָּה animal(s) (s or pl collective) – Ch. 40: 97

חַיִל strength, power; wealth; army – Ch. 24: 246

חָכָם wise (adj), wise man (noun) – Ch. 8: 138

חָכְמָה wisdom – Ch. 3: 152

(1) חֵלֶב fat, (by extension) choice part – Ch. 39: 92

(1) חלל Piel: חִלֵּל defile, profane – Ch. 23: 134

חָלָל pierced, slain, struck dead – Ch. 40: 94

חֵמָה heat, poison, rage, wrath – Ch. 35: 126

(1) חֲמֹור donkey – Ch. 27: 97

חָמֵשׁ five – Ch. 13: 478

(1) חנה Qal: חָנָה encamp, lay siege to – Ch. 35: 143

(2) חֶסֶד loyalty, steadfast love, devotion, faithfulness – Ch. 20: 250

(1) חפץ Qal: חָפֵץ desire, enjoy, want the qatal 3ms is חָפֵץ, but other forms are normal, e.g., qatal 2ms is חָפַצְתָּ – Ch. 11: 86

חֲצִי half, middle – Ch. 38: 123

חָצֵר courtyard, village – Ch. 1: 193

חֹק rule, statute, law – Ch. 16: 128

חֻקָּה statute, regulation – Ch. 32: 104

חֶרֶב sword – Ch. 16: 407

(1) חרה Qal: חָרָה be(come) hot, be(come) burning, (by extension) be(come) angry – Ch. 39: 94

חֶרְפָּה disgrace, shame, taunt – Ch. 39: 73

חשׁב Qal: חָשַׁב regard, assume, plan; Niphal: נֶחְשַׁב be regarded – Ch. 30: 124

חֹשֶׁךְ darkness – Ch. 16: 82

ט

טָהוֹר clean (ritually) – Ch. 15: 95

טהר Qal: טָהֵר be clean (usually ceremonially); Piel: טִהַר cleanse, purify, declare clean (ceremonially) – Ch. 39: 94

טוב Qal: טוֹב be good – Ch. 39: 90

טמא Qal: טָמֵא be unclean; Piel: טִמֵּא defile, declare unclean – Ch. 23: 161

(1) טוֹב good – Ch. 15: 612

טָמֵא ; טְמֵאָה (ceremonially) unclean – Ch. 25: 88

י

יבשׁ Qal: יָבֵשׁ be(come) dry, wither – Ch. 37: 55

יָד hand – Ch. 12: 1,580

(2) ידה Hiphil: הוֹדוּ (qatal 3cp) praise, thank – Ch. 35: 115

ידע Qal: יָדַע know – Ch. 16; Niphal: נוֹדַע reveal, become known; Hiphil: הוֹדִיעַ make known, inform – Ch. 28 Update 924

יהוה Yahweh, the LORD – Ch. 12: 5766

(1) יוֹם day (irregular plural יָמִים) – Ch. 5: 2,241

יַחַד ; יַחְדּוּ uniting, community (noun); together, at the same time (adv) – Ch. 33: 142

יטב Qal: יִיטַב (yiqtol 3ms) go well, do well; Hiphil: הֵיטִיב treat well – Ch. 26: 120

יַיִן wine – Ch. 31: 141

יכל Qal: יָכֹל be able to, be capable of (stative) – Ch. 21: 194

ילד Qal: יָלַד give birth, beget – Ch. 19; Niphal: נוֹלַד be born; Pual: יֻלַּד be born; Hiphil: הוֹלִיד beget – Ch. 27 Update 488

יֶלֶד (ms) young male offspring, boy; יַלְדָּה (fs) young female offspring, girl – Ch. 27: 92

יָם sea (plural = יַמִּים) – Ch. 13: 392

(1) יָמִין right side, south – Ch. 30: 139

יסף Qal: יָסַף add, continue to do; Hiphil: הוֹ(וֹ)סִיף add, increase, do again – Ch. 24: 212

יַעַן because of, on account of (prep); because (conjunction) – Ch. 35: 93

יעץ Qal: יָעַץ advise, plan; Niphal: נוֹעַץ consult, decide – Ch. 41: 82

יצא Qal: יָצָא go out – Ch. 19; Hiphil: הוֹצִיא lead, cause to go out – Ch. 30 Update 1,055

(1) ירא Qal: יָרֵא fear, be afraid; Niphal: נוֹרָא (= ptc) be feared – Ch. 20: 377

ירד Qal: יָרַד go down, descend – Ch. 12; Hiphil: הוֹרִד bring down, cause to fall – Ch. 27 Update 380

ירשׁ Qal: יָרַשׁ possess, inherit, dispossess; Hiphil: הוֹרִישׁ take possession of, dispossess, drive out – Ch. 20: 231

יֵשׁ there is – Ch. 2: 139

ישׁב Qal: יָשַׁב sit, dwell – Ch. 10; Hiphil: הוֹשִׁיב set, inhabit, cause to dwell – Ch. 25 Update 1,078

יְשׁוּעָה salvation, also seen as יְשׁוּעָתָה – Ch. 5: 78

יָשַׁע Niphal: נוֹשַׁע receive help, be victorious, be rescued; Hiphil: הוֹשִׁיעַ help, save – Ch. 25: 205

יָשָׁר upright (adj), upright man (noun) – Ch. 8: 119

יָתַר Niphal: נוֹתַר be left, remain; Hiphil: הוֹתִיר leave over/behind, have left over – Ch. 33: 106

(1) יֶתֶר remainder, the rest, what is left behind – Ch. 33: 93

כ

כְּ as, like (attached directly to a noun, as in כְּדָוִד ["like David"]) – Ch. 5: 5,000+

כַּאֲשֶׁר (כְּ+אֲשֶׁר) as, just as, because, when – Ch. 26: 504

כָּבֵד Qal: כָּבֵד be heavy, weighty, honored; Niphal: נִכְבַּד be honored, enjoy honor, appear in one's glory; Piel: כִּבְּדוּ (*qatal* 3cp) honor – Ch. 29: 114

כָּבוֹד heaviness, honor, glory – Ch. 21: 200

כֶּבֶשׂ ; כִּבְשָׂה young ram; ewe-lamb – Ch. 28: 129

כֹּה thus – Ch. 14: 554

כֹּהֵן priest – Ch. 3: 749

כּוּן Niphal: נָכוֹן be firm, be established, be fixed; Polel: כּוֹנֵן establish, set up, fix solidly; Hiphil: הֵכִין prepare, set up, make firm – Ch. 24: 219

(1) כֹּחַ strength, power – Ch. 36: 125

(2) כִּי because, although, indeed, that, rather, instead – Ch. 10: 4,395

כֹּל all, whole, every (in construct with Maqqeph כָּל־) – Ch. 14: 5,000+

(1) כָּלָה Qal: כָּלָה stop, be finished; perish; Piel: כִּלָּה complete, finish; destroy – Ch. 23: 204

כְּלִי vessel, tool, weapon, thing – Ch. 2: 324

כְּמוֹ like, as – Ch. 27: 139

כֵּן thus – Ch. 11: 707

כָּנָף wing, extremity, edge – Ch. 36: 110

כִּסֵּא throne, chair – Ch. 33: 136

כָּסָה Piel: כִּסָּה cover – Ch. 24: 157

כֶּסֶף silver – Ch. 4: 399

כַּף palm of hand *or* sole of foot – Ch. 29: 192

כָּפַר Piel: כִּפֶּר cover, appease, (by extension) make atonement – Ch. 32: 102

(1) כְּרוּב cherub – Ch. 41: 92

(1) כֶּרֶם vineyard – Ch. 18: 93

כָּרַת Qal: כָּרַת cut, cut off (when used with בְּרִית, it means "make a covenant" – Ch. 14; Niphal: נִכְרַת be cut off, eliminated; Hiphil: הִכְרִית exterminate – Ch. 21 Update 287

כָּתַב Qal: כָּתַב write – Ch. 9; Niphal: יִכָּתֵב (*yiqtol* 3ms) be written – Ch. 20 Update 222

ל

לְ to, for – Ch. 6: 5,000+

לֹא no, not, never – Ch. 7: 4,973

לֵב heart (a "by-form" or alternative form of this word is לֵבָב) – Ch. 8: 844

לְבַד alone (adv); besides (prep) – Ch. 28: 155

לָבַשׁ Qal: לָבַשׁ put on, clothe – Ch. 38: 113

(1) לחם Niphal: נִלְחַם fight – Ch. 29: 171

לֶחֶם bread – Ch. 8: 296

לַיְלָה night – Ch. 10: 231

לָכַד Qal: לָכַד seize, capture; Niphal: נִלְכַּד get trapped, be overpowered, be selected – Ch. 31: 121

לָכֵן therefore – Ch. 25: 196

לָמַד Qal: לָמַדְתִּי (*qatal* 1cs) learn; Piel: לִמַּד teach – Ch. 40: 85

לָמָה ; לָמֶה why? – Ch. 28: 173

לְמַעַן for the sake of, in order that, so that – Ch. 6: 269

לִפְנֵי before, in the presence of – Ch. 13: 1,099

לקח Qal: לָקַח take, grasp, capture – Ch. 21: 964

לָשׁוֹן tongue (as part of the body, a language, or the shape) – Ch. 37: 117

מ

מְאֹד very, very much – Ch. 20: 287

(1) מֵאָה hundred – Ch. 12: 577

מִגְרָשׁ pastureland, outskirts – Ch. 34: 115

(1) מָגֵן shield (as weapon, ornament, or protection) – Ch. 29: 59

(1) מִדְבָּר desert, wilderness – Ch. 9: 271

מָה what? why? – Ch. 17: 760

(1) מהר Piel: מִהַר hasten, hurry – Ch. 40: 83

מוֹעֵד appointed place or time, season – Ch. 25: 223

מות Qal: מֵת die; Hiphil: הֵמִית cause to die, kill; Hophal: הוּמַת be killed – Ch. 36: 737

מָוֶת death – Ch. 4: 159

מִזְבֵּחַ altar – Ch. 5: 401

מַחֲנֶה camp, army – Ch. 12: 219

מָחָר tomorrow, next day – Ch. 36: 52

מַטֶּה tribe; rod, staff – Ch. 19: 252

מִי who? – Ch. 17: 406

מַיִם water – Ch. 4: 574

(1) מכר Qal: מָכַר sell – Ch. 41: 81

מלא Qal: מָלֵא be full, fill up; Niphal: יִמָּלֵא (= impf) be filled; Piel: מִלֵּא fill, endow, devote, fulfill – Ch. 21: 250

מָלֵא full (adj); fullness (noun) – Ch. 40: 67

מַלְאָךְ messenger, angel – Ch. 12: 213

מְלָאכָה work, service, fruit of labor – Ch. 29: 167

מִלְחָמָה war, battle – Ch. 11: 319

(1) מלט Niphal: נִמְלַט escape, flee to safety; Piel: מִלֵּט save, deliver, rescue – Ch. 34: 95

(1) מלך Qal: מָלַךְ be king, rule – Ch. 9; Hiphil: הִמְלִיךְ install someone as king – Ch. 20 Update 347

(1) מֶלֶךְ king – Ch. 1: 2,522

מַלְכָּה queen – Ch. 2: 35

מַלְכוּת kingdom; dominion – Ch. 41: 91

מַמְלָכָה kingdom – Ch. 23: 117

מִן from, than – Ch. 13: 1,279

מִנְחָה gift, present; offering – Ch. 21: 211

מִסְפָּר number – Ch. 19: 134

מְעַט little, in small amount (adj); a little (noun) – Ch. 34: 96

(2) מַעַל above; מַעְלָה = "upwards" – Ch. 19: 138

מַעֲשֶׂה work, labor, accomplishment – Ch. 24: 235

מצא Qal: מָצָא find, seek; Niphal: נִמְצָא be found – Ch. 20: 451

מִצְוָה command (plural מִצְוֹת with consonantal ו) – Ch. 5: 181

מָקוֹם place – Ch. 18: 399

מַרְאֶה appearance, sight, visage – Ch. 26: 103

מִשְׁכָּן dwelling place, abode (often of the abode of YHWH = tabernacle, central sanctuary) – Ch. 28: 139

(2) משל Qal: מָשַׁל rule – Ch. 41: 82

מִשְׁפָּחָה family – Ch. 11: 300

מִשְׁפָּט judgment, justice – Ch. 2: 425

נ

נָא (particle used with commands or requests; do not translate) – Ch. 26: 401

נְאֻם utterance, declaration – Ch. 21: 378

נבא Niphal: נִבָּא prophesy, behave like a prophet – Ch. 31: 115

נבט Hiphil: הִבִּיט look, look at, behold; (by extension) accept favorably – Ch. 30: 70

נָבִיא prophet – Ch. 4: 313

נגד Hiphil: הִגִּיד tell; Hophal: הֻגַּד be told – Ch. 24: 369

נֶגֶד opposite, in front of, corresponding to – Ch. 39: 151

נגע Qal: נָגַע touch, strike; Piel: וַיְנַגַּע (Wayyiqtol 3ms) afflict; Hiphil: הִגִּיעַ touch, hurl, happen – Ch. 27: 150

נֶגַע blow, wound, plague (noun) – Ch. 27: 78

נגש Qal: נָגַשׁ approach, step forward, draw near; Hiphil: הִגִּישׁוּ (qatal 3cp) bring near, present – Ch. 35: 125

נָהָר river, stream – Ch. 32: 117

(1) נוח Qal: נָחָה (qatal 3fs) rest, settle down; Hiphil (2 forms): הֵנִיחַ cause to rest, secure repose, pacify; הִנִּיחַ place, set, leave (untouched) – Ch. 30: 143

נוס Qal: נָס flee – Ch. 28: 160

(1) נַחַל river valley, wadi, stream, trench – Ch. 32: 138

(1) נַחֲלָה inheritance, possession – Ch. 18: 223

נחם Niphal: נִחַם/נִחָם regret, be sorry; Piel: נִחַם comfort – Ch. 32: 108

נְחֹשֶׁת bronze, copper – Ch. 36: 139

נטה Qal: נָטָה reach out, spread out, stretch out, turn aside; Hiphil: הִטָּה stretch out, extend, guide away – Ch. 21: 215

נטע Qal: נָטַע plant – Ch. 40: 57

נכה Hiphil: הִכָּה strike, smite, injure – Ch. 24: 504

נסע Qal: נָסַע tear/pull out; journey, depart – Ch. 36: 146

נַעַר boy, youth – Ch. 16: 240

נפל Qal: נָפַל fall – Ch. 11; Hiphil: הִפִּיל drop, throw down – Ch. 25 Update 433

נֶפֶשׁ life, self, person, soul – Ch. 16: 753

(1) נצב Niphal: נִצְּבָה (qatal 3fs) stand; Hiphil: הִצִּיב place, set up – Ch. 36: 75

נצל Niphal: נִצַּל be rescued; Hiphil: הִצִּיל snatch away, deliver – Ch. 24: 208

נשא Qal: נָשָׂא carry, lift up; Niphal: נִשָּׂא be carried – Ch. 20: 651

(1) נָשִׂיא prince – Ch. 37: 133

נתן Qal: נָתַן give, place – Ch. 10; Niphal: נִתַּן be given – Ch. 25 Update 1,994

ס

סבב Qal: סָבַב turn round, go around, surround; Hiphil: הֵסֵב make to go around, bring around, turn away – Ch. 28: 162

סָבִיב surrounding(s), circuit – Ch. 24: 309

סגר Qal: סָגַר shut, close; Hiphil: הִסְגִּיר surrender, deliver; separate – Ch. 40: 90

(1) סוּס horse – Ch. 2: 139

סור Qal: סָר turn away, turn aside; Hiphil: הֵסִיר remove – Ch. 22: 298

ספר Qal: סָפַר count, number, write; Piel: סִפַּרְתִּי (qatal 1cs) count up, announce, report – Ch. 30: 162

סֵפֶר scroll, book – Ch. 16: 185

סתר Niphal: נִסְתַּר hide oneself, be hidden; Hiphil: הִסְתִּיר hide, conceal – Ch. 37: 83

ע

עבד Qal: עָבַד serve, work, accomplish – Ch. 31: 289

(1) עֶבֶד servant, slave – Ch. 1: 800

עֲבֹדָה service, work, labor – Ch. 31: 143

(1) עבר Qal: עָבַר pass over/through/by, cross; transgress – Ch. 16; Hiphil: הֶעֱבִיר allow to pass over, overlook – Ch. 26 Update 539

(1) עֵבֶר side, edge – Ch. 41: 91

(2) עַד until, as far as, unto – Ch. 13: 1,246

(1) עֵדָה congregation – Ch. 11: 149

עוֹד still, yet – Ch. 7: 481

(1) עוֹלָה whole burnt offering – Ch. 5: 288

עוֹלָם , עֹלָם remote time; eternity, forever – Ch. 18: 434

עָוֹן sin, transgression; guilt caused by sin – Ch. 23: 231

עוֹר skin (of a person or animal), leather – Ch. 39: 99

עֹז ; עַז strength, might (noun); strong, mighty (adj) – Ch. 40: 94

עֵז goat, goat hair – Ch. 30: 74

(1) עזב Qal: עָזַב leave, abandon; Niphal: נֶעֱזַב be abandoned – Ch. 23: 212

(1) עזר Qal: עָזַרְתָּ (*qatal* 2ms) help, assist – Ch. 41: 82

עַיִן eye, spring (of water) – Ch. 4: 867

(1) עִיר city – Ch. 2: 1,080

(2) עַל upon, over, against – Ch. 9: 4,898

עַל־כֵּן therefore – Ch. 35: 149

עלה Qal: עָלָה go up – Ch. 18; Hiphil: הֶעֱלָה lead up, cause to rise, offer (sacrifice) – Ch. 25 Update 879

(1) עַם people – Ch. 3: 1,827

עִם with – Ch. 13: 1,076

עמד Qal: עָמַד stand – Ch. 12; Hiphil: הֶעֱמִיד set in position, erect, cause to

stand – Ch. 26 Update 519

עַמּוּד pillar, upright support – Ch. 38: 111

(1) ענה Qal: עָנָה answer – Ch. 13: 314

(2) ענה Piel: עִנָּה afflict, oppress – Ch. 31: 79

עָנִי poor, wretched – Ch. 20: 76

עָפָר dust – Ch. 8: 110

עֵץ tree, wood – Ch. 15: 330

(1) עֵצָה advice – Ch. 9: 89

(1) עֶצֶם bone, skeleton – Ch. 38: 123

(2) עֶרֶב evening, sunset – Ch. 19: 134

ערך Qal: עָרַךְ arrange, set in order, make ready – Ch. 34: 75

עשה Qal: עָשָׂה do, make, build – Ch. 9; Niphal: נַעֲשָׂה be done, be prepared – Ch. 24 Update 2,573

עֶשֶׂר ten; in numbers eleven through nineteen, עָשָׂר as in אַחַד עָשָׂר, "eleven" – Ch. 19: 173

עֵת time, season – Ch. 14: 282

עַתָּה now – Ch. 22: 432

פ

פֶּה mouth – Ch. 12: 492

פֹּה ; פֹּו ; פֹּא here, at this place – Ch. 33: 68

(1) פַּחַד dread, trembling, deep fear – Ch. 20: 49

(2) פלל Hithpael: הִתְפַּלֵּל make intercession, pray – Ch. 34: 80

פֶּן־ lest – Ch. 24: 133

פנה Qal: פָּנָה turn, turn about, turn aside – Ch. 34: 134

פָּנִים face, front; (when linked with preps) before, away from (plural in form but usually singular in meaning) – Ch. 13: 2,120

פעל Qal: פָּעַל do – Ch. 21: 57

פַּעַם foot, step; time – Ch. 38: 111

פקד Qal: פָּקַד inspect, attend to, urge, muster, call to account, visit, punish – Ch. 13; Niphal: נִפְקַד be missed, be punished; Hiphil: הִפְקִיד appoint – Ch. 21 Update 301

פַּר ; פָּרָה steer, young bull (m), cow (f) – Ch. 28: 159

פְּרִי fruit – Ch. 14: 119

פֶּשַׁע crime, rebellion, revolt, wrongdoing – Ch. 41: 93

(1) פתח Qal: פָּתַח open; Piel: פִּתַּח break open, let loose – Ch. 27: 144

פֶּתַח opening, entrance, gateway – Ch. 27: 163

צ

צֹאן flock (of sheep or goats) (s or pl collective) – Ch. 1: 275

(1) צָבָא army, host; service in war – Ch. 4: 485

צֶדֶק righteousness: what is right, just, accurate, normal – Ch. 29: 116

צוה Piel: צִוָּה command, instruct, send – Ch. 28: 494

צַדִּיק righteous – Ch. 11: 206

צְדָקָה righteousness, justness, justice, communal loyalty – Ch. 29: 157

(1) צָפוֹן north; mountain of the gods (in the north) – Ch. 30: 153

ק

קבץ Qal: קָבַץ collect, assemble, gather; Niphal: נִקְבְּצוּ (*qatal* 3cp) assemble, be assembled; Piel: קִבְּצָה (*qatal* 3fs) gather together – Ch. 31: 127

קבר Qal: קָבַר bury; Niphal: יִקָּבֵר (*yiqtol* 3ms) be buried – Ch. 32: 132

קָדוֹשׁ holy – Ch. 15: 115

קדשׁ Piel: קִדַּשׁ sanctify, dedicate; Hiphil: הִקְדִּישׁ mark or treat as holy – Ch. 22: 172

קֹדֶשׁ holiness, holy thing – Ch. 14: 430

קָהָל contingent, assembly, congregation – Ch. 31: 123

קוֹל voice – Ch. 12: 499

קום Qal: קָם rise, get up; Hiphil: הֵקִים erect, raise up, keep, confirm – Ch. 24: 624

קָטֹן small – Ch. 15: 54

(1) קטר Piel: קִטְּרוּ (*qatal* 3cp) send (an offering) up in smoke; Hiphil: הִקְטִיר cause (a sacrifice) to go up in smoke – Ch. 32: 116

קלל Qal: קַלּוֹתָ (*qatal* 2ms) be small, be insignificant; swift; Piel: קִלֵּל belittle, curse, declare cursed – Ch. 37: 82

קֵץ end; boundary – Ch. 37: 67

קָצֶה edge, end (spatial); end (temporal) – Ch. 37: 90

(1) קרא Qal: קָרָא call, summon, proclaim – Ch. 18; Niphal: נִקְרָא be summoned, be proclaimed – Ch. 27 Update 739

(2) קרא Qal: קָרָאת (*qatal* 3fs) meet, encounter, happen; לִקְרַאת over against, opposite (special use of the infinitive construct as a prep) – Ch. 31: 139

קרב Qal: קָרַב draw near, approach – Ch. 14; Hiphil: הִקְרִיב bring (near), take, offer – Ch. 21 Update 291

קֶרֶב inward part, midst; בְּקֶרֶב in the midst of (prep) – Ch. 34: 227

קֶרֶן horn – Ch. 35: 76

ר

ראה Qal: רָאָה see, inspect – Ch. 9; Niphal: נִרְאָה appear, present oneself; Hiphil: הֶרְאָה show someone, cause to experience – Ch. 24 Update 1,294

(1) רֹאשׁ head, top, leader – Ch. 4: 593

רִאשׁוֹן first – Ch. 19: 182

רַב much, many – Ch. 16: 475

רֹב abundance, multitude – Ch. 35: 153

(1) רבה Hiphil: הִרְבָּה make numerous, multiply – Ch. 24: 226

רְבִיעִי fourth, one-fourth – Ch. 32: 55

רֶגֶל foot – Ch. 14: 252

רדף Qal: רָדַף pursue – Ch. 21: 143

רוּחַ wind, breath, spirit, (divine) Spirit – Ch. 3: 376

רום Qal: רָם be high above, be exalted, rise, go up, be haughty; Polel: רוֹמַמְתִּי (*qatal* 1cs) bring up, exalt; Hiphil: הֵרִים raise up, lift up, erect – Ch. 25: 195

רוץ Qal: רָץ run – Ch. 38: 103

רֹחַב breadth, expanse – Ch. 36: 101

רָחוֹק far, distant, remote (adj); distance (noun) – Ch. 33: 85

רֶכֶב chariot, group of chariots (s or pl collective) – Ch. 38: 120

רַע , רָע ; רָעָה evil, bad, wicked, trouble (adj, noun) – Ch. 15: 661

רֵעַ counterpart, companion, friend – Ch. 31: 195

רָעָב famine, hunger – Ch. 26: 103

(1) רעה Qal: רָעָה feed, graze, nourish, protect as a shepherd; (often as a substantive in the participle: רֹעֶה) shepherd – Ch. 27: 171

(1) רעע Qal: רָע ;רַע be bad, wicked; Hiphil: הֵרַע do evil, treat badly – Ch. 39: 99

(2) רַק only, however, nevertheless – Ch. 34: 108

רָשָׁע wicked – Ch. 9: 264

שׂ

שבע Qal: שָׂבַע consume one's fill, satisfy oneself – Ch. 38: 97

שָׂדֶה field – Ch. 3: 332

(1) שִׂים Qal: שָׂם set, put, place – Ch. 25: 584

(1) שכל Hiphil: הִשְׂכִּיל understand, have insight, behave wisely, achieve success – Ch. 22: 75

שמח Qal: שָׂמַח rejoice, be merry; Piel: שִׂמַּח gladden, make (someone) merry, cause to rejoice – Ch. 25: 156

שִׂמְחָה joy (its feeling and display) – Ch. 40: 94

שנא Qal: שָׂנֵא hate; (often as substantive in the participle: שֹׂנֵא) one who hates, enemy – Ch. 36: 148

שָׂפָה lip; (by extension) edge, border – Ch. 35: 178

שַׂר ruler, leader, prince – Ch. 1: 412

שרף Qal: שָׂרַף burn – Ch. 36: 117

שׁ

שֶׁ־ ;שַׁ־ (+ Daghesh in following consonant) who, which, that – Ch. 29: 139

שאל Qal: שָׁאַל ask, consult, demand – Ch. 28: 173

שאר Niphal: נִשְׁאַר/נִשְׁאָר remain, be left, survive; Hiphil: הִשְׁאִיר leave over, allow to survive, preserve – Ch. 33: 133

שֵׁבֶט rod, staff, scepter; tribe – Ch. 25: 190

שְׁבִיעִי seventh – Ch. 32: 96

שבע Niphal: נִשְׁבַּע swear (an oath); Hiphil: הִשְׁבִּיעַ make (someone) swear (an oath), implore – Ch. 26: 186

שֶׁבַע seven – Ch. 14: 492

(1) שבר Qal: שָׁבַר shatter, smash, break; Niphal: נִשְׁבַּר be smashed, be broken, be destroyed; Piel: שִׁבַּר smash (into fragments) (of things not easily broken in a single action—e.g., stone, metal, trees) – Ch. 32: 149

שַׁבָּת sabbath, rest – Ch. 37: 106

שׁוּב Qal: שָׁב return; Hiphil: הֵשִׁיב bring back – Ch. 22: 1,055

(1) שחט Qal: שָׁחַט slaughter, kill (usually of a cultic sacrifice) – Ch. 34: 85

שחת Piel: שִׁחֵת ruin, destroy; Hiphil: הִשְׁחִית ruin, destroy, corrupt – Ch. 22: 161

שׁיר Qal: שָׁר sing; Polel: שׁוֹרְרוּ (*qatal* 3cp) burst into song, sing about; (the participle forms of both the Qal שָׁרִים and Polel מְשֹׁרְרִים are often used as substantives) singers – Ch. 35: 88

שִׁיר; שִׁירָה song – Ch. 41: 91

שׁית Qal: שָׁת set, stand, place; ordain; direct towards – Ch. 40: 87

שכב Qal: שָׁכַב lie (down), have sexual intercourse – Ch. 14: 211

(1) שכח Qal: שָׁכַח forget – Ch. 38: 102

שכם Hiphil: הִשְׁכִּים do (something) early (e.g., rise early, set out early) – Ch. 33: 65

שכן Qal: שָׁכַן reside, dwell, settle – Ch. 28: 130

שָׁלוֹם peace, well-being, wholeness – Ch. 23: 242

שלח Qal: שָׁלַח send, stretch out – Ch. 18; Piel: שִׁלַּח stretch out, let go, expel – Ch. 22 Update 839

שְׁלִישִׁי third, one-third – Ch. 33: 106

שלך Hiphil: הִשְׁלִיךְ throw, hurl, cast – Ch. 33: 125

שלם Piel: שִׁלֵּם make complete, make restitution – Ch. 32: 117

שָׁלֹשׁ three; with feminine noun like שָׁלֹשׁ סוּסוֹת; with masculine noun like שְׁלֹשָׁה סוּסִים – Ch. 11: 586

שָׁם there – Ch. 7: 817

(1) שֵׁם name – Ch. 14: 862

שמד Niphal: נִשְׁמַד be destroyed, be exterminated, be rendered unusable; Hiphil: הִשְׁמִיד exterminate – Ch. 40: 90

שָׁמַיִם heaven(s), sky – Ch. 4: 416

שמם Qal: שָׁמֵם be desolate, deserted; be astonished, shudder; Niphal: נָשַׁמָּה (*qatal* 3fs) be uninhabited, tremble; Hiphil: הֲשִׁמּוֹתָ (*qatal* 2ms) cause to be deserted, cause to be desolated – Ch. 29: 95

שֶׁמֶן oil – Ch. 37: 193

שְׁמֹנֶה eight – Ch. 18: 147

שמע Qal: שָׁמַע hear, listen – Ch. 10; Niphal: נַשְׁמַע be heard; Hiphil: הִשְׁמִיעַ cause to hear, summon – Ch. 24 Update 1,136

שמר Qal: שָׁמַר keep, guard, observe – Ch. 10; Niphal: נִשְׁמַר be kept, be guarded – Ch. 20 Update 465

שֶׁמֶשׁ sun – Ch. 31: 134

שָׁנָה year – Ch. 12: 871

שֵׁנִי second – Ch. 34: 156

שְׁנַיִם; שְׁתַּיִם two – Ch. 4: 739

(1) שַׁעַר gate – Ch. 3: 368

שִׁפְחָה slave-girl, handmaid, maidservant – Ch. 27: 63

שפט Qal: שָׁפַט judge, rule – Ch. 9: 203

שֹׁפֵט judge, leader – Ch. 1: 58

שפך Qal: שָׁפַךְ pour out; Niphal: נִשְׁפַּךְ be poured out – Ch. 22: 116

שֶׁקֶר lie, falsehood, deceit – Ch. 38: 113

שרת Piel: שֵׁרֵת serve, minister – Ch. 34: 98

שֵׁשׁ six – Ch. 19: 272

(2) שתה Qal: שָׁתָה drink – Ch. 16: 217

ת

תָּוֶךְ middle, midst – Ch. 13: 416

תּוֹלֵדוֹת official records of descendants from an ancestor, often translated "generations" or "account" – Ch. 19: 39

תּוֹעֵבָה abomination, abhorrence – Ch. 34: 118

תּוֹרָה instruction, teaching, law – Ch. 5: 220

(1) תַּחַת under, instead of – Ch. 12: 490

תָּמִים complete, without blemish, perfect, honest, impeccable (adj); honesty, blamelessness (noun) – Ch. 30: 91

תָּמִיד continuance (noun); lasting, continually (adv) – Ch. 39: 104

תֵּשַׁע nine – Ch. 18: 77

APPENDIX 8
PRINCIPAL PARTS AND FINITE VERB PARADIGMS

Appendix Table 8.1. The Principal Parts of the Qal Stem

קטל	Qatal קָטַל	Yiqtol יִקְטֹל	Inf. Con. קְטֹל	Participle קֹטֵל
בנה	בָּנָה	יִבְנֶה	בְּנוֹת	בּוֹנֶה
עמד	עָמַד	יַעֲמֹד	עֲמֹד	עֹמֵד
בחר	בָּחַר	יִבְחַר	בְּחֹר	בֹּחֵר
שמע	שָׁמַע	יִשְׁמַע	שְׁמֹעַ	שֹׁמֵעַ
מצא	מָצָא	יִמְצָא	מְצֹא	מֹצֵא
חטא	חָטָא	יֶחֱטָא	חֲטֹא	חוֹטֵא
נפל	נָפַל	יִפֹּל	נְפֹל	נֹפֵל
שוב	שָׁב	יָשׁוּב	שׁוּב	שָׁב
סבב	סָבַב	יָסֹב	סְבֹב	סֹבֵב
ישב	יָשַׁב	תֵּשֵׁב | יֵשֵׁב	שֶׁבֶת	יֹשֵׁב
ירש	יָרַשׁ	יִירַשׁ	רֶשֶׁת	יוֹרֵשׁ
אמר	אָמַר	יֹאמַר	לֵאמֹר	אֹמֵר
אהב	אָהַב	יֶאֱהַב	אַהֲבַת	אֹהֵב

Appendix Table 8.2. The III-ה Principal Parts in Various Stems

	Root	Qatal	Yiqtol	Inf. Con.	Participle
Qal	בנה	בָּנָה	יִבְנֶה	בְּנוֹת	בּוֹנֶה
Niphal	בנה	נִבְנָה	יִבָּנֶה	הִבָּנוֹת	נִבְנֶה
Piel	כסה	כִּסָּה	יְכַסֶּה	כַּסּוֹת	מְכַסֶּה
Hiphil	רבה	הִרְבָּה	יַרְבֶּה	הַרְבּוֹת	מַרְבֶּה
Hithpael	כסה	הִתְכַּסָּה	יִתְכַּסֶּה	הִתְכַּסּוֹת	מִתְכַּסֶּה
Pual	כסה	כֻּסָּה	יְכֻסֶּה	כֻּסּוֹת	מְכֻסֶּה

Appendix Table 8.3. The Principal Parts of the Derived Stems

	Qatal		Yiqtol	Inf. Con.	Participle
Niphal	נִקְטַל		יִקָּטֵל	הִקָּטֵל	נִקְטָל
עבד	נֶעֱבַד		יֵעָבֵד	הֵעָבֵד	נֶעֱבָד
בנה	נִבְנָה		יִבָּנֶה	הִבָּנוֹת	נִבְנֶה
נצל	נִצַּל		יִנָּצֵל	הִנָּצֵל	נִצָּל
ישב	נוֹשַׁב		יִוָּשֵׁב	הִוָּשֵׁב	נוֹשָׁב
כון	נָכוֹן		יִכּוֹן	הִכּוֹן	נָכוֹן
Piel	קִטֵּל	קִטַּלְתָּ	יְקַטֵּל	קַטֵּל	מְקַטֵּל
כסה	כִּסָּה	כִּסִּיתָ	יְכַסֶּה	כַּסּוֹת	מְכַסֶּה
ברך	בֵּרַךְ	בֵּרַכְתָּ	יְבָרֵךְ	בָּרֵךְ	מְבָרֵךְ
Hiphil	הִקְטִיל	הִקְטַלְתָּ	יַקְטִיל	הַקְטִיל	מַקְטִיל
רבה	הִרְבָּה	הִרְבִּיתָ	יַרְבֶּה	הַרְבּוֹת	מַרְבֶּה
עבד	הֶעֱבִיד	הֶעֱבַדְתָּ	יַעֲבִיד	הַעֲבִיד	מַעֲבִיד
נפל	הִפִּיל	הִפַּלְתָּ	יַפִּיל	הַפִּיל	מַפִּיל
ישב	הוֹשִׁיב	הוֹשַׁבְתָּ	יוֹשִׁיב	הוֹשִׁיב	מוֹשִׁיב
שוב	הֵשִׁיב	הֲשִׁיבוֹת	יָשִׁיב	הָשִׁיב	מֵשִׁיב
Hithpael	הִתְקַטֵּל	הִתְקַטַּלְתָּ	יִתְקַטֵּל	הִתְקַטֵּל	מִתְקַטֵּל
כסה	הִתְכַּסָּה	הִתְכַּסִּיתָ	יִתְכַּסֶּה	הִתְכַּסּוֹת	מִתְכַּסֶּה
ברך	הִתְבָּרֵךְ	הִתְבָּרַכְתָּ	יִתְבָּרֵךְ	הִתְבָּרֵךְ	מִתְבָּרֵךְ
שמר	הִשְׁתַּמֵּר	הִשְׁתַּמַּרְתָּ	יִשְׁתַּמֵּר	הִשְׁתַּמֵּר	מִשְׁתַּמֵּר
Pual	קֻטַּל		יְקֻטַּל	קֻטַּל	מְקֻטָּל
כסה	כֻּסָּה		יְכֻסֶּה	כֻּסּוֹת	מְכֻסֶּה
ברך	בֹּרַךְ		יְבֹרַךְ	בֹּרַךְ	מְבֹרָךְ
Hophal	הָקְטַל		יָקְטַל	הָקְטַל	מָקְטָל
ירד	הוּרַד		יוּרַד	הוּרַד	מוּרָד
שוב	הוּשַׁב		יוּשַׁב	הוּשַׁב	מוּשָׁב
נגד	הֻגַּד		יֻגַּד	הֻגַּד	מֻגָּד

Appendix Table 8.4. Qal Stem Paradigms

Conjug	PGN	Strong	I-Gutt	I-א	II-Gutt	III-ח/ע	III-א	III-ה	I-נ	Orig. I-י	True I-י	Hollow
Qatal	3ms											
	3fs											
	2ms											
	2fs											
	1cs											
	3cp											
	2mp											
	2fp											
	1cp											
Yiqtol	3ms											
	3fs											
	2ms											
	2fs											
	1cs											
	3mp											
	3fp											
	2mp											
	2fp											
	1cp											

1. This pattern is for active verbs only; *qatal* statives in triconsonantal roots follow one of two patterns: כָּבֵד or קָטֹן. In every form other than 3ms, כָּבֵד-type statives use a Pathach stem vowel, except in III-א statives, which use a Tsere stem vowel in every form. Similarly, קָטֹן-type statives use a Holem stem vowel throughout.
2. Strong triconsonantal stative *yiqtols* follow the pattern of II/III-ח/ע *yiqtols*.
3. In the Hebrew Bible, the following five verbs follow this pattern: אָבַד, אָבָה, אָכַל, אָמַר, and אָפָה; all other I-א *yiqtols* following the pointing for the I-guttural חָזַק.

Conjug	PGN	Strong	I-Gutt		I-א	II-Gutt	III-ה/ע	III-א	III-ה	I-נ		Orig. I-'	True I-'	Hollow
Impv	ms	קְטֹל[1]	עֲמֹד	חֲזַק	אֱמֹר	בְּחַר	שְׁמַע	מְצָא	בְּנֵה	נְפֹל	גַּשׁ[2]	שֵׁב[2]	רֵד	קוּם
	fs	קִטְלִי	עִמְדִי	חִזְקִי	אִמְרִי	בַּחֲרִי	שִׁמְעִי	מִצְאִי	בְּנִי	נִפְלִי	גְּשִׁי	שְׁבִי	רְדִי	קוּמִי
	mp	קִטְלוּ	עִמְדוּ	חִזְקוּ	אִמְרוּ	בַּחֲרוּ	שִׁמְעוּ	מִצְאוּ	בְּנוּ	נִפְלוּ	גְּשׁוּ	שְׁבוּ	רְדוּ	קוּמוּ
	fp	קְטֹלְנָה	עֲמֹדְנָה	חֲזַקְנָה	אֱמֹרְנָה	בְּחַרְנָה	שְׁמַעְנָה	מְצֶאןָה	בְּנֶינָה	נְפֹלְנָה	גַּשְׁנָה	שֵׁבְנָה	רֵדְנָה	קֹמְנָה
Inf Con		קְטֹל	עֲמֹד		אֱמֹר	בְּחֹר	שְׁמֹעַ	מְצֹא	בְּנוֹת	נְפֹל	גֶּשֶׁת[3]	שֶׁבֶת	רֶדֶת	קוּם
Inf Abs		קָטוֹל	עָמוֹד		אָמוֹר	בָּחוֹר	שָׁמוֹעַ	מָצוֹא	בָּנֹה	נָפוֹל		יָשׁוֹב	יָרֹד	קוֹם
PtcA	ms	קֹטֵל	עֹמֵד		אֹמֵר	בֹּחֵר	שֹׁמֵעַ	מֹצֵא	בֹּנֶה	נֹפֵל		יֹשֵׁב	יֹרֵד	קָם
	fs	קֹטֶלֶת[5]	עֹמֶדֶת		אֹמֶרֶת	בֹּחֶרֶת	שֹׁמַעַת	מֹצֵאת	בֹּנָה	נֹפֶלֶת		יֹשֶׁבֶת	יֹרֶדֶת	קָמָה
	mp	קֹטְלִים	עֹמְדִים		אֹמְרִים	בֹּחֲרִים	שֹׁמְעִים	מֹצְאִים	בֹּנִים	נֹפְלִים		יֹשְׁבִים	יֹרְדִים	קָמִים
	fp	קֹטְלוֹת	עֹמְדוֹת		אֹמְרוֹת	בֹּחֲרוֹת	שֹׁמְעוֹת	מֹצְאוֹת	בֹּנוֹת	נֹפְלוֹת		יֹשְׁבוֹת	יֹרְדוֹת	קָמוֹת
PtcP	ms	קָטוּל[6]	עָמוּד		אָמוּר	בָּחוּר	שָׁמוּעַ	מָצוּא	בָּנוּי[7]	נָפוּל		יָשׁוּב	יָרוּד	
WA	3ms	וַיִּקְטֹל	וַיַּעֲמֹד	וַיֶּחֱזַק	וַיֹּאמֶר[8]	וַיִּבְחַר	וַיִּשְׁמַע	וַיִּמְצָא	וַיִּבֶן	וַיִּפֹּל	וַיִּגַּשׁ	וַיֵּשֶׁב	וַיֵּרֶד	וַיָּקָם
WQ	2ms	וְקָטַלְתָּ	וְעָמַדְתָּ	וְחָזַקְתָּ	וְאָמַרְתָּ	וּבָחַרְתָּ	וְשָׁמַעְתָּ	וּמָצָאתָ	וּבָנִיתָ	וְנָפַלְתָּ	וְנִגַּשְׁתָּ	וְיָשַׁבְתָּ	וְיָרַדְתָּ	וְקַמְתָּ
Jussive	3ms	יִקְטֹל	יַעֲמֹד	יֶחֱזַק	יֹאמַר	יִבְחַר	יִשְׁמַע	יִמְצָא	יִבֶן	יִפֹּל	יִגַּשׁ	יֵשֵׁב	יֵרֵד	יָקֹם

1. An alternate form with paragogic ה is קָטְלָה.
2. Alternate longer forms are seen in many I-נ and orig. I-' verbs—e.g., the ms impv. of נסע can be either סַע (short) or סְעָה (long); the ms impv of ישׁב can be either שֵׁב (short) or שְׁבָה (long).
3. The I-נ/III-א verb נשׂא has three possible infinitive construct forms: שְׂאֵת, שֵׂאת, and נְשׂא.
4. An alternate form is נְתֹן.
5. An alternate form is קֹטְלָה.
6. קְטֻלָּה (fs); קְטוּלִים (mp); קְטוּלוֹת (fp).
7. בְּנוּיָה (fs); בְּנוּיִם (mp); בְּנוּיוֹת (fp).
8. The pattern וַיֹּאבַד is also found.

Appendix Table 8.5. Niphal Stem Paradigms

Conjug	PGN	Strong	I-Gutt	II-Gutt	III-ח/ע	III-א	III-ה	I-נ	Orig. I-ו	Hollow
Qatal	3ms	נִקְטַל	נֶעֱזַב	נִבְרַךְ	נִשְׁלַח	נִמְצָא	נִבְנָה	נִגַּשׁ	נוֹשַׁב	נָכוֹן
	3fs	נִקְטְלָה	נֶעֶזְבָה	נִבְרְכָה	נִשְׁלְחָה	נִמְצְאָה	נִבְנְתָה	נִגְּשָׁה	נוֹשְׁבָה	נָכוֹנָה
	2ms	נִקְטַלְתָּ	נֶעֱזַבְתָּ	נִבְרַכְתָּ	נִשְׁלַחְתָּ	נִמְצֵאתָ	נִבְנֵיתָ	נִגַּשְׁתָּ	נוֹשַׁבְתָּ	נְכוּנוֹתָ
	2fs	נִקְטַלְתְּ	נֶעֱזַבְתְּ	נִבְרַכְתְּ	נִשְׁלַחַתְּ	נִמְצֵאת	נִבְנֵית	נִגַּשְׁתְּ	נוֹשַׁבְתְּ	נְכוּנוֹת
	1cs	נִקְטַלְתִּי	נֶעֱזַבְתִּי	נִבְרַכְתִּי	נִשְׁלַחְתִּי	נִמְצֵאתִי	נִבְנֵיתִי	נִגַּשְׁתִּי	נוֹשַׁבְתִּי	נְכוּנוֹתִי
	3cp	נִקְטְלוּ	נֶעֶזְבוּ	נִבְרְכוּ	נִשְׁלְחוּ	נִמְצְאוּ	נִבְנוּ	נִגְּשׁוּ	נוֹשְׁבוּ	נָכוֹנוּ
	2mp	נִקְטַלְתֶּם	נֶעֱזַבְתֶּם	נִבְרַכְתֶּם	נִשְׁלַחְתֶּם	נִמְצֵאתֶם	נִבְנֵיתֶם	נִגַּשְׁתֶּם	נוֹשַׁבְתֶּם	נְכוּנוֹתֶם
	2fp	נִקְטַלְתֶּן	נֶעֱזַבְתֶּן	נִבְרַכְתֶּן	נִשְׁלַחְתֶּן	נִמְצֵאתֶן	נִבְנֵיתֶן	נִגַּשְׁתֶּן	נוֹשַׁבְתֶּן	נְכוּנוֹתֶן
	1cp	נִקְטַלְנוּ	נֶעֱזַבְנוּ	נִבְרַכְנוּ	נִשְׁלַחְנוּ	נִמְצֵאנוּ	נִבְנֵינוּ	נִגַּשְׁנוּ	נוֹשַׁבְנוּ	נְכוּנוֹנוּ
Yiqtol	3ms	יִקָּטֵל	יֵעָזֵב	יִבָּרֵךְ	יִשָּׁלַח	יִמָּצֵא	יִבָּנֶה	יִנָּגֵשׁ	יִוָּשֵׁב	יִכּוֹן
	3fs	תִּקָּטֵל	תֵּעָזֵב	תִּבָּרֵךְ	תִּשָּׁלַח	תִּמָּצֵא	תִּבָּנֶה	תִּנָּגֵשׁ	תִּוָּשֵׁב	תִּכּוֹן
	2ms	תִּקָּטֵל	תֵּעָזֵב	תִּבָּרֵךְ	תִּשָּׁלַח	תִּמָּצֵא	תִּבָּנֶה	תִּנָּגֵשׁ	תִּוָּשֵׁב	תִּכּוֹן
	2fs	תִּקָּטְלִי	תֵּעָזְבִי	תִּבָּרְכִי	תִּשָּׁלְחִי	תִּמָּצְאִי	תִּבָּנִי	תִּנָּגְשִׁי	תִּוָּשְׁבִי	תִּכּוֹנִי
	1cs	אֶקָּטֵל	אֵעָזֵב	אֶבָּרֵךְ	אֶשָּׁלַח	אֶמָּצֵא	אֶבָּנֶה	אֶנָּגֵשׁ	אִוָּשֵׁב	אֶכּוֹן
	3mp	יִקָּטְלוּ	יֵעָזְבוּ	יִבָּרְכוּ	יִשָּׁלְחוּ	יִמָּצְאוּ	יִבָּנוּ	יִנָּגְשׁוּ	יִוָּשְׁבוּ	יִכּוֹנוּ
	3fp	תִּקָּטַלְנָה	תֵּעָזַבְנָה	תִּבָּרַכְנָה	תִּשָּׁלַחְנָה	תִּמָּצֶאנָה	תִּבָּנֶינָה	תִּנָּגַשְׁנָה	תִּוָּשַׁבְנָה	תִּכּוֹנֶינָה
	2mp	תִּקָּטְלוּ	תֵּעָזְבוּ	תִּבָּרְכוּ	תִּשָּׁלְחוּ	תִּמָּצְאוּ	תִּבָּנוּ	תִּנָּגְשׁוּ	תִּוָּשְׁבוּ	תִּכּוֹנוּ
	2fp	תִּקָּטַלְנָה	תֵּעָזַבְנָה	תִּבָּרַכְנָה	תִּשָּׁלַחְנָה	תִּמָּצֶאנָה	תִּבָּנֶינָה	תִּנָּגַשְׁנָה	תִּוָּשַׁבְנָה	תִּכּוֹנֶינָה
	1cp	נִקָּטֵל	נֵעָזֵב	נִבָּרֵךְ	נִשָּׁלַח	נִמָּצֵא	נִבָּנֶה	נִנָּגֵשׁ	נִוָּשֵׁב	נִכּוֹן

1. An alternate form is אֶקָּטֵל.

Conjug	PGN	Strong	I-Gutt	II-Gutt	III-ח/ע	III-א	III-ה	I-נ	Orig. I-י	Hollow
Impv	2ms	הִקָּטֵל	הֵעָמֵד	הֵרָאֵה	הִמָּצֵא	הִגָּלֵה	הִנָּצֵל	הִוָּשֵׁב	הִכּוֹן
	2fs	הִקָּטְלִי	הֵעָמְדִי	הֵרָאִי	הִמָּצְאִי	הִגָּלִי	הִנָּצְלִי	הִוָּשְׁבִי	הִכּוֹנִי
	2mp	הִקָּטְלוּ	הֵעָמְדוּ	הֵרָאוּ	הִמָּצְאוּ	הִגָּלוּ	הִנָּצְלוּ	הִוָּשְׁבוּ	הִכּוֹנוּ
	2fp	הִקָּטֵלְנָה	הֵעָמֵדְנָה	הֵרָאֶינָה	הִמָּצֶאנָה	הִגָּלֶינָה	הִנָּצֵלְנָה	הִוָּשֵׁבְנָה	הִכּוֹנֶנָה
Inf Con		הִקָּטֵל	הֵעָמֵד	הֵרָאֵה	הִמָּצֵא	הִגָּלוֹת	הִנָּצֵל	הִוָּשֵׁב	הִכּוֹן
Inf Abs		הִקָּטֹל	הֵעָמֹד	הֵרָאֹה	הִמָּצֹא	הִגָּלֹה	הִנָּצֹל	הִוָּשֵׁב	הִכּוֹן
		נִקְטֹל	נַעֲמֹל			נִגְלֹה		נוֹשֵׁב	
Ptc	ms	נִקְטָל	נֶעֱמָד	נִבְחָר	נִמְצָא	נִגְלֶה	נִצָּל	נוֹשָׁב	נָכוֹן
	fs	נִקְטָלָה	נֶעֱמָדָה	נִבְחֶרֶת	נִמְצֵאת	נִגְלָה	נִצֶּלֶת	נוֹשָׁבָה	נְכוֹנָה
	mp	נִקְטָלִים	נֶעֱמָדִים	נִבְחָרִים	נִמְצָאִים	נִגְלִים	נִצָּלִים	נוֹשָׁבִים	נְכוֹנִים
	fp	נִקְטָלוֹת	נֶעֱמָדוֹת	נִבְחָרוֹת	נִמְצָאוֹת	נִגְלוֹת	נִצָּלוֹת	נוֹשָׁבוֹת	נְכוֹנוֹת
WA	3ms	וַיִּקָּטֵל	וַיֵּעָמֵד	וַיִּבָּחֵר	וַיִּמָּצֵא	וַיִּגָּל	וַיִּנָּצֵל	וַיִּוָּשֵׁב	וַיִּכּוֹן
WQ	2ms	וְנִקְטַלְתָּ	וְנֶעֱמַדְתָּ	וְנִבְחַרְתָּ	וְנִמְצֵאתָ	וְנִגְלֵיתָ	וְנִצַּלְתָּ	וְנוֹשַׁבְתָּ	
Jussive	3ms	יִקָּטֵל	יֵעָמֵד	יִבָּחֵר	יִמָּצֵא	יִגָּל	יִנָּצֵל	יִוָּשֵׁב	יִכּוֹן

1. Alternate forms for the Niphal participle include נִקְטְלָה (fs), נִקְטָלִים (mp), and נִקְטָלוֹת

Appendix Table 8.6. Piel Stem Paradigms

Conjug	PGN	Strong (Act)	II-Gutt	II-Gutt	III-ע/ח	III-א	III-ה
Qatal	3ms	קִטֵּל	בֵּרַךְ	מֵאֵן	שִׁלַּח	מִלֵּא	גִּלָּה
	3fs	קִטְּלָה	בֵּרְכָה	מֵאֲנָה	שִׁלְּחָה	מִלְאָה	גִּלְּתָה
	2ms	קִטַּלְתָּ	בֵּרַכְתָּ	מֵאַנְתָּ	שִׁלַּחְתָּ	מִלֵּאתָ	גִּלִּיתָ
	2fs	קִטַּלְתְּ	בֵּרַכְתְּ	מֵאַנְתְּ	שִׁלַּחַתְּ	מִלֵּאת	גִּלִּית
	1cs	קִטַּלְתִּי	בֵּרַכְתִּי	מֵאַנְתִּי	שִׁלַּחְתִּי	מִלֵּאתִי	גִּלִּיתִי
	3cp	קִטְּלוּ	בֵּרְכוּ	מֵאֲנוּ	שִׁלְּחוּ	מִלְאוּ	גִּלּוּ
	2mp	קִטַּלְתֶּם	בֵּרַכְתֶּם	מֵאַנְתֶּם	שִׁלַּחְתֶּם	מִלֵּאתֶם	גִּלִּיתֶם
	2fp	קִטַּלְתֶּן	בֵּרַכְתֶּן	מֵאַנְתֶּן	שִׁלַּחְתֶּן	מִלֵּאתֶן	גִּלִּיתֶן
	1cp	קִטַּלְנוּ	בֵּרַכְנוּ	מֵאַנּוּ	שִׁלַּחְנוּ	מִלֵּאנוּ	גִּלִּינוּ
Yiqtol	3ms	יְקַטֵּל	יְבָרֵךְ	יְמָאֵן	יְשַׁלַּח	יְמַלֵּא	יְגַלֶּה
	3fs	תְּקַטֵּל	תְּבָרֵךְ	תְּמָאֵן	תְּשַׁלַּח	תְּמַלֵּא	תְּגַלֶּה
	2ms	תְּקַטֵּל	תְּבָרֵךְ	תְּמָאֵן	תְּשַׁלַּח	תְּמַלֵּא	תְּגַלֶּה
	2fs	תְּקַטְּלִי	תְּבָרְכִי	תְּמָאֲנִי	תְּשַׁלְּחִי	תְּמַלְאִי	תְּגַלִּי
	1cs	אֲקַטֵּל	אֲבָרֵךְ	אֲמָאֵן	אֲשַׁלַּח	אֲמַלֵּא	אֲגַלֶּה
	3mp	יְקַטְּלוּ	יְבָרְכוּ	יְמָאֲנוּ	יְשַׁלְּחוּ	יְמַלְאוּ	יְגַלּוּ
	3fp	תְּקַטֵּלְנָה	תְּבָרֵכְנָה	תְּמָאֵנָּה	תְּשַׁלַּחְנָה	תְּמַלֶּאנָה	תְּגַלֶּינָה
	2mp	תְּקַטְּלוּ	תְּבָרְכוּ	תְּמָאֲנוּ	תְּשַׁלְּחוּ	תְּמַלְאוּ	תְּגַלּוּ
	2fp	תְּקַטֵּלְנָה	תְּבָרֵכְנָה	תְּמָאֵנָּה	תְּשַׁלַּחְנָה	תְּמַלֶּאנָה	תְּגַלֶּינָה
	1cp	נְקַטֵּל	נְבָרֵךְ	נְמָאֵן	נְשַׁלַּח	נְמַלֵּא	נְגַלֶּה

1. An alternate form is לְקַד.

Conj	PGN	Strong (Act)	II-Gutt	III-ח/ע	III-א	III-ה
Impv	2ms	קַטֵּל	בָּרֵךְ	שַׁלַּח	מַלֵּא	גַּלֵּה
	2fs	קַטְּלִי	בָּרְכִי	שַׁלְּחִי	מַלְּאִי	גַּלִּי
	2mp	קַטְּלוּ	בָּרְכוּ	שַׁלְּחוּ	מַלְּאוּ	גַּלּוּ
	2fp	קַטֵּלְנָה	בָּרֵכְנָה	שַׁלַּחְנָה	מַלֶּאנָה	גַּלֶּינָה
Inf Con		קַטֵּל	בָּרֵךְ	שַׁלֵּחַ	מַלֵּא	גַּלּוֹת
Inf Abs		קַטֵּל	בָּרֵךְ	שַׁלֵּחַ	מַלֵּא	גַּלֵּה
Ptc	ms	מְקַטֵּל	מְבָרֵךְ	מְשַׁלֵּחַ	מְמַלֵּא	מְגַלֶּה
	fs	מְקַטְּלָה	מְבָרֶכֶת	מְשַׁלַּחַת	מְמַלְּאָה	מְגַלָּה
	mp	מְקַטְּלִים	מְבָרְכִים	מְשַׁלְּחִים	מְמַלְּאִים	מְגַלִּים
	fp	מְקַטְּלוֹת	מְבָרְכוֹת	מְשַׁלְּחוֹת	מְמַלְּאוֹת	מְגַלּוֹת
WA	3ms	וַיְקַטֵּל	וַיְבָרֶךְ	וַיְשַׁלַּח	וַיְמַלֵּא	וַיְגַל
WQ	2ms	וְקִטַּלְתָּ	וּבֵרַכְתָּ	וְשִׁלַּחְתָּ	וּמִלֵּאתָ	וְגִלִּיתָ
Jussive	3ms	יְקַטֵּל	יְבָרֵךְ	יְשַׁלַּח	יְמַלֵּא	יְגַל

1. An alternate form is קַטְּלָה.
2. An alternate form is מִלֵּאת.
3. Daghesh forte is absent in the Yod preformative of Piel *wayyiqtol* forms.

Appendix Table 8.7. Hiphil Stem Paradigms

Conjug	PGN	Strong (Act)	I-Gutt	III-ח/ע	III-א	III-ה	I-נ	Orig. I-ו	True I-י	Hollow
Qatal	3ms									
	3fs									
	2ms									
	2fs									
	1cs									
	3cp									
	2mp									
	2fp									
	1cp									
Yiqtol	3ms									
	3fs									
	2ms									
	2fs									
	1cs									
	3mp									
	3fp									
	2mp									
	2fp									
	1cp									

1. Frequently, one or both of the pointed vowel letters is written defectively. An alternate paradigm does not have the linking Holem-Waw in the *qatal*.

2. Alternate forms for the *qatal* 3fs and 2mp III-ה verbs are הִקְרְתָה and הִקְרִיתֶם, respectively.

3. Alternate forms for the *yiqtol* 3fp III-ה and Hollow verbs are תַּקְרֶינָה and תְּקִימֶינָה, respectively.

Conjug	PGN	Strong (Act)	I-Gutt	III-ה/ע	III-א	III-ה	I-נ	Orig. I-ו	True I-י	Hollow
Impv	2ms	קְטֹל	עֲמֹד	שְׁמַע	מְצָא	בְּנֵה	גַּשׁ	רֵד	יְטַב	קוּם
	2fs	קִטְלִי	עִמְדִי	שִׁמְעִי	מִצְאִי	בְּנִי	גְּשִׁי	רְדִי	יִטְבִי	קוּמִי
	2mp	קִטְלוּ	עִמְדוּ	שִׁמְעוּ	מִצְאוּ	בְּנוּ	גְּשׁוּ	רְדוּ	יִטְבוּ	קוּמוּ
	2fp	קְטֹלְנָה	עֲמֹדְנָה	שְׁמַעְנָה	מְצֶאנָה	בְּנֶינָה	גַּשְׁנָה	רֵדְנָה	יְטַבְנָה	קֹמְנָה
Inf Con		קְטֹל	עֲמֹד	שְׁמֹעַ	מְצֹא	בְּנוֹת	גֶּשֶׁת	רֶדֶת		קוּם
Inf Abs		קָטוֹל	עָמוֹד	שָׁמוֹעַ	מָצוֹא	בָּנֹה	נָגוֹשׁ	יָרוֹד		קוֹם
Ptc	ms	קֹטֵל	עֹמֵד	שֹׁמֵעַ	מֹצֵא	בֹּנֶה	נֹגֵשׁ	יֹרֵד		קָם
	fs	קֹטֶלֶת[2]	עֹמֶדֶת	שֹׁמַעַת	מֹצֵאת	בֹּנָה	נֹגֶשֶׁת	יֹרֶדֶת		קָמָה
	mp	קֹטְלִים	עֹמְדִים	שֹׁמְעִים	מֹצְאִים	בֹּנִים	נֹגְשִׁים	יֹרְדִים		קָמִים
	fp	קֹטְלוֹת	עֹמְדוֹת	שֹׁמְעוֹת	מֹצְאוֹת	בֹּנוֹת	נֹגְשׁוֹת	יֹרְדוֹת		קָמוֹת
WA	3ms	וַיִּקְטֹל	וַיַּעֲמֹד	וַיִּשְׁמַע	וַיִּמְצָא	וַיִּבֶן	וַיִּגַּשׁ	וַיֵּרֶד	וַיִּיטַב	וַיָּקָם
WQ	2ms	וְקָטַלְתָּ	וְעָמַדְתָּ	וְשָׁמַעְתָּ	וּמָצָאתָ	וּבָנִיתָ	וְנִגַּשְׁתָּ	וְיָרַדְתָּ	וְיָטַבְתָּ	וְקַמְתָּ
Jussive	3ms	יִקְטֹל	יַעֲמֹד	יִשְׁמַע	יִמְצָא	יִבֶן	יִגַּשׁ	יֵרֵד	יִיטַב	יָקֹם

1. An alternate form is קָטְלָה.
2. An alternate form is קֹטְלָה.

Appendix Table 8.8. Pual, Hophal, Hithpael, Polel, and Pilpel Stem Paradigms

Conjug	PGN	Pual Strong	Hophal Strong	Hithpael Strong	Hithpael I-S	Polel כון	Pilpel כול
Qatal	3ms	קֻטַּל	הָקְטַל	הִתְקַטֵּל	הִשְׁתַּמֵּר	כּוֹנֵן	כִּלְכֵּל
	3fs	קֻטְּלָה	הָקְטְלָה	הִתְקַטְּלָה	הִשְׁתַּמְּרָה	כּוֹנְנָה	כִּלְכְּלָה
	2ms	קֻטַּלְתָּ	הָקְטַלְתָּ	הִתְקַטַּלְתָּ	הִשְׁתַּמַּרְתָּ	כּוֹנַנְתָּ	כִּלְכַּלְתָּ
	2fs	קֻטַּלְתְּ	הָקְטַלְתְּ	הִתְקַטַּלְתְּ	הִשְׁתַּמַּרְתְּ	כּוֹנַנְתְּ	כִּלְכַּלְתְּ
	1cs	קֻטַּלְתִּי	הָקְטַלְתִּי	הִתְקַטַּלְתִּי	הִשְׁתַּמַּרְתִּי	כּוֹנַנְתִּי	כִּלְכַּלְתִּי
	3cp	קֻטְּלוּ	הָקְטְלוּ	הִתְקַטְּלוּ	הִשְׁתַּמְּרוּ	כּוֹנְנוּ	כִּלְכְּלוּ
	2mp	קֻטַּלְתֶּם	הָקְטַלְתֶּם	הִתְקַטַּלְתֶּם	הִשְׁתַּמַּרְתֶּם	כּוֹנַנְתֶּם	כִּלְכַּלְתֶּם
	2fp	קֻטַּלְתֶּן	הָקְטַלְתֶּן	הִתְקַטַּלְתֶּן	הִשְׁתַּמַּרְתֶּן	כּוֹנַנְתֶּן	כִּלְכַּלְתֶּן
	1cp	קֻטַּלְנוּ	הָקְטַלְנוּ	הִתְקַטַּלְנוּ	הִשְׁתַּמַּרְנוּ	כּוֹנַנּוּ	כִּלְכַּלְנוּ
Yiqtol	3ms	יְקֻטַּל	יָקְטַל	יִתְקַטֵּל	יִשְׁתַּמֵּר	יְכוֹנֵן	יְכַלְכֵּל
	3fs	תְּקֻטַּל	תָּקְטַל	תִּתְקַטֵּל	תִּשְׁתַּמֵּר	תְּכוֹנֵן	תְּכַלְכֵּל
	2ms	תְּקֻטַּל	תָּקְטַל	תִּתְקַטֵּל	תִּשְׁתַּמֵּר	תְּכוֹנֵן	תְּכַלְכֵּל
	2fs	תְּקֻטְּלִי	תָּקְטְלִי	תִּתְקַטְּלִי	תִּשְׁתַּמְּרִי	תְּכוֹנְנִי	תְּכַלְכְּלִי
	1cs	אֲקֻטַּל	אָקְטַל	אֶתְקַטֵּל	אֶשְׁתַּמֵּר	אֲכוֹנֵן	אֲכַלְכֵּל
	3mp	יְקֻטְּלוּ	יָקְטְלוּ	יִתְקַטְּלוּ	יִשְׁתַּמְּרוּ	יְכוֹנְנוּ	יְכַלְכְּלוּ
	3fp	תְּקֻטַּלְנָה	תָּקְטַלְנָה	תִּתְקַטֵּלְנָה	תִּשְׁתַּמֵּרְנָה	תְּכוֹנֵנָּה	תְּכַלְכֵּלְנָה
	2mp	תְּקֻטְּלוּ	תָּקְטְלוּ	תִּתְקַטְּלוּ	תִּשְׁתַּמְּרוּ	תְּכוֹנְנוּ	תְּכַלְכְּלוּ
	2fp	תְּקֻטַּלְנָה	תָּקְטַלְנָה	תִּתְקַטֵּלְנָה	תִּשְׁתַּמֵּרְנָה	תְּכוֹנֵנָּה	תְּכַלְכֵּלְנָה
	1cp	נְקֻטַּל	נָקְטַל	נִתְקַטֵּל	נִשְׁתַּמֵּר	נְכוֹנֵן	נְכַלְכֵּל

Conj	PGN	Pual Strong	Hophal Strong	Hithpael Strong	Hithpael I-S	Polel כּוֹן	Pilpel כּוּל
Impv	2ms		הָקְטַל	הִתְקַטֵּל	הִשְׁתַּמֵּר	כּוֹנֵן	
	2fs			הִתְקַטְּלִי	הִשְׁתַּמְּרִי	כּוֹנְנִי	
	2mp			הִתְקַטְּלוּ	הִשְׁתַּמְּרוּ	כּוֹנְנוּ	
	2fp			הִתְקַטֵּלְנָה	הִשְׁתַּמֵּרְנָה	כּוֹנֵנָּה	כַּלְכֵּל
Inf Con		קֻטַּל	הָקְטַל	הִתְקַטֵּל	הִשְׁתַּמֵּר	כּוֹנֵן	מְכַלְכֵּל
Inf Abs			הָקְטֵל	הִתְקַטֵּל	הִשְׁתַּמֵּר		
Ptc	ms	מְקֻטָּל	מָקְטָל	מִתְקַטֵּל	מִשְׁתַּמֵּר	מְכוֹנֵן	
	fs	מְקֻטֶּלֶת	מָקְטֶלֶת	מִתְקַטֶּלֶת	מִשְׁתַּמֶּרֶת	מְכוֹנֶנֶת	
	mp	מְקֻטָּלִים	מָקְטָלִים	מִתְקַטְּלִים	מִשְׁתַּמְּרִים	מְכוֹנְנִים	
	fp	מְקֻטָּלוֹת	מָקְטָלוֹת	מִתְקַטְּלוֹת	מִשְׁתַּמְּרוֹת	מְכוֹנְנוֹת	
WA	3ms	וַיְקֻטַּל	וַיָּקְטַל	וַיִּתְקַטֵּל	וַיִּשְׁתַּמֵּר	וַיְכוֹנֵן	וַיְכַלְכֵּל
WQ	2ms	וְקֻטַּל	וְהָקְטַל	וְהִתְקַטֵּל	וְהִשְׁתַּמֵּר		וְכִלְכַּלְתָּ
Jussive	3ms			יִתְקַטֵּל	יִשְׁתַּמֵּר